ISBN 978-1-330-75777-2
PIBN 10101552

Jurisdiction and Procedure

OF THE

Federal Courts

BY

JOHN C. ROSE

United States District Judge for the District of Maryland

SECOND EDITION

ALBANY, N. Y.

MATTHEW BENDER & COMPANY

INCORPORATED

1922

CORRIGENDA

Since the early part of the text was printed, the Act of September 14, 1922, has been passed, and is found incorporated in the Judicial Code in the appendix. It changes Sections 53, 55 and 65 as follows:

Section 53, page 67, add at end:

"Besides the special provision for additional judges made by the Act of September 14, 1922." (See Act of September 14, 1922, Appendix, p. 551.)

Section 55, page 70, add at end:

"which, while this book was passing through the press has been done by the Act of September 14, 1922." (See Act of September 14, 1922, Appendix, p. 557.)

Section 65, page 81, the first sentence of the second paragraph of the section should read:

"In all the circuits, the number of Circuit Judges has been increased, so that in the Second, Seventh and Eighth, there are now four, and in all others, three."

The Act of September 19, 1922, requires the following addition to Section 266, on page 241:

"Until September 19, 1925, any civil suit brought by the United States, or any of its officers, authorized by law to sue, may be brought in any district in which any necessary defendant is an inhabitant, or in any district wherein the cause of action or any part thereof arose." (See Section 51 J. C., Appendix, page 575.)

PREFACE

The first edition of this book was published in 1915. It was intended to state and illustrate the fundamental principles governing the jurisdiction and procedure of the Federal Courts concisely and clearly, so that it would be of use both to those who had previously had little familiarity with Federal practice, and to those who, frequently engaged in the Courts of the United States, wanted readily at hand a precise and accurate statement of the basic rules, with references to the leading cases in which they had been laid down and applied.

The present second edition is enlarged and brings the work down to date. The appendix contains the Judicial Code, with all amendments made to it up to the adjournment of Congress in September, 1922.

The author is indebted to Mr. Robert France of Baltimore for a verification of the references. Everything else in it has been personally prepared by him.

JOHN C. ROSE.

Baltimore, Md.,
December, 1922.

TABLE OF CONTENTS

[References are to Pages.]

ABBREVIATIONS.

C. C. A..................... Circuit Courts of Appeals.

Fed. . . .. Federal Reporter.

Fed. Cases................. Federal Cases.

Fed. Stat. Ann.............. Edw. Thompson Company's second edition.

Fed. Stat. Ann. Sup......... Supplement to the second edition of the Fed. Stat. Ann. for the year indicated.

J. C....................... Judicial Code.

L. Ed....,................. Lawyer's Edition of the Supreme Court Reports, Lawyer's Co-operative Publishing Co.

R. S....................... Revised Statutes.

Sup. Ct.................... Supreme Court Reporter, West Publishing Company.

U. S. Comp. Stat............ United States Compiled Statutes, West Publishing Company.

U. S. Comp. Stat. Sup....... Two volume supplement of 1919 West Publishing Company.

Jurisdiction and Procedure

OF THE

COURTS OF THE UNITED STATES

CHAPTER I.

THE ORIGIN AND THE LIMITS OF THE JURISDICTION OF THE FEDERAL COURTS.

1. Introduction.

In an ideal State there would be only one set of courts. If a controversy is one with which the law can deal at all, there should be no room for difference of opinion as to what tribunal may pass upon it. If there are different kinds of Courts, the limits of their jurisdiction with respect to each other must be defined. The affairs of men are of infinite variety. No one can foresee all their possible complexities and combinations. No statute can draw the line which separates the cases of which one Court may

take cognizance from those which may be passed upon
only by another, so accurately and so minutely as to foreclose the possibility of dispute as to whether a particular
controversy lies upon one side or the other of it. Time,
money, learning and professional experience and skill will
be spent in finding out, not what the substantial rights of
the parties are, but merely what Court may pass upon
them. When there are two or more systems of Courts, it
is almost inevitable that their procedure will differ in
some respects. Their pleading and practice will not be
quite the same. Moreover, mutually independent tribunals will, sometimes come to different conclusions as to
what is the substantive law. Each will be prone to hold
to its own view. It may follow that the result of a particular suit will turn altogether upon whether it is tried
in one Court or in another. It is possible to conceive of
a case which the plaintiff will be bound to win in a State
Court sitting on one side of a street and which he will
as certainly lose if it be determined by the United
States Court which may hold its sessions on the other side
of the same thoroughfare. Such a state of things does
not increase popular respect for either the law or the
persons or tribunals administering it.

This book seeks to state and briefly to explain the general rules which determine the jurisdiction of the Federal
Courts; to give some account of the organization of the
Federal judicial system; to point out the more important
respects in which the procedure of these tribunals differs
from those of the States; and to say a little about those
subjects of general law upon which they do not feel themselves bound to follow the decisions of the State Courts,
and in which in consequence they may upon the same state
of facts reach an opposite conclusion.

A number of volumes, every one larger than this, have
been written on these subjects, and many others will be.

Thousands of decisions relate to them. Most industrial
processes are, in a scientific sense, wasteful. They fail
to turn to the best theoretical advantage much of the material consumed and much of the energy exerted. The
money, the time, the learning, the ability and the nervous
force which have been laid out in answering such questions as those with which this treatise deals represent in
a way, the same sort of economic loss as that which is
incurred when all the power, which for countless centuries
has been stored up in a ton of coal, is expended in order
that a small percentage of it may be put to the use of
man. Within the present limits of our knowledge we can
do no better. Waste is part of the cost of use. So the
necessity of dealing with the problems herein discussed
is a portion of the price we pay for our dual system of
government. That system has been worth all that in this
and other ways it has cost us. Without Federal Courts
independent of those of the States, and, in the case of the
Supreme Court when dealing with a certain class of questions paramount to them, our Federal Government would
not be what it today is. Very probably it would ere this
have been dissolved.

Nevertheless, no good purpose can be served by shut-
ting our eyes to the fact that in some respects that system
is costly. The activities of the Federal Government are
now far greater than they formerly were. It is not un-
likely that for some time to come they will still further
increase. It does not necessarily follow that there must
be a proportionate expansion of the volume of litigation
in the Federal Courts. The duty of enforcing Federal
rights may by Congress be imposed upon the State
Courts.[1] Local and sectional prejudice is much less general and intense than it once was. Doubtless it will still

1. Second Employers' Liability Cases, 223 U. S. 1; 56 L. Ed. 327; 32
Sup. Ct. 169; 38 L. R. A. (N. S.) 44.

further abate. There will be correspondingly less occasion to seek protection from it in the Federal Courts.

We have become in fact one people. We none the less still clearly recognize the paramount importance of maintaining and, if possible, of developing every existing instrument of local self government even though it be at the cost of some temporary sacrifice of efficiency in administration. No considerable body of opinion in this country has ever sought centralization for its own sake. There are no longer any large number of persons who cherish any intense jealousy of the Federal Government. It should be easier than it has been to agree upon what should be the limits of the respective jurisdictions of the State and of the Federal Courts.

The pages which follow deal with the Courts of the United States as they now are. Such reference is made to past conditions as may help to a more accurate understanding of those at present existing.

2. Nature of the Questions Discussed.

Questions of jurisdiction, of pleading and of practice are not usually interesting. They deal with none of those touches of nature, whether great or trivial, which make all the world akin. Nor have they interest of another kind. Practical considerations usually determine the limits of the jurisdiction of a particular Court and the ways in which cases are brought into it and tried before it. The rules which govern in such matters are arbitrary rather than logical. The topics here discussed cannot therefore have that fascination which the ordered and reasoned unfolding of an abstract idea exerts upon well-trained minds. It is none the less necessary that those who are to practice law in these United States shall know something about the national Courts as distinguished from those of the States. A member of the Bar should know when he may and when he may not assert or defend the rights of his clients in the Federal tribunals.

3. Principles More Important Than Details.

The subject is arbitrary. In some respects it is highly technical. It abounds in nice distinctions. The law student cannot hope to get all of them into his head. It is just as well that he should not try. There are a number of general principles. These he should master. He should do more than remember them. He should understand them. To help him to do so is the purpose of this book. Details cannot be altogether avoided. Without some reference to them it would not be easy to make clear how in practice the principles work. The exceptions and qualifications which the statutes and the decisions have grafted upon the general rules must be stated. They are the rocks and the shoals which make legal navigation dangerous.

4. All Federal Courts Creatures of Written Law.

The great principle which lies at the bottom of all the law as to the jurisdiction of the Federal courts is that they owe their existence and their jurisdiction to certain written enactments. These may be constitutional or legislative. Whether they are one or the other, they are alike written. They are the original authorities. Behind them you need not look. Indeed, you may not for any purpose other than that of finding out what they mean.

5. All Federal Courts of Limited Jurisdiction.

No Federal Court may deal with any controversy, over which it has not been given authority by some constitutional or statutory grant.[2]

2. M. C. & L. M. Ry. Co. vs. Swan, 111 U. S. 382; 28 L. Ed. 462; 4 Sup. Ct. 510; Hanford vs. Davies, 163 U. S. 279; 41 L. Ed. 157; 16 Sup. Ct. 1051.

It follows that the Federal Courts, from the Supreme Court to the Courts of the Referees in Bankruptcy, and the Courts, if they may be so called, of the United States Commissioners, are one and all Courts of limited jurisdiction. In this they differ radically from the superior Courts of the States. The latter are, for the most part at least, Courts of general jurisdiction. It is true that all our States have written Constitutions. In most of them the judicial tribunals as they now exist are the creatures of those Constitutions or of statutes. Even the English Courts of today are the offspring of Victorian legislation. Nevertheless, the State Courts and the English Courts, no matter how recently created, are in some way given powers which make them Courts of general jurisdiction in a sense in which no Federal Court is.

6. Superior State Courts are of General Jurisdiction.

An illustration of what is meant may be found in Maryland. The Circuit Courts in the several counties date from the Constitution of 1851. In the form in which they actually exist today they were created by the Constitution of 1867, which declares they shall have "all the power, authority and jurisdiction * * * which the present Circuit Courts now have and exercise, or which may hereafter be prescribed by law."[3] The Constitution of 1864 used like language.[4]

The Constitution of 1851, which for the first time created Circuit Courts, gave them all the power, authority and jurisdiction of the former County Courts, and their judges, within their respective circuits all the jurisdiction of the old Court of Chancery.[5]

When by constitutional amendment adopted in 1805, the

---

3. Constitution of Maryland, 1867, Art. IV, Sec. 20.
4. Constitution of Maryland, 1864, Art. IV, Sec. 25.
5. Constitution of Maryland, 1851, Art. IV, Sec. 8.

judicial system of the State was reorganized, similar language was used to show that the new County Courts were the successors of the old.[6]

These County Courts were far older than the Revolution. The first State Constitution, that of 1776, recognized their existence.[7] It did not define their jurisdiction. It has long been the settled law of Maryland that those Courts acquired before the Declaration of Independence all the jurisdiction and powers of the Superior Courts of Westminster, except in so far as such powers and jurisdiction were obviously out of place under the political system or organization of the Province. Such powers and jurisdiction the Maryland Courts still have unless

(a) they have been taken away by some constitutional or legislative enactment; or

(b) are incompatible with the form of government set up by the constitution formed by the people of Maryland for themselves.

An important consequence follows. If you wish to dispute the jurisdiction of a Circuit Court of a Maryland county or of the Superior Court of Baltimore City, over any suit which could have been brought in any one of the three great Courts in Westminster Hall, you must affirmatively show how and why it is that the Maryland tribunal has not the right to entertain that suit. If you cannot point out some valid enactment, legislative or constitutional, which has taken away jurisdiction over that class of controversies, you must try the case in the Court in which it has been brought, unless you can demonstrate that judicial settlement of such issues as are raised by it is not consistent with the political system under which we live or the organization of our form of government.[8]

6. Amendment to Constitution of 1776, 1 Poore's Constitution and Charters, 830.

7. Constitution of 1776, Art. XL, XLVII.

8. Tomlinson's Lessee vs. DeVore, 1 Gill, 345.

As Courts of general jurisdiction, the presumption is that whatever they have done they have rightfully and legally done.

The origin and the limits of the jurisdiction of the Maryland Courts have been compared with those of the Federal tribunals because a concrete illustration may make clearer the abstract rule. The doctrine is one of general application and could be illustrated as well from the constitutions and statutes of any other State.

It was clearly stated by CHIEF JUSTICE TANEY in his opinion in an historic case. Speaking of the higher Courts of the several States, he said:—

> "Where they are what the law terms Courts of general jurisdiction, they are presumed to have jurisdiction unless the contrary appears. No averment in the pleadings of the plaintiff is necessary in order to give jurisdiction. If the defendant objects to it he must plead it specially, and unless the fact on which he relies is found to be true by a jury or admitted to be true by the plaintiff, the jurisdiction cannot be disputed in an Appellate Court."[9]

It follows that even on a direct appeal from one of the Superior Courts of a State, or upon a review of its proceedings upon writ of error, the appellant or plaintiff in error must affirmatively show upon the face of the record or by his bill of exceptions that error has been committed.

The presumption is that whatever jurisdiction was taken and whatever was done was properly taken and done, unless the contrary appears.[10]

7. Federal Courts of Limited Jurisdiction.

On the other hand, the Courts of the United States are Courts of *limited jurisdiction.*[11] If a case comes up from

9. Dred Scott vs. Sanford, 19 How. 401; 15 L. Ed. 691.
10. Schulze vs. State, 43 Md. 295.
11. Hanford vs. Davies, 163 U. S. 279; 41 L. Ed. 157; 16 Sup. Ct. 1051.

one of the State Courts of general jurisdiction to a higher Court of the State, the latter does not search the record for allegations sufficient to show the jurisdiction of the former. It assumes that there was jurisdiction unless one of the parties says that there was not, and shows from the record not that jurisdiction might not have existed, but that it did not. On the other hand, if a record comes up from a District Court of the United States to a United States Circuit Court of Appeals or to the Supreme Court, the appellate tribunal will of its own motion look through the record to find out whether from all facts therein set forth it clearly appears that the District Court had jurisdiction. If for anything shown by the record the Court below may or may not have had jurisdiction, the Appellate Court will proceed no further with the case, unless and until by appropriate amendment, sufficient jurisdictional allegations are introduced.

8. Record in Federal Courts Must Affirmatively Show Jurisdiction.

There are no presumptions in favor of the jurisdiction of Courts of the United States.[12] At a very early date in the history of the Government under the Constitution, the Bank of North America brought suit in a Circuit Court of the United States against one Turner as administrator of a certain Stanley upon a promissory note drawn by the deceased to the order of Biddle & Co., and by that firm endorsed over to the plaintiff. The declaration alleged that the plaintiff was a citizen of Pennsylvania; that Stanley and Turner were citizens of North Carolina. It said that Biddle & Co. used trade and merchandise in partnership together at Philadelphia or North Carolina. Under a statute the Circuit Court had no

12. Ex Parte Smith, 94 U. S. 456; 24 L. Ed. 165; Robertson vs. Cease, 97 U. S. 648; 24 L. Ed. 1057.

jurisdiction of a suit brought by an endorsee of a promissory note against the maker unless it would have had jurisdiction had the suit been brought by the original payee. In this case it will be noted that the citizenship of Biddle & Co., the original payees, was not alleged. The partners in that firm might, so far as anything appeared, have been citizens of any State or aliens. In the Court below there was a judgment for the plaintiff. In the Supreme Court this judgment was reversed. The Court, speaking through CHIEF JUSTICE ELLSWORTH, said:

"A Circuit Court * * * is of limited jurisdiction and has cognizance not of cases generally but only of a few specially circumstanced, amounting to a small proportion of the cases which an unlimited jurisdiction would embrace. And the fair presumption is (not as with regard to a Court of general jurisdiction, that a cause is within its jurisdiction unless the contrary appears, but rather) that a cause is without its jurisdiction until the contrary appears. This renders it necessary, inasmuch as the proceedings of no Court can be deemed valid further than its jurisdiction appears, or can be presumed, to set forth upon the record of a Circuit Court the facts or circumstances which give jurisdiction either expressly or in such manner as to render them certain by legal intendment."[13]

It is not necessary that the absence of the proper jurisdictional averments shall be set up by one of the parties. The Appellate Court will of its own motion notice the omission.

A bill in equity was filed in a United States Circuit Court. The caption of the bill was

"THOMAS JACKSON, a Citizen of the State of Virginia; WILLIAM GOODWIN JACKSON and MARIE CONGREVE

13. Turner vs. Bank of North America, 4 Dallas, 11; 1 L. Ed. 718.

JACKSON, Citizens of Virginia, Infants, by Their Father and Next Friend, the said THOMAS JACKSON,

vs.

The REV. WILLIAM ASHTON, a Citizen of the State of Pennsylvania.''

- ˙ In the body of the bill the Virginia citizenship of the plaintiffs was directly alleged. All that was said in that connection of the defendant was that he "was of the City of Philadelphia." The Court below passed upon the merits of the case and entered a decree in favor of the defendant. There was an appeal to the Supreme Court. The case was there set down for argument. The latter of its own motion called attention to the fact that the bill did not allege the citizenship of the defendant. The parties wished to have a decision of the Supreme Court upon the merits. They united in asking the Court to waive the point. CHIEF JUSTICE MARSHALL said:—

"The title or caption of the bill is no part of the bill and does not remove the objection to the defects in the pleadings. The bill and the proceedings should state the citizenship of the parties to give the Court jurisdiction of the case. The only difficulty which could arise to the dismissal of the bill presents itself upon the statement that the defendant is of Philadelphia. This, it might be answered, shows that he is a citizen of Pennsylvania. If this were a new question the Court might decide otherwise, but the decision of the Court in cases which have heretofore been before it has been expressed upon the point.''[14]

The general principle was fully discussed in the famous case which bulked so large in the constitutional and poli-

14. Jackson vs. Ashton, 8 Peters, 148; 8 L. Ed. 898.

(By the later practice and now by Statute, the plaintiff would, even in the Supreme Court, have been permitted to amend his bill by inserting the allegations that the reverend defendant was a citizen of Pennsylvania, as he doubtless was. Act March 5, 1915, 38 Stat. 956.) 5 Fed. Stat. Ann. 1059; U. S. Comp. Stat. Sec. 1251.

tical discussions of the years immediately preceding the Civil War.

Dred Scott, a negro, alleged that he was free. He said he was unlawfully held as a slave. He brought suit in a United States Circuit Court to recover his freedom. He asserted that he was a citizen of Missouri. By plea the defendant set up that the plaintiff was not a citizen and could not be, because he was of African and servile descent. The plaintiff demurred. The demurrer was sustained. The defendant pleaded over. In the Supreme Court the plaintiff claimed that the defense of no jurisdiction was no longer open to the defendant. By pleading over on the merits after his plea was held bad he had admitted jurisdiction. Under the then recognized rules such an admission once made could not be recalled. CHIEF JUSTICE TANEY said:—

"But in making this objection we think that the peculiar and limited jurisdiction of the Courts of the United States has not been adverted to. This peculiar and limited jurisdiction has made it necessary in these Courts to adopt different rules and principles of pleading so far as jurisdiction is concerned from those which regulate Courts of common law in England and in the different States of the Union which have adopted the common law rules. * * * Under the Constitution and laws of the United States the rules which govern the pleadings in its Courts in questions of jurisdiction stand on different principles and are regulated by different laws. This difference arises * * * from the peculiar character of the Government of the United States, for although it is sovereign and supreme in its appropriate sphere of action, yet it does not possess all the powers which usually belong to the sovereignty of a nation. Certain specified powers enumerated in the Constitution have been conferred upon it; and neither the legislative, executive nor judicial departments of the government can lawfully exercise any authority beyond the limits marked out by the Constitution. And in regulating the judicial department the cases in which the Courts of the United States shall have jurisdiction are particularly and specifically enumerated and defined; and they are not authorized to take cognizance of any case which does not come within the description therein specified. Hence, when a plaintiff sues in a Court of the United States it is necessary that he should show in his pleading that the suit he brings is within the jurisdiction of the Court and that he is entitled to sue there. And if he omits to do this and should by any oversight of the Circuit Court obtain a judgment in his favor, the judgment would be reversed in the Appellate Court for want of jurisdiction in the Court below. The jurisdiction would not be presumed, as in the case of a common law English or State Court unless the contrary appeared. But the record when it comes before the Appellate Court must show affirmatively that the inferior Court had authority under the Constitution to hear and determine the case. And if the plaintiff claims a right to sue in a Circuit Court of the United States under that provision of the Constitution which gives jurisdiction in controversies between citizens of different States, he must distinctly aver in his pleading that they are citizens of different States, and he cannot maintain his suit without showing this fact in his pleadings.'"[15]

The Court held that the plaintiff in this great case had shown that he was not a citizen of Missouri. He was a negro and had been a slave. In the view of the majority of the Court those facts were inconsistent with citizenship.

9. Duty of Every Federal Court to Make Sure it Has Jurisdiction.

It is the duty of every Court of the United States before which a case comes, whether originally or upon appeal or writ of error, to satisfy itself that upon the face

15. Dred Scott v. Sanford, 19 How. 401; 15 L. Ed. 691.

of the record facts appear giving it jurisdiction. If they do not the case may not be further proceeded with until the omission has been supplied.[16] So soon as the absence of any of the necessary jurisdictional averments is noticed the case must be stopped, it matters not how far it has gone,[17] provided final judgment or decree has not been entered up by the Court before which it is pending.

10. District Courts Not Inferior Courts in Common Law Sense.

The Constitution says that Congress may from time to time ordain and establish "inferior" Courts. It is under this grant of authority that all the Federal Courts, other than the Supreme Court, have been created.

The word "inferior" in connection with the word "Courts" has two meanings. At common law the word so used had a technical significance. An "inferior" Court was one whose judgments or decrees could not be set up even collaterally without showing affirmatively by the record the existence of all the circumstances necessary to give jurisdiction.

A Maryland case will illustrate this rule. A defendant in ejectment claimed under title originating in a sale under an execution issued on a magistrate's judgment. The law then required that such sales should be reported to the Superior Court and by it ratified. This was done. In the record of the magistrate, however, nothing appeared to show that the person against whom judgment had been given had ever been summoned. Even after final judgment no presumption could be made in support of the jurisdiction of such an inferior Court as that of a

16. Grace vs. American Central Ins. Co., 109 U. S. 283; 27 L. Ed. 932; 3 Sup. Ct. 207; Robertson vs. Cease, 97 U. S. 648; 24 L. Ed. 1057; Bors vs. Preston, 111 U. S. 255; 28 L. Ed. 419; 4 Sup. Ct. 407; M. C. & L. M. Ry. Co. vs. Swan, 111 U. S. 382; 28 L. Ed. 462; 4 Sup. Ct. 510.

17. Brown vs. Keene, 8 Peters, 112; 8 L. Ed. 885.

Justice of the Peace. The defendant in the ejectment case relied solely upon the execution sale. It was held that he had acquired no title thereby.[18]

It would be easy to multiply authorities on this point.[19]

More than a century ago the Supreme Court, speaking through the mouth of CHIEF JUSTICE ELLSWORTH, declared that the Circuit and District Courts of the United States were not inferior Courts in this common law sense. The word inferior as used in the Constitution has another meaning. It serves merely to mark their relation to the Supreme Court. Their proceedings are "not subject to the scrutiny of those narrow rules which the caution or jealousy of the Courts at Westminster long applied to Courts of that denomination, but are entitled to as liberal intendments, or presumptions in favor of their regularity as those of any Supreme Court."[20]

The Chief Justice did not mean that the same presumptions would be raised in favor of the jurisdiction of a Federal Court as in support of that of a superior Court of one of the States. Indeed the very case from which the quotation is made is an authority to the contrary. The judgment was reversed for failure of the record to disclose diversity of citizenship between the plaintiff and the defendant, a circumstance which would not have had to have been alleged had the proceeding been in a State tribunal.

11. Objection to the Absence of Jurisdictional Allegations Cannot be Made After the Judgment or Decree Itself Can No Longer Be Directly Attacked.

In the case last cited it was held that where on a direct appeal or writ of error the record does not affirmatively show that the Court of first instance had jurisdiction, the

18. Fahey vs. Mottu, 67 Md. 252; 10 Atl. 63.

19. Cooley Constitutional Limitations, p. 585, note 2; Argument of Stockton in Kempe vs. Kennedy, 5 Cranch, 179; 3 L. Ed. 70.

20. Turner vs. Bank of North America, 4 Dallas, 11; 1 L. Ed. 718.

appellate tribunal will order the case dismissed, and that is still the practice if the necessary allegations cannot be supplied by amendment. There, however, comes a time after which the binding force of the judgment or decree can no longer be assailed on the ground that the record does not affirmatively show jurisdiction.

If a suit proceeds to final judgment or decree, and the time in which an appeal can be taken or a writ of error sued out goes by without action, the judgment or decree is presumed to be valid and binding to the same extent as under like circumstances that of a State Court of analogous rank would be. If an appeal has been taken or a writ of error sued out, and the case has been heard and disposed of by the Appellate Court, and its mandate has been issued, it will thereafter be too late to raise an objection that the record does not affirmatively show the existence of jurisdiction.

A bill in equity had been filed in the United States Circuit Court for the District of Kentucky. The cause was prosecuted to final decree. An appeal was taken to the Supreme Court. The decree below was there reversed and the cause sent back with instructions to the Circuit Court to re-enter it in different terms. After the mandate had gone down the defeated party for the first time called attention to the fact that the record did not contain all the necessary jurisdictional averments. Their absence had not been noted theretofore. The Supreme Court held that it was then too late to make the point. Its mandate was final. The case could not be reopened.[21]

12. Validity of Judgment Cannot be Collaterally Attacked Because of Absence of Jurisdictional Allegations.

From the principle stated in the last paragraph, it logically follows that the regularity and binding force of

21. Skillern's Executors vs. May's Executors, 6 Cranch, 266; 3 L. Ed. 215.

a judgment or decree of a United States District Court cannot be collaterally attacked because the record of the cause does not on its face show that the Court had jurisdiction. The fact that the District Court has taken jurisdiction raises under the conditions stated a presumption that it acted rightfully in so doing.

A bill in equity was filed praying discovery and a decree for the conveyance of certain lands. The answer alleged that a similar bill had been filed in the United States Court for the District of Ohio, that a decree had there been made in favor of the defendant and the bill dismissed. The complainant objected that the decree of the United States Court was not binding because the record of the proceedings in that Court did not contain the necessary allegations of diverse citizenship. The Supreme Court, however, said:—

> "The reason assigned by the replication why that decree cannot operate as a bar is that the proceedings in that suit do not show that the parties to it, plaintiffs and defendants, were citizens of different States and that consequently the suit was *coram non judice* and the decree void. But this reason proceeds upon an incorrect view of the character and jurisdiction of the inferior Courts of the United States. They are all of limited jurisdiction; but they are not, on that account, inferior Courts in the technical sense of those words, whose judgments taken alone are to be disregarded. If the jurisdiction be not alleged in the proceedings their judgments and decrees are erroneous, and may upon writ of error or appeal be reversed for that cause. But they are not absolute nullities. * * * We are, therefore, of opinion that the decree of dismissal relied upon in this case, whilst it remains unreversed is a valid bar of the present suit as to the above defendants."[22]

22. McCormick vs. Sullivant, 10 Wheat. 199; 6 L. Ed. 300; see also Evers vs. Watson, 156 U. S. 533; 39 L. Ed. 520; 15 Sup. Ct. 430.

Under the present bankrupt law a petition was filed against a corporation asking that it be adjudged an involuntary bankrupt. It came in and consented. Adjudication followed. None of its creditors objected. A holder of much of its stock was indebted to a third person, who thought that the adjudication of the corporation injured him by lessening the value of the stock belonging to his debtor. He came into the Court of Bankruptcy, asserting that the decree of adjudication was void and should be set aside. He pointed out that the creditors' petition by which the proceedings were begun did not contain the necessary jurisdictional averments. The Court answered that he was not a person interested within the meaning of the bankrupt law, and consequently could not be a party to the bankruptcy proceedings. None but a party can attack a decree, passed by a Court of limited but not of inferior jurisdiction.[23]

13. A Federal Court Can Entertain No Suit Except By Authority of an Express Written Enactment.

The fact that a presumption in favor of the regularity of the proceedings of a Federal Court may be sufficient to sustain its judgments or decrees against collateral attack, is in no sense a limitation upon or an exception to the general rule that no Court of the United States may exercise any jurisdiction not given to it by the Constitution or some statute. Every one who brings any suit in such a Court should first examine the written enactment which gives to it jurisdiction over that particular kind of controversy.

---

23. In re Columbia Real Estate Co., 101 Fed. 970; Cutler vs. Huston, 158 U. S. 430; 39 L. Ed. 1040; 15 Sup. Ct. 868.

14. No Federal Court Can Exercise Any Jurisdiction Not Given to the United States by the Second Section of the Third Article of the Constitution.

The second great principle to which the students' attention should be directed is that no Federal Court has, or by possibility can have, any jurisdiction over any case unless it is one included within the grant of judicial power made by the second section of the Third Article of the Constitution of the United States. That section declares that

> "Judicial power shall extend to all cases in law and equity arising under this Constitution, the laws of the United States and the treaties made, or which shall be made, under their authority; to all cases affecting ambassadors and other public ministers and consuls; to all cases of admiralty and maritime jurisdiction; to controversies to which the United States shall be a party; to controversies between two or more States; between a State and citizens of another State; between citizens of different States; between citizens of the same State claiming lands under grants of different States, and between a State or the citizens thereof and foreign States, citizens or subjects."

In an early case coming up to the Supreme Court from a Circuit Court of the United States the defendants were described in the record as "late of the District of Maryland, merchants." Nothing else was said as to their citizenship. The plaintiffs were alleged to be aliens and subjects of the King of the United Kingdom of Great Britain and Ireland. Luther Martin, who appeared above for the defendants, contended that the Court below had no jurisdiction. It was nowhere alleged that the defendants were citizens of any State. Lee, who represented the plaintiffs, pointed out that the judiciary act expressly gave jurisdiction to the Circuit Court of all suits to which an alien was a party. CHIEF JUSTICE

MARSHALL said: "Turn to the article of the Constitution of the United States, for the statute cannot extend the jurisdiction beyond the limits of the Constitution." The words of the Constitution where aliens are concerned give jurisdiction only when the suit is between them on the one hand and citizens of a State on the other. The omission from the record of the important allegation was a clerical oversight. It was by consent supplied by amendment.[24]

15. Neither Congress Nor Consent of Parties Can Extend Jurisdiction of Federal Courts Beyond Constitutional Grant.

If Brown and Jones are citizens of the same State, they cannot have a controversy between them tried in the Federal Courts unless their dispute arises under the Constitution, the law or treaties of the United States, or is a matter of admiralty and maritime jurisdiction, or relates to the title of land which they each claim under grants from different States. They could not try out their quarrel in those Courts even if an express statute of Congress said they might. The statute would itself be void as attempting to extend the jurisdiction of the Federal Courts beyond the limits of the judicial power given to the United States by the Constitution.

16. Federal Courts Careful to Exercise No Jurisdiction Not Clearly Theirs.

From the beginning the Federal Courts have been careful to confine their activities within the very letter of the constitutional grant. They have never attempted to extend their jurisdiction by indirection. They have, with one exception to be fully discussed in a later chapter,

24. Hodgson vs. Bowerbank, 5 Cranch, 303; 3 L. Ed. 308.

never resorted to legal fictions to get over, under or around the barriers erected by the Constitution.

In many countries at some periods in the development of their legal procedure, every Court struggled to extend its own jurisdiction and to limit that of all competing tribunals. To accomplish those ends resort was had to the most barefaced fictions. The Court of Exchequer was a Court which had jurisdiction over matters affecting the royal revenues, and over them alone. It became a Court of concurrent jurisdiction with the Court of Common Pleas by the simple expedient of allowing the plaintiff to say that he was a debtor to the King. It followed that the King's revenue was concerned in his securing his rights against the defendant, for if the defendant was forced to pay the plaintiff, the plaintiff would be the better able to pay the King. The Court forbade the defendant to deny that the plaintiff in truth owed the King anything or ever intended to pay His Majesty a farthing.

The Court of King's Bench in like manner permitted a plaintiff to allege that the defendant was in the custody of its marshal, and was therefore suable only before it. This statement was almost always untrue, but the Court would never let the defendants dispute it. The Federal Courts, on the other hand, from the beginning of the Government have been inclined to limit rather than to extend their jurisdiction. .

17. Congress Always Anxious to Restrict Jurisdiction of Federal Courts.

Congress itself has been very unwilling to extend the jurisdiction of the United States Courts. That which they now exercise or have ever exercised is but a very small part of that which Congress might constitutionally confer upon them if it was so minded. It never has been. Quite naturally, therefore, Congress has seldom attempted to give those Courts any jurisdiction which it had no constitutional right to bestow upon them.

18. Congress Cannot Extend Jurisdiction of Federal Courts Beyond Constitutional Grant.

Nevertheless, some acts have been passed which purported to give the Federal Courts jurisdiction not included within the judicial power conferred on the United States by the Constitution.[25] Usually when this has been done, it has been due either to careless draftsmanship or to a more or less confused or muddled understanding of some of the provisions of the Constitution itself. Very seldom have the members of the Federal Legislature had any deliberate intention unduly to enlarge the jurisdiction of the Courts of the United States.

The language of the original Judiciary Act by which the Courts were given jurisdiction over all suits to which an alien was a party was a case in which the statute literally interpreted went farther than the Constitution authorized.[26]

19. Congress May Not Enlarge the Original Jurisdiction Which the Constitution Gives the Supreme Court.

The Constitution says that "in all cases affecting Ambassadors, other public Ministers and consuls, and in those in which a State shall be a party, the Supreme Court shall have original jurisdiction. In all other cases," to which the judicial power of the United States shall extend, "the Supreme Court shall have appellate jurisdiction both as to law and fact, with such exceptions and under such regulations as the Congress shall make."

By Section 13 of the original Judiciary Act, the Supreme Court was authorized to issue writs of mandamus "in cases warranted by the principles and usages

25. Trade Mark Cases, 100 U. S. 82; 25 L. Ed. 550.
26. Hodgson vs. Bowerbank, 5 Cranch. 303; 3 L. Ed. 308.

of law * * *   to persons holding office under the authority of the United States.'' Every case, in which such writ could properly be granted, would necessarily arise under the constitution, laws or treaties of the United States, and the right of Congress to empower some Federal Court to issue it is not open to question. But can the Supreme Court be authorized to entertain an application for it in an original proceeding to which a State is not a party, and by which no diplomatic or consular official is affected?

The question was first considered when Mr. Marbury and three other gentlemen asked the Supreme Court to command James Madison, Secretary of State, to give them their commissions as Justices of the Peace for the District of Columbia. President Adams had appointed them, the Senate advising and consenting thereto. Their commissions had been made out and signed by Adams, who gave them to John Marshall, then Secretary of State as well as Chief Justice, to be handed to them. Before delivery was actually made, Adams went out, and Madison replaced Marshall as Secretary of State. Perhaps because the appointees were Federalists, Madison refused to let them have their commissions. The Court, speaking through CHIEF JUSTICE MARSHALL, held that it was Madison's clear ministerial duty to deliver the commissions, and that by the principles and usages of law, a mandamus should issue to compel him to do so, if there was any Court validly vested with jurisdiction to grant it. It was clear that Congress had said that the Supreme Court might do so, but in so saying, the Court held that the Federal Legislature had attempted to extend its original jurisdiction beyond the limits fixed by the constitution, and to that extent, the statute was of none effect.[27]

---

27. Marbury vs. Madison, 1 Cranch, 137; 2 L. Ed. 60.

Marshall's latest biographer believes that he seized the opportunity given by the wording of the constitution on this relatively minor matter of the distribution of original jurisdiction among the various Federal Courts, to lay down the far reaching principle that it was the duty of the judiciary to strike down legislation not in its view sanctioned by the constitution, and to announce that doctrine, under such conditions that it could not be effectively challenged until the lapse of time had buttressed it against successful attack.[28] It is scarcely true, however, that in the opinion then delivered, the Court reversed or overruled any of its earlier decisions. The cases[29] which Mr. Beveridge cites as showing that the Court had previously recognized the constitutionality of the provision it then declared void, were applications for writs of mandamus or prohibition to judges of inferior Federal Courts. Such proceedings were then and are now recognized as an exercise of the appellate jurisdiction of the Supreme Court. The holding in Marbury vs. Madison that the limits of its original jurisdiction are fixed by the constitution is in harmony with the more natural construction of the words used by its framers and has ever since been accepted as law.[30]

20. Constitutional Grant of Original Jurisdiction to the Supreme Court Is Not Exclusive.

Congress may not add to the original jurisdiction of the Supreme Court as defined in the Constitution. Is the

28. 3 Beveridge's Marshall, 131.

29. U. S. vs. Lawrence, 3 Dallas, 42; 1 L. Ed. 502; U. S. vs. Peters, 3 Dallas, 121; 1 L. Ed. 535.

30. U. S. vs. Ferreira, 13 Howard, 40-53; 14 L. Ed. 42; California vs. Southern Pacific Co., 157 U. S. 229-261; 39 L. Ed. 683; 15 Sup. Ct. 591; B. & O. vs. Interstate Commerce Com., 215 U. S. 216-224; 54 L. Ed. 164; 30 Sup. Ct. 86; Mushrat vs. U. S., 219 U. S. 346-355; 55 L. Ed. 250; 31 Sup. Ct. 250; dissenting opinion of Mr. Justice Curtis in Florida vs. Georgia, 17 Howard, 478-505; 15 L. Ed. 181.

converse true? May Congress confer any of that jurisdiction on other Federal Courts? In several of the great
opinions of CHIEF JUSTICE MARSHALL, the power to do so
was denied.[31] In none of them was the question directly
involved. Whenever it has been, the Supreme Court has
held that the constitutional grant to it of original jurisdiction is not exclusive.

As early as 1793 the Genoese consul at Philadelphia
was indicted in the United States Circuit Court for the
District of Pennsylvania for sending a threatening letter
to the British Minister. Quite clearly within the constitutional, as within every other sense, he was affected by
the prosecution. He contended that the Supreme Court
was the only tribunal in which it could be lawfully instituted. The Circuit Court, presided over by JUSTICE
CHASE, ruled against him.[32]

The first two sentences of Section 13 of the original
Judiciary Act[33] now form, almost without change of
verbiage, section 233 of the Judicial Code,[34] which reads:

"The Supreme Court shall have exclusive jurisdiction of all controversies of a civil nature where a
State is a party, except between a State and its
citizens, or between a State and citizens of other
States, or aliens, in which latter cases it shall have
original but not exclusive jurisdiction. And it shall
have exclusively all such jurisdiction of suits or proceedings against ambassadors or other public
ministers, or their domestics or domestic servants,
as a Court of law can have consistently with the law
of nations; and original, but not exclusive, jurisdic-

31. Marbury vs. Madison, 1 Cranch, 137; 2 L. Ed. 60; Osborn vs. U. S.
Bank, 9 Wheat. 820; 6 L. Ed. 204.

32. U. S. vs. Ravara, 2 Dallas, 297; 1 L. Ed. 388.

33. Act Sept. 24, 1789; 1 Stat. 73; 5 Fed. Stat. Ann. 709; U. S. Comp.
Stat., Sec. 1210.

34. Act March 3, 1911, in force Jan. 1, 1912; 36 Stat. 1156; 5 Fed. Stat.
Ann. 708; U. S. Comp. Stat., Sec. 1210; U. S. vs. Louisiana, 123 U. S. 32;
31 L. Ed. 69; 8 Sup. Ct. 17.

tion of all suits brought by ambassadors or other public ministers, or in which a consul or vice-consul is a party."

In terms it gives other Federal Courts concurrent jurisdiction over some classes of cases of which the Constitution says the Supreme Court shall have original jurisdiction. In 1883 it was expressly decided that such legislation was constitutional. Suits against foreign consuls could be instituted in the District Courts.[35]

The Supreme Court has repeatedly held that its original jurisdiction over suits in which a State is a party is not necessarily exclusive of any which Congress may see fit to confer upon other Federal tribunals.[36]

The construction of the Constitutional grant of original jurisdiction to the Supreme Court is therefore now settled. Congress may not add to it. Other Courts may be permitted to share it.

Practical considerations have had much to do with giving to this clause of the Constitution the construction which it has received. It is not well that the Supreme Court shall be made a tribunal of first instance in any cases other than those expressly mentioned in the Constitution. It may be convenient that many of them shall be first instituted elsewhere.

As CHIEF JUSTICE TANEY pointed out in a case he heard on circuit, it hardly could have been the intention of the statesmen who framed our Constitution to require that one of our citizens, who had a claim of even less than five dollars against another citizen, clothed by some foreign government with the consular office, should be compelled to go into the Supreme Court to have a jury summoned in order to enable him to recover it; nor could it have been intended that the time of that Court, with all its

35. Bors vs. Preston. 111 U. S. 252; 28 L. Ed. 419; 4 Sup. Ct. 407.
36. Ames vs. Kansas. 111 U. S. 449; 28 L. Ed. 482; 4 Sup. Ct. 437.

high duties, should be taken up with the trial of every petty offense that might be committed by a consul in any part of the United States, that consul, too, being often one of our own citizens.[37]

21. The First Three Rules Limiting Jurisdiction of Federal Courts.

Thus far three general rules have been stated and illustrated:

1. That the Courts of the United States have no jurisdiction except that given them by the Constitution or by statutes passed under the Constitution.

2. That no statute can extend the jurisdiction of any one of these Courts beyond the limits of the grant of judicial power made in the Constitution.

3. That the original jurisdiction of the Supreme Court is fixed by the Constitution itself and cannot be extended by Congress, although it may be shared by other tribunals, State or Federal.

22. Except as to Original Jurisdiction of Supreme Court, the Jurisdiction of Every Federal Court is Statutory.

The fourth great rule is that no Court of the United States, except the Supreme Court, can claim any jurisdiction unless it can point to the particular Act of Congress conferring such jurisdiction upon it.[38] This rule is of great practical importance. The jurisdiction which Congress has in fact given to the Federal Courts is but a very small fraction of that which Congress might grant if it would.

---

37. Gittings vs. Crawford, 10 Fed. Cases, 447.
38. Sheldon vs. Sill, 8 Howard, 448; 12 L. Ed. 1147.

23. The Constitutional Grant of Judicial Power is Not Self Executing.

Is the grant of judicial power in the Constitution self executing?

In the case of Turner vs. Bank of North America, the suit was between a citizen of Pennsylvania and a citizen of North Carolina. The Constitution declares that the judicial power shall extend to controversies between citizens of different States. The parties to the case actually instituted were citizens of different States. Congress had, however, said that no suit might be brought in the Federal Courts by an assignee of a chose in action unless such suit could have been brought in those Courts had no assignment been made. Could Congress lawfully say that no Court of the United States should exercise jurisdiction over a class of cases clearly within the constitutional grant of judicial power? JUSTICE CHASE in 1799 answered:—

> "The notion has frequently been entertained that the Federal Courts derive their judicial power immediately from the Constitution, but the political truth is that the disposal of the judicial power (except in a few specified instances) belongs to Congress. If Congress has given the power to this Court we possess it, not otherwise; and if Congress has not given the power to us or to any other Court, it still remains at the legislative disposal. * * * Congress is not bound, and it would perhaps be inexpedient to enlarge the jurisdiction of the Federal Courts to every subject in every form which the Constitution might warrant."[39]

A half century later the point was elaborately discussed. It arose in the same way as in the earlier case.

39. Turner vs. Bank of North America, 4 Dallas, 10; 1 L. Ed. 718; Symonds vs. St. Louis & S. E. Ry. Co., 192 Fed. 353.

The suit was to recover upon a chose in action. The plaintiff acquired it by assignment. He and the defendant were citizens of different States. The original holder of the chose in action was a citizen of the same State as the defendant. If the statute already referred to was a valid exercise of congressional power, the suit could not be maintained, for the case could not have been brought in the Federal Court had no assignment been made. If it was invalid as limiting a jurisdiction given by the Constitution, the suit was properly instituted. The Supreme Court said:—

"It has been alleged that this restriction of the judiciary act * * * is in conflict with * * * the Constitution and therefore void. It must be admitted that if the Constitution had ordained and established the inferior Courts and distributed to them their respective powers, they could not be restricted or divested by Congress. But as it has made no such distribution, one of two consequences must result— either that each inferior Court created by Congress must exercise all the judicial powers not given to the Supreme Court, or that Congress having the power to establish the Courts must define their respective jurisdictions. The first of these inferences has never been asserted and could not be defended with any show of reason, and if not, the latter would seem to follow as a necessary consequence. And it would seem to follow also that having a right to prescribe, Congress may withhold from any Court of its creation jurisdiction of any of the enumerated controversies. Courts created by statute can have no jurisdiction but such as the statute confers. No one of them can assert a just claim to jurisdiction exclusively conferred on another or withheld from all. The Constitution has defined the limits of the judicial power of the United States, but has not prescribed how much of it shall be exercised by the Circuit Courts; consequently the statute which does prescribe the limits of their jurisdiction cannot be in conflict with the Constitution, unless it confers powers not enumerated therein.''[40]

24. Congress Has Never Provided for the Exercise of More Than a Part of the Judicial Power Given by the Constitution.

The political history of the United States under the Constitution is often summed up as a struggle between those who believe in a strict, and those who favor a liberal, construction of the powers granted the Federal Government by the Constitution. So stated and taken with the limitations, qualifications and exceptions to which all such general and easy summaries of history must always be subject, it was, until about 1913, roughly accurate. Sometimes, however, it was said that the contest was between those who wanted a strong and centralized government and those who did not. That never was true. No better proof of its falsity need be given than to tell the story of the way in which Congress has dealt with the jurisdiction of the Federal Courts.

The Federal Government has been for long periods under the control of political parties which did not make strict construction a part of their creed. Nevertheless, there probably never has been an extension of Federal jurisdiction for the mere purpose of extending it. There has always been a real or supposed reason for any enlargement of it which has been made. Usually when the supposed reason has proved to be a bad reason or no reason at all, or has been found no longer to exist, the jurisdiction once given has been withdrawn. National banks are created under the authority of an Act of Congress. As early as 1824 the Supreme Court held[41] that a controversy to which a corporation holding a Federal

40. Sheldon vs. Sill, 8 How. 448; 12 L. Ed. 1147.
41. Osborne vs. U. S. Bank, 9 Wheat. 738; 6 L. Ed. 204.

charter is a party, arises under an Act of Congress.
Jurisdiction over such controversies may therefore be
lawfully given to the Federal Courts. Our present national banking system dates from the period of the Civil
War. It was a time when political feeling ran high. The
banks were new institutions. There was much hostility
to them. In certain portions of the country there was
reason to fear that they would get scant justice from
State Court juries. The Act of June 3, 1864, gave to the
Federal Courts jurisdiction over all suits to which a national bank was a party. By 1887 national banks were
familiar things. Serious hostility on the part of any
great number of people had everywhere died out. Congress then provided that national banks should, so far as
actions by or against them are concerned, be regarded as
citizens of the State in which they are respectively located; and that the Federal Courts shall not have jurisdiction over suits by or against them unless such Courts
would have it had the national bank been in fact a citizen
of the State in which it was located.

Congress could provide that every controversy between
citizens of different States should be tried in the United
States Courts. Actually it has always left concurrent
jurisdiction over all such cases to the State Courts. It
might declare that no matter how trifling may be the
amount in dispute between the citizens of different
States, the case might at the will of either of them be
taken into the Federal Courts. In the original Judiciary
Act, it said that no such case in which the amount in
controversy did not exceed $500, exclusive of interest and
costs, should be within their jurisdiction. In 1875, $2,000
was substituted for $500, and since the first of January,
1912, $3,000 has taken the place of $2,000.

25. Unnecessary Extension of Jurisdiction of Federal Courts Undesirable.

The unwillingness to extend, the wish to restrict the jurisdiction of the Federal Courts, is natural. Litigation in them is usually more expensive than in the State tribunals. To many suitors it is more inconvenient. It consumes more of their time and is in that way more burdensome. It costs more and is more inconvenient because the Federal Courts never sit at more than a relatively few places in a State. There are State Courts in every county. The lawyers living at the county towns at which the Federal Courts do not hold sessions are reluctant to see the jurisdiction of those Courts extended. Since 1787 local prejudice or local patriotism has greatly diminished. There would not now perhaps be any very fierce and unreasoning objection to the transfer of much litigation from the State to the Federal Courts. But just because there is nothing like so much State jealousy there is far less reason than there was a hundred and thirty years ago to take from the State Courts the disposition of cases with which they can more cheaply and conveniently deal.

If a New York suitor feels that in a Maryland State Court he may meet a Maryland adversary on equal terms, he will care little whether he may or may not bring his case into a Federal Court.

26. Federal Courts Have No Common Law Criminal Jurisdiction.

As the inferior Federal Courts have no jurisdiction except that expressly given them by statute, they cannot punish as a crime anything which is not made an offense by an act of Congress. In Maryland, as in a number of other States, men are frequently sentenced for acts which are not forbidden by any statute, but which were crimes at common law. In the years immediately following the adoption of the Constitution, there were those who thought that the Federal Courts might exercise a like jurisdiction. A common law offense had been committed; its effect and perhaps its purpose might have been to obstruct the operations of the Federal Government. Could not the doer be prosecuted in the Federal Courts? One who similarly transgressed against the peace and dignity of a State could be held to answer for his misdeed in the tribunals of the latter.

Libel is a common law misdemeanor punishable by fine and imprisonment. It has never been forbidden by any Act of Congress.

The Connecticut Current was a Federalist paper. On May 7, 1806, it said that the President and Congress had in secret voted a present of $2,000,000 to Napoleon Bonaparte for permission to make a treaty with Spain. The Federal Grand Jury indicted the proprietors for libel. The defendants demurred. · The judges of the trial Court were divided in opinion. They asked the instructions of the Supreme Court. It said:—

> "the only question which this case presents is whether the Circuit Courts of the United States can exercise a common law jurisdiction in criminal cases. We state it thus broadly because a decision on a case of libel will apply to every case in which jurisdiction is not vested in those Courts by statute. * * * Of all the Courts which the United States may under their general powers constitute, one only, the Supreme Court, possesses jurisdiction derived immediately from the Constitution, and of which the legislative power cannot deprive it. All other Courts created by the general Government possess no jurisdiction but what is given them by the power that creates them * * *. The only ground on which it has ever been contended that this jurisdiction could

be maintained, is that upon the formation of any political body an implied power to preserve its own existence and promote the end and object of its creation necessarily results to it. * * * If admitted as applicable to the state of things in this country, the consequence would not result from it which is here contended for. If it may communicate certain implied powers to the general Government it would not follow that the Courts of that Government are vested with jurisdiction over any particular act done by an individual in supposed violation of the peace and dignity of the sovereign power. The legislative authority of the Union must first make an act a crime, affix a punishment to it and declare the Court that shall have jurisdiction of the offense.''[42]

The doctrine then laid down has never been since seriously questioned, although, as recited in the next succeeding section, there has been at least one attempt to limit its application.

27. Independent of Statute, Federal Courts Have No Criminal Jurisdiction Over Offenses Punishable in Admiralty.

In 1847 in the United States Court for the District of Massachusetts, an indictment was returned against the New Bedford Bridge Co. charging it with obstructing the navigation of the Acushnet River. Congress had not then passed any act forbidding the obstruction of navigable waters and providing for the punishment of one who in that respect transgressed. It has since done so. In the case in question it was claimed that an obstruction to navigation was by the general law of the admiralty a nuisance, criminally punishable. It was argued that admiralty jurisdiction had been given to the United States and that it extended to punishment of crimes and offenses committed upon navigable waters.

42. U. S. vs. Hudson & Goodwin, 7 Cranch, 32; 3 L. Ed. 259.

Mr. Justice Woodbury, who, on circuit, sat in the case, answered that while Congress might constitutionally provide penalties for offenses of that character, it had not done so. Until it did, the Federal Courts could not require anyone to answer for them.[43]

28. Federal Courts Have Some Implied Power to Punish.

The Judicial, as well as the Legislative and Executive Departments have implied powers, although the occasion for their exercise by the first named is of comparatively minor importance. The Supreme Court has said "Certain implied powers must necessarily result to our Courts of justice from the nature of their institution * * *. To fine for contempt, imprison for contumacy, enforce the observance of order, etc., are powers which cannot be dispensed with in a Court, because they are necessary to the exercise of all others and so far our Courts no doubt possess powers not immediately derived from the statute."[44]

There has been little call to act upon this statement of the law, for Section 17 of the original Judiciary Act in so many words gave the Courts of the United States power to punish by fine or imprisonment, at their discretion, all contempts of their authority in any case or proceeding before them.[45] For ninety years, Congress has assumed that it had the right to limit and regulate the exercise by the Courts of their power to deal with contempts.[46] As all the inferior Federal Courts are the

43. U. S. vs. New Bedford Bridge Co., 27 Fed. Cases, 91 (No. 15867); 1 W. & M. 401.

44. U. S. vs. Hudson, 7 Cranch, 32; 3 L. Ed. 259.

45. 1 Stat. 83; 5 Fed. Stat. Ann. 1009; U. S. Comp. Stat., Sec. 1245a.

46. 4 Stat. 487; 5 Fed. Stat. Ann. 1009; U. S. Comp. Stat., Sec. 1245a; J. C. Sec. 268; 38 Stat. 730; 5 Fed. Stat. Ann. 1009; U. S. Comp. Stat., Sec. 1245a.

creatures of Congress, the latter has the right to restrict their jurisdiction over contempts as well as over other matters, provided it leaves them still able to function as Courts. The constitution itself provides for a Supreme Court, and by so doing, may be held to have given to it all the authority necessarily inherent in a Court. The question of whether Congress may impose limitations upon its right to deal with contempts has been mooted but never decided.[47]

29. What Constitutes Contempt.

Some forty years after the enactment of the Judiciary Act, United States District Judge Peck sent a lawyer to jail for sharp and contemptuous criticism of his conduct in a case which had terminated before the comment was made. This proceeding aroused widespread feeling, and resulted in the House of Representatives exhibiting to the Senate formal articles of impeachment. As there had been precedents which, if sound, sustained his action, and as there was no conclusive evidence that he was actuated by malicious or other improper motives, he was acquitted. It was nevertheless felt that the recurrence of such an incident should be guarded against by making it clear that in a land of free speech and of a free press, judges, like other public officials, were subject to adverse comment when interference with the due administration of justice in a pending case could not result therefrom. In consequence Congress enacted a law,[48] drawn by the then Senator, afterwards, President Buchanan, incorporating part of a statute which for a number of years had been in force in his State of Pennsylvania. It now forms Section 268 of the Judicial Code and declares that the power

47. Ex Parte Robinson, 19 Wallace, 505; 22 L. Ed. 205; U. S. vs. Shipp, 203 U. S. 563; 51 L. Ed. 323; 27 Sup. Ct. 165; 8 Ann. Cas. 265.

48. 4 Stat. 487; 5 Fed. Stat. Ann. 1009; U. S. Comp. Stat., Sec. 1245a.

to punish for contempts shall not be construed to extend to any cases except (1) misbehavior of any person in the presence of the Court or so near thereto as to obstruct the administration of justice; (2) misbehavior of any officer of the Court in his official transactions; (3) disobedience or resistance by such an officer or by any party, juror, witness or other person, to any lawful writ, process, order, rule or decree of the Court. The act in question was after all probably nothing more than a re-enactment in plain and concise terms of what the better considered cases had always held to be law,[49] although ill advised judges had sometimes gone farther. It has been many times construed.

Within its meaning, the court, when in session, is held to be present in every part of the place set apart for its own use or that of its officers, jurors or witnesses, so that an attempt to bribe a witness in a hallway or room adjoining the Court is a contempt committed in the presence of the Court.[50]

Any act or conduct which, in a material degree, is calculated to make difficult the right determination of a pending case may be held to have been committed so near the presence of the Court as to obstruct the administration of justice by it. Thus it was held that a punishable contempt had been committed when, during a fare controversy between a municipality and a trolley car company, the Court had under consideration an application for an injunction, and a newspaper publisher persistently attacked and ridiculed the judge before whom the case was tried in such manner as to suggest that the purpose was either to intimidate him or to stir up forcible resistance

49. Toledo Newspaper Co. vs. U. S., 247 U. S. 402; 62 L. Ed. 1186; 38 Sup. Ct. 560.

50. Savin, Petitioner, 131 U. S. 267; 33 L. Ed. 150; 9 Sup. Ct. 699.

to any order he might make.[51] Nevertheless except under peculiar conditions and in exceptional circumstances, it will be the part of wisdom to leave such attacks to the judgment of public opinion rather than to seek to repress or punish them by fine or imprisonment.

30. Federal Courts Have Implied Power to Make Rules.

In addition to preserving order, compelling obedience and punishing for contempt, the Courts of the United States have other implied powers. Of necessity they have the right to make rules and regulations for the conduct of proceedings before them.

"Such a jurisdiction is essential to, and is inherent in, the organization of Courts of justice."[52]

31. Meaning of Statement That Federal Courts Have No Common Law Jurisdiction.

It is sometimes said the Federal Courts have no common law jurisdiction. This is true in the sense which has already been explained. The Federal Courts have only that jurisdiction which has been given them and to the extent to which it has been conferred. The statement that they have no common law criminal jurisdiction is absolutely accurate. Like other Courts, they can punish only offenses against the sovereignty by whom they are created. That sovereign cannot be offended against in any other way than by breaking the laws made by its legislature, to wit, Congress. Whether breaches of common law rules are in any particular State punishable crimes, is a matter which concerns the State and its Courts. It is no affair of the Federal tribunals.

51. Toledo Newspaper Co. vs. U. S., 247 U. S. 402; 62 L. Ed. 1186; 38 Sup. Ct. 560.
52. Elberly et al. vs. Moore. 24 How. 158; 16 L. Ed. 612.

32. Federal Courts May Have Jurisdiction in Civil Cases to Give Common Law Relief.

None of the Federal Courts, other than the Supreme Court, has any jurisdiction not expressly given it by some Act of Congress. No one of them can say, this controversy is one over which the Court of King's Bench always had jurisdiction, therefore we have it. In this sense the Federal Courts have no common law civil jurisdiction. Nevertheless, in civil cases it may be their duty to apply and in a sense to enforce State laws, written and unwritten.

The Constitution declares that the judicial power of the United States shall extend "to controversies between citizens of different States; and to controversies between a State or the citizens thereof and foreign States, citizens and subjects."

The citizenship of the parties and not the nature of the controversy gives it jurisdiction. If the dispute may be fought out in the State Courts and arises between the persons described in the Constitution, Congress may give the Federal Courts jurisdiction over it. In many of the States, Maryland being one, most of the suits at law are common law actions. They are in assumpsit or in debt, in trespass or in case, in trover or in replevin. The rights of parties to them are still largely governed by common law principles, more or less modified by statute. Congress has given to its Courts jurisdiction over civil suits between citizens of different States or between citizens of a State and foreign States, citizens or subjects when the amount in controversy exceeds a fixed sum. Such a controversy may and often does take the form of a common law action. The law applied by the Federal Court to its determination may be the common law. If the common law has been changed by the statutes of the

State whose law governs the transaction, the Federal Court will apply it as it has been so modified.

In the sense above stated, therefore, the Federal Courts have and daily exercise a common law civil jurisdiction.

Whenever a citizen of one State has upon a citizen of another State what is in the State Courts an actionable demand, whether made so by statute or because it was so at common law, he may seek redress in the Federal Courts, provided the amount in controversy is sufficiently large.[53]

33. There is a Federal Common Law on Some Subjects.

The common law is always in the making. Decisions add new rules and change old. This process is in operation in every State in which the common law itself exists. All Courts cannot see everything in quite the same light; consequently the common law is no longer the same in all the States; in none of them, perhaps, is it precisely what the common law of England now is. In determining what is the applicable common law, the Federal Courts on many subjects will follow the decisions of the highest Court of that State to whose law the particular transaction under consideration is subject. The same Court of the United States may, on Monday, hold that the common law requires a particular case to be decided in one way, and, on Tuesday, that another controversy in which the facts are legally identical shall be determined in another; there may be no other difference than that Monday's suit is governed by Maryland law and Tuesday's by that of Virginia.

There are, however, some classes of questions upon which the Federal Courts will take their own view as to what the common law is, irrespective of any decisions of

53. State of Pennsylvania vs. Wheeling Bridge Co., 13 How. 563; 14 L. Ed. 249.

the State Courts. On such matters, the Supreme Court has the last word. Through its deliverances, the rulings of the Federal Courts are kept uniform throughout the country. So far as concerns the subjects upon which the Courts of the United States do not feel bound to follow the State Courts, there has in this way been built up something which may not inaptly be called Federal common law.

Further discussion of this interesting and important topic is postponed to a later chapter.

34. Common Law Definitions Are Accepted by the Federal Courts.

The Federal Courts habitually look to the common law for definition of the words used by Congress and by the legislatures of the various States.[54]

If Congress says that larceny or embezzlement from the United States, or from anyone, within a place under the exclusive jurisdiction of the United States, shall be punished, the Courts turn to the common law to find out what the crimes of larceny and embezzlement are.[55] Persons accused of crime, and parties to civil actions at law where the amount involved is twenty dollars or upwards, are entitled to trial by jury.[56] In determining what a trial by jury is,[57] and what the respective provinces of Court and jury are, the common law governs.[58]

Some of these qualifications of the two rules—first, that the Federal Courts have no common law jurisdiction, and, second, that there is no Federal common law—are important. They will be hereafter discussed.

54. Rice vs. R. R. Co., 1 Black, 374; 17 L. Ed. 147.
55. Moore vs. U. S., 160 U. S. 268; 40 L. Ed. 422; 16 Sup. Ct. 294.
56. Sixth and Seventh Amendments to the Constitution.
57. Thompson vs. Utah, 170 U. S. 349; 42 L. Ed. 1061; 18 Sup. Ct. 620; Callan vs. Wilson, 127 U. S. 549; 32 L. Ed. 223; 8 Sup. Ct. 1301.
58. Sparf & Hansen vs. U. S., 156 U. S. 51; 39 L. Ed. 343; 15 Sup. Ct. 273; Freeman vs. United States, 227 Fed. 741; 142 C. C. A. 256.

35. Federal Courts in Equity Cases Administer a Common Law of Chancery.

What has thus far been said as to the common law has been said with reference to law as distinguished from equity. The Constitution recognizes the difference between the two. By its amendments the right to trial by jury is secured to parties to civil actions at common law involving more than twenty dollars. This provision is not applicable to proceedings in equity.

It follows that in the Federal Courts the distinction between law and equity must be maintained. Even prior to the adoption of the Constitution, there were States which did not keep the two systems separate. In all, or nearly all, of the States, statutes have since, to a greater or less extent, broken down the barriers between them. The Supreme Court, under these conditions, was compelled to determine how the constitutional distinction could be preserved.

36. In the Federal Courts the Line Separating Law From Equity is Drawn Where it was in England in 1789.

It solved the problem by declaring that the framers of the Constitution must have had in mind the contemporary English practice, and that in the Federal Courts the line of division between law and equity must be drawn where in 1789 the High Court of Chancery drew it.

Massachusetts had no Court of Equity. A bill which revealed a case of equity jurisdiction was filed in the Circuit Court of the United States for the District of Massachusetts. The Supreme Court by the mouth of CHIEF JUSTICE MARSHALL, said:—

"As the Courts of the Union have a chancery jurisdiction in every State and the Judiciary Act confers the same chancery powers on all and gives the same rule of decision, its jurisdiction in Massachusetts must be the same as in other States."[59]

The same doctrine is more elaborately stated in the case already cited of State of Pennsylvania vs. Wheeling Bridge Co.[60]

It was there said:—

"Chancery jurisdiction is conferred on the Courts of the United States with the limitation that 'suits in equity shall not be sustained in any of the Courts of the United States in any case where plain, adequate and complete remedy may be had at law. The rules of the High Court of Chancery of England have been adopted by the Courts of the United States. * * * In exercising this jurisdiction the Courts of the Union are not limited by the chancery system adopted by any State, and they exercise their functions in a State where no Court of Chancery has been established. The usages of the High Court of Chancery in England whenever the jurisdiction is exercised govern the proceedings. This may be said to be the common law of chancery, and since the organization of the Government it has been observed."

59. United States vs. Howland, 4 Wheat, 115; 4 L. Ed. 526.
60. 13 How. 563; 14 L. Ed. 249.

CHAPTER II.

THE SUPREME COURT AND ITS ORIGINAL JURISDICTION.

37. The Supreme Court.

The Constitution provides for a Supreme Court and defines the limits of its original jurisdiction.

38. The Appellate Jurisdiction of the Supreme Court is Such as Congress Sees Fit to Give.

The Constitution declares that in all cases of which the Supreme Court has not original jurisdiction it "shall have appellate jurisdiction both as to law and fact with such exceptions and under such regulations as the Congress shall make.'' That is to say, it has such appellate jurisdiction as Congress sees fit to give it. It follows that what Congress has given, Congress may take away.

One McCardle, after the close of the Civil War, was arrested by the military authorities of the United States. Under the alleged sanction of the Reconstruction Acts, he was held in custody for trial by a military commission, for disturbances of the public peace in inciting to insurrection, disorder and violence, for libel and for impeding reconstruction. He applied for a writ of habeas corpus to the Circuit Court of the United States for the District of Mississippi. He was remanded to the custody of the military authorities. He appealed to the Supreme Court of the United States. The Government moved to dismiss his appeal; contending that an order of a Circuit Court denying a writ of habeas corpus was not appealable. The Supreme Court denied the motion; holding that by statute the right to appeal was expressly given.[1] It fully heard the case upon the merits. The argument, which lasted over four days, was not concluded until the 9th of March, 1867. Congress was at the very height of its conflict with President Johnson. It wished to be free to make further use of military commissions for the maintenance of order and for the enforcement of its policies in what it was then in the habit of calling "the States lately in rebellion.''

On the 27th of March, 1868, that is eighteen days after the conclusion of the argument in the case, but before the Court had announced any decision, Congress, over the veto of the President, repealed the Act which the Supreme Court had held gave it jurisdiction. The Court thereupon announced that it was "not at liberty to inquire

1. In re McCardle, 6 Wall. 318; 18 L. Ed. 816.

into the motives of the legislature. We can only examine into its power under the Constitution; and the power to make exceptions to the appellate jurisdiction of this Court is given by express words.'' The Court cited with approval its own language in a much earlier case[2] to the effect that while the appellate powers of the Supreme Court are not given by the Judiciary Act, but by the Constitution, they are, nevertheless, limited and regulated by that Act and by such other Acts as have been passed on the subject. The Judiciary Act was an exercise of the power given by the Constitution to Congress of making exceptions to the appellate jurisdiction of the Supreme Court. Congress had described affirmatively the jurisdiction of the Court, and this affirmative description was understood to imply a negation of the exercise of such appellate powers as were not comprehended within it.

The Court concluded ''it is quite clear, therefore, that this Court cannot proceed to pronounce judgment in this case, for it has no longer jurisdiction of the appeal; and judicial duty is not less fitly performed by declining ungranted jurisdiction than in exercising firmly that which the Constitution and the laws confer.''[3]

39. The Organization of the Supreme Court.

By the original Judiciary Act[4] the Supreme Court was composed of one Chief Justice and five Associate Justices.

The Federalists, on the eve of their going out of power, with the hope of keeping Jefferson from putting any of his followers on the bench of the Supreme Court, passed an Act providing that the number of Associate Justices

2. Durousseau vs. United States, 6 Cranch, 312; 3 L. Ed. 232.

3. In re McCardle, 7 Wall. 506; 19 L. Ed. 264.

4. Sept. 24, 1789, 1 Stat. 73; 5 Fed. Stat. Ann. 701; U. S. Comp. Stat., Sec. 1191.

after the next vacancy should occur, should be but four.[5] This Act was speedily repealed by a Democratic Congress.[6]

By the Act of February 24, 1807,[7] the number of Associate Justices was fixed at six, thus giving the Court seven members.

Thirty years later,[8] the number of Associate Justices was raised to eight, and by the Act of March 3, 1863,[9] to nine.

Congress on the 23rd day of July, 1866,[10] provided that no vacancy in the office of Associate Justice of the Supreme Court should be filled by appointment until the number of Associate Justices should be reduced to six, and that thereafter the Supreme Court should consist of a Chief Justice and six Associates.

The purpose of this last enactment was to prevent President Johnson making any appointments to the Supreme bench during the remainder of his term. His successor had been only five weeks in the White House when the number of Associate Justices was raised to eight, at which it has ever since remained.[11]

40. Original Jurisdiction of the Supreme Court Does Not Extend Beyond the Grant of Judicial Power to the United States.

The second and third sentences of the second section of the third article of the Constitution define the character of the jurisdiction to be exercised by the Supreme

5. Act Feb. 13, 1801, 2 Stat. 89.

6. Act March 8, 1802, 2 Stat. 132.

7. 2 Stat. 420, Sec. 5.

8. March 3, 1837, 5 Stat. 176.

9. 12 Stat. 794.

10. 14 Stat. 209.

11. April 10, 1869, 16 Stat. 44; 5 Fed. Stat. Ann. 701; U. S. Comp. Stat., Sec. 1191.

Court over the cases to which the first sentence of the section declares the judicial power of the United States· shall extend, and do not add to the grant therein made. In order that the Supreme Court shall have original jurisdiction over a case to which a State is a party, it must appear that it is one affecting an ambassador, other public minister or a consul, or to which the United States is a party, or is between two or more States, or is between a State and citizens of another State, or is between a State and foreign States, citizens or subjects.[12] It will be noted that it is not sufficient that a State is a party; if it were, the Supreme Court might be called upon to take original jurisdiction of all the countless suits, civil and perhaps criminal, that the several States are of necessity continually bringing against their own citizens.

It follows that the Court has no jurisdiction of a suit in which a State sues one of its own citizens and another State, because the judicial power of the United States does not extend to a controversy between a State· and one of its own citizens, unless that controversy arises under the Constitution, treaties or laws of the United States.[13]

41. The Supreme Court's Original Jurisdiction is Self Executing.

The constitutional grant of original jurisdiction to the Supreme Court is so far self executing that in the absence of legislation, it may be exercised without any statutory prescription or regulation of procedure. The

12. Cohens vs. Virginia, 6 Wheaton, 398; 5 L. Ed. 257; Minnesota vs. Hitchcock, 185 U. S. 383; 46 L. Ed. 954; 22 Sup. Ct. 650; Louisiana vs. Texas, 176 U. S. 15; 44 L. Ed. 347; 20 Sup. Ct. 251; U. S. vs. Texas, 143 U. S. 643; 36 L. Ed. 285; 12 Sup. Ct. 488.

13. Pennsylvania vs. Quicksilver Co., 10 Wall. 553-556; 19 L. Ed. 998; California vs. Southern Pacific Co., 157 U. S. 229-261; 39 L. Ed. 683; 15 Sup. Ct. 591; Minnesota vs. Northern Securities Co.. 184 U. S. 199; 46 L. Ed. 499; 22 Sup. Ct. 308.

power of Congress to regulate such procedure is clear, but many of the ordinary statutory provisions dealing with pleading, practice and process in the Federal courts have obviously no application to such cases. In practice, they are governed by the general rules of the Court or by special orders made by it.[14]

42. Original Jurisdiction of the Supreme Court Over Suits or Proceedings Against Diplomatic Personages.

It is not easy to conceive of any suit or legal proceeding which consistently with the well-settled principles of international law, may be brought against an ambassador or other public minister, or against his domestics or domestic servants. It is therefore probable that the principal, if not the sole purpose of the constitutional convention in conferring original jurisdiction upon the Supreme Court over such cases, and of Congress in making that jurisdiction exclusive, was to ensure that no less learned and responsible tribunal, State or Federal, should ever be tempted to exercise it. The Supreme Court itself, so far as I am aware, has never had any occasion during the more than one hundred and thirty years of its existence, to do so. The only litigated questions have been whether a defendant proceeded against in a District or Circuit Court was in fact entitled to the diplomatic privilege. Whether he is or is not does not depend upon what title he bears. He may be styled an ambassador, or an envoy, or a minister, or a plenipotentiary, extraordinary or resident, or a procurator, or legate, or nuncio, or internuncio, or deputy, or commissioner, or a *chargé*

14. Commonwealth of Kentucky vs. Dennison, 24 Howard, 66-98; 16 L. Ed. 717; Chisholm vs. Georgia, 2 Dallas, 419-450; 1 L. Ed. 440; Grayson vs. Virginia, 3 Dallas, 320; 1 L. Ed. 619; New Jersey vs. New York, 5 Peters, 284-287; 8 L. Ed. 127; Florida vs. Georgia, 17 Howard, 478-491, 15 L. Ed. 181.

d'affaires, or merely an agent, or be given some other name. It is the function he discharges and not what he is called, which determines whether he is in fact a public minister.[15]

There is to be noted a clear distinction between diplomatic personages and consular officers. The latter may be sued, and often are. This is true although they may be permitted by the State Department to bring diplomatic questions to its attention.[16] Whether any one is or is not entitled to the diplomatic immunity, depends upon whether he is recognized as a diplomatic personage by the Executive of this country, and the usual and convenient, if not the sole way of proving the fact is by a certificate from the Department of State.[17]

A case does not affect a public minister merely because he may have a sentimental interest in its outcome. For example, Congress has made it a penal offense to assault an ambassador or other public minister of a foreign government, or his servants, but the prosecution for such an assault is not a case affecting him. He is not a party to the litigation, and is in no legal sense concerned in its outcome.[18]

43. Original Jurisdiction of the Supreme Court May Extend to Any Case in Which a State May Properly Be Made a Party Whether as Plaintiff or Defendant.

While a State may not be sued by an individual,[19] it

15. Opinion of Atty. Gen. Cushing, 7 Opinions Atty. Gen. 186.

16. In re Baiz, 135 U. S. 403; 34 L. Ed. 222; 10 Sup. Ct. 854.

17. In re Baiz, 135 U. S. 403; 34 L. Ed. 222; 10 Sup. Ct. 854; U. S. vs. Ortega, 27 Fed. Cases, 359; 6 L. Ed. 521; 11 Wheaton, 466; U. S. vs. Benner, 24 Fed. Cases, 14,568; Bald. 234; Ex Parte Hitz, 111 U. S. 766; 28 L. Ed. 592; 4 Sup. Ct. 698.

18. U. S. vs. Ortega, 11 Wheaton, 466; 6 L. Ed. 521.

19. Eleventh Amendment Constitution; Hans vs. Louisiana, 134 U. S. 1; 33 L. Ed. 842; 10 Sup. Ct. 504.

may be by another State, or by the United States,[20] and it may sue individuals as well as States, and also the United States, with [21] but not without the latter's consent.[22] In all such cases, the Supreme Court has original jurisdiction, which is exclusive, except in those cases in which a State sues its citizens or citizens of other States or aliens, or is, by its own consent, sued by them or some of them in a State court.[23]

44. When Is a State a Party?

A State is none the less a party when the proceedings are brought by or against its governor, its attorney-general or other of its officials as such, if the relief sought is for or against it. In a number of the earlier cases, the suit was instituted by the Governor of the State as such, and in some it was brought against the Governor in his official capacity. In them it was clear upon the face of the pleadings that the State was the party, and not the individual who, at the time, was filling the office of governor, even within the rule declared by Chief Justice Marshall to be without exception that in all cases in which jurisdiction depends upon the party, the latter is the one named in the record.[24] Later decisions have pointed out that the Chief Justice spoke too broadly, for there have been many cases in fact against a State in which the omission to name it as a defendant was deliberate, either because the plaintiff was an individual and could not sue the State, or in rare instances, because there was a ques-

20. U. S. vs. Texas, 143 U. S. 621-641; 36 L. Ed. 285; 12 Sup. Ct. 488.

21. Minnesota vs. Hitchcock, 185 U. S. 373-378; 46 L. Ed. 954; 22 Sup. Ct. 783.

22. Oregon vs. Hitchcock, 202 U. S. 60-70; 50 L. Ed. 935; 26 Sup. Ct. 568.

23. Judicial Code, Secs. 256, 233; 5 Fed. Stat. Ann. 921-708; U. S. Comp. Stat., Secs. 1233-1210.

24. Gov. of Georgia vs. Madrago, 1 Peters, 110; 7 L. Ed. 73; Osborne vs. Bank of U. S., 9 Wheaton, 738, 851; 6 L. Ed. 204.

tion of whether the Federal court had, as against the State, power to give the relief sought.

In such case, the judgment or decree asked by the plaintiff would often in substance be against the State, and, Marshall to the contrary notwithstanding, when that is true, it will be held that the suit is in fact one against the State, or what will amount to the same thing, that the State is an indispensable party, and that jurisdiction fails when it is brought in.[25]

Nevertheless, a State may be bound by the determination of a suit brought by an individual against its officials, if it has voluntarily come into the case by taking part in its defense. Where a corporation brought suit in the Federal court against a county treasurer to enjoin the collection of taxes under color of a State statute which the plaintiff claimed to be in conflict with the Constitution of the United States, and the State directed its law officers to defend the case, it was held that it had voluntarily submitted itself to the jurisdiction of the court, and was bound by the decree in subsequent litigation between it and the plaintiff and those in privity with the latter as to all issues adjudged in the first suit.[26]

45. The Supreme Court Has No Original Jurisdiction of Any Proceeding by a State to Enforce Its Penal Laws.

Both in form and in substance the State is a party to every criminal prosecution instituted within its bounds and to most, if not all of those of a quasi criminal character. It frequently happens that the defendants are citizens of other States, or are aliens. Literally such cases are included in the constitutional grant of judicial

25. In re Ayres, 123 U. S. 443, 487; 31 L. Ed. 216; 8 Sup. Ct. 164.

26. Gunter vs. Atlantic Coast Line, 200 U. S. 273; 50 L. Ed. 477; 26 Sup. Ct. 252.

power to the Federal Government, but it has always been obvious that the framers of the Constitution could never have intended that the United States should have anything to do with such prosecutions, as for example, of sailors from foreign ships who may commit offenses in our ports, or citizens of one State who transgress against the laws of another, in which they transiently are.

As early as 1793 it was held that despite the broad language of the Constitution, the cases and controversies over which the Federal Government was declared to have judicial power because of the citizenship or the nationality of the parties, or by reason of a State being a party to them, were limited to those of a civil nature,[27] and this conclusion was affirmed and illuminated by what Chief Justice Marshall said in Cohens vs. Virginia.[28]   In Wisconsin vs. Pelican Insurance Company,[29] the Supreme Court, after a full view of the authorities, held the principle applicable to proceedings by a State on the civil side of its courts to recover pecuniary penalties for infractions of its laws.   Such suits are so far civil that in them verdicts may be properly given upon a fair preponderance of the evidence, or may be directed.

In the last cited case, the defendant was a Louisiana insurance company which had carried on business in Wisconsin and had there subjected itself to certain pecuniary penalties for which the State, in its own courts, had recovered a judgment for fifteen thousand dollars.   The company had no assets in Wisconsin.   The State brought suit upon the judgment in the Supreme Court of the United States.   The Court said it would look through form to substance; and as the claim was in essence for a penalty, it must decline to take jurisdiction.   For the

27. Chisholm vs. Georgia, 2 Dal. 419; 1 L. Ed. 440.
28. 6 Wheat. 264-398; 5 L. Ed. 257.
29. 127 U. S. 265; 32 L. Ed. 239; 8 Sup. Ct. 1370.

same reason, the Federal courts will not take cognizance of suits in which a State seeks to enforce its penal legislation by suing out injunctions against citizens or corporations of other States or aliens, as for example, to enjoin railroad companies from bringing intoxicating liquors into a State in contravention of its laws.[30] In accordance with this principle, it was held that the State of Oklahoma could not sustain an original bill in the Supreme Court of the United States to restrain railroad companies from charging unreasonable rates within its jurisdiction.[31] Those rights must be asserted by the shippers injured.

46. Original Jurisdiction of the Supreme Court of Suits by One State Against Another.

By the first sentence of the second section of the third article of the Constitution the judicial power of the United States is expressly declared to extend to controversies between two or more States, and as a State is necessarily a party thereto, by the second sentence of the same section, original jurisdiction over them is given to the Supreme Court, and the Judicial Code makes such jurisdiction exclusive.[32]

The Supreme Court recognizes that such suits are quasi international controversies, which are not governed by any municipal code and that it is called upon to adjust differences which cannot be dealt with by Congress or disposed of by the Legislature of either State alone. It will apply Federal, State or international law as the cir-

30. Oklahoma vs. Gulf. Colorado & Santa Fe Ry.. 220 U. S. 290; 55 L. Ed. 469; 31 Sup. Ct. 437.

31. Oklahoma vs. A.. T. & Santa Fe Ry., 220 U. S. 277; 55 L. Ed. 465; 31 Sup. Ct. 434.

32. Secs. 233 and 256, Judicial Code; 5 Fed. Stat. Ann. 708, 921; U. S. Comp. Stat. Secs. 1210-1233.

cumstances of the particular case may demand.[33]   It will
deal with such cases in a broad and non-technical spirit,
declining to consider objections as to procedure except
insofar as they bear upon the merits.[34]   If each of the
States be really parties, and the controversy is justiciable, the Court will hear it.   Where jurisdiction of
the Federal courts depends entirely upon the character
of the parties, it is immaterial what may be the subject of
the controversy.   Be it what it may, these parties have
a constitutional right to come into the courts of the Union,
and a State, as a quasi sovereign and representative of
the interests of the public, has a standing in court to
protect the atmosphere, the water and the forests within
its limits.[35]

47. A State Is Not a Party Unless Its Interest Is Other than the Mere Vindication of the Rights of Its Citizens in Their Individual Capacity.

It was early held that a State had no standing to intervene in an ejectment suit between individuals, although
the case turned upon the true location of the boundary
between the States of New York and Connecticut.   New
York had no proprietary interests in the lands in con-

33. Kansas vs. Colorado, 185 U. S. 125; 46 L. Ed. 838; 22 Sup. Ct. 552.

34. Virginia vs. West Virginia, 220 U. S. 1; 55 L. Ed. 353; 31 Sup. Ct.
330; Kansas vs. Colorado, 206 U. S. 46; 51 L. Ed. 956; 27 Sup. Ct. 585;
Missouri vs. Illinois, 200 U. S. 496; 50 L. Ed. 572; 26 Sup. Ct. 268; Rhode
Island vs. Massachusetts, 14 Peters, 210; 10 L. Ed. 423.

35. Cohens vs. Virginia, 6 Wheaton, 264; 5 L. Ed. 257; Kansas vs.
Colorado, 185 U. S. 125; 46 L. Ed. 838; 22 Sup. Ct. 552; Kansas vs.
Colorado, 206 U. S. 46; 51 L. Ed. 956; 27 Sup. Ct. 585; Missouri vs.
Illinois, 180 U. S. 208; 45 L. Ed. 497; 21 Sup. Ct. 331; Georgia vs. Copper
Co., 206 U. S. 230; 51 L. Ed. 1038; 27 Sup. Ct. 618; U. S. vs. Texas, 143
U. S. 621; 36 L. Ed. 285; 12 Sup. Ct. 488; U. S. vs. North Carolina, 136
U. S. 211; 34 L. Ed. 336; 10 Sup. Ct. 290; U. S. vs. Michigan, 190 U. S.
379; 47 L. Ed. 1103; 23 Sup. Ct. 742; R. I. vs. Massachusetts, 14 Peters,
210; 10 L. Ed. 423; Hudson County Water Co. vs. McCarter, 209 U. S. 349;
52 L. Ed. 828; 28 Sup. Ct. 475.

troversy, and no outcome of the suit between other parties could conclude its sovereign rights over the disputed territory, if in fact it had any,[36] nor was it entitled to an injunction to restrain the prosecution of such actions.

Many years later, New Hampshire and New York brought suit in the Supreme Court against Louisiana to recover upon certain bonds of the defendant State which were held by citizens of the plaintiffs. They had been assigned to the States which brought the suit for purposes of collection only. It was held that the plaintiffs were not in fact parties in any substantial sense. To their contention that as sovereign States, they had a right to assert and collect the claims of their citizens, in accordance with international practice often followed if not always considered to be sound, it was answered that as the Constitution originally adopted had declared that the judicial power should extend to controversies "between a State and citizens of other States" it was clear that it was the intention of the framers to take from the States the right to act for their individual citizens in such cases, and that the subsequent adoption of the Eleventh Amendment had not the effect of restoring to the States the right which conceivably they had before the Constitution was adopted.[37] The decision was of great importance, for had it been otherwise, the Supreme Court would have been called on to require a number of the Southern States to pay large quantities of bonds issued in their names and by their officials during the reconstruction period, the validity of which the States had subsequently declined to recognize.

Still later it was intimated that a State would have no

36. New York vs. Connecticut, 4 Dallas, 1; 1 L. Ed. 715.

37. New Hampshire vs. Louisiana; New York vs. Louisiana, 108 U. S. 76-91; 27 L. Ed. 656; 2 Sup. Ct. 176.

right to sue to prevent an unlawful interference with the commerce of its principal city, the rest of its citizens not being specially affected.[38]   The actual point decided was that it did not appear that the State of Texas had ever authorized the acts complained of.   It was, however, held that if the health officer of Texas had in fact exceeded the authority given him by the Texas statute, he could not be sued by Louisiana.   The remedy would have to be sought from his State.   There was an implication perhaps that if Texas had been asked to restrain his unlawful interference with the commerce of Louisiana, and had refused or failed to act, a controversy between the States might have arisen.   This reasoning is not altogether satisfactory, and subsequent cases already cited have shown that a State may seek redress for tangible material injuries which do harm to portions of its territory, and to those of its citizens who live therein, and do not in any direct or measurable way affect those who do not, as where Illinois was charged with fouling the waters of the Mississippi so as to endanger the health of the citizens of Missouri, who dwelt upon its banks,[39] or Colorado was alleged to have diverted the waters of the Arkansas River with the effect of making a desert of what had been a tillable section of Kansas.[40]

48. Original Jurisdiction of the Supreme Court Extends to a Suit by One State Against Another to Recover on a Pecuniary Demand Owned by the Plaintiff State Although Assigned to It by an Individual.

Certain individual holders of bonds of North Carolina, which the State had declined to pay, gave some of them outright to the State of South Dakota, which

38. Louisiana vs. Texas, 176 U. S. 1; 44 L. Ed. 347; 20 Sup. Ct. 251.
39. Missouri vs. Illinois, 200 U. S. 496; 50 L. Ed. 572; 26 Sup. Ct. 268.
40. Kansas vs. Colorado, 185 U. S. 125; 46 L. Ed. 838; 22 Sup. Ct. 552.

brought suit against North Carolina on them in the United States Supreme Court.[41] The Court, by a vote of five Justices against four, maintained its jurisdiction and entered a decree in favor of the plaintiff. In that case the prayer of the bill was for an ascertainment of the amount due on the bonds and for foreclosure of certain property pledged for them.

In the subsequent case of Virginia vs. West Virginia, the Court expressly decided that it had the authority to render a money judgment or decree against a defendant State at the suit of another State. The facts were that upon the division of Virginia at the outbreak of the Civil War, the new State, with the assent of Congress, agreed with the old, to pay its equitable proportion of the existing debt. This obligation had never been discharged in whole or in part. Virginia had declined to pay one-third of the debt it owed, on the ground that that portion should be paid by West Virginia, and it issued certificates to the holders of its debt for one-third of their claims, setting forth in substance that they were to be paid by West Virginia. Then it brought suit against West Virginia to compel the payment of this part of its debt. The case was long pending before the Supreme Court and many times figured in the reports.[42] There was much hesitation and delay on the part of West Virginia in complying with the decree. Throughout, the Supreme Court "considered the case in the untechnical spirit proper for dealing with a quasi-inter-

41. South Dakota vs. North Carolina, 192 U. S. 286; 48 L. Ed. 448; 24 Sup. Ct. 269.

42. Virginia vs. West Virginia. 206 U. S. 290; 51 L. Ed. 1068; 27 Sup. Ct. 732; 209 U.·S. 514; 52 L. Ed. 914; 28 Sup. Ct. 614; 220 U. S. 1; 55 L. Ed. 353; 31 Sup. Ct. 330; 222 U. S. 17; 56 L. Ed. 71; 32 Sup. Ct. 4; 231 U. S. 89; 58 L. Ed. 135; 34 Sup. Ct. 29; 234 U. S. 117; 58 L. Ed. 1243; 34 Sup. Ct. 889; 238 U. S. 202; 59 L. Ed. 1272; 35 Sup. Ct. 795; 241 U. S. 531; 60 L. Ed. 1147; 36 Sup. Ct. 719; 246 U. S. 565; 62 L. Ed. 883; 38 Sup. Ct. 400.

national controversy, remembering that there is no municipal code governing the matter, and that this Court may be called on to adjust differences that cannot be dealt with by Congress or disposed of by the Legislature of either State alone." Therefore it said "we shall spend no time on objections as to multifariousness, laches and the like, except so far as they affect the merits," and further that "this case is one that calls for forbearance upon both sides. Great States have a temper superior to that of private litigants, and it is to be hoped that enough has been decided for patriotism, the fraternity of the Union, and mutual consideration to bring it to an end." [43]

The litigation lasted many years but the Court proceeded with great patience. It said "a State cannot be expected to move with the celerity of a private business man. It is enough if it proceeds, in the language of the English Chancery, with all deliberate speed." [44]

In the end, West Virginia not having paid the decree, Virginia moved for a mandamus upon the Legislature of West Virginia directing it to levy a tax to pay the judgment. The motion was not granted at the time, but the Supreme Court, speaking through Chief Justice White, held that Congress had power to legislate to secure the enforcement of a contract between the States, and reserved for further consideration the question as to whether a mandamus should issue, or whether the Court, in the absence of legislation, would have a right to direct its issue, in order that full opportunity might be afforded to Congress to exercise the power which it undoubtedly possessed. As an earnest that indefinite delay might not be permitted, the Court put down the question of whether the mandamus should issue for argument at the next

43. 220 U. S. 27-36; 55 L. Ed. 353; 31 Sup. Ct. 330.
44. 222 U. S. 19-20; 56 L. Ed. 71; 32 Sup. Ct. 4.

term, and reserved the right, if it deemed it advisable before the time fixed for the hearing, to open the motion, for the purpose of examining and reporting the amount and method of taxation essential to be put into effect, whether by way of order to the State Legislature or direct action to secure the full execution of the judgment.[45] As the result of this determined tone, West Virginia finally provided for its payment.

49. Original Jurisdiction of the Supreme Court in Boundary Controversies Between States.

Boundary disputes have been the most fruitful source of litigation between States in the Supreme Court. More than one-half of all the forty-eight States have at one time or another figured as plaintiff or defendant in such cases. Sometimes the controversy grew out of real or alleged mistakes of early surveyors in running lines prescribed by charter, treaty or act of Congress.[46] In other instances it had its origin in the shifting channels of great boundary rivers, such as the Ohio,[47] the Missis-

45. Virginia vs. West Virginia, 246 U. S. 565; 62 L. Ed. 883; 38 Sup. Ct. 400.

46. New York vs. Connecticut, 4 Dallas, 1; 1 L. Ed. 715; New Jersey vs. New York, 5 Peters, 284; 8 L. Ed. 127; Rhode Island vs. Massachusetts, 12 Peters, 657; 9 L. Ed. 1233; 13 Peters, 23; 10 L. Ed. 41; 14 Peters, 10; 10 L. Ed. 335; 15 Peters, 233; 10 L. Ed. 948; 4 Howard, 591; 11 L. Ed. 1116; Missouri vs. Iowa, 7 Howard, 660; 12 L. Ed. 861; Florida vs. Georgia, 11 Howard, 293; 13 L. Ed. 702; 17 Howard, 478; 15 L. Ed. 181; Alabama vs. Georgia, 23 Howard, 505; 16 L. Ed. 556; Iowa vs. Illinois, 147 U. S. 1; 37 L. Ed. 55; 13 Sup. Ct. 239; 202 U. S. 59; 50 L. Ed. 934; 26 Sup. Ct. 571; Virginia vs. Tennessee, 148 U. S. 503; 37 L. Ed. 537; 13 Sup. Ct. 728; 158 U. S. 267; 39 L. Ed. 976; 15 Sup. Ct. 818; 190 U. S. 64; 47 L. Ed. 956; 23 Sup. Ct. 827; Maryland vs. West Virginia, 217 U. S. 1; 54 L. Ed. 645; 30 Sup. Ct. 32; 217 U. S. 577; 54 L. Ed. 888; 30 Sup. Ct. 630; 225 U. S. 1; 56 L. Ed. 955; 32 Sup. Ct. 672; North Carolina vs. Tennessee, 235 U. S. 1; 59 L. Ed. 97; 35 Sup. Gt. 8; 240 U. S. 652; 60 L. Ed. 847; 36 Sup. Ct. 604.

47. Indiana vs. Kentucky, 136 U. S. 479; 34 L. Ed. 329; 10 Sup. Ct. 1051.

sippi,[48] the Missouri,[49] or the Columbia.[50]   In one case
the sovereignty over valuable oyster reefs in the Gulf of
Mexico was in issue,[51] and in another, the right of Georgia,
in conjunction with the United States, to improve the
navigation of the Savannah River with the incidental
effect of somewhat narrowing the South Carolina half of
the channel.[52]   The case which was best calculated to
raise feeling, and which doubtless did, was that in which
Virginia sought to recover from West Virginia the
counties of Jefferson and Berkley.[53]   The plaintiff State
knew that whatever legal assumption there might have
been to the contrary, she had never in fact consented to
her own dismemberment.   Whether justified or not, she
believed that the elections, in which the voters of the
two counties of the eastern panhandle of West Virginia
had apparently signified their wish to become citizens of
the new State, were farces.   The questions involved
were political in almost every sense.   Yet in that, as in
all other boundary cases, the judgment of the Supreme
Court was gracefully and promptly accepted as final.

Given such conditions as here exist, boundary controversies present purely justiciable issues.   With us
they are not complicated, as in other lands they often
have been and still are, by the fact that the dividing lines

48. Missouri vs. Kentucky, 11 Wall. 395; 20 L. Ed. 116; Iowa vs. Illinois, 147 U. S. 1; 37 L. Ed. 55; 13 Sup. Ct. 239; 202 U. S. 59; 50 L. Ed.
934; 26 Sup. Ct. 571; Arkansas vs. Tennessee, 246 U. S. 158; 62 L. Ed.
638; 38 Sup. Ct. 301; 247 U. S. 461; 62 L. Ed. 1213; 38 Sup. Ct. 557;
Arkansas vs. Mississippi, 250 U. S. 39; 63 L. Ed. 832; 39 Sup. Ct. 422.

49. Nebraska vs. Iowa, 143 U. S. 359; 36 L. Ed. 186; 12 Sup. Ct. 396;
Missouri vs. Nebraska, 196 U. S. 33; 49 L. Ed. 374; 25 Sup. Ct. 155;
Missouri vs. Kansas, 213 U. S. 78; 53 L. Ed. 706; 29 Sup. Ct. 417.

50. Washington vs. Oregón, 211 U. S. 127; 53 L. Ed. 118; 29 Sup. Ct. 47;
214 U. S. 205; 53 L. Ed. 969; 29 Sup. Ct. 631.

51. Louisiana vs. Mississippi, 202 U. S. 1; 50 L. Ed. 913; 28 Sup. Ct. 408;
202 U. S. 58; 50 L. Ed. 934; 26 Sup. Ct. 571.

52. South Carolina vs. Georgia, 93 U. S. 4; 23 L. Ed. 782.

53. Virginia vs. West Virginia, 11 Wallace, 39; 20 L. Ed. 67.

between sharply antagonistic racial, religious or linguistic groups do not always coincide with national boundaries. The precautions by which the constitution sought to prevent war between adjoining States have worked so well that its very possibility has now become unthinkable to us. There is complete freedom of trade among all our States. It follows that no one of them ever has cause to believe that the possession of any strip of territory is vital either to its strategic or to its economic safety. There has therefore been no real reason why the Supreme Court should not pass upon their boundary differences although in the cases which came before it, what was in issue was seldom the property in the soil or indeed any other right of the kind about which individuals can ever go to law. What was in dispute was " sovereignty and jurisdiction." The controversy was therefore political, and as late as 1838, Chief Justice Taney declared in a dissenting opinion:[54] "Contests for rights of sovereignty and jurisdiction between states over any particular territory are not, in my judgment, the subjects of judicial cognizance and control, to be recovered and enforced in an ordinary suit, and are, therefore, not within the grant of judicial power contained in the constitution." Fortunately, the majority of his colleagues differed with him, and in many subsequent cases coming before the Court during the more than a quarter of a century he afterwards remained upon the Bench he appears to have acquiesced in what had become the accepted view, and indeed in one case[55] where he spoke for the Court he said: "The question of boundary between States is necessarily a political question, to be settled by compact made by the political departments of the government. * * * But under our

54. Rhode Island vs. Massachusetts, 12 Peters, 752; 9 L. Ed. 1272.
55. Florida vs. Georgia, 17 Howard, 478; 15 L. Ed. 181.

form of government, a boundary between two States may become a judicial question, to be decided in this court." It is stated by Mr. Justice Baldwin, who delivered the opinion in the case in which Chief Justice Taney dissented, that "title, jurisdiction, sovereignty, are therefore dependent questions, necessarily settled when boundary is ascertained, which being the line of territory, is the line of power over it, so that great as questions of jurisdiction and sovereignty may be, they depend on facts." Because, however, the issue in these cases is never mere ownership as proprietor of the soil, they are not brought on the law side of the Court as they would be if they were simple actions of ejectment or something in the nature of such actions. They are instituted by a bill in equity in accordance with the English practice where questions of boundary as distinct from questions of title to the soil were in controversy.[56]

56. Penn vs. Baltimore, 1 Ves. Sr. 446; Rhode Island vs. Massachusetts, 12 Peters, 657-787; 9 L. Ed. 1232.

CHAPTER III.

50. The District Courts of the United States.

By the original Judiciary Act of 1789, District Courts were created, one for each of the thirteen districts into which, by the Act, the eleven States then in the Union

were divided.   From time to time the number of districts, and with them the number of District Courts, has
been increased.   At the present time there are eighty,
or more than six times as many as there were in 1789.

No district crosses State lines and no district ever has
crossed States lines—that is, each district is now, as
always, wholly within the boundaries of a single State.
Maryland and twenty-three other States have only one
district each; Virginia and seventeen others are divided
into two each; Pennsylvania and three others into three
each, while in New York, as in Texas, there are four.

51. Division of Districts.

Congress has in various ways sought to send the Federal Courts to litigants rather than to compel the latter
to travel long distances to prosecute or defend suits in
them.   To this end, in nearly two-thirds of the districts
there have been established what are legally known as
divisions, and which, for some purposes, are in fact sub-
districts.   In some districts there are as many as seven,
and in the country as a whole, more than one hundred
and forty.   Each of them has usually been created by a
separate act of Congress.   These enactments varied
greatly in their terms.   By some of them the creation of
a division amounted to little more than a designation of
the counties, the litigation originating in which would
ordinarily be tried at a particular place.   By others the
divisions were made so distinct that each of them was
in fact a sub-district, a status which it has been held[1] the
enactment of the judicial code [2] gave to all of them.   The
special problems arising out of the existence of divisions
will be later discussed.[3]

1. U. S. vs. Chennault, 230 Fed. 942.
2. Sec. 53.
3. Sec. 282, infra.

52. Terms of Court at More than One Place in a District or Division.

In a further attempt to make litigation in the Federal Courts less burdensome to suitors, Congress has very generally required that District Courts should hold sessions at more than one place in a district or in a division of the district. There are probably less than a half dozen districts in which the District Court does not in consequence sit at more than one place, and the aggregate number of cities, towns and villages in which regular terms of such courts are now required to be held, exceed three hundred. In most of these places a permanent clerk's office is maintained in charge of a resident clerk or his deputy. In some instances, a desire to flatter local pride, to help along a real estate boom, or to create a pretext for getting an appropriation for a Federal building, has led to legislation which entails inconvenience upon the Judges, delay to the litigants and a burden upon the Treasury out of all proportion to any good done.

53. District Judges.

As a rule, there is a separate District Judge for each district. In two States there is, however, only one District Judge for two districts; he is the District Judge in and for each. Until relatively recently there was never more than one District Judge in a single district. When the business in a district became too large to be handled by one Judge, the old practice was to divide it. With the great modern concentration of population in limited areas, it has been found more convenient in some instances to appoint two or more District Judges for the same district. In each of a dozen or more districts there are now two District Judges; in New Jersey three, and in the Southern District of New York four.

54. Who Decides when Judges of Same District Differ.

The purpose of having more than one judge in a district is that each of them shall separately devote himself to the dispatch of its business. Judges are not expected to preside jointly over the trial of cases, and the occasions, if any, upon which they do so are so rare that it has been unnecessary to make provision as to what shall happen when they differ as to the rulings to be made. It should be said, however, that in some limited although important classes of proceedings the statutes require three judges to sit in the District Court.[4] When they do, the majority rule.

The judges of the district may not be able to agree among themselves as to the division of work between or among them, or as to how particular cases or classes of cases shall be assigned for trial. If so, the senior *Circuit* Judge of the Circuit makes such orders as he thinks best.[5] If the majority of them are not of one mind as to the appointments to be made by the Court, or by the Judge thereof, such as of clerks, criers, commissioners, referees in bankruptcy, and so on, they may be made by the senior *District* Judge of the district. He is ordinarily, of course, the one whose commission bears the earliest date.[6] One exception is that if a judge exercises the privilege of retiring, or is demoted by the President, he becomes junior to all the other Judges of his district, or if he be a Circuit Judge, of his Circuit. He cannot retire nor can he be demoted until he has reached the age of seventy years and has been for ten years continuously on the Federal Bench. A Federal Judge, once appointed, confirmed and qualified, stays in office until he is impeached, resigns or dies. He may, however, outlive his

4. Secs. 559 to 561, infra.

5. J. C., Sec. 23; 4 Fed. Stat. Ann. 838; U. S. Comp. Stat. Sec. 990.

6. Act Feb. 25, 1919; Sec. 260, J. C., 40 Stat. 1157; Fed. Stat. Ann. 1919 Supplement; 228 U. S. Comp. Stat. Sec. 1237 (1919 Supp.).

physical or mental fitness without having committed any high crime or misdemeanor. In the event of his becoming incapacitated, it is scarcely fair to ask him to resign, for if he has ever been fit for his work he has usually served the government at a very much smaller compensation than he could have earned at the Bar. For the first eighty years, under the constitution, a judge, no matter how seriously he was unfitted by age for the discharge of his duties, was almost forced to remain on the bench. The public inconvenience occasioned thereby in some conspicuous instances led Congress in 1869 to provide that a judge who had held his commission for ten years, and had attained the age of seventy years, might resign his office, and should still, during the remainder of his life, continue to receive his salary.[7] Occasionally, however, a judge who had become incapacitated did not realize it, and in other instances judges who knew that they were capable of some good work were reluctant to be put altogether on the shelf. Therefore, in 1919,[8] Congress provided that a judge qualified to resign on full pay might, instead of doing so, retire, in which case he was not compelled to do any work, but remained eligible at any time to do any which he was willing to do and which he might be called upon to do either by the senior Circuit Judge of his Circuit or the Chief Justice of the United States, or by the presiding or senior judge of any district or circuit, and that the President might, with the advice and consent of the Senate, appoint an additional judge whenever he found a judge of seventy years of age, or upwards, with ten years of continuous service, incapable of performing efficiently all the duties of his office, by reason of mental

7. Act April 10, 1869, 16 Stat. 45; 5 Fed. Stat. Ann. 926; U. S. Comp. Stat. Sec. 1237.

8. Act Feb. 25, 1919, 40 Stat. 1152; Fed. Stat. Ann. 1919 Supp. 230; U. S. Comp. Stat. Sec. 1237 (1919 Supp.).

or physical disability of a permanent character. The retired or disabled judge thereafter ranks as the junior judge in the district.

55. When a District Judge Is Incapacitated or Disqualified or Business Has Accumulated or Is Urgent.

A judge may become ill or he may be personally interested in some case pending in his Court, or be closely related by blood or affinity to some one who is, or he may be a material witness for one of the parties, or before he went on the Bench may have been of counsel in it or for some other reason may feel that he may not be able to act impartially with relation to it, or an objection to his trying it may be made by a party who sets forth under oath facts tending to show that he has a personal prejudice or bias against the affiant, or in favor of his adversary, or conceivably there may be other circumstances in which it is well that some other Judge shall sit, or he may be in health, and there may be no reason why he should not deal with every cause on his docket, other than that there are so many of them awaiting trial that it is physically impossible for him in any reasonable length of time to dispose of them, or that two or more of them may be simultaneously urgent. In every one of these contingencies it is desirable that some other Judge shall be authorized to act, and in some it is necessary if justice is to be done without damaging delay.

In many of the districts there is but one Judge, and some one must be called in from the outside. Congress has made provision by which this may be done. There is much general similarity in the ways it has provided for dealing with each of the occasions for outside assistance, but as it has acted at different times by separate statutes, and usually with reference to one or a few contingencies, there are differences.

Section 6 of the Judiciary Act of 1789 contented itself with providing that when a Judge was unable to hold his Court at the appointed time, he might give a written order to the Marshal to adjourn it to a named day. If a Judge died, all proceedings were to be continued until the next stated session after the appointment and acceptance of his successor. Both provisions are still law with the qualification that in the case of death the continuance may be only until another Judge from the outside has been designated to hold the Court until the vacancy is permanently filled.[9]

At various times other provisions now embodied in Sections 13 to 20 of the Judicial Code, both inclusive, have been made for dealing with the exigencies already mentioned, as well as for any others which lead the senior Circuit Judge present in the Circuit to believe that the public interest requires the services of another judge. In some instances the appointment may be made by any Circuit Judge of the Circuit; in others, by the Circuit Justice assigned to the Circuit or by the Chief Justice. There does not appear to be any special reason why these distinctions have been made, but they exist and for them reference should be had to the sections of the Judicial Code named.

Section 18 of it authorizes the senior Circuit Judge of the Circuit or the Circuit Justice, or the Chief Justice, when the public interest requires, to name a Circuit Judge of the Circuit to hold a District Court, and under section 13, under some circumstances the Chief Justice may appoint a District Judge of another Circuit to hold a District Court. It would be desirable to recast and simplify these provisions, and perhaps to make them a little more elastic than they now are.

9. J. C. Sec. 22; 4 Fed. Stat. Ann. 837; U. S. Comp. Stat. Sec. 989.

56. Recusing or Challenging a Judge.

Conceivably a judge may dislike one man so much or
be so attached to another that it will be difficult for him
to do justice in a case to which either is a party.   He
may not appreciate the intensity of his own feeling, and
in consequence know of no reason why he should not sit.
Such cases are probably rare, especially in the Federal
Courts, in which, from the nature of things, very few of
the litigants are personally known to the judges, but
doubtless they arise once in a while.   It was not until
the adoption of the Judicial Code that any attempt was
made to provide for them, and section 21 was the result.
It authorizes a party to make and file an affidavit that
the judge who is to try the case has a personal bias or
prejudice either against him or in favor of any opposite
party.   The facts and reasons for the belief must be
stated.   In order to minimize the delay and other inconvenience which may be occasioned by such action, the
Act requires that the affidavit shall be filed not less than
ten days before the beginning of the term, or good cause
shown for the delay.   Counsel must certify that it is
filed in good faith, and nobody is entitled to file more than
one such affidavit.

The express terms of the statute applies to any proceeding, civil or criminal.   It has, however, been intimated and perhaps decided that motions to disbar, at
least when based upon a criminal contempt committed
in the presence of the Court, are not within its scope.[10]
The Court may have been right in the particular case
referred to, but, generally speaking, there is a greater
probability of a judge having an adverse personal bias
in disbarment proceedings than in most others.   There
can be little question of the soundness of the decision of
the Circuit Court of Appeals for the First Circuit that

10. In re Ulmer, 208 Fed. 465.

the whole frame of the section shows that it was not intended to relate to appellate cases.[11]

The bias alleged must be personal. The statute cannot be evoked because the judge holds strong views on some legal proposition involved in the case, or because his cast of mind is such that he may give more weight than others would do to certain kinds of testimony or to take off the Bench a judge who has been led by what he has heard in the course of the case to a conclusion adverse to the party making the affidavit.[12] It cannot be filed after the verdict, in order to compel the turning over to another judge of the hearing of the motion for a new trial.[13] The facts stated must be such as would lead a rational man to believe that they indicated bias.[14] The counsel who gives the certificate must be on the rolls of the Court at the time.[15]

It has not been easy to administer this statute, largely because no provision is made by which the sufficiency of the affidavit, either in form or in fact, can, in the first instance, he passed upon by any one except the judge assailed in it. It is his duty to determine whether it fulfills the conditions prescribed by the statute for his disqualification.[16] In so doing, he must assume the truth of all the facts stated in the affidavit as ground for the belief of bias, although they are avowedly made, not upon personal knowledge, but only upon information and be-

11. Kinney vs. Plymouth Rock Co., 213 Fed. 449; 130 C. C. A. 586.

12. Ex Parte American Steel Barrel Co., 230 U. S. 35; 57 L. Ed. 1379; 33 Sup. Ct. 1007; In Re Equitable Trust Co., 232 Fed. 836; 147 C. C. A. 30; Henry vs. Harris, 191 Fed. 868.

13. Ex Parte Glasgow, 195 Fed. 780.

14. Ex Parte N. K. Fairbanks Co., 194 Fed. 978; Henry vs. Speer, 201 Fed. 869; Ex Parte American Steel Barrel Co., 230 U. S. 35; In Re Equitable Trust Co., 232 Fed. 836; 147 C. C. A. 30.

15. Ex Parte N. K. Fairbanks Co., 194 Fed. 978.

16. Henry vs. Speer, 201 Fed. 869; 120 C. C. A. 207; Ex Parte American Steel Barrel Co., 230 U. S. 35.

lief, and although he may personally know them to be false.[17] The task is so delicate that in practice many affidavits which would be held bad by a disinterested arbiter, accomplish their purpose.

57. The Supreme Court and the District Courts Have Been Permanent.

Since the first organization of the judicial system of the United States there have always been a Supreme Court and District Courts. The organization of each has remained substantially unchanged.

58. The Circuit Courts.

By the origninal Judiciary Act Circuit Courts were established in each district. They had an uninterrupted existence of more than one hundred and twenty years. The Act which abolished them became effective January 1, 1912. The title of these Courts was not actually a misnomer, but it was capable of giving a false impression. It often did. The country has always been divided into circuits of considerable size, extending over several States, sometimes over many. From 1789 to 1869, with the exception of a little over twelve months, between February, 1801, and March, 1802, the only Federal Judges were the Justices of the Supreme Court and the District Judges. If there were to be Courts of higher rank than those of the District, their work had to be done in whole or in part by the Justices of the Supreme Court. In order that this duty might be apportioned in some orderly fashion among them it was expedient that the country should be divided and particular Justices assigned to each of such divisions—that is to say, each of such divisions constituted the circuit of a particular Supreme Court Justice. The appellation "Circuit Court" suggests that such tribunal

17. Berger vs. U. S., 255 U. S. 22; 65 L. Ed. 277; 41 Sup. Ct. 230.

had jurisdiction throughout the circuit. That, in point of fact, it never had. Its writs and processes did not run beyond the district in which it was held. The full and accurate title of the Circuit Court in Maryland was the Circuit Court of the United States for the District of Maryland. For many years Maryland and Virginia have formed part of the same Federal circuit. Nevertheless, the Circuit Court for the District of Maryland was as distinct in every way from that for either of the districts into which Virginia is divided as it was from the Circuit Court for the District of Oregon.

The word circuit had no reference whatever to the territorial extent of the Court's jurisdiction. It was purely arbitrary, so far as concerned the Court itself, as distinguished from the Judges who might hold it.

59. Circuit Courts From 1789 to 1801.

At first there were only three circuits, the Eastern, the Middle and the Southern. The last-named comprised but two States, South Carolina and Georgia. It is significant of the essentially frontier conditions which one hundred and thirty years ago prevailed throughout the greater part of those Commonwealths that the assignment to the Southern Circuit was universally held to be burdensome. To ride circuit in that part of the country was very hard work. It is true there was not much to be done by a Federal Judge when he reached any one of his various Court houses. To get to them at all required long and exhausting journeys which to elderly men were dangerous.

Originally the Supreme Court had six members. Two of them were accordingly assigned to each circuit. These two, together with the District Judge of the district, were required to hold in each district a Circuit Court twice in each year. To make a Court at least two of the three had

to be present. Under the conditions of travel then prevailing, the Supreme Court Justices must have spent the
larger part of their time in public or private conveyances
or on horse-back. It is not surprising that at this period
many gentlemen declined appointments to the Supreme
Bench; one citizen of Maryland preferred to take the post
of Chancellor of that State, and many of the earlier Justices of the Supreme Court resigned after a few months
or a few years of service. If there had been any considerable number of cases to be disposed of either on circuit or
by the Supreme Court the system would have been utterly
unworkable. As a matter of fact, the Supreme Court had
hardly anything to do and the Circuit Courts not much
more. John Jay while Chief Justice was also Minister
to England, and Oliver Ellsworth, while holding the same
high judicial post, represented us in France. John Marshall for some little while was both Secretary of State
and Chief Justice. Samuel Chase, of Maryland, found
time while an Associate Justice to canvass his State in
advocacy of the re-election of President Adams.

As originally constituted the Circuit Courts exercised
both original and appellate jurisdiction. In 1891 the
latter was taken from them and for the remaining twenty
years of their existence they were Courts of first instance
and nothing more.

It will be unnecessary here to discuss the jurisdiction,
both original and appellate, which at different times they
had. It will tend to clearness if attention be confined to
the changes which from time to time were made in their
organization.

60. Circuit Courts Under the Act of February 13, 1801.

As has been said, the conditions under which circuit
work had to be done were very trying. As a rule, the
Supreme Court Justices heartily disliked it. There was a

doubt as to whether under a strict construction of the Constitution a Justice of the Supreme Court could be required to sit in an inferior tribunal. It was often impossible for either of the Justices of the Supreme Court to get to the place fixed for holding the Circuit Court in a particular district at the time designated by law. Some changes in the original scheme had by 1801 become necessary. The Federalists were about to lose control of the Presidency and of Congress. They wished to insure that for an indefinite time to come the Courts of the United States would be in the hands of those whom they would have described as men of "sound principles"—that is, good Federalists. On February 13, 1801, less than three weeks before they went out of power; as it turned out forever, they passed an Act for the more convenient organization of the Courts of the United States.[18] By it the Circuit Court system was radically altered. It increased the number of districts to twenty-two and directed the establishment of a district Court in each. It doubled the number of the circuits. The geographical grouping of the States, then made, is very similar to that now in force. The first six of the present circuits are today constituted very much as they were by the Act of 1801. For each of these circuits, except the sixth, they directed that there should be appointed three new Judges to be called Circuit Judges. In the Sixth Circuit there was to be only one such Judge. The Justices of the Supreme Court were no longer to sit in the Circuit Courts. This was not a bad system. If all original jurisdiction had been given to the District Courts and the Circuit Courts made appellate tribunals purely, the organization would have been substantially the same as that which now exists. It was then doubtless far more elaborate than the needs of the country required. The Federal Courts were very un-

18. 2 Stat. 89.

popular with the party about to come into power. The appointment of a large number of distinguished Federalists to life positions was even less to its liking. President Adams promptly exercised the powers conferred on him by this Act. New District and Circuit Judges were appointed and promptly confirmed by a Federal Senate. These were the gentlemen whom the Jeffersonians dubbed the "Midnight Judges."

61. Circuit Courts Under the Act of April 29, 1802.

A year later the victorious Democrats, or Republicans as they then called themselves, repealed the Act of 1801.[19] By the express provisions of this statute all laws relating to the Federal judiciary changed by the Act of February 13, 1801, were re-enacted. Thus things were put back precisely where they had been thirteen months earlier, but some changes in the organization prescribed by the original Judiciary Act had become absolutely necessary. They were made a couple of months later by the Act of April 29, 1802.[20] By it six circuits were again established, although with different boundaries. The Circuit Courts no longer consisted of two Justices of the Supreme Court and of a District Judge. Only one Justice was assigned to each circuit. He and the District Judge might hold the Court together, or either could act alone, except that the appellate jurisdiction of the Circuit Court could be exercised only by the Circuit Justice, as a Justice of the Supreme Court sitting on circuit has always been styled. When in other cases the District Judge differed from the Circuit Justice, the question upon which they disagreed was certified to the Supreme Court for its determination. With the growth of the business of the Supreme Court itself, with the expansion

19. March 2, 1802, 2 Stat. 132.
20. 2 Stat. 156.

of the country, and therefore with the increase in the number of districts, more and more of the work of holding the Circuit Courts fell upon the District Judges. Except for additions to the number of circuits, this system remained unchanged for sixty-seven years.

62. Justices of the Supreme Court Can Be Constitutionally Assigned to Circuit Duty.

In 1803 the Supreme Court was called on to say whether its members could constitutionally be assigned to sit in the Circuit Courts without being specially appointed and commissioned as Judges of the latter. It held that "practice, and acquiescence under it, for a period of several years, commencing with the organization of the judicial system, affords an irresistible answer and has indeed fixed the construction. It is a contemporary interpretation of the most forcible nature. This practical exposition is too strong and obstinate to be shaken or controlled."[21]

63. Circuit Courts Under the Act of April 10, 1869.

In the nearly three score years and ten which elapsed between the close of the administration of the first Adams and the beginning of that of General Grant, the area of the country more than trebled and its population multiplied seven-fold. The great changes which the Civil war had brought about in the relations of the States and the Nation, and the enormous increase of interstate business which followed upon the development of our railroad system, had combined to add immensely to the volume and importance of the business which the Federal Courts were called upon to transact. These Courts were still organized as they had been at the beginning of the century. There were more districts and there were nine

21. Stuart vs. Laird, 1 Cranch, 298; 2 L. Ed. 115.

circuits where there had been but six, but beyond that no provision had been made for disposing of the greatly increased work which had to be done.

By the Act of April 10, 1869,[22] the President was authorized to appoint a Circuit Judge in each of the nine circuits. He was to have within his circuit all the powers which had been exercised by the Circuit Justice assigned to it. It was not the intention of Congress that the latter should be altogether relieved from circuit duty. He was to continue to sit, when he could, in the Circuit Court. A special section of the Act provided that it should be the duty of the Chief Justice and of each Justice of the Supreme Court to attend at least one term of the Circuit Court in each district of his circuit during every period of two years. This requirement remained on the statute book for more than forty years. During most of the latter part of that period it was little regarded.

The distinguished Justices of the Supreme Court were law-abiding citizens. As a rule they were hard workers, yet their days were only twenty-four hours long. The burdens of the Supreme Court became more and more onerous. It was simply impossible for its members to do circuit duty without neglecting the still more important work of the Supreme Court itself. A third of a century ago that Court was taxed beyond its capacity. In ordinary course it was several years after a case was docketed before it was reached for argument. Every year the Court fell farther and farther behind. Something had to be done. By the Act of March 3, 1891[23] intermediate Courts of Appeal were established, one in each circuit.

The same Act took from the Circuit Courts all appellate jurisdiction.

22. 16 Stat. 44.
23. 26 Stat. 826; 5 Fed. Stat. Ann. 600; U. S. Comp. Stat. Sec. 1108.

After the passage of the Circuit Courts of Appeals Act there was, therefore, in each district two distinct Courts —the Circuit and the District—each of which was a Court of original jurisdiction only.

64. The Abolition of the Circuit Courts.

In nearly all of the circuits the time and strength of the Circuit Judges were largely taken up by the work of the Circuit Court of Appeals. The Circuit Courts were ordinarily held by District Judges. In every district both the Circuit and District Courts had the same Marshal. In most of them the same clerk. There was no substantial reason for their separate existence. Accordingly, the Judicial Code provided that on the 31st of December, 1911, the Circuit Courts should be abolished. All their business and jurisdiction were transferred to the District Courts.

While they existed the Circuit Courts had original jurisdiction exclusive of that of the District Courts, of all the more important civil causes cognizable in the Federal Courts, other than those in admiralty and in bankruptcy.

65. Circuit Courts of Appeals.

As before stated, Circuit Courts of Appeals were created by the Act of March 3, 1891. There is one of them. in each circuit. The Act which established them provided for the appointment of an additional Circuit Judge in each circuit. The Circuit Court of Appeals was to be composed of three Judges. If the Circuit Justice was present and both the Circuit Judges and no one of them was disqualified, the Court was made up of those three. The Circuit Justice was seldom at hand—perhaps not oftener than at one hearing out of a hundred. The Circuit Judges still occasionally sat in the Circuit Courts. It sometimes happened that the appeals to be heard were

6

from decisions or orders made by them. In such cases
they could not sit in the appellate tribunal. It was therefore provided by law that the District Judges within each
circuit should be competent to sit in the Court according
to such order or provision among them as either by general or particular assignment should be designated by
the Court. In this, and doubtless in the other circuits, it
has been the practice of the Circuit Court of Appeals to
designate the District Judges of the Circuit to sit in
turn in the appellate tribunal.

In all the Circuits, except the Fourth, the number of
Circuit Judges has been increased, so that in the Second
and Eighth, there are now four, and in all the other Circuits, except the Fourth, three. In addition, four Circuit
Judges originally appointed to the Commerce Court have
since its abolition, been assigned to various Circuits.

By law never more than three Judges sit in the Circuit
Court of Appeals. The Court may be held by two Judges
and occasionally is. It is far better that three shall sit.
If a case is heard by two and they happen to differ in
opinion, either the decree below is affirmed by a divided
Court, or, more usually, a re-argument is ordered.
Neither alternative is in itself desirable.

66. No Judge May in a Circuit Court of Appeals Hear an Appeal from Himself.

When Justices of the Supreme Court went on circuit
and heard cases in the Circuit Courts, there was no rule
of law which forbade their taking part in the hearing
and decision of an appeal or writ of error from their
judgment or decree. In earlier years it was not unusual for them to do so. Now they seldom sit below at
all. In our day when Circuit and District Judges have
been promoted to the Supreme Bench they usually have
been careful to have nothing to do with appeals in any

case in which they sat below. They have the legal right so to do if they wish. They have usually thought it well to refrain. When the Circuit Courts of Appeals were created, it was expressly provided that no Justice or Judge before whom a cause or question may have been tried or heard in a District or Circuit Court, should sit on the trial or hearing of such cause or question in the Circuit Court of Appeals. The Supreme Court has held that this means that no judge shall sit in the Circuit Court of Appeals in any case in which there is to be reviewed any order or decision made by him below.[24]

67. Jurisdiction of the Circuit Courts of Appeals.

These Courts were intended primarily to relieve the Supreme Court. Accordingly, most, though not all, appeals from the District Courts are taken to the Circuit Court of Appeals. A few cases may still be taken directly from the District Court to the Supreme Court.

A discussion of the appellate jurisdiction of the Federal Courts is reserved for a later chapter.

68. The Circuits.

There are at present nine circuits. Since 1802 there have always been precisely as many circuits as there were Justices of the Supreme Court. Since 1837, as we have seen, that number has been nine, except for a period of about six years from 1863 to 1869, when it was ten. The present nine circuits are very unequal, both in population and in area. Thus, the First, is made up of Maine, New Hampshire, Massachusetts, Rhode Island and Porto Rico. It has an area of a little more than fifty-five thousand square miles. Its population is about seven millions. As it has only four District Judges, it may be

---

24. Rexford vs. Brunswick-Balke Collender Co., 228 U. S. 339; 57 L. Ed. 875; 33 Sup. Ct. 548.

assumed that the volume of Federal litigation in it is not great. The Eighth Circuit, however, comprises twelve States, the smallest of which is nearly as large as the entire First Circuit. It extends from the Canadian boundary of Minnesota and North Dakota to the line which separates New from Old Mexico. It has more than sixteen million inhabitants. There are eighteen District Judges in it. Some re-arrangement of the circuits would seem to be desirable.

69. The Fourth Circuit.

Maryland is in the Fourth Circuit, which includes beside it the Virginias and the Carolinas. It is divided into nine districts—that of Maryland, the Eastern and the Western Districts of Virginia, the Northern and Southern of West Virginia, the Eastern and Western of North Carolina, and the Eastern and Western of South Carolina.

70. Federal Courts of Special Jurisdiction.

Although the jurisdiction of a District Court is limited to its District, and a Circuit Court of Appeals to its Circuit, there are other inferior Courts of the United States whose jurisdiction is without territorial restriction, and whose writs run throughout the Union.[25]

There are at present two of these: The Court of Claims and the Court of Customs Appeals. Each of them deals with a special class of cases, to every one of which the United States is a party.

A Court of Claims' judgment, given in favor of the United States, upon a counterclaim against a plaintiff petitioner, by the simple process of being filed in the Clerk's Office of any District Court and entered upon the

25. U. S. vs. Borcherling, 185 U. S. 223-234; 46 L. Ed. 884; 22 Sup. Ct. 607.

latter's records, becomes a judgment of that Court, and may be enforced as its other judgments are.[26]

The Court of Claims may issue subpoenas to any part of the United States, commanding the attendance of witnesses before Commissioners of the Court, and may enforce obedience as a District Court might do under similar circumstances.[27]

Witnesses are protected by the provision that testimony shall be taken in the County in which the witness resides, when that can be conveniently done.[28]

And the Court of Claims has, in construing this statute, said that while witnesses residing or found in the District of Columbia may be called to testify at the Bar of the Court, when they are at a distance, their evidence must be taken by commission.[29]

71. The Court of Claims.

The Court of Claims was originally established by the Act of February 24, 1855,[30] for the purpose of hearing and determining all claims founded upon any law of Congress or upon any regulation of an executive department, or upon any contract, express or implied, with the Government of the United States; or which might be referred to it by either House of Congress. It was created for the "triple purpose of relieving Congress and of protecting the Government by regular investigation and of benefiting the claimants by affording them a certain mode of examining and adjudicating upon their claims."[31] Origi-

26. Judicial Code, Sec. 146; 5 Fed. Stat. Ann. 660; U. S. Comp. Stat. Sec. 1137.

27. Judicial Code, Sec. 168; 5 Fed. Stat. Ann. 676; U. S. Comp. Stat. Sec. 1159.

28. Judicial Code, Sec. 167; 5 Fed. Stat. Ann. 676; U. S. Comp. Stat. Sec. 1158.

29. Elting vs. U. S., 27 Ct. Clms., 158.

30. 10 Stat. 612; 5 Fed. Stat. Ann. 646; U. S. Comp. Stat. Sec. 1127.

31. United States vs. Klein, 13 Wall. 144; 20 L. Ed. 519.

nally it was a Court merely in name, for its power extended only to the preparation of bills to be submitted to Congress.[32] In 1863 the number of its Judges were increased from three to five. Its jurisdiction was somewhat enlarged. Instead of being required to prepare bills for Congress, it was authorized to render final judgment, subject to appeal to the Supreme Court, and to an estimate by the Secretary of the Treasury of the amount required to pay each claimant.[33]

Subsequent to the passage of the Act of 1863, the Supreme Court held that the Court of Claims was not one of the inferior Courts of the United States within the constitutional meaning of that phrase.

That Act had provided that a claimant whose claim had been allowed by the Court, or upon appeal by the Supreme Court, should be paid out of any general appropriation made by law for the payment and satisfaction of private claims, but no payment was to be made until the claim allowed had been estimated for by the Secretary of the Treasury, and Congress upon such estimate had made an appropriation for its payment.

Neither Court could by any process enforce its judgment. Whether that should be paid or not did not depend on the decision of either Court, but upon the future actions of the Secretary of the Treasury and of Congress. There was no question that Congress could create the Court of Claims. No harm was done by calling it a Court. Congress can establish tribunals with special powers to examine testimony and decide in the first instance upon the validity and justice of any claim against the United States. It may lawfully subject the decisions of such

32. United States vs. Klein, supra; Gordon vs. United States, 2 Wall. 561; 17 L. Ed. 971.

33. Act March 3, 1863, 12 Stat. 765; 5 Fed. Stat. Ann. 646; U. S. Comp. Stat. Sec. 1127.

tribunals to the supervision and control of Congress or of the head of any of the executive departments.

The Supreme Court said that by the Constitution, Congress may authorize appeals to it only "from such inferior Courts as Congress may ordain or establish to carry into effect the judicial power specifically granted to the United States. The inferior Court, therefore, from which the appeal is taken must be a judicial tribunal authorized to render a judgment which will bind the rights of the parties litigating before it unless appealed from." * * * "Congress cannot extend the appellate power" of the Supreme Court "beyond the limits prescribed by the Constitution, and can neither confer nor impose on it the authority and duty of hearing and determining an appeal from a commissioner or auditor or any other tribunal exercising only special powers under an Act of Congress, nor can Congress authorize and require the Supreme Court to express an opinion on a case where its judicial power could not be exercised and where its judgment could not be final and conclusive upon the rights of the parties."

Subsequently the objectionable part of the Act of 1863 was repealed.[34] Thereafter judgments of the Court of Claims were held to be final judgments, subject to be affirmed or reversed on appeal to the Supreme Court. It is true that they cannot be enforced against the United States, if Congress does not see fit to appropriate money for their payment, because there is no other process known to the law by which money in the treasury of the United States can be taken out of it. The fact that a suitor before a Court may be execution proof does not make the investigation and determination of a claim against him any less a judicial matter. The Court of

34. Act March 17, 1866; 14 Stat. 9; 5 Fed. Stat. Ann. 646; U. S. Comp. Stat. Sec. 1127.

Claims is now one of the inferior Courts of the United States.[35] Its jurisdiction will be later discussed.

72. The Court of Customs Appeals.

The Court of Customs Appeals was established by the Act of August 5, 1909.[36] It consists of a presiding judge and four associates, three of whom will constitute a quorum, but as the concurrence of at least three is required for any decision, in case of a vacancy or of a temporary disability or disqualification of one or two of the judges, the President may designate a Circuit or District Judge to act.[37] The Court was created for the purpose of reviewing on appeal final decisions of the Board of General Appraisers as to the construction of the law and the facts respecting the classification of merchandise, the rate of duty imposed thereon under such classification and the fees and charges connected therewith, and all appealable questions as to the jurisdiction of such board, and as to the law and regulations governing the collection of the customs revenue. The decisions of the Court of Customs Appeals are in most cases final; in some of exceptional importance, its action may be reviewed by the Supreme Court.[38] The purpose of its creation was to relieve the then existing Circuit Courts of the United States of the labor of passing upon questions as to the classification of merchandise under the tariff Acts and the rates of duty to which various articles were liable. The Circuit Courts in different circuits and the Circuit Courts of Appeals therein might well give different answers to the same question. Uniformity in customs administration could in that event be secured only by

35. U. S. vs. Klein, 13 Wall. 144; 20 L. Ed. 519.
36. 36 Stat. 105; 5 Fed. Stat. Ann. 685; U. S. Comp. Stat. Sec. 1179.
37. J. C. Section 188; 5 Fed. Stat. Ann. 686; U. S. Comp. Stat. Sec. 1179.
38. Act of Aug. 22, 1914, 38 Stat. 703; 5 Fed. Stat. Ann. 689; U. S. Comp. Stat. Sec. 1186.

carrying the controversy to the Supreme Court of the United States. Its time is too valuable for much of it to be taken up with such questions. In matters of taxation it ordinarily does not make so much difference what the rate is, as it does whether it is certain and uniform. The Court usually sits in Washington but may hold sessions in any of the judicial circuits at such place as it may designate.[39]

73. Commerce Court.

This Court was created by the Act of June 18, 1910.[40] It had jurisdiction over most proceedings to enforce, and over all to enjoin, set aside, annul or suspend, any order of the Interstate Commerce Commission. It was composed of five judges, specially appointed in the first instance by the President. They became by virtue of such appointment, Circuit Judges of the United States.

There had been not a little popular as well as partisan opposition to its creation in the first place, inspired by the belief that the railroad companies desired it, as, for a number of altogether proper reasons, they doubtless did. Some of its early decisions were sharply criticized. One of its judges was impeached for personal misconduct, and the political complexion of Congress having changed, the Court was abolished by a provision of the deficiency appropriation bill of October 22, 1913.[41] It was provided that the Judges of the Court should remain Circuit Judges of the United States, and should, from time to time, be designated by the Chief Justice of the United States to sit in different districts or circuits.

39. J. C. Section 189; 5 Fed. Stat. Ann. 686; U. S. Comp. Stat. Sec. 1180.
40. 36 Stat. 539; 5 Fed. Stat. Ann. 1105; U. S. Comp. Stat. Sec. 993.
41. 38 Stat. 219; 5 Fed. Stat. Ann. 1108; U. S. Comp. Stat. Sec. 992.

CHAPTER IV.

THE CRIMINAL JURISDICTION AND PROCEDURE OF THE FEDERAL COURTS.

74. Jurisdiction of the Several Courts of the United States.

The organization of the United States Courts has been sufficiently discussed. The jurisdiction of each of them must next be considered.

75. The District Courts.

The District Courts are, for most matters, the only Federal Courts of original jurisdiction. The Supreme Court has original jurisdiction over the few cases named in the Constitution. The Court of Customs Appeals does not, it is true, hear appeals from other Courts, but it deals only with matters or issues which have been previously passed upon by the Board of General Appraisers. The last named is technically an administrative board. Its functions and modes of proceeding are not unlike those of a Court. The Court of Claims is not in any sense an appellate tribunal, but it has jurisdiction of only one class of controversies.

There are certain kinds of actions and proceedings within the grant of judicial power to the United States, which may not be brought in the State Courts at all. There are others which at the option of the parties may be instituted in either the State or the Federal tribunals.

76. The Exclusive Jurisdiction of Courts of the United States.

By the Judicial Code the jurisdiction of the Courts of the United States is made exclusive in eight classes of cases, viz:—

1. Crimes and offenses cognizable under the laws of the United States.

2. Penalties and forfeitures under those laws.

3. Civil causes of admiralty and maritime jurisdiction.

4. Seizures under the laws of the United States otherwise than in admiralty and prizes brought into the United States.

5. Cases under the patent or copyright laws.

6. All matters and proceedings in bankruptcy.

7. All controversies of a civil nature where a State is a party, except between a State and its citizens or between a State and citizens of other States or aliens.

8. (*a*) All such suits and proceedings against ambassadors or other public ministers, their domestics or domestic servants as may consistently with the law of nations be entertained by a Court of law.

(*b*) Suits and proceedings against consuls or vice-consuls.

Exclusive original jurisdiction over the first six of these is conferred upon the District Courts. The Supreme Court is given such exclusive original jurisdiction over the seventh class and over "a" subdivision of the eighth, while the Supreme and the District Courts have concurrent original jurisdiction over cases within its "b" subdivision.[1]

---

1. Judicial Code, Sections 256 and 233; 5 Fed. Stat. Ann. 921-708; U. S. Comp. Stat. Secs. 1233-1210.

77. District Courts Have Exclusive Jurisdiction to Enforce the Criminal, Penal and Quasi Penal Legislation of the United States.

It is only in its own Courts that the United States may proceed to enforce its criminal, penal or quasi penal legislation. The District Courts have, therefore, exclusive jurisdiction of all crimes and offenses against the United States, of all suits for penalties and forfeitures incurred, and of all seizures made under the laws of the United States.

78. Every Criminal Prosecution in the United States Court Must Charge the Violation of a Specific Federal Statute.

Because the Federal Courts have no common law criminal jurisdiction, every prosecution in them must charge the violation of some specific Federal statute, and accordingly the District Attorney usually endorses on the indictment or information a reference to the statute under which it is framed. This endorsement is, however, not a part of the indictment. The District Attorney may make a mistake. He may suppose that what is charged in the indictment is a violation of a particular statute when it is not. The indictment will be good for all that, if what it says the accused did constitutes a violation of some other Federal statute.[2]

79. Such Statute Must Be Constitutional.

Not only must an indictment or information charge the defendant with having broken a Federal statute, but that statute must be one which Congress had the constitutional power to enact. The right of the United States to punish at all depends either upon the nature of the

2. Williams vs. United States, 168 U. S. 382; 42 L. Ed. 509; 18 Sup. Ct. 92; 93 Fed. 396; 35 C. C. A. 369.

thing done or upon its having been done in a particular place.

80. Congress Can Provide for the Punishment of One Who Anywhere Interferes with the Exercise of a Power Given to the Federal Government.

Most of the powers granted the Federal Government may be exercised without other territorial limitations than those imposed by international law. Congress can declare that anyone who anywhere interferes with the exercise of any of its powers will commit a crime, and it can fix the punishment therefor. For example: Congress has the power to establish postoffices and post roads. It may provide for the punishment of anyone who in any way interferes with the mails or who tries to send, through them, things which it says shall not be so sent. Congress has no power to punish one man for obtaining property from another by false pretenses, unless, perhaps, the transaction is a part of interstate commerce. It can say that no one with intent to cheat another shall put any letter into the mails anywhere. It will make no difference whether the letter so mailed is directed to an address in the same city or to one at the other extremity of the country. The offense against the Federal laws has been equally committed in either case.

81. How Far May Congress Go to Prevent Interference With the Exercise of Federal Power?

How far may Congress go to prevent interference with the proper exercise of a Federal power? For example, may it punish anyone who at any place assaults a Federal official who is not at the moment engaged in any official duty?

Immediately after the assassination of President McKinley this question was much discussed. The controversy is referred to now merely because it illustrates the rule that an act done within territory over which the exclusive jurisdiction of the United States does not extend cannot be made a crime by Congress unless it may in the fair exercise of legislative discretion be supposed to obstruct the exercise of some of the powers committed to the Federal Government.

Not long before we went to war with Germany, and when there was much apprehension as to what unbalanced individuals might attempt, Congress provided for the punishment of anyone who threatened to take the life of the President or to do him bodily harm.[3] In one District Court case, it was held that the statute must be construed as limited to threats made against the President in his official capacity.[4] In other cases, in which prosecutions under it have been sustained, that question does not appear to have been considered, the facts doubtless showing that official acts or omissions of the President had aroused the anger of the accused.[5]

82. Power of Congress to Punish Crimes Committed in Particular Localities.

Over the territories of the United States, the District of Columbia and all those numerous places ceded to the United States by the consent of the States for the purposes of the Federal Government, Congress has exclusive jurisdiction. As to them it has all the powers of any other sovereign legislature, limited only by the restrictions in favor of individual liberty imposed by the Constitution of the United States. By the express language of the Constitution its jurisdiction is exclusive. If two men get into an altercation in the Postoffice Building in Baltimore, or if a civilian commits any offense within

3. Act Feb. 14, 1917; 39 Stat. 919; Fed. Stat. Ann. 1918 Supp. 667; U. S. Comp. Stat. Sec. 10200a (1919 Supplement).

4. U. S. vs. Metzdorf, 252 Fed. 933.

5. Clark vs. U. S., 250 Fed. 449.

the grounds of the Naval Academy at Annapolis, the offenders are punishable by the United States District Court for the District of Maryland, and by it alone.

83. Offenses Against Federal Laws Can Be Punished by the District Court Only.

It is quite possible that Congress might confer upon the United States Commissioners powers to deal summarily with petty offenses;[6] out of tender regard for the liberty of the citizen it has never done so. One who commits a trivial assault or breach of the peace in any place within the exclusive jurisdiction of the United States must be proceeded against in the United States District Court for the district. He cannot be put on trial until an indictment or information has been returned against him. A fine of from $1 to $5 may be adequate punishment for anything that he has done. It may be impossible for the Government to punish him at all unless at an expenditure fifty or a hundred times as great. The national legislature may in this matter have acted wisely. In exceptional cases the result may be unfortunate. A poor and friendless person may be charged with some trifling offense; and may be unable to give bail; it may be days, weeks or, in exceptional circumstances, months before his case can be disposed of. If the committing magistrate were authorized to pass upon the issues involved, the guilt or innocence of the accused might be at once determined. If found guilty he would doubtless be less severely punished than he will in fact be, if he be held in prison until he is acquitted by the District Court.

6. Callan vs. Wilson, 127 U. S. 555; 32 L. Ed. 223; 8 Sup. Ct. 1301; Lawton vs. Steele, 152 U. S. 141; 38 L. Ed. 385; 14 Sup. Ct. 499; Schick vs. U. S., 195 U. S. 65; 49 L. Ed. 99; 24 Sup. Ct. 826.

84. Places Within the Jurisdiction of the Federal Government Rapidly Increasing.

At every session of Congress there is a determined effort to pass what is known as a Public Buildings Bill; that is a bill providing for the erection of Federal buildings in many different cities and towns. It is frequently successful and sometimes in a single session, provision is made for upwards of a hundred new structures. The Federal Government acquires exclusive criminal jurisdiction over all sites purchased for such purposes with the consent of the State legislature.

85. Whether a Crime Has Been Committed Within State or Federal Jurisdiction is Sometimes a Difficult Question of Fact.

In a particular case it may be difficult to determine whether the State or the Federal Government has jurisdiction.

There is in the grounds of the State House at Annapolis a statue of the Baron de Kalb. It was erected by the United States. The State of Maryland[7] ceded to the United States as a site for it a plot of ground 24 feet square. It might not always be easy to say whether an offense was committed within or without the narrow confines of this piece of land.

86. Whether a Crime Has Been Committed Within the Exclusive Jurisdiction of the United States is Sometimes an Important Question.

That may be the very question which it is important to determine. For example: A group of men may be standing near the DeKalb statue. The pocket of one of them may be picked. The offender may be caught. He may be sentenced to fifteen years in the State penitentiary if the

7. Acts of General Assembly of Md. of 1884, Chapter 339.

offense was committed outside of the 24 feet square. If within it the maximum penalty will be ten years.

Before January 1st, 1910, when the Federal Penal Code went into effect, one year's imprisonment was the severest punishment which could have been inflicted upon any one convicted of larceny within the exclusive jurisdiction of the United States.

Some years earlier, a famous professional criminal while in the Postoffice in Baltimore, stole the satchel of a runner of the Merchants National Bank. He was arrested, tried and convicted. He received the maximum penalty. That was only one year. Had he taken the same satchel on the west side of Calvert Street instead of on the east he might have been sent to the penitentiary for fifteen years.

Other interesting questions of jurisdiction arise. For example: A number of years ago a somewhat intoxicated sailor from a United States war ship provoked a controversy with two residents of Annapolis. While he was scuffling with one of them the other shot him. He died in a few minutes. When the bullet struck him, he was on one of the grass plots forming part of the Postoffice site of Annapolis. The man who fired was at the moment outside of the lines of that lot on one of the public streets of the town and therefore within the jurisdiction of the State of Maryland. It is a principle of the common law that in such cases the offense is committed where it takes effect.[8] The man who fired the fatal shot was accordingly tried in the United States Court for the District of Maryland. If his trial had taken place in a State Court he doubtless would have been convicted of murder in the second degree. That was punishable by imprisonment in the penitentiary for from five to eighteen years.

Prior to 1897 any one convicted in the United States

8. United States vs. Davis, 25 Fed. Cases, 786 (No. 14932); 2 Sum. 482.

Courts of murder was punished with death. Between 1897 and 1910 the jury was allowed to return a verdict of guilty of murder, but without capital punishment. If they did the convict was sent to the penitentiary for life. In this Annapolis case the jury found a verdict of guilty of murder, without capital punishment. The prisoner was necessarily given a life sentence.

Since the Penal Code went into effect, a person indicted for murder may be found guilty in either the first or the second degree.[9] The penalty for the former is death unless the jury qualify their verdict by the addition of the words "without capital punishment." For the latter it cannot be less than ten years' imprisonment, it may be life-long confinement.[10]

87. Congress Has Made Some State Criminal Laws Applicable to Places Within Exclusive Federal Jurisdiction.

The character and the consequences of an act should not ordinarily depend upon whether it was committed a foot or two on one side or the other of the boundary line of a lot upon which a Federal building stands. Many years ago Congress attempted to limit the occasions upon which anything of this kind can happen by providing that any one who commits in any place which has been ceded to or is under the jurisdiction of the United States, an offense which is not prohibited, or the punishment for which is not specially provided for by any law of the United States, shall be liable to and receive the same punishment as the laws of the State in which such place is situated, at the time Congress acted, provided for the like offense when committed within the jurisdiction of

9. Section 273, 35 Stat. 1143; 7 Fed. Stat. Ann. 905; U. S. Comp. Stat. Sec. 10446.

10. Sections 275, 330, 35 Stat. 1143, 1152; 7 Fed. Stat. Ann. 917, 983; U. S. Compiled Stat. Sections 10448, 10504.

such State. It was further declared that no subsequent repeal of any such State law should affect any prosecution for such offense in any Court of the United States. This Act is constitutional. Congress could in the very language used by the State legislature have enacted all or any such State laws. It can, if it wishes, do the same thing by adopting them all in general terms.

88. Congress May Not Adopt in Advance Such Laws as a State May Pass.

It was quite early ruled, however, that Congress could not make State laws to be subsequently passed, applicable to territory within the jurisdiction of the United States.[11] It cannot delegate its exclusive jurisdiction, or any part of it, to a State legislature. It follows that when, after the passage of a congressional Act adopting State legislation the State creates a new offense or increases or diminishes the punishment for an old one, its commission in a place within the exclusive jurisdiction of the United States will be punished differently than if committed on the other side of the boundary line of the Government's property. Congress, therefore, at short intervals re-enacts the Act and adopts all State legislation up to the time of its latest enactment.

The statute now in force is section 289 of the Penal Code.[12]

89. When Congress Has Exclusive Jurisdiction.

The constitutional provision is that Congress shall have power to exercise exclusive jurisdiction in all cases whatsoever over all places purchased with the consent of the legislature of the State in which the same shall be

11. United States vs. Paul, 6 Peters, 139; 8 L. Ed. 348.

12. Acts of 1909, Ch. 321; 35 Stat. 1145; 7 Fed. Stat. Ann. 938; U. S. Comp. Stat. Sec. 10462.

for the erection of forts, magazines, arsenals, dockyards and other needful buildings.[13]

Whenever, for any of the purposes named, the legislature having consented, the property is bought, the United States *ipso facto* acquires exclusive jurisdiction over it. The reservation by the State of concurrent jurisdiction to serve civil and criminal process within lands so purchased does not limit or affect the exclusive right of the United States to punish crimes and offenses therein committed. Sometimes the State attaches to its consent to the purchase conditions which, if effective, restrict the jurisdiction of the United States and make it less than the Constitution says it shall have. What the effect of such attempted limitation by the State legislature is has not been clearly determined. Probably a consent so limited is no consent at all, and the land remains in the same situation it would have been, had it, without the consent of the State legislature, been purchased by the Government for the purpose in question.

The United States may acquire land without the consent of a legislature when such land is purchased for a proper governmental purpose. Over lands so obtained the Government has no other jurisdiction than that sufficient to prevent the State or anyone else from interfering with its use by the Government for Federal purposes. Over such of them as are acquired for purposes other than those specially named in the constitutional provision already referred to, the State may grant such extent of jurisdiction as to it may seem fit. The United States when admitting a State into the Union may retain exclusive jurisdiction over land then owned by the United States.

A review of this whole subject will be found in the very interesting case of Fort Leavenworth R. R. Co. vs. Lowe.[14]

13. Constitution, Art. 1, Sec. 8.
14. 114 U. S. 525; 29 L. Ed. 264; 5 Sup. Ct. 995.

90. When Offenses Against State Laws Are Not Offenses Against Federal Laws, Although Committed Within the Exclusive Jurisdiction of the United States.

In 1908, the New York World charged that Charles Taft, a brother of Judge Taft, at the time a candidate for the Presidency of the United States, and Douglas Robinson, a brother-in-law of President Roosevelt, had been improperly interested in the sale, by the French Panama Canal Company, of its property to the United States. By the law of the State of New York libel is an indictable offense.

The New York World is habitually sold within the limits of the West Point military reservation, which is in Orange County in the State of New York, and one or more copies are regularly mailed to the Postoffice Building in New York City; both places are within the Southern District of New York. It is printed in the defendant's printing establishment in the City of New York. The Grand Jury of the United States for the Southern District of New York indicted the publishers of the World for publishing the libel in a place within the exclusive jurisdiction of the United States. The case was taken to the Supreme Court. CHIEF JUSTICE WHITE pointed out that "where acts are done on reservations which are expressly prohibited and punished as crimes by a law of the United States, that law is dominant and controlling. Yet, on the other hand, where no law of the United States has expressly provided for the punishment of offenses committed on reservations, all acts done on such reservations which are made criminal by the laws of the several States are left to be punished under the applicable State statutes."

The law of New York which made libel punishable, provided that where a person libelled was a resident of the State, the prosecution should be either in the county of such residence or in the county where the paper was published, and where the person libelled was a non-resident the prosecution should be in the county in which the paper on its face purported to be published, or if it did not so indicate, in any county in which it was circulated, and that the accused could not be indicted or tried for a publication of the same libel against the same person in more than one county. To allow a prosecution in the United States Court for the circulation of that libel upon a Government reservation would have been using a State law for the prosecution of an offense in a manner forbidden by that law. The indictment should have been found by the State Grand Jury for the County of New York, where the paper was published. It was therefore held that the prosecution could not be sustained.[15]

The judges of the Supreme Court were careful to say that they "do not intimate that the rule which in this case has controlled our decision would be applicable to a case where an indictment was found in a court of the United States for a crime which was wholly committed on a reservation, disconnected with acts committed within the jurisdiction of the State, and where the prosecution for such crime in the Courts of the United States instead of being in conflict with the applicable State law was in all respects in harmony therewith."

Such a case as that upon which the Supreme Court declined to intimate their opinion would be raised if some-one within a United States reservation published and circulated a libel, such reservation being either the sole, or the primary and most important place of publication.

91. Offenses on the High Seas.

The Constitution[16] empowers Congress to define and punish piracies and felonies on the high seas. The high

15. United States vs. Press Pub. Co., 219 U. S. 1; 55 L. Ed. 65; 31 Sup. Ct. 209.

16. Article 1, Sec. 8, Cl. 10.

seas are open waters without the body of a county and which are in fact free to the navigation of all nations and peoples. They do not include the waters surrounded by or enclosed between narrow headlands or promontories.[17] Within this definition are included the waters of the Great Lakes.[18] Congress has exercised this power and has made punishable a number of offenses when committed on the high seas.

92. Offenses Upon Navigable Waters.

Much navigable water does not form a part of the high seas within the definition above given. There is no express grant to Congress of power to make offenses committed on such waters punishable, but the Constitution does declare that the judicial power of the United States shall extend to all cases of admiralty and maritime jurisdiction. All waters which are in fact navigable either by themselves or in connection with other waters for purposes of interstate or foreign commerce, are within the admiralty jurisdiction.[19]

Congress has always assumed that it has the power to provide for the punishment of offenses committed thereon. The Courts have held this assumption well founded.[20]

It has legislated with reference to such waters only so far as has been necessary to prevent serious inconvenience and scandal. It has provided for the punishment of offenses committed upon waters within the admiralty and maritime jurisdiction of the United States and out of the jurisdiction of any particular State, or when committed within the admiralty and maritime jurisdiction of the United States and out of the jurisdiction of any par-

17. United States vs. Brailsford, 5 Wheat. 184; 5 L. Ed. 65.

18. United States vs. Rodgers, 150 U. S. 255; 37 L. Ed. 1071; 14 Sup. Ct. 109.

19. The Robert W. Parsons, 191 U. S. 26; 48 L. Ed. 73; 24 Sup. Ct. 8.

20. Imbrovek vs. Hamburg-American Steam Packet Co., 190 Fed. 234.

ticular State on board any vessel belonging in whole or in part to the United States, or to any citizen thereof, or to any corporation created by or under the laws of the United States or of any State, territory or district thereof,[21] or when committed upon any vessel licensed, registered or enrolled under the laws of the United States and being on a voyage upon the waters of any of the Great Lakes, or any of the waters connecting any of them, or upon the River St. Lawrence where it constitutes the international boundary line.[22] It has also made punishable certain offenses when committed on board an American vessel although within the jurisdiction of a particular State, as, for example, assaults by the master upon the crew.[23] It is under these statutes that the masters of vessels engaged in dredging oysters in Maryland waters have, in the United States District Court for the District of Maryland, been tried and convicted for beating and otherwise cruelly treating their dredgers.

93. Federal Criminal Procedure.

While the criminal procedure of the Federal and of the State Courts is very similar in most respects, there are differences both in form and in substance.

94. United States Commissioners.

There are no Federal Justices of the Peace. The original Judiciary Act authorized United States Judges and certain State officers to give preliminary hearings to persons accused of offenses against the United States and to admit them to bail or to commit them for trial.[24]

21. Act March 4, 1909,.Sec. 272; 35 Stat. 1142; 7 Fed. Stat. Ann. 890; U. S. Comp. Stat. Sec. 10445.

22. Ibid.

23. Ibid, Sec. 291; 35 Stat. 1145; 7 Fed. Stat. Ann. 943; U. S. Comp. Stat. Sec. 10464.

24. Sec. 33, 1 Stat. 91; 5 Fed. Stat. Ann. 1056; U. S. Comp. Stat. Sec. 1247.

It was speedily found that prisoners were sometimes taken into custody at places which were not within a convenient distance of any person empowered to take bail. In such cases the Circuit Courts were directed to appoint, for that purpose, one or more discreet persons learned in the law.[25] Various statutes from time to time added to the powers and duties of these appointees. For a great many years they were known as Commissioners of the Circuit Courts. In 1896 their official title was changed to United States Commissioners;[26] and it was provided that they were for the future to be appointed by the District and not by the Circuit Courts. Their term of office is now four years. They have always been removable at the will of the appointing power. The District Court may appoint as many of them as it sees fit. They receive no salary. They are compensated exclusively by fees. They have a number of miscellaneous powers and duties, most of which are enumerated by the Supreme Court in the case of United States vs. Allred.[27]

95. Warrant of Arrest.

There are not many United States Commissioners. There are many places in the United States from which you would have to go a hundred miles or more before you could find one. Even near where one ordinarily resides there may be frequent occasions when he is not accessible at the moment when immediate action is necessary. The Federal law, therefore, provides that "for any crime or offense against the United States, the offender may, by any Justice or Judge of the United States," or by any United States Commissioner, "or by any Chancellor,

25. Act March 2, 1793, 1 Stat. 334; 5 Fed. Stat. Ann. 1056; U. S. Comp. Stat. Sec. 1247.

26. Act May 28, 1896; 29 Stat. 184; 4 Fed. Stat. Ann. 631; U. S. Comp. Stat. Sec. 1333.

27. 155 U. S. 594; 39 L. Ed. 273; 15 Sup. Ct. 231.

Judge of a Supreme or Superior Court, Chief or first Judge of Common Pleas, Mayor of a city, Justice of the Peace, or other magistrate, of any State where he may be found, and agreeably to the usual mode of process against offenders in such State, and at the expense of the United States, be arrested and imprisoned, or bailed, as the case may be, for trial before such Court of the United States as by law has cognizance of the offense.''[28]

In practice State Justices of the Peace are occasionally called on to issue warrants and hold the prisoner to bail or commit him for the action of the United States Court. As a rule, however, the preliminary hearings are had before a United States Commissioner. Sometimes, as under the State practice, proceedings are first instituted by an indictment or presentment by the Grand Jury, or by information presented by the Attorney of the United States.

96. Where Offender Must Be Tried.

The Sixth Amendment to the Constitution of the United States provides that the accused shall enjoy the right of a speedy and public trial by an impartial jury of the State and District where the crime has been committed. It is not always easy to tell where that is. The offense may have been begun in one district and completed in another. In such case the Act of Congress provides that it may be prosecuted in either.[29] When committed out of the jurisdiction of any district, as on the high seas, or in some of the guano islands belonging to the United States, the statute provides that the trial shall be in the district in which the offender is found, or in the district into which he may be first brought.[30] It was under this provision that the Circuit Court for the District of Maryland

28. Rev. Stat. Sec. 1014.
29. Rev. Stat., Sec. 731.
30. Rev. Stat , Sec. 730, Sec. 5576.

some thirty years ago tried thirty or more negroes who, on the Island of Navassa, a barren guano rock in the West Indies, rose in mutiny and murdered a number of the white men in charge of the work there carried on.[31]

97. When an Offense Begun in One District Has Been Finished in Another.

In applying the statute which provides that when an offense has been begun in one district and has been completed in another the offender may be prosecuted in either, it is necessary to keep clearly in mind what is the precise offense charged. How important this may be is shown by comparison of section 5480 of the Revised Statutes, as it stood before section 215 of the Penal Code was substituted for it, with section 3894 of the Revised Statutes as amended by the Act of September 19, 1890.[32]

Section 5480 defined and punished what in ordinary parlance was referred to as the fraudulent use of the United States mails. In substance it provided that any person who had devised a scheme or artifice to defraud to be effected by means of the postoffice establishment of the United States and who should, for executing such scheme, place or cause to be placed any letter in the mails, or should take any letter therefrom, should be punished by fine or imprisonment.

On the other hand, section 3894 as amended provided, among other things, for the punishment of any person who should knowingly cause to be delivered by mail any lottery ticket.

In the first statute the offense was the putting into the mails or the taking out of the mails. This could be committed only in one district—that is the district in which the letter was put in the mail or the district in which it was taken out of the mail. It followed that all prosecu-

31. Jones vs. United States, 137 U. S. 202; 34 L. Ed. 691; 11 Sup. Ct. 80.
32. 26 Stat. 465; 7 Fed. Stat. Ann. 805; U. S. Comp. Stat. Sec. 10383.

tions for violations of section 5480 had necessarily to be brought at the place at which the offender had sent out his mail or at which he had received it. In such cases the accused might have sent letters into every State in the Union. There was only one district in which he could be prosecuted.

The second statute mentioned makes it an offense knowingly to cause to be delivered a lottery ticket or a circular relating to a lottery.

One, Horner, in New York, deposited in the mail a lottery circular addressed to a person in the Southern District of Illinois. Such circular was in due course of mail delivered to the individual to whom it had been directed. The Supreme Court of the United States held that the offense was the causing to be delivered by the mails; that it was not completed until the delivery took place, and as that delivery was in the Southern District of Illinois the District Court of the United States for that district had jurisdiction.[33] To prevent misapprehension, it should be said that section 215 of the Penal Code, which has taken the place of old section 5480 of the Revised Statutes, now makes it an offense for anyone, for the purpose of executing a scheme or artifice to defraud, knowingly to cause to be delivered by mail any letter according to the direction thereon. Doubtless under the decision in Horner vs. United States, *supra,* one who now uses the mails in furtherance of a fraudulent scheme may be prosecuted in the district in which he mails the letter or in any district into which he sends it. In that case many businesslike offenders will be liable to indictment in half the judicial districts of the United States.

There thus may be a constructive, as distinguished from a personal, presence in a district. A man may cause a crime to be committed at a place in which he never was.

33. Horner vs. U. S., 143 U. S. 207; 36 L. Ed. 126; 12 Sup. Ct. 407.

If he does he may be prosecuted where the crime was so consummated.

The whole subject has been fully reviewed by the Supreme Court of the United States.[34]

98. Prosecutions in Districts in Which There Is More Than One Division.

Where the District has more than one division, the indictment must be returned by the grand jury sitting in the division in which the offense was committed.[35] Before the enactment of the Judicial Code, this was not necessarily so.[36]

99. When Accused is Arrested in Another District.

When a prosecution is instituted, it often happens that the accused is not in the district in which the offense is said to have been committed. In such case he may be arrested wherever he happens to be. He will be brought back to the district having jurisdiction of the offense upon a warrant of removal signed by the District Judge of the district in which he is found. This warrant is never issued until after the accused has had a hearing before a United States Commissioner or other committing magistrate, or has waived it.

100. Removal Proceedings After Indictment Found.

If an indictment has been found against him in the district in which the offense is alleged to have been committed, the Government produces at the hearing a certified copy of the indictment and a witness or witnesses who can prove that the man under arrest is the man whom

34. Hyde & Schneider vs. U. S., 225 U. S. 347; 56 L. Ed. 1114; 32 Sup. Ct. 793.

35. J. C. Section 53; United States vs. Chennault, 230 Fed. 942.

36. Barrett vs. U. S., 169 U. S. 218-31; 32 L. Ed. 723; 18 Sup. Ct. 327; also 32 L. Ed. 727; 18 Sup. Ct. 332.

the Grand Jury intended to indict. As a rule, this is all that need be done.[37]

An indictment if valid on its face raises a presumption of probable cause. The Supreme Court has said that

"the extent to which a Commissioner in extradition may inquire into the validity of the indictment put in evidence before him, as proof of probable cause of guilt, has never been definitely settled, although we have had frequent occasion to hold generally that technical objections should not be considered, and that the legal sufficiency of the indictment is only to be determined by the Court in which it is found. Of course, this rule has its limitations. If the indictment were a mere information, or obviously, upon inspection, set forth no crime against the United States, or a wholly different crime from that alleged as the basis for proceedings, or if such crime be charged to have been committed in another district from that to which the extradition is sought, the Commissioner could not properly consider it as ground for removal. In such case resort must be had to other evidence of probable cause. * * * An Extradition Commissioner is not presumed to be acquainted with the niceties of criminal pleading. His functions are practically the same as those of an examining magistrate in an ordinary criminal case, and if the complaint upon which he acts or the indictment offered in support thereof contains the necessary elements of the offense, it is sufficient, although a more critical examination may show that the statute does not completely cover the case."[38]

The indictment is, however, not conclusive evidence that there is probable cause to believe the accused guilty. He may rebut the presumption it raises. He may offer testimony to show that he did not do what was charged against

37. Beavers vs. Haubert, 198 U. S. 87; 49 L. Ed. 950; 25 Sup. Ct. 573.
38. Benson vs. Henkel, 198 U. S. 10; 49 L. Ed. 919; 25 Sup. Ct. 569.

him in the indictment. If he does, the testimony must be heard and considered.

The Grand Jury of the United States for the Middle District of Tennessee indicted a number of firms, corporations and individuals, for a violation of the Sherman Act. Some of the defendants were arrested in Virginia. They offered to produce testimony that they had not and could not have committed in the Middle District of Tennessee, the offense charged in the indictment. The offer was refused on the ground that in Virginia no examination before a committing magistrate can be had after the defendant has been indicted. The Supreme Court held that the refusal constituted reversible error.[39]

101. Removal Proceedings Before Indictment Found.

Frequently the accused is arrested before it has been possible to obtain an indictment. In such case it is necessary to send to the district in which he is in custody witnesses who can show that there is probable cause to believe that he has committed the offense charged against him. He has precisely the same kind of hearing in that district as he would have had had he been arrested in the district in which the offense was committed.

102. Removal Hearings Usually Held by United States Commissioner.

Section 1014 of the Revised Statutes already quoted provides that the Commissioners and the other officers therein named may arrest and imprison or bail offenders for trial before such Court of the United States as by law has cognizance of the offense. In point of fact, these hearings, whether the accused has already been indicted or not, are usually held before a United States Commissioner. If he finds there is probable cause to believe the

---

39. Tinsley vs. Treat, 205 U. S. 20; 51 L. Ed. 639; 27 Sup. Ct. 430.

prisoner guilty he so certifies to the Judge of the district,. who thereupon, and ordinarily without further hearing, issues a warrant of removal.

103. Duty of District Judge in Removal Proceedings.

But "in such cases the Judge exercises something more than a mere ministerial function involving no judicial discretion. He must look into the indictment to ascertain whether an offense against the United States is charged, find whether there was probable cause and determine whether the Court to which the accused is sought to be removed, has jurisdiction of the same."[40]

"Doubtless the action of the committing magistrate is prima facie sufficient for the basis of the warrant, but it is not conclusive, and while the Judge should not necessarily require another or preliminary examination, if in his judgment it is expedient that the prisoner be further heard in defense, it is his duty to pass fully upon the case and determine for himself whether the removal should be ordered."[41]

104. Proceedings May Be First Taken in District in Which Prisoner is Arrested.

Ordinarily the order of removal is not made until some criminal proceedings have been begun in the district in which it is alleged the offense has been committed, but it is not absolutely necessary that such proceeding shall have been so instituted. CHIEF JUSTICE MARSHALL, after a hearing in the Virginia District before him as committing magistrate, committed Aaron Burr for trial in Ohio for an offense alleged to have been there committed,. although up to that time no steps had been taken in the matter in the latter district.

40. Tinsley vs. Treat, 205 U. S. 29; 51 L. Ed. 689; 27 Sup. Ct. 430.
41. Price vs. McCarty, 89 Fed. 84; 32 C. C. A. 162.

105. When Indictment Necessary Before Accused May Be Tried.

The charge upon which a person accused of crime is tried, is regularly embodied either in an indictment or in an information. The Constitution declares that no one shall be held to answer for a capital or other infamous crime except upon an indictment by a Grand Jury. "Infamous," as applied to crimes, means, in different connections, different things. Thus, under the Constitution of Maryland, conviction of an adult for larceny or other infamous crime involves perpetual disfranchisement unless there is a pardon from the Governor. The taking of an apple or an ear of corn which does not belong to one is an infamous crime. The committing of an assault with intent to rape is not. Conviction for the former entails perpetual disfranchisement; for the latter no disfranchisement at all.[42]

By a State statute such an assault may be punished by death or by long confinement in the penitentiary. Nevertheless, the Court of Appeals of Maryland has held that it is not even a felony.[43]

Here the State follows the classification of crimes which the common law made for the purpose of determining the competency of witnesses. It held those offenses infamous which were not likely to be committed by any one whose evidence could be safely relied on. The Supreme Court of the United States has said that the Fifth Amendment was intended for the protection of the accused. "Whether a man shall be put upon his trial for crime without a presentment or indictment by a Grand Jury of his fellow-citizens depends upon the consequences to himself if he shall be found guilty." By the law of England, informations by the Attorney-Gen-

42. State vs. Bixler, 62 Md. 360.
43. Dutton vs. State, 123 Md. 373; 91 Atl. 417.

eral without the intervention of a Grand Jury were not allowed for capital crimes nor for any felony; by which was understood any offense which at common law occasioned a total forfeiture of the offender's lands or goods, or both. The question whether the prosecution must be by indictment or may be by information thus depended upon the consequences to the convict himself. "The Fifth Amendment * * * manifestly had in view that rule of the common law, rather than the rule on the very different question of the competency of witnesses." "The question is whether the crime is one for which the statutes authorize the Court to award an infamous punishment, not whether the punishment ultimately awarded is an infamous one. When the accused in in danger of being subjected to an infamous punishment if convicted, he has the right to insist that he shall not be put upon his trial except upon the accusation of a Grand Jury." The Court concluded: For more than a century imprisonment at hard labor in the State prison or penitentiary or other similar institution has been considered an infamous punishment in England and America."[44]

106. All Offenses Against the United States Punishable by More Than One Year's Imprisonment Are Both Infamous Crimes and Felonies.

Whenever a convict is sentenced to imprisonment for more than one year he may be sent to a penitentiary.[45] It follows that where an offense may possibly be punished by more than one year's imprisonment it is an infamous crime. The person charged with it can be prosecuted by indictment only. All offenses against the United States punishable by death or imprisonment for more than one

---

44. Ex parte Wilson, 114 U. S. 417; 29 L. Ed. 89; 5 Sup. Ct. 935.
45. R. S., Sec. 5541.

year are felonies.[46] All offenses for which no such punishment can be inflicted are misdemeanors. It follows that the line of demarcation between infamous and non-infamous crimes is now in the Federal practice the same as between felonies and misdemeanors. There are two possible exceptions to this rule. It may be that there are offenses punishable by not more than one year's imprisonment in which hard labor may be added as part of the penalty. If there are such they are infamous crimes.[47]

In *Ex parte* Wilson,[48] the Supreme Court intimated that there may be crimes the commission of which would be in public opinion so disgraceful that they would be held "infamous" within the purpose of the Fifth Amendment, independent of the punishment which may be prescribed for them.

107. When Accused May Be Prosecuted Upon an Information.

As a rule, however, all offenses for which the offender upon conviction cannot lawfully be punished by an imprisonment exceeding one year, may be prosecuted upon information. An indictment is not necessary. An information is filed by the District Attorney under his official oath of office.

At common law, the King, through his Attorney-General, might file informations in certain classes of cases without any evidence and against all evidence.

The Fourth Amendment to the Constitution of the United States provides, among other things, that no warrants shall issue, but upon probable cause supported by oath or affirmation. It follows that no warrant may issue upon an information filed by a United States Dis-

46. Penal Code, Sec. 335, 35 Stat. 1152; 7 Fed. Stat. Ann. 987; U. S. Comp. Stat. Sec. 10509.
47. U. S. vs. Moreland, decided April 17, 1922.
48. 114 U. S. 417; 29 L. Ed. 89; 5 Sup. Ct. 935.

trict Attorney, except it be supported by a statement made under oath or affirmation by some one having actual knowledge as to facts which if true, show probable cause to believe the accused guilty.[49]   If the latter is already in custody upon a warrant duly issued by a United States Commissioner upon a complaint in ordinary form, it is not necessary for the District Attorney to have new complaints or affidavits made.   He may annex to his information the affidavits made to the complaint before the Commissioner or the evidence of the witnesses given at the preliminary hearing before the committing magistrate.[50] Contrary to what has been sometimes held[51] and to what was stated in the first edition of this book, leave of Court is not necessary before the filing of an information.[52]   In late years, informations have been much more freely used, Congress having made the maximum punishment for many offenses a year or less, so that it should be possible to save the expense and delay involved in Grand Jury proceedings.   To prevent misapprehension, it should be stated that an indictment may be returned whenever an information can be exhibited, although as already stated, the reverse is not true.

108. Either Indictment or Information Necessary Before Accused Can Be Put Upon His Trial for Anything Other than a Petty Offense.

No one can be tried, upon a criminal charge, unless he has been indicted by the Grand Jury or an information has been filed against him by the District Attorney. Prosecutions for what at common law were known as petty offenses are exceptions to this rule.   In all other

49. U. S. vs. Tureaud, 20 Fed. 621; Johnston vs. U. S., 97 Fed. 187.

50. U. S. vs. Baumert, 179 Fed. 739.

51. U. S. vs. Schurman, 177 Fed. 581.

52. U. S. vs. Thompson, 251 U. S. 407; 64 L. Ed. 333; 40 Sup. Ct. 289; Weeks vs. U. S,. 216 Fed. 292; 132 C. C. A. 436.

cases the prosecution may begin with a complaint to, and a warrant of arrest from the committing magistrate. The accused is given a hearing before the latter. The indictment or information is a subsequent step in the proceedings. The Grand Jury may, however, itself investigate the case before a warrant has been sworn out against anybody. The first paper filed before any legal tribunal may be the presentment. In like manner the District Attorney may without giving the accused a previous hearing, exhibit an information against him.

109. An Indicted Person Arrested in the District in Which the Indictment Has Been Found, Cannot Demand a Preliminary Hearing.

Mr. Hughes in his book on Federal Procedure[53] says "the preliminary examination is a valuable right, and the prisoner can have it either on prosecutions instituted by complaint or by indictment." For this the case of United States vs. Farrington[54] is cited. An examination of the opinion in that case shows that the particular point was not involved. The Supreme Court appears to have definitely ruled that the absence of the preliminary examination is no ground for objection to the indictment.[55] An earlier case[56] on circuit was to the same effect.

110. Persons Accused of Anything More Serious Than Petty Offenses Cannot in Federal Courts Waive Jury Trials.

There is one marked distinction in the trial of criminal cases between the practice of the Federal and some of the State Courts. For example, in the Courts of Maryland a

---

53. 2nd Ed. 32, 33.
54. 5 Fed. 343.
55. Goldsby vs. U. S., 160 U. S. 73; 40 L. Ed. 343; 16 Sup. Ct. 216.
56. U. S. vs. Fuers, 25 Fed. Cases No. 15174.

prisoner may in any case whatever elect to be tried by the Judge without a jury. In the United States Courts he may do so only when charged with the so-called petty offenses.[57] Among them are the violations of the navigation laws referred to in sections 4300 to 4304 of the Revised Statutes. These latter may be prosecuted without either indictment or information upon a written complaint verified by oath and presented to the Court. It is read to the accused. He may plead to or answer it or make a counter statement. The trial is then proceeded with in a summary manner before the Court. The accused may at the time of pleading or answering demand a jury trial. If he does a plea of not guilty is entered on his behalf, and a jury is impaneled. The complaint takes the place of an indictment or information. To detain the accused until a jury can be gotten together to try him may sometimes inflict upon him a greater punishment than is merited by the offense with which he is charged. At one time many Federal Judges doubted whether even under such circumstances a defendant could constitutionally waive a jury trial. Whenever it was possible a jury was impaneled even when the traverser was willing to go to trial without one.[58] I have in a few cases in this district tried such cases without a jury.

The doubt as to the constitutionality of such proceedings was removed by Shick vs. United States.[59] That was an action by the Government to recover a penalty of $50 under section 11 of the Oleomargarine Act. The parties in writing waived a jury trial and agreed to submit the issues to the Court. This was something they had a clear statutory right to do if the proceeding was a civil one. The Supreme Court, however, held that the case was in

57. Thompson vs. Utah, 170 U. S. 343; 42 L. Ed. 1061; 18 Sup. Ct. 620.
58. In re Smith, 13 Fed. 25; U. S. vs. Smith, 17 Fed. 510.
59. 195 U. S. 65; 49 L. Ed. 99; 24 Sup. Ct. 826.

its nature criminal, though it was one of the class known to the common law as petty offenses and did not necessarily involve any moral delinquency. It was not a crime within the meaning of the third clause of section 2 of Article 3 of the Constitution, which provides that the trial of all crimes, except in cases of impeachment, shall be by jury. Consequently the defendant could lawfully and effectually waive his right to such a trial.

111. An Accused Does Not Have a Jury Trial Unless the Jury is Constituted as Required by the Common Law.

The constitutional jury must have twelve members, so that an agreement by the accused to go on before a jury of eleven or any smaller number is not binding on him.[60] Moreover, it has been held by at least one Circuit Court of Appeals that the accused has not had a jury trial unless the court is constituted as it was at common law. In that case the trial of certain defendants indicted for using the mails in furtherance of a scheme to defraud had been going on for many weeks. Much testimony had been taken at great expense to both traversers and the government. The presiding judge was taken ill. It was clear that an interval of indefinite duration, but certain to be a long one, must elapse before he would be able to resume his seat on the Bench. By the agreement another qualified judge of the District took his place, reading from the stenographer's transcript, all the testimony that had been given. The jury returned a verdict of guilty, but on writ of error, the Circuit Court of Appeals set aside the conviction on the ground that the defendant had not had a jury trial as known to the common law.[61]

60. Thompson vs. Utah, 170 U. S. 343; 42 L. Ed. 1061; 18 Sup. Ct. 620.
61. Freeman vs. U. S., 227 Fed. 732; 142 C. C. A. 256.

112. The Trial.

In what respects may the procedure in a criminal trial in a Federal differ from that in a State Court?

113. Accused May Be Tried at One Time for Several Crimes or Offenses of the Same Class.

In Maryland, as in many other States, one accused of several offenses may ordinarily demand a separate trial upon each of them. He may do so even when the different charges are of the same general character and are in a sense at least all parts of one continuous transaction. Thus, a clerk in the employ of the City of Baltimore was said to have embezzled or stolen a very large sum from it. It was stated that, as usual in such cases, the money had been taken on many different occasions. The Grand Jury made each of these asserted takings the basis of a distinct indictment. He had several trials. At each of them he was called upon to answer a single charge only. The evidence for the State was confined with more or less strictness, to matters relevant to the alleged abstraction of the particular sum named in the indictment the jury was sworn to try. Had he been in the employ of the Federal Government and accused of stealing from it, the case would have taken a different course. In all probability the Federal Grand Jury would have combined all the accusations against him in a single indictment of many counts. Each of these counts would have charged the taking of a particular sum. It is possible that separate indictments would have been found against him as they were in the State Court. In either event he would in all likelihood have been tried on all the charges at the same time.

Section 1024 of the Revised Statutes provides, that whenever there are several charges against any person growing out of the same act or transaction, or for two or more acts or transactions connected together, or for two or more acts or transactions of the same class of crimes or offenses which may be properly joined, instead of having several indictments, the whole may be joined in one indictment and in separate counts. If two or more indictments are found the Court may order them to be consolidated.

The language is permissive, not mandatory. The question of whether indictments for offenses which may be joined shall be consolidated, is therefore left to the sound judicial discretion of the Court.

·It is not easy to lay down any precise rule as to what offenses may be joined in one indictment or tried together upon the consolidation of separate indictments, or as to when the prosecutor will be compelled to elect between or among the counts of the indictment. Such election will be compelled at any stage of the trial when it becomes apparent to the Court that otherwise the prisoner may be embarrassed in his defense.[62]

The accused demurs or pleads precisely as he does in the State Courts.

114. Challenge of Jurors.

Assuming that a plea of not guilty has been interposed, the next step is the selection of a jury.

State law or practice has nothing to do with the number of peremptory challenges allowed either the Government or the accused. That is fixed by Federal statute.[63] In trials for treason and capital felonies, the prisoner is entitled to twenty; for felonies not punishable by death to ten. In each of the above classes of cases the Government has six. In all other cases, civil and criminal, each party has three.

62. Pointer vs. U. S., 151 U. S. 403; 38 L. Ed. 208; 14 Sup. Ct. 410.
63. Sec. 287, Judicial Code, 5 Fed. Stat. Ann. 1078; U. S. Comp. Stat. Sec. 1264.

The parties on either side, no matter how numerous they may be, are for the purpose of challenging considered as one. Five defendants jointly tried will have no more peremptory challenges than if only one of them stood at the bar.

115. Laws of Evidence in Criminal Trials in Federal Courts.

After the jury has been selected and sworn and the opening statements made, the witnesses are examined. By what laws of evidence are the Federal Courts governed in the trial of criminal cases?

116. State Statutes Cannot Control Rules of Evidence in Criminal Cases in Federal Courts.

More than seventy years ago, the Supreme Court declared "that no law of a State made since 1789 can affect the mode of proceeding or the rules of evidence in criminal cases," in the Federal Courts.[64] This ruling was made in spite of the Federal Statute declaring that the laws of the several States, except where the constitution, treaties or statutes of the United States otherwise require or provide, should be regarded as rules of decision in trials at common law in Courts of the United States, for as CHIEF JUSTICE TANEY said:—

"It could not be supposed * * * that Congress intended to give to the States the power of prescribing the rules of evidence in trials for offenses against the United States, for this construction would in effect place the criminal jurisprudence of one sovereignty under the control of another."

Four decades later, it was held[65] that the provision of 858 of the Revised Statutes, which says that with some

64. U. S. vs. Reid, 12 Howard, 361; 13 L. Ed. 1023.
65. Logan vs. U. S., 144 U. S. 299; 36 L. Ed. 429; 12 Sup. Ct. 617.

exceptions, the laws of the State in which the Court is held shall be the rule of decision as to the competency of witnesses in the Courts of the United States in trials at common law and in equity and admiralty, has no reference to criminal cases. In each of these cases the State statute in question had been passed long subsequent to the admission of the State into the Union. As late as 1921, the Supreme Court held that a wife could not be called as a witness for her husband in a criminal prosecution against him in a Federal Court in Pennsylvania, in spite of the fact that had he been on trial in a Court of that State, a State Statute, passed in 1887, would have made her a competent witness for him although she would not have been permitted to testify against him.[66]

117. Congress May Change Rules of Evidence in the Federal Courts.

Congress may at any time alter the rules of evidence governing trials in the Federal Courts. It has from time to time done so. It has made the accused a competent witness. His failure to take the stand does not create any presumption against him; and the prosecuting counsel may not comment upon it.[67]

118. In Criminal Cases in Federal Courts, Husbands or Wives Are Not Competent Witnesses For or Against Each Other.

In spite of the sweeping character of some of the language used in United States vs. Rosen,[68] in the Federal Courts the common law rule which, with certain carefully

---

66. Jim Euey Moy vs. U. S., 254 U. S. 195; 65 L. Ed. 89; 41 Sup. Ct. 98; Pa. Statutes, Secs. 1 and 2, Act May 23, 1887; Sahms vs. Brown, 4 Pennsylvania County Court Reports, 488.

67. Act March 16, 1878, 20 Stat. 30; 9 Fed. Stat. Ann. 1434; U. S. Comp. Stat. Sec. 1465.

68. Rosen vs. U. S., 245 U. S. 467; 62 L. Ed. 406; 38 Sup. Ct. 148.

limited exceptions, rendered a husband or wife incompetent to testify in a criminal case either for or against the other, still remains in force.[69]   Congress, it is true, has provided that in certain kinds of prosecutions, such as for bigamy, polygamy and unlawful cohabitation, the lawful husband or wife of the accused shall be a competent witness, but may not be compelled to testify.[70]

119. No Person Disqualified as a Witness by Reason of Race, Color or Previous Condition of Servitude.

By statute all disqualifications on the ground of color, race or previous condition of servitude have been removed.

120. What Rule Determines the Competency of Witnesses in Criminal Cases in Federal Courts.

In the language of CHIEF JUSTICE TANEY, some "certain and established rule upon the subject" is "necessary to enable the courts to administer the criminal jurisprudence of the United States."[71]   It was in the same case held that it was not controlled by the common law which existed at the time of the emigration to the colonies, nor by that which prevailed in England at the time of the adoption of the Act of 1787, but by that which was in force in the respective States when the Judiciary Act was passed, subject to whatever changes Congress, but not the States, might subsequently make in it.   It was later apparently decided that in a State admitted to the Union after 1789, the law which governed was that in force in the State at the time of its admission.[72]

Until recently, it was generally assumed that the law

69. Jim Fuey Moy vs. U. S., 254 U. S. 195; 65 L. Ed. 89; 41 Sup. Ct. 98.

70. Act March 3, 1887, 24 Stat. 635; 1 Fed. Stat. Ann. 1225; U. S. Comp. Stat. Sec. 1466.

71. U. S. vs. Reid, 12 Howard, 361; 13 L. Ed. 1023.

72. Logan vs. U. S., 144 U. S. 299; 32 L. Ed. 429; 12 Sup. Ct. 617.

was as above stated, namely, that all questions as to competency of witnesses in criminal cases in Federal Courts was to be determined by the law prevailing in the particular State at the time of the adoption in 1789 of the Judiciary Act, if such State was one of the original thirteen, or if it was not, when it was admitted into the Union.

In 1918, the Supreme Court had before it a case coming up from a Federal Court in New York in which the government, over the objection of the defendant, had offered as a witness against him, a person who had been convicted of perjury in a State Court of New York, had been sentenced to imprisonment, served his sentence, and had never been pardoned. It was assumed that by the common law which was administered in New York in 1789, a person found guilty of perjury and sentenced, was thereby rendered incompetent as a witness until pardoned. The Court held that the modern rule is that the witness is not incompetent merely because he had been formerly convicted of crime, and concluded "that the dead hand of the common law rule of 1789 should no longer be applied to such cases as we have here."[73]

It is therefore clear that no matter what may have been the law in any State at the time of its admission into the Union, no witness is disqualified from testifying in the Federal Courts because of previous conviction of crime, Congress it may be noted, in enacting the Penal Code in 1909, repealed the Federal disqualification resulting from a conviction of perjury. Perhaps what really was decided was that in respect to the matter in question, the Courts had the same right they have often exercised in other matters to modify the unwritten law and that the trend of both legislative and judicial authority authorized and required such modification in the case mentioned.

73. Rosen vs. U. S., 245 U. S. 467; 62 L. Ed. 406; 41 Sup. Ct. 98.

121. Evidence Admissible in Cases of Disputed Handwriting.

Formerly, in the Federal Courts, the genuineness of a disputed handwriting could not be determined by a comparison of it with other handwriting of the party, unless the paper admitted to be in his handwriting, or to have been physically subscribed by him, was in evidence for some other purpose in the cause. If it was, it might be compared by the jury with the disputed writing. This comparison could be made either with or without the aid of expert witnesses.[74] In most of the States, this common law rule was years ago changed by statute. The Act of Congress of February 26, 1913,[75] declares that any admitted or proved handwriting of a person by whom the disputed writing is alleged to have been written, shall be competent for comparison by witnesses, judge or jury.

122. Evidence Procured by Search of Accused's Premises.

The Fourth Amendment to the Constitution provides that "the right of the people to be secure in their persons, houses, papers and effects, against unreasonable searches and seizures, shall not be violated; and no warrants shall issue, but upon probable cause, supported by oath or affirmation, and particularly describing the place to be searched, and the persons or things to be seized." The Fifth Amendment, among other things, declares that "no person * * * shall be compelled, in any criminal case, to be witness against himself." The Supreme Court has had a number of occasions to construe these provisions, and the rules it has laid down are enforced

---

74. Hickory vs. United States, 151 U. S. 305; 38 L. Ed. 170; 14 Sup. Ct. 334.

75. 37 Stat. 683; 3 Fed. Stat. Ann. 227; U. S. Comp. Stat. Sec. 1471.

in every Court of the United States, irrespective of what may be the State practice.

Where a search, if made by Government officers, would be unreasonable, and therefore illegal, if entrance were obtained by threats or the show of force, it is equally illegal if admission is obtained by stealth. Thus where a Government agent, who was a business acquaintance of the accused, under pretext of making a friendly call, secured admission to the accused's office, and in his absence, without warrant of any kind, seized and carried away documents, it was held prejudicial error to permit their introduction in evidence over the defendant's protest.[76] The Court held that not only was the consideration of the evidence so obtained forbidden in effect by the Fourth Amendment, but that it was compelling the accused to be a witness against himself in defiance of the fifth as well, a conclusion which, although perhaps not necessarily required by the language of the latter amendment, was quite in harmony with earlier decisions.[77]

Of course a search permitted by the accused is not unreasonable, but the courts will scrutinize carefully all the circumstances before they will hold that his consent was genuine and not a mere yielding to a demand which he supposed he might not refuse.[78] Nor can everything which may tend to prove guilt be taken under any warrant, no matter how regularly issued and executed. The primary right to such search and seizure must be found in the interest which the public or the complainant may have in the property to be seized or in the right to the possession of it, or where the valid exercise of the police

76. Gouled vs. U. S., 255 U. S. 298; 65 L. Ed. 311; 41 Sup. Ct. 261.
77. Boyd vs. U. S., 116 U. S. 616; 29 L. Ed. 746; 6 Sup. Ct. 524.
78. Amos vs. U. S., 255 U. S. 313; 65 L. Ed. 316; 41 Sup. Ct. 266.

power renders possession of the property by the accused unlawful, and provides that it may be taken.[79]

It is not easy to lay down any precise rule as to what may be searched for and seized. The practice existing at the time the amendment was ratified may doubtless be decisive in a case otherwise close. But where the article, whether it be a paper or something else, is of evidentiary value only, and is not the property of the public or the complainant, was not something the possession of which by the defendant was legally forbidden, or had not been used and was not intended to be used in the perpetration of an offense, or was not of like character with such things, or some of them, it may not be searched for or seized, and if it is, it may not be produced in evidence against the objection of the defendant from whose possession it has been taken.[80]

123. How and When an Objection to the Production in Evidence of Articles Procured by Illegal Search or Seizure Should Be Made.

The inquiry into all the circumstances under which an article or a document offered in evidence has been procured by the government, may often require an investigation almost as long, troublesome and difficult of determination as the main issue itself. For that reason, even the Supreme Court has held or has seemed to hold that the fact that papers pertinent to the issue may have been illegally taken from the possession of the party against whom they are offered, is not a valid objection to their admissibility. The Court, in the trial of a criminal case, it was said, should consider the competency of the evidence and not the method by which it was obtained.[81] The

79. Gouled vs. U. S., supra.
80. Gouled vs. U. S., supra.
81. Adams vs. New York, 192 U. S. 585; 48 L. Ed. 575; 24 Sup. Ct. 372.

defendant, however, can secure the return of the papers by a seasonable application in advance of trial.[82] If such petition is improperly denied, and the papers are subsequently, over defendant's objection, admitted in evidence at his trial, error has been committed.[83] The latest cases have gone still farther in protecting the accused by holding that his objection is not too late if made for the first time at his trial, if it was not until then he learned that the government had obtained possession of the property or article offered in evidence.[84] Even when he had previous knowledge of the fact and had, in advance of his trial, done nothing to secure its return to him, it is inadmissible if the Government's own proof as to the source of what is produced shows that it had been illegally obtained.[85]

It should be noted that the constitutional amendments in question are limitations upon Federal and not upon State authority, and it is no valid ground of objection that articles offered in evidence in the United States Court were obtained by police officers of the State acting under their own initiative, and not at the instance of any officer of the United States, or in collusion with him.[86]

124. All Who Take Part in Violating a Federal Law Are Principal Offenders.

All who participate in a violation of a Federal law are principals. Section 332 of the Penal Code provides that whoever directly commits any act constituting an offense defined in any law of the United States, or aids, abets, conceals, commands, induces or procures its commission,

82. Weeks vs. U. S., 232 U. S. 383; 58 L. Ed. 652; 34 Sup. Ct. 341.
83. Weeks vs. U. S., supra.
84. Gouled vs. U. S., 255 U. S. 298; 65 L. Ed. 311; 41 Sup. Ct. 261.
85. Amos vs. U. S., 255 U. S. 313; 65 L. Ed. 316; 41 Sup. Ct. 266.
86. Weeks vs. U. S., supra, at page 398.

is a principal. The common law rule governing the participants in the commission of misdemeanors has, therefore, been extended by Congress to all those who are in anywise concerned in the commission of a felony.

125. In Criminal Trials in the Federal Courts Juries Are Not Judges of the Law.

After the evidence is all in, it becomes necessary to determine what the applicable law is. In Maryland and in some other States, the jury in criminal cases are the judges both of the law and of the facts. In the Federal Courts this is not so. In both civil and criminal cases the judge instructs the jury as to what the law is. It is his duty so to do. It is their duty to accept the law as he declares it to be. This duty is however, a moral one only. It may be that the facts in the case are practically undisputed. They may make out a' clear case of guilt. The judge, however, cannot instruct the jury to find a verdict of guilty. He cannot set aside a verdict of not guilty if they return it. A person who has been once put in jeopardy cannot for the same offense be again tried, unless the first verdict is set aside at his instance.

In spite of the fact that a jury may ignore the instructions, the power to instruct is of great importance. In the overwhelming majority of cases juries accept the law as the Court declares it.

In Sparf vs. United States[87] JUSTICE HARLAN for the majority of the Court, and JUSTICE GRAY for the minority, brought a wealth of historical and legal learning to the discussion of the relation of the jury to the Court in criminal cases. The opinions will richly repay careful reading.

87. 156 U. S. 51; 39 L. Ed. 343; 15 Sup. Ct. 273.

126. A Federal Judge May Comment Upon the Facts.

A Judge of the Federal Court may also review the facts of the case. He may make such a charge as an English judge may and does. The Federal judges habitually charge their juries even in criminal cases and in so charging review the facts more or less elaborately. They can comment on the evidence as they see fit provided they do not do so in an intemperate or argumentative manner. They must, however, make it perfectly clear to the jury that although they are bound by what the Court says as to the law, they are under no obligation to take the Court's view of the facts. A judge may intimate or express his opinion as to the guilt or innocence of the prisoner provided he leaves no doubt in the jury's mind that they are free to come to another conclusion if they are so disposed.[88]

It has been decided, however, that the judge may not, after the jury have retired and have reported their inability to agree, tell them that in his opinion the prisoner is guilty. It has been thought by a Circuit Court of Appeals that an expression of opinion by the judge at such a time is likely to have an undue influence upon the action of the jury.[89]

127. Excepting to Judge's Charge.

The prisoner may except to anything in the judge's charge which he regards as wrong. In order that the exception shall avail him, it is necessary that his counsel at the time it is taken shall point out specifically what particular portion of the charge is alleged to be erroneous.[90] The object of this rule is obvious. A judge may

88. Rucker vs. Wheeler, 127 U. S. 85, 93; 32 L. Ed. 102; 8 Sup. Ct. 1142; Starr vs. U. S., 153 U. S. 624; 38 L. Ed. 841; 14 Sup. Ct. 919.

89. Foster vs. U. S., 188 Fed. 305; 110 C. C. A. 283.

90. Gardner vs. U. S., 230 Fed. 575; 144 C. C. A. 629.

consume an hour in charging the jury. By a slip of the tongue he may say something or several things which are not good law. If the prisoner's counsel is free to put in a general exception to the entire charge, the judge will not have his attention called to those matters in which it was supposed he was wrong. If they were brought to his notice he would have had an opportunity before the jury retired to correct the mistakes he had inadvertently made.

128. The Jurisdiction of District Courts Over Suits for Federal Penalties, Forfeitures and Seizures.

As we have seen, the District Courts are given jurisdiction exclusive of the Courts of the States of all suits for penalties and forfeitures incurred under the laws of the United States and of all seizures under the laws of the United States on land or on waters not within the admiralty and maritime jurisdiction.

129. Suits for Penalties and Forfeitures and to Enforce Seizures Are Civil Proceedings.

There are a number of statutes of the United States which impose pecuniary penalties for various breaches of the Federal law and provide that such penalties may be enforced by suit; as, for example, the penalty for importing under contract an alien laborer;[91] and the penalties imposed upon a railroad for violating the Safety Appliance Act or the Hours of Service Act.[92] A suit to collect such a penalty is, when the liberty of the defendant is not imperiled, a civil proceeding. A verdict should be given upon a preponderance of evidence. The Court may instruct the jury to find for one party or the

91. Hepner vs. U. S., 213 U. S. 103; 53 L. Ed. 720; 29 Sup. Ct. 474.
92. C. B. & Q. R. R. Co. vs. U. S., 220 U. S. 559; 55 L. Ed. 582; 31 Sup. Ct. 612.

other, but the defendant, if an individual cannot be compelled to testify against himself.[93]

The latter constitutional guarantee has no application to corporations. They may be forced to furnish evidence of their own guilt.[94]

Under the customs and revenue laws of the United States, under the Food and Drug Act, the Insecticide Act and the Volstead Act, and perhaps under other statutes, real or personal property may become liable to forfeiture to the United States. Such forfeiture is not incurred unless somebody has done something by law forbidden. It usually cannot be enforced unless somebody has committed a criminal act. Nevertheless, a suit for its enforcement is a civil proceeding. The judge may instruct a verdict. The jury may upon a preponderance of the evidence find in favor of the Government.[95]

93. Hepner vs. U. S., supra.

94. B. & O. R. R. Co. vs. Interstate Commerce Commission, 221 U. S. 612; 55 L. Ed. 878; 31 Sup. Ct. 621.

95. Gr. Distillery No. 8 vs. U. S., 204 Fed. 429; 122 C. C. A. 615; Lilienthal's Tobacco vs. U. S., 97 U. S. 237; 24 L. Ed. 901; Four Packages vs. U. S., 97 U. S. 404; 24 L. Ed. 1031.

CHAPTER V.

CIVIL CONTROVERSIES OVER WHICH THE JURISDICTION OF THE DISTRICT COURTS IS EXCLUSIVE OF THAT OF THE STATES.

130. The District Courts Have Exclusive Jurisdiction in Admiralty.

No State Court may exercise jurisdiction in admiralty. Every case in which it is sought to use the distinctive processes of the admiralty for the vindication of a maritime right is within the admiralty jurisdiction and therefore must be brought in a District Court of the United States and not elsewhere.

What processes are peculiar to a Court of Admiralty and what rights are in their nature essentially maritime are inquiries which may be most profitably made in connection with the study of the admiralty law.[1] Their discussion here would carry us too far afield. It should, however, be noted that the fact that a controversy may be cognizable in the admiralty does not necessarily mean that the parties to it may not properly carry it into a Court of Law of a State or, in some cases, of the United States. If they are content to seek only the relief which such other Court is competent to give, they may there

1. The Moses Taylor, 4 Wall., 427; 18 L. Ed. 397; Martin vs. West, 222 U. S. 191; 56 L. Ed. 159; 32 Sup. Ct. Rep. 42; Richardson vs. Harmon, 222 U. S. 96; 56 L. Ed. 110; 32 Sup. Ct. 27; Knickerbocker Ice Co. vs. Stewart, 253 U. S. 149; 64 L. Ed. 834; 40 Sup. Ct. 438; Act June 10, 1922.

try out the differences between them, despite the fact that the disputes have their origin in a maritime transaction.[2]

Matters of prize are so peculiarly of admiralty jurisdiction that it is hard to conceive of any common law proceeding applicable to them. Exclusive jurisdiction over all such cases is expressly given to the Courts of the United States. The closely analogous proceedings taken to enforce seizures on land made by the authority of the laws of the United States, are in fact, a part of the penal or *quasi*-penal jurisdiction of the Federal Courts. Something has already been said about them. Jurisdiction over them is necessarily vested exclusively in the Courts of the sovereign for the vindication of whose laws, they are decreed.

131. The District Courts Have Exclusive Jurisdiction Over All Cases Arising Under the Patent and Copyright Laws.

The law of patents and of copyrights cannot be here discussed. A case does not arise under the patent or the copyright laws unless it is brought to assert a right given by them, as distinguished from a right arising out of a contract relating to them. Thus the Courts of the United States do not have jurisdiction of suits to recover royalties due by a licensee under a patent or a copyright,[3] or to enforce a specific execution of a contract relating to one,[4] or to rescind an assignment of one,[5] or to enforce an agreement that the licensee or purchaser of a patented article shall use, in connection with it, only such unpatented goods as are purchased from his vendor,

2. Leon vs. Galceran, 11 Wall., 185; 20 L. Ed. 74.
3. Albrecht vs. Teas, 106 U. S. 613; 27 L. Ed. 295; 1 Sup. Ct. 550.
4. Wade vs. Lawder, 165 U. S. 624; 41 L. Ed. 851; 17 Sup. Ct. 425.
5. Brown vs. Shannon, et al., 20 Howard, 55; 15 L. Ed. 826.

or licensor,[6] on the ground that such controversies arise under the patent or copyright laws; nor do they obtain jurisdiction merely because it may become necessary in the case to inquire into the scope or validity of a patent.[7] Whether the Court has or has not jurisdiction largely depends on the plaintiff's statement of his own case. If that, made in good faith from his own standpoint, discloses a controversy under the patent or copyright laws, the Court will have jurisdiction in spite of the fact that the defendant denies the plaintiff's jurisdictional allegations.[8]

132. The District Courts Have Exclusive Jurisdiction in Bankruptcy.

The jurisdiction of the District Courts to adjudge a debtor a bankrupt, to administer his estate in bankruptcy, and to grant or to refuse him a discharge from such of his debts as are dischargeable in bankruptcy, is exclusive of all other Courts. Moreover, whenever a Federal bankruptcy law is in force, the operation of all State insolvency laws is suspended, so far as concerns persons and transactions coming within the purview of the Bankruptcy Act. It is, however, true that certain rights created by the bankrupt law, as, for example, the right of the trustee in bankruptcy to vacate a preferential conveyance, may be enforced in State Courts. The consideration of this very important branch of the jurisdiction of the District Court forms a part of all treatises on the law of bankruptcy and may not with profit be here further considered.

6. Motion Picture Patents Co. vs. Universal Film Mfg. Co., 243 U. S. 502; 61 L. Ed. 871; 37 Sup. Ct. 416.

7. Albrecht vs. Teas, supra.

8. Fair vs. Kohler Die & Specialty Co., 228 U. S. 22; 57 L. Ed. 716; 33 Sup. Ct. 410.

133. Federal Courts and Judges Have Exclusive Jurisdiction to Release by Habeas Corpus Persons Held in Federal Custody.

The power of Federal Courts and judges to issue writs of *habeas corpus* and the procedure under such writs are considered in another chapter. It is sufficient here to point out that no State Court or judge has any power to discharge any one from Federal custody.

The whole question was reviewed by CHIEF JUSTICE TANEY in an opinion of great interest and ability.[9] One Booth had been arrested under a warrant issued by a United States commissioner for a violation of the Fugitive Slave Law. He was charged with having assisted a negro slave to escape from the custody of a United States deputy marshal. He had been committed by a United States commissioner for the action of the United States District Court for the District of-Wisconsin. He applied for a writ of *habeas corpus* to a State judge. The judge granted it and upon hearing released him. The Supreme Court of the State affirmed the action of the judge below. Subsequently he was indicted by the United States Grand Jury, again arrested by the Federal authorities, tried, convicted and sentenced to imprisonment. The State Court on *habeas corpus* a second time discharged him from the custody of the Federal authorities. The Supreme Court of the United States said:—

"We do not question the authority of State Court or Judge who is authorized by the laws of the State to issue the writ of *habeas corpus*, to issue it in any case where the party is imprisoned within its territorial limits, provided it does not appear, when the application is made, that the person imprisoned is in custody under the authority of the United States. The Court or judge has a right to inquire, in this mode of proceeding, for what cause and by what

9. Abelman vs. Booth, 21 How. 506; 16 L. Ed. 169.

authority the prisoner is confined within the territorial limits of the State sovereignty. And it is the duty of the marshal, or other person having the custody of the prisoner, to make known to the Judge or Court, by a proper return, the authority by which he holds him in custody. * * * But after the return is made and the State Judge or Court judicially apprised that the party is in custody under the authority of the United States, they can proceed no further. They then know that the prisoner is within the dominion and jurisdiction of another Government, and that neither the writ of *habeas corpus*, nor any other process issued under State authority, can pass over the line of division between the two sovereignties. He is then within the dominion and exclusive jurisdiction of the United States. If he has committed an offense against their laws, their tribunals alone can punish him. If he is wrongfully imprisoned, their judicial tribunals can release him and afford him redress. And although, as we have said, it is the duty of the marshal, or other person holding him, to make known, by a proper return, the authority under which he detains him, it is at the same time imperatively his duty to obey the process of the United States, to hold the prisoner in custody under it, and to refuse obedience to the mandate or process of any other Government. And consequently it is his duty not to take the prisoner, nor suffer him to be taken, before a State judge or Court upon a *habeas corpus* issued under State authority. No State Judge or Court, after they are judicially informed that the party is imprisoned under the authority of the United States has any right to interfere with him or to require him to be brought before them. And if the authority of a State, in the form of judicial process or otherwise, should attempt to control the marshal or other authorized officer or agent of the United States, in any respect, in the custody of his prisoner, it would be his duty to resist it, and to call to his aid any force that might be necessary to maintain the authority of law against illegal interference. No judicial process, whatever form it may assume, can have any lawful authority outside of the limits of the jurisdiction of the Court or Judge by whom it is issued; and an attempt to enforce it beyond these boundaries is nothing less than lawless violence.''

134. The Original Jurisdiction of the District Courts Which is Exclusive of that of the States But Concurrent With That of the Supreme Court.

As already stated, section 233 of the Judicial Code gives the District Courts original jurisdiction over suits against consuls and vice-consuls, concurrent with that conferred by the Constitution upon the Supreme Court, but exclusive of that of the State Courts.

135. Suits Against Consuls and Vice-Consuls.

A suit against a consul or vice-consul cannot be safely brought elsewhere than in a Court of the United States. If sued in a State Court the defendant may, at any time, in the course of the proceedings, raise the question of jurisdiction; and a new suit in a Federal Court may then be subject to the bar of the Statute of Limitations.

The privilege of being sued in the Courts of the United States and not in those of the States is not a personal one which may be waived by the defendant. It is an immunity of his government. He cannot surrender it. A consul who has been sued in a State Court does not by going to trial therein on the merits waive a right to object to the jurisdiction. · He may, in the Appellate Court, for the first time, set up his claim for exemption from suit in the State tribunals.[10] The Supreme Court of New York has, in recent years, held that a State Court has no jurisdiction over an action for separation brought against a consul by his wife.[11]

10. Davis vs. Packard, 7 Peters, 276; 8 L. Ed. 684; Bors vs. Preston, 111 U. S. 252; 28 L. Ed. 419; 4 Sup. Ct. 807.

11. Higginson vs. Higginson, 158 N. Y. Supp. 92.

136. Where a Consul is a Defendant, District Court Has Jurisdiction Irrespective of Citizenship or Status of His Co-defendants.

As we shall see, when the jurisdiction of the District Court depends upon diverse citizenship, every party on one side must be competent to sue, in the United States Court, every party on the other. Such is not the rule where one of the defendants is a consul or vice-consul. Then the District Court has jurisdiction in spite of the fact that if he were not joined with his co-defendants they could not be there sued.[12]

137. In Suits Against a Consul Amount in Controversy Immaterial.

Nor in such cases is the amount in controversy material. If the plaintiff claims that a consul owes him any sum, however small, any legal proceeding to coerce payment must be taken in a Court of the United States.

138. The Privilege is That of Foreign, Not American, Consuls.

Consuls and vice-consuls, as the words are used in the statute under consideration, mean the consular representatives of foreign governments. An American consul whose station is abroad is not exempt from suits in the State Courts of this country.[13]

139. Federal Courts Have Exclusive Jurisdiction of Suits Against the United States.

Section 256 of the Judicial Code, which enumerates the cases in which jurisdiction, vested in the Courts of the United States, shall be exclusive of the Courts of the several States, does not mention suits against the United States. It was unnecessary to do so. The United States

12. Froment vs. Duclos, 30 Fed. 385.
13. Milward vs. McSaul, 17 Fed. Cases, 425 (No. 9624).

cannot be sued except by its own consent. It has consented to be sued under some circumstances, but only in its own Courts.

140. Jurisdiction of the Court of Claims.

The Judicial Code[14] confers jurisdiction upon the Court of Claims over claims, except for pensions, or arising under a treaty, (1) founded upon the Constitution of the United States or any law of Congress, or upon any regulation of an executive department, or upon any contract, express or implied, with the Government of the United States, or for damages, liquidated or unliquidated, in cases not sounding in tort, in respect to which claims, the party would, if the United States were suable, be entitled to redress in a Court of law, equity or admiralty; (2) of disbursing officers for relief from responsibility; (3) of patentees whose inventions have, without their consent, been used by the United States, provided, however, that the claimant, or any assignor of him, has, in no court, sued any person who at the time the cause of action arose, was acting or professing to act for the United States.[15]

There are circumstances in which there may be a question as to whether an individual out of whose actions the claim arose, was validly authorized to act for the United States. If he was not, he may himself be personally liable for their consequences, and the United States may not be, but the claimant cannot sue the United States while he has a suit pending against such individual.

Various acts confer upon the Court powers to pass upon certain questions arising out of the conditions brought about by the World War, as, for example, the amount of fair and just compensation to any person, who, during that war, entered into an agreement, express

14. Sections 145, 153, J. C.
15. J. C., Sec. 154; 5 Fed. Stat. Ann. 667; U. S. Comp. Stat. Sec. 1145.

or implied, with some one acting under the authority of the President or the Secretary of War, or who suffered damage by reason of a notice from the Government that it intended to take his property,[16] or to determine what is just compensation for buildings in the District of Columbia taken over by the Secretary of Agriculture,[17] or for the use by the Government of an invention, the issue of a patent for which was suspended during the war by order of the President.[18] An Executive Department may refer to the Court any contractual claim involving controverted questions of law or fact pending before it, and when such reference is made, the Court proceeds with the case substantially as if it had been brought by the claimant.[19]

The Government may claim that some one owes it money. He does not deny that something is or may be due. What he wants to know is precisely how much, and that is what no one can or will tell him. If three years have elapsed after he has applied for such information without being able to get it, and without the Government having brought suit against him, he may apply to the Court of Claims to fix it.[20]

From time to time, by special acts, various claims by or against the Indian wards of the Government are submitted to the Court, and either House of Congress may refer any claim to it for investigation. In this last mentioned instance, the Court, however, does not render a judgment. It merely makes a report.[21]

---

16. 40 Stat. 1272; U. S. Com. St. Sec. 3115, 14-15a; Fed. Stat. Ann. 1919 Supp. 304.

17. 40 Stat. 1048; U. S. Com. St. Sec. 839c; Fed. Stat. Ann. 1919 Supp. 3.

18. 40 Stat. 395-420; U. S. Com. Stat. Sec. 9465; Fed. Stat. Ann. 1918 Supp. 577.

19. J. C. Sec. 148; 5 Fed. Stat. Ann. 662; U. S. Comp. Stat. Sec. 1139.

20. J. C. Sec. 180; 5 Fed. Stat. Ann. 681; U. S. Comp. Stat. Sec. 1171.

21. J. C. Sec. 151; 5 Fed. Stat. Ann. 665; U. S. Comp. Stat. Sec. 1142.

10

141. Contractual Claims Against the Government, Jurisdiction Over Which is Withheld from the Court of Claims.

The Court of Claims has no jurisdiction to hear and determine claims growing out of the late Civil War, known as "war claims," nor may it reopen any claim which had been rejected or reported on adversely prior to the 3d day of March, 1887, by any Court, department or commission authorized to hear and determine the same.

142. Aliens Suing in the Court of Claims.

Aliens may sue in the Court of Claims on the same footing as citizens, provided they are citizens or subjects of a Government which accords to citizens of the United States, the right to prosecute claims against it in its courts.[22]

143. How a Suit is Brought in the Court of Claims.

The initial pleading in the Court of Claims is called a petition. The statute requires that in it the claimant shall fully set forth the claim, and the action of Congress or any department concerning it, if any such action there has been. It must state the persons who own the claim or are interested in it, and when and upon what consideration each of them became interested. It should allege that there has been no assignment or transfer except as stated in it, and that the claimant is justly entitled to the amount he claims, after allowing all just credits and offsets. It must contain an allegation that the claimant and every previous owner of the claim, if it has been assigned, did, if a citizen of the United States, at all times bear true allegiance to the Government of the United States, and whether a citizen or not, did not,

22. J. C. Sec. 155; 5 Fed. Stat. Ann. 668; U. S. Comp. Stat. Sec. 1146.

in any way, voluntarily aid, abet or give encouragement to rebellion against the Government. The petition must state that the claimant believes the allegations in it to be true and it must be verified either by his affidavit or by that of his agent or attorney.[23]

144. Government May Examine Claimant.

A privilege not enjoyed by an ordinary defendant, but which the Government reserves to itself, as a condition to its right to be sued at all in the Court of Claims, is that it may compel any claimant to submit to an examination, under oath, in advance of trial, without being under any obligation to put his deposition in evidence. If he refuses to testify at all, or does not answer fully and fairly, the Court may, if it thinks proper, decline to try the case until he does.[24]

145. Forfeiture of Claim for Fraud.

One who sues the United States must be careful, if he has a claim good in whole or in part, not to practice any fraud to secure its allowance, or to swell its amount, for if he does it becomes the duty of the Court of Claims to declare the entire claim forfeited to the Government.[25]

146. Court of Claims May Tax Costs Against the Government.

As a rule the Government may not be required to pay costs, but the statute provides that if the Government in the Court of Claims puts in issue the right of any claimant to recover therein, costs although on rather a restricted scale may, in the discretion of the Court, be allowed the prevailing party.[26]

23. J. C. Sec. 160; 5 Fed. Stat. Ann. 673; U. S. Comp. Stat. Sec. 1151.
24. J. C. Sec. 166; 5 Fed. Stat. Ann. 675; U. S. Comp. Stat. Sec. 1157.
25. J. C. Sec. 172; 5 Fed. Stat. Ann. 677; U. S. Comp. Stat. Sec. 1163.
26. J. S. Sec. 152; 5 Fed. Stat. Ann. 667; U. S. Comp. Stat. Sec. 1143.

147. Court of Claims May Grant Government a New Trial After an Appeal and Affirmance.

An unusual provision as to suits in the Court of Claims is that which authorizes the Court, on motion of the United States, to grant a new trial at any time while any claim is pending before it, or on appeal from it, or within two years next after its final disposition. To entitle the Government to such a new trial, it must present such evidence, cumulative or otherwise, as will satisfy the Court that some wrong or injustice in the premises has been done the United States.[27]

The provision that a new trial may be allowed in the lower Court while the record is on appeal from the higher, is rare, if not unprecedented, and still more out of the ordinary is the provision that such new trial may be allowed even after an affirmance by the Supreme Court of the judgment below. Indeed the two years during which such trial may be granted will, in the case of appeal, date from the final determination of the appeal.[28] The wrong or injustice alleged must result from some error of fact, and not from some erroneous decision as to the law curable on appeal.[29]

148. Jurisdiction of District Courts Over Suits Against the United States.

Many people have claims of comparatively small amount against the United States. To prosecute them in the Court of Claims is sometimes inconvenient and expensive, and by a statute passed in 1887,[30] jurisdiction, concurrent with the Court of Claims, is conferred upon the District Court of all claims not exceeding Ten Thousand Dollars, and of the class numbered 1 in Section 140,

27. J. C. Sec. 175; 5 Fed. Stat. Ann. 678; U. S. Comp. Stat. Sec. 1166.

28. Ex parte Walker, 13 Wallace, 664; 20 L. Ed. 632; Ex parte U. S., 16 Wall., 699; 21 L. Ed. 507.

29. Purcell Envelope Co. vs. U. S., 45 Court of Claims, 66.

30. 24 Stat. 505; 5 Fed. Stat. Ann. 650; U. S. Stat. Com. Sec. 1136 (1); Nov. 23, 1921, Sec. 1310c, 42 Stat. 311.

supra, and also for the recovery of any internal revenue tax alleged to have been erroneously or illegally assessed or collected, or of any penalty claimed to have been collected without authority or any sum alleged to have been excessive or in any manner wrongfully collected, under the internal revenue laws, even if the claim exceeds $10,000, if the collector of internal revenue by whom such tax, penalty or sum was collected, is dead at the time such suit or proceeding is commenced.

Ordinarily suits to recover taxes illegally collected are brought against the collector who wrongfully collected them, and there is no limitation upon the amount for which such suits may be brought in the District Court, the case technically not being against the United States, but against the individual who, under color of official place, did the wrong. In fact, the United States pays any judgment which is recovered against him, but when he is dead there are difficulties in the way of the usual procedure, and for that reason the Revenue Act of November 23, 1921, makes the provision just cited.[30a]

149. Claims for Fees, Salaries or Compensation for Official Services May Not Be Brought in the District Court.

The District Court no longer has jurisdiction of actions brought to recover fees, salaries or compensation for official services of officers of the United States. Under the original Tucker Act, the District Court might entertain such suits, but since 1898,[31] they are cognizable in the Court of Claims only. From the Government's standpoint, it is inexpedient to submit such claims to the determination of a Court of which the claimants may be officers.

150. Neither the Court of Claims nor the District Court Has Jurisdiction Over Claims for the Collection of which, Other Machinery is Specially Provided.

There are statutes which provide ways in which, under

30a. Sec. 13100, 42 Stat. 311.

certain circumstances, claims against the Government for internal revenue taxes or customs duties paid under protest, may be recovered—in some instances by suit against the collector of internal revenue or of customs, and in others by an appeal to the Board of General Appraisers, and from thence to the Customs Court.

Where by statute the Government has specifically provided a method of determining the validity of a claim and a way of collecting it, the claimant cannot seek redress in any other manner.[32] This doctrine has its limitations. They have been clearly set forth by the Supreme Court.[33]

151. How Suit May Be Brought in the District Court Upon a Claim Against the United States.

The Act which gave concurrent jurisdiction to the District Court with the Court of Claims of contractual demands against the Government, is usually referred to as the Tucker Act.[34] It requires the plaintiff to bring suit by petition under oath. He must cause a copy of it to be served upon the district attorney of the United States for the district wherein he sues.

He is required to send another copy by registered mail to the Attorney-General of the United States. He must make and file with the clerk of the Court, an affidavit that such service has been made and such copy mailed.

152. District Court Must in Suits Upon Claims Against the United States File an Opinion as Well as Findings of Fact and Conclusions of Law.

In this class of cases the Court must file a written opinion. In it there must be specific findings of fact and distinct statements of all conclusions of law involved in the case. If the suit be in equity or admiralty, the Court is directed to proceed according to its ordinary rules.[35]

32. Nichols vs. U. S., 7 Wall., 122; 19 L. Ed. 125.
33. Dooley vs. U. S., 182 U. S. 222; 45 L. Ed. 1074; 21 Sup. Ct. 762.
34. 24 Stat. 506, 5 Fed. Stat. Ann. 650; U. S. Comp. Stat. Sec. 1136 (1).
35. Sec. 7, 24 Stat. 506; 5 Fed. Stat. Ann. 650; U. S. Comp. Stat. Sec.

153. Court Has Jurisdiction of All Claims by the Government Against the Claimant.

The District Court, like the Court of Claims has jurisdiction of all set-offs, counter claims, claims for damages, whether liquidated or unliquidated, or other demands whatsoever on the part of the United States against any claimant who in such Court sues the Government.[36]

The right of set-off or counter claim given the United States by this statute is far broader than that which exists between private parties in any suit at law or in equity in the Courts of Maryland or of the United States within Maryland, and indeed is broader than any usually given by the set-off statutes of other States.

154. In Cases Under the Tucker Act, the District Courts Sit Without a Jury as the Court of Claims Always Does.

In suits against the United States, the District Court and the Court of Claims sit without a jury to determine not only the claim against the United States but the counter claim preferred by it.

The Government may not be sued without its own consent. If it consents to be sued at all, it has the right to say in what way the trial shall be conducted. The claimant is deprived of no constitutional privilege when Congress says "we will let you sue the United States provided the case is tried without a jury, and we will not let you sue otherwise."

At the time the seventh amendment was adopted he could not sue at all. He could not now sue if the statute were repealed. It is open to him to sue or not to sue as he sees fit. If he does sue he must do so in the manner and subject to the limitations prescribed by law.

36. March 3, 1863, 12 Stat. 765; 4 Fed. Stat. Ann. 1034; U. S. Comp. Stat. 991.

So much is clear enough. How is it when the Government seeks an affirmative judgment against him? Its right to sue him is not the creature of statute. That right has always existed. If the demand for which it brought suit was legal rather than equitable it could not deprive him of his right to a jury trial. The Supreme Court answers, Congress tells him in advance that if he avails himself of the privilege of suing the Government in the special Court organized for that purpose, he may be met with a set-off, counter claim or other demand of the United States upon which judgment may go against him without the intervention of a jury. If he makes use of the privilege thus granted, he must do so subject to the conditions annexed by the Government to its exercise.[37]

155. No Relief Other Than a Judgment for Money May Be Given Against the United States.

Certain petitioners sought to have the United States compelled specifically to perform contracts for the conveyance of timber lands. The Court below held that they were entitled to the relief prayed. The Supreme Court reversed the judgment and decided that Congress had not given the Courts power to decree any relief other than the payment of money.[38]

156. Limitation as to Suits Against the United States.

Suits against the United States must be brought within six years after the cause of action arose.

Married women and infants whose claims first accrued during coverture or minority, and idiots, lunatics, insane persons and persons beyond the seas at the time the claim accrued, may bring suit within three years after the

37. McEllrath vs. U. S., 102 U. S. 426; 26 L. Ed. 189.
38. United States vs. Jones, 131 U. S. 1; 33 L. Ed. 90; 9 Sup. Ct. 669.

disability has ceased. None of such disabilities operate cumulatively.

157. The United States Cannot Be Sued for a Tort.

Congress did not intend to make the United States liable to suits for torts. Such torts can be committed only by officers, agents or employees of the United States. It is not willing to assume the responsibility for their actions. There are many reasons of public policy why it should not do so. Courts, in applying the statute, will give effect to the obvious intent of Congress. They will, therefore, look through the form of the pleadings to see what the actual origin of the claim is. If the claimant is attempting to hold the Government liable for a tort, he will fail, no matter how ingeniously his contentions may be stated.

Someone was hurt in a Government elevator in the postoffice building in New York. He brought suit against the United States, alleging that the Government had contracted to carry him safely and had broken its contract. The Supreme Court said:—

"Nothing short of an Act of Congress can make the United States responsible for a personal injury done to a citizen by one of its employees who, while discharging his duties, fails to exercise such care and diligence as a proper regard to the rights of others required." "Causing harm by negligence is a tort" * * * "A party may in some cases waive a tort; that is, he may forbear to sue in tort and sue in contract, where the matter out of which his claim arises has in it the elements both of contract and tort. But it has been well said that a right of action in contract cannot be created by waiving a tort, and the duty to pay damages for a tort does not imply a promise to pay them upon which assumpsit can be maintained."[39]

39. Bigby vs. United States, 188 U. S. 400; 47 L. Ed. 519; 23 Sup. Ct. 468.

CHAPTER VI.

OF WHAT CONTROVERSIES DISTRICT COURTS HAVE JURISDICTION CONCURRENT WITH STATE COURTS.

158. Jurisdiction of District Court Concurrent With That of Courts of the States.

In some classes of cases the plaintiff may at his election bring suit either in a District Court of the United States or in a State Court. In legal phrase the jurisdiction of the District Courts is as to such cases concurrent with the Courts of the several States. Many of the most important controversies which are brought before the Federal Courts might have been taken into the State tribunals had the parties so wished.

The first paragraph of section 24 of the Judicial Code enumerates the classes of controversies which most frequently arise and in which there is this concurrent jurisdiction, as

"All suits of a civil nature, at common law or in equity, brought by the United States, or by an officer thereof authorized by law to sue, or between citizens of the same State claiming lands under grants from different States; or, where the matter in controversy exceeds, exclusive of interest and costs, the sum or value of three thousand dollars, and" (a) "arises under the Constitution or laws of the United States, or treaties made, or which shall be made, under their authority, or" (b) "is between citizens of different States, or" (c) "is between citizens of a State and foreign States, citizens or subjects."

This section is modeled upon and is an amplification and in some respects an amendment of section 11 of the original Judiciary Act. That section has been many times amended, the more important of such amendments prior to the adoption of the Judicial Code having been made by the Acts of March 3, 1875,[1] of March 3, 1887,[2] and of August 13, 1888.[3]

159. Jurisdiction Over These Classes of Cases Formerly in Circuit Court.

It is only since the abolition of the Circuit Courts that the District Courts have had any jurisdiction over the more important classes of cases mentioned in the first paragraph of section 24. Formerly such suits, if instituted in the Federal Courts at all, had to be brought in the Circuit Courts.

160. Jurisdiction Under Section 24, Paragraph 1, Limited to Suits of a Civil Nature at Law or in Equity.

The first paragraph of section 24 limits the proceedings over which it gives jurisdiction to the District Courts to suits of a civil nature at common law or in equity. This same limitation couched in this precise language was made by section 11 of the original Judiciary Act and by every revision thereof. Every one of these words has been judicially construed many times. It has been said that every line of the Statute of Frauds is worth a subsidy, by which, of course, is meant that before any line of that famous enactment received its final interpretation a sum equal to a subsidy had been spent in litigation over it. Very much the same may be said of each one of the phrases now under consideration. Each of them will be briefly discussed.

161. What is a Suit?

A beginning may be made with the word "suits." What is a "suit" within the meaning of the first paragraph of section 24?

1. 18 Stat. 470; 5 Fed. Stat. Ann. 525; U. S. Stat. Compiled, Sec. 1010.
2. 24 Stat. 552; 5 Fed. Stat. Ann. 525; U. S. Stat. Compiled, Sec. 1010.
3. 25 Stat. 433; 5 Fed. Stat. Ann. 525; U. S. Stat. Compiled, Sec. 1010.

CHIEF JUSTICE MARSHALL said:—

"The term is certainly a very comprehensive one, and is understood to apply to any proceeding in a Court of justice by which an individual pursues that remedy" * * * "which the law affords him. The modes of proceeding may be various, but if a right is litigated between parties in a Court of justice the proceeding by which the decision of the Court is sought is a suit."[4]

The definition is broad. It has been much relied on. It is as sound and as accurate today as it ever was. It is true, nevertheless, that there are legal controversies which everybody calls suits, and which fully answer to Marshall's definition, and yet which may not be taken into the Federal Courts. They are clearly proceedings in a Court of justice. Individuals there pursue the remedy which the law gives them. Rights are therein litigated between parties, who seek to obtain the decision of the Court, yet the Federal tribunals may not pass upon them. It has been sometimes said that the Courts of the United States have no jurisdiction over them because they are not suits, as in this connection Congress intended to use the words. Some nice and finely drawn reasoning has been used, to distinguish them from similar proceedings which everybody admits to be suits in every sense of that word. Much legal ingenuity and acumen has been exhibited in discovering, if not in creating, these distinctions. One may still believe that their real or supposed existence is not the reason why the Federal Courts have no jurisdiction over such matters. The Supreme Court has kept steadily before it the dual nature of our Government. It has been careful to reduce to a minimum the opportunities for clashing

4. Weston vs. The City Council of Charleston, 2 Peters, 464; 7 L. Ed. 481.

between State and Federal sovereignty. It has believed, and has been right in believing, that Congress was anxious that there should be no unnecessary friction, albeit Congress might not always have used words of precision. It has therefore habitually construed the general language of statutes in such manner as to avoid or reduce the chance of collision, and has thereby given effect to what it felt was the real intention of the law-makers. It has accordingly held that when Congress made a general grant to the Federal tribunals of jurisdiction over all suits of a civil nature between certain classes of litigants, or in which certain issues were involved, it intended to except some controversies which could not be carried on in the Federal Courts without seriously and unnecessarily embarrassing the management by the States of matters which were peculiarly within their province.

162. Federal Courts Have No Jurisdiction Over Probate Proceedings.

The authority to make wills is derived from the State. The requirement of probate is but a regulation to make a will effective.

> "Jurisdiction as to wills and their probate as such is neither included in, nor excepted out of, the grant of judicial power to the Courts of the United States. So far as it is *ex parte* and merely administrative, it is not conferred and it cannot be exercised by them at all until in a case at law or in equity its exercise becomes necessary to settle a controversy of which a Court of the United States may take cognizance by reason of the citizenship of the parties."[5]

Matters of pure probate in the strict sense of the word are not within the jurisdiction of the Courts of the United States.

5. Ellis vs. Davis, 109 U. S. 485; 27 L. Ed. 1006; 3 Sup. Ct. 327.

Now, what are matters of pure probate? They include all proceedings which by the law of the State may be taken to determine the right to probate, at the time of application therefor, or to settle any such question thereafter in an ancillary probate proceeding. The State law may provide for a form of notice on an application to probate a will and may authorize a contest before the admission of the writing to probate, or it may authorize a will to be proved in common form, that is without notice, and may allow a supplementary probate proceeding by which the probate in common form can be contested. All such proceedings are matters of probate purely. It follows that the trial in Maryland of issues sent from the Orphans' Court to a Court of law to determine whether the testator was of sound mind, whether the signature to his will was his signature, whether the execution of the will was procured by undue influence or fraud, are proceedings ancillary to probate. Over such controversies the Courts of the United States have no jurisdiction, even when there is a diversity of citizenship between the parties to them.[6]

163. Federal Courts May Have Jursidiction of Suits Inter Partes Involving the Validity of a Will.

The rule which prohibits Federal Courts from exercising what is essentially a probate jurisdiction extends no further than the reason for it. Where the "State law, statutory or customary, gives to the citizens of the State in an action or suit *inter partes* the right to question at law the probate of a will or to assail probate in a suit in equity, the Courts of the United States in administering the rights of citizens of other States or aliens will enforce such remedies."[7]

6. Farrell vs. O'Brien, 199 U. S. 89; 50 L. Ed. 101; 25 Sup. Ct. 727.

7. Farrell vs. O'Brien, 199 U. S. 89, 110; McDermott vs. Hannon, 203 Fed. 1015; Gaines vs. Fuentes, 92 U. S. 10; 23 L. Ed. 524.

Thus, when the State law gives one who wishes to assail the validity of a will, the right to institute in a State Court either at law or in equity, an independent suit not ancillary to the probate proceedings, he may exercise the like privilege in a Federal Court, provided there is the necessary diversity of citizenship and amount in controversy.

164. Federal Courts May Have Jurisdiction to Construe a Will.

Even where the executor is in possession of the estate and therefore the estate itself is in the custody of a Probate Court, a Federal Court of Equity, where the necessary diversity of citizenship exists, may entertain a bill to construe the will. Its decree passed in such suit will be binding upon the executor.[8]

165. Federal Court May Have Jurisdiction of a Suit Against an Administrator or an Executor on a Debt Due by the Deceased.

It is well settled law that where the necessary diversity of citizenship and amount in controversy exists, a suit may be brought in the Federal Court against an executor or administrator upon a debt alleged to be due by the testator or intestate.[9] If the plaintiff recovers a judgment in such suit, the fact that he was a creditor of the decedent is conclusively established. The Probate Court must give that judgment full faith and credit. The plaintiff cannot, however, by virtue of a decree of the United States Court seize any part of the decedent's estate. He must file his judgment in the State Probate Court and therein assert his rights.[10]

8. Waterman vs. Canal-Louisiana Bank Co., 215 U. S. 33; 54 L. Ed. 80; 30 Sup. Ct. 10.

9. Hess vs. Reynolds, 113 U. S. 73; 28 L. Ed. 927; 5 Sup. Ct. 377.

10. Yonly vs. Lavender, 21 Wall., 276; 22 L. Ed. 536.

166. Federal Courts Disclaim all Jurisdiction of Divorce or the Allowance of Alimony.

As early as Barber vs. Barber[11] the Supreme Court said:—

"We disclaim altogether any jurisdiction in the Courts of the United States upon the subject of divorce, or for the allowance of alimony, either as an original proceeding in chancery or as an incident to divorce *a vinculo*, or to one from bed and board.

This statement has been several times reiterated.[12] In the Burros Case, the reason for this disclaimer was stated to be that, within the States of the Union, the whole subject of the domestic relations of husband and wife, and parent and child belong to the laws of the State and not to the laws of the United States.

It is not true that the United States Courts will not take jurisdiction over any case which requires them to pass on questions of law peculiarly within the control of the States. The latter regulate, as they will, titles to the lands within them. All questions of real property law are governed by them, yet that fact has never been considered as any reason why a Federal Court will not take jurisdiction of an ejectment case, where the parties to it are of diverse citizenship.

In none of the cases above cited was it strictly necessary to decide whether the Courts of the United States could take jurisdiction of a suit for a divorce and alimony where the parties to the controversy were citizens of different States and the alimony claimed was large enough. Under the Statutes of the United States as they now are and always have been, a suit for divorce only cannot be maintained in the Federal Courts, because the question in controversy cannot be reduced to a pecuniary stand-

11. Barber vs. Barber, 21 Howard, 582; 16 L. Ed. 226.
12. In re Burros, 136 U. S. 586; 34 L. Ed. 500; 10 Sup. Ct. 850.

11

point. It is, however, clearly established that the Courts of the United States will not under any circumstances take jurisdiction of a suit for a divorce or for alimony as incident to a divorce proceeding.

While the controversy is *inter partes,* it also partakes largely of the nature of a proceeding *in rem* by which the future status of the married pair is to be determined. It is in the latter aspect analogous to a probate proceeding.

There are cogent reasons of public policy why Federal Courts should not interfere in such matters—reasons which have no application to land titles and the like, although the latter are, of course, subject to State regulation and control. In spite of all this, it is possible to conceive of a proceeding for divorce in which a District Court would have original jurisdiction, provided the defendant is a consul of a foreign State.[13]

167. Courts of the United States May Have Jurisdiction of Suits to Recover Arrears of Alimony.

Where a State Court of competent jurisdiction has decreed that the husband shall pay the wife alimony, and he fails to comply with that decree, and the parties are citizens of different States, and the amount due by him is sufficient to give jurisdiction to the Federal Court, such Court may entertain an action by the wife to compel its payment.[14]

168. District Courts May Take Jurisdiction of Condemnation Suits Under State Laws.

Federal Courts are sometimes asked to try condemnation cases where there is a diversity of citizenship between the parties and the necessary amount is in contro-

13. Higginson vs. Higginson, 158 N. Y. Supp. 92.
14. Barber vs. Barber, 21 How., 582; 16 L. Ed. 226.

versy. In gainsaying their right so to do, it has been argued that the proceeding to take private property for public use is an exercise by the State of its sovereign right of eminent domain, with which the United States, a separate sovereignty, has no right to interfere.

To this reasoning the Supreme Court answered:—

"This position is undoubtedly a sound one so far as the act of appropriating the property is concerned. The right of eminent domain, that is the right to take private property for public uses, appertains to every independent government. It requires no constitutional recognition; it is an attribute of sovereignty. * * * When the use is public, the necessity or expediency of appropriating any particular property is not a subject of judicial cognizance. The property may be appropriated by an Act of the Legislature, or the power of appropriating it may be delegated to private corporations, to be exercised by them in the execution of works in which the public is interested. But notwithstanding the right is one that appertains to sovereignty, when the sovereign power attaches conditions to its exercise, the inquiry whether the conditions have been observed is a proper matter for judicial cognizance. If that inquiry take the form of a proceeding before the Courts between parties, the owners of the land on the one side and the company seeking the appropriation on the other, there is a controversy which is subject to the ordinary incidents of a civil suit, and its determination derogates in no respect from the sovereignty of the State."[15]

Ordinarily such proceedings are in their inception in the nature of an inquest to ascertain the value of the land, and they are not then a suit in the ordinary sense of that word. Usually at some stage they may, at the instance of either party, be transferred to a Court of law and may under the laws of the State take the form of a suit. They

15. Boom Co. vs. Patterson, 98 U. S. 406; 25 L. Ed. 206.

then become a matter of which the Federal Courts may assume jurisdiction, if the other necessary conditions exist.

The question as to whether these special proceedings are or are not suits, comes up most frequently in connection with the removal of cases from the State to the Federal Courts. The word "suit," however, is used in the same sense in those sections of the statute which confer original jurisdiction and in those which authorize removals.

169. Federal Courts May not Under Section 24, Paragraph 1, of the Judicial Code, Entertain an Original Petition for a Mandamus.

It has always been held that a mandamus proceeding is not included within the suits of a civil nature at common law of which the Federal Courts, by section 11 of the original Judiciary Act and its various revisions, were given jurisdiction. There are two reasons for so holding. At common law mandamus was a prerogative writ. A private suitor had no right to ask for it. It was applied for by the Attorney-General. He might, if he saw fit, make such request at the instance of some individual and in reliance upon the latter's relation of the facts. The approved form of petition for the writ in many jurisdictions is "the State upon the relation of John Doe." In modern times, even where the old forms of pleading are more or less completely retained, a mandamus proceeding has become an ordinary suit which anyone may institute. A hundred years ago it still had more of its ancient seeming, even if most of its antique substance had passed away. There was, therefore, a real question in the minds of lawyers as to whether Congress intended to include mandamus proceedings within the word "suits" as used in the eleventh section. It was held that such was not its purpose, because a comparison of the language of section 14 of the same Act, now section 716 of the Revised Statutes, led to that conclusion. That section reads: "The Supreme Court and the Circuit and District Courts shall have power to issue writs of *scire facias*. They shall also have power to issue all writs not specifically provided for by statute which may be necessary for the exercise of their respective jurisdiction and agreeable to the principles and usages of law." It was held that the writ of mandamus was included within the writs thus described, and that the obvious purpose of the section was to give to the Courts power to issue them as ancillary to the exercise of some jurisdiction specifically conferred.[16]

There was doubtless a practical reason of public policy for reaching that conclusion—a reason which probably explains why the Courts have always adhered to the determination they first reached and why Congress has never authorized the Federal Courts, except in some specially enumerated cases, to entertain petitions for mandamus otherwise than in aid of their other jurisdiction.

Under our dual system of government, there are many opportunities for collision between State and Federal authorities. It is not to the public interests that private litigants should be in a position to force them. If a citizen of one State conceived that he had the right to the exercise of some purely ministerial function by a public official of another, he might go into the Federal Courts and apply for a writ of mandamus to compel that State official to do his duty. In the long run it is probably better that he be forced to seek relief of this kind from a State tribunal. Doubtless State prejudice or partiality sometimes stands in the way of his getting what he

16. Rosenbaum vs. Bauer, 120 U. S. 453; 30 L. Ed. 743; 7 Sup. Ct. 633.

should have. If it does, it is a lesser evil than to arouse the antagonisms always so easily stirred up when a Federal Court undertakes to order a State officer to do anything.

Occasionally, where the writ of mandamus is used as a writ of execution, the Federal Courts have issued it to municipal officials. In this way judgments recovered against cities and counties have been enforced. The tax-levying officials of the defendant municipality have been commanded to levy a tax sufficient to pay the judgment.[17]

Congress has in a few special cases conferred upon the District Courts power to issue the writ as an original one—as, for example, to compel interstate carriers to furnish equal facilities to shippers,[18] or to enforce obedience to orders of the Interstate Commerce,[19] the Tariff[20] or the Federal Trade Commissions,[21] to require Federal Court Clerks to make returns required by law,[22] or to compel the Union Pacific Railroad company to operate its road.[23]

170. What Does "Of a Civil Nature" Mean?

By the first paragraph of Section 24 of the Judicial Code, the District Courts are given jurisdiction over such suits only as are "of a civil nature." The constitutional

17. Riggs vs. Johnson County, 6 Wall., 166; 18 L. Ed. 768.

18. Sec. 10, Act March 2, 1889; 25 Stat. 862; 4 Fed. Stat. Ann. 544; U. S. Comp. Stat. Sec. 8593; U. S. vs. Norfolk & Western R. R. Co., 143 Fed. 266; 74 C. C. A. 404.

19. Act March 1, 1913, Sec. 19a, Par. 15; 37 Stat. 701; 4 Fed. Stat. Ann. 495; U. S. Comp. Stat. Sec. 8591; Act Feb. 4, 1887, Sec. 20, Par. 9 as amended; 4 Fed. Stat. Ann. 499; U. S. Comp. Stat. Sec. 8592.

20. Act Sept. 8, 1916, Sec. 706, 39 Stat. 797; 1918 Supp. Fed. Stat. Ann. 147; U. S. Comp. Stat. Sec. 5326g.

21. Act Sept. 26, 1914, Sec. 9, 38 Stat. 722; 4 Fed. Stat. Ann. 581; U. S. Comp. Stat. Sec. 8836i.

22. Act Feb. 22, 1875, Sec. 4, 18 Stat. 333; 4 Fed. Stat. Ann. 773; U. S. Comp. Stat. Sec. 1327.

23. R. S. 5262.

provision defining the extent of the Federal judicial power nowhere used the word "civil" or any word of like import. Nevertheless as was pointed out in Chisholm vs. Georgia,[24] and as CHIEF JUSTICE MARSHALL demonstrated in his opinion in Cohens vs. Virginia,[25] under the dual system established by the Constitution, the *original* jurisdiction of the Federal Courts, except when they are called upon to enforce the laws of Congress, is necessarily limited to cases of a civil nature. Any other construction would have extended Federal jurisdiction to criminal prosecutions against persons not citizens of the prosecuting State. The Supreme Court, in Wisconsin vs. The Pelican Insurance Co.,[26] said that it had repeatedly held that even its original jurisdiction was confined to proceedings of a civil nature. In that case, the defendant, a Louisiana corporation, had carried on business in Wisconsin, and had there subjected itself to certain pecuniary penalties, for which the State in its own Courts recovered a judgment for $15,000. The company had no assets within the State. In the Supreme Court of the United States Wisconsin brought, as an original action, a civil suit upon the judgment. The Court said it would look through form to substance. The claim was in essence for a penalty. On the other hand, quite in conformity with the conclusion there reached, it subsequently declared that the test is not what name the statute is given by the Legislature or by the Courts of the State in which it was passed, but whether it appears to the tribunal which is called upon to enforce it to be, in its essential character and effect, a punishment of an offense against the public or a grant of a civil right to a private person.[27]

24. 2 Dallas, 419; 1 L. Ed. 440.
25. 6 Wheat. 264; 5 L. Ed. 257.
26. 127 U. S. 265; 32 L. Ed. 239; 8 Sup. Ct. 1370.
27. Huntington vs. Attrill, 146 U. S. 683; 36 L. Ed. 1123; 13 Sup. Ct. 224; Boston & M. R. R. vs. Hurd. 108 Fed. 116; 47 C. C. A. 615.

171. In What Sense Does Paragraph 1, Section 24, Use the Words "At Common Law"?

What construction is to be put upon the words "at common law" as used in the paragraph now under consideration?

A suit may be a suit at common law without necessarily being a suit which could have been carried to a successful conclusion in one of the Superior Courts at Westminster. The jurisdiction is not restricted to old and settled forms. The words are used in contradistinction to proceedings in equity, on one hand, and to admiralty and criminal cases, on the other. They include all suits in which legal, as distinguished from equitable, rights are to be ascertained and determined. "Wherever by either the common law or the statute law of a State a right of action has become fixed and a legal liability incurred, that liability may be enforced and the right of action pursued in any Court which has jurisdiction of such matters and can obtain jurisdiction of the parties."[28]

172. Suits Under Lord Campbell's Act Are Suits "At Common Law."

The Federal Courts, where the proper diversity of citizenship exists, can take jurisdiction of suits under the Lord Campbell's Acts of the States, although at common law no such suit could have been maintained. When the liability has been fixed by the law of one State, a Court of the United States sitting in another may enforce it;[29] it is not penal.[30]

28. Dennick vs. Railroad Co., 103 U. S. 11; 26 L. Ed. 439.
29. Dennick vs. The R. R. Co., 103 U. S. 17; 26 L. Ed. 439.
30. Texas & Pacific Railway Co. vs. Cox, 145 U. S. 604; 36 L. Ed. 829; 12 Sup. Ct. 905.

173. In What Sense Does Paragraph 1, Section 24, Use the Phrase "In Equity"?

The jurisdiction applies not only to suits at common law, but also to suits in equity. What is meant by those words here? A case in equity is a case over which at the time of the adoption of the Federal Constitution the High Court of Chancery in England would have had jurisdiction in accordance with the principles and practices then recognized and followed by it.[31]

174. State Legislation Cannot Limit the Equitable Jurisdiction of Federal Courts.

This jurisdiction cannot be diminished by any legislation of the States.

Wood & Lee were a firm, each of the partners of which was a citizen of the State of Missouri. They obtained a judgment in the State Courts of Louisiana against one Cohn, a citizen of the latter commonwealth. They filed their bill in equity in the Circuit Court of the United States for the Western District of Louisiana against Cohn, his wife and his wife's mother, all citizens of Louisiana. The bill sought to set aside as fraudulent a judgment in favor of Mrs. Cohn against Cohn; and asked that property standing in the name of Mrs. Cohn's mother and alleged to be in fact the property of Cohn, should be subject to the payment of the firm's judgments. The Court below dismissed the bill on the ground that equity had no jurisdiction, there being a well-known and adequate remedy at law. The Supreme Court said:—

> "We are unable to concur in these views. It is well settled that the jurisdiction of the Federal Courts, sitting as Courts of Equity, is neither enlarged nor diminished by State legislation. Though by it, all differences in forms of actions be abolished, though all remedies be administered in a single action

31. Payne vs. Hook, 7 Wall., 425; 19 L. Ed. 60.

at law, so far at least as form is concerned, all distinction between equity and law be ended, yet the jurisdiction of the Federal Court, sitting as a Court of Equity, remains unchanged." * * * "That jurisdiction, as has often been decided, is vested as a part of the judicial power of the United States in its Courts by the Constitution and Acts of Congress in execution thereof. Without the assent of Congress, that jurisdiction cannot be impaired or diminished by the statutes of the several States regulating the practice of their own Courts." * * * "So conceding it to be true as stated by the learned Judge, that the full relief sought in this suit could be obtained in the State Courts in an action at law, it does not follow that the Federal Court, sitting as a Court of Equity, is without jurisdiction. The inquiry rather is whether by the principles of common law and equity, as distinguished and defined in this and the mother country at the time of the adoption of the Constitution of the United States, the relief here sought was one obtainable in a Court of law or one which only a Court of Equity was fully competent to give."[32]

Further stating the facts in the case, the Court said:—

"It will be seen from this statement that these bills were substantially creditors' bills to subject property—in fact the property of the defendant, but fraudulently standing in the name of a third party— to the payment of those judgments, and to remove a fraudulent judgment which might stand as a cloud upon the title of the debtor. Such suits have always been recognized as within the jurisdiction of equity."

175. State Legislation Cannot Extend the Equitable Jurisdiction of the Federal Courts Over Legal Demands.

The converse proposition that no State legislation can extend that jurisdiction to matters essentially legal has been quite as clearly ruled.

32. Mississippi Mills vs. Cohn, 150 U. S. 202; 37 L. Ed. 1052; 14 Sup. Ct. 75.

176. A Federal Court of Equity May Not Set Aside a Conveyance in Fraud of Creditors at Suit of a Creditor Who Has Not a Lien.

The State of Mississippi has a statute substantially like that which forms a part of the Codes of many other States, and which provides that in case of a proceeding in equity to vacate any conveyance or contract or other act as fraudulent against creditors, it shall not be necessary for any creditor to have obtained a judgment at law on his demand in order to be entitled to the relief sought.

Certain citizens of Missouri, Alabama and Louisiana claiming to be creditors of Cates & Co., citizens of Mississippi, filed a bill against the latter in the District Court of the United States for the Northern District of the last named State. The bill said the defendants had assigned their property with the fraudulent intent to hinder, delay and defraud the complainants and other creditors. The Supreme Court held that the United States Courts, as Courts of equity, had no jurisdiction. "The Constitution of the United States, in creating and defining the judicial power of the general government," "established the distinction between law and equity." "Equitable relief in aid of demands, cognizable in the Courts of the United States only on their law side, could not be sought in the same action, although allowable in the State Courts by virtue of State legislation." "The Code of Mississippi in giving to a simple contract creditor a right to seek in equity in advance of any judgment or legal proceedings upon his contract the removal of obstacles to the recovery of his claim caused by fraudulent conveyances of property whereby the whole suit involving the determination of the validity of the contract and the amount due thereon is treated as one in equity to be heard and disposed of without a trial by jury, could not be enforced in the Courts of the United States because in conflict with the provision of the Seventh Amendment by which the right to a trial by jury is secured."[33]

177. In Federal Courts Right of Trial by Jury Must Be Held Inviolate in What Were Cases at Common Law.

That amendment declares that in suits at common law where the value in controversy shall exceed $20, the right of trial by jury shall be preserved. In the Federal Court this right may, it is true, be waived by the parties entitled to it, but it is otherwise absolute and cannot be impaired or evaded by blending with a claim, properly cognizable at law, a demand for equitable relief in aid of the legal action or during its pendency. "Such aid in the Federal Courts must be sought in separate proceedings, to the end that the right to a trial by a jury in the legal action may be preserved intact. * * * All actions which seek to recover specific property, real or personal, with or without damages for its detention, or a money judgment for breach of a simple contract, or as damages for injury to person or property, are legal actions, and can be brought in the Federal Courts only on their law side."[34]

Important practical consequences follow. Suppose a citizen of New York has a claim for $3,500 against a Maryland debtor. The creditor is satisfied he can show that the debtor has made a fraudulent transfer of property. He wants very much to attack at once the *bona fides* of the conveyance. It is important to keep the person in whose name or in whose possession the property is from transferring it for value to some innocent third party. The creditor needs an injunction without delay. Perhaps the Maryland man has large local influence. The New Yorker

33. Cates vs. Allen, 149 U. S. 451; 37 L. Ed. 804; 13 Sup. Ct. 883.
34. Scott vs. Neely, 140 U. S. 106; 35 L. Ed. 358; 11 Sup. Ct. 712.

may at the time be personally unpopular in the particular county in which the defendant resides. He has in that event a more or less unpleasant choice to make. He will have to take the chance of local prejudices influencing the State Court against him or else he will have to lose the time necessarily consumed in first securing in the Federal Courts a judgment at law.

178. Federal Courts May Enforce in Equity New Rights Given by State Legislation When Such Rights Are Essentially Equitable.

Although no State legislation can take from a Federal Court the right to give equitable relief when, under the circumstances, equitable relief would have been given by the High Court of Chancery in 1789, and while no State legislation can authorize a Federal Court of Equity to dispose of a controversy which, at that date, would have been one of common law cognizance, yet it is not true that State legislation cannot, in anywise, extend the jurisdiction of Federal Courts of Chancery. Those Courts have jurisdiction where a new remedy in equity is given by the State statutes in cases of the same general character as those of which the High Court of Chancery took jurisdiction, provided that they are not cases in which the defendant at common law would have been entitled to a jury trial.

Put in another way—no State legislation can change the boundary line between the legal and equitable jurisdiction of the Federal Courts, but it may on either side of that boundary extend the area of that jurisdiction. Where there has been a legal wrong without, at common law, a corresponding legal remedy, State legislation may supply one, and the Federal Courts will enforce it. Similarly State legislation may provide an equitable remedy for an equitable wrong, although the High Court of Chancery in 1789 would not or could not have furnished relief. When that remedy has been given, a Federal Court, under proper circumstances, may apply it.[35]

179. The Effect of Modern Legislative and Judicial Action Upon the Distinction Between Cases at Law and in Equity.

Prior to 1913, a mistake as to the proper side of the Court upon which to bring a proceeding was a serious matter. All that could be done was to drop the first case and bring a second one on the other side. Not infrequently, limitations had run before the error was discovered. The Twenty-second Equity Rule of the Supreme Court, in force from February 1, 1913, directs that whenever in the prosecution of a suit in equity it appears that it should have been brought as an action of law, it shall be transferred to the law side and there prosecuted, with only such alterations in the pleadings as are essential. That was as far as the Courts could go, but two years later, Congress dealt more comprehensively with the whole subject,[36] and provided that whenever a suit at law should have been brought in equity, or a suit in equity at law, the Court should order such amendments to the pleadings as might be necessary to conform them to proper practice. At any stage of the proceeding, any party has the right to amend his pleadings so as to obviate the objection that the suit was not brought on the right side of the Court. The case then goes on and is determined upon the amended pleadings. All testimony theretofore taken, if it has been preserved, will be still treated as in the case. These provisions are altogether sensible and are not likely to prove difficult of applica-

35. Louisville & Nashville R. R. Co. vs. Western Union Tel. Co., 234 U. S. 369; 58 L. Ed. 1356; 34 Sup. Ct. 810.

36. Section 274a, Judicial Code, March 3, 1915, 38 Stat. 956; 5 Fed. Stat. Ann. 1059; U. S. Comp. Stat. Sec. 1251a.

tion. They alter nothing of substance. They simply provide the means by which a client can escape from paying a high price for his lawyer's blunder.

Another statutory reform will make it difficult to keep rigid the line dividing law from equity, even in things which count. By the same statute, equitable defenses may now be interposed in actions at law[37] by answer, plea or replication. When they are, certain procedural problems are necessarily raised. These will be discussed in a later chapter. Here it is sufficient to point out that some blending of the two systems will be the almost inevitable result with the probable effect of somewhat extending the number of issues to be passed on by the jury. The constitution will prevent any appreciable encroachment of equity upon law, but there is nothing to prevent the chancellor from taking the opinion of the jury upon any issue of fact, and although their finding may not be technically binding upon him, it is not likely to be ignored when it is more or less bound up or associated with those issues at law upon which their verdict is final.

37. Judicial Code, Section 274b, Act March 3, 1915, 38 Stat. 956; 5 Fed. Stat. Ann. 1061; U. S. Comp. Stat. Sec. 1251b.

CHAPTER VII.

THE AMOUNT IN CONTROVERSY.

180. A Minimum Amount in Controversy.

We may now pass to the consideration of another condition which may be necessary to give jurisdiction to a District Court of the United States over a suit of a civil nature at common law or in equity—that is to say that there shall be a certain minimum sum in controversy.

181. Where United States or One of Its Officers Sues, Amount in Controversy Immaterial.

When suit is brought by the United States or by one of its officers authorized by law to sue, the amount in controversy is immaterial. The United States ought not to be compelled to go into any other Court than its own to assert a right belonging to it, merely because the sum or value in controversy may be small.[1]

The same reason applies when a suit is brought by an officer of the United States acting in his official capacity.[2]

182. When Controversy is Between Citizens of the Same State Claiming Lands Under Grants of Different States Amount in Controversy is Immaterial.

To provide impartial tribunals for the determination of disputes growing out of the grant of the same land by different States was one of the reasons for the adoption of the Constitution. Both New York and New Hampshire had claims to Vermont. Before the Revolution, what is now the last named State was familiarly known in New England as the "New Hampshire grants." The "Green Mountain Boys" first became famous by their irregular resistance to the asserted rights of New York. There had been actual blood shed as the result of the grants made by Connecticut in what is now, and was then claimed to be, Northern Pennsylvania. The tribunals of either

1. Postmaster General vs. Early, 12 Wheat., 136; 6 L. Ed. 577.
2. Henry vs. Sowles, 28 Fed. 481.

of the States concerned were ill fitted to deal with such disputes. Fortunately, litigation of this particular sort is now extremely rare. If any such case shall arise, it may be brought in a Federal Court irrespective of the pecuniary value of the land in controversy.

183. District Courts Have No Jurisdiction in Other Cases Mentioned in Paragraph 1, Section 24, Judicial Code, Unless Upwards of $3,000 is in Controversy.

None of the other suits mentioned in the first paragraph of section 24 can, under the authority given by it, be brought in a District Court of the United States unless the matter in controversy exceeds, exclusive of interest and costs, the sum or value of $3,000, except the bills of interpleader filed by insurance companies or fraternal societies referred to in Section 199, *infra*. This statement requires some explanation. Among the suits mentioned in this paragraph are those arising under the Constitution or laws of the United States or treaties made, or which shall be made, under their authority. There are twenty-four other paragraphs in the section. Each of them gives the District Court jurisdiction of one or more descriptions of cases, all of which arise under the Constitution, laws or treaties of the United States. Most of them are suits of a civil nature either at common law or in equity. Over some of them the jurisdiction of the Courts of the United States is exclusive, and of course in them the amount in controversy is immaterial. Over some the State Courts have concurrent jurisdiction, but it is expressly provided that the requirement as to a minimum sum or value in controversy shall not apply to any of the proceedings mentioned in those other twenty-four paragraphs. Accordingly, therefore, it should be said that upwards of $3,000 in controversy is required to give the District Court jurisdiction of a case arising under the Constitution, laws or treaties of the United States, unless it is a case included in the grants of jurisdiction made by paragraphs 2 to 25, inclusive, of section 24, or is one over which jurisdiction is given by some other Act of Congress.

Where an amount in controversy is required, no suit, the purpose of which cannot be expressed in terms of pecuniary value, may be brought. For example: Suppose there is a question as to the custody of a child between those who had been husband and wife, but who have been divorced? They may be citizens of different States. The United States Courts have no jurisdiction to issue a writ of *habeas corpus* to determine the right to the possession of the child.[3]

184. Changes in the Amount Required to be in Controversy.

Congress has always been unwilling to permit suits for small sums to be brought into its own Courts, not because it specially wanted to save those Courts labor, or even because it wished to uphold their dignity, but principally, if not solely, for the protection of litigants. Where the amounts at issue are not large, litigation in the Federal Courts may be unduly burdensome.

By the first Judiciary Act none of the suits which are now under consideration could be brought into the Federal Courts unless there was upwards of $500 in controversy. In spite of the great increase in wealth in the country, this figure remained unchanged for nearly a century. By the Act of March 3, 1887, it was quadrupled, being fixed at upwards of $2,000. It was again

3. Barry vs. Mercien, 5 How. 103; 12 L. Ed. 70; Kurtz vs. Moffitt, 115 U. S. 487; 29 L. Ed. 458; 6 Sup. Ct. 148.

raised by the Judicial Code on January 1, 1912, to upwards of $3,000. The amounts named were to be exclu-
sive of interest and costs.

185. In Determining Amount in Controversy, Interest is Excluded Only When it is Claimed as Accessory to a Principal Demand.

The statute declares that the amount in controversy
must be upwards of $3,000, exclusive of interest and
costs. This language does not mean that under no circumstances shall interest be taken into account in determining whether the required amount is in controversy.
Conceivably the only thing in dispute may be interest.
A may have lent B $100,000 for five years at six per cent
interest, payable annually. A year's interest may be in
arrears. The contract may not have contained any provision by which failure to pay the interest when due
made the principal immediately demandable. Under
such circumstances A's only remedy would be to sue B
for the amount of the overdue interest, viz: $6,000. If
there was the necessary diversity of citizenship, the case
might be brought in the United States Court, although
the only thing sued for would be interest. It would be
itself the principal demand and not accessory to something else, the recovery of which was sought.

This principle has been applied to suits upon interest
coupons. These coupons are each independent contracts.
Suit to recover upon them is not in any just sense accessory to any other demand, but is in itself principal and
primary.

When upwards of $2,000, exclusive of interest and
costs, was the amount required to be in controversy, suit
was brought upon two bonds for $1,000 each and upon
overdue interest coupons attached to such bonds. The

Supreme Court held that the amount in controversy exceeded $2,000, exclusive of interest and costs.[4]

The same principle had shortly before been applied to another kind of case. The defendant had, a number of years prior to the suit, sold the plaintiff a tract of Nebraska land for $1,200. He gave a general warranty deed. Subsequently the plaintiff was ousted by third parties whose title was paramount to that of either plaintiff or defendant. Plaintiff then brought suit to recover upwards of $2,000 from the defendant for breach of warranty. The State statute fixed the amount of recovery in such action at the price paid for the land with interest thereon until suit brought. The Supreme Court, in an opinion by JUSTICE WHITE, held that the sum demanded was not the price and the interest thereon as such, but damages for the breach of the covenant of warranty. It was, in the view of the Supreme Court immaterial that one element of such damage was interest. The suit was none the less a demand for what was in law a legal unit, viz: damages suffered by the plaintiff. The interest formed part of the principal demand and was not a mere accessory thereto.[5]

186. An Attorney's Fee Provided for in the Contract is Part of Sum in Controversy and not of the Costs.

A debtor often promises to pay an attorney's fee if he does not discharge the debt when due. The amount of such fee, if fixed by the debtor's promise or when it is not, the sum alleged by the plaintiff to be reasonable, is included in the amount in controversy, and is not part of the costs.[6]

4. Edwards vs. Bates County, 163 U. S. 269; 41 L. Ed. 155; 16 Sup. Ct. 967.

5. Brown vs. Webster, 156 U. S. 329; 39 L. Ed. 440; 15 Sup. Ct. 377.

6. Springstead vs. Crawfordsville State Bank, 231 U. S. 541; 58 L. Ed. 354; 34 Sup. Ct. 195.

187. Difficulty of Precisely Valuing the Right or Thing in Controversy Does Not Necessarily Defeat Jurisdiction.

The pecuniary value of particular rights is often difficult of ascertainment. It may be that there are no certain standards for measuring their worth in money; it does not follow that they are valueless even in terms of dollars and cents.

When the minimum sum required was upwards of $2,000, the Supreme Court ruled that the Circuit Court had jurisdiction over an action brought by a voter to recover $2,500 from the election officials who wrongfully, as he alleged, rejected his vote for a representative in the Congress of the United States. The Court said:—

> "What amount of damages the plaintiff shall recover in such an action is peculiarly appropriate for the determination of a jury, and no opinion of the Court upon that subject can justify it in holding that the amount in controversy was insufficient to support the jurisdiction of the Circuit Court."[7]

188. Impossibility of Putting Any Pecuniary Value on the Right or Thing in Controversy is Fatal to Jurisdiction.

Unless, however, the right or thing in controversy is translatable in some fashion into terms of money, there is no pecuniary amount in· controversy, as there is not where one seeks by *habeas corpus* to be discharged from custody in which he is being held for a criminal offense,[8] or where it is sought specifically to enforce an arbitration agreement under a State statute.[9]

7. Wiley vs. Sinkler, 179 U. S. 65; 45 L. Ed. 84; 21 Sup. Ct. 17.
8. Cross vs. Burke, 146 U. S. 82; 36 L. Ed. 896; 13 Sup. Ct. 22.
9. In re Red Cross Line, 277 Fed. 853.

189. In Suits for Unliquidated Damages the Amount in Controversy is Ordinarily the Sum Claimed by Plaintiff.

Wiley vs. Sinkler[10] is an illustration of the rule that, in actions for unliquidated damages, the sum in controversy is ordinarily the amount claimed by the plaintiff. It is not that which he ultimately recovers.

The whole subject was carefully considered by the Supreme Court of the United States a number of years ago.[11]

The plaintiff Barry was a citizen of Virginia. In the year 1884 a tax of $56.34 had been properly levied upon his property. The State of Virginia then had outstanding a great many coupon bonds. When they were issued the State had agreed that the coupons should be receivable in payment of all taxes. A majority of its people came to the conclusion that it was not able to pay these bonds in full. A long contest between the State and the bondholders ensued. Various laws were passed intended to make it difficult for a bondholder to use his coupons in payment of taxes. The plaintiff had tendered coupons for the tax assessed against him. The defendant had refused to receive them, and, in spite of a decision of the Supreme Court that they must be so received, had levied upon the property of the plaintiff and carried it away. The plaintiff asserted that the defendant's purpose in so doing was to make an example of him and to injure his credit. The Supreme Court said:—

> "The cause of action stated in the declaration is a willful and malicious trespass in seizing and taking personal property, with circumstances of aggravation and averments of special damage." * * * "The plaintiff is not limited in his recovery to the mere value of the property taken. That would not neces-

10. 179 U. S. 65; 45 L. Ed. 84; 21 Sup. Ct. 17.
11. Barry vs. Edmunds, 116 U. S. 550; 29 L. Ed. 729; 6 Sup. Ct. 501.

sarily cover his actual, direct and immediate pecuniary loss. In addition, according to the settled law
of this Court, he might show himself, by proof of the
circumstances, to be entitled to exemplary damages
calculated to vindicate his right and protect it against
future similar invasion.'"[12]

190. Even in a Suit for Unliquidated Damages, Plaintiff's Claim Not Necessarily Conclusive of the Amount in Controversy.

This rule has its limits. There was a period when the
State of South Carolina saw fit to monopolize the retail
liquor trade within its borders. The State established
certain dispensaries. No one other than the State's
officers in charge of these institutions was lawfully entitled to sell liquors. Much litigation arose. A plaintiff
had shipped some packages of wines and brandies into
the State. They were seized by some of the defendants
for an alleged violation of its laws. Another of the defendants subsequent to the seizure, and with knowledge
of its wrongful nature, received the packages into his
custody, and refused to return them when demanded.
The declaration alleged that the malicious trespass of
the defendants and their continuation in the wrongful
detention of the liquors had greatly damaged the plaintiff's business. It was further alleged that the goods
had been seized wrongfully, knowingly, wilfully and
maliciously, with intent to oppress, humiliate and intimidate the plaintiff, and make him afraid to rely upon the
Constitution and laws of the United States. Judgment
was prayed for the value of the goods, which was said to
be $1,000, and for $10,000 damages. The Supreme Court
said that this was nothing more than an action of trover;
that in South Carolina the measure of damage in that
kind of action is the value of the property converted;

12. Barry vs. Edmunds, supra.

consequential damages are not recoverable. The amount claimed by the plaintiff, omitting the consequential damages, was, therefore, less than the sum necessary to give the Circuit Court jurisdiction.[13]

191. In an Action Ex Contractu for Liquidated Damages the Amount in Controversy is the Liquidated Sum.

In an action *ex contractu* upon a liquidated claim, the Court has no jurisdiction unless such liquidated sum exceeds $3,000. It makes no difference what damage the plaintiff may demand if his declaration shows that the amount in controversy cannot exceed a sum which is below that required to give the Court jurisdiction.

At a time when the statute authorized the Circuit Court to take jurisdiction of controversies in which the amount involved exceeded $500, and when it limited the right of appeal to the Supreme Court of the United States, to cases in which $2,000 was involved, there was an action in which the writ and the original declaration showed that the amount in controversy did not exceed $1,000. The evidence offered at the trial by the plaintiff proved that it did not exceed $700. The plaintiff at the close of his declaration claimed $2,100 damages. It was held that the amount in controversy was $1,000.[14]

192. The Amount Recovered Does Not Determine Jurisdiction.

It was so ruled because where the amount in controversy, as it has been defined, is sufficient to give the Court jurisdiction, it is immaterial on the jurisdictional question that the trial may show that the defendant does not owe the plaintiff so much. The amount in controversy is

13. Vance vs. Vandercook, 170 U. S. 468; 42 L. Ed. 1111; 18 Sup. Ct. 645.
14. Lee vs. Watson, 1 Wall., 337; 17 L. Ed. 557.

that which the plaintiff seeks to make the defendant pay; not the amount which the judgment says he must pay.

In another one of the dispensary cases from South Carolina suit was brought for a malicious trespass. The declaration averred such facts as, if true, would have justified the jury in awarding punitive damages. The Supreme Court held that the Circuit Court had jurisdiction, in spite of the fact that the plaintiff recovered only $300.[15]

193. Jurisdiction May Exist Although Plaintiff's Declaration Shows That There May Be a Defense to His Claim.

The mere fact that the plaintiff's declaration on its face shows that there may be a defense, and even a perfect defense, to so large a part of his claim as will leave the balance below the jurisdictional amount, is not sufficient to oust the jurisdiction.

Thus, in the Circuit Court of the United States for the District of Nebraska, a citizen of Ohio, to whom a Nebraska corporation was indebted in the sum of $2,100, only $500 of which was due at the time the action was instituted, brought suit and applied for an attachment on the ground that the debtor was conveying its property with intent to defraud his creditors. It was objected that there being but $500 due, the amount in controversy did not exceed $2,000. A Nebraska statute provided that where a debtor had made a fraudulent conveyance, a creditor might bring an action on a claim before it became due and have an attachment against the debtor's property. The Supreme Court said:—

"The fact of a valid defense to a cause of action, although apparent on the face of the petition, does not diminish the amount that is claimed, nor deter-

15. Scott vs. Donald, 165 U. S. 58; 41 L. Ed. 632; 17 Sup. Ct. 265.

mine what is the matter in dispute; for who can say in advance that that defense will be presented by the defendant, or, if presented, sustained by the Court?"[16]

The Court was careful to add:—

"We do not mean that a claim, evidently fictitious and alleged simply to create a jurisdictional amount, is sufficient to give jurisdiction." * * * "It may be laid down as a general proposition that no mere pretense as to the amount in dispute will avail to create jurisdiction. But here there was no pretense. The plaintiff, in evident good faith and relying upon the express language of a statute, asserted a right to recover over $2,000."

194. If Plaintiff Recovers Less Than $500 He Cannot Be Given Costs and May Have to Pay Them.

Congress has discouraged the bringing in the Federal Courts of suits in which it is not likely that any considerable recovery can be had, by providing[17] that when a plaintiff or petitioner in equity, other than the United States, recovers less than the sum or value of $500, exclusive of costs, he shall not be allowed costs, but at the discretion of the Court may be adjudged, to pay them.

195. What is the Amount in Controversy When an Injunction Is Sought?

Where the suit is in equity and the relief prayed is an injunction, the amount in controversy may be the value of the right or thing which the complainant seeks to have enjoined. It is not necessarily the damage suffered by the complainant. Thus, a part owner of three steamboats and commander of one of them, engaged in

16. Schunk vs. Moline, Milburn & Stoddard Co., 147 U. S. 505; 37 L. Ed. 255; 13 Sup. Ct. 416; Smithers vs. Smith, 204 U. S. 642; 51 L. Ed. 659; 27 Sup. Ct. 297.

17. R. S., Sec. 968.

the navigation of the Mississippi River between St. Louis and St. Paul, filed his bill of complaint alleging that navigation was much obstructed and delayed by a bridge of the defendant, which he said was a permanent nuisance. His bill prayed for no damages, but only for an abatement of the nuisance. The Supreme Court said:—

> "The want of a sufficient amount of damage having been sustained to give the Federal Courts jurisdiction will not defeat the remedy, as the removal of the obstruction is the matter of controversy and the value of that object must govern."[18]

In many cases, however, the test will be the value of the right which the complainant seeks to protect.[19] Thus where a taxpayer sought to enjoin a bond issue the amount in controversy was the amount of taxes the plaintiff would have to pay for the interest and sinking fund of the bonds.[20]

196. Distinct Claims Against Different Parties Cannot Be United to Give Jurisdiction.

Separate demands against different parties on distinct causes of action or on a single cause of action in which there are distinct liabilities, cannot be joined to give the Court jurisdiction.

A Vermont agent for four different insurance companies, in one policy, insured the property of the plaintiff for $12,000, each company severally assuming one-fourth of the obligation. Loss having occurred, the plaintiff brought a single suit against the four defendants and recovered a judgment for $3,000 and interest

18. Mississippi & Missouri R. R. Co. vs. Ward, 2 Black, 492; 17 L. Ed. 311.

19. Board of Trade vs. Cella Commission Co., 145 Fed. 28; 76 C. C. A. 28; Scott vs. Donald, 165 U. S. 107; 41 L. Ed. 648; 17 Sup. Ct. 262.

20. Colvin vs. Jacksonville, 158 U. S. 456; 39 L. Ed. 1053; 15 Sup. Ct. 866.

against each one of them. The defendants wanted to take the case to the Supreme Court of the United States, which then had jurisdiction to entertain appeals in such cases where the amount in controversy exceeded $5,000. It was held that the liability of each defendant was distinct, and as it did not exceed $5,000, without interest, the Supreme Court had no jurisdiction.[21]

197. Claims of Different Plaintiffs Against a Common Defendant Cannot Ordinarily Be United to Give Jurisdiction.

Several plaintiffs, each having claims less than the jurisdictional amount, cannot unite together in one joint suit so as to bring the amount in controversy up to the required sum.

Two judgment creditors of the same defendant each had a claim less than the jurisdictional amount. The sum of the two exceeded that amount. They filed a bill in the United States Court to subject a particular fund, itself greater than the sum necessary to give jurisdiction, to the liens of their respective judgments. It was held that the Court had no jurisdiction.[22]

198. When Plaintiffs Must Join, the Amount in Controversy is the Aggregate of Their Claims.

This whole subject was carefully considered by the Supreme Court in Gibson vs. Shufeldt.[23] In another case it said:—

"The general principle * * * is, that if several persons be joined in a suit in equity or admiralty, and have a common and undivided interest, though separable as between themselves, the amount of their

21. Ex parte Phoenix Ins. Co., 117 U. S. 369; 29 L. Ed. 923; 6 Sup. Ct. 772.
22. Seaver vs. Bigelows, 5 Wall., 208; 18 L. Ed. 595.
23. 122 U. S. 28; 30 L. Ed. 1083; 7 Sup. Ct. 1066.

joint claim or liability will be the test of jurisdiction; but where their interests are distinct, and they are joined for the sake of convenience only, and because they form a class of parties whose rights or liabilities arose out of the same transaction, or have relation to a common fund or mass of property sought to be administered, such distinct demands or liabilities cannot be aggregated together for the purpose of giving" * * * "jurisdiction."[24]

One of the tests as to whether a creditor's claim is a distinct one, or whether all the creditors stand together, is whether the suit as brought by the creditor is a suit which he could bring for himself individually, or whether it is a suit which he can only bring for himself and all other creditors.[25]

On this principle, in a number of cases, jurisdiction has been sustained of a creditor's bill, filed by a number of creditors whose claims aggregate more than the jurisdictional amount, though none of them by itself equalled that sum.[26] When jurisdiction has been taken of such bills, they have been filed on behalf of the complainants and of all other creditors who might come in and contribute to the expenses of the suit. The bills were such as could not have been filed by an individual creditor on his own behalf.

199. Five Hundred Dollars Jurisdictional Amount for Bills of Interpleader by Insurance Companies or Fraternal Societies.

Sometimes there is more than one claimant for the money payable by a life insurance company or a fraternal or mutual benefit society. Occasionally these rival claimants are citizens of different States, and may each sue in

24. Clay vs. Field, 138 U. S. 479; 34 L. Ed. 1044; 11 Sup. Ct. 419.
25. Hanley vs. Stutz, 137 U. S. 366; 34 L. Ed. 706; 11 Sup. Ct. 117.
26. Jones et al. vs. Mutual Fidelity Co., 123 Fed. 506.

his own State. In consequence, once in a while, the defendant was compelled to pay twice. To prevent the possibility of such injustice, Congress has permitted the company or society to file a bill of interpleader in a District Court of the United States when the claimants are citizens of different States, and the amount payable is as much as Five Hundred Dollars.

CHAPTER VIII.

CASES ARISING UNDER THE CONSTITUTION, TREATIES OR LAWS OF THE UNITED STATES.

200. Only Certain Classes of Suits May Be Brought in Federal Courts Under Paragraph 1, Section 24, Judicial Code.

The analysis heretofore made of the very important first paragraph of section 24 of the Judicial Code has shown what a suit is; what kind of suits are of a civil nature; when a suit is at common law and when in equity, and what are the principles which determine whether the amount in controversy, exclusive of interest and costs, exceeds the sum or value of $3,000.

It also appeared that when the United States or one of its officers authorized to sue is the plaintiff, or when the litigation is between citizens of the same State claiming lands under grants from different States, the amount in controversy is immaterial. But even though a suit be of a civil nature at common law or in equity, and the amount in controversy exceed $3,000, yet this paragraph does not give the District Courts jurisdiction over it unless it (a) arises under the Constitution, treaties or laws of the United States, or (b) is between parties of diverse citizenship. For brevity the former class are customarily referred to as cases which raise a Federal question.

201. Cases Raising a Federal Question—History.

The paragraph provides that the District Court shall have original jurisdiction of all suits of a civil nature at common law or in equity, when the matter in controversy exceeds, exclusive of interest and costs, the sum or value of $3,000, and arises under the Constitution or laws of the United States or treaties made or which shall be made

13

under their authority. No similar provision is to be found in the original Judiciary Act. It first made its appearance in the amendment of 1875. Prior to that time such suits, unless the parties were of diverse citizenship or unless the controversy itself was one of a special class, jurisdiction over which had been conferred upon the Circuit Courts had to be brought before a State tribunal.

202. What Cases Raise a Federal Question.

The Supreme Court has said that "when it appears that some title, right, privilege or immunity on which the recovery depends will be defeated by one construction of the Constitution or a law of the United States, or sustained by the opposite construction," the case is one arising under the Constitution or laws of the United States within the meaning of that term as used in the Act of 1875, otherwise not.[1]

203. Existence of Federal Question Must Appear From Plaintiff's Statement of His Own Case.

Where the only ground of jurisdiction is the existence of the Federal question, that there is such question must appear from the plaintiff's statement of his own case, in his declaration or bill. There may be many cases in which a plaintiff so setting up his claim does not state, and cannot state, that it arises under any Federal law. The case may actually turn upon a Federal question. In the end that may be the only thing decided, yet under the authorities it may not be a case arising under the Constitution or laws of the United States in such sense that the District Court will have jurisdiction over it.

For example—a defendant gives his promissory note

1. Starin vs. New York, 115 U. S. 248; 29 L. Ed. 388; 6 Sup. Ct. 28.

to the plaintiff and does not pay it. When the plaintiff demands payment the defendant asserts that the note was given in furtherance of a combination to restrain interstate trade or to monopolize that trade in violation of the Sherman Anti-Trust Act. He frankly tells the plaintiff he will not pay it and that he will, on the ground stated, defend any suit brought against him. The plaintiff cannot bring such a case in the Federal Courts on the ground that a Federal question is involved. His statement of his own cause of action will show nothing more than that the defendant is indebted to him on the promissory note and has not paid him. No possible question under the Constitution, laws or treaties of the United States is raised.

204. Plaintiff Cannot Show Existence of Federal Question by Alleging What Defenses Will Be.

The plaintiff cannot give jurisdiction by alleging that the defendant sets up, or will set up, by way of defense, rights or pretensions which turn upon a Federal question. The Supreme Court says "where diversity of citizenship does not exist, a suit can only be maintained in the Circuit Court of the United States on the ground that it arises under the Constitution or laws of the United States, and it does not so arise unless it really and substantially involves a controversy as to the effect or construction of the Constitution or some law or treaty of the United States on the determination whereof the result depends. This must appear from plaintiff's statement of his own claim, and cannot be aided by allegations as to defenses which may be interposed."[2]

The construction of the statement is for the Courts. If they do not see that it raises a Federal question the

2. Devine vs. Los Angeles, 202 U. S. 313; 50 L. Ed. 1046; 26 Sup. Ct. 652.

fact that the defendant thinks that such question is raised is immaterial.[3]

205. Court Has Jurisdiction if Plaintiff in Good Faith Sets Up a Federal Question.

If there is a Federal question actually in the case, that is to say, if the plaintiff in good faith sets up one as the basis of his claim, then the Federal Court has jurisdiction. It is immaterial that other questions are also involved.[4] It makes no difference that in the end the case is determined upon some other issue; precisely as it makes no difference that the judgment or decree may be for less than the jurisdictional amount.[5]

206. Whoever in a State Court Unsuccessfully Relies Upon the Constitution, Treaties or Laws of the United States, May Carry the Question to the Supreme Court.

A plaintiff cannot give jurisdiction to a Federal Court by anticipating in his complaint the raising by the defendant of a Federal question. He can, however, usually secure an ultimate ruling upon it by a Court of the United States. After the case has been fought through to the highest State Court having jurisdiction of it, and the Federal question has been there decided adversely to his contention, he can, in some cases, carry the controversy to the Supreme Court by writ of error, and in others, that Court may, if it thinks fit, grant a writ of certiorari. With such proceedings we are not now concerned. We are considering the original jurisdiction of

3. N. J. Central R. Co. vs. Mills, 113 U. S. 257; 28 L. Ed. 949; 5 Sup. Ct. 456.

4. R. R. Co. vs. Mississippi, 102 U. S. 135; 26 L. Ed. 96.

5. City Railway Co. vs. Citizens R. R. Co., 166 U. S. 562; 41 L. Ed. 1114; 17 Sup. Ct. 653.

the District Court and that alone. The books are full of cases in which the existence of the Federal question is one of the matters of dispute.[6] It will profit little to discuss their details. Sometimes a question so clearly arises under some Federal law or under some provision of the Constitution as to make it impossible seriously to question the jurisdiction of the Federal Court. Unless that be so, before assuming that a case raises a Federal question, it will be expedient to consider carefully the authorities and their bearing on its particular facts.

207. Federal Court May Have Jurisdiction Whether the Case Arises Under the Constitution, the Laws or the Treaties of the United States.

The clause of the first paragraph of section 24 of the Judicial Code now under consideration includes cases arising under

(a) The Constitution of the United States.

(b) A law of the United States.

(c) A treaty of the United States.

In Cohens vs. Virginia, CHIEF JUSTICE MARSHALL declared that a case arises under the Constitution or a law of the United States whenever its correct decision depends on the construction of either.[7] The same test will determine whether it arises under a treaty.

208. Cases Arising Under the Constitution.

One individual may, through official position or otherwise, be so placed that he can prevent another from exercising some constitutional right. The injured party may, if the amount in controversy is sufficient, sue the wrongdoer, in the District Court of the United States, on the ground that the case arises under the Constitu-

6. City Railway Co. vs. Citizens R. R. Co., 166 U. S. 562; 41 L. Ed. 1114; 17 Sup. Ct. 653.

7. 6 Wheaton, 379; 5 L. Ed. 257.

tion. For example, the right to vote for a member of the House of Representatives of the United States is one given by the Constitution. It is true that the Constitution, in giving the right, confines it to those persons who are qualified, by the laws of the State in which they live, to vote for the members of the most numerous branch of its legislature; nevertheless, the right to vote for a member of Congress is derived from the Constitution. An election officer who improperly prevents a person so entitled to vote from casting his ballot may be sued in a District Court of the United States.[8]

Perhaps the most numerous class of cases which are said to arise under the Constitution are those in which the plaintiff claims that the obligation of a valid contract with him is being impaired, or that he is being deprived of his life, liberty or property without due process of law, or is being denied the equal protection of the laws. The prohibition against such impairment or deprivation is directed solely at State action. It has no reference to what individuals may do, and, in order to show that a case of this class arises under the Constitution of the United States the plaintiff must allege that the defendant is acting under color of some State law. Such is the case where a railroad company sets up that some legislative act or some proceeding of a public service commission acting under authority of such an act, is depriving it of its property without due compensation, by requiring it to perform public service at a rate so unremunerative as to cause practical confiscation.[9] The District Court has jurisdiction where a public service corporation complains that a municipality, acting under

8. Wiley vs. Sinkler, 179 U. S. 61; 45 L. Ed. 84; 21 Sup. Ct. 17.

9. Willcox vs. Consolidated Gas Co., 212 U. S. 19; 53 L. Ed. 382; 29 Sup. Ct. 192.

the authority of State legislation, is taking steps which impair the obligation of a contract validly entered into with it at some previous time.[10]

It will serve no good purpose to give further illustrations of this particular class of questions. The one distinction already mentioned must be kept steadily in mind; viz: that where one seeks redress for the breach of some prohibition which the Constitution imposes upon the States, he must show that the act of which he complains is being done under color of State law, but where he is being deprived of some positive privilege or immunity conferred upon him by the Constitution, it is immaterial whether the State is or is not involved.

209. Cases Arising Under a Law of the United States.

There are many cases which arise under some act of Congress. Thus, any suit which seeks to assert a right given by the Interstate Commerce Act, is clearly one arising under the laws of the United States.[11]

The liability of the stockholders of a national bank, which has gone into liquidation, to the creditors of the bank is one which is created by the laws of the United States;[12] a suit by a creditor to enforce such liability is therefore a suit arising under them.

210. Suits Upon Official Bonds of Officers of the United States or Upon Bonds Taken in the Course of Judicial Proceedings in the United States Courts.

In a series of cases, the United States Supreme Court has held that suits by private individuals upon the offi-

10. Vicksburg vs. Vicksburg Water Works Co., 202 U. S. 453; 50 L. Ed. 1102; 26 Sup. Ct. 660.

11. Macon Grocery Co. vs. Atlantic Coast Line R. R. Co., 215 U. S. 501; 54 L. Ed. 300; 30 Sup. Ct. 184.

12. Wyman vs. Wallace, 201 U. S. 230; 50 L. Ed. 738; 26 Sup. Ct. 495.

cial bonds of United States marshals or clerks of Courts are cases arising under the laws of the United States.[13]

It is clear that the Federal Courts have jurisdiction of suits brought upon *supersedeas,* injunction or attachment bonds taken in proceedings before them.[14]

211. Suits Against United States Officers for Acts Done Under Color of Their Office.

When a United States officer is sued for something which he did under color of his official duties, the case is one which arises under the laws of the United States. Thus, when suit is brought against a United States Marshal for seizing goods under an execution from a United States Court, the case so arises,[15] at least, if the declaration shows upon its face that when the defendant did that for which he is sued he was acting or claiming to act in his official capacity.[16]

212. Whenever a Federal Corporation is a Party the Case Arises Under the Laws of the United States.

Whenever a corporation created by Federal law is a party to an action, the case arises under a law of the United States. It was so ruled many years ago[17] and is still the unquestioned law.

213. Statutory Exception of National Banks.

Congress has declared that national banks shall, for purposes of actions by or. against them, be held to be citizens of the States in which they are respectively located. Suits by or against a national bank cannot be

13. Howard vs. U. S., 184 U. S. 676; 46 L. Ed. 754; 22 Sup. Ct. 543.

14. Lamb vs. Ewing, 54 Fed. 269; 4 C. C. A. 320; Leslie vs. Brown, 90 Fed. 171; 32 C. C. A. 556.

15. Bock vs. Perkins, 139 U. S. 628; 35 L. Ed. 314; 11 Sup. Ct. 650.

16. Sonnentheil vs. Moerlein Brewing Co., 172 U. S. 404; 43 L. Ed. 492; 19 Sup. Ct. 233.

17. Osborn vs. United States Bank, 9 Wheat., 738; 6 L. Ed. 204.

brought in the Federal Courts unless they could have been brought by or against it had it been a corporation incorporated under the laws of the State in which it is located.[18]

It should be borne in mind, however, that this legislation does not apply to receivers of such banks. They may, because they are officers of the United States, sue in the Federal Courts irrespective of the amount in controversy. In the Circuit Court for the Western District of Pennsylvania, a receiver of a national bank brought suit for about $60.[19]

214. Statutory Exception of Railroad Companies Incorporated by Congress.

Still more recently, Congress has provided that no Court of the United States shall have jurisdiction of any action or suit by or against any railroad company upon the ground that it was incorporated under an Act of Congress.[20] This provision goes farther than that relating to national banks. A federal corporation is not a citizen of any State, and therefore the Courts of the United States have, on the ground of diverse citizenship, no jurisdiction over any action to which such a corporation is a party. A railroad company holding its charter from Congress can sue or be sued in the Federal Courts only when it can, upon other grounds than its Federal incorporation, show that the controversy arises under the constitution, treaties or laws of the United States.

215. Cases Arising Under a Treaty of the United States.

To give jurisdiction to the Courts of the United States on the ground that the case is one arising under a treaty

18. Judicial Code, Sec. 24, Par. 16; 4 Fed. Stat. Ann. 842; U. S. Compiled Stat. Sec. 991.

19. Murray vs. Chambers, 151 Fed. 142.

20. Act Jan. 28, 1915, Sec. 5, 38 Stat. 804; 6 Fed. Stat. Ann. 238; U. S. Comp. Stat. Sec. 1233a.

of the United States, plaintiff's right, as stated by him, must depend upon the construction or application of some provision of the treaty. Such cases are not common. Occasionally one is instituted, as for example, when a Canadian corporation sought to have a Michigan municipality enjoined from enforcing a tax upon the operation of a ferry between Sault Sainte Marie and the Ontario shore, on the ground that to do so would violate a treaty with Great Britain.[21] Every now and then it is true some one seeks to invoke the jurisdiction of the Federal Court on the ground that his case arises under a treaty, but it is seldom that the Courts sustain the contention. Thus, a plaintiff claimed that he had succeeded to the rights of one who had obtained a valid grant of land from the Spanish Governor of Louisiana and that by the treaty with France by which Louisiana was ceded to the United States, the latter bound itself to respect the grants theretofore made by the Spanish or French Governments, and that the defendants were in wrongful possession of the land and would not surrender it. The Supreme Court said that there was involved no question as to the construction of the treaty or its application. The only question in the case even remotely connected with the treaty was one of fact as to whether the plaintiff's ancestor had ever received a grant which under the laws and regulations of the province of Louisiana was valid when it was made. Such inquiry raised no question under the treaty.[22]

216. Cases Involving a Federal Question and Not Dependent Upon the Amount in Controversy.

There are twenty-four paragraphs of section 24 devoted to an enumeration of cases arising under the Constitu-

21. Sault Ste. Marie vs. International Transit Co., 234 U. S. 333; 58 L. Ed. 1337; 34 Sup. Ct. 826.

22. Muse vs. Arlington Hotel Co., 168 U. S. 430; 42 L. Ed. 531; 18 Sup. Ct. 109.

tion, laws or treaties of the United States or in which the national or official character of some of the parties involved brings the controversy within the constitutional grant of judicial power to the United States. In none of. these does the jurisdiction of the District Court in anywise depend upon the amount in controversy. It will not be necessary here to say a great deal about any of them.

217. Subjects Already Discussed.

The criminal, penal and quasi-penal jurisdiction of the District Court as conferred by paragraphs 2, 3 and 9 has already been sufficiently discussed, as has the power to hear and determine claims against the United States given by paragraph 20, and the right, exclusive of the State Courts and concurrent with the Supreme Court, to take cognizance of suits against consuls and vice-consuls granted by paragraph 18.

218. Subjects Not to Be Here Discussed.

The admiralty, patent, copyright, trade-mark and bankruptcy jurisdiction as conferred by paragraphs 3, 7 and 19 can be most profitably studied in connection with the substantive law of those topics.

219. Cases Under the Revenue and Postal Laws.

Two of the paragraphs of this section, viz: 5 and 6, give jurisdiction over cases arising under the internal revenue, the customs and the postal laws. Under these grants, District Courts may take original jurisdiction of suits brought against collectors of customs, or of internal revenue, to recover taxes illegally exacted irrespective of the citizenship of the parties or the amount in controversy.[23] Closely related to these is the grant of jurisdic-

23. Downes vs. Bidwell, 45 L. Ed. 1088; 21 Sup. Ct. 770.

tion contained in paragraph 10 over suits by assignees of debentures for draw-backs of duty against previous holders of such debentures.

By section 80 of the Act to Regulate the Collection of Duties on Imports and Tonnage,[24] it was provided that an importer of dutiable goods might under regulations therein prescribed receive a debenture for the amount of draw-back to which he might become entitled upon the re-export of such goods. Such debentures were often used by the holder for the purpose of raising money. If any question arose upon such assignment, it was desirable that the case should be tried in the United States Court. I do not find reference by any of the annotators of the statutes to a decision under this grant of jurisdiction. It is probably, therefore, of small practical importance.

220. Cases Concerning Government Interest in Land.

The 21st and 25th paragraphs are intended to give to the United States Courts jurisdiction of some cases in which the United States is concerned as a landlord. The 21st paragraph refers to suits to restain the unlawful enclosure of public lands. As the United States will in all such cases be the complainant, the special grant of jurisdiction would be unnecessary except that the paragraph also provides that service of process may be had upon any agent or employee having charge or control of the enclosure. The 25th paragraph gives the District Court jurisdiction of any suit brought by a co-tenant of the United States for a partition of lands held in joint tenancy or tenancy in common, and grants a like privilege to the United States. Such suit must be brought in the district in which the land lies.

24. Act March 2, 1799, 1 Stat. 687; 2 Fed. Stat. Ann. 1149; U. S. Comp. Stat. Sec. 5741.

221. Jurisdiction for the Protection of Aliens and Indians.

The 17th paragraph gives jurisdiction of a suit by an alien for a tort in violation of the law of nations or of a treaty of the United States, and the 24th of all actions, suits or proceedings involving the right of anyone with Indian blood to an allotment of land under law or treaty.

222. Jurisdiction for the Protection of the Privileges and Immunities of Citizens of the United States.

Paragraphs 11, 12, 13, 14 and 15 give the District Courts power to take cognizance of suits authorized by Federal law to protect or vindicate the rights and privileges of citizens of the United States. Only one portion of these statutes antedates the Civil War, and that is the part of paragraph 11, which authorizes the District Court to take jurisdiction of suits brought by any person to recover damages for any injury to his person or property on account of an act done by him under law of the United States for the protection or collection of its revenues. This is from section 2 of the famous Force Bill, passed in view of the threatened nullification by South Carolina of the tariff of 1828.[25] It was a part of Gen. Jackson's answer to that State.

The other provisions all originated after the Civil War. They are intended more effectually to secure the rights guaranteed by the 13th, 14th and 15th amendments. The 15th section gives jurisdiction over suits at law or in equity authorized by law to be brought by any person to redress the deprivation, under color of any law, statute, ordinance, regulation, custom or usage of any State, of any right, privilege or immunity, secured by the Constitution of the United States, or of any right secured

25. Act March 2, 1833, 4 Fed. Stat. Ann. 1034; U. S. Comp. Stat. Sec. 991, Par. 11.

by any of its laws providing for equal rights of its citizens, or of all persons within its jurisdiction. It was in a suit brought under this provision by some colored citizens of Maryland, residing in Annapolis, against registrars of voters, for refusing them registration because they could not comply with certain requirements of the State law, that the Supreme Court held the so-called Grandfather clauses of some Southern constitutions and statutes invalid, as contrary to the Fifteenth Amendment.[26]

223. Jurisdiction for Enforcing Rights Under the Laws Regulating Commerce, the Immigration of Aliens and Protecting Trade and Commerce Against Restraints and Monopolies.

Paragraph 8 confers upon the District Court jurisdiction over all suits and proceedings arising under any law regulating commerce. Under this head are included suits brought for deaths or personal injuries under the Employer's Liability Act of April 22, 1908.

Section 22 confers like jurisdiction of suits or proceedings arising under any law regulating the immigration of aliens or under the contract labor laws, and section 23 of all suits and proceedings arising under any law to protect trade and commerce against restraints and monopolies.

224. Jurisdiction of Certain Proceedings Under the National Banking Acts.

Paragraph 16 gives jurisdiction of proceedings by the United States or of its officers against national banking associations and for winding up the affairs of such banks, and of suits brought by a national bank to enjoin the Comptroller of the Currency or any receiver acting under

26. Myers vs. Anderson, 238 U. S. 369; 59 L. Ed. 1349; 35 Sup. Ct. 932.

his direction. Suits by receivers[27] of a national bank appointed by the Comptroller of the Currency, or by agents[28] of such bank selected by stockholders to liquidate the bank, can be brought in the Federal Court without respect to diversity of citizenship, or to the amount in controversy, both because they are suits by officers of the United States and because they are for the winding up of the affairs of such banks, and on the latter ground, Federal Courts have jurisdiction of suits brought against such receivers or agents.[29]

27. McCartney vs. Earle, 115 Fed. 462; 53 C. C. A. 392.

28. McConville vs. Gilmour, 36 Fed. 277.

29. International Trust Co. vs. Weeks; 203 U. S. 364; 51 L. Ed. 224, 27 Sup. Ct. 69.

CHAPTER IX.

DIVERSITY OF CITIZENSHIP.

225. Suits Which May Be Brought in the Federal Courts Because of the State or National Character of the Parties to Them.

We have seen that a suit of a civil nature at law or in equity in which upwards of $3,000 is in controversy may be brought in a District Court of the United States no matter what may be the nationality or citizenship of any of the parties, provided it arises under the Constitution, the laws or the treaties of the United States. We have now to consider those suits which may be there instituted because there are certain kinds of diversity of citizenship or nationality between the opposing parties. When such diversity of citizenship exists, the Courts of the United States will have jurisdiction, although the dispute does not involve any Federal question. Jurisdiction so arising is commonly spoken of as that dependent upon diversity of citizenship; but not every kind of such diversity suffices to make the controversy one of Federal cognizance.

14

226. What Kinds of Diverse Citizenship Are Constitutionally Sufficient to Give Jurisdiction to the Federal Courts.

The Constitution declares that the judicial power of the United States shall extend, among other matters, to (a) "controversies between a State and citizens of another State;" (b) "between citizens of different States" * * * and (c) "between a State and the citizens thereof and foreign States, citizens or subjects."[1] It is only when some one of the kinds of diversity of citizenship or nationality so enumerated exists that a controversy may on that ground be brought into the Courts of the United States.

227. District Courts Have No Jurisdiction of Suits Between a State and Citizens of Another State or Aliens.

Subject to the limitations imposed by the Eleventh Amendment, which "recalled" the decision of the Supreme Court in Chisholm vs. Georgia,[2] the Supreme Court has original jurisdiction of all suits of a civil nature to which a State is a party. This jurisdiction is exclusive, except as to controversies between a State and its citizens, or between a State and citizens of other States or aliens, in which cases the Supreme Court has original jurisdiction concurrent with the Courts of the States, but not with the District Courts.

It is to be remembered what is now being discussed is jurisdiction on the ground of the status of the parties, and not jurisdiction which depends upon a case arising under the constitution, treaties or laws of the United States. The Federal Courts may have jurisdiction of a suit instituted by a State against its own citizens, or

1. Constitution, Art. 3, Sec. 2.
2. 2 Dallas, 419; 1 L. Ed. 440.

citizens of another State or aliens, when the controversy arises under the constitution, treaties or laws of the United States.[3]

228. District Courts May Have Jurisdiction of Suits Between Citizens of Different States.

Suits between citizens of different States are expressly within the grant of judicial power to the United States and by the Judicial Code original, but not exclusive, jurisdiction of such suits when upwards of $3,000 is in controversy is conferred upon the District Courts.[4]

229. What Does the Constitution Mean by a "State"?

In the second section of the third article of the Constitution declaring the extent of the judicial power of the United States, the word "State" is used either in the singular or in the plural eight times. In one of these it is preceded by the limiting adjective "foreign;" in the other seven it is unqualified. It was early settled that when the Constitution speaks of a State it means a State of the American Union unless the context clearly shows that another meaning is intended.[5] Citizenship which is neither of a State of the Union or of some foreign country cannot give jurisdiction to the Courts of the United States. A citizen of the District of Columbia or of one of the territories is, accordingly, not a citizen of a State. Suits to which he is a party may not be brought in the Federal Courts if the jurisdiction of those Courts is invoked solely on the ground of diverse citizenship.[6]

Once in a while, a Federal Court has apparently as-

3 Ames vs. Kansas, 111 U. S. 449; 28 L. Ed. 482; 4 Sup. Ct. 437.

4. Judicial Code, Sec. 24, Par. 1, cl. b., 4 Fed. Stat. Ann. 842; U. S. Comp. Stat. Sec. 991.

5. Hepburn vs. Elzey, 2 Cranch, 445; 2 L. Ed. 332.

6. Hepburn vs. Elzey, supra; Corporation of New Orleans vs. Winter, 1 Wheat., 92; 4 L. Ed. 44.

sumed jurisdiction of such a case.[7] When this has been done, it is believed it has always been an oversight. The question was not suggested by the parties, and the Court becoming interested in the other issues which were discussed, overlooked the jurisdictional point.

230. What Makes One a Citizen of a State?

To be a citizen of a particular State one must be a citizen of the United States by birth or naturalization, and he must at one time have been an actual resident of the State in question with intent at the time of such residence to make it either his permanent home or his home for an indefinite period.

The only possible exception to the last statement may be in the case of a child, born abroad, to citizens of the United States and of a particular State, or born elsewhere in the United States while its parents were on a journey, or as government officers, were temporarily stationed somewhere else. In each of these cases, it is probable that such child would be a citizen of the State although he had never been in it.

231. Citizenship Not Synonymous With Residence.

Residence in a State does not necessarily make one a citizen of it. It follows that the statement that one is a resident of a particular State, is not equivalent, in its legal effect to the allegation that he is a citizen of that State.

A plaintiff was described as a resident of Ohio in the County of Richland. The Supreme Court held that this was not a sufficient allegation that he was a citizen of Ohio.[8]

7. Addison vs. Alexander Milburn Co., 275 Fed. 148.

8. Neel vs. Pennsylvania Company, 157 U. S. 153; 39 L. Ed. 654; 15 Sup. Ct. 566.

232. Citizenship Not Dependent Upon Length of Residence.

It does not require any particular time to make one who is already a citizen of the United States, a citizen of a State into which he moves. Doubtless he may become a citizen of such State as soon as he has taken up residence therein with intent to make it his permanent home or his home for an indefinite period. This, of course, does not mean that he will be entitled to vote in that State before he has lived in it the length of time prescribed by its Constitution or laws as a qualification for suffrage. One may be a citizen without having the right to vote; for example, women were citizens before they had the franchise.

233. Citizenship Dependent Upon Intent to Acquire Domicile.

While one may become a citizen of a State so soon as he moves into it, he does not become a citizen no matter how long he remains in it, unless when he comes into it, or at some subsequent period he in good faith forms an intention to take up his domicile therein.

Thus, one Gilmer, then a citizen of Alabama, had a suit in the State Courts of that State against the members of the firm of Josiah Morris & Co. They also were citizens of Alabama. He lost his case. The decision below was affirmed by the Supreme Court of the State on the 27th of January, 1886. Shortly thereafter he went to Tennessee. In the following September, he brought suit in the Circuit Court of the United States for the Middle District of Alabama against the same defendants; alleging that he was a citizen of Tennessee. In May or June, 1887, he came back to Montgomery, Alabama, with the intent to reside there permanently. There were other facts shown which satisfied the Supreme Court that he had gone to Tennessee for no other purpose than that of bringing the suit, intending to return to Alabama so soon as he could without imperilling his standing as a plaintiff in the United States Court. The Court held that upon the evidence it could "not resist the conviction that the plaintiff had no purpose to acquire a domicile or settled home in Tennessee, and that his sole object in removing to that State was to place himself in a situation to invoke the jurisdiction of the Circuit Court of the United States. He went to Tennessee without any present intention to remain there permanently or for an indefinite time, but with a present intention to return to Alabama as soon as he could do so without defeating the jurisdiction of the Federal Court to determine his new suit. He was, therefore, a mere sojourner in the former State when his suit was brought." His case was within the rule that "if the removal be for the purpose of committing a fraud upon the law and to enable the party to avail himself of the jurisdiction of the Federal Courts and that fact be made out by his acts, the Court must pronounce that his removal was not with the bona fide intention of changing his domicile, however frequent and public his declarations to the contrary may have been.'"[9]

234. Motive for Change of Domicile Immaterial.

There is a distinction here which must not be lost sight of. If the change of residence and domicile is actually made, the motive or combination of motives inducing the party to make it is not material. It may be that he has moved from one State to another for the purpose of qualifying himself to bring his case in the Federal Court. If the removal was with the *bona fide* intention of taking up his permanent domicile in the new State he, so soon as

9. Morris vs. Gilmer, 129 U. S. 315; 32 L. Ed. 690; 9 Sup. Ct. 289.

he arrives there, becomes a citizen of it; and his right to sue is a "legitimate, constitutional and legal consequence not to be impeached by the motive of his removal."[10]

235. A State is Not a Citizen.

It would seem from the nature of the case, as well as from the language of the Constitution and of the Judiciary Act, to be sufficiently plain that a State is not a citizen within the meaning here intended. The Supreme Court had, however, to decide the point.

The State of Alabama brought suit against the Postal Cable and Telegraph Co. for taxes alleged to be due by it. There was the necessary jurisdictional amount involved. The defendant removed the case to the Circuit Court of the United States for the Middle District of Alabama, where the State won its suit, recovering judgment for nearly $4,000. The defendant appealed to the Supreme Court of the United States. The latter held that, as the State was not a citizen, the case was improperly removed into the Federal Court. It reversed the judgment, and remanded the cause to the Circuit Court with instructions to send it back to the State Court. It imposed the costs, both in the Circuit and the Supreme Courts, on the Telegraph Company because it had improperly removed the suit.[11]

This case illustrates the vigor with which the Supreme Court represses any attempt to extend the jurisdiction of the Courts of the United States beyond the limits fixed by the statutes. Apparently both parties were willing that the case should be finally disposed of in the Federal Courts. The Supreme Court none the less held that they had no jurisdiction.

10. Briggs vs. French, 4 Fed. Cases, 117.

11. Postal Telegraph Cable Co. vs. Alabama, 155 U. S. 482; 39 L. Ed. 231; 15 Sup. Ct. 192.

236. Diverse Citizenship Does Not Exist Unless Every Plaintiff is of Different Citizenship From Any Defendant.

One of the most interesting, as well as practically important, questions in the law of jurisdiction as dependent upon diverse citizenship, is as to the status of corporations. It is impossible to understand the history of the law in this connection, without bearing in mind that the Supreme Court early held that diverse citizenship does not exist unless every plaintiff is a citizen of a different State from that of any defendant, or, as the same rule is otherwise expressed, jurisdiction on the ground of diverse citizenship cannot be sustained unless every plaintiff is entitled to sue every defendant.[12] It is sufficient here to state the rule. It will be more fully discussed later.

237. Citizenship of Corporations.

Corporations are continually suing and being sued in the United States Courts. In many cases, the only ground of jurisdiction is the diversity of citizenship, yet, from many important standpoints, corporations are not citizens. How is it, that if they are not, the Federal Courts, on the ground of diverse citizenship, take jurisdiction of suits by or against them? The explanation requires the telling of a somewhat long story.

238. Federal Jurisdiction Because of Diversity of Citizenship in Suits to Which Corporations Are Parties Based on Legal Fiction.

It has been said that with one exception Federal Courts have never extended their jurisdiction by resort to a legal fiction, although in other countries, and at other

12. Strawbridge vs. Curtiss, 3 Cranch, 267; 2 L. Ed. 435.

times, such fictions were habitually used to such an end. We come now to that exception.

239. The Genesis of this Modern Fiction.

For some fifteen years or thereabouts after the adoption of the Constitution, it appears to have been assumed that the corporations of a particular State were citizens of it within the meaning of the Third Article of the Constitution. As such they sued or were sued in the Federal Courts. The cases were heard and decided without any question of jurisdiction being raised. In 1805, however, the State of Georgia attempted to tax the Savannah branch of the bank of the United States. The bank said that it was not liable to State taxation, and refused to pay the taxes levied upon it. The Georgia officials thereupon seized $2,000 of its money, and it sued for trespass. In its declaration, it said it was a citizen of Pennsylvania and the defendants were citizens of Georgia. The defendants pleaded in abatement that the president, directors and company of the Bank of the United States averred themselves to be a body politic and corporate and that in that capacity they could not sue or be sued, plead or be impleaded, in that Court by anything contained in the Constitution and laws of the United States. To this plea the plaintiff demurred. The Circuit Court held the plea good. The bank took a writ of error to the Supreme Court. In an elaborate opinion CHIEF JUSTICE MARSHALL said: ''That invisible, intangible and artificial being, that mere legal entity, a corporation aggregate, is certainly not a citizen; and consequently cannot sue or be sued in the Courts of the United States, unless the rights of the members in this respect can be exercised in their corporate name.'' The Court held, however, that for such purposes the Courts will disregard the separate existence of the corporation and will look to see who actually compose it, and that if its members be all citizens of one State, it acting for them, may maintain an action in the Courts of the United States against citizens of another State. The Court said that when the plaintiff described itself as a citizen of Pennsylvania it was tantamount to an averment that those who composed it were citizens of Pennsylvania. The plea of the defendants in abatement was therefore held bad.[13]

240. Presumption of Identical Citizenship of Corporation and Stockholders Held Rebuttable.

In 1839 certain citizens of Louisiana sued the president, directors and company of the Commercial and Railroad Bank of Vicksburg, citizens of Mississippi, incorporated by its legislature. The defendant pleaded, in abatement, that it was a corporation aggregate, and that the incorporators and stockholders of the company were citizens of other and different States, to wit, that Wm. F. Lambeth and Wm. E. Thompson were citizens of the State of Louisiana. Plaintiffs demurred to the plea. The Court below sustained the demurrer. On appeal the Supreme Court reaffirmed the rule that where there are two or more joint plaintiffs and two or more joint defendants, each of the plaintiffs must be capable of suing each of the defendants in the Courts of the United States, if those Courts are to have jurisdiction on the ground of diverse citizenship. Upon the same principle, it was held that all the incorporators must be citizens of a different State from that of the party sued if the corporation aggregate be the plaintiff, or from that of the party suing where it is the defendant. The plea was held good, and the judgment of the Court below reversed.[14]

13. Bank of the United States vs. Deveaux, 5 Cranch, 61; 3 L. Ed. 38.

14. Commercial & Railroad Bank of Vicksburg vs. Slocomb, 14 Peters, 60; 10 L. Ed. 354.

241. Corporations May Be Treated as Citizens.

At the January Term, 1844, the question again came before the Supreme Court. This time suit was brought by a citizen of New York against the Louisville, Cincinnati & Charleston Railway Co., a corporation of the State of South Carolina. The defendant pleaded that the Court ought not to have or take further cognizance of the action because some of the members of the corporation were not citizens of South Carolina, but were citizens of North Carolina; that the Bank of Charleston, a body corporate, was one of the members of the defendant corporation, and that some of the stockholders of the bank were citizens of New York—that is citizens of the same State as the plaintiff. To this plea the defendants demurred. The demurrer was sustained. There was a verdict and judgment for the plaintiff, and the defendant appealed to the Supreme Court. By a unanimous decision it held that its former rulings were wrong. The opinion was delivered by MR. JUSTICE WAYNE. He reviewed the earlier cases and said that the case of Strawbridge vs. Curtiss, which, as has been stated, decided that where there are two or more joint plaintiffs and two or more joint defendants each of the plaintiffs must be capable of suing each of the defendants, in the Courts of the United States in order to support the jurisdiction, and the case of the Bank vs. Deveaux, already cited,

> "have never been satisfactory to the Bar, and that they were not, especially the last, entirely satisfactory to the Court that made them. They have been followed always most reluctantly and with dissatisfaction. By no one was the correctness of them more questioned than by the late Chief Justice, who gave them. It is within the knowledge of several of us that he repeatedly expressed regret that those decisions had been made, adding, whenever the subject was mentioned, that if the point of jurisdiction was an original one the conclusion would be different.

We think we may safely assert that a majority of
the members of this Court have at all times partaken
of the same regret, and that whenever a case has
occurred on the circuit involving the application of
the case of the Bank vs. Deveaux it was yielded to
because the decision had been made and not because
it was thought to be right." * * * "The case of the
Bank of Vicksburg vs. Slocomb was most reluctantly
given upon mere authority. We are now called upon,
upon the authority of those cases alone, to go further
in this case than has yet been done. It has led to a
review of the principles of all the cases. We cannot
follow further, and upon our maturest deliberation
we do not think the cases relied upon for a doctrine
contrary to that which the Court will here announce
are sustained by a sound and comprehensive course
of professional reasoning."[15]

The Court then expressly decided that

"a corporation created by and doing business in a
particular State is to be deemed as a person, although
an artificial person, an inhabitant of the same State
for the purposes of its incorporation, and capable of
being treated as a citizen of that State as much as a
natural person."

242. Presumption of Identical Citizenship of Corporations and Members Held Irrebuttable.

Nine years later the subject was again fully considered
by the Supreme Court. One Marshall, a citizen of Virginia, brought suit against the **B. & O. R. R. Co.** in the
Circuit Court of the United States for the District of
Maryland. He claimed that the company owed him
$50,000 under a special contract for services in procur-
ing the passage, by the Virginia Legislature, of an Act
granting it a right of way. In his declaration he said the
defendant was a body corporate by the Act of the General Assembly of Maryland. His description of it was of

15. Louisville R. R. Co. vs. Letson, 2 How., 550; 11 L. Ed. 353.

precisely the same character as that which had been held insufficient by the Supreme Court some forty-four years before.[16] The Court, however, three of the judges dissenting, said:—

"It is contended that, notwithstanding the Court in deciding the question of jurisdiction, will look behind the corporate or collective name given to the party to find the persons who act as the representatives, curators or trustees of the association, stockholders or *cestui que* trusts, and in such capacity are the real parties to the controversy, yet the declaration contains no sufficient averment of their citizenship." * * * "If the declaration sets forth facts from which the citizenship of the parties may be presumed or legally inferred, it is sufficient. The presumption arising from the habitat of a corporation in the place of its creation being conclusive as to the residence or citizenship of those who use the corporate name and exercise the faculties conferred by it, the allegation that the 'defendants are a body corporate by the Act of the General Assembly of Maryland' is a sufficient averment that the real defendants are citizens of that State.'"[17]

243. The Modern Doctrine.

The Supreme Court has not thought it best to carry the case of the Louisville R. R. Co. vs. Letson, above cited, to its logical conclusion and to hold that a corporation is a citizen. Such a ruling might embarrass both the States and the Federal Government in dealing with corporate problems. On the other hand, it is highly desirable that the Federal jurisdiction shall extend to cases in which corporations are parties. The Court has solved the difficulty by resorting to the fiction already alluded to. The present doctrine of the Court was stated by it more than forty years ago. It is to the effect that a suit may be

16. Hope Insurance Co. vs. Boardman, 5 Cranch, 57; 38 L. Ed. 36.
17. Marshall vs. B. & O. R. R. Co., 16 How., 328; 14 L. Ed. 953.

brought in the Federal Courts by or against a corporation. In such case it is regarded as a suit by or against
the stockholders. For the purposes of jurisdiction, it
is conclusively presumed that all of them are citizens of
the State which by its laws created the corporation.[18]

This is precisely the same sort of irrebuttable presumption which the Court of King's Bench made that its
suitors were in the custody of the warden of the Marshal-
sea, or the Court of Exchequer that they were debtors to
the King. The legal presumption is sometimes very far
away from the actual facts.

244. Jurisdiction Cannot Be Created by Organizing a Sham Corporation.

The Supreme Court has, however, intimated that there
is such a thing as riding even a good fiction to death.

A couple of ingenious Georgia attorneys thought they
could increase their practice if they were in a position to
take any ejectment case into the United States Court.
They entered into communication with another ingenious
and energetic person. He was a South Dakota lawyer.
In three years he had secured for non-residents 985
charters under the laws of his State. Part of his business was to furnish South Dakota incorporators when
necessary. Under the name of the Southern Realty Investment Co., a South Dakota corporation was formed
which had a president and a board of directors, all of
whom were citizens of Georgia. Two of the five directors
were the Georgia attorneys; one was their female
stenographer. The president and a majority of the directors were the holders each of only one share of stock; and
that donated. They recognized it to be their duty to
represent the Georgia attorneys and to obey their will
implicitly. The company, in respect of all its business,

18. Muller vs. Dows, 94 U. S. 445; 24 L. Ed. 207.

was the agent of those attorneys to do their bidding. Its president testified that he did not know for what purpose the company was really organized, or that it had ever done any business except to bring certain ejectment suits in the United States Court, or that it had any money. Its place of business in Georgia was in the office of the Georgia attorneys. Its pretended place of business in South Dakota was in what is called a domiciliary office, maintained by the attorney who procured its charter in that State. In the latter office the Supreme Court remarked there could have been found, no doubt, a desk and a chair or two, but no business. The company's president never knew of its doing any business in South Dakota. The Supreme Court held, that it must be deemed a mere sham; that the actual parties to the suit were the citizens of Georgia for whose real benefit the litigation was being carried on, and that the United States Court had no jurisdiction.[19]

245. The Fiction Does Not Extend to Joint Stock Companies or Limited Partnerships.

The Supreme Court has, moreover, shown that it is not willing to extend the legal fiction to organizations which are not corporations in every sense of the word. It has expressly decided that joint stock companies and limited partnerships are not entitled to the benefit of the presumption.

The United States Express Company brought a suit in the United States Circuit Court for the Northern District of Illinois. It described itself as a joint stock company organized under the laws of the State of New York and a citizen of that State. The defendant was described

19. Southern Realty Investment Co. vs. Walker, 211 U. S. 603; 53 L. Ed. 346; 29 Sup. Ct. 211.

as a citizen of Illinois. The question of jurisdiction was not raised below. Neither of the parties suggested it in the Supreme Court, but the latter of its own motion held that there was no jurisdiction. It said the

> "allegation that the company was organized under the laws of New York is not an allegation that it is a corporation. In fact, the allegation is that the company is not a corporation, but a joint stock company —that is, a mere partnership." * * * "Although it may be authorized by the laws of the State of New York to bring suit in the name of its president, that fact cannot give the company power by that name to sue in a Federal Court. The company may have been organized under the laws of the State of New York and may be doing business in that State, yet all the members of it might not be citizens of that State. The record does not show the citizenship" * * * "of any of the members of the company. They are not shown to be citizens of some State other than Illinois."[20]

246. Suits Against Unincorporated Labor Unions.

In at least one case it has been held that in a suit against an unincorporated labor union, the citizenship of the members must be alleged,[21] but the reasoning of the Supreme Court in the recent Coronado case[22] would apparently point to an opposite conclusion, although as diversity of citizenship was not the ground of jurisdiction there relied on, this precise question was not discussed and may not have been considered.

---

20. Chapman vs. Barney, 129 U. S. 677; 32 L. Ed. 800; 9 Sup. Ct. 426; Great Southern Fire Proof Hotel Co. vs. Jones, 177 U. S. 450; 44 L. Ed. 842; 20 Sup. Ct. 690.

21. Wise vs. Brotherhood of Locomotive F. & En., 252 Fed. 961; 164 C. C. A. 469.

22. United Mine Workers of America vs. Coronado Coal Co., decided June 5, 1922.

247. New Equity Rule 37.

New Equity Rule 37 provides among other things, that every action shall be prosecuted in the name of the real party in interest, but that an executor, administrator, guardian, trustee of an express trust, a party with whom or in whose name a contract has been made for the benefit of another, or a party expressly authorized by statute, may sue in his own name without joining with him the party for whose benefit the action is brought.

Possibly under this rule it will be held that on the equity side a suit may hereafter be maintained by someone authorized by a State statute to sue on behalf of a joint stock company or a limited partnership, provided the citizenship of such plaintiff be different from that of any of the defendants. The rule may be construed to make the citizenship of the persons for whom he sues immaterial.

248. Municipal Corporations Treated as Citizens of Their State.

Municipal corporations chartered by a State are, for the purposes of the jurisdiction of the United States Courts, held to be composed solely of its citizens; where the amount in controversy is sufficient, they may be sued in the United States Courts by a citizen of another State.[23]

249. Controversies Between Citizens of States and Foreign States, Citizens or Subjects.

In addition to conferring jurisdiction upon the District Courts of civil suits at law or in equity between citizens of different States and in which the matter in controversy exceeds $3,000, the first paragraph of section 24 of the Judicial Code gives jurisdiction to those Courts

23. Cowles vs. Mercer County, 7 Wall., 118; 19 L. Ed. 86.

15

over such suits when they are between citizens of a State
and foreign States, citizens or subjects.

250. Place of Actual Residence of Alien Immaterial.

If one of the parties to the controversy is a citizen or
subject of a foreign power, the place of his actual residence is immaterial.

Many years ago two citizens of the Republic of Switzer-
land, residing and trading in the City of New Orleans,
brought suit against certain citizens of Louisiana in the
District Court of the United States for that district. It
was objected that the United States Court had no jurisdiction because the plaintiffs, though aliens, were residents of Louisiana. CHIEF JUSTICE MARSHALL said:—

> "The residence of aliens within the State consti-
> tutes no objection to the jurisdiction of the Federal
> Courts."[24]

251. No Length of Residence Will in Itself Turn an Alien Into a Citizen.

A foreign citizen or subject remains an alien until he
has been completely naturalized by the granting of his
final papers.

A native born subject of the Grand Duchy of Mecklenburg immigrated to the United States many years before
the case arose. Shortly after his arrival he declared his
intention to become a citizen of the United States—that
is to say, in common phrase, he took out his first papers.
For fifteen years thereafter he resided in Minnesota, and,
as its Constitution authorized, had frequently voted at
its elections. Under that Constitution he was eligible to
State office. He sued a citizen of Minnesota. It was
objected that the United States Court was without jurisdiction. MR. JUSTICE MILLER, then on Circuit, said:—

24. Breedlove vs. Nicolet, 7 Peters, 428; 8 L. Ed. 731.

"The plaintiff is undoubtedly a subject of the Grand Duke of Mecklenburg, having been born such, unless something has been done since his coming to this country to change that relation. It will hardly be contended that length of residence, even with the intention never to return, can have that effect, nor can the incomplete movement toward naturalization under the laws of the United States. The moving counsel then must rely on the Constitution of the State of Minnesota and the action of plaintiff under it to change his citizenship. I am of opinion that no State can make the subject of a foreign prince a citizen of the State in any other mode than that provided by the naturalization laws of Congress." * * * "But I do not place the decision of the present case on that ground. The State of Minnesota has not attempted to make the plaintiff a citizen of that State, nor do the provisions of her Constitution when applied to the condition of the plaintiff have that effect. The error has arisen from the same confusion of ideas which induced the advocates of female suffrage to assert in the Supreme Court the right of women to vote. That assertion is based upon the proposition that citizenship and the right to vote are inseparable. Therefore, females who are citizens must be allowed to vote. This was unanimously overruled by this Court. The present case is based upon the same idea."[25]

252. All Stockholders of a Foreign Corporation Conclusively Presumed Aliens.

The same legal fiction is applied to foreign as to domestic corporations.

All the stockholders of a corporation chartered by a foreign country are conclusively presumed to be citizens or subjects thereof.

The United States Court has jurisdiction of suits brought by citizens of any State against a corporation

25. Lanz vs. Randall, 4 Dillon, 425; 14 Fed. Cases, 1131.

chartered by a foreign country and of suits by such corporation against a citizen of any of the States, provided the proper jurisdictional amount be involved. Such suits are controversies between citizens of a State and foreign States, citizens or subjects.[26]

253. Foreign State or Sovereign May Sue in Federal Courts.

Both the Constitution and the Judicial Code authorize a foreign State to sue in the Courts of the United States.

In the harbor of San Francisco in December, 1867, the American ship Sapphire collided with a French transport. Two days later, in the District Court of the United States, a libel against the Sapphire was filed in the name of Napoleon III, Emperor of the French, as the owner of the transport. A decree was entered in favor of the Emperor for $15,000. An appeal was taken to the Supreme Court. While the case was there pending Napoleon was deposed. A Republic was established and recognized by the United States. The Supreme Court said:—

> "A foreign sovereign as well as any other foreign person who has a demand of a civil nature against any person here may prosecute it in our Courts." * * * "The reigning sovereign represents the national sovereignty, and that sovereignty is continuous and perpetual, residing in the proper successors of the sovereign for the time being. Napoleon was the owner of the transport, "not as an individual, but as sovereign of France." * * * "On his deposition the sovereignty does not change, but merely the person or persons in whom it resides. The foreign State is the true and real owner of its public vessels of war."[27]

26. Steamship Co. vs. Tugman, 106 U. S. 118; 27 L. Ed. 87; 1 Sup. Ct. 58.
27. The Sapphire, 11 Wall., 164; 20 L. Ed. 127.

The case cited was a libel in admiralty. The jurisdiction did not, of course, depend upon the first paragraph of section 24 of the Judicial Code, which we have been particularly considering, but the principles there laid down are applicable to cases brought thereunder. It was under it the Republic of Colombia filed a bill of complaint in the Circuit Court for the District of West Virginia against the Cauca Company to set aside an award under a submission made by that Republic and the defendant company.[28]

254. Record Must Show Alienage.

In cases brought under this clause of the statute the record must clearly show that the alien is a citizen or subject of a foreign power; precisely as in cases in which the ground of jurisdiction is the diverse State citizenship of the parties, the citizenship of every party must be clearly stated.

255. Every Plaintiff Must Be of Diverse Citizenship From Any Defendant.

As already stated, in order that there shall be jurisdiction in the Federal Courts on the ground of diversity of citizenship, each plaintiff must be capable of suing each of the defendants in the Courts of the United States. More than a century ago the Supreme Court so ruled.[29]

Nearly forty years afterwards JUSTICE WAYNE, speaking for the Court, said that CHIEF JUSTICE MARSHALL regretted having ever made the decision. It remains, however, the unquestioned law. It is one of the cardinal principles governing the jurisdiction of the Federal Courts and must be kept steadily in mind by every prac-

28. Colombia vs. Cauca Co., 190 U. S. 524; 47 L. Ed. 1159; 23 Sup. Ct. 704.

29. Strawbridge vs. Curtiss, 3 Cranch, 267; 2 L. Ed. 435.

titioner in them. It has been constantly applied, and, at times, with what must have seemed to disappointed litigants, remorseless logic.

A citizen of the State of Kentucky and a citizen of the Mississippi territory united, as plaintiffs, in a suit in the District Court of the United States for the District of Louisiana, against a Louisiana corporation. It was held that the Court had no jurisdiction because a citizen of a territory is not a citizen of a State. The Court said:—

> "it has been doubted whether the parties might elect to sue jointly or severally. However this may be, having elected to sue jointly, the Court is incapable of distinguishing their case so far as respects jurisdiction from one in which they were compelled to unite."[30]

Wherever any party to a case is incapable of suing in the Federal Court any party on the opposite side, the Court is without jurisdiction. If the suit is brought by a person or persons who, or each of whom, is capable of suing all the defendants, and it appears that there is an indispensable party who has been omitted, then the case fails because of his omission.[31] If his citizenship is such that if he were joined the Court would not have jurisdiction, and it is attempted to join him by amendment, the case will also fail, because it will then be manifest that the Court is without jurisdiction.

In the case last cited, the bill was filed originally in the Supreme Court of the United States by the State of California against the Southern Pacific Co., a corporation of Kentucky. The issues involved in the litigation, in the opinion of the Supreme Court, affected the rights of the City of Oakland and the Oakland Water Front Co. The

---

30. Corporation of New Orleans vs. Winter, 1 Wheat., 91; 4 L. Ed. 44.
31. California vs. Southern Pacific Co., 157 U. S. 229; 39 L. Ed. 683; 15 Sup. Ct. 591.

Court held that it ought not to proceed in their absence. If they were brought in, then the suit would be between the State of California on the one side and a citizen of another State and citizens of California on the other, and the Federal Courts would not have jurisdiction.

256. Parties Not Indispensable Need Not Be Joined.

If any person whose presence upon the record would destroy jurisdiction, is not an indispensable party, he need not be joined and jurisdiction may be maintained.

Under a statute of Alabama every joint promissory note had the same effect in law as if it were joint and several. Whenever a writ issued against two or more joint and several drawers of a promissory note, it was lawful, at any time after the return, to discontinue the action against any one or more of the defendants on whom the writ had not been executed and to proceed to judgment against the others.

A suit was brought in the United States Circuit Court for the District of Alabama on a joint promissory note against the two makers. One was summoned; the other was not found. The declaration was filed against the one who had been served with process and alleged him to be a citizen of Alabama, the plaintiff being described as a citizen of New York; nothing was said as to the citizenship of the other defendant. The Supreme Court held that, under the laws of Alabama, the plaintiff might proceed solely against the maker who was found, and his citizenship and that of the plaintiff were alone material.[32]

257. Section 50, Judicial Code.

Shortly before the case last cited was decided, Congress had legislated upon the subject. The act in question now constitutes section 50 of the Judicial Code. It

32. Smith vs. Clapp, 15 Peters, 125; 10 L. Ed. 684.

provides that when there are several defendants in any
suit at law or in equity and one or more of them are
neither inhabitants of, nor found within, the district in
which the suit is brought, and do not voluntary appear,
the Court may entertain jurisdiction and proceed to trial
and adjudication between the parties who are properly
before it. The non-joinder of parties who are neither
inhabitants of, nor found within, the district, does not
constitute matter of abatement or objection to the suit.
Of course, no judgment or decree will bind anyone who
is not a party.

The Thirty-ninth Equity Rule of the Supreme Court is
very similar. It provides that in all cases where it shall
appear to the Court that persons, who might otherwise
be deemed necessary and proper parties to the suit, cannot be made parties by reason of their being out of the
jurisdiction of the Court or incapable otherwise of being
made parties, or because their joinder would oust the
jurisdiction; the Court may, in its discretion, proceed
without them, and the decree shall be without prejudice
to their rights.

258. Difference Between Necessary and Indispensable Parties.

It follows that, in the Federal Courts, many persons
who under the old chancery practice would have been held
to be necessary, are not considered indispensable parties.
Whenever either at law or in equity the Federal Courts
can do justice as between the parties before them, they
will not refuse to proceed because other parties have not
been brought in, provided those other parties could not
have been joined without defeating jurisdiction.

A citizen of Illinois brought suit against co-partners
who were doing business in Wisconsin. He alleged they
were citizens of the latter. He caused their partnership

property to be attached. They all appeared. Two of them set up that they were citizens of Illinois. Under the State practice, he was entitled, at this stage of the proceedings, to discontinue against such of the defendants as were without the jurisdiction of the Court. He did discontinue as to the two citizens of Illinois. The Supreme Court thought he had the right so to do. The Federal Court had jurisdiction to hear and determine the controversy and to hold the property for the debt for which it was attached. Service on one partner when one partner is alone within the jurisdiction is sufficient to bind the partnership property. The judgment recovered in the case did not affect the property of the partners against whom the proceedings had been discontinued other than that of the partnership actually within the jurisdiction of the Court.[33]

259. Parties Without Whose Presence Justice Cannot Be Done Are Indispensable.

Nevertheless, a Federal Court will not decide a controversy when it can make no decision going to the real root of the matter, without necessarily affecting the rights of parties not before it. The Supreme Court has said:—

> "We do not put the case upon the ground of jurisdiction, but upon a much broader ground which must equally apply to all Courts of Equity, whatever may by their structure as to jurisdiction. We put it on the ground that no Court can adjudicate directly upon a person's right without the party being either actually or constructively before it."[34]

260. Whose Citizenship Controls Where Suit in Name of One Person, But for Benefit of Another?

In some cases suits are, by statute or custom, required to be brought for one person in the name of another. In

33. Imbush vs. Farwell, 1 Black, 566; 17 L. Ed. 188.
34. Mallow vs. Hinde, 12 Wheat., 198; 6 L. Ed. 599.

other cases, while the suit is brought by one person in his own name, it is another individual who will really gain or lose by the result of the litigation. In such cases it is necessary to know whose citizenship it is which determines whether the parties to the litigation are or are not citizens of different States.

261. Citizenship of Purely Nominal Parties Immaterial.

In Maryland, the bonds of trustees, administrators and executors, as well as of various officials, are given to the State of Maryland. They are for the protection and benefit of whomsoever may be interested in the proper discharge of the duties of the trustee, the administrator or the officer. The persons so interested may be citizens of Maryland, or they may be citizens of other States or of foreign countries. If the bond is breached and the injured parties are all citizens of States other than Maryland, or are aliens, has the Federal Court jurisdiction? The nominal plaintiff is the State of Maryland. It is not a citizen. If it were a citizen in any sense it would be a citizen of the same State with the defendants, assuming that the principal and the sureties on the bond were all Marylanders.

This question came before the Supreme Court a hundred years ago. In Virginia, executors then gave bonds to the justices of the peace of the county. A citizen of Virginia died, indebted to a British subject. Letters testamentary were granted to a citizen of Virginia, who, with another Virginian as his surety, gave bond to the justices of the peace for the county of Stafford. The executor wrongfully withheld the payment of the debt due the British subject. The latter began suit in the United States Court for the District of Virginia. His declaration was filed in the name of the justices of the peace of the county of Stafford to his use. The Supreme

Court said the suit was properly brought. The Federal Court had jurisdiction.[35]

The ground of the decision was that the justices of the peace were nominal parties only; that the real contest was between the British subject and the citizen of Virginia, and of such a controversy the Federal Court had jurisdiction. For this reason, when an infant sues by his next friend it is the citizenship of the infant and not of the next friend which determines whether there is a diversity of citizenship between the plaintiff and the defendant. The next friend is in some sort an officer of the Court. He is appointed merely to look after the interests of the infant. The judgment is binding on the latter, who cannot, when he attains full age, maintain a fresh proceeding founded on the same cause of action.

262. Citizenship of Representative Parties Controlling.

A plaintiff who brings a suit may be a good deal more than a nominal party, although other persons may have a more direct personal interest in the outcome of the litigation. Such is the case with executors, administrators and trustees.

A Georgia citizen died. His administrator and his residuary legatee were French subjects. They brought suit against a citizen of Georgia. It was held that the United States Court had jurisdiction. The plaintiffs were aliens. They sued as trustees, it is true, but they were something more than nominal parties. They had actual title in themselves, although the beneficial interest may have been in someone else.[36]

In another case a suit was brought in the Federal Court by the executor of the surviving partner of a firm. The declaration said that the executor was a citizen of Mary-

---

35. Browne vs. Strode, 5 Cranch, 303; 3 L. Ed. 108.
36. Chappedelaine vs. Dechenaux, 4 Cranch, 308; 2 L. Ed. 629.

land. The defendants were alleged to be citizens of Tennessee. Nothing was said as to the citizenship of the persons who originally composed the firm or of those who were entitled to share in the estate of the surviving partner. The Court held that no such allegations were necessary. The citizenship of the executor was all that was material on his side of the case.[37]

A citizen of New York and a citizen of Pennsylvania brought suit in the Federal Court against a Pennsylvania corporation. They described themselves as trustees who sued solely for the use of an alien, a subject of Great Britain and of a citizen of New Jersey. The Supreme Court held that the Federal Courts were without jurisdiction. Distinguishing the case from such as **Browne vs. Strode**, it said:—

"There is no analogy between these cases and the case at bar. The nominal plaintiffs in those cases were not trustees and held nothing for the use or benefit of the real parties in interest. They could not" * * * "prevent the institution or prosecution of the actions or exercise any control over them." * * * "In the case at bar the plaintiffs are the real prosecutors of the suit. They are parties to the mortgage contract negotiating its terms and stipulations, and to them the usual rights and powers of mortgagees are reserved and to them the usual obligations of mortgagors are made."[38]

263. Citizenship at Time Suit Brought Controls.

At the time a contract is entered into or a tort committed, one of the parties may be a citizen of a particular State. By the time the suit is brought, he may be a citizen of another. Before judgment is rendered, he may move again and become a citizen of a third, or after suit brought one of the parties may die and his executor or

---

37. Childress vs. Emory, 8 Wheat., 668; 5 L. Ed. 705.
38. Coal Co. vs. Blatchford, 11 Wall., 174; 20 L. Ed. 179.

administrator may be a citizen of a State other than his. At what time must the parties be citizens of different States in order to give the Federal Courts jurisdiction? The only time of importance is that at which the suit is brought. It matters not of what State the parties were citizens when the contract was made or the tort committed, or of what State they become citizens after the suit is instituted. If they are citizens of different States at the time of the institution of the action, the Federal Court has jurisdiction, and, once properly taken, no subsequent change of citizenship or of parties may oust it.

Citizens of Ohio brought suit in the United States Circuit Court for the District of Kentucky against citizens of Kentucky. Before decree, one of the complainants removed from Ohio and became a citizen of Kentucky. The Supreme Court held that change of residence did not divest the jurisdiction.[39]

264. Citizenship at Time of Bringing Original and Not Ancillary or Supplemental Suit Controls.

In the Circuit Court of the United States for the District of Rhode Island, a citizen of Connecticut filed a bill in equity against certain citizens of Rhode Island. During the pendency of the proceeding, he died, and a Rhode Island administrator for his estate was appointed. The latter filed a bill of revivor. The Circuit Court dismissed the bill for want of jurisdiction on the ground that both the parties to the new bill were citizens of Rhode Island. The Supreme Court said:—

"We are of opinion that the Court erred. The bill of revivor was in no just sense an original suit, but was a mere continuation of the original suit. The parties to the original bill were citizens of different

39. Morgan's Heirs vs. Morgan, 2 Wheat., 297; 4 L. Ed. 242.

States and the jurisdiction of the Court completely attached to the controversy. Having so attached, it could not be divested by any subsequent events."[40]

Citizens of Pennsylvania brought an action of eject-ment in the United States Circuit Court for the District of Missouri against the tenant in possession, a citizen of Missouri. Under a State statute the landlord of the de-fendant, who was a citizen of Pennsylvania, applied to be admitted as a co-defendant. The permission was granted. The defendants then moved to dismiss the case for want of jurisdiction because there were citizens of Pennsylvania on each side of the record. The Supreme Court said:—

"It was quite proper" * * * "for the Circuit Court to admit the landlord as a party for the purpose of defending his tenant's possession and through that, his own title; and to this end he might not only be permitted to appear as a party to the record and co-defendant, but to control the defense as *dominus litis,* raising and conducting such issues as his own rights and interests might dictate. And this need not arrest or interfere with the jurisdiction of the Court, already established by the plaintiffs against the tenant in possession. For such proceedings should be treated as incidental to the jurisdiction thus acquired and auxiliary to it."[41]

40. Clarke vs. Mathewson, 12 Peters, 171; 9 L. Ed. 1041.
41. Phelps vs. Oaks, 117 U. S. 240; 29 L. Ed. 888; 6 Sup. Ct. 714.

CHAPTER X.

VENUE OF ACTIONS IN THE FEDERAL COURTS WHEN THEIR
JURISDICTION IS CONCURRENT WITH THAT OF
STATE COURTS.

265. Consideration of the Provisions of Paragraph 1, Section 24, of Judicial Code Limiting Jurisdiction of Suits By Assignees Postponed.

The paragraph so long under discussion contains another provision of much practical importance. By it the jurisdiction of the District Courts over suits brought by assignees is greatly limited. The Court is forbidden to take jurisdiction of a suit upon a chose in action unless such suit could have been prosecuted in such Court, had no assignment been made.

We shall hereafter see that by a construction put upon this provision by some authorities, no assignee can sue in any particular District Court unless suit could have been there brought had no assignment been made.[1]

It will tend to clearness, therefore, if we first inquire in what District Court or Courts a plaintiff is required to bring his suit.

266. In What District or Districts a Plaintiff May Sue— Statutory Rules.

The United States is a very large country. It has many Federal judicial districts. If a plaintiff, in a case

1. Waterman vs. C. & O. R. R. Co., 199 Fed. 667.

in which the State Court has concurrent jurisdiction, might sue a defendant in any of them he chose, he would have an instrument of oppression ready to his hands. Congress has been careful to prevent any such abuse. When the original Judiciary Act was passed, and for many years afterwards, arrest of the person was a common method of beginning many civil suits. The 11th section of the original Judiciary Act provided that

"no person shall be arrested in one district for trial in another, in any civil action, * * * and no civil suit shall be brought * * * against an inhabitant of the United States, by any original process in any other district than that whereof he is an inhabitant, or in which he shall be found at the time of serving the writ."

By the Act of March 3, 1887, the possible venue of civil actions in the Federal Courts was still further limited. The provision then made is substantially reproduced in section 51 of the Judicial Code, which declares that, with certain exceptions, to be hereafter alluded to

"no person shall be arrested in one district for trial in another in any civil action before a District Court," and that (1) "no civil suit shall be brought in any District Court against any person by any original process or proceeding in any other district than that whereof he is an inhabitant," (2) "but where the jurisdiction is founded only on the fact that the action is between citizens of different States, suit shall be brought only in the district of the residence of either the plaintiff or the defendant."

267. Statutory Rules as to Venue Not Applicable to Suits Against Aliens.

In section 11 of the original Judiciary Act, the provisions protecting defendants from being sued except in particular districts were expressly limited to "inhabitants of the United States." In subsequent revisions and changes those words have been omitted, but the

16

Courts have held that such omission was not intended to change the meaning. To hold otherwise would be to decide that Congress had in effect directed that many aliens should not be suable at all in the Courts of the United States.

In the language of the Supreme Court,

"to construe the provision as applicable to all suits between a citizen and an alien would leave the Courts of the United States open to aliens against citizens, and close them to citizens against aliens. Such a construction is not required by the language of the provision, and would be inconsistent with the general intent of the section as a whole."[2]

268. Aliens and Alien Corporations Suable in Any Federal District in Which Service Can Be Had.

One Michael Kane, a resident of New Jersey, was a passenger on the Devonia, belonging to the Barrow Steamship Co., a British corporation. When in the port of Londonderry, Ireland, and while on the ship, he was assaulted and beaten by one of its officers. He brought suit against the Company in the Circuit Court of the United States for the Southern District of New York and had the summons served on its duly appointed agents in New York, where it had property. The Supreme Court held that the Circuit Court had jurisdiction; the action was for a personal tort committed abroad, such as would have been actionable if committed in the State of New York or elsewhere in this country, and an action for which might be maintained in any Circuit Court of the United States which acquired jurisdiction of the defendant. The action was within the general jurisdiction conferred by Congress upon the Circuit Courts of the United States.[3]

2. In re Hohorst, 150 U. S. 660; 37 L. Ed. 1211; 14 Sup. Ct. 221.

3. Barrow Steamship Co. vs. Kane, 170 U. S. 100; 42 L. Ed. 964; 18 Sup. Ct. 526.

269. Rule I.—If Jurisdiction Exists on Any Ground Other Than Diversity of State Citizenship, Suit Can Be Brought Only in the District of Defendant's Residence.

It will be perceived that where the ground of jurisdiction is anything other than that the action is between citizens of different States, there is only one district in which the suit can be brought, viz: the district of which the defendant is an inhabitant. Where the jurisdiction is founded only on the fact that the action is between citizens of different States, suit may be brought in the district in which either the plaintiff or the defendant resides. What will happen if the plaintiff, a citizen of one State, sues the defendant, a citizen of another, in the district of the residence of the plaintiff upon a cause of action arising under a Federal law?

Certain citizens of Georgia filed a bill in equity against the Atlantic Coast Line and a number of other railroad companies, all of which did business in Georgia, but were incorporated under the laws of other States. The suit was brought in the district of the residence of the plaintiffs. Diverse citizenship existed between them and defendants, but the object of the bill was to assert rights under the Interstate Commerce and Anti-Trust Acts. Jurisdiction, consequently, did not rest solely upon diverse citizenship, although, upon the facts in the case, that would have been sufficient to have sustained the jurisdiction of the Court. Nevertheless, had the parties been all citizens of the same State, the suit could still have been brought in a Federal Court. A Federal question was involved. The Supreme Court held that the Circuit Court for the Southern District of Georgia was without jurisdiction as against the objections of the defendants.[4]

4. Macon Grocery Co. vs. Atlantic Coast Line, 215 U. S. 501; 54 L. Ed. 300; 30 Sup. Ct. 184.

270. Rule II. Where Sole Ground of Jurisdiction is Diverse State Citizenship Suit May Be Brought in the District of the Residence of Either Plaintiff or Defendant.

Where the jurisdiction rests on diverse State citizenship only, the action may be brought in the district of the residence of either the plaintiff or the defendant; but a suit instituted in the residence of the plaintiff can effect nothing unless he is able there to secure the service of process on the defendant.

If a citizen of Maryland in the District Court of the United States for the District of Massachusetts sues a citizen of the latter State, he ordinarily will have no difficulty in securing service of process and in carrying the case through to an end. The plaintiff has the right, however, to bring his suit in the District Court of the United States for the District of Maryland, but the case will not make any progress unless the defendant either comes into the District of Maryland and is summoned therein, or voluntarily instructs counsel to enter an appearance for him.

271. Of What District Defendant is an Inhabitant.

Resident and inhabitant in this clause of the statute mean the same thing. A natural person is an inhabitant of the district in which he has his regular home or domicile. A corporation is a resident or inhabitant of the State by which it is incorporated; if that State is divided into more than one district, it is an inhabitant of the district in which its general business is carried on, and in which it has its headquarters and general offices. It cannot be said to be an inhabitant of the other Federal districts, although it may operate a line of railroad through them and maintain therein freight and ticket offices and stations.[5]

272. Defendant's Right to Object to Suit in Wrong District May Be Waived.

An objection to the right of the Court to entertain the action on the ground that the case itself is not one over which the Court has jurisdiction, is of a very different kind from the contention that the defendant is not properly suable in that particular district.

If a citizen of one State sues a citizen of the same State in the Federal Court, and there is no Federal question involved, the Court has not jurisdiction and never can get it. No possible consent of the parties, and no waiver by one or both of their rights can confer it. The same consequences would follow if the suit was between a citizen of a State and a citizen of the District of Columbia or of a territory.

On the other hand, an objection based solely on the ground that a defendant is not properly suable in the particular district in which suit has been brought against him, does not go to the constitutional, nor, in a sense, to the statutory, jurisdiction of the Court over the cause of action. The right not to be sued outside of the districts described in the statute is a privilege conferred upon the defendant. He may waive it. He does waive it by appearing generally to the action.

273. General Appearance by Defendant Waives It.

Thus, when the statute provided that suit must be brought in the district of which the defendant was an inhabitant, or in which he could be found, suit by process of foreign attachment was brought by a citizen of Penn-

5. Galveston Railway Co. vs. Gonzales, 151 U. S. 496; 38 L. Ed. 248; 14 Sup. Ct. 404.

sylvania, in the Circuit Court of the United States for the Eastern District of Pennsylvania, against a citizen of Massachusetts then residing abroad at Gibraltar. The defendant entered a general appearance and afterwards objected to the jurisdiction. The Supreme Court said:—

> "It appears that the party appeared and pleaded to issue. Now, if the case were one of a want of jurisdiction in the Court, it would not, according to well-established principles, be competent for the parties, by any act of theirs, to give it. But that is not the case. The Court had jurisdiction over the parties and the matter in dispute, the objection was, that the party defendant, not being an inhabitant of Pennsylvania, nor found therein, personal process could not reach him. This was a personal privilege or exemption, which it was competent for the party to waive."[6]

274. Objection Not Waived by Defendant Appearing Specially to Object.

Of course, the objection to jurisdiction is not waived by filing a demurrer for the special and single purpose of objecting to the jurisdiction nor by answering to the merits upon that demurrer being overruled.[7]

A plaintiff was a citizen of Texas and a resident of the Eastern District thereof. The defendant was a Kentucky corporation doing business in the Western District of Texas and having an agent in that district qualified under the State law to accept service of process. The suit was brought in the Circuit Court of the United States for the Western District of Texas. The Supreme Court held that a corporation is not a citizen or resident of a State in which it is not incorporated, and there being no

---

6. Toland vs. Sprague, 12 Peters, 330; 9 L. Ed. 1093.

7. Southern Pacific Co. vs. Denton, 146 U. S. 203; 36 L. Ed. 942; 13 Sup. Ct. 44.

waiver by general appearance or otherwise, the Court never acquired jurisdiction.

275. When Service May Be Obtained on a Corporation Sued in District of Plaintiff's Residence.

Where jurisdiction is exclusively based on diverse citizenship a corporation incorporated by one State may be sued in the district of another State in which the plaintiff resides, provided service of process can be secured upon it in the latter district; which is possible when the corporation carries on business therein.

The plaintiff was a citizen of New York. The defendant was a corporation of Virginia. Suit was brought in the Circuit Court of the United States for the Southern District of New York. Service was had upon two of the directors of the defendant corporation, residing in the City of New York. The corporation was not doing any business in that State. The Supreme Court held that the residence of an officer of a corporation does not necessarily give the corporation a domicile in the State. He must be there officially representing the corporation in its business. In other words, the corporation must be doing business there, either generally or specially.[8]

276. When is a Corporation Doing Business in a District so That it May be Sued Therein?

It is not always easy to say whether a corporation is doing business in a particular district to such an extent and in such a way that it is liable to be sued therein. For example—a Pennsylvania corporation made a contract in Maryland with a Maryland corporation to do work in Illinois. The Maryland corporation alleged that the Pennsylvania corporation broke its agreement. The vice-

8. Conley vs. Mathieson Alkali Works, 190 U. S. 406; 47 L. Ed. 1113; 23 Sup. Ct. 728.

president of the latter had acted for it in making the contract. It sent him to Baltimore to confer with the Maryland corporation as to the dispute. While in that city on that errand he was served with a summons upon his company in a suit which the Maryland corporation had brought upon the contract in the United States District Court for Maryland. It was clear that the Pennsylvania corporation was not doing business generally in Maryland. With much doubt and hesitation, it was held that it was not there doing business specially, of a character which rendered it liable to suit therein.[9]

In this case the authorities are reviewed.

Reference may also be had to a later decision of the Circuit Court of Appeals for the Ninth Circuit.[10]

Upon the facts the two cases may be distinguished. It is, however, doubtful whether the Circuit Court of Appeals for the Ninth Circuit would have deemed the differences material.

277. Each Plaintiff Must Be Entitled to Sue Any Defendant in District in Which Suit is Brought.

Where there are two defendants, each citizens of different States, and two plaintiffs, each citizens of different States, if all the parties are indispensable parties, it will be impossible to find any District Court of the United States which will have jurisdiction, because there is no district which is the place of residence of both the plaintiffs and there is no district which is the place of residence of both the defendants. The Supreme Court has decided that the suit can be brought only in a district in which either all the plaintiffs or all the defendants reside.[11]

9. Noel Construction Co. vs. George W. Smith & Co., 193 Fed. 492.

10. Premo Specialty Mfg. Co. vs. Jersey Creme Co., 200 Fed. 352; 118 C. C. A. 458.

11. Strawbridge vs. Curtiss, 3 Cranch, 267; 2 L. Ed. 435.

A citizen of Missouri and a citizen of Arkansas, as plaintiffs in the Circuit Court for the Eastern District of Missouri, brought suit against a defendant, who was a citizen of the State of Texas. The defendant objected that the Court had no jurisdiction because the district was not the district of the residence of one of the plaintiffs and was not the residence of the single defendant. The Supreme Court held that the objection was well taken; that Congress had shown in the Acts of 1887 and 1888 no intention to enlarge, but rather to diminish, the jurisdiction of the United States Courts, and that the language used by it in defining that jurisdiction must be understood in the light of the construction put upon similar phrases in Strawbridge vs. Curtiss, and adhered to for ninety years thereafter.[12]

It should be noted, however, that if both the defendants are citizens of the same State, but reside in different districts thereof, the suit may, as stated in Section 281 (*infra*) be brought in either district.[13]

278. Two Plaintiffs Residing in Different Districts May Sue Defendant in a Third District of Which He is a Resident.

On the other hand, where there are two plaintiffs, each residents of different States, and there is a single defendant, resident in a third, the two plaintiffs may sue him in the district of his residence.

A citizen of New York and a citizen of Pennsylvania as plaintiffs sued in the Northern District of West Virginia a defendant corporation organized under the laws of the State of West Virginia. The Supreme Court held, that the suit was properly brought. It follows, there-

---

12. Smith vs. Lyon, 133 U. S. 315; 33 L. Ed. 635; 10 Sup. Ct. 303; Camp vs. Gress, 250 U. S. 308; 63 L. Ed. 997; 39 Sup. Ct. 528.

13. J. C. Sec. 52; 5 Fed. Stat. Ann. 518; U. S. Comp. Stat. Sec. 1034.

fore, that if there is a single plaintiff and there are two indispensable defendants, each residing in a different State, he cannot sue either of them in the district of such defendant's residence. He can sue them in the district of his own residence provided he can there get service upon both of them. If there are any number of plaintiffs, all residents of different States from the defendant, they can bring suit in the district in which the defendant resides.[14]

279. Federal Courts Can Seldom Issue Non-resident Attachments.

Because of the statutory limitation on the venue of actions, the process of non-resident attachment in a case originally brought in the United States Court, is practially unknown.

The Supreme Court years ago held that an attachment cannot be sued out against a non-resident in any district in which he cannot be sued. When this decision was made the districts in which he could be sued were that of his residence and any other in which he might be found.

An Iowa corporation brought suit in the United States Circuit Court for the District of Iowa against a citizen of Massachusetts. It claimed he was indebted to it in a sum of about $100,000. He was not within the district of Iowa. The plaintiff attempted to attach his property in the manner in which such an attachment could have been sued out in the State Courts of Iowa. The Supreme Court said:—

> "No civil suit, not local in its nature, can be brought in the Circuit Court of the United States, against an inhabitant of the United States, by original process, in any other State than that of which

14. Sweeney vs. Carter Oil Co., 199 U. S. 252; 50 L. Ed. 178; 26 Sup. Ct. 55.

he is an inhabitant, or in which he is found at the time of serving the writ." "It is conceded," the Court continued, "that the person against whom this suit was brought in the Circuit Court was an inhabitant of the State of Massachusetts, and was not found in or served with process in Iowa. Clearly, then, he was not suable in the Circuit Court of the District of Iowa, and unless he could be sued no attachment could issue from that Court against his property."[15]

Since then the statute has been amended, as we have seen, so that when the ground of jurisdiction is diverse citizenship the suit can be brought in the district of the residence of either the plaintiff or of the defendant.

It has been contended that the District Court of the district of plaintiff's residence now has jurisdiction to attach defendant's property found therein, but the Supreme Court has said that

"the amendment to the statute was not intended to do away with the settled rule that, in order to issue an attachment, the defendant must be subject to personal service or voluntarily appear in the action. If Congress had intended any such radical change, it would have been easy to have made provision for that purpose, and doubtless a method of service by publication in such cases would have been provided. We think the rule has not been changed; that an attachment is still but an incident to a suit, and that, unless jurisdiction can be obtained over the defendant, his estate cannot be attached in a Federal Court."[16]

These rulings rest on the language of the Federal Statutes. They are of little real value to a defendant. His property can be validly attached in the Courts of the State in which as a non-resident, he may occasionally be

15. Ex parte Railway Co., 103 U. S. 794; 26 L. Ed. 461.

16. Big Vein Coal Co. of West Va. vs. Read, 229 U. S. 31; 57 L. Ed. 1053; 33 Sup. Ct. 694.

at a disadvantage. If he seeks to put himself upon a more equal footing by removing the case to a Federal Court, the lien secured by the attachment remains unaffected, and will, if the merits be decided against him, be there enforced.[17] The defendant by moving the case, has entered his voluntary submission to the jurisdiction of the Federal Court, and there is no reason that the attachment should not be binding upon his property.[18]

280. Attachments Can Be Issued by the District Court When Other Suit Could Be Prosecuted Therein.

A non-resident defendant may be temporarily in the district of the residence of the plaintiff. Such defendant may have attachable property in that district. I see no reason why he may not be there sued and his property there attached if under the State law a non-resident attachment could under such circumstnaces be sued out; nor does there appear to be any reason why an attachment, upon an original process for fraud, when authorized by the State law, could not be brought against a defendant in the United States Court of the district in which he lives and in which property to be attached can be found.

281. Special Provisions as to Venue in States in Which there is More than One District.

The Judicial Code,[19] provides that in States in which there are two or more districts, every suit, not of a local nature, must be brought in the District in which the defendant resides, unless there are two or more defendants

17. J. C. Sec. 36, 5 Fed. Stat. Ann. 387; U. S. Comp. Stat. Sec. 1018; Clark vs. Wells, 203 U. S. 164; 51 L. Ed. 138; 27 Sup. Ct. 43.

18. Hatcher vs. Hendrie & Bolthoff Mfg. & Sup. Co.. 133 Fed. 267; 68 C. C. A. 19.

19. Section 52 J. C., 5 Fed. Stat. Ann. 518; U. S. Comp. Stat. Sec. 1034.

living in different districts of the State, and in that case, it may be brought in any of the Districts. A duplicate writ of summons issues to the marshal of any other district in which a defendant resides.

282. Venue Where District Contains More than One Division.

Many districts are divided into two or more divisions. When this is the case, any action not of a local nature must be brought in the division in which the defendant resides unless there are two or more defendants living in different divisions. In that case, the suit may be brought in either division.[20] A plaintiff residing in one division of a district may sue in another a defendant who is a citizen of another State. There is no statute precluding a plaintiff from suing in a division in which he does not live.[21] In criminal cases,[22] the Court may, upon the application of the defendant, and in civil cases,[23] upon the written stipulation of both parties, or their attorneys, order a transfer from one division of a district to another.

283. District in Which Local Actions May Be Brought.

Sometimes a plaintiff wants to bring a suit which is of a local nature; as, for example, an action of trespass *q. c. f.* The land lies in one district. The defendant or defendants live in another of the same State. In such case the suit may be brought in that one in which the land lies.[24]

Where the land is in one State and neither plaintiff nor defendant resides therein, it does not appear that the

20. Section 53 J. C., 5 Fed. Stat. 520; U. S. Comp. Stat. Sec. 1035.
21. Merchants Nat. Bank vs. Chattanooga Construction Co., 53 Fed. 314.
22. Section 53 J. C., 5 Fed. Stat. 520; U. S. Comp. Stat. Sec. 1035.
23. Section 58 J. C., 5 Fed. Stat. Ann. 537; U. S. Comp. Stat. Sec. 1040.
24. J. C. Sec. 54, 5 Fed. Stat. Ann. 523; U. S. Comp. Stat. Sec. 1036.

suit can be brought in the United States Court at all. This last statement is true only of those cases which although they grow out of something which has happened with reference to tangible property and are local in their nature, are still actions in which nothing is sought but the recovery of personal damages against the defendant.

Technical to the last degree as the rule itself is, the leading case upon it in this country is full both of historic and human interest. The plaintiff was Edward Livingston of the great New York family of that name. In the course of his long career, he had been the leader of what was then called the Republican party in the House of Representatives. He became Mayor of New York, in which office, while ill with yellow fever, he was pecuniarily ruined by the defalcation of a clerk. He removed to New Orleans, recast the Code Napoleon to adapt it to Louisiana conditions, and years afterwards, as Jackson's Secretary of State, drafted the famous proclamation against nullification. The defendant was the still greater and more celebrated Thomas Jefferson.

Livingston claimed to be the owner of certain land formed by the deposits of the Mississippi. Jefferson, while president, made up his mind that the tract belonged to the United States. He was not willing to await the orderly processes of litigation, but directed the United States Marshal summarily to eject Livingston. This was done by force, and the work which Livingston was doing upon the land stopped, to his great damage, as he claimed. Subsequently the courts upheld his title and after Jefferson went out of office, Livingston brought, in the United States District Court for the District of Virginia, suit against him to recover for the wrong done. Jefferson objected that the action was in its nature local, and could be instituted only in the district of Louisiana where the land lay. He of course had no intention of ever going to

Louisiana so if his point was well taken, no recovery could ever be had against him. When the objection came on for argument, the Court was being held by Chief Justice Marshall as Circuit Justice, and by District Judge John Tyler, the elder, the father of the future President. One was no admirer of Jefferson, and the other had been appointed at Jefferson's instance. They were both of opinion, however, that they were without jurisdiction. Marshall commented nevertheless upon the lack of reason in the rule and the injustice which might result from it, but said he felt constrained by authority to follow it.[25] More than eighty years later the Supreme Court recognized its continued existence[26] and as late as 1914 I personally had to apply it.[27]

284. Section 57 of the Judicial Code—Jurisdiction to Enforce Liens and Remove Encumbrances.

There is a statutory provision dealing with cases which are brought "to enforce any legal or equitable lien upon, or claim to, or to remove any encumbrance or lien or cloud upon the title to real or personal property within the district where such suit is brought," although "one or more of the defendants therein shall not be an inhabitant of or found within the said district, or shall not voluntarily appear thereto." In such case section 57 of the Judicial Code declares that "it shall be lawful for the Court to make an order directing such absent defendant" * * * "to appear, plead, answer or demur by a day certain to be designated, which order shall be served on such absent defendant" * * * "if practicable, wherever found, and also upon the person or persons in pos-

25. Livingston vs. Jefferson, 15 Fed. Cas. 8411; 4 Beveridge's Marshall, 100-116.

26. Ellenwood vs. Marietta Chair Co., 158 U. S. 106; 39 L. Ed. 913; 15 Sup. Ct. 771.

27. Potomac Milling & Ice Co. vs. B. & O. R. R., 217 Fed. 665.

session or charge of said property, if any there be, or where such personal service upon the absent defendant" * * * "is not practicable such order shall be published in such manner as the Court may direct, not less than once a week for six consecutive weeks." If the defendant "shall not appear, plead, answer or demur within the time so limited or within some further time to be allowed by the Court in its discretion," the Court may entertain jurisdiction and proceed with the case as if the absent defendant had been served with process within the district. It is declared that what is done shall, as regards the absent defendant not appearing, "affect only the property which shall have been the subject of the suit and under the jurisdiction of the Court therein, within such district.

Where actual service upon the absent defendant is attempted, it should be made by the marshal[28] of the district in which the defendant is found. That which is served by him must be the order of the Court directing the defendant to appear, plead, answer or demur by a day certain, and the ordinary subpoena will not suffice.[29] It will be noted that substituted service by publication is authorized only when actual service is not practicable, and before an order for it can rightfully issue, it must be made to appear that such actual service is not practicable, and why.[30]

285. Do.—Defendant Not Personally Served May Have Decree Set Aside at Any Time Within a Year of Its Entry.

There is a further proviso that any defendant not actually served as above provided may at any time within

---

28. Evans vs. Scribners' Sons, 58 Fed. 303.
29. Jennings vs. Johnson, 148 Fed. 337; 78 C. C. A. 329.
30. McDonald vs. Cooper, 32 Fed. 745.

one year after final judgment in any such suit enter his appearance to it and thereupon the Court shall make an order setting aside the judgment and permitting him to plead, on payment of such costs as the Court shall deem just.

One Fernandez in the United States District Court for the District of Porto Rico brought suit against a certain Perez and other citizens and residents of Spain, to set aside certain mortgages and sales of real property in Porto Rico. Personal service was never had on Perez and an order of publication was issued. The order was published and due proof thereof made. The bill was thereupon taken as confessed against him. After further proceedings, all *ex parte,* the mortgages and sales were held to be void. The marshal was directed to sell the land under an execution upon the judgment held by the complainant. Within two months after the decree and before the property had been sold, Perez entered his appearance. He applied for leave to defend the suit on the ground that he had not been personally notified. It appeared that he actually had learned of the pendency of the proceedings. The Supreme Court said that the defendant had an absolute right to have the decree set aside at any time within twelve months after its entry upon applying so to do, provided he had not actual personal notice resulting from the service on him outside of the district of an order of the Court directed to him and requiring him to appear and defend within a time stated.[31]

286. Do.—Suits to Partition Lands and Remove Clouds.

The authority given by this section of the Code is one of much importance. Without it the Federal jurisdiction would be greatly restricted. It enables the United States Court to entertain partition suits when there is diversity

31. Perez vs. Fernandez, 220 U. S. 224; 55 L. Ed. 443; 31 Sup. Ct. 412.

of citizenship. For example—the plaintiff, who was a citizen of New Hampshire, claimed to be seized as tenant in common in fee simple and to be in actual possession of some 10,000 acres of land in the Northern District of Florida. Some of the defendants—130 in all—were citizens of Florida; others of Georgia, South Carolina, North Carolina, Alabama, Mississippi, Texas, Illinois, New York and New Jersey. The bill was to quiet title and for partition. It was held that this was a case of which the Court for the Northern District of Florida had jurisdiction and in which it might proceed by service of actual process or by publication, so as to bring in the absent defendants and bind their interests in the land in controversy.[32]

287. Do.—Suits to Enforce Trusts.

The section is applicable to suits to enforce trusts in, and liens upon funds or property within the territorial jurisdiction of the Court. A citizen of a State other than either Indiana or New York filed a bill in the Circuit Court of the United States for the District of Indiana against the administrator of a decedent, claiming that a fund of $150,000 in the hands of the administrator was subject to a trust for the payment of some $31,000 to the complainant. The trustees were citizens of New York. The Supreme Court held that they were indispensable parties, but that the complainant could have them brought in by actual service of process or by publication in the manner prescribed in the statute.[33]

288. Do.—Suits to Enforce Rights in Shares of Stock.

It has been held that an action to enforce rights in shares of stock of a corporation whose legal habitation is

32. Greeley vs. Lowe, 155 U. S. 58; 39 L. Ed. 69; 15 Sup. Ct. 24.
33. Goodman vs. Niblack, 102 U. S. 563; 26 L. Ed. 229.

within the district, is authorized by the section. It is a proceeding to remove a cloud upon the title to personal property.

In a case which went to the Supreme Court the plaintiffs were all stockholders in a Michigan mining company. They were citizens of States other than Michigan. They alleged that officers and directors of the corporation, some of whom were citizens of Michigan and some of Massachusetts, had fraudulently conspired together to cause the stock belonging to the plaintiffs to be sold for the non-payment of assessments alleged to have been fraudulently levied for the purpose of bringing about such sales. The plaintiffs said that they were the equitable owners of the stock, although the legal title was in certain of the defendants. The relief asked was a decree establishing their rightful title and ownership. The corporation was properly summoned. The individual defendants residing in Boston had process actually served upon them, but they had not appeared, answered, pleaded or demurred. The Circuit Court for the Northern District of Michigan thought that it was without jurisdiction and dismissed the bill. The Supreme Court reversed the decree below. It held, that by the statutes of Michigan, shares of stock were personal property. As the habitation or domicile of the company is and must be in the State that created it, the property represented by its certificates of stock may be deemed to be held by it within the State, whose creature it is, whenever it is sought by suit to determine who is the owner. The property represented by the shares of stock was held by the corporation in Michigan.[34]

34. Jellenik vs. Huron Copper Mining Co., 177 U. S. 1; 44 L. Ed. 647; 20 Sup. Ct. 559.

289. Section 57 of Judicial Code Rather Strictly Construed.

The Federal Courts strictly construe the statutes conferring jurisdiction upon them. In the case of Ladew vs. Tennessee Copper Co.[35] the Court refused to hold that the physical cloud of fumes and gases which was damaging plaintiff's property was such a cloud as could be dealt with under section 57 of the Federal Code.

A citizen of Florida, brought suit in the United States Court for the Eastern District of North Carolina against A, a resident of such district, and B, a resident of Tennessee. He charged that B had been his confidential agent; had induced him to buy land from A for a large sum of money and had pretended himself to pay one-twentieth of the purchase price. The fact was that B was acting as the agent of A. With A's knowledge and at A's procurement he had made to the plaintiff many false and material representations about the land. Plaintiff paid A $38,000 for it and understood that **B** paid A $2,000. The land was conveyed by A to the plaintiff, A undertaking to hold one-twentieth of it in trust for B. In point of fact, B never paid A anything. He received one-twentieth of it from A as a part of his commission for swindling the plaintiff. Plaintiff sought to rescind the sale and he made B a party to the suit for the purpose of removing the cloud raised by B's equitable title to the one-twentieth. The Circuit Court of Appeals for the Fourth Circuit held that the case made by the bill did not come under the provisions of section 57. The plaintiff was not trying to perfect or clear title to land; all that he asked was to get back his $38,000.[36]

A bill for the specific performance of a contract to con-

---

35. 218 U. S. 357; 54 L. Ed. 1069; 31 Sup. Ct. 81.
36. Camp vs. Bonsal, 203 Fed. 913; 122 C. C. A. 207.

vey land cannot be brought under this section,[37] as in its nature, such a proceeding is *in personam*. But if the contract which forms the basis of the controversy creates a lien upon the property, then the suit for specific performance may be in effect to enforce a lien or claim upon it, and if so, section 57 is applicable.[38]

290. Actions Under the Employers' Liability Act.

Actions under the Federal Employers' Liability Act may be brought in the district of the residence of the defendant, or in the district in which the cause of action arose, or in any district in which the defendant is doing business at the time such action is commenced.[39]

291. Actions for Personal Injuries or Death Under Section 33 of the Merchant Marine Act.

The Act of Congress, approved June 5, 1920, officially designated as the Merchant Marine Act of 1920, but more commonly referred to as the Jones Act,[40] gives to seamen and their personal representatives the right to recover for personal injuries or death suffered in the course of their employment, by an action for damages at law, with the right to trial by jury, and gives them the benefit of the statutes of the United States conferring or regulating the right of action for death in the case of railroad employees. Such actions may be brought in the Court of the district in which the defendant employer resides or in which its principal office is located.

292. Venue of Bills of Interpleader Filed by Insurance Companies or Fraternal Beneficial Societies.

Bills of Interpleader by insurance companies or fraternal beneficial societies permitted to be filed as hereto-

37. Nelson vs. Husted, 182 Fed. 921.
38. Texas Co. vs. Central Fuel Oil Co., 194 Fed. 1; 114 C. C. A. 21.
39. 36 Stat. 291; 8 Fed. Stat. Ann. 1369; U. S. Comp. Stat. Sec. 1010.
40. 41 Stat. 1007; Fed. Stat. Ann. 1920; Sup. 227.

fore stated,[41] may be brought in any district in which one or more of the persons *bona fide* claiming against the company or society reside, with the limitation that wherever a beneficiary or beneficiaries are named in the policy of insurance or certificate of membership, or where such policy or certificate has been assigned, and written notice thereof given to the company or society, the bill must be filed in the district where the beneficiary or beneficiaries reside.

There is a difference of opinion in the District Courts as to whether, if there has been a beneficiary named, and there is a subsequent assignment to an assignee living in another district, the law requires that the bill shall be filed in the district of the beneficiary or in that of the assignee.[42]

293. Actions to Recover for Negligence or Wanton Injury to Submarine Cables.

Suits to recover damages for negligence or wanton injury to submarine cables may be brought in any district in which the defendant may be found and served with process.[43]

41. Sec. 199, supra.

42. Penn Mutual Life Ins. Co. vs. Henderson, 244 Fed. 877; N. Y. Life Ins. Co. vs. Kennedy, 253 Fed. 287.

43. Act Feb. 29, 1888, Sec. 13, 25 Stat. 42; 9 Fed. Stat. Ann. 534; U. S Comp. Stat. Sec. 1099.

CHAPTER XI.

VENUE WHERE JURISDICTION OF FEDERAL COURTS IS EXCLUSIVE

294. General Venue Provisions Now Found in Section 51 of the Judicial Code Apply Only to Cases in Which the Jurisdiction of the District Court is Concurrent With That of the States.

In former acts the special provisions of the Judicial Code, by which ordinarily a defendant may not be sued in any district except that in which he resides, with the exception that if the sole ground of jurisdiction is diversity of citizenship, the suit may be brought in the district of the residence of either the plaintiff or of the defendant, applied only to cases in which the jurisdiction of the Courts of the United States was concurrent with that of the States.[1]

In the Judicial Code, section 51 is preceded by a number of sections, dealing with some, but not all of the cases in which the jurisdiction of the Courts of the United States is exclusive. In them, various and varying provisions are made as to venue, and then section 51 exempts from its provisions cases provided for in the succeeding six sections only. All of them include cases in which there may be concurrent jurisdiction in the Courts of the States, although perhaps they are not in terms necessarily limited to such cases. It would appear therefore that section 51 should receive the construction given to the earlier statutes by the Supreme Court in the Hohorst case.[2]

Doubtless, however, where any case is within the exclusive jurisdiction of the Courts of the United States, and no special venue provision is made for it, it will be safest for the plaintiff to institute his proceeding in the district of which the defendant is a resident.

295. Venue of Prosecution for Crimes and Offenses Cognizable Under the Laws of the United States.

This subject has already been fully discussed in sections 96 to 104, *supra*.

296. Venue of Proceedings to Enforce Penalties and Forfeitures Under the Laws of the United States.

The Judicial Code[3] provides that all pecuniary penalties and forfeitures may be sued for and recovered either

1. In re Hohorst, 150 U. S. 653; 37 L. Ed. 1211; 14 Sup. Ct. 221.
2. 150 U. S. 653; 37 L. Ed. 1211; 14 Sup. Ct. 221.
3. Section 43 J. C.

in the district where they accrue or in the district where the offender is found. The constitutional provision requiring crimes to be prosecuted in the district in which they were committed, is not applicable to such suits.[4]

297. Venue of Civil Causes of Admiralty and Maritime Jurisdiction.

An Admiralty proceeding *in rem* must be brought in the district in which the *res* is.[5] One *in personam* may be instituted in any district in which the respondent may be found,[6] or in any district in which he has property which may be attached, for what has been said in sections 248 and 249 (*supra*) has no application to proceedings in Admiralty.[7]

298. Venue of Proceedings to Enforce Seizures.

If property is seized upon the high seas, its forfeiture may be enforced in any district into which it is brought and in which proceedings are instituted.[8] But when a seizure is made in any district, it must be prosecuted therein unless other statutory provision is made for it. In a case quite interesting upon its facts, involving as they did the seizure of two American merchant ships engaged in transporting slaves from Havana to Pensacola, when both were under Spanish sovereignty, but when the latter was in the temporary possession of the military forces of the United States under the command of General Jackson, and when the seizure had been made in the harbor of Pensacola and not upon the high seas, it was held that the general principles of the admiralty law

4. St. Louis & S. F. R. Co. vs. U. S., 169 Fed. 69; 94 C. C. A. 437.

5. The Slavers, 2nd Wallace, 383; 17 L. Ed. 911.

6. In re Louisville Underwriters, 134 U. S. 488; 33 L. Ed. 991; 10 Sup. Ct. 587.

7. Atkins vs. The Disintegrating Co., 18 Wallace, 272; 21 L. Ed. 841.

8. J. C. Sec. 45; 5 Fed. Stat. Ann. 476; U. S. Comp. Stat. Sec. 1027.

permitted the filing of a libel in any district into which the property was brought, whether it had been seized upon the high seas or within the harbors of a foreign State.[9] To support the jurisdiction at all, there must first be a valid seizure. It is not enough that it may appear to the Court that the property seized was subject to forfeiture if the seizure itself had not been lawfully made.[10]

299. Venue of Suits to Recover Internal Revenue Taxes.

Suits for internal revenue taxes may be brought either in the district in which the liability for the tax accrues, or in that in which the delinquent resides.[11]

300. Venue of Suits for Infringement of Patents.

Suits, whether at law or in equity, for the infringement of patents, may be brought in the district of which the defendant is an inhabitant, or in any district where the defendant, whether a person, partnership or corporation, shall have committed acts of infringement, and have a regularly established place of business.[12]

Before a suit can be brought in a district in which a defendant does not live, it must be shown both that completed acts of infringement have been committed in the district at some time,[13] and that at the time suit is brought, the defendant has a regularly established place of business in the district.[14]

It is not essential that the acts of infringement shall

9. The Merino, 9 Wheaton, 391; 6 L. Ed. 118.

10. U. S. vs. Larkin, 208 U. S. 333; 52 L. Ed. 517; 28 Sup. Ct. 417.

11. J. C. 44; 5 Fed. Stat. Ann. 476; U. S. Comp. Stat. Sec. 1026.

12. J. C. 48; 5 Fed. Stat. Ann. 478; U. S. Comp. Stat. Sec. 1030.

13. Westinghouse Elec. & Mfg. Co. vs. Stanley Elec. Mfg. Co., 116 Fed. 641.

14. Tyler vs. Ludlow Saylor Wire Co., 236 U. S. 725; 59 L. Ed. 808; 35 Sup. Ct. 458.

be continuing at the time suit is brought, but it is necessary that defendant have at that time a regularly established place of business in the district.[15]

301. Venue of Suits for Infringement of Copyrights.

Proceedings for the infringement of a copyright may be taken in the district of which the defendant or his agent is an inhabitant, or in which he may be found, and it has apparently been held that service on an agent in the district in which the agent resides or is found is sufficient.[16]

302. Venue of Proceedings in Bankruptcy.

Voluntary or involuntary petitions in bankruptcy may be filed in any district in which the alleged bankrupt has had his principal place of business, residence or domicile for the greater part of the preceding six months, or in which, if he has none of them within the United States, he has property, or who, having been adjudged a bankrupt by a foreign court of competent jurisdiction, has property within the district. If the alleged bankrupt be a partnership, the petition in bankruptcy may be filed in any district which would have jurisdiction over any one of the partners.[17]

Suits by trustees in bankruptcy on claims of the bankrupt against third persons cannot, without the defendant's consent, be brought in any district in which such suit could not have been maintained by the bankrupt.[18]

For a more detailed discussion of these questions, reference may be had to any of the standard works on bankruptcy.

15. Underwood Typewriter Co. vs. Fox Typewriter Co., 158 Fed. 476.

16. Wagner vs. Wilson. 225 Fed. 912.

17. Bankruptcy Act, Sections 1 and 5; 1 Fed. Stat. Ann. 509-578; U. S. Comp. Stat. 9585.

18. Bankruptcy Act. Section 23; 1 Fed. Stat. Ann. 759; U. S. Comp. Stat. Sec. 9588.

303. Venue of Suits Against Consuls or Vice Consuls.

There is no special statutory provision as to the venue of suits against consuls or vice consuls. A consul or vice consul may of course be sued either in the Supreme Court or in the District Court of the district in which he resides. If it be held that section 51 has no relation to cases within the exclusive jurisdiction of the United States, it is possible that a consul or vice consul may be suable in any district in which he is found.

304. Venue of Suits Under the Anti-Trust Acts.

Anybody injured in his business or property by anything forbidden by the anti-trust laws, may, irrespective of the amount in controversy, sue in any district in which the defendant resides, is found, or has an agent.[19] If the defendant is a corporation, the suit may be brought in any district of which it is an inhabitant or is found or transacts business.[20] There is some conceivable difficulty in construing these provisions. If the defendant be an individual, can the suit proceed against him in the district in which he neither resides or is found and in which he does not voluntarily appear merely because he has an agent therein? There is no provision for serving him with process in any district, other than that in which the suit is brought. In the case of a corporate defendant, this particular question cannot arise, for provided it is suable in the district in which suit is brought, process may be served upon it in any district of which it is an inhabitant or in which it may be found. I have elsewhere had occasion to discuss rather fully some of the questions which may arise in this connection and to suggest that a determination of them may easily be made unneces-

19. 38 Stat. 731; 9 Fed. Stat. Ann. 730; U. S. Comp. Stat. Sec. 8835.
20. 38 Stat. 736; 9 Fed. Stat. Ann. 744; U. S. Comp. Stat. Sec. 8836k.

sary[21] where the defendant is a corporation, as in this class of cases it almost always is.

305. Venue of Suits to Enforce, Suspend or Set Aside Orders of the Interstate Commerce Commission.

Suits to enforce, suspend or set aside an order of the Interstate Commerce Commission may be brought in any district in which reside any of the parties upon whose petition the order was made, except when an order does not relate either to transportation or to a matter so complained of, the matter covered by the order is deemed to arise in the district where one of the petitioners in Court has either its principal office or its principal operating office.[22]

Suits to enjoin, set aside, annul or suspend any order of the Interstate Commerce Commission must be brought against the United States,[23] which has consented to be sued in that connection, but only in the district specified by the statute.

State officials of Illinois had threatened action, under State laws, against certain railroad companies, if they carried out an order of the Interstate Commerce Commission which had originally been passed upon the petition of a resident of the Eastern District of Missouri. The defendants filed a cross bill in which they sought to have the Commission's order set aside. The Supreme Court held that the original bill was not one to enforce an order of the Interstate Commerce Commission, and that therefore it had been filed in the proper district, being that in which the defendants resided, but that the cross bill was a proceeding to set aside an order of the Commission, and could be brought nowhere else than in

21. Frey & Son vs. Cudahy Packing Co., 228 Fed. 209.
22. 38 Stat. 219; 5 Fed. Stat. Ann. 1108; U. S. Comp. Stat. Sec. 994.
23. J. C. Sec. 208; 5 Fed. Stat. Ann. 1110; U. S. Comp. Stat. Sec. 997.

the Eastern District of Missouri in which the party upon whose petition the Commission made its order, had its residence.[24]

306. Venue of Actions on Bonds of Contractors for Public Works.

Actions upon bonds given to the United States by contractors for public works, must be brought in the district in which the work is to be performed, and not elsewhere.[25] There is no special statutory provision for the service of process when the defendants are residents of other districts, as they frequently are. The Supreme Court has, however, said that the provision restricting the place of suit operates *pro tanto* to displace the provision upon that subject in the general jurisdiction act, and authorizes the Court in the district wherein the action is required to be brought to obtain jurisdiction of the person of the defendants through the service upon them of its process in whatever district they may be found.[26]

307. Venue of Actions Against the United States to Recover War Risk Insurance.

The United States issued many war risk insurance policies on the lives of its soldiers and sailors, and it is provided that wherever there is disagreement as to such a contract of insurance between the Bureau of War Risk Insurance and any beneficiary or beneficiaries, an action may be brought on the claim against the United States in the District Court in and for the district in which such beneficiaries, or any one of them reside, and it has

24. Ill. Cent. R. R. Co. vs. Public Utilities Comm., 245 U. S. 493; 62 L. Ed. 425; 38 Sup. Ct. 170.

25. Act Feb. 24, 1905; 33 Stat. 811; 8 Fed. Stat. Ann. 375; U. S. Comp. Stat. Sec. 6923.

26. U. S. vs. Congress Construction Co., 222 U. S. 199; 56 L. Ed. 163; 32 Sup. Ct. 44.

been held that the suit cannot be brought elsewhere, the United States having consented to be sued in the district or districts named, and in no others.[27]

It may be worth while to add that in such suits, the Court fixes the attorney fees, which cannot exceed 5% of the amount recovered. If the payments to the beneficiary himself are to be made in instalments, as is sometimes the case, the attorney may have to take his fee in like manner, because not more than one-tenth of any payment may be deducted for his compensation.[28]

308. Venue of Proceedings to Recover Penalty for Violation of Anchorage Regulations.

A vessel violating the anchorage regulations made by the Secretary of War may be proceeded against in any district in which it may be found.[29]

309. Venue of Proceedings to Review or Enforce Orders of the Federal Trade Commission.

Proceedings to enforce, set aside or modify orders of the Federal Trade Commission must be taken in the Circuit Court of Appeals for the circuit in which the method of competition condemned by the Commission was used, or where the person, partnership or corporation failing or neglecting to obey the order of the Commission resides or carries on business.[30]

27. U. S. vs. Forbes, 278 Fed. 331.

28. Act May 20, 1918; 40 Stat. 555; 9 Fed. Stat. 1305; U. S. Comp. Stat. Sec. 514kk.

29. 38 Stat. 1053; 9 Fed. Stat. Ann. 78; U. S. Comp. Stat. Sec. 9959a.

30. 38 Stat. 720; 4 Fed. Stat. Ann. 577; U. S. Comp. Stat. Sec. 8836e.

CHAPTER XII.

JURISDICTION OF FEDERAL COURTS AS AFFECTED BY ASSIGNMENTS AND TRANSFERS.

310. Introduction.

We have seen of what cases District Courts have jurisdiction and in what districts suits may be brought. We have thus far been dealing with proceedings which have been instituted by the original party to the contract or by the one actually injured by the tort, or by some one who succeeded by operation of law to his rights. Sometimes would-be plaintiffs would like to go into the Federal Court. They are citizens of the same State with the defendants, and have not the right to take their cases there. Under such circumstances they are tempted to transfer their claims to assignees who are citizens of another State.

311. Sham Assignments Will Not Confer Jurisdiction.

Sometimes the assignment is a pure form. It is not made with intent to make the assignee the real owner of that which is assigned to him. In such cases, independently of any statutory provisions, the Courts will hold that they have no jurisdiction; the plaintiff has no interest in the subject-matter of the controversy.

A citizen of Pennsylvania, without consideration, made a conveyance of land to a citizen of Maryland. The

18

latter, to accommodate the grantor, allowed his name to be used in the Federal Court as a plaintiff in an action of ejectment against another citizen of Pennsylvania. The Court held that the conveyance was entirely colorable and collusive, and therefore incapable of laying a foundation for jurisdiction.[1]

Citizens of the District of Columbia wished to have certain litigation concerning land in which they were interested prosecuted in the United States Court for the District of Maryland. They conveyed their interest in the lands to a citizen of that State. The conveyance was without consideration and the grantee was on the request of the grantors to reconvey to them. The complainant in the proceeding was a citizen of Delaware. The Supreme Court said:—

> "If the conveyance" * * * "had really transferred the interest" of the grantor to the grantee, "although made for the avowed purpose of enabling the Court to entertain jurisdiction of the case, it would have accomplished that purpose" * * * "But in point of fact that conveyance did not transfer the real interest of the grantors. It was made without consideration, with a distinct understanding that the grantors retained all their real interest, and that the deed was to have no other effect than to give jurisdiction to the Court" * * * "The Court will not, under such circumstances, give effect to what is a fraud upon the Court, and is nothing more.'"[2]

312. If Assignment Genuine, Motive Immaterial.

The Supreme Court said, it will be noted, that if the conveyance had been real, transferring the interest in the land to the grantee, it would have been immaterial what the motive of the grantor was.

A citizen of Alabama filed a bill in the United States

1. Maxwell's Lessee vs. Levy, 2 Dallas, 381; 1 L. Ed. 424.
2. Barney vs. Baltimore City, 6 Wall., 288; 18 L. Ed. 825.

Court for the District of Ohio, against certain citizens of the latter State, to compel them to convey to him certain land, which had been granted to him by a citizen of Ohio. The grantor feared that his title would not be sustained in the Ohio State Courts. He was indebted to the plaintiff in the sum of $1,100. He offered to sell and convey the land to the latter in payment of this debt. He said that he thought the title was good; that it would most probably be established in the Courts of the United States, but would fail in those of the State. In his opinion the property was worth much more than the sum he was willing to take for it, but in consequence of the difficulties attending the title he would convey it in satisfaction of the debt. He offered to render any service in his power to the grantee in the prosecution of his claim in the Courts of the United States. The testimony showed a sale and conveyance binding on both parties. The title of the grantor was extinguished. The Supreme Court thought that the motives which induced him to make the contract, whether justifiable or censurable, could not affect its validity. It said: "The conveyance appears to be a real transaction, and the real as well as nominal parties to the suit are citizens of different States."[3] The jurisdiction was therefore upheld.

When one or the other of the parties to the controversy claims under a deed, grant or assignment from some one else, if the conveyance is a real conveyance by which the grantor parts with the property and the grantee gets it, then if the Court will have jurisdiction, if the grantee be a party to the suit, it will, except where statute otherwise directs, have jurisdiction although the motive for the transfer was the desire to have the case tried in the United States Court. On the other hand, if the grantor still remains the real owner, the Court will

3. McDonald vs. Smalley, 1 Peters, 623; 7 L. Ed. 309.

not have jurisdiction unless it would have were the grantor himself a party to the suit.

313. Special Statutory Jurisdictional Test as to Assigned Choses in Action—District Court Has No Jurisdiction Unless it Would Have, Had There Been No Assignment.

But Congress has never felt that it was wise to leave the law in this state.

There are many classes of contracts, nominal title to which can be transferred with facility. In many, if not most, cases it is impossible to determine whether the assignment was an actual transfer of the beneficial interests or was merely colorable, and even where it was genuine and complete there was a feeling that bonds and notes given in the usual course of business by citizens of the same State to each other, should not be sued upon in the Federal Courts.[4] Therefore, the original Judiciary Act provided that except in cases of foreign bills of exchange, no District or Circuit Court should have cognizance of any suit to recover the contents of any promissory note or other chose in action in favor of an assignee unless the suit might have been prosecuted in such Court to recover the said contents if no assignment had been made. With slight changes in phraseology, which have not been intended to alter its legal effect,[5] this provision has remained the law ever since. In the Judicial Code it forms a sentence of that same first paragraph of section 24, about which so much has been said. As there worded, it reads:—

> "No District Court shall have cognizance of any suit (except upon foreign bills of exchange) to recover upon any promissory note or other chose in action in favor of any assignee, or of any subsequent holder

4. U. S. vs. Planters Bank, 9 Wheaton, 908; 6 L. Ed. 244.
5. Brown vs. Fletcher, 235 U. S. 589; 59 L. Ed. 374; 35 Sup. Ct. 154.

if such instrument be payable to bearer and be not made by any corporation, unless such suit might have been prosecuted in such Court to recover upon said note or other chose in action if no assignment had been made.''

314. At What Time Must Court Have Had Jurisdiction Had There Been No Assignment.

The Code provides that the assignee may not sue in a Federal Court unless suit could have been brought in that Court if no assignment had been made. As of what time does the statute here speak? Suppose a citizen of Maryland gives his promissory note to another citizen of the same State. The payee endorses it over to a citizen of Pennsylvania. After its endorsement and maturity, the payee moves to Delaware. The Pennsylvania holder brings suit against the Maryland maker in the United States Court for the District of Maryland. Has the Court jurisdiction? At the time suit was brought that Court would have had jurisdiction had no assignment been made, for the original payee was then a citizen of Delaware and competent to sue the maker in the Federal Court. Or does the restriction relate to the time when the assignment became effective? If it does, the Federal Court would have no jurisdiction because at that time both the maker and the payee were citizens of the same State. The law is settled that, if at the time the action was instituted, the assignor could have brought suit in the Federal Court, it is immaterial whether he could have done so when the assignment was made.[6]

315. When There Have Been Several Successive Assignments, to Which Does the Statute Refer?

Suppose that a citizen of Maryland gives his promissory note to a citizen of Delaware. The citizen of Dela-

6. Emsheimer vs. New Orleans, 186 U. S. 33; 46 L. Ed. 1042; 22 Sup. Ct. 770.

ware endorses the note over to another citizen of Maryland. The endorsee endorses it to a citizen of Pennsylvania, who endorses it over again to a citizen of New York. Can the citizen of New York sue the original maker in the Federal Courts? The original payee could have sued because he was of Delaware, and if the assignment referred to in the statute is the first assignment, suit could have been brought in the Federal Courts had no such assignment been made. On the other hand, the holder of the note at the time suit was instituted, traced his title to it through mesne assignment from a person incapable of suing in the Federal Courts, viz: the Maryland holder.

This question has been fully considered by the Circuit Court of Appeals for the Seventh Circuit.[7]

It reached the conclusion that when there are a number of successive assignments, not more than two of them at the most need be taken into account; the statute has no reference to any which are intermediate between the first and the last. If the original payee and the immediate assignor of the plaintiff are both at the time suit is brought competent to sue the maker in the Federal Courts, the jurisdiction of those Courts is not defeated by the fact that some intermediate assignor or endorser is not.

Suppose at the time suit is brought the plaintiff is a citizen of another State than that of the maker. At that time the original payee might have sued the maker in the Federal Court. The plaintiff himself claims under an assignment made directly to him by an intermediate holder, who at the time suit is brought is not competent to sue the maker. Has a Federal Court jurisdiction of the case? The Court of Appeals for the Seventh Circuit in the opinion last cited did not find it necessary to decide

7. Farr vs. Hobe-Peters Land Co., 188 Fed. 10; 110 C. C. A. 160.

that question and reserved it. The authorities are there reviewed.

All hold that unless the Federal Courts would at the time suit is brought have had jurisdiction of an action between the original parties they will not have it as between the then holder and the maker; whether they will have it when the plaintiff's immediate assignee is not one competent to sue the maker in the Federal Courts, although the original payee could have done so, is still an open question.

316. What, in the Statutory Sense, is a Chose in Action?

The words of the statute refer only to a chose in action based upon a contract. "The restriction on jurisdiction is limited to cases where A is indebted to B on an express or implied promise to pay; B assigns this debt or claim to C, and C, as assignee of such debt sues A thereon or to foreclose the security. Or where A has contracted with B, and B assigns the contract to C who sues to enforce his rights, by bill for specific performance, or by an action for damages for breach of the contract."[8]

317. Mortgages.

A citizen of Michigan owed money to a Michigan corporation. He gave his bond therefor and secured its payment by a mortgage on land. The mortgagee assigned the bond, the mortgage, the money secured, and the estate created to a citizen of New York. The latter subsequently filed a bill in the Circuit Court of the United States for the District of Michigan for the foreclosure of the mortgage. The Supreme Court said that the term

" 'chose in action' is one of comprehensive import. It includes the infinite variety of contracts, covenants and promises, which confer on one party a

8. Brown vs. Fletcher, 235 U. S. 598; 59 L. Ed. 374; 35 Sup. Ct. 154.

right to recover a personal chattel or a sum of money from another, by action. It is true, a deed or title for land does not come within this description. And it is true, also, that a mortgagee may avail himself of his legal title to recover in ejectment, in a court of law. Yet, even there, he is considered as having but a chattel interest, while the mortgagor is treated as the true owner." * * * "In equity, the debt or bond is treated as the principal, and the mortgage as the incident. It passes by the assignment or transfer of the bond, and is discharged by its payment." * * * "The complainant in this case is the purchaser and assignee of a sum of money—a debt, a chose in action —not of a tract of land. He seeks to recover by this action a debt assigned to him. He is therefore 'the assignee of a chose in action' within the letter and spirit of the Act of Congress under consideration, and cannot support this action in the Circuit Court of the United States, where his assignor could not."[9]

Later cases have qualified some of the language used. They have held that the statute does not apply to rights of action arising out of the ownership of an assigned chattel any more than it does to those incident to the ownership of granted land.[10]

318. Contracts for the Conveyance of Lands.

The School Fund Commissioners of Black Hawk County, Iowa, entered into contracts with a number of individuals, all citizens of Iowa, to convey to them some of the school lands of that county. Part of the purchase money was paid in cash and the balance was to be paid thereafter at times stipulated in the agreements. It was provided that if the subsequent payments were not forthcoming those previously made should be forfeited. There-

9. Sheldon vs. Sill, 8 How. 449; 12 L. Ed. 1147.
10. Deshler vs. Dodge, 16 Howard, 622; 14 L. Ed. 1084.

after, the lands and all interests under these contracts were conveyed to the plaintiff, a citizen of New York. He filed a bill alleging a tender of the amount still due and praying that his title to the land might be cleared, and that all conveyances made in fraud of his rights might be cancelled. There was a very ingenious attempt so to frame the bill as to avoid all appearance of asking for the specific performance of the contract and to make it seem as if the real controversy was over the title to the land, but it was held that the Federal Court had no jurisdiction.[11]

319. An Action for a Tort Unconnected With Contract, Not Within the Statute.

The Supreme Court has said that a consideration of the mischief which the statute was intended to prevent warrants the conclusion that it has no application to mere naked rights of action founded on some wrongful act, or some neglect of duty to which the law attaches damages.[12] Whether the assignee of a judgment can sue thereon when the person in whose favor the judgment was rendered could not have done so, depends upon whether the cause of action for which the judgment was obtained was within the statute or not, for where justice requires, it is permissible to inquire into the nature of the demand on which the judgment was rendered.[13]

320. Right of Assignee to Sue as Affected by the Requirement of a Minimum Amount in Controversy.

Suppose a plaintiff claims as the assignee of a number of separate payees? The holder, at the time suit is brought, is himself a citizen of another State than that of

11. Corbin vs. County of Black Hawk, 105 U. S. 659; 26 L. Ed. 1136.
12. Bushnell vs. Kennedy, 9 Wall., 387; 19 L. Ed. 736.
13. Walker vs. Powers, 104 U. S. 248; 26 L. Ed. 729.

the maker, as is also each one of the payees to whose rights he has succeeded. The aggregate of his claim exceeds $3,000. No one of his assignees had a claim for so much. Would the Federal Court have jurisdiction? Although the suit could not have been brought had no assignment been made, the Supreme Court[14] has held that the statute has no application to such a case.

The provision that the United States Courts shall not have jurisdiction unless the amount in controversy exceeds a certain sum, is intended merely to prevent cases in which the amount involved is not large being brought in Courts in which as a rule litigation is more expensive than it is in the State tribunals. If when the case gets into Court the required amount is in controversy, the purpose of Congress has been attained.

321. Does the Assignment Statute Have Any Relation to the Venue of Actions?

Suppose A, a citizen of Maryland, gives his promissory note to B, a citizen of Pennsylvania, and B endorses the note over to C, a citizen of the Southern District of New York. A does not pay the note at maturity, is in New York and is there sued by C. Can he object to the jurisdiction on the ground that, if no assignment had been made he could not have been sued in that particular Court, because, if the note had remained in the hands of B, B could have sued on it only in the Eastern District of Pennsylvania, in which he lived, or in the District of Maryland, in which A lived?[15]

The decided cases differ on the question. The earlier

14. Emsheimer vs. New Orleans, 186 U. S. 33; 46 L. Ed. 1042; 22 Sup. Ct. 770.

15. Bolles vs. Lehigh Valley R. Co., 127 Fed. 884; Consolidated Rubber Tire Co. vs. Ferguson, 183 Fed. 756; 106 C. C. A. 330; Waterman vs. C. & O. R. Co., 199 Fed. 667.

say that such a suit can be maintained. The later that it cannot.

322. Exceptions—Foreign Bills of Exchange.

From this assignment provision foreign bills of exchange are expressly excepted. What is a foreign bill of exchange?

In 1819 Finley & Van Lear of this city drew a bill of exchange in favor of one Rosewell L. Colt, also of Baltimore, on Stephen Dever of New Orleans. The payee endorsed the bill for value to one Buckner, a citizen of New York. It was not paid at maturity and was properly protested. Suit was brought on it by Buckner as a citizen of New York against Finley & Van Lear as citizens of Maryland in the United States Circuit Court for the District of Maryland. It was contended on one side that the bill in question was not a foreign bill of exchange; that in order that it should be, it would necessarily have had to have been drawn by persons residing abroad, but the Supreme Court was of a different opinion. It held that bills of exchange drawn in one State of the Union on persons living in another, partake of the character of foreign bills and ought to be so treated in the Courts of the United States.[16]

The reason for this exception was discussed by the Supreme Court in that case. It was there suggested that the purpose of the assignment statute was

> "to prevent frauds upon the jurisdiction of the" Federal Courts, "by pretended assignments of bonds, notes and bills of exchange, strictly inland; and as these evidences of debt generally concern the internal negotiation of the inhabitants of the same State, and would seldom find their way fairly into the hands of persons residing in another State, the prohibition as to them would impose a very trifling

16. Buckner vs. Finley & Van Lear, 2 Peters. 586; 7 L. Ed. 528.

restriction, if any, upon the commercial intercourse
of the different States with each other. It is quite
otherwise as to the bills drawn in one State upon
another. They answer all the purposes of remit-
tances, and of commercial facilities, equally with bills
drawn upon other countries, or *vice versa* and if a
choice of jurisdiction be important to the credit of
bills of the latter class, which it undoubtedly is, it
must be equally so, to that of the former. Nor does
the reason for restraining the transfer of other
choses in action, apply to bills of exchange of this
description; which, from their commercial character,
might be expected to pass fairly into the hands of
persons residing in the different States of the
Union.''

323. Instruments Payable to Bearer Made by a Corporation Also Excepted From Assignment Proviso.

The provision prohibiting suits by assignees unless the
suit could have been brought had no assignment been
made, is expressly made applicable to instruments payable to bearer, with the exception of such as are made by
corporations.

The City of New Orleans issued a number of certificates
of indebtedness payable to bearer. One Quinlan, a citizen
of New York, brought suit in the United States Court for
the Eastern District of Louisiana against the City of New
Orleans. The declaration contained no averment that
the suit could have been maintained by the assignors of
the certificates sued upon. The Supreme Court said that
was immaterial; that the certificates were payable to
bearer, they were made by a corporation; "they were
transferable by delivery; they were not negotiable under
the law merchant, but that was immaterial; they were
payable to any person holding them in good faith, not by
virtue of any assignment of the promisee, but by an
original and direct promise, moving from maker to the

bearer." It was, therefore, held that they were not subject to the assignment restrictions and that the Circuit Court had jurisdiction.[17]

324. The Statute Has No Application to Suits Brought by an Assignee to Recover Possession of a Thing or Damages for its Detention.

The recovery of the contents of the assigned chose in action must be the object of the suit; otherwise the statute does not apply. The tax collector of Cuyahoga County, Ohio, distrained upon some of the banks of that county. He seized certain bank notes in their possession. He said the banks owed taxes and he took the notes because the taxes were due and to pay the taxes with them. The banks thereupon sold those very notes to a citizen of New York. The latter, in the Circuit Court of the United States for the Northern District of Ohio, brought an action of replevin against the tax collector, who, of course, was an Ohio citizen. The Supreme Court, five judges against four, said:—

"We are of opinion that this clause of the statute has no application to the case of a suit by the assignee of a chose in action to recover possession of the thing in specie, or damages for its wrongful caption or detention; and that it applies only to cases in which the suit is brought to recover the contents, or to enforce the contract contained in the instrument assigned. In the case of a tortious taking, or wrongful detention of a chose in action against the right or title of the assignee, the injury is one to the right of property in the thing, and it is therefore unimportant as it respects the derivation of the title; it is sufficient if it belongs to the party bringing the suit at the time of the injury. The distinction, as it respects the application of the 11th section of the

17. New Orleans vs. Quinlan, 173 U. S. 191; 43 L. Ed. 664; 9 Sup. Ct. 329.

Judiciary Act to a suit concerning a chose in action is this: where the suit is brought to enforce the contract, the assignee is disabled unless it might have been brought in the Court, if no assignment had been made; but if brought for a tortious taking or a wrongful detention of the chattel, then the remedy accrues to the person who has the right of property or of possession at the time, the same as in case of a like wrong in respect to any other sort of personal chattel.''[18]

325. The Assigned Chose in Action Must Be the Cause of Action.

In order that this proviso of the statute shall apply, there must have been something assigned, and that something must constitute the cause of action.

Citizens of New York sued citizens of Oregon as makers of a promissory note. On its face, it was payable to another citizen of Oregon and was endorsed by him. The plaintiffs in their declaration alleged that the transaction was a loan by them to the endorser; that the defendants executed the note for the accommodation of the endorser to enable him to procure the loan, and that he was in fact the maker of the notes and never himself had any cause of action thereon against the defendants. The Supreme Court affirmed a judgment in favor of the plaintiffs. It said:—

"The plaintiffs below were the first and only holders of the note for value." * * * "It is quite plain that the plaintiff's action did not offend the spirit and purpose of this section of the Act. The purpose of the restriction as to suits by assignees was to prevent the making of assignments of choses in action for the purpose of giving jurisdiction to the Federal Court." * * * "The true meaning of the restriction in question was not disturbed by per-

18. Deshler vs. Dodge, 16 How., 630; 14 L. Ed. 1084.

mitting the plaintiffs to show that, notwithstanding the terms of the note, the payee was really a maker or original promisor, and did not, by his endorsement, assign or transfer any right of action held by him against the accommodation makers.''[19]

326. Suits by Drawers Against Acceptors Are Not Within Statute.

A municipal corporation of Nebraska contracted with citizens of that State for the construction of waterworks. The contractors gave certain citizens of Missouri an order upon the city for $5,750. The municipality accepted the order and undertook to withhold its amount from the final payment that might become due the contractors. The city was sued by the holders of the order. The Supreme Court said:—

"This acceptance was a contract directly between the city and the plaintiffs below, upon which the city was immediately chargeable as promisor to the plaintiffs. Nothing is better settled in the law of commercial paper than that the acceptance of a draft or order in favor of a certain payee, constitutes a new contract between the acceptor and such payee, and that the latter may bring suit upon it without tracing title from the drawer. From the moment of acceptance, the acceptor becomes the primary debtor, and the drawer is only contingently liable, in case of nonpayment by the acceptor." * * * "It has been the settled law of this Court that the Circuit Court has jurisdiction of a suit, brought by the endorsee of a promissory note against his immediate endorser, whether a suit would lie against the maker or not, upon the ground, as stated by CHIEF JUSTICE MARSHALL, 'that the endorsee does not claim through an assignment. It is a new contract entered into by the endorser and endorsee.' ''[20]

---

19. Holmes vs. Goldsmith, 147 U. S. 150; 37 L. Ed. 118; 13 Sup. Ct. 288.
20. Superior City vs. Ripley, 138 U. S. 96; 34 L. Ed. 914; 11 Sup. Ct. 288.

327. Suits by Endorsees Against Endorsers Are Not Within Statute.

The case referred to in the opinion of the Supreme Court last cited was a case in which citizens of Pennsylvania in the United States Circuit Court for the District of Tennessee sued a citizen of Tennessee as the endorser of a promissory note drawn by another citizen of Tennessee and endorsed to the plaintiffs.[21]

328. Suits by Those Claiming Through Subrogation Are Not Within Statute.

Subrogation is not assignment. The subrogated creditor, by operation of law represents the persons to whose rights he is subrogated. The administrator of that famous litigant, Mrs. Gaines, brought suit in the United States Court against the City of New Orleans. He claimed to be subrogated to the rights of certain citizens of Louisiana. It was held that the United States Court had jurisdiction on the ground of diverse citizenship, the administrator being a citizen of another State than Louisiana, although the persons to whose rights he was subrogated were citizens of Louisiana. The Court said:—

"We have repeatedly held that representatives may stand upon their own citizenship in the Federal Courts, irrespectively of the citizenship of the persons whom they represent,—such as executors, administrators, guardians, trustees, receivers, etc. The evil which the law was intended to obviate was the voluntary creation of Federal jurisdiction by simulated assignments. But assignments by operation of law creating legal representatives, are not within the mischief or reason of the law. Persons subrogated to the rights of others by the rules of equity are within this principle. When, however, the State or the Governor of a State, is a mere figurehead or

21. Young vs. Bryan, 6 Wheat., 146; 5 L. Ed. 228.

nominal party in a suit on a sheriff's or administrator's bond, the rule does not apply. There the real party in interest is taken into account on a question of citizenship."[22]

329. Suits Upon Novations Are Not Within Statute.

Citizens of Illinois entered into a contract of employment with an Illinois corporation and assumed certain obligations in connection therewith. The Illinois corporation sold all its property, including such contracts, to a New Jersey corporation. The defendants, with knowledge of the sale, remained in the service of the purchaser in the same capacities and with the same salaries. Subsequently it sued them for breach of the contract of employment. The Supreme Court held that the rights of the New Jersey corporation and of the defendants depended not upon the original contract, but upon its adoption by the New Jersey corporation and the defendants as the contract between them; and that therefore the New Jersey corporation was not assignee of the rights of the Illinois corporation under the contract, but was an original contracting party with the Illinois defendants.[23] The Federal Court had jurisdiction.

330. Suits by Lessors Against Assignees of Lessees Are Not Within Statute.

A citizen of one State brought suit against a citizen of another on the covenants contained in a lease made by the plaintiff to an assignor of the defendant. In the declaration the plaintiff did not allege the citizenship of the original lessee. The Court held that his citizenship

---

22. New Orleans vs. Gaines Admr., 138 U. S. 606; 34 L. Ed. 1102; 11 Sup. Ct. 428; affirmed in Mexican Central Ry. Co. vs. Eckman, 187 U. S. 429; 42 L. Ed. 245; 23 Sup. Ct. 211.

23. American Colortype Co. vs. Continental Co., 188 U. S. 104; 47 L. Ed. 404; 23 Sup. Ct. 265.

was immaterial; that the statute only applied to the assignee of the right of action, and had no reference to interest in specific things acquired by the defendant by assignment; such interests and the rights resulting from them were within neither the purpose nor the letter of the statute."[24]

331. Suits by Party to Contract Against Assignee of Other Are Not Within Statute.

A contract was made between two citizens of Florida. One of them assigned his rights under the contract to citizens of France. The other subsequently brought suit against those citizens of France in the United States Court. It was held that independently of the question whether there had not been necessarily a novation upon which the plaintiff was suing, the assignment statute had no application to an assignment made by an assignee of the defendant and not by an assignee of the plaintiff.[25]

332. Suits for Trespass to Property Are Not Within Statute.

The statute relates solely to such suits as grow out of the contracts of the original parties. It has no reference to actions brought to recover damages for trespass to property.

A plaintiff, a citizen of New York, brought an action in his own right and as assignee of another, whose citizenship was not stated, against citizens of Florida, to recover as damages $6,000, the alleged value of 3,000 trees and pine logs cut by the defendants upon the lands in Florida of the plaintiff and one Russell, and carried away and converted to the use of the defendants. Russell had assigned all his interests in the logs and in the claim to

24. Adams vs. Shirk, 105 Fed. 659; 44 C. C. A. 653.
25. Brooks vs. Laurent, 98 Fed. 647; 39 C. C. A. 201.

the plaintiff. The Supreme Court held that the suit could be maintained and that the statute did not apply to claims of that character.[26]

333. Duty of Court to Dismiss Suits Not Involving a Controversy Within Its Jurisdiction.

Congress and the Courts are zealous to prevent the bringing in the United States Courts of suits of which those Courts would not have had jurisdiction had the real facts been set forth by the plaintiff. The Judicial Code provides:—

"If in any suit commenced in a District Court, or removed from a State Court to a District Court of the United States, it shall appear to the satisfaction of the said District Court, at any time after such suit has been brought or removed thereto, that such suit does not really and substantially involve a dispute or controversy properly within the jurisdiction of said District Court, or that the parties to said suit have been improperly or collusively made or joined, either as plaintiffs or defendants, for the purpose of creating a case cognizable or removable under this chapter, the said District Court shall proceed no further therein, but shall dismiss the suit or remand it to the Court from which it was removed, as justice may require, and shall make such order as to costs as shall be just."[27]

334. History of the Statutory Provision.

The history of this section and the reasons for it have been fully stated by the Supreme Court of the United States.[28] Under the Act of 1789, as it originally stood, because of the then commercial and industrial conditions

26. Ambler vs. Eppinger, 137 U. S. 480; 34 L. Ed. 765; 11 Sup. Ct. 173.
27. Sec. 37, Judicial Code, 5 Fed. Stat. Ann. 398; U. S. Comp. Stat. Sec. 1019.
28. Farmington vs. Pillsbury, 114 U. S. 141; 29 L. Ed. 114; 5 Sup. Ct. 807.

of the country, there were, apparently, not very many
cases of colorable transfers for the purpose of giving
jurisdiction. As we have seen, it was uniformly held that
if the transfer was real and actually conveyed to the
assignee or grantee all the title and interest of the assignor or grantor in the thing assigned or granted, it
was a matter of no importance that the assignee or
grantee could sue in the Courts of the United States when
his assignor or grantor could not, except, of course, in
that very large class of cases in which the statute provided that the assignee could not sue unless the original
party to the contract could have done so.

"But it was equally well settled that if the transfer
was fictitious, the assignor or grantor continuing to
be the real party in interest, and the plaintiff on
record but a nominal or colorable party, his name
being used only for purposes of jurisdiction, the suit
would be essentially a controversy between the assignor or grantor and the defendant, notwithstanding
the formal assignment or conveyance, and that the
jurisdiction of the court would be determined by their
citizenship rather than that of the nominal plaintiff."

Under the Act of 1789, it early became the law that if
jurisdiction was shown on the face of the plaintiff's pleading, the defendant could attack the truth of the jurisdictional allegations only by a plea in abatement, and
that such plea, in accordance with the general rule governing pleas of that character, must be filed before the
filing of a plea to the merits. The Act of 1875 largely
extended the jurisdiction of the United States Courts
over a class of cases in which it was exceedingly easy to
make colorable transfers under such circumstances that
it would be difficult for the defendant to know the facts
sufficiently early to plead them in abatement. This provision of the statute as to collusive assignment was therefore incorporated in the Act. It was carried forward

into the Act of 1888, although the purpose and effect of the latter statute was to restrict the jurisdiction of the United States Courts. The Supreme Court said:—

> "it does not, any more than did the Act of 1789, prevent the courts from taking jurisdiction of suits by an assignee when the assignment is not fictitious, and actually conveys all the interest of the assignor in the thing assigned, so that the suit when begun involves really and substantially a dispute or controversy in favor of the assignee for himself and on his account against the defendant; but it does in positive language provide that, if the assignment is collusive and for the purpose of enabling the assignee to sue in the courts of the United States for the benefit of the assignor, when the assignor himself could not bring the action, the court shall not proceed in the case."[29]

335. Application of the Statutory Provision to Concrete Cases.

A citizen of Indiana brought suit in the United States Court against a Michigan township on certain negotiable bonds for $100 each, payable to bearer. He owned only three of them. Three more had been assigned to him for purposes of collection only by one Toban, whose citizenship was not disclosed. The rest of those sued on had been transferred to him for like purposes by certain citizens of Michigan. At that time the statute required that the amount in controversy should be upwards of $500. The Court gave judgment for the plaintiff for the amount due on the bonds belonging to him, and on those owned by Toban and for the defendant on the others. He carried the case to the Supreme Court. It was there held that the Court below should have dismissed the suit. It was true that the defendant had not appealed, but the

29. Farmington vs. Pillsbury, 114 U. S. 141; 29 L. Ed. 114; 5 Sup. Ct. 807.

plaintiff had, and the case was still before the Court. It had been brought contrary to the provisions of the Act; the judgment was reversed and the suit dismissed.[30]

In the case of Farmington vs. Pillsbury,[31] already referred to, certain citizens of Maine transferred overdue coupons, detached from the bonds of a Maine municipal corporation held by them, to a citizen of Massachusetts, who gave them a promissory note for $500. The face value of coupons was nearly $8,000. The promissory note was payable two years after date. He made an agreement with them that he would give them 50% of the net amount he could collect upon the coupons. Nearly two years before the suit was brought the highest Court of Maine had decided that the bonds were void. The Supreme Court held that under all the circumstances it was apparent that the transfer was purely collusive and only for the purpose of giving jurisdiction.

There was a case in which Sacramento County, California, was very much interested. It arose out of the fouling of one of the California rivers by the debris thrown into it by certain processes of hydraulic mining. For some reason the county preferred to have the case determined in the United States rather than in the State Courts. It accordingly arranged with an alien who owned land along the river to bring the suit in his name. It guaranteed that it would furnish the lawyers and pay all the expenses, and he promised not to compromise, settle or dismiss the case without its consent. The Supreme Court held that from the very beginning the suit was in reality the suit of the county with a party plaintiff collusively made for the purpose of creating a case cognizable by the Circuit Court of the United States. While, therefore, the dispute or controversy involved

30. Williams vs. Nottawa, 104 U. S. 209; 26 L. Ed. 719.
31. 114 U. S. 141; 29 L. Ed. 114; 5 Sup. Ct. 807.

was nominally between an alien and the defendants, citizens of California, it was really and substantially between one of the counties of California and citizens of that State, and was not properly within the jurisdiction of the Circuit Court.[32]

336. Plaintiff's Alignment of Parties Does Not Bind the Court.

In a chancery suit it is often possible properly to make a particular person either a plaintiff or a defendant. Ordinarily under the flexible rules governing the giving of equitable relief it may not make much difference whether a particular person appears on one side or upon the other. When the jurisdiction of a Federal Court on the ground of diversity of citizenship is involved, the alignment of the parties on the respective sides of the controversy may be of great moment, because, as we have seen, those Courts may not entertain the suit on such grounds unless every plaintiff is of diverse citizenship from any defendant.

A plaintiff who wishes to bring his suit in the Federal Court will have every motive so to arrange the parties that there shall not be citizens of the same State on opposite sides. His action in this matter is not now binding upon the Court. Prior to the passage of the Act of 1875 it was.[33]

Since then the Court will re-align the parties for itself, whenever justice requires it. A defendant who is really on the same side as the plaintiff will be put there, although the result is to defeat the jurisdiction.

32. Cashman vs. Amador & Sacramento Canal Co., 118 U. S. 58; 30 L. Ed. 72; 6 Sup. Ct. 926.

33. Removal Cases, 100 U. S. 457; 25 L. Ed. 493.

337. Suits by a Stockholder Against a Corporation and Others.

A Court of Equity has jurisdiction to prevent a threatened breach of trust in the misapplication or diversion of the funds of a corporation by illegal payments out of its capital or profits.[34]

A stockholder may under this doctrine wish to test in the United States Court the validity of some statute, which he thinks injurious to the corporation. He accordingly makes the corporation one of the defendants and joins on the same side all the officials and other parties who are citizens of that State.

Such, for example, was a bill filled by a citizen of New York, a stockholder in a California corporation, against that corporation, its directors and the City of Oakland. The complaint stated that the city claimed the right to have water furnished it free for all municipal purposes; that it had no such right, but the corporation and its directors had furnished water free, and, despite the protests of the stockholders, proposed to continue so to do.[35]

Another is a case in which an Alabama stockholder in an Illinois gas company filed a bill against the company and the City of Quincy, alleging that the City of Quincy owed the company large sums for gas and would not pay them, and the corporation, though urged by the stockholders, would not bring suit.[36]

338. How Collusion is Sought to Be Prevented in Suits by a Stockholder Against a Corporation and Others.

Cases frequently arise in which a stockholder plaintiff makes both the corporation and other parties residing in

34. Pollock vs. Farmers Loan & Trust Co., 157 U. S. 553; 39 L. Ed. 759; 15 Sup. Ct. 673.

35. Hawes vs. Oakland, 104 U. S. 450; 26 L. Ed. 827.

36. Quincy vs. Steel, 120 U. S. 241; 30 L. Ed. 624; 7 Sup. Ct. 520.

the same State as that from which the corporation has its charter, defendants, and in which the relief sought by the plaintiff would clearly benefit the corporation.[37]

A corporation will be held to be opposed to the plaintiff stockholder whenever the persons controlling it are in fact antagonistic to the relief for which he asks.[38]

A citizen of New York, a stockholder in a Massachusetts corporation, filed a bill against it, its directors, another corporation, and the City of Boston, alleging that the State Legislature and the City of Boston had attempted to repeal its charter and to grant its property to the other corporation; that its directors had refused to bring any action in the State Courts, and that he was remediless except in equity. The Supreme Court held that this bill presented "so strong a case of the total destruction of the corporate existence, and of the annihilation of all corporate powers" that "we think complainant as a stockholder comes within the rule laid down in" Hawes vs. Oakland, "which authorizes a shareholder to maintain a suit to prevent such a disaster, where the corporation peremptorily refuses to move in the matter."[39]

On the other hand, when the officers of the corporation are in fact in sympathy with the stockholder, the Federal Courts will re-align the parties so as to put the plaintiff and the corporation on the same side, and by so doing will usually oust their jurisdiction.

339. Equity Rule 27.

In Hawes vs. Oakland (*supra*), certain rules to prevent collusive suits of this character were laid down. They are

37. Pittsburgh, C. & St. L. Ry. Co. vs. Baltimore & O. R. Co., 61 Fed. 705; 10 C. C. A. 20.

38. Street's Federal Equity Practice, sec. 562.

39. Greenwood vs. Fruit Co., 105 U. S. 16; 26 L. Ed. 961.

now substantially embodied in Equity Rule 27, which provides that every bill brought by a stockholder in a corporation against the corporation and other parties, founded on rights which may properly be asserted by the corporation, must be verified by oath and must contain an allegation that the plaintiff was a shareholder at the time of the transaction of which he complains, or that his shares had devolved on him since by operation of law, and that the suit is not a collusive one to confer on a Court of the United States jurisdiction of a case of which it would not otherwise have cognizance. The bill must also set forth with particularity the efforts of the plaintiff to secure such action as he desires on the part of the managing directors or trustees, and if necessary, of the shareholders, and the causes of his failure to obtain such action, or the reasons for not making such effort. Most of the requirements of this rule speak for themselves.

A corporation has some controversy with the municipality in which it is doing business. All the stockholders are citizens of the same State, or if there are any who reside elsewhere they are not willing to bring suit. It is highly inexpedient that it shall be in the power of some resident of another State to buy a few shares of stock in the corporation for the very purpose of promoting litigation.

340. Removal to Federal Courts Cannot Be Prevented by False Alignment of Parties by State Court Plaintiff.

The plaintiff, instead of desiring to bring his case in a Federal Court, may wish to keep it out of that Court, and to defeat the right of removal thereto which may sometimes be exercised by a defendant. Under such circumstances he may in the State Court unite as a defendant one who is a citizen of the same State with himself.

A Kansas mortgagor wished to contest the validity of a mortgage previously made by him to a Missouri corporation. He had strong reasons to wish that the litigation should be carried on in the State and not in the Federal Courts. He accordingly made a new or second mortgage to another citizen of Kansas. The debt secured by this second mortgage was made payable in ten days. At the end of that time the second mortgagee filed in the State Court a bill to foreclose and for other relief against the mortgagor and the first mortgagee. The relief asked against the latter was a declaration of the invalidity of its mortgage.

It will be perceived that as the holder of the second mortgage was the plaintiff and the mortgagor was a defendant, there was a citizen of Kansas on each side of the record. The first mortgagee sought to remove the case to the Federal Court. The Circuit Court of Appeals for the Eighth Circuit held that the cause was removable. In the real controversy the mortgagor and the second mortgagee were on one and the same side, the first mortgagee on the other.[40]

341. How and When Objection to Jurisdiction Should be Taken.

The Court is not entitled to dismiss the suit merely upon suspicion, even though it be strong enough to make the judge feel that the case does not properly belong in the United States Court. The discretion he is called upon to exercise is a judicial one. It must be founded upon evidence, the sufficiency of which may be reviewed upon appeal or writ of error.[41]

The question may be suggested by the Court at any time during the course of the proceedings, but it must be

---

40. Boatmen's Bank vs. Fritzlen, 135 Fed. 650; 68 C. C. A. 288.
41. Barry vs. Edmunds, 116 U. S. 560; 29 L. Ed. 729; 6 Sup. Ct. 501.

raised in some distinct way, so that the parties shall have opportunity to present evidence concerning it.[42]   If one of the parties seeks to raise the issue, he must do so by some appropriate pleading.[43]   The general issue will not suffice.   A subject of Holland, in the United States Court, sued one whom he described as a citizen of Illinois, and the latter pleaded the general issue and limitations.   During the progress of the case, the defendant, testifying on his own behalf, said he was a citizen of Great Britain. The verdict was for the plaintiff, and before judgment was entered, the defendant moved to dismiss the case on the ground that as both parties were aliens, there was no jurisdiction.   The Supreme Court said that neither party has the right, however, without pleading to the jurisdiction at the proper time and in the proper way, to introduce evidence, the only purpose of which is to make out a case for dismissal.   The evidence raised "must be pertinent either to the issue made by the parties, or to the inquiry instituted by the Court."[44]

342. Necessary Allegations in Suits by Assignees.

In suits in the Federal Court by an assignee upon a chose in action, it is necessary that the declaration or complaint shall set forth, on its face, such facts as will show affirmatively that the Court would have had jurisdiction of the suit had no assignment been made.[45]

42. Hartog vs. Memory, 116 U. S. 591; 29 L. Ed. 725; 6 Sup. Ct. 521.
43. Hartog vs. Memory, supra.
44. Hartog vs. Memory, supra.
45. Turner vs. Bank of North America, 4 Dallas, 8; 1 L. Ed. 718.

CHAPTER XIII.

REMOVAL OF CASES FROM STATE TO FEDERAL COURTS.

343. Introductory.

The jurisdiction given to the District Courts by section 24 of the Judicial Code is for the greater part not exclusive, but is concurrent with the Courts of the States;[1]

1. Chap. VI, supra.

that is to say, the plaintiff has the option of bringing his suit either in a State or in a Federal Court.

344. Why Removal is Permitted.

A defendant may be as much exposed to the dangers of local prejudice as a plaintiff. He may be as much interested in setting up the Federal view of some right claimed under the Constitution and laws of the United States. If he is compelled to remain in the Court into which the plaintiff brought him, he has no such choice between the State and the Federal tribunals as was exercised by his adversary. If opportunity is afforded him of removing to a Court of the United States, cases in which Federal questions are involved, or in which diversity of citizenship exists, he will stand on an equal footing with his opponent.

In some cases removal statutes give him this option; in others, in which it would seem to be as necessary to the protection of his interests, it is withheld, either because of the manifest intent of the lawmakers or because of the somewhat narrow construction the Courts have put upon the language of the statutes.

There are sound reasons for carefully restricting the jurisdiction which may be exercised by the Federal Courts over litigation between individuals. It is to be regretted that many of the limitations imposed are of so arbitrary a character. This is especially true with reference to those which hedge about the right of removal from State to Federal tribunals.

Whether a case is or is not removable, often depends upon incidental or accidental circumstances having little discoverable bearing upon anything of real moment.

345. Rules Regulating Removals—Ordinarily No Suit Can Be Removed Unless it Could Have Been Brought Originally in the District Court.

The statutory provisions governing removals of cases from State to Federal Courts will be found in sections 28 to 39, both inclusive, of the Judicial Code. Section 28 provides that "any suit of a civil nature, at law or in equity, arising under the Constitution or laws of the United States, or treaties made, or which shall be made, under their authority, of which the District Courts of the United States are given original jurisdiction by this title * * * brought in any State Court, may be removed by the defendant or defendants therein to the District Court of the United States for the proper district."

Under this provision no suit can be removed unless it might have been brought in the District Court in the first instance.

346. Right of Removal Because Federal Question Involved—Existence of Such Question Must Be Shown By Plaintiff's Statement of His Own Case.

Where jurisdiction is based on the existence of a Federal question the right of removal does not in anywise depend on diversity of citizenship. Such a suit may be brought in the District Court, although all the parties to it are citizens of the same State. The District Court has no jurisdiction on the ground that there is a Federal question involved, unless the plaintiff's statement of his own case raises it.[2] It is not sufficient for him to allege what the defendant's defense will be. The Courts have held that it follows that where the plaintiff's declaration or bill does not disclose the existence of a Federal question, the defendant cannot remove, however much his defense may in fact turn upon it.

2. Sec. 203, supra.

20

The State of Tennessee, in one of its Chancery Courts, sued the Union & Planters Bank for taxes. The bank said that by an irrepealable contract, the State had exempted it from taxation, and alleged that the statutes by which taxes were imposed upon it, impaired the obligation of this contract and were null and void. The sole issue in the case was this Federal question, but as the State's bill was founded entirely upon its own laws, the Supreme Court held that the defendant could not remove the case to the United States Court.[3]

There is one exception to this rule. A corporation created by the United States when made a defendant in a State Court, may, if the Federal incorporation is not stated in the plaintiff's pleading, set up the fact in its petition and demand a removal.[4]

To say, as does the statute, that a suit which could originally be brought may be removed, is easy—far easier, perhaps, than it would be in any other way, to describe cases which Congress is willing to have removed from the State to the Federal Courts. Nevertheless, such simple form of statement has its disadvantages. It makes irremovable cases which it is impossible to distinguish for any practical reason from some of those which are removable. For example, if a plaintiff may bring his case into the Federal Court because it rests upon a claim of right under the Constitution, laws or treaties of the United States, why should not a defendant, who bases his defenses on rights given him by the same enactments, be equally entitled to have that case tried out in the Federal Court? There is no answer except that Congress has not allowed him to do so.

3. Tennessee vs. Union Planters' Bank, 152 U. S. 454; 38 L. Ed. 511; 14 Sup. Ct. 654.

4. Texas & Pacific R. R. Co. vs. Cody, 166 U. S. 606; 41 L. Ed. 1132; 17 Sup. Ct. 703.

347. Cases Which Are Not Removable Although They Involve a Federal Question—Under the Employer's Liability Act.

There are cases which, though they involve a Federal question and may be brought in the District Court, cannot, if originally instituted in a State Court, be removed to a Federal.

The District Courts have concurrent jurisdiction with the Courts of the States over suits brought by railroad employees against a railroad company engaged in interstate commerce for injuries received by them while employed in such commerce. Congress has expressly declared that when such suit has been instituted in any State Court of competent jurisdiction it may not be removed into the Federal Court.[5]

It makes no difference that the right of removal would exist independently of the nature of the case—as, for example, that the plaintiff and the defendant are citizens of different States. If it arises under the Employer's Liability Act and is first brought in a State Court it cannot be removed at all.[6]

Section 33 of the Merchant Marine Act,[7] gives to a seaman suffering personal injury in the course of his employment, the right, at his election, to maintain an action for damages at law, with the right of trial by jury, and in such action, all statutes of the United States modifying or extending the common law right or remedy in cases of personal injury to railway employees, shall apply; and the same right is given to his representatives in case of his death, as the result of such injuries. It is further provided that in such action, all statutes of the

---

5. Proviso at end of sec. 28, Judicial Code; 5 Fed. Stat. Ann. 17; U. S. Comp. Stat., sec. 1010.

6. Stafford vs. Norfolk & Western Ry. Co., 202 Fed. 605.

7. 41 Stat. 1007; 1920 Supp. Fed. Stat. Ann. 227.

United States conferring or regulating the right of action for death in the case of railway employees, shall be applicable. It has been held that the statutes so made applicable do not include those prohibiting removal,[8] a decision which finds at least some support in the fact as already noted that a different venue provision is made with reference to actions brought under the Merchants Marine Statute from those which govern the bringing of actions under the Employers' Liability Act.[9]

348. Do.—Against Common Carriers to Recover Damages for Delay, Loss of, or Injury to, Property Unless Upwards of $3,000 in Controversy.

Another statute provides that suits brought in State Courts against common carriers to recover damages for delay, loss of, or injury to, property received for transportation by such common carriers under various Acts to regulate commerce, shall not be removable into the United States Court, unless the matter in controversy exceeds, exclusive of interest and costs, the sum or value of $3,000.[10]

349. Do.—Suits Against Receivers Appointed by Federal Courts.

A suit by or against a receiver appointed by a Federal Court is ancillary to the administration of the estate in his hands. It may for reasons stated in the next chapter be brought in the Court whose officer he is, no matter what the citizenship of the parties, the nature of the issues or the amount in controversy may be.[11]

8. Wenzler vs. Robin Line S. S. Co., 277 Fed. 812.

9. Secs. 290-291, supra.

10. Act of Jan. 20, 1914; 5 Fed. Stat. Ann. 16; U. S. Comp. Stat, sec. 1010.

11. Betts vs. Fisher, 213 Fed. 581; 130 C. C. A. 161.

Apart from statute, a receiver may not be sued without the consent of the Court which appointed him. Prior to the Act of March 3, 1887,[12] as amended by that of August 3, 1888,[13] the Federal Courts rigidly enforced this rule. Some hardships resulted. The Courts of the United States were from time to time called upon to appoint receivers for large corporations, some of which operated great railway systems, extending into many States. Usually the receivers continued the business of the insolvent concern. Their employees negligently injured others. Disputes arose as to the meaning or as to the performance of some of the countless agreements they made in the course of their daily operations. Many persons who had, or who thought they had, causes of action against them, greatly disliked being forced to seek, in a relatively distant Federal Court, recovery of what was often a trifling sum. Congress, accordingly, in the third section of the Act mentioned, declared that every receiver or manager of any property appointed by any Court of the United States may be sued, in respect of any act or transaction of his in carrying on the business connected with such property, without the previous leave of the Court in which he is appointed.

Unless the receiver is himself individually negligent, an action against him is not personal, and does not affect any property other than that of the estate in his hands. It follows that no suit can be brought against him after his receivership is at an end.[14]

In some of the cases decided shortly after the passage of these Acts, language was used which intimated that a suit against a Federal receiver was a suit arising under

12. 24 Stat. 552; 5 Fed. Stat. Ann. 17; U. S. Comp. Stat., sec. 1010.
13. 25 Stat. 433; 5 Fed. Stat. Ann. 17; U. S. Comp. Stat., sec. 1010.
14. Gray vs. Grand Trunk Western Ry. Co., 156 Fed. 736; 84 C. C. A. 392.

the laws of the United States, and as such removable into the Federal Courts whenever a sufficient amount was in controversy. Subsequent cases, however, have said that such statements were inadvertent and unsound.[15] It follows that if a suit be brought against such a receiver in a State Court and his authority as receiver or the validity of his appointment as such is not drawn in question, the case is not one arising under the laws of the United States and cannot therefore be removed by the defendant on that ground to the Federal Courts, although it might have been brought originally in those Courts had the plaintiff so wished. In Matarazzo vs. Hustis,[16] Judge Ray held that by the Act of August 23, 1916,[17] which amended section 33 of the Judicial Code, by giving the right of removal to any officer of the Courts of the United States, for or on account of any act done under color of his office, or in the performance of his duties as such officer, suits in State Courts against receivers as such had again been made removable. His suggestion that the act was passed because of conflicting decisions as to suits against receivers and their removability, however, has no support in the report of the committee upon whose recommendation the act was passed.[18] There is however, no statutory prohibition of the removal of such suits when there is a sufficient amount in controversy and some other Federal question is involved, or diversity of citizenship exists.

15. Gablemann vs. Peoria, etc. Ry. Co., 179 U. S. 335; 45 L. Ed. 220; 21 Sup. Ct. 171.

16. 256 Fed. 882.

17. 39 Stat. 532; Fed. Stat. Ann. 1918 Supp. 401; U. S. Comp. Stat., sec. 1015.

18. House of Representatives Reports, No. 776, First Session, 64th Congress, Volume 3.

350. Practice Where Removal is Sought of Suits Brought in Equity Under the State Practice Although in 1789 Relief Would Have Had to be Sought at Law.

In many States, a creditor who has not reduced his claim to judgment may file a bill to vacate as fraudulent his debtor's conveyance of property. It had been well settled law that when such a suit was instituted in a State Court, it could not be removed into a Federal Court, because the latter, as a Court of Equity, could not entertain it.[19] Very possibly, this may still be the law, in spite of the new equity rules and of the statute permitting the transfer of a case from the law to the equity side of the Federal Court, or vice versa, because in the Courts of the United States, under the circumstances supposed, there must first be an action at law tried to a jury, if either party wishes, and not until afterwards may the suit in equity be disposed of, and it is by no means certain that there is as yet any machinery by which all this can be done in one case. Of course when the cause is brought over into the Federal Court, it might be divided into two, one in equity, and the other at law, but the trouble is that until there is a judgment in the law case in favor of the plaintiff, equity has no jurisdiction to entertain his bill. There are cases, however, in which this objection would not apply and when one of them is removed to the Federal Court, there is no reason why it should not be divided into two.[20]

Still more clearly, where adequate relief can be had at law, the fact that in accordance with State practice, an equity suit has been instituted in the State Court will not preclude its removal to the Federal Court. There the case will simply be transferred to the law

19. Cates vs. Allen, 149 U. S. 451; 37 L. Ed. 804; 13 Sup. Ct. 883.
20. Hatcher vs. Hendrie & Bolthoff Mfg. & Supply Co., 133 Fed. 267; 68 C. C. A. 19.

side of the Court, with such amendments to the plead
ings as may be necessary.[21]

351. Removal on the Ground of Diversity of Citizenship.

Section 28 provides that any suit, other than one
arising under the Constitution, laws or treaties of the
United States of which the District Courts of the United
States are given jurisdiction, and which is first brought
in a State Court, may be removed into the District
Court of the United States for the proper district by
the defendant or defendants, being non-residents of the
State.

A defendant who is sued in his own State Court by a
resident of another State has no right under the present
statutes to remove his case into the Federal Court. It
is true that there is a controversy between citizens of
different States, the determination of which is within
the constitutional grant of judicial power to the United
States, but this is one of the many grants of which Congress does not at present see fit to avail itself. Under
ordinary circumstances, there is no reason why it
should. A resident of a particular State ought not to
fear that its Courts will be prejudiced against him in
favor of some one who lives elsewhere.

352. Do.—When Suit Brought and Removal Sought.

A defendant is not entitled to have a case removed
on the ground that there is diversity of citizenship between him and the plaintiff unless such diversity existed
both at the time the suit was brought and at the time
the removal was asked for.[22]

21. City of Knoxville vs. Southern Paving & Con. Co., 220 Fed. 236.
22. Stevens vs. Nichols; 130 U. S. 230; 32 L. Ed. 914; 9 Sup. Ct. 518.

353. Do.—Owner of Property Sought to be Condemned is Treated as Defendant.

In some States when a condemnation proceeding is carried into Court the owner of the property sought to be condemned is treated as the plaintiff. This practice does not make him such within the meaning and purpose of the Removal Acts. As the condemnation proceedings have been instituted against him, the Federal Courts will treat him as the defendant. As such, he may remove the case, if he be a non-resident and the amount in controversy be sufficient.[23]

354. Right of Removal in Cases Between Citizens and Aliens—An Alien Defendant May Remove His Case Whether the Plaintiff Be or Be Not a Resident of the District.

It has been contended that an alien, individual or corporate, who is sued in a State Court by a plaintiff who does not reside in the Federal district in which the suit is brought, may not remove the case to the United States Court, but that contention has been held unfounded.[24]

355. Do.—May a Defendant Who is Sued By An Alien in a State Court of a District of Which Such Defendant is a Non-Resident Remove His Case?

On general principles, there would seem to be no reason why a defendant who is sued by an alien in a State Court of a district in which he does not live, should not have the right to remove his case to the Federal Court. The removal is by the citizen, for whose pro-

23. Mason City & Fort Dodge R. R. Co. vs. Boynton, 204 U. S. 570; 51 L. Ed. 629; 27 Sup. Ct. 321.

24. Wind River Lumber Co. vs. Frankfort Ins. Co., 196 Fed. 340; 116 C. C. A. 160.

tection, venue provisions exist, and he has thereby waived any claim to rely upon them, and the plaintiff never had any,[25] but there are cases to the contrary.[26]

356. Right of Removal of Cases Involving Separable Controversies.

The general purpose of the removal statutes, as has already been pointed out, is to put the defendant on an equal footing with the plaintiff as to the choice of Courts. This result is, by no means, as·fully attained in practice now as it was before the Acts of 1887 and 1888. Nevertheless, that is the theory which underlies all the provisions for removals. We have already seen that a plaintiff, if he wishes to bring his suit in the Federal Court, may avoid ousting the jurisdiction of the Court by refusing to join as defendants those who, under the ordinary equity rule, would be necessary parties, but who, from the standpoint of absolute justice, are not strictly indispensable.

357. Do.—Under Act of July 27, 1866.

While from a relatively early period it was recognized that the plaintiff might do so, it was not until the Act of July 27, 1866,[27] that a corresponding privilege was given to the defendant. Before that time, a suit could be removed only in the event that every party plaintiff to it, as originally brought, was ·a citizen of a different State from any of the defendants. By that act it was provided that if the suit, so far as it relates to a defendant who is a citizen of a State other than that in which it is brought, is such that there can be a final deter-

---

25. In Re Red Cross Line, 277 Fed. 853; Guarantee Trust Co. of New York vs. McCabe, 250 Fed. 703; 163 C. C. A. 31.

26. Sagara vs. Chicago, R. I. & P. Ry. Co., 189 Fed. 220.

27. 14 Stat. 306; 5 Fed. Stat. Ann. 387; U. S. Comp. Stat., sec. 1018.

mination of the controversy, so far as it concerns him, without the presence of the other defendants as parties in the cause, he should have the right to remove. It was held that under the act what was removed to the Federal Court was only such part of the dispute as concerned the particular defendant who had applied for the removal.

After its amendment the Supreme Court said:—

"Much confusion and embarrassment, as well as increase in the cost of litigation, had been found to result from the provision in the former Act permitting the separation of controversies arising in a suit, removing some to the Federal court, and leaving others in the State court for determination. It was often convenient to embrace in one suit all the controversies which were so far connected by their circumstances as to make all who sue, or are sued, proper, though not indispensable, parties. Rather than split up such a suit between courts of different jurisdictions, Congress determined that the removal of the separable controversy to which the judicial power of the United States was, by the Constitution, expressly extended, should operate to transfer the whole suit to the Federal Court.'"[28]

358. Do.—Under Act of March 3, 1875.

The determination alluded to by the Supreme Court was evidenced by the Act of 1875, which contained the language now found in section 28 of the Judicial Code.

359. Do.—Whole Case Now Removed.

The Act of 1875 came before the Supreme Court in the case of Barney vs. Latham, already cited. That suit had been brought in a State Court of Minnesota by plaintiffs who were citizens respectively of Minnesota and Indiana. There were in all ten defendants. Nine of

28. Barney vs. Latham, 103 U. S. 205; 26 L. Ed. 514.

them were individual citizens of different States other than Minnesota or Indiana. The tenth was a Minnesota corporation. The individual defendants sought to remove the case to the United States Court. The removal was made and a petition to remand was denied. The Supreme Court held that there was a controversy which could be decided between the individual plaintiffs and the individual defendants, and that therefore the latter had the right to remove the case, but the effect of such removal was to carry over the entire cause, including such part of the controversy as concerned the Minnesota corporation only.[29]

360. Do.—Right of Removal Restricted by Construction.

The Federal Courts have by construction, restricted rather than enlarged the classes of cases in which the right of removal can be exercised on the ground that there is a separable controversy. Since the passage of the Act of 1887, they have steadily sought to limit rather than to extend their jurisdiction. The separable controversy must be one which is wholly between citizens of different States. If an alien is a party the case is not removable.[30]

361. Do.—What Controversies Are Separable.

The Supreme Court has said "a separate and distinct cause of action, on which a separate and distinct suit might properly have been brought and complete relief afforded as to such cause of action, with all the parties on one side of that controversy citizens of different States from those on the other," is a separable controversy and nothing else is. "To say the least, the

---

29. Connell vs. Smiley, 156 U. S. 336; 39 L. Ed. 443; 15 Sup. Ct. 353.

30. King vs. Cornell, 106 U. S. 395; 27 L. Ed. 60; 1 Sup. Ct. 312; Creagh vs. Equitable Life Assur. Soc., 88 Fed. 1.

case must be one capable of separation into parts, so that, in one of the parts, a controversy will be presented with citizens of one or more States on one side and citizens of other States on the other, which can be fully determined without the presence of any of the other parties to the suit as it has been begun.''[31]

An example of a case held to include a separable controversy was where stockholders of a corporation brought suit against it and its directors and also against another corporation to which it had conveyed its property. The bill sought to set aside the conveyance as *ultra vires* and as in fraud of complainant's rights and to compel the directors to respond in damages. It was held that the latter were not necessary parties to the relief sought against the corporations. The controversy as to them was separable. They had a right to remove.[32]

362. Do.—Existence of Separable Controversy Must Be Shown By Plaintiff's Statement of His Own Case.

A controversy is not separable unless it appears so to be from the plaintiff's own allegations. The rule here is the same as it is with reference to the existence of a Federal question.[33] It has one necessary qualification. As the plaintiff in bringing an action in a State Court is not required to allege the citizenship of either himself or the defendant, and usually does not do so, the fact of diverse citizenship may be set up by the defendant in his petition for removal. In all other respects, however, the rule is strictly enforced.

31. Fraser vs. Jennison, 106 U. S. 191; 27 L. Ed. 131; 1 Sup. Ct. 171.
32. Geer vs. Mathieson Alkali Works, 190 U. S. 428; 47 L. Ed. 1122; 23 Sup. Ct. 807.
33. Ayres vs. Wiswall, 112 U. S. 187; 28 L. Ed. 693; 5 Sup. Ct. 90.

363. Right of Removal Because of Prejudice or Local Influence.

Section 28 of the Judicial Code makes provision for removal under still other conditions. It declares that

"where a suit is now pending, or may hereafter be brought, in any State court, in which there is a controversy between a citizen of the State in which the suit is brought and a citizen of another State, any defendant, being such citizen of another State, may remove such suit into the District Court of the United States for the proper district, at any time before the trial thereof, when it shall be made to appear to said District Court that from prejudice or local influence he will not be able to obtain justice in such State court, or in any other State court to which the said defendant may, under the laws of the State, have the right, on account of such prejudice or local influence, to remove said cause."

364. Do.—A Case Which Could Not Have Been Brought in a Federal Court May Not Be Removed Thereto on the Ground of Prejudice and Local Influence.

It has been held[34] that a case may be removed on the ground of prejudice or local influence, although it was a case which could not have been brought originally in the United States Court, as, for example, where citizens of the same State were on opposite sides of the controversy. This view, however, has been definitely determined to be unsound. The Supreme Court has said that the clause of the statute permitting removal on the ground of prejudice and local influence does not furnish a separate and independent ground of Federal jurisdiction, but describes only a special case comprised in the preceding clauses.[35]

34. Boatmen's Bank vs. Fritzlen, 135 Fed. 650; 68 C. C. A. 274.

35. Cochran vs. Montgomery County, 199 U. S. 260; 50 L. Ed. 182; 26 Sup. Ct. 58.

365. Right of Removal of Cases Between Parties Claiming Lands Under Grants of Different States.

Provision is made by section 30 of the Judicial Code for the removal of cases in which plaintiff and defendants though both citizens of the same State, are claiming lands under grants of different States. Such a case may doubtless still sometimes arise, but not very often.

366. Right of Removal Because of Denial of Equal Civil Rights.

Section 31 of the Judicial Code provides for the removal of any civil suit or criminal prosecution commenced in a State Court against any person who is denied or cannot enforce in the judicial tribunals of the State, or in the part of the State where such suit or prosecution is pending, any right secured to him by any law providing for the equal civil rights of citizens of the United States or of all persons within the jurisdiction of the United States.

This provision of law has been held constitutional.

In West Virginia in the early seventies all colored men were by law ineligible for jury service. A negro was there indicted for murder. It was held that he was entitled to have his case removed to the United States Court for trial.[36]

The section is applicable only to cases in which such right is denied by the Constitution or laws of the State and not to cases where the denial results from the action of officers of the State, not authorized by the latter's Constitution or statutes.

The whole subject has been very thoroughly reviewed by the Supreme Court of the United States.[37]

36. Strauder vs. West Virginia, 100 U. S. 303; 25 L. Ed. 664.
37. Kentucky vs. Powers, 201 U. S. 1; 50 L. Ed. 633; 26 Sup. Ct. 387.

367. Right of Removal of Suits or Prosecutions Against Certain Classes of Persons in the Service of the United States.

Section 33 of the Judicial Code as amended[38] provides:

"That when any civil suit or criminal prosecution is commenced in any court of a State against any officer appointed under or acting by authority of any revenue law of the United States, now or hereafter enacted, or against any person acting under or by authority of any such officer, on account of any act done under color of his office or of any such law, or on account of any right, title or authority claimed by such officer or other person under any such law, or is commenced against any person holding property or estate by title derived from any such officer and affects the validity of any such revenue law, or against any officer of the courts of the United States, for or on account of any act done under color of his office, or in the performance of his duties as such officer, or when any civil suit or criminal prosecution is commenced against any person for or on account of anything done by him while an officer of either House of Congress in the discharge of his official duty in executing any order of such House, the said suit or prosecution may at any time before the trial or final hearing thereof be removed for trial to the District Court next to be holden in the district where the same is pending, upon the petition of such defendant to said District Court."

By section 28 of the so-called Volstead Act,[39] all officers of the United States charged with the enforcement of its criminal laws, are apparently given the right to claim the protection of the above provision, whenever they are attacked in the State Courts for any-

38. 39 Stat. 532; 5 Fed. Stat. Ann. 380; U. S. Comp. Stat., sec. 1015.
39. 41 Stat. 316; 1919 Supp. Fed. Stat. Ann. 215.

thing done in enforcing the national prohibition law.[40]
Years ago it was held by some judges at least that the
postal statutes were revenue laws and that postal officials might avail themselves of the same removal privileges.[41] Some of the provisions of the present section
33 of the Judicial Code have been in force ever since
they were enacted in 1833, as part of section 3[42] of the
Force Bill which was Andrew Jackson's reply to South
Carolina's threatened nullification of the Tariff Act of
1828,[43] known to heated partisans of that day as the
"Tariff of Abominations." This third section was in
its turn modeled upon the eighth section of the still
earlier statute[44] passed in view of the intense hostility
in some portions of the country, particularly in sections
of New England, to the War of 1812. It was avowedly
a temporary measure, to expire with the War, which
unknown to Congress, had come to an end before, in
February, 1815, it had received Presidential approval,
and for that reason, it appears never to have been
availed of. The immediate occasion for the Force Bill
itself speedily passed away, but the right to remove
civil suits against collectors of customs was at once
found convenient to everybody concerned, and was
habitually exercised.[45] Thirty years, however, elapsed,
so far as the reports disclose, before any one attempted
to remove a criminal prosecution from a State to the
Federal tribunal, and that was under a Civil War
statute, since repealed.[46] A little later, some liquor
sellers, prosecuted for violations of State laws, unsuc-

40. State of Oregon vs. Wood, 268 Fed. 975.
41. Warren vs. Fowler, 29 Fed. Cases, 255.
42. 4 Stat. 632; 5 Fed. Stat. Ann. 387; U. S. Comp. Stat., sec. 1018.
43. 4 Stat. 270.
44. 3 Stat. 198.
45. Elliott vs. Swartwout, 10 Peters, 138; 9 L. Ed. 373.
46. Pennsylvania vs. Artman, 19 Fed. Cas. 10,952.

21

cessfully sought a removal to the Federal Courts.[47] During the war and the reconstruction period, a number of acts,[48] now expired or repealed, gave a right of removal to officials charged with war duties, or with the enforcement of reconstruction or election legislation. In 1875, Congress empowered its own officers to remove cases brought against them in the State Courts for anything done by them under the orders of either House.[49] In 1916, the protection was extended to officials of the Federal Courts when sued or prosecuted for something done by them in the discharge of their official duties,[50] and in 1920, the same privilege was given to officers engaged in enforcing the prohibition act.[51]

For more than a century, Congress has felt that it must open to officials charged with the duty of enforcing unpopular Federal legislation, a door of escape from what may possibly be hostile State Courts.

368. Criminal Cases, as Well as Civil, May Be Constitutionally Removed.

When during the reconstruction era, Federal officials first sought to remove criminal cases against them, their constitutional right to do so was vigorously, but unavailingly assailed.[52] When one accused of crime says that he did what is charged against him, in performance of a duty imposed upon him by a Federal statute, there arises a controversy under the laws of the United States.

47. Commonwealth vs. Casey, 12 Allen, 214; State vs. Elder, 54 Maine, 381.

48. 12 Stat. 756; 5 Fed. Stat. Ann. 377; U. S. Comp. Stat., sec. 1013; 14 Stat. 27; 5 Fed. Stat. Ann. 377; U. S. Comp. Stat., sec. 1013; 16 Stat. 144; 5 Fed. Stat. Ann. 377; U. S. Comp. Stat., sec. 1013.

49. 18 Stat. 401; 5 Fed. Stat. Ann. 38; U. S. Comp. Stat. Sec. 1015.

50. 39 Stat. 532; 5 Fed. Stat. Ann. 380; U. S. Comp. Stat., sec. 1015.

51. 41 Stat. 316; 1919 Supp. Fed. Stat. Ann. 215.

52. Tinley vs. Satterfield, 9 Fed Cas. 67; Tennessee vs. Davis, 100 U. S. 257; 25 L. Ed. 648.

That it happens to be a criminal prosecution, does not prevent the judicial power of the Federal Government extending to it. Nor is it material that Congress may not have prescribed any penalty for the offense charged. The prosecution is by the State—not by the United States. The latter merely supplies the tribunal to pass upon the controversy precisely as it does when it disposes of those civil cases arising under State statutes, but over which the diverse citizenship of the parties gives it jurisdiction.

369. May a Federal Officer, Who Denies that He Did What Is Charged Against Him, Remove His Case?

If a Federal official, prosecuted in a State Court, never did what is charged against him by the State, he logically did not do it under color of official duty, and many years ago Judge Gresham held that under such circumstances, he might not remove.[53] That ruling would seem to smack overmuch of formal logic and to give little weight to practical considerations of compelling force; whether the accused officer did or did not commit the act with which he is charged, is the very issue upon which local hostility to the Federal enactments, it was his duty to enforce, might prove most irreparably prejudicial to him, and Judge Ervin in 1918 expressly declined to follow the earlier case.[54]

370. Amount in Controversy and Character of State Court Not Material to Right of Removal of Civil Suits Under Section 33.

A defendant otherwise entitled to the benefits of section 33 may remove a civil suit against him irrespective of the amount in controversy or the character of the

---

53. State of Ill. vs. Fletcher, 22 Fed. 776.
54. State of Alabama vs. Peak, 252 Fed. 306.

State Court in which he has been sued. Thus a revenue officer sued before a Vermont Justice of the Peace for the return of a seized horse worth less than Ten Dollars was held entitled to remove, it appearing that in such cases, the magistrate's decision was under the State practice, final.[55]

371. Removal Can Be Had to the District Court of that District Only in Which the State Court Suit is Pending.

Section 28 of the Judicial Code says that the removal shall be to the District Court of the proper district. It has been contended that when neither the plaintiff nor the defendant are citizens of that district, the suit may be removed to the district of the residence of one or the other on the ground that they are the only proper districts, and several cases have so held.[56] Thé first and the last of them were decided by Judge Ray in the Northern District of New York, and the second was largely, if not altogether, based upon the first. Judge Ray has himself conceded that he was wrong and that a removal, if it can be made at all, can be made only to the District Court of the district in which the State suit was brought.[57] An illustration of the extremes to which the contrary doctrine might lead was presented where a citizen of Wyoming sued a Maryland corporation in a Montana State Court. The defendant sought to remove the case to the United States District Court for the District of Maryland. The State Court refused to order the removal. Defendant then filed a transcript

55. Wood vs. Matthews, 30 Fed. Cases, 17,955.

56. Mattison vs. B. & M. R. R., 205 Fed. 821; Stewart vs. Cybur Lumber Co., 211 Fed. 343; Park Square Automobile Station vs. American Locomotive Co., 222 Fed. 979.

57. Matarazzo vs. Hustis, 256 Fed. 882.

of the record in the United States District Court for Maryland. The latter held that it had no jurisdiction, pointing out that section 29 of the Judicial Code, which tells how the right of removal given by section 28 shall be exercised, specifically says that the petition shall ask for the removal of the suit into the District Court to be held in the district where such suit is pending; and calling attention to the fact that such provision had been embodied in all the Federal statutes from the original Judiciary Act to the Judicial Code.[58]

Judge Rellstab, in a much more thorough examination of the question, has reached the same conclusion,[59] and I think there is no question that his view is now accepted as the settled law.

372. Removal to a District in Which There Is More than One Division.

If the case is removed from the State Court of a county to the United States District Court of a district in which there is more than one division, it must go to the Court of the division in which such county is.[60]

373. The Right to Remove a Case Cannot Be Given by Consent.

A case may be removed only when the Federal statute so provides. It can never be removed merely because both parties are willing that it shall be.[61]

374. The Right to Remove May Be Waived.

On the other hand, as it is a mere right of the parties, and under the present statute, a right confined to the

58. St. John vs. U. S. F. & G. Co., 213 Fed. 685.

59. Ostrom vs. Edison, 244 Fed. 228.

60. Section 53 J. C. 5 Fed. Stat. Ann. 520; U. S. Comp. Stat., sec. 1035.

61. Parker vs. Ormsby, 141 U. S. 81; 35 L. Ed. 654; 11 Sup. Ct. 912.

defendant, he can exercise it or not as he sees fit. He may so act as to show that he has elected not to do so. This election he will conclusively evidence by not making his motion to remove within the time limited by law. It is easy to conceive of many other ways in which even before the expiration of the time in which, if at all, he must exercise this right, he may so act as to estop himself from so doing, upon the theory that what he has done shows that he has agreed not to avail himself of it.

375. Right to Remove Not Waived By Contesting Case in State Court After Latter Has Refused Permission to Remove.

No such presumption can arise where the defendant has done all in his power to remove the case and has been held in the State Court against his will.

An Ohio administratrix sued an insurance company of New York in the Court of Common Pleas of Hamilton County, Ohio. The Insurance Company took the proper proceedings to remove the case to the United States Circuit Court for the Southern District of that State. The State Court refused to permit the removal. The Supreme Court held the subsequent proceedings of the Common Pleas Court to be a clear case of usurped jurisdiction, and that the defendant was not estopped by having defended itself in the State Court as best it could, after permission to remove had been refused.[62]

In a subsequent case the Supreme Court said, in answer to the objection that the defendant had gone on with his case after the State Court had refused to permit it to be removed and had thereby waived his right to remove.

"Indeed, it is difficult to see what more he could have done than he did to get out of court and take

62. Insurance Co. vs. Dunn, 19 Wall. 214; 22 L. Ed. 68.

his suit with him. He remained simply because he was forced to remain, and is certainly now in a condition to have the original error of which he complained corrected in any court having jurisdiction for that purpose.''[63]

376. Right to Remove Waived By Asking Affirmative Relief From State Court After Latter Has Refused Permission to Remove.

A defendant who has tried to remove his case and has been refused permission to do so, may, if the final judgment or decree be against him, sue out a writ of error from the Supreme Court and there assert that, as the denial of his petition to remove was erroneous, the subsequent proceedings are not binding upon him. He may, however, by his conduct estop himself from contesting the jurisdiction of the State Court. He will do so if, after his case has been wrongfully retained, he asks for affirmative relief, as, for example, if he should bring a third party into the litigation.[63a]

377. Defendant Cannot Waive in Advance His Right to Remove All Cases.

While a defendant can in a particular case so act as to waive his right of removal, he cannot in advance make any agreement by which he waives this right generally. The question as to the power to do so has most frequently arisen in connection with attempted removals by non-resident corporations of suits against them.

378. State Law Requiring Corporations to Agree Not to Remove Into Federal Courts Invalid.

There has always been a desire on the part of many of the States to prevent corporations of other States or

63. Removal Cases, 100 U. S. 475; 25 L. Ed. 593.

63a. Texas & Pacific Ry. Co. vs. Eastin & Knox, 214 U. S. 153; 53 L. Ed. 946; 29 Sup. Ct. 564.

countries, doing business within them, from taking their litigation into the Courts of the United States. The efforts of the States to attain this end have often come before the Supreme Court.

It was settled nearly a half century ago that any statute which requires a non-resident corporation as a condition of doing business in the State to agree that it will not remove any case into the Federal Court is invalid. Such a consent to forego its constitutional rights may not be exacted of a corporation whether it is or is not engaged in interstate commerce.[63b]

One of the cases already cited was that of an insurance company, which was not conducting commerce between the States; the other of a railroad, which was.

379. A State May Not Revoke a License to do Business of a Nonresident Corporation Because it Removes a Case Into the Federal Courts.

There were, however, cases which held that as a State had a right to refuse to permit a corporation of another State or of a foreign country to do business within its borders for any reason which seemed good to it, and under most circumstances, at its pleasure to withdraw permission once granted, it might, after such a corporation had removed its case into the Federal Court, prevent it from doing business within its borders.[64]

In course of time it was made clear that this right did not exist with reference to corporations engaged in interstate commerce[65] and finally the Supreme Court has

63b. Insurance Co. vs. Morse, 20 Wall. 445; 22 L. Ed. 365; Barron vs. Burnside, 121 U. S. 186; 30 L. Ed. 915; 7 Sup. Ct. 931.

64. Doyle vs. Continental Insurance Co., 94 U. S. 535; 24 L. Ed. 148; Security Mutual Life Ins. Co. vs. Prewitt, 202 U. S. 246; 50 L. Ed. 1013; 26 Sup. Ct. 619.

65. Harrison vs. St. Louis & San Francisco R. R. Co., 232 U. S. 318; 58 L. Ed. 621; 34 Sup. Ct. 333.

unequivocably declared that a State may not, in imposing conditions upon a foreign corporation's doing business in a State, exact from it a waiver of the exercise of its constitutional right to resort to the Federal Courts, or thereafter withdraw the privilege of doing business because of its exercise of such right, whether waived in advance or not.[66] This principle, it is declared, protects as well corporations which are not engaged in interstate commerce as those which are, and Doyle vs. Continental Insurance Company and Security Mutual vs. Prewitt, are expressly overruled.

380. State Laws Prohibiting the Removal of Certain Classes of Suits Invalid.

Sometimes the States have attempted to provide that certain kinds of actions, or actions in which certain classes of corporations are defendants, shall be brought in a particular Court only. Thus—

The State of Nevada authorized Lincoln County to issue bonds and provided that litigation concerning them should be carried on in a particular State Court and not elsewhere. A holder of the bonds brought suit against the county in the Circuit Court of the United States for the District of Nevada, and the Supreme Court held that he had the right to do so. The power to contract with citizens of other States implies liability to suit by them, and no statutory limitation of that liability imposed by a State, can defeat a jurisdiction given by the Constitution.[67]

In Iowa the Probate Court had exclusive jurisdiction to determine the validity of claims against the estate of a deceased person. The proceeding involved a judicial

66. Terral vs. Burke Construction Co., decided February 27, 1922.

67. Lincoln County vs. Luning, 133 U. S. 529; 33 L. Ed. 766; 10 Sup. Ct. 363.

determination as to the liability of the estate for the amount of the claim, with parties before the Court to contest all questions of law and fact. It was clearly a suit within the meaning of the Removal Acts. A claimant had a case removed from the Probate Court to the Circuit Court of the United States. The Supreme Court said:—

"The removal in this case was, therefore, proper, unless it be competent for a State, by legislative enactment conferring upon its own courts exclusive jurisdiction of all proceedings or suits involving the settlement and distribution of the estates of deceased persons, to exclude the jurisdiction of the courts of the United States even in cases where the constitutional requirement as to citizenship is met. But this court has decided, upon full consideration, that no such result can be constitutionally effected by State legislation."[68]

381. Right of Removal as Affected by Venue Provisions.

The provision that a defendant may not be sued except in a particular district or districts is a personal privilege given him which he may waive, and he does waive it by entering a general appearance.[69]

A defendant who seeks to remove a case from a State to a Federal Court of a district in which he could not have been sued without his consent, waives the objection to the jurisdiction of the latter Court. If the plaintiff takes any other action in the United States Court than to move to remand, he, also, waives his right to object to its jurisdiction. Both of them are thereafter estopped to question the propriety of the District Court's proceeding with the case.[70]

68. Clark vs. Bever, 139 U. S. 102; 35 L. Ed. 88; 11 Sup. Ct. 468.

69. Western Loan & Savings Co. vs. Butte & Boston Consolidated Mining Co., 210 U. S. 368; 52 L. Ed. 1101; 28 Sup. Ct. 720.

70. In re Moore, 209 U. S. 490; 52 L. Ed. 904; 28 Sup. Ct. 585.

382. Can a Plaintiff Suing in the Courts of a State of Which Neither He Nor the Defendant is a Citizen, Prevent Removal to Federal Court?

The plaintiff may bring suit against the defendant in the Courts of a State, in the Federal Court of which he could not have sued the defendant against defendant's objection, either because the defendant is not a resident of that district, in cases in which such residence is the test, or because neither the plaintiff nor the defendant are residents of it, in those cases in which the residence of either would give the Federal Court jurisdiction in the original suit. May the defendant remove the case to the United States Court for the district? A number of judges have held that he may; that the limitation as to the district in which suit may be brought is for the protection of the defendant, and operates upon the plaintiff alone; that when the defendant sued in a State Court in a district in which he was not subject to suit in the Federal Court, seeks to remove his case to the latter, he has waived his objection, and plaintiff has no right to make any; and that the very language of section 51 of the Judicial Code relied on by those who hold to the contrary view—"That no civil suit shall be brought in any District Court against any person by any *original* process or proceeding in any other district than that whereof he is inhabitant, but where the jurisdiction is founded only on the fact that the action is between citizens of different States, suit shall be brought only in the district of the residence of the plaintiff or defendant" shows that the framers of it did not intend that it should apply to removed cases. One of the best and latest expositions of this point of view is by Judge Ervin in the Southern District of Alabama.[71] The great majority of the cases, however, hold that such suits are not remov-

---

71. Hohenberger & Co. vs. Mobile Liners, 245 Fed. 169.

able either where the sole ground of jurisdiction is diversity of State citizenship, and the suit is brought by a plaintiff in a district of which neither he nor the defendant is a resident,[72] or in which the jurisdiction depends upon the fact that the case arises under the laws of the United States, and the suit is brought in a district in which the defendant does not live.[73]

That the question has remained a disputable one so long is largely due to the fact that section 28 of the Judicial Code denies an appeal from a decision of a District Court remanding a removed case to a State Court. An attempt to evade this provision by seeking a mandamus from the Supreme Court to compel the judge of the District Court to retain jurisdiction failed.[74] A case in which a remand has been denied may get to the Supreme Court and doubtless sometime will.

383. Right of Removal as Affected by Assignment Provisions.

Prior to 1887 the provision that an assignee of a chose in action could not sue in the Federal Court unless the original contracting party to whose rights he had succeeded could have there sued, had no application to cases originally brought in a State Court and which the defendant sought to remove to the Federal. Such cases were not within the mischief against which the assignment provision was directed. It was the defendant who exercised the right of removal. He, of course, had nothing to do with any collusive transfer of the contract to the person who was seeking to hold him liable. It might be that the assignment had actually been made for the

72. Coalmont Monshannon Coal Co. vs. Matthew Addy S. & C. Corp., 271 Fed. 114.

73. Orr vs. B. & O. R. R., 242 Fed. 608.

74. Ex parte in the Matter of Matthew Addy S. & C. Corp., 256 U. S. 417; 65 L. Ed. 299; 41 Sup. Ct. 317-321.

purpose of putting the claim in the name of one who would have local bias in his favor. Whether it had been or not, the defendant would be quite as likely to suffer from State or sectional prejudice as he would, had the contract originally been made with the assignee.

All the earlier decisions distinctly recognized that if "A," a citizen of New York, contracted with "B," a citizen of the same State, and "A" assigned his rights to "C," a citizen of Pennsylvania, and "C" sued "B" in the Courts of Pennsylvania, "B" could remove the case to the Circuit Court of the United States for that district of Pennsylvania in which the suit was brought. But the Act of 1888 laid down a new rule. It provided that no case could be removed unless it was a case which originally could have been brought in the Court of the United States to which removal was sought. It is clear that "C" could not have sued "B" in the Federal Court. It follows that such a case cannot now be removed.

A Colorado corporation had certain claims of large amount against another Colorado corporation. It assigned those claims to a citizen of New York, who brought suit against the defendant corporation in one of the State Courts of New York. The defendant sought to remove the case into the United States Circuit Court for the Eastern District of New York. It was held that it could not do so.[75]

384. Actual Plaintiff May Prevent Removal by Making Fictitious Assignment.

A plaintiff may so arrange matters as to make it impossible for a defendant to remove a case. Two Iowa corporations had claims against a citizen of New York. They transferred those claims to another citizen of New

75. Mexican Nat'l R. R. Co. vs. Davidson, 157 U. S. 201; 39 L. Ed. 672; 15 Sup. Ct. 563.

York under an agreement by which he was to exercise reasonable diligence to enforce them, and after deducting all costs and expenses incurred in so doing he was to hold the amounts collected in trust for the use and benefit of the parties owning the same. He brought suit in an Iowa State Court. The defendant attempted, under an earlier statute, to remove the case into the United States Court, alleging that the plaintiff was only a nominal party and had no interest therein whatever, but was prosecuting the suit for the sole and exclusive use and benefit of the Iowa corporations, which employed counsel to prosecute it and were directing and controlling it. The Supreme Court said:—

"It may, perhaps, be a good defense to an action in a State court, to show that a colorable assignment has been made to deprive the United States Court of jurisdiction; but * * * it would be a defense to the action, and not a ground of removing that cause into the Federal Court."[76]

385. How Plaintiff May Prevent Removal by Joining as a Defendant a Resident of the State.

A much more common way, however, of preventing the removal of a case from the State to the Federal Courts is for the plaintiff to join in one action the non-resident defendant with others who are residents. This has become not unusual in negligence cases. Where, for example, some one has suffered an injury upon a railroad operated by a non-resident corporation, the plaintiff may bring suit against the railroad, uniting as defendants some of its employees who happen to be citizens of the State.

A woman was killed by a train of the Alabama Great Southern Railway, an Alabama corporation. Her ad-

76. Oakley vs. Goodnow, 118 U. S. 43; 30 L. Ed. 61; 6 Sup. Ct. 944.

ministrator, a citizen of Tennessee, brought suit in a Court of the latter State against the Railway Company and against two citizens of Tennessee, respectively, the conductor and engineer of the train. In his complaint he charged that the accident was the result of the joint negligence of all the defendants. The Railway Company attempted to remove the case to the United States Court. The Supreme Court held that the right to remove depended upon the case alleged by the complaint. It said: "The fact that by answer the defendant may show that the liability is several cannot change the character of the case made by the plaintiff in his pleading so as to affect the right of removal." The Court added:—

> "It is to be remembered that we are not now dealing with joinders, which are shown by the petition for removal, or otherwise, to be attempts to sue in the State courts with a view to defeat Federal jurisdiction. In such cases entirely different questions arise, and the Federal courts may and should take such action as will defeat attempts to wrongfully deprive parties entitled to sue in the Federal courts of the protection of their rights in those tribunals." * * * "In good faith, so far as appears in the record, the plaintiff sought the determination of his rights in the State court by the filing of a declaration in which he alleged a joint cause of action. Does this become a separable controversy within the meaning of the act of Congress because the plaintiff has misconceived his cause of action and had no right to prosecute the defendants jointly?"

The Court thought not.[77]

Whether the declaration makes out a case of joint liability of the defendants, is a matter of State law, and the Federal Courts will not attempt to go behind the

77. Alabama Great Southern Ry. Co. vs. Thompson, 200 U. S. 206; 50 L. Ed. 441; 26 Sup. Ct. 161.

decision of the highest Court of the State before whom
the question would come.[78] If by that test the cause of
action is a joint one, so that the plaintiff may, in good
faith, believe that he has a joint claim, it makes no difference that the resident may be pecuniarily irrespon-
sible, and that the plaintiff's only reason for joining him
is to preclude removal to the United States Court. If
the plaintiff has a right to sue the resident jointly with
the non-resident, his motive for doing so may not be
inquired into.[79]

386. Defendant May Show Joinder of Resident to Be Fraudulent.

If the defendant proves that the joinder is fraudulently made for the purpose of defeating removal, he can
remove.

The plaintiff attempted to prevent a removal by joining as co-defendants with the principal defendant one of
the latter's employees, a citizen of plaintiff's State. Defendant filed its petition for removal and submitted affidavits tending to show that the employee sued had no
possible connection with the matter and had been joined
for the mere purpose of preventing a removal. The
State Court ordered the removal. In the Federal Court
the plaintiff moved to remand and filed counter affidavits. The Court reached the conclusion that the
joinder was fraudulent and denied the motion. The
Supreme Court affirmed the ruling below.[80]

It is necessary in such cases that the defendant in the

78. Chicago, R. I. & Pacific R. R. Co. vs. Schwyhart, 227 U. S. 193; 57
L. Ed. 473; 33 Sup. Ct. 250.

79. Chicago, R. I. & Pacific R. R. Co. vs. Schwyhart, supra.

80. Wecker vs. National Enameling & Stamping Co., 204 U. S. 176;
51 L. Ed. 430; 27 Sup. Ct. 184.

petition for removal shall allege facts which, if true, will show the joinder to have been fraudulent.[81]

387. Filing of Petition for Removal Does Not Waive Objection to Jurisdiction of State Court.

Very frequently a non-resident defendant wishes to claim that he has never been properly served with process in the State Court. He prefers to have the Federal Court determine whether he has or has not. It has been contended that when he comes into the State Court and files his petition for removal he waives the objection that he has not been properly summoned. It is, however, clearly settled that no such waiver is thereby made. He can, and frequently does, successfully assert in the Federal Court his claim that the State Court never secured any jurisdiction over him.[82]

388. How a Case May Be Removed.

Section 29 of the Judicial Code specifies what a defendant, who wishes to remove one of the more ordinary kind of removable cases, on grounds other than for prejudice or local influence, shall do. He must prepare a duly verified petition setting forth facts which entitle him to remove and praying the State Court to direct the removal. This petition should contain all the necessary jurisdictional averments. If any of them are omitted, but are to be found in the previous record of the case, the omission may not necessarily be fatal. To omit any of them is, however, to run unnecessary risk. He must make and execute a bond with a sufficient surety that he will cause a certified copy of the record to be

81. C. & O. Ry. Co. vs. Cockrell, 232 U. S. 146; 58 L. Ed. 544; 34 Sup. Ct. 278.

82. Wabash Western Ry. Co. vs. Brow, 164 U. S. 271; 41 L. Ed. 431; 17 Sup. Ct. 126.

entered in the United States District Court within thirty days, and that he will pay all costs if the District Court shall hold that the removal was improperly made.

389. Defendant Must Give Plaintiff Written Notice of Intent to Present Removal Petition and Bond.

The Judicial Code for the first time required that a defendant, intending to ask for removal, must give prior written notice to the adverse party or parties that he intends to present the petition for removal and a removal bond to the State Court. The statute says nothing else on the subject. The requirement is however so far mandatory that its omission, if not waived by the plaintiff, requires a remand.[83] It can be waived, and a substantial compliance with it is all that appears to be necessary. Thus the presentation of the petition and bond to the State Court, in the presence of plaintiff's counsel, who accepted service of a rule to show cause why the case should not be removed[84] and the delivery to plaintiff's counsel of a copy of the petition in advance of its presentation,[85] were held sufficient. The purpose of the requirement appears to be principally, if not solely, to let the plaintiff know that the defendant is about to remove, and it is not necessary that it shall advise him when the petition will be presented or to which judge, if there be more than one qualified to pass upon it.[86]

390. For Prejudice or Local Influence.

The application to remove a case on the ground of prejudice or local influence is made not to the State

---

83. Arthur vs. Md. Casualty Co., 216 Fed. 386.
84. Lewis vs. Erie R. Co., 257 Fed. 868.
85. Chase vs. Ehrhardt, 198 Fed. 365.
86. Potter vs. General Baking Co., 213 Fed. 697.

Court, but to the District Court of the United States. The affidavits in its support, should set forth the facts which tend to show the existence of prejudice or local influence to such an extent as to make it probable that the defendant seeking to remove will not be able to obtain justice in the State Court or in any other State Court to which he would have the right to remove the case. The plaintiff may appear in the District Court and file rebutting affidavits or the Court may hear oral testimony in support of the petition and in opposition thereto. If the United States Court decides that the allegations of the petition have been sustained, it orders its clerk to certify to the State Court the order of removal, together with copies of the petition, bond and affidavit. The State Court is thereby advised of the action of the Federal Court and of its order of removal. It is the duty of the former to proceed no further with the suit and to direct its clerk to make a full and complete transcript of the record and certify the same to the United States Court for trial.[87]

391. Except Where There Is a Separable Controversy or Prejudice or Local Influence, All Defendants Must Join in the Petition for Removal.

All the substantial defendants must join in the petition for removal[88] unless there is a separable controversy or prejudice or local influence is alleged,[89] or the case is one in which citizens of the same State claim land under grants from different States. Purely nominal or formal parties need not.[90] Parties who are sued,

87. Southern Railway Co. vs. Allison, 190 U. S. 326; 47 L. Ed. 1078; 23 Sup. Ct. 713.

88. Wilson vs. Oswego Township, 151 U. S. 63; 38 L. Ed. 70; 14 Sup. Ct. 259.

89. J. C. Section 30; 5 Fed. Stat. Ann. 375; U. S. Comp. Stat., sec. 1012.

90. Bacon vs. Rives, 106 U. S. 99; 27 L. Ed. 69; 1 Sup. Ct. 3.

but who are not served with process are not defendants
in the action. It suffices if all who are summoned join in
the application.[91]

392. A Single Defendant May Remove on Ground of Prejudice or Local Influence.

In order to remove on the ground of prejudice or local
influence, the defendant seeking such removal must be a
non-resident of the State in whose Courts the suit has
been brought. On the other hand, he may remove upon
this ground without his co-defendants uniting in the
petition for removal, and although there may be no
separable controversy. The proviso following this portion of the section makes this clear. It says: "Provided, that if it further appear that said suit can be
fully and justly determined as to the other defendants
in the State Court, without being affected by such prejudice or local influence, and that no party to the suit will
be prejudiced by a separation of the parties, said District Court may direct the suit to be remanded, so far
as relates to such other defendants, to the State Court."
That is to say, a single non-resident defendant against
whom prejudice or local influence operates, has the right
to remove the case, whether it contains a separable controversy or not. When it gets over into the United
States Court, if it then be made to appear that there is
a separable controversy and that one or more of those
separable controversies may be remanded to the State
Court for separate trial without danger of injustice, such
order will be made.

393. In Cases of Removal Because of Denial of Civil Rights.

In cases where removal is sought under the provisions
of Section 31 of the Judicial Code, the petition for re-

91. Bowles vs. Heinz Co., 188 Fed. 937.

moval should be filed in the State Court and need not be accompanied by a bond.

394. In Cases Removable Because They Are Against Persons Acting Under Certain Federal Laws.

Petitions for removal by officers of the United States entitled to remove, must be filed in the United States and not in the State Court. The petition must set forth the nature of the suit or prosecution. It must be verified by affidavit, and be supported by a certificate of an attorney or counsellor of some court of record of the State in which the case is pending, or of the United States, stating that he has, as counsel for the petitioner, examined into the proceedings and carefully inquired as to all matters set forth in the petition, and that he believes them to be true.

The petition is presented to the Court, if it be in session, and if not, to the clerk at his office. All bail and other security given in the State Court continue in full force. If the case has been commenced by process other than that directing the arrest of the defendant, the clerk of the United States Court issues a writ of certiorari to the State Court requiring it to send to the United States Court the record and proceedings. When a personal arrest has been ordered, the clerk of the United States Court issues a writ of *habeas corpus cum causa,* a duplicate of which is to be delivered to the State Court clerk or left at his office by the marshal. If the defendant is in actual custody on *mesne* process, the marshal, under the writ, takes him into his custody to be dealt with according to law and the order of the District Court, or in its vacation, of any judge thereof. A criminal case cannot be removed until a prosecution has been instituted. That is to say, under ordinary circumstances, not until an indictment has been found or

an information exhibited.[92]   Doubtless in cases in which
the defendant may be punished without his ever having
been either indicted or in a technical sense informed
against, as when a justice of the peace has jurisdiction
to hear and determine finally, the general rule will not
apply, and the defendant may remove so soon as the
proceedings against him have been instituted.

395. State Court Must in First Instance Decide Whether Upon the Record the Case is Removable.

The State Court, where the application for removal
is made to it, must of necessity before passing the order,
determine whether upon the face of the record the case
is removable, assuming the verity of all defendant's
assertions of fact.   If it concludes that it clearly is not,
the order for removal should be refused and the case
proceeded with.[93]   The defendant may, however, procure a transcript of the record and file it in the Federal
Court.   In this way he can secure a decision of the latter
on the question of removability.   If such decision is in
the affirmative he may have further proceedings in the
State Court enjoined.   It is therefore expedient that the
latter direct a removal unless it is clear either that the
case is one, the removal of which is not authorized by
law, or that the defendant has failed in some material
respect to do all that the law requires to entitle him to
remove.

Nor can a plaintiff, no matter how well he may be
satisfied of the defect in the defendant's petition for
removal, safely ignore the filing by the latter of the
transcript of the record in the United States Court, for
that Court has jurisdiction to decide whether the case

92. Virginia vs. Paul, 148 U. S. 107; 37 L. Ed. 386; 13 Sup. Ct. 536.
93. Madisonville Trac. Co. vs. St. Bernard Mining Co., 196 U. S. 239; 49
L. Ed. 462; 25 Sup. Ct. 251.

is properly before it, and if it holds that it is, and he does not move to remand, and does not appeal from a judgment against him, he will be bound in spite of the fact that the failure to remand is clearly wrong.[94]

396. State Court Need Not Permit a Removal on Defective Petition.

If the petition is defective, the State Court may permit it to be amended,[95] but will doubtless be justified in refusing to order the removal of the case, if leave to amend is not sought, even although it may think it possible that by amendment the shortcoming could be supplied.

397. When and How Far the Petition for Removal is Amendable.

It was once doubted whether the District Court could permit the amendment of a petition for removal. Such a petition alleged that the "plaintiff is a citizen of Missouri and the defendants are citizens of the State of New York." No question was made by any of the parties either in the Court below or in the Supreme Court as to the propriety of a removal. The latter of its own motion, nevertheless, held that as the petition for removal did not allege the citizenship of the parties except at the date when it was filed, and as it was not shown elsewhere in the record that the defendants were, at the commencement of the action, citizens of a State other than the one of which the plaintiff was at that date a citizen, the Circuit Court had no jurisdiction. The Supreme Court refused to pass upon the merits of the appeal, and reversed the judgment and remanded

94. C. & O. R. R. Co. vs. McCabe, 213 U. S. 207; 53 L. Ed. 765; 29 Sup. Ct. 430.
95. Roberts vs. Pacific & A. Ry. & Nav. Co., 104 Fed. 577.

the case to the Circuit Court with directions to send it back to the State Court.[96]

The history of a subsequent case was as follows:— On August 24, 1899, plaintiff commenced suit in the District Court of Salt Lake County, Utah. On September 2, 1899, the defendant filed a petition and bond for removal to the Circuit Court of the United States for the District of Utah. That petition alleged "that the controversy in said suit is between citizens of different States, and that your petitioner, the defendant in the above entitled suit, was at the time of the commencement of the suit and still is a resident and citizen of the City of Denver, in the State of Colorado." On December 30, 1899, the plaintiffs moved to remand on the ground that the diverse citizenship of the parties at the time of the commencement of the suit and at the time of its removal from the jurisdiction of the State Court did not appear upon the record. On January 2, 1900, the defendant gave notice of a motion to amend its petition for removal by adding this allegation:—"That the plaintiffs, and each of them, were, at the time of the commencement of this suit, and still are, citizens and residents of the City of Salt Lake and State of Utah." The Supreme Court held that the amendment could be made, it having been offered before any action had been had in the Federal Court on the merits of the case. Upon the actual facts the appellee was entitled to remove, as nothing to prejudice the rights of the plaintiff had been done before the petition for removal was perfected.[97]

Congress has since removed all obstacles in the way of amendments required to show the existence of the

96. Stevens vs. Nichols, 130 U. S. 230; 32 L. Ed. 914; 9 Sup. Ct. 518.

97. Kinney vs. Columbia Svgs. & Loan Asso., 191 U. S. 78; 48 L. Ed. 103; 24 Sup. Ct. 30.

necessary diversity of citizenship, at the time the suit was brought or removed. Where the facts justify it, such amendments may be made even in an Appellate Court.[98]

398. Determination of All Disputed Questions of Fact as to the Right to Remove is with the Federal Court.

The State Court is bound to accept as true the averments of fact contained in the petition for removal. If the plaintiff would dispute them, he must do so in the Federal and not in the State Court.[99]

399. Defendant May Remove Without Consent of State Court.

A defendant, who has been improperly denied the removal for which he has asked, need not await a judgment or decree against him. He may file a transcript of the record in the proper United States District Court and may then ask it to enjoin further proceedings in the State tribunal.

Section 39 of the Judicial Code makes elaborate provision to insure that a defendant who is entitled to remove his case shall not be prevented from so doing. The clerk of a State Court who will not, upon tender of proper fees, make out a transcript of the record, commits an offense against the United States, and upon conviction may be fined not more than $1,000 or imprisoned not more than a year, or both. The District Court to which the case is removable is empowered to issue a writ of *certiorari* to the State Court commanding the latter to make a return of the record.

By section 35, if the clerk refuses or neglects, upon

98. Sec. 274c, Judicial Code; March 3, 1915, 38 Stat. 956; 5 Fed. Stat. Ann. 1061; U. S. Comp. Stat., sec. 1251.

99. C. & O. Ry. Co. vs. Cochrell, 232 U. S. 146; 58 L. Ed. 544; 34 Sup Ct. 278.

payment or tender of the legal fees, to furnish the transcript, the United States District Court may direct such record to be supplied by affidavit or otherwise, as the circumstances of the case may require and allow.

In suits or prosecutions under section 33, if no copy of the record and proceedings in the State Court can be obtained, the District Court may allow and require the plaintiff to proceed anew, and upon failure to do so, judgment of *non pros* with costs may be entered against him.

400. When Removal Becomes Effective.

Upon the filing of a petition for removal, after proper notice and in due form accompanied by the required bond, the State Court ceases to have any jurisdiction over the controversy beyond that of entering a formal order that it has been removed, and although such order be never entered, its power to do anything further in the case is at an end. The jurisdiction of the Federal Court attaches from the filing of the transcript of the record therein, and it must determine whether the removal should have been made.[100] In those cases in which the petition for removal is in the first instance filed in the Federal Court, as it must be when removal is sought on the ground of local prejudice or influence, or under section 33, the jurisdiction of the State Court ceases so soon as the writ of certiorari or of habeas corpus *cum causa* has been served upon or filed in the State Court or with its clerk.[101]

401. Federal Court May Enjoin Plaintiff From Proceeding in State Court.

When a defendant has presented his petition for removal and the State Court has improperly refused it

100. C. & O. vs. McCabe, 213 U. S. 207; 53 L. Ed. 765; 29 Sup. Ct. 430.
101. Virginia vs. Paul, 148 U. S. 107; 37 L. Ed. 386; 13 Sup. Ct. 536.

and he has caused a transcript of the record to be filed
in the Federal Court, the latter will at his request enjoin the plaintiff from further prosecuting his action
in the former.[102]

402. When Petition for Removal Must Be Filed.

In all cases covered by section 28, except those in
which the removal is asked for on the ground of prejudice or local influence, the defendant must make and file
his petition for removal in the State Court at or before
he is required by the laws of the State or the rules of the
Court in which such suit is brought to answer or plead
to the declaration or complaint of the plaintiff.

403. Required to Answer or to Plead Means Earliest Time Defendant is Required to Make Any Kind of Plea or Answer.

Under the rules of practice prevailing in most of the
States, a defendant if he wishes to plead limitations or
in abatement must do so at a somewhat earlier period
than that at which he is required to plead to the merits.
A Maryland corporation was sued in a West Virginia
Court by a citizen of that State. If it had desired to
plead to the jurisdiction or in abatement it would have
had to do so at the April rule day. After that date, but
while it still might plead to the merits, it filed its petition
for removal. The Supreme Court held that under the
language of the statute the petition for removal must
be filed at or before the time the defendant is required
to make any defense whatever in the State Court, so
that if the case be removed, the validity of any or all
defenses may be tried and determined in the Federal

---

102. Madisonville Traction Co. vs. Saint Bernard Mining Co., 196 U. S.
239; 49 L. Ed. 462; 25 Sup. Ct. 251; Donovan vs. Wells Fargo & Co., 169
Fed. 363; 94 C. C. A. 609.

tribunal. It followed that the defendant's petition had not been filed in time.[103]

404. Time in Which Removal Must Be Sought Does Not Begin to Run Until Suit Becomes for the First Time Removable.

A plaintiff may in his declaration claim a sum not exceeding $3,000. He may bring his action against two defendants, only one of whom is a citizen of another State. He may not base his claim to recover upon any Federal right. Later, and after the time at which the defendant is required to plead, and after the non-resident defendant has in fact pleaded, plaintiff may amend by increasing his claim for damages to upwards of $3,000, by discontinuing as to the resident defendant, or by setting up a Federal right. If the declaration or bill had originally been framed in its amended form the non-resident defendant would have been entitled to remove the case to the Federal Court. As it was in fact first drawn, the case made was a non-removable one. Does the defendant lose his right to have the case sent to the Federal Court, because he did not ask to have it removed before the time at which he was required to plead to or answer the original declaration or complaint? If he does, a plaintiff has always at his command an easy way of preventing the possibility of removal. The Supreme Court, in accordance with obvious justice and common sense, has held that a defendant's petition for removal is filed in time if it be filed so soon as the cause assumes a removable form.[104]

It should be noted, however, that this result follows

103. Martin vs. B. & O. R. R. Co., 151 U. S. 684; 38 L. Ed. 311; 14 Sup. Ct. 533.

104. Powers vs. Chesapeake & Ohio R. Co., 169 U. S. 92; 42 L. Ed. 673; 18 Sup. Ct. 264.

only when the voluntary act of the plaintiff has made the case removable. It may not be removed when, over the objection of the plaintiff, the case has been dismissed against the resident defendant.[105]

405. When Petition to Remove on Ground of Prejudice or Local Influence Must Be Filed.

Section 29 says that the petition to remove on the ground of prejudice and local influence may be filed at any time before trial. The defendant therefore may ask for a removal on this ground at a later date than he could on some others. He must, however, make the application, as the statute directs, before trial, and that means before the first trial of the cause. He cannot apply for a removal after the case has been once tried, although the verdict and judgment has been set aside or even though the jury failed to arrive at a verdict at all.[106]

406. When Petition for Removal Must be Filed, Because of Denial of Civil Rights or Under Section 33 of the Judicial Code or Section 28 of the National Prohibition Act.

Petitions for removal under section 31 of the Judicial Code, because of the denial of civil rights, or by Federal officials under section 33 or under section 28 of the National Prohibition Act, may be filed at any time before the final hearing. These last words are the same as used in earlier removal acts. They were there held to refer to the final trial. It follows that if there has been a mistrial, the petition for removal, if filed before the new trial begins, will be filed in time.[107]

105. American Car Company vs. Kettlehake, 236 U. S. 311; 59 L. Ed. 594; 35 Sup. Ct. 355.

106. Fisk vs. Henarie, 142 U. S. 459; 35 L. Ed. 1080; 12 Sup. Ct. 207.

107. Ins. Co. vs. Dunn, 19 Wal. 214; 22 L. Ed. 68; B. & O. vs. Bates, 119 U. S. 467; 30 L. Ed. 436; 7 Sup. Ct. 285.

407. Right to Object that Petition for Removal is Not Made in Time May Be Waived.

It is, however, clearly settled that the "time for the filing of a petition for removal is not essential to the jurisdiction; the proviso is * * * but modal and formal, and a failure to comply with it may be the subject of waiver or estoppel."[108] The waiver may be express,[109] but it is much more frequently implied. Thus where a State Court ordered a removal upon a petition filed too late, and the plaintiff did not at once move the Federal Court to remand, but went on with the trial of the case, it was held that he had waived all right to set up that the removal had not been properly made.[110] In the case last cited, the Supreme Court said that the requirement as to the time in which the petition for removal shall be filed, is "more analogous to the direction that a civil suit * * * shall be brought in a certain district, a non-compliance with which is waived by a defendant who does not seasonably object that the suit is brought in the wrong district." It would appear, therefore, that a plaintiff who wishes to remand on the ground that the petition for removal was not filed in time, must ask for it before taking any other step in the Federal Court.

408. Does an Extension of Time to Plead, by Order of Court or Agreement of the Parties, Extend the Time in Which Removal May Be Asked For?

The lower Federal Courts are in irreconcilable conflict as to whether an extension of time to plead, either by order of the Court, or by agreement of the parties,

108. Powers vs. C. & O. Ry., 169 U. S. 398; 42 L. Ed. 793; 18 Sup. Ct. 396.

109. Bryan vs. Barriger, 251 Fed. 330.

110. Martin vs. B. & O. R. R., 151 U. S. 684; 38 L. Ed. 311; 14 Sup. Ct. 533.

correspondingly extends the time in which the defendant may ask for removal, and the Supreme Court has not yet had occasion to settle the controversy.

In the Circuit and District Courts, some of the earlier cases holding that the time was not extended, were decided before the Court of last resort held that the requirement as to the time for removal was not of the essence of jurisdiction, and their reasoning seems to have given to that provision of the statute greater rigidity than can now be attributed to it,[111] but others are of quite recent date.[112]

In the Second Circuit it has been long settled that the petition for removal is in time if filed before the expiration of any extension to plead given by special order of the Court, or by stipulation of the parties.[113]

All the reported decisions in the Fourth Circuit are to the same effect.[114]

In the Eighth Circuit,[115] the right to remove under such circumstances has been almost uniformly denied. A single decision in each of the Third,[116] Fifth[117] and Seventh[118] Circuits also so holds.

In the Ninth Circuit, all the earlier cases refuse to permit the removal, but in three districts, it is now

111. Ruby Canyon Mining Co. vs. Hunter, 60 Fed. 305.

112. Pilgrim vs. Aetna Life Ins. Co., 234 Fed. 958.

113. Mayer vs. Fort Worth & D. C. R. R. Co., 93 Fed. 601; Lord vs. Lehigh Valley R. R. Co., 104 Fed. 929; Russell vs. Harriman Land Co., 145 Fed. 745.

114. People's Bank vs. Aetna Insurance Co., 53 Fed. 161; Sandelin vs. People's Bank, 140 Fed. 191; Avent vs. Deep River Lumber Co., 174 Fed. 298.

115. Velie vs. Manufacturers' Ins. Indemnity Co., 40 Fed. 345; Spangler vs. Atchison, T. & S. F. R. Co., 42 Fed. 305; Ruby Canyon Mining Co. vs. Hunter, supra; Waverly Stone & Granite Co. vs. Waterloo, C. F. & N. Ry. Co., 239 Fed. 561.

116. Pilgrim vs. Aetna Life Ins. Company, supra.

117. Wayt vs. Standard Nitrogen Co., 189 Fed. 231.

118. Rock Island National Bank vs. Keator Lumber Co., 52 Fed. 897.

allowed.[119] In the district of Oregon[120] and in that of Idaho,[121] the removal is not permitted after the expiration of the earliest date at which the defendant is required to plead by the regular standing rules of Court.

All that can be said on either side of the question can be found in the opinions in some of the cases cited. Nothing can be added except perhaps an expression of the author's personal opinion that the Second Circuit's rule would seem to be more in harmony with the views of the Supreme Court, as expressed in Martin vs. B. & O. R. R.,[122] and Powers vs. C. & O. Ry.[123]

409. How Issues Arising Upon Motion to Remand Are Tried.

Motions to remand are often, perhaps are usually based upon matters apparent upon the face of the record, such for example, that the case does not involve any Federal question; that there is no separable controversy, although citizens of the same State are to be found on each side of the record and the like. Such issues of law are of course determined by the judge, but the plaintiff may object to the case remaining in the Federal Court on the ground that some jurisdictional allegation of the defendant is untrue in fact. If the cause be one in equity, the issue thus raised will like those arising in the course of the proceeding, be tried by the Court.[124]

All this is simple enough, but is either party entitled

119. Tevis vs. Palatine Ins. Co., 149 Fed. 560; State Imp.-Development Co. vs. Leininger, 226 Fed. 884; Chiatovich vs. Hanchett, 78 Fed. 193; Hansford vs. Stone-Ordean Wells Co., 201 Fed. 185.

120. Heller vs. Ilwaco Mill & Lumber Co., 178 Fed. 111.

121. Williams vs. Wilson Fruit Co., 222 Fed. 467.

122. 151 U. S. 674; 38 L. Ed. 311; 14 Sup. Ct. 533.

123. Powers vs. C. & O. Ry., 168 U. S. 398; 42 L. Ed. 515; 18 Sup. Ct. 87.

124. Morris vs. Gilmer, 129 U. S. 315; 32 L. Ed. 690; 9 Sup. Ct. 289.

to have the disputed question tried to a jury when the suit is at law, and the case has been removed on the ground of diversity of citizenship, and the plaintiff moves for remand because he says the defendant is in truth a citizen of the same State with him, or that the defendant, when the plaintiff is an alien, is himself not a citizen, although he says he is, or that the allegation that plaintiff fraudulently joined a citizen of plaintiff's State with the defendant seeking to remove is false, or where removal has been asked on the ground of prejudice or local influence and the plaintiff says that there is no such prejudice or local influence, or where a Federal officer removes a suit or prosecution against him on the ground that he is being attacked for something done in the course of his official duty, and the plaintiff claims that the act in question had no legal connection with such duty? The ordinary practice is unquestionably for the judge to pass upon the issue, upon affidavits or oral testimony or both. There can of course be no question of the right to do so if both sides assent, either expressly or tacitly, but there have been cases in which there have been jury trials.[125] In most such cases, though probably not in all, a jury trial will be inconvenient,[126] a circumstance which doubtless explains the rarity of the use of that method, but upon principle, it would be doubtless difficult to deny the right of either party to a jury trial of an issue of fact.

410. No Appeal from Order of District Court Remanding Case to State Court.

By section 28 of the Judicial Code, it is provided that if the District Court shall decide that a cause has been

125. Chicago & Northwestern Ry. Co. vs. Ohle, 117 U. S. 123; 29 L. Ed. 837; 6 Sup. Ct. 632.
126. State of Virginia vs. Feltz, 133 Fed. 90.

improperly removed into it from the State Court, and order the same to be remanded, such remand shall be immediately carried into execution and no appeal or writ of error from the remanding decision shall be allowed, nor will the Supreme Court entertain a petition for a writ of mandamus to compel the District Court to retain the case.[127]

127. Ex parte Matthew Addy S. & C. Corp., 256 U. S. 417; 65 L. Ed. 299; 41 Sup. Ct. 317-321.

CHAPTER XIV.

ANCILLARY JURISDICTION OF THE FEDERAL COURTS.

411. Ancillary Jurisdiction.

The principal heads of the original jurisdiction of the District Courts, whether exclusive or concurrent have been enumerated. Many of them have been discussed in some detail. Something has been said about the jurisdiction which may be acquired by removal of cases from State tribunals.

All the jurisdiction of the Federal Courts thus far discussed depends either upon the character of the parties or upon the kind of questions in controversy. They exercise, however, another jurisdiction, usually referred to as ancillary or dependent.

In spite of the terms of the statutes, and of all that has been said as to the limited jurisdiction of the United States Courts, there are cases in which they can properly decree the payment of a debt, perhaps of a few cents, due by a Maryland citizen to another citizen of that State.

412. What Ancillary Jurisdiction Means.

It has been suggested that the ancillary jurisdiction in the Federal Court is exercised in supplemental proceedings, (a) to protect from interference with, and to determine conflicting claims to assets, within its administrative control, and (b) to control and regulate suits brought before it and to restrain or enforce its judgments, or to further deal with the subject-matter thereof.[1]

413. Illustrations—Creditor's Bills.

For example, a corporation of one State, say Maryland, may be indebted in the sum of more than $3,000 to a citizen of another, for example, say New York. The Maryland corporation is insolvent. The citizen of New York, in the United States Court for the District of Maryland, may file a creditor's bill against it. He prays that receivers be appointed for its property, and that the latter shall be reduced to money and divided

1. Venner vs. Pennsylvania Steel Co., 250 Fed. 296.

among its creditors. The corporation appears, admits the allegations of the bill, and consents to the passage of the decree asked for. It has thus waived its right to insist that plaintiff must first secure a judgment at law.[2] Receivers are accordingly appointed. The Court, through them, takes possession of the corporate property. Ultimately all its assets are sold under an order of Court. Notice is given to all creditors to come in and file their claims. They do so, many of them being Maryland individuals, firms or corporations. Their claims may vary in amount from a dollar or two to many thousands. If any of them are disputed, the question as to whether they are or are not owing and what is their amount may and doubtless will be tried out by the Court sitting in equity. As to them there is no diversity of citizenship. No Federal question of any kind is involved. Many of the claims are for less than $3,000.

414. Ancillary Jurisdiction Dependent Upon the Possession of the Res.

Upon what did the jurisdiction of the Court to pass upon these claims and to allow them, rest? Briefly, upon the fact that it had in its possession the property of the defendant, and was required to dispose of that property in accordance with equity and good conscience. It is a well settled principle of law that so long as one Court has possession of property, no other Court of co-ordinate jurisdiction can exercise control over it. The Federal Courts have been unusually careful to observe this rule in their relations with the State Courts and to insist that the State Courts in turn shall observe it with respect to them. It makes very little difference whether

2. Hollins vs. Brierfield Coal & Iron Co., 150 U. S. 371; 37 L. Ed. 1113; 14 Sup. Ct. 127.

custody was rightfully or wrongfully taken; in any case the redress must be sought from the custodian Court itself or from such appellate tribunal as has the right to review its proceedings. It follows as an almost necessary consequence that those persons who cannot seek redress anywhere but in a particular Court, shall have the right there to demand it, no matter what their citizenship, or how small, from a pecuniary standpoint, their interest in the litigation.

415. Illustrative Cases—Freeman vs. Howe.

There have been some interesting applications of this doctrine.

A citizen of New Hampshire had a pecuniary claim against a Massachusetts corporation. He instituted suit in the United States Circuit Court for the District of Massachusetts, and, as was permitted under the State practice, took out an attachment. Under this attachment a large quantity of property belonging to the defendant corporation was seized by the marshal. It was subject to the lien of a mortgage given to certain citizens of Massachusetts as trustees for bondholders. These trustees sued out a writ of replevin in the State Court. The Supreme Judicial Court of Massachusetts held that the property was properly taken under the writ. On writ of error from the Supreme Court of the United States, this decision was reversed. The Court distinctly held that, although the writ of attachment authorized the marshal to seize nothing but property of the defendant corporation, yet, as he had actually seized this other property under the writ, it was in the custody of the United States Court.[3] The Supreme Court said the Massachusetts Court was in error in supposing that the plaintiffs in the replevin suit, being citizens of Massa-

---

3. Freeman vs. Howe, 24 How. 450; 16 L. Ed. 749.

chusetts, as was the marshal, were remediless in the Federal Courts. It pointed out that the "principle is, that a bill filed on the equity side of the court to restrain or regulate judgments or suits at law in the same court, and thereby preventing injustice, or an inequitable advantage under mesne or final process, is not an original suit, but ancillary and dependent, supplementary merely to the original suit, out of which it had arisen, and is maintained without reference to the citizenship or residence of the parties."

416. Buck vs. Colbath.

There are, of course, limitations upon this doctrine. In **Buck** vs. Colbath,[4] suit was brought by a citizen of Minnesota against another citizen of that State for trespass *d. b. a.* The defendant pleaded that he was marshal of the United States for the District of Minnesota and that he took the goods under a writ of attachment against certain parties other than the plaintiff in the suit against him. He did not aver in his plea that they were the goods of the defendant to the writ of attachment. At the trial the plaintiff made proof of his ownership. The defendant relied solely on the fact that he was marshal and held the goods under the writ in the attachment suit. The Supreme Court said:—

> "It is only while the property is in possession of the court, either actually or constructively, that the court is bound, or professes to protect that possession from the process of other courts. Whenever the litigation is ended, or the possession of the officer or court is discharged, other courts are at liberty to deal with it according to the rights of the parties before them, whether those rights require them to take possession of the property or not. The effect to be given in such cases to the adjudications of the court

4. 3 Wall. 341; 18 L. Ed. 257.

first possessed of the property, depends upon principles familiar to the law; but no contest arises about the mere possession, and no conflict but such as may be decided without unseemly and discreditable collisions." * * * "It is obvious that the action of trespass against the marshal in the case before us, does not interfere with the principle thus laid down and limited." * * * "Property may be seized by an officer of the court under a variety of writs, orders, or processes of the court. For our present purpose, these may be divided into two classes. First, those in which the process or order of the court describes the property to be seized, and which contain a direct command to the officer to take possession of that particular property." * * * "Second, those in which the officer is directed to levy the process upon property of one of the parties to the litigation, sufficient to satisfy the demand against him, without describing any specific property to be thus taken." * * * "In the first class he has no discretion to use, no judgment to exercise, no duty to perform but to seize the property described. It follows from this, as a rule of law of universal application, that if the court issuing the process had jurisdiction in the case before it to issue that process, and it was a valid process when placed in the officer's hands, and that, in the execution of such process, he kept himself strictly within the mandatory clause of the process, then such writ or process is a complete protection to him, not only in the court which issued it, but in all other courts. In addition to this, in many cases the court which issued the process will interfere directly to protect its officers from being harassed or interfered with by any person, whether a party to the litigation or not." * * * "In the other class of writs to which we have referred, the officer has a very large and important field for the exercise of his judgment and discretion. First, in ascertaining that the property on which he proposed to levy, is the property of the person against whom the writ is directed; secondly, that it is property which, by law, is subject to be taken under the writ; and thirdly, as to the quantity of such property necessary to be seized in the case in hand. In all these particulars he is bound to exercise his own judgment, and is legally responsible to any person for the consequences of any error or mistake in its exercise to his prejudice." * * * "The Court can afford him no protection against the parties so injured; for the court is in no wise responsible for the manner in which he exercises that discretion which the law reposes in him, and in no one else."

It was held that the marshal was liable. It will be noticed, however, that there was no attempt by State Court process to take the property seized out of his hands.

417. Jurisdiction in Original Suits Extends to Ancillary and Supplementary Proceedings.

The doctrine in Freeman vs. Howe, as limited by Buck vs. Colbath, has been consistently adhered to. Thus, where a railroad property was in the possession of a receiver of the United States Circuit Court for the District of Wisconsin, it was held that any litigation for the possession of the property must take place in that Court, no matter what the citizenship of the parties might be. There it was sought to test the question as to the right of possession by what was called a supplemental bill. It was said that it was brought in violation of the rules of equity pleading; that the subject-matter and the new parties made by it were not such as could properly be brought before the Court by that class of bills. The Supreme Court said:—

"But we think that the question is not whether the proceeding is supplemental and ancillary or is independent and original, in the sense of the rules of equity pleading; but whether it is supplemental and ancillary or is to be considered entirely new and original, in the sense which this court has sanctioned with reference to the line which divides the jurisdiction of the Federal courts from that of the State Courts. No one, for instance, would hesitate to say that, according to English chancery practice, a bill to enjoin a judgment at law, is an original bill in the chancery sense of the word. Yet this court has decided many times, that when a bill is filed in the Circuit Court, to enjoin a judgment of that court, it is not to be considered as an original bill, but as a continuation of the proceeding at law; so much so, that the court will proceed in the injunction suit without actual service of subpoena on the defendant, and though he be a citizen of another State, if he were a party to the judgment at law. The case before us is analogous. An unjust advantage has been obtained by one party over another by a perversion and abuse of the orders of the court."[5]

The Circuit Court of the United States for the Southern District of Illinois had taken possession of a railroad under a bill filed to foreclose a mortgage, and had placed it in the hands of a receiver. Subsequently an Illinois creditor sued out an attachment in the State Court and seized some of its property, whereupon the original complainants intervened and applied for the removal of the case to the Federal Court. The parties entered into an agreement which was silent as to their citizenship, but which provided for the removal of the proceedings to the United States Court. The Supreme Court held that the removal was not only permissible, but that it was the proper thing to do. The jurisdiction of the Circuit Court of the United States did not "depend on the citizenship of the parties, but on the subject-matter of the litigation. That was in the actual possession of that Court when the State Court attempted to levy its writ of attachment on the property. It was for

5. Minnesota Co. vs. St. Paul Co., 2 Wall. 632; 17 L. Ed. 886.

the Court having such possession to determine how far it would permit any other Court to interfere with that possession.''[6]

A judgment recovered in a suit brought against a Federal receiver for a transaction growing out of his conduct of business, as permitted by Act of Congress,[7] cannot be enforced by execution upon the property in his hands. Satisfaction of it can be obtained only through the order of the Court, under which the defendant is acting.[8]

418. Even When Possession of Res Is Irregularly Acquired Exclusive Jurisdiction May Attach.

Citizens of States other than Louisiana obtained from the United States Circuit Court for the District of Louisiana certain writs of attachment. These writs were sued out and issued on Sunday, and by the law and practice in Louisiana they were for that reason invalid. The marshal, however, acted under them and seized the property, such seizure also being made on Sunday. A few minutes after midnight—that is, on the following Monday morning,—a citizen of Louisiana got out an attachment from the State Court, but the sheriff was not allowed to serve it by the marshal who held possession under the Sunday attachments. A little later on Monday morning the original plaintiffs sued out new writs of attachment in the Federal Court, and under them the marshal continued to hold the property. Subsequently the creditor who had attempted to proceed in the State Court filed his petition in the Federal, and asked to be given a preference out of the proceeds of the goods to the amount of the claim for which he had

6. People's Bank vs. Calhoun, 102 U. S. 256; 26 L. Ed. 101.

7. Sec. 299, supra.

8. Gableman vs. Peoria, etc., Ry. Co., 179 U. S. 335; 45 L. Ed. 220; 21 Sup. Ct. 171.

attached. The Supreme Court held that he was entitled to this preference; that the marshal had no right to hold the property under the Sunday attachments; yet as they were not absolutely void on their face, and as he actually held it, the creditor who had sought the aid of the State Court had been compelled to come into the Federal, but that the latter would give him all the rights that he would have had, if the marshal had acted properly.[9]

419. Citizenship of Intervenors Usually Immaterial.

Certain non-resident creditors filed a creditors' bill in a State Court of Mississippi, and subsequently removed it to the Circuit Court of the United States for the Southern District of that State. Afterwards other creditors who were citizens of Mississippi intervened in the case and were admitted as parties plaintiff. It was objected that, as thereafter there were citizens of Mississippi on both sides of the controversy, the Court was without jurisdiction. The Supreme Court answered: "The right of the Court to proceed to decree between the appellants and the new parties did not depend upon difference of citizenship; because, the bill having been filed by the original complainants on behalf of themselves and all other creditors choosing to come in and share the expenses of the litigation, the Court, in exercising jurisdiction between the parties, could incidentally decree in favor of all other creditors coming in under the bill."[10]

420. Federal Courts of Equity Have Exclusive Jurisdiction to Enjoin Enforcement of Federal Judgments.

An amusing illustration of how much difference it may make whether the proceeding is in essentials an original

---

9. Gumbel vs. Pitkin, 124 U. S. 131; 31 L. Ed. 374; 8 Sup. Ct. 379.

10. Stewart vs. Dunham, 115 U. S. 64; 29 L. Ed. 329; 5 Sup. Ct. 1163.

one or merely ancillary or dependent, is afforded by the case of Johnson vs. Christian.[11]

In that case the bill was filed to release certain lands from a deed of trust and to remove a cloud upon the title growing out of a sale and deed. On April 16, 1888, the Supreme Court announced that on looking into the record "we can find no evidence of the jurisdiction of the Circuit Court. The bill commences in this way: 'The complainants, George Christian and Jerry Steuart, citizens of the County of Chicot and State of Arkansas, would respectfully represent,' etc. Joel Johnson is the sole defendant, but there is no allegation as to his citizenship, nor does that appear anywhere in the record." The decree below in favor of the plaintiffs was accordingly reversed. Thereupon the attention of the Court was called to the fact that a paragraph of the bill set forth that by virtue of the sale which it was sought to set aside, the defendant had instituted a suit in ejectment on the law side of the United States Court for the District of Arkansas, and "your complainants, not being admitted to interpose their equitable defense to the same he did" * * * "obtain judgment in ejectment against them." On the 14th of May in the same year the Supreme Court admitted that it had overlooked this allegation; that it was sufficient to give the Circuit Court jurisdiction of the case without any averment of the citizenship of the parties; the suit in equity was merely an incident of, and ancillary to, the ejectment suit, and no other Court than the one which rendered the judgment in ejectment could interfere with it or stay process in it on the ground set forth in the bill.

In the case of Compton vs. Jesup, the whole subject

11. 125 U. S. 642; 31 L. Ed. 820; 8 Sup. Ct. 989.

was ably reviewed by the then JUDGE TAFT, speaking for the Circuit Court of Appeals for the Sixth Circuit.[12]

421. Federal Court Has Jurisdiction of Suits by Its Receivers Irrespective of Citizenship or Amount in Controversy.

The Supreme Court of the United States has recognized a logical extension of this doctrine to a subject of great practical importance. It has held that a Circuit Court of the United States has jurisdiction, in a general creditors' suit properly pending therein for the collection, administration and distribution of the assets of an insolvent corporation, to hear and determine an ancillary suit instituted in the same Court by its receivers, in accordance with its order against debtors of such corporation, although in such suit the receiver claims the right to recover from the debtor a sum less than the amount required by Par. 1 of Sec. 24 of the Judicial Code. The Supreme Court said:—

> "it is insisted that there is a distinction between cases were parties are brought before the court for the purpose of the payment to them of claims they may hold against the estate, and cases where it is sought to recover of them claims which the receiver insists they owe the estate; that the receiver stands in the shoes of the company, and has no higher rights than the corporation, and having sued for less than the jurisdictional amounts, that as to them the cases must be dismissed. This position is entirely correct, so far as the right of the receiver to recover upon the merits is concerned; but it has no bearing whatever upon the question of the jurisdiction of the court to pass upon such merits." * * * "In this case, however, the court proceeds upon its own authority to collect the assets of an estate, with the administration of which it is charged; and, if the receiver in

12. Compton vs. Jesup, 68 Fed. 263; 15 C. C. A. 397.

such cases appears as a party to the suit, it is only because he represents the court in its inherent power to wind up the estate of an insolvent corporation, over which it has by an original bill obtained jurisdiction.'' * * * ''There is just as much reason for questioning the jurisdiction of the court in this case upon the ground of the want of diverse citizenship, as upon the ground that the requisite amount is not involved.''[13]

In that case there was a single suit in equity brought against a number of alleged debtors of the corporation. None of them objected to the form of the proceeding, and those who contested the case at all, did so upon the ground that they were not liable in any form of action. In a subsequent case,[14] the Supreme Court has pointed out that as against the objections of a defendant, there would be no jurisdiction to bring such suits in equity, and that under the present bankruptcy law, unlike its predecessor of 1867, a trustee in bankruptcy has no right to bring the suit in the Federal Court unless the bankrupt could have done so. Apparently, however, a receiver might, under White vs. Ewing, bring such suit in the Federal Court at law irrespective of the amount in controversy or diversity of citizenship.

422. Federal Courts May Not Ordinarily Enjoin Proceedings in State Courts.

One of the best established heads of equity jurisdiction is the issue of injunctions to prohibit the institution or prosecution of suits at law. In the Federal Courts of Equity that jurisdiction, so far as it relates to suits in the Federal Courts, remains unimpaired, but Congress, having in view the dual nature of our Government, and for the purpose of preventing unseemly conflicts of

13. White vs. Ewing, 159 U. S. 36; 40 L. Ed. 67; 15 Sup. Ct. 1018.
14. Kelly vs. Gill, 245 U. S. 116; 62 L. Ed. 185; 38 Sup. Ct. 38.

jurisdiction between State and Federal Courts, has provided that "the writ of injunction shall not be granted by any court of the United States to stay proceedings in any court of a State except in cases where such injunction may be authorized by any law relating to proceedings in bankruptcy.[15]

423. Neither State Court Nor Its Suitors May Be Enjoined.

While the language of the statute simply forbids injunctions to stay proceedings in the State Courts, it means that such writs of injunction are not to be issued to the parties to those proceedings, and not merely that the Federal Court shall not enjoin State Courts. The method of enjoining proceedings in other tribunals has always, or nearly always, been by enjoining the parties from prosecuting, and therefore an injunction from a Federal Court to prohibit an individual from instituting or prosecuting a suit in a State Court is within the mischief intended to be guarded against by the statute.[16] With the exception of cases in bankruptcy, or those arising under the limited liability Acts of Congress relating to ship owners, or those in which an injunction is necessary for the protection of its own suitors, and the enforcement of its own decrees, a Federal Court may not grant a writ of injunction restraining individuals from instituting or prosecuting suits in the State Courts.

424. Federal Court May Enjoin State Court Proceedings When Necessary to Enforce Its Own Decrees or Judgments.

In spite of this sweeping prohibition, it has been decided that where a case is properly pending in a Court

15. R. S., sec. 720.

16. Central National Bank vs. Stevens, 169 U. S. 461; 42 L. Ed. 815; 18 Sup. Ct. 499.

of the United States, and that Court has proceeded to judgment or decree therein, it may, if necessary to give effect thereto, enjoin parties from instituting or prosecuting actions in State Courts.

Thus, a replevin proceeding was instituted in a State Court for Cook County, Ill., a replevin bond given and the property seized. The plaintiffs, who under the then existing statutes had the right to remove filed a proper petition for the removal of the case to the Circuit Court for the Northern District of Illinois. The defendants opposed the removal and the State Court refused to order it. The plaintiffs, however, as they were authorized by law to do, filed a transcript of the record in the Circuit Court of the United States for the District of Illinois. That Court held that it had jurisdiction, and upon appeal to the Supreme Court of the United States its decree was affirmed. Before the appeal was heard the State Court had gone ahead with the case, which it held to be still pending before it, and decided in favor of the defendants and ordered a return to them of the property replevied. This order was not obeyed. Thereupon the defendants began suit on the replevin bond.

The United States Circuit Court for the Northern District of Illinois enjoined the prosecution of this proceeding in the State Courts. Upon appeal the Supreme Court held that it was right in so doing. The Court said:

"The bill in this case was, therefore, ancillary to the replevin suit, and was in substance a proceeding in the Federal court to enforce its own judgment by preventing the defeated party from wresting the replevied property from the plaintiffs in replevin, who, by the judgment of the court, were entitled to it, or what was in effect the same thing, preventing them from enforcing a bond for the return of the property to them. A court of the United States is

24

not prevented from enforcing its own judgments by the statute which forbids it to grant a writ of injunction to stay proceedings in a State court." * * * "The original plaintiff in the action on the replevin bond, represented the real parties in interest, and he was a party to the action of replevin, which had been pending, and was finally determined in the United States Circuit Court. That Court had jurisdiction of his person, and could enforce its judgment in the replevin suit against him, or those whom he represented, their agents and attorneys. The bill in this case was filed for that purpose and that only."[17]

425. Enjoining State Court Judgments on the Ground That They Were Procured by Fraud, Accident or Mistake.

The jurisdiction of a Court is not exhausted by the rendition of a judgment; it continues until the judgment is satisfied.[18]

Ordinarily, therefore, a Federal Court has no jurisdiction to enjoin the holder of a State Court judgment from enforcing it. To this rule there is no exception where the inequity of allowing the enforcement is based upon an error in the proceedings of the State Court itself. The Supreme Court has held, however, that where a defendant was prevented by fraud from setting up in a State Court a meritorious defense which he had, the Federal Court may, in spite of the statute, enjoin the enforcement of such judgment provided there is the necessary diversity of citizenship between the parties.[19]

The Circuit Court of Appeals for the Eighth Circuit in a very able opinion has held that the exception applies

---

17. Dietzsch vs. Huidekoper, 103 U. S. 496; 26 L. Ed. 497.

18. Central National Bank vs. Stevens, 169 U. S. 464; 42 L. Ed. 807; 18 Sup. Ct. 403.

19. Marshall vs. Holmes, 141 U. S. 589; 35 L. Ed. 870; 12 Sup. Ct. 62.

as well to cases where the defendant was prevented from making his defense by accident or mistake.[20]

In that case the defendant in the State Court suit was a non-resident corporation. In accordance with the laws of the State, the State Auditor had been appointed its attorney to accept service of process. Suit had been brought against it upon a claim as to which it had a perfect and conclusive defense. Process was served on the State Auditor and he, by mistake, failed to notify the defendant of the suit. It knew nothing about it and of course never appeared. Judgment was given against it for $7,800. Some years later it learned of the judgment. It brought suit in the United States Circuit Court to enjoin the enforcement of it. It was held that the court had jurisdiction to grant the relief prayed. It is still more clear that a Federal Court of equity may enjoin the enforcement of an absolutely void State judgment,[21] although it may not use its process to restrain further prosecution of a case still actually being litigated in a State Court.[22]

426. Ancillary Jurisdiction in Aid of Another Federal Court.

In addition to the jurisdiction of a District Court over proceedings which are ancillary to other proceedings properly pending before that Court, there is still another kind of ancillary jurisdiction which it is sometimes called on to exercise. The occasion for it usually arises where property involved in litigation is found in two or more districts.

20. National Surety Co. vs. State Bank, 120 Fed. 593; 56 C. C. A. 657.

21. Simon vs. Southern R. R. Co., 236 U. S. 115; 59 L. Ed. 492; 35 Sup. Ct. 255.

22. Essanay Film Mfg. Co. vs. Kane, Supreme Court, April 10, 1922.

427. Do.—Ancillary Receivers.

It is especially important to exercise ancillary jurisdiction when it becomes necessary to appoint a receiver for property. The powers of a receiver do not ordinarily extend beyond the jurisdiction of the Court which appoints him. Where receivers are needed for a great railroad corporation, such as the Northern Pacific, it becomes necessary to obtain appointments from the Court in each district through which the road runs or in which it has property. Such a corporation may have property lying in a number of different districts in the same circuit. Section 56 of the Judicial Code makes provision for such a case. It declares that the appointment of a receiver in one district of the circuit and his qualification gives him "full jurisdiction and control over all the property, the subject of the suit, lying or being within such circuit, subject, however, to the disapproval of such order within thirty days thereafter by the Circuit Court of Appeals for such circuit, or by a Circuit Judge thereof, after reasonable notice to adverse parties and an opportunity to be heard upon the motion for such disapproval." If it is disapproved the receiver is divested of jurisdiction over all the property not lying or being within the State in which the suit was brought. It will be noted that the statute gives no power to a Circuit Judge or to the Circuit Court of Appeals to vacate in this summary way a receivership, or to change a receiver for the District in which he was appointed. If in any of these respects the District Judge errs, the remedy is by appeal.[23]

The section also requires that within ten days after the filing of the order in the District Court of original jurisdiction, a duly certified copy of the bill and of the order of appointment shall be filed in the District Court

23. In re Brown, 242 Fed. 452; 155 C. C. A. 228.

of each district of the circuit in which any of the property lies.

It is declared that where a receiver is appointed under the authority so given, process may issue and be executed within any district of the circuit in the same manner and to the same extent as if the property were wholly within the same district. Orders affecting such property shall be entered of record in each district in which the property affected may lie or be.

428. Do.—Ancillary Receivers When Property Lies in Different Circuits.

But in some cases, as where a large railroad system is involved, the property may not only be in several districts of one circuit but in a number of different circuits. In such cases an ancillary bill should be filed in some district of each circuit in which the property is found. Usually the judge of the Court of such district appoints as ancillary receivers the same persons as were appointed original receivers. All orders are obtained from the Court of original jurisdiction. Such of them as apply to the property in any other circuit are obtained also in the proper District Court of the latter circuit.

429. Do.—Administration Under Ancillary Receiverships.

The assets realized in a district in which the jurisdiction has been ancillary, after paying the necessary expenses and Court costs in that district, and making proper reservations to protect the rights and liens of the creditors living in it, are turned over to the Court of primary jurisdiction for distribution among the general creditors.

430. Do.—Court of Ancillary Jurisdiction May Select Its Own Receivers.

There is no binding obligation, however, upon the District Court of another circuit, when application is made to exercise this ancillary jurisdiction, to do so, in the precise manner which is usual and most convenient. If it sees fit it can decline to appoint receivers at all, or it can, and it sometimes does, appoint other receivers, or having appointed in the first instance the same receivers as those of the Court of primary jurisdiction, it may afterwards remove them and appoint others in their place.

431. Do.—Ordinarily Expedient That Original Receivers Be Made Ancillary.

Sometimes very serious difficulties result from these varying views of different Courts. For example—In 1893 the Northern Pacific Railroad Company, which then operated a railroad in seven States and eight or nine Federal districts, was put in the hands of receivers on a bill filed in the Circuit Court of the United States for the Eastern District of Wisconsin. The same receivers were appointed in the other districts. Subsequently, however, the Circuit Courts for the Districts of Washington and Idaho revoked these appointments and appointed other persons. This led to so much confusion and trouble that, after various other efforts had been made to restore the control of the properties to a single set of hands, all parties agreed to submit the matter to the four justices of the Supreme Court who were assigned to the four circuits in which the receivers had been appointed. Those four judges by agreement sat to hear the case in Washington, outside of any of the circuits, and decided that the Circuit Court for the Eastern District of Wisconsin should be regarded as the Court of primary jurisdiction, and that the receivers appointed by it should be appointed in all the other districts. The Court said:

"We are of opinion that proceedings to foreclose a mortgage placed by a railroad company upon its lines extending through more than one district should, to the end that the mortgaged property may be effectively administered, be commenced in the Circuit Court of the district in which the principal operating offices are situated, and in which there is some material part of the railroad embraced by the mortgage; that such court should be the court of primary jurisdiction and of principal decree, and the administration of the property in the Circuit Courts of the other districts should be ancillary thereto."

Now it so happened that in this case the principal offices of the company were in the District of Minnesota, and there was some question whether it actually operated any railroad in the Eastern District of Wisconsin, for it had leased all the property it there owned to another company for ninety-nine years. The justices, however, concluded, that because in point of fact the primary jurisdiction had been taken by the Court for the Eastern District of Wisconsin and its action in the matter had been acquiesced in for sometime thereafter, it was expedient to regard the Eastern District of Wisconsin as the primary district.[24]

24. Farmers Loan & Trust Co. vs. Northern Pacific R. R. Co., 72 Fed. 30.

CHAPTER XV.

HABEAS CORPUS.

432. Power of Federal Courts and Judges to Issue Writ of Habeas Corpus.

Federal Courts and Federal Judges may under some circumstances issue writs of *habeas corpus.*

It has been stated that the District Court has no power under the first clause of section 24 to issue the writ, because no money or money's worth is in controversy; but by sections 751 and 752 of the Revised Statutes, which were not repealed by the enactment of the Judicial

Code, the Supreme Court and the District Courts, and their several Justices and Judges within their respective jurisdictions, have power to grant it for the purpose of inquiring into the cause of restraint of liberty.

433. Federal Court May Issue Writ Only When Petitioner is in Custody Under Color of Federal Authority or in Violation of Federal Right.

The writ, it is provided by section 753, "shall in no case extend to a prisoner in jail unless where he is in custody (1) under or by color of the authority of the United States, or is committed for trial before some Court thereof, or (2) is in custody for an act done or omitted in pursuance of a law of the United States or of an order, process or decree of a Court or judge thereof, or (3) is in custody in violation of the Constitution or of a law or treaty of the United States, or (4) being a subject or citizen of a foreign State and domiciled therein is in custody for an act done or omitted under any alleged right, title, authority, privilege, protection or exemption claimed under the commission or order or sanction of any foreign State or under color thereof, the validity and effect whereof depends upon the law of nations, or (5) unless it is necessary to bring the prisoner into Court to testify."

434. Supreme Court, Except in Connection With Cases in Which it Has Original Jurisdiction, May Issue the Writ Only in the Nature of an Appellate Proceeding.

To prevent misapprehension it should be mentioned that the Supreme Court, except in connection with the limited class of cases over which it is given by the Constitution original jurisdiction, may issue the writ only when the questions raised are of an appellate nature.

A certain member of the City Council of Cincinnati

who, as such, was by the State law a judge of election, was indicted in the United States Court under the Federal election laws, now repealed, for an offense committed at a congressional election. He was sentenced to be imprisoned for twelve months and to pay a fine of $200 and costs. He applied for a writ of *habeas corpus* to Mr. JUSTICE STRONG of the Supreme Court, who made the same returnable before him at the Catskill Mountain House, in the State of New York. On the petitioner being brought before him, he made an order transferring the hearing of the cause into the Supreme Court, and fixing such hearing for the second Tuesday of October, 1879. He admitted the prisoner meanwhile to bail. The point was made by the Government that the matter could not be considered by the Supreme Court, as that Court had no original jurisdiction. The Court said:—

> "It is clear that the writ, whether acted upon by the Justice who issued it or by this court, would in fact require a revision of the action of the Circuit Court by which the petitioner was committed, and such revision would necessarily be appellate in its character. This appellate character of the proceeding attaches to a large portion of cases on *habeas corpus*, whether issued by a single Judge or by a Court." * * * "The Justice who issued it could undoubtedly have disposed of the case himself, though not at the time, within his own circuit. A Justice of this court can exercise the power of issuing the writ of *habeas corpus* in any part of the United States where he happens to be. But as the case is one of which this court also has jurisdiction, if the Justice who issued the writ found the questions involved to be of great moment and difficulty, and could postpone the case here for consideration of the whole court without injury to the petitioner, we see no good reason why he should not have taken this course, as he did."[1]

1. Ex parte Clarke, 100 U. S. 399; 25 L. Ed. 715.

435. Habeas Corpus is a Civil and Not a Criminal Writ.

The writ of *habeas corpus* is a civil, and not a criminal procedure. The petitioner asserts his civil right of personal liberty against the respondent who is holding him in custody, and the inquiry is into his right to the liberty for which he asks. A person convicted of murder and sentenced to death by the Supreme Court of the District of Columbia applied for a writ of *habeas corpus* to the Supreme Court of the United States. The latter held that its jurisdiction depended not upon the general statute already mentioned, but upon some legislation local to the District of Columbia, which limited the jurisdiction of the Supreme Court on appeals from the highest Court of the District to civil cases in which the matter in dispute, exclusive of costs, exceeded the sum of $5,000. In order to give the Supreme Court jurisdiction under the statute the matter in dispute had to be money or some right the value of which in money could be calculated or ascertained, and as the matter in dispute had no money value, there was no appeal.[2]

436. Habeas Corpus May Not Serve Purpose of Writ of Error.

It has been decided over and over again that this writ cannot be used as a writ of error. If the Court or tribunal below had jurisdiction over the subject matter and to enter the special order complained of, then the defendant's remedy, if any, must be sought by appeal or writ of error.[3]

437. Federal Courts Issue Writ Only When Federal Question is Involved.

The Federal Courts, because they are Federal Courts, on petition for the writ of *habeas corpus* or a return

2. Cross vs. Burke, 146 U. S. 82; 36 L. Ed. 896; 13 Sup. Ct. 22.
3. Charlton vs. Kelly, 229 U. S. 456; 57 L. Ed. 1274; 33 Sup. Ct. 945.

thereto, take cognizance of such questions only as arise under the Constitution, treaties or laws of the United States, or in connection with the proceedings of the United States Courts, or of Federal officers in their official capacity. Since the passage of the Fourteenth Amendment, which declares that no State shall deprive any person of life, liberty or property without due process of law, nor deny to any person within its jurisdiction the equal protection of the laws, repeated attempts have been made to get the Federal Courts to exercise general powers of jail delivery of criminals arrested, indicted or convicted under the State laws. The theory advanced is that the law under which the petitioner is arrested or prosecuted was not validly passed by the State Legislature, or is not constitutional or does not mean what the State authority says it does, and that consequently he has been deprived of his liberty without due process of law or has been denied the equal protection of the laws.

Such was the case of *In re* Duncan.[4] Duncan was a convicted murderer. He applied to the United States Circuit Court for the Western District of Texas for a writ of *habeas corpus*, averring among other things, that the pretended law under which he was convicted was not a law at all, as it had not been read on the number of days and in the manner required by the Constitution of Texas; that it had not been enrolled, etc.; that the judges of the Texas Court were interested in upholding the law, because the same statute fixed their salaries, etc. The Supreme Court said:—

"The State of Texas is in full possession of its faculties as a member of the Union, and its legislative, executive and judicial departments are peacefully operating by the orderly and settled methods

4. 139 U. S. 449; 35 L. Ed. 219; 11 Sup. Ct. 573.

prescribed by its fundamental law. Whether certain statutes have or have not binding force, it is for the State to determine, and that determination in itself involves no infraction of the Constitution of the United States, and raises no Federal question giving the courts of the United States jurisdiction.''

438. Federal Court Will Not Always Issue Writ Even Where Federal Question is Involved.

Ordinarily, even if there is a Federal question involved, the rule of the Federal Courts is not to interfere until the highest Court of the State that can consider the question has finally passed on it and has decided it adversely to the claim which the prisoner sets up under the Constitution, laws or treaties of the United States. At that stage he can always have his remedy by writ of error to the Supreme Court. To this policy of non-interference there are some exceptions. For example, in the famous case of Neagle,[4a] the Supreme Court interfered to discharge him from custody before he was tried by the California Court. It was felt that the obligation resting upon the United States to protect the lives of its judges from assaults committed upon them, because of the manner in which they discharged their official duties was so imperative that the Federal officials who gave this protection should, in their turn, be defended to the full power of the Federal Government so soon as any proceedings were taken against them.

439. Federal Courts Will Issue Writ to Protect Federal Jurisdiction.

Somewhat similar principles controlled the action of the Court in *In re* Loney.[5] Loney, in the City of Richmond, had testified in a case of a contested election for

4a. In re Neagle, 135 U. S. 1; 34 L. Ed. 55; 10 Sup. Ct. 658.
5. 134 U. S. 372; 33 L. Ed. 949; 10 Sup. Ct. 584.

a seat in the House of Representatives of the United States. He was charged before a State magistrate with having perjured himself in the testimony so given. He was arrested by the State authorities. He applied to the Circuit Court of the United States for the Eastern District of Virginia for a writ of *habeas corpus*. He was discharged by that Court and the respondent appealed to the Supreme Court of the United States. The latter said:

> "The power of punishing a witness for testifying falsely in a judicial proceeding belongs peculiarly to the Government in whose tribunals that proceeding is had. It is essential to the impartial and efficient administration of justice in the tribunals of the nation, that witnesses should be able to testify freely before them, unrestrained by legislation of the State, or by fear of punishment in the State courts. The administration of justice in the national tribunals would be greatly embarrassed and impeded if a witness testifying before a court of the United States, or upon a contested election of a member of Congress, were liable to prosecution and punishment in the courts of the State upon a charge of perjury, preferred by a disappointed suitor or contestant, or instigated by local passion or prejudice." * * * "The Courts of Virginia having no jurisdiction of the matter of the charge on which the prisoner was arrested, and he being in custody, in violation of the Constitution and laws of the United States, for an act done in pursuance of those laws by testifying in the case of a contested election of a member of Congress, law and justice required that he should be discharged from such custody, and he was rightly so discharged by the Circuit Court on writ of *habeas corpus*."

In 1907 the Legislature of North Carolina passed certain Acts providing for radical reductions in the fares of passengers on railroads. The Southern Railroad Company applied to the United States Court to enjoin their enforcement on the ground that they deprived it of its property, the prescribed rates being so low as in their practical effect to be confiscatory. JUDGE PRITCHARD granted the injunction. In his order he directed that the railroad should give bond in a large sum to repay the excess fares, if upon final hearing the validity of the State legislation was upheld. Each passenger agent in selling a ticket was required to give the purchaser a coupon for the difference between the old fare and that which the Act fixed. The ticket agent at Asheville continued in accordance with the order to sell tickets at the former rate issuing the coupons to their purchasers. He was arrested by the State authorities, tried, convicted, and sentenced to thirty days in the chain gang. JUDGE PRITCHARD released him on *habeas corpus* and the Supreme Court affirmed the action. It said the agent was held in custody by the State authorities for an act done pursuant to an order, process or decree of a Court or judge of the United States.[6]

440. Federal Courts Will Issue Writ to Protect Federal Officers in Discharge of Their Duties.

In the case of Boske vs. Comingore,[7] the Supreme Court upheld the action of a District Court of the United States in discharging on *habeas corpus* a United States Collector of Internal Revenue who had been committed for contempt of a State Court in refusing to produce records of his office. He had acted by direction of his official superiors given under the authority of a valid law of the United States. The Court said:—

"When the petitioner is in custody by State authority for an act done or omitted to be done in pursuance

6. Hunter vs. Wood, 209 U. S. 205; 52 L. Ed. 747; 28 Sup. Ct. 472.
7. 177 U. S. 459; 44 L. Ed. 1150; 20 Sup. Ct. 976.

of a law of the United States, or of an order, process or decree of a court or judge thereof; or where, being a subject or citizen of a foreign State, and domiciled therein, he is in custody, under like authority, for an act done or omitted under any alleged right, title, authority, privilege, protection or exemption claimed under the commission, or order, or sanction of any foreign State, or under color thereof, the validity and effect whereof depend upon the law of nations; in such and like cases of urgency, involving the authority and operations of the General Government, or the obligations of this country to, or its relation with, foreign nations, the courts of the United States have frequently interposed by writs of *habeas corpus* and discharged prisoners who were held in custody under State authority." The Court added: "The present case was one of urgency, in that the appellee was an officer in the revenue service of the United States, whose presence at his post of duty was important to the public interests, and whose detention in prison by the State authorities might have interfered with the regular and orderly course of the business of the Department to which he belonged."

In other words, while the Federal Courts have the power to release persons held in custody by State authorities, contrary to the Constitution or laws of the United States, they will ordinarily refuse to pass the order of discharge unless they feel that, if they do not, some great public interest will suffer or be imperiled, or, in exceptional cases, that great private injustice and hardship will result.

441. An Alleged Fugitive From the Justice of One State May Have Federal Writ to Inquire Into the Lawfulness of His Detention.

One State may in its Courts begin a prosecution against "A." He may at the time be in another State.

The Governor of the prosecuting State makes requisition upon the Governor of the other for his return as a fugitive from justice. The latter Governor may issue his warrant for the delivery of "A" to the agent of the prosecuting State. "A" may deny that he is a fugitive from the justice of the demanding State, or he may, perhaps, assert that the proceedings under which he is held in custody are for other reasons so irregular or improper as to afford no legal ground for his detention. If he wishes he may apply for a writ of *habeas corpus* to a United States District Court or to a Federal judge. Upon what does his right to do so rest? He is not in the custody of any Federal official or under any process of its Courts. He has not been charged with any violation of its laws. It is possible that the proceedings against him may be so wanting in all regularity that his detention under them may be without due process of law, and therefore in violation of the Fourteenth Amendment; but, as has been stated, it is, even under such circumstances, ordinarily the policy of the Federal Court to avoid precipitate interference with the action of the State authorities. Proceedings for interstate extradition are, however, not in legal theory taken altogether or even principally under State laws. The duty to return fugitives from the justice of other States is imposed by the Federal Constitution upon each of the States, and it has been held that the statement in the constitution as to when a State should return such fugitives is in effect a declaration that it may not return them or may not permit their extradition under other circumstances, although as an independent sovereignty before the adoption of the constitution, it could have done so.[8]

Therefore it follows that the constitution protects one who is not a fugitive from the justice of one State from

8. Innes vs. Tobin, 240 U. S. 127; 60 L. Ed. 622; 36 Sup. Ct. 274.

being delivered up to that State by the other in which he is found.[9]   Congress has power to provide by law machinery for executing this constitutional duty.   It has done so, but its statutory provisions are not necessarily exclusive of State action in any case within the constitutional provision but not covered by the Federal Statute, so that where one, found in Oregon, was returned to Texas as a fugitive from its justice and there acquitted, she could be lawfully delivered to Georgia upon a requisition from the Governor of the last named State, although the Statute provides only for the surrender by the executive authority of a State to which the fugitive has fled. It was argued in this case that as the prisoner had never voluntarily gone into Texas, she had of course not fled into that State, but the Supreme Court held the contention unavailing.[10]   A prisoner held for delivery by one State to another is, in a sense, in custody under color of the Constitution and laws of the United States.   The Federal Courts, therefore, may and should inquire into the regularity of his detention.[11]   It is, however, only in a limited sense that the prisoner is held under color of a Federal law.   If he were in custody of any officer of the United States, or were detained under any process from its Courts, they, and they alone, could inquire into the lawfulness of his detention as has been more fully stated elsewhere;[12] but being in custody of State officers, State Courts and State judges have concurrent jurisdiction to issue the writ.   He may accordingly invoke the protection of either the State or the Federal Courts.   If in the former he asserts that he is held in violation of some right given him by the Constitution or statutes of the

9. Hyatt vs. Corkran, 188 U. S. 711; 47 L. Ed. 657; 23 Sup. Ct. 456.

10. Innes vs. Tobin, supra.

11. Ex parte Thaw, 214 Fed. 423.

12. Sec. 133, supra.

United States, and the decision is against him, he may, after having fought the case to and through the highest Court of the State to which he may carry it, appeal to the Supreme Court of the United States.

The scope of the inquiry of either State or Federal Courts in such cases is quite limited. They may not ordinarily review the Governor's decision on any disputed question upon which it was his duty to pass, and upon which there was conflicting evidence.[13] Nor will the Courts inquire as to the technical sufficiency of the indictment.[14] It is sufficient if it shows that the defendant is substantially charged with the crime; for the case is not to be tried on habeas corpus.[15]

The cases cited show that the petitioner ought not to be returned to the demanding State if it be clearly established that he was not physically present in that State at any time at which he did anything towards effectuating the crime charged against him, but that it is not necessary to his return that he shall have been present in the State when the offense was actually consummated.

442. The Petition for the Writ.

The Revised Statutes prescribe that the application for the writ shall be made by complaint in writing signed by the person for whose benefit it is intended, setting forth the facts concerning the detention of the party restrained, in whose custody he is detained, and by virtue of what claim or authority, if known. The facts set forth in the complaint are to be verified by the oath of the person making the application. It is further provided that the Court, justice or judge to whom the application is made shall forthwith award a writ of *habeas corpus*,

13. Hyatt vs. Corkran, 188 U. S. 711; 47 L. Ed. 657; 23 Sup. Ct. 456.
14. Drew vs. Thaw, 235 U. S. 432; 59 L. Ed. 302; 35 Sup. Ct. 137.
15. Strassheim vs. Daily, 221 U. S. 282; 55 L. Ed. 735; 31 Sup. Ct. 558.

unless it appears from the petition itself that the applicant is not entitled thereto.

443. Federal Court May Issue Rule to Show Cause Why Writ Should Not Issue.

A practice, sanctioned by the Supreme Court, has grown up whereby in many cases the Court, instead of granting the writ, requires the person, to whom it would otherwise be issued, to show cause why it should not be granted.

An application was made to the Supreme Court for a writ of *habeas corpus,* alleging that the petitioners were confined in the jail of Fulton County, Georgia, in the custody of the United States Marshal for the Northern District of Georgia, under sentence of the Circuit Court for that district, and that the trial, conviction and sentence under which they were held were illegal, null and void. On the filing of the petition, the Court issued a rule on the Marshal, or on any person in whose custody the prisoners might be found, to show cause why the writ should not issue for their release. The superintendent of the Albany penitentiary, in the State of New York, made return that the prisoners had been sentenced to that institution for two years and were then confined there. A transcript of the proceedings of the Circuit Court for the Northern District of Georgia was annexed. The Supreme Court said:—

> "As this return is precisely the same that the superintendent would make if the writ of *habeas corpus* had been served on him, the court here can determine the right of the prisoners to be released on this rule to show cause, as correctly and with more convenience in the administration of justice, than if the prisoners were present under the writ in the custody of the superintendent; and such is the practice of this court."[16]

16. Ex parte Yarborough, 110 U. S. 651; 28 L. Ed. 274; 4 Sup. Ct. 152.

This method of procedure is obviously convenient, especially when, as often happens, the Court is sitting at some considerable distance from the place at which the prisoner is confined. Moreover, where the petitioner is in the custody of State officials, it is more courteous to the State to lay such a rule than to issue the writ in the first instance.

The petition may very well itself show, and indeed very often does show, that the applicant is not entitled to release. Where this appears there is no necessity for issuing the writ. The petitioner cannot retry his case. He cannot in this collateral way attack the proceedings of the Court by which he was indicted or under the order of which he is held in custody, but he can show facts which do not contradict the record, if they are material to the question he wishes to raise.

444. Appeals in Habeas Corpus Cases.

From the grant or refusal of a writ of *habeas corpus* an appeal lies. Whether it should be taken to the Circuit Court of Appeals, or directly to the Supreme Court, depends upon the kind of question raised by the proceeding. If such question belongs to the class which goes directly to the Supreme Court, the appeal from the *habeas corpus* proceeding will take the same course; while if the issue passed upon is of the kind over which appellate jurisdiction is given to the Circuit Court of Appeals, the appeal from the grant or refusal of the writ will be taken to that Court.

445. Habeas Corpus ad Testificandum.

A Federal Court may issue the writ of *habeas corpus ad testificandum* to bring into Court a person whose testimony is required, but who is in lawful custody, either State or Federal. That power should not be exercised unless there is some obvious necessity for it.[17]   He is, of course, returned to that custody so soon as the occasion for his presence in the Federal Court has passed.[18]

17. In re Thaw, 172 Fed. 288.
18. In re Hamilton, 11 Fed. Cases, 5976.

CHAPTER XVI.

CIVIL PROCEDURE OF THE FEDERAL COURTS WHEN SITTING AS COURTS OF LAW.

446. Civil Procedure as Distinguished From Civil Jurisdiction of Federal Courts.

The preceding chapters have treated of those cases which may be instituted in the Federal Courts, or which may be removed into them; that is to say, of the jurisdiction of those Courts. Something has been said about their procedure when dealing with criminal charges. Now attention must be given to the way in which they handle those civil cases which are properly brought in them or which are removed to them from State Courts. In other words, their civil procedure as distinguished from their civil jurisdiction is to be discussed.

447. Pleading in Federal Courts Should Affirmatively Show Existence of Jurisdictional Facts.

As has already been pointed out, it is necessary, in the Federal Courts, that the record shall affirmatively show that the Court has jurisdiction of the controversy. It follows that the plaintiff should distinctly allege such facts, as, if true, will confer jurisdiction upon the Court. This rule was early established and has been consistently adhered to. It is a requirement to which, ordinarily, pleading in the State Courts need not conform. Formerly it was enforced with great rigidity, as, for example, when the Supreme Court dismissed for want of jurisdiction, the case in which the defendant in the body of the bill was described merely as of Philadelphia, although in its caption he had been spoken of as a citizen of Pennsylvania.[1]

448. In the Federal Appellate Courts it is Sufficient if the Record Anywhere Affirmatively Shows Jurisdiction in the Lower Court.

It is, however, well settled that the Appellate Court, in determining whether it sufficiently appears that the Court of first instance had jurisdiction, does not restrict its examination to those pleadings in which jurisdictional facts should properly be alleged and ordinarily are. It is sufficient after verdict or decree below, that they distinctly and affirmatively appear somewhere in the record.[2] Appear, however, they must, and that clearly, in what is properly a part of the record; it is not

1. Jackson vs. Ashton, 8 Peters, 148; 8 L. Ed. 898.
2. Railway Co. vs. Ramsay, 22 Wall., 322; 22 L. Ed. 523.

enough that from something therein, it may be gathered, that they probably exist. They must be unambiguously set forth.[3]

449. Averments of Jurisdictional Allegations Inadvertently Omitted May Be Inserted by Amendment Even After Final Judgment or Decree.

Until within the last few decades, the Supreme Court, when it found that the record did not disclose jurisdiction, directed that the case should be dismissed[4] unless both parties agreed to amend the record so as to show it.[5] To take such course was to inflict a grievous punishment upon the client for the mistake of his counsel, a punishment, moreover, which was not required by any public policy, and to prevent which it became the established practice of the Supreme and other Appellate Federal Courts to remand the case to the District Court, with directions to allow the plaintiff to amend his pleadings so as to show the existence of the necessary jurisdictional requirements, if the facts justified his so doing, or to permit the amendment to be made in the Court above, provided both parties united in the request.[6]

In a further effort to mitigate the consequences of such mistakes, it was held that if after the amendment was made, the defendant did not traverse the truth of the new jurisdictional allegations, or if having done so, they were nevertheless proven to be true, a judgment or decree on the merits might be entered upon the old verdict or findings of fact, without retrying the whole case.[7]

3. Robertson vs. Cease, 97 U. S. 646; 24 L. Ed. 1035.

4. Jackson vs. Ashton, 8 Peters, 148; 8 L. Ed. 898.

5. Hodgson vs. Bowerbank, 5 Cranch, 303; 3 L. Ed. 108.

6. Kennedy vs. Georgia State Bank, 8 Howard, 586; 12 L. Ed. 1209.

7. Grand Trunk Western Ry. Co. vs. Reddick, 160 Fed. 898; 88 C. C. A. 80; Parker Washington Co. vs. Cramer, 201 Fed. 878; 120 C. C. A. 216.

In 1915, Congress,[8] gave either party the right, at any stage of the proceeding, and in the Appellate as well as in the Trial Court, to amend so as to show the existence of the necessary diversity of citizenship upon such terms as the Court might impose. The amendment, when made, relates back to the institution of the suit or to the filing of the petition for removal.

450. Distinction Between Law and Equity.

In some States the difference between the Federal and State procedure is more marked than it is in Maryland. In many, if not in most of the States of the Union, the larger part of the distinctions between law and equity have been broken down. Probably it is only in a minority of them that separate Courts of equity still exist.

The distinction between law and equity and between Courts of law and of equity, is still maintained in the Federal tribunals.

As has previously been pointed out,[9] the latter understand a case in equity to be a case of the same kind, class and general nature as those proceedings which were held, by the practice of the English High Court of Chancery in 1789, to be of equitable cognizance.

451. Legal and Equitable Procedure May Not Be Intermingled.

The rule that legal and equitable procedure may not be intermingled was formerly rigidly adhered to. Texas, from the time of its admission into the Union, had no separate Courts of equity and no distinct equity procedure.

A citizen of New York brought suit in the United States Court for the District of Texas against a citizen of Texas by filing a petition in that Court in which he

8. 38 Stat. 956; 5 Fed. Stat. Ann. 1059; U. S. Comp. Stat. 1251c.
9. Section 36, supra.

described himself as lawfully possessed of four negroes, slaves for life, to-wit, Billy, a negro man of dark complexion, aged about 12 years, of the value of $500; Lindsay, a negro man of dark complexion, aged 22 years, of the value of $1,000; Betsy, a mulatto woman of light complexion, aged about 30 years, and of the value of $800, and Alexander, a boy of very light complexion, aged about 4 years, and of $400 value. His petition went on to say that he casually lost the same out of his possession and that they came into the possession of the defendant by finding, and that the defendant, though often requested so to do, had refused to deliver them to the plaintiff. The plaintiff alleged his damage to be $5,000. Thus far the petition was strictly a declaration in trover. It contained a prayer for process and that upon trial of the cause "your petitioner may have a judgment in specie for the said negroes, together with damages for the detention of the same and also the costs of suit," and then ended with a prayer for such other and further relief as should be in accordance with right and justice. In other words, to a common law declaration in trover were annexed prayers for equitable relief.

The defendant pleaded that the title of these negroes had been arbitrated between the plaintiff and the person under whom defendant claimed them and had been decided in favor of the latter. The plaintiff in reply alleged that the award was not binding. The jury found a verdict for the plaintiff for $1,200; the value of the negro slaves in the suit, with six and a quarter cents damages. The plaintiff then released the judgment for $1,200 and the Court ordered that the defendant return to the plaintiff the four negroes and pay him six and a quarter cents damages and costs of suit. The defendant appealed to the Supreme Court. CHIEF JUSTICE TANEY delivered the decision; he said:—

"The common law has been adopted in Texas, but the forms and rules of pleading in common law cases have been abolished, and the parties are at liberty to set out their respective claims and defenses in any form that will bring them before the court. And as there is no distinction in its courts between cases at law and equity, it has been insisted in this case, on behalf of the defendant in error, that this court may regard the plaintiff's petition either as a declaration at law or as a bill in equity. Whatever may be the laws of Texas in this respect, they do not govern the proceedings in the Courts of the United States. And although the forms of proceedings and practice in the State courts have been adopted in the district Court, yet the adoption of the State practice must not be understood as confounding the principles of law and equity, nor as authorizing legal and equitable claims to be blended together in one suit. The Constitution of the United States, in creating and defining the judicial power of the general government, establishes this distinction between law and equity; and a party who claims a legal title must proceed at law, and may undoubtedly proceed according to the forms of practice in such cases in the State court. But if the claim is an equitable one, he must proceed according to rules which this court has prescribed (under the authority of the Act of August 23, 1842), regulating proceedings in equity in courts of the United States.. There is nothing in these proceedings which resembles a bill or answer in equity according to the rules prescribed by this court, nor any evidence stated upon which a decree in equity could be revised in an appellate court. Nor was any equitable title set up by" * * * "the plaintiff in the court below. It was a suit at law to try a legal title." * * * "Here the matter in issue was the property in these negroes. The verdict does not find that they are the property of the plaintiff or the defendant, but finds for the plaintiff their value, which was not an issue. It ought, therefore, to have been set aside upon motion of either party, as no judgment could be lawfully entered upon it.''[10]

452. By Recent Statutes, Equitable Defenses Can Now Be Made at Law in the Federal Courts.

There can now be made directly at law many defenses which formerly could be set up only in equity. When the change in common law practice was brought about by decisions in effect holding that the earlier rulings prohibiting such defenses were erroneous, there was in principle no reason why they might not be made in the Courts of the United States, when sitting at law and not as chancery tribunals, but State legislation permitting the setting up at law of equitable defenses generally did not affect Federal procedure. In the Courts of the United States, the general principle that equitable and legal rights and remedies are to be kept separate, and enforced in distinct proceedings was clearly recognized, and on the whole, firmly adhered to.[11] Even the Federal equity rule No. 22, which went into effect February 1, 1913,[12] providing that ''if at any time it appears that a suit commenced in equity should have been brought as an action on the law side of the Court, it shall be forthwith transferred to the law side and be there proceeded with, with only such alteration in the pleadings as shall be essential,'' and the new Section 274a of the Judicial Code, dated March 3, 1915,[13] which permits any party, at any stage of any case in law or in equity, to amend his pleadings so as to obviate the objection that his suit was not brought upon the right side of the Court, and

10. Bennett vs. Butterworth, 11 How. 669; 13 L. Ed. 859; Fenn vs. Holme, 21 How. 481; 16 L. Ed. 198.

11. Platte Valley C. Co. vs. Gosserman-Gates Live S. & L. Co., 202 Fed. 693; 121 C. C. A. 102.

12. 198 Fed. XXIV.

13. 38 Stat. 956; 5 Fed. Stat. Ann. 1059; U. S. Comp. Stat., sec. 1251a.

which gives to the testimony previously taken, if it has been preserved, the same effect as if the original pleadings had been in the amended form, of themselves, merely prevented a useless waste of time and expense, by providing that a proceeding originally begun as an action at law, might be turned into a suit in equity, or vice versa, but in the end it became definitely one or the other, and the pleadings were to be so reformed as to make clear which it was.

Another section of the last mentioned act amending section 274b of the Judicial Code, made a great breach in the rigid rule of demarcation maintained for a century and a quarter, for it was there enacted that in all actions at law, equitable defenses might be interposed by answer, plea or replication, without the necessity of filing a bill on the equity side of the Court. The defendant has, in such case, the same rights as if he had claimed them by a bill in chancery. In case affirmative relief is asked for, the plaintiff files a replication thereto.

453. Does the Act Permit a Plaintiff to Interpose a Replication on Equitable Grounds to Defendant's Bill.

If a plaintiff sues at law, and defendant pleads release under seal, is the plaintiff entitled to reply that the release is not binding upon him because given in ignorance of a material fact? The Court of Appeals for the Second Circuit, one judge dissenting, answered in the negative. In its view the division between legal and equitable procedure was still to be preserved by the Federal Courts, except in the special cases for which the statute spoke, and in law cases, it gave the privilege of setting up equitable defences to defendants, and to them alone.[14]   On the other hand, before the decision in the Second Circuit, in a case pending in the Circuit Court of

14. Keatley vs. U. S. Trust Co., 249 Fed. 296; 161 C. C. A. 304.

Appeals for the Eighth Circuit, in which the facts were
almost identical, all the parties assumed that the plaintiff
could, by replication, set up that the release was void,[15]
and such has been the express determination of the Circuit Court of Appeals for the First Circuit,[16] which
declined to follow Keatley vs. United States Trust Company, *supra*. It is quite possible that what was the
dissenting view in the last mentioned case may before
long become the accepted law.

454. A Defendant in an Action at Law May Not as an Equitable Defense Require Interpleading by Persons Not Parties to the Original Cause.

The Circuit Court of Appeals for the Second Circuit
has held that the statute authorizing the making of an
equitable defense at law does not authorize the filing of
a plea in the nature of a bill of interpleader intended to
bring in other parties.[17]

455. A Defendant May Now in an Action at Law Obtain Affirmative Equitable Relief Such as the Reformation of a Contract.

There would seem to be no question that in a suit at
law brought upon a written instrument, the defendant
may obtain a reformation of the instrument by an appropriate plea, on equitable grounds.[18]

456. How and When Are Equitable Defenses to be Passed Upon.

The Circuit Court of Appeals for the Eighth Circuit,
in an opinion of great ability, has held that in view of

15. Union Pac. R. Co. vs. Syas, 246 Fed. 562; 158 C. C. A. 531.

16. Plews vs. Burrage, 274 Fed. 881.

17. Sherman Nat. Bank vs. Shubert Theatrical Co., 247 Fed. 256; 159
C. C. A. 350.

18. Upson Nut Co. vs. American Shipbuilding Co., 251 Fed. 707.

the constitutional recognition of the division between law and equity, it will not be supposed that Congress intended to bring about any confusion as to what issues were legal and what were equitable, nor did it purpose to require that the method of trial of either should be changed. The Court accordingly ruled that where defenses on equitable grounds are set up, the issues raised by them should be first disposed of by the Court in the same manner as if they would be if the suit were in equity, and then if after their determination there are any material issues left, they will be tried, if the parties desire, to a jury, as at common law.[19] In a law case, the Circuit Court of Appeals for the First Circuit has said that it is not able to accord with the view that the issue calling for equitable relief must first be tried by the Court alone, sitting as a Court of equity.[20] It held that whether that course should be followed or not was, in its opinion, a question of judicial discretion, and when the equitable issue is simple and one eminently fit for submission to a jury, it thought that that was the preferable practice and the one most consonant with the spirit and purpose of the statute. In this connection it may perhaps be noted that the Circuit Court of Appeals for the Fourth Circuit, about a month after the enactment of section 274b, said incidently, for it had no occasion so to decide, that this section had substantially abolished all technical distinctions between proceedings at law and in equity.[21] In view of the sharpness with which legal and equitable proceedings had so long been differentiated in the Federal Courts it is not surprising that there has been much difference of opinion as to the consequences which will

19. Union Pacific R. Co. vs. Syas, 246 Fed. 561; 158 C. C. A. 531; Fay vs. Hill, 249 Fed. 415; 161 C. C. A. 389; followed in Cavender vs. Virginia Bridge & Iron Co., 257 Fed. 877.
20. Plews vs. Burrage, 274 Fed. 881.
21. U. S. vs. Richardson, 223 Fed. 1010; 139 C. C. A. 386.

follow the enactment of a statute which goes so little
into detail.

457. Federal Legal Procedure.

It is expedient in actions at law if not in equity that
the differences between the procedure of the Federal
Court sitting in any particular State and the State
Courts therein shall be few. The more nearly they are
alike, the more likely it is that justice will be furthered.

The great diversity among the several States themselves in matters of pleading and practice is unfortunate.
It has been thought that greater uniformity and greater
simplicity and despatch might be brought about if Congress authorized the Supreme Court to prescribe rules
governing pleading and practice in the Federal Courts
on their law side as it now does with reference to their
equitable jurisdiction. The adoption by the several
States of these Federal rules, would result in uniformity
of procedure, not only between the Courts of the States
and of the United States, but among the former as well.

458. Federal Process Prior to Conformity Act.

Up to this time the problem has been approached from
the other side. As early as 1789 Congress made temporary provision for assimilating Federal to State process. In 1792 a permanent statute on the subject was
enacted. By it the process in the Federal Courts was to
be the same in each State, respectively, as had in 1789
been used by the highest Courts of the latter. Many
years afterwards what is now known as the Conformity
Act was adopted.

459. The Conformity Act.

That enactment prescribes that the practice, pleading,
forms and modes of proceeding in civil causes, other

than those in equity and admiralty, in the Federal Courts of original jurisdiction shall conform as nearly as may be to the practice, pleading, forms and modes of proceeding existing at the time in like causes in the Courts of record of the State in which the District Courts are held, any rule of Court to the contrary notwithstanding.

The Supreme Court said:

"The purpose of the provision is apparent upon its face. No analysis is necessary to reach it. It was to bring about uniformity in the law of procedure in the Federal and State courts of the same locality. It had its origin in the code-enactments of many of the States. While in the Federal tribunals the common law pleadings, forms and practice were adhered to, in the State courts of the same district the simpler forms of the local code prevailed. This involved the necessity on the part of the bar of studying two distinct systems of remedial law, and of practicing according to the wholly dissimilar requirements of both. The inconvenience of such a state of things is obvious. The evil was a serious one. It was the aim of the provision in question to remove it."[22]

460. Conformity Statute Does Not Affect Province of Judge and Jury.

By the law of Illinois a judge is required to give all his instructions in writing, and he may not otherwise add to or modify them. The jury are permitted to take the written instructions with them to the jury room. In Nudd vs. Burrows, one of the parties had requested the judge to give his charge and all of it in writing and to refrain, as the Illinois judges are required to do, from any comment on the facts. The Supreme Court, after using the language quoted in the preceding section, said:—

22. Nudd vs. Burrows, 91 U. S. 441; 23 L. Ed. 286.

"The personal administration by the judge of his duties while sitting upon the bench was not complained of. No one objected, or sought a remedy in that direction. We see nothing in the Act to warrant the conclusion that it was intended to have such an application. If the proposition of the counsel for the plaintiff in error be correct, the powers of the judge, as defined by the common law, were largely trenched upon." * * * "The personal conduct and administration of the judge in the discharge of his separate functions is, in our judgment, neither practice, pleading, nor a form nor mode of proceeding within the meaning of those terms as found in the context."

461. Conformity to Be Only as Near as May Be.

In a subsequent case the Court pointed out that

"the conformity is required to be 'as near as may be'—not as near as may be possible, or as near as may be practicable. This indefiniteness may have been suggested by a purpose: it devolved upon the judges to be affected the duty of construing and deciding, and gave them the power to reject, as Congress doubtless expected they would do, any subordinate provision in such State statutes which, in their judgment, would unwisely encumber the administration of the law, or tend to defeat the ends of justice, in their tribunals. While the act of Congress is to a large extent mandatory, it is also to some extent only directory and advisory.' "[23]

462. Conformity Statute and Rules of Court.

A rule of the United States Court for the District of Colorado provided that the defendant should appear, demur or answer within ten days from the day of service, if such service be made within the county from which the summons is issued. A subsequent statute of Colorado extended the time to twenty days. A defendant

23. Indianapolis R. R. Co. vs. Horst, 93 U. S. 301; 23 L. Ed. 898.

appeared within ten days and moved to quash the return on the ground that the process was not the process required by the Act of Congress, in that it did not give the defendant the number of days in which to appear and answer or demur accorded by the State law. The Supreme Court held that the summons was in proper form and said:—

"We think * * * while it was the purpose of Congress to bring about a general uniformity in Federal and State proceedings in civil cases, and to confer upon suitors in Courts of the United States the advantages of remedies provided by State legislation, yet that it was also the intention to reach such uniformity often largely through the discretion of the Federal courts, exercised in the form of general rules, adopted from time to time, and so regulating their own practice as may be necessary or convenient for the advancement of justice and the prevention of delays in proceedings."[24]

Any other construction would involve an unconstitutional delegation of congressional power to State legislatures.

463. The Conformity Statute Yields to the Constitution and to Any Specific Federal Statute.

The separation of law and equity, and the requirement that in trials at common law when a sum greater than $20 is at issue, either party is entitled to a trial by jury, by which is meant a trial conducted substantially as jury trials were conducted at the time of the adoption of the Constitution, necessarily in many features make radical distinctions between the State and Federal procedure. Nor will the Courts assume that Congress by the Conformity Act intended to repeal or change any specific

24. Sheppard vs. Adams, 168 U. S. 625; 42 L. Ed. 602; 18 Sup. Ct. 214.

provision it had already made for the government of the procedure of the Federal Courts, much less can it be supposed that Congress by enacting it attempted to tie its hands for the future. It follows that the Conformity Act must yield to the other legislation of Congress.[25]

464. The Conformity Act Does Not Adopt for Federal Courts State Statutes as to Service of Process Inconsistent With the General Principles of Jurisprudence.

It sometimes happens that State statutes go very far in attempting to extend the jurisdiction of their Courts over persons who, according to the general principles of jurisprudence, are not subject thereto. This tendency is especially manifested with reference to corporations. In some States a corporation may be bound by service on one of its agents or employees found in the State, although it was not incorporated therein and is not at the time of such service doing business within it, either generally or specially. The Conformity Statute does not require or permit the Federal Courts to hold such service valid when under general principles of jurisprudence it would not have been. This rule applies as well to cases instituted in the United States Courts as to those brought in the State tribunals and thence removed to the Federal.[26]

465. Conformity Statute Does Not Control Mode of Proof in Federal Courts.

Congress has prescribed the mode of proof in actions in the Federal Courts. It has said that this shall be by

25. Southern Pacific Co. vs. Denton, 146 U. S. 202; 36 L. Ed. 942; 13 Sup. Ct. 44.

26. Mechanical Appliance Co. vs. Castleman, 215 U. S. 437; 54 L. Ed. 272; 30 Sup. Ct. 125.

the oral examination of witnesses in open Court and has provided that, under certain specific exceptional circumstances, depositions taken elsewhere may be admitted in evidence. It is not in the power of State legislation to add to or withdraw from those exceptions. Congress, it is true, has provided that in addition to the other modes of taking depositions prescribed by the Revised Statutes, it shall be lawful to take them in the manner fixed by State law. This permission, however, relates merely to the way in which a deposition may be taken when such deposition is under the Federal law admissible at all. It does not extend the cases in which depositions may be admitted.[27]

466. Whether a Plaintiff in a Personal Injury Case May Be Required to Submit to Physical Examination Depends on the State Law.

At common law the Court had no power to require a plaintiff in a personal injury case to submit to a physical examination.[28]

A statute of New Jersey authorized the Court in a litigation of that character, upon the application of the defendant to order one. The question arose as to whether the United States Court, sitting in that State, could do the like. The Supreme Court held that the statute was one of the laws of the State which by section 721 of the Revised Statutes, as we shall later see, were to be regarded as a rule of decision of the Courts of the United States when not in conflict with the Federal Constitution, treaties or statutes; and that there is nothing in the laws of the United States to prohibit such an ex-

27. Hanks Dental Assn. vs. Tooth Crown Co., 194 U. S. 310; 48 L. Ed. 989; 24 Sup. Ct. 700.

28. Union Pacific Ry. Co. vs. Botsford, 141 U. S. 250; 35 L. Ed. 734; 11 Sup. Ct. 1000.

amination, when made at the trial, although under them it could not have been required against the plaintiff's consent in advance thereof.[29]

467. State Statutes or Usages as to Continuances Are Not Binding on the Federal Courts.

The statute law of Texas under certain circumstances gives a party an absolute right to at least one continuance. The defendant in a case depending before the United States Court sitting in Texas sought to avail itself of this privilege. The Circuit Court of Appeals for the Fifth Circuit held that such State law was not binding on the Federal Courts, and that whether a continuance should or should not be granted rested in the sound discretion of the trial judge.[30]

468. Amendment of Pleadings Freely Permitted.

The framers of the original Judiciary Act of 1789 were far ahead of their contemporaries in the liberality of their provisions for amendment. Indeed it is doubtful whether in any modern State Code there is any more liberal and enlightened provision for amendment than was then made. In most of the States, even today, the right to correct errors in pleadings is by no means as extensive as it is under this Federal law passed more than one hundred and thirty years ago. The provisions which formed section 32 of the Judiciary Act of 1789 are now codified as section 954 of the Revised Statutes. They direct the Federal Courts in civil cases to ignore all defects of form except those attacked by demurrer and substantially assigned in the demurrer itself as grounds therefor. The Court is, in the broadest way, authorized

29. Camden & Suburban Ry. Co. vs. Stetson, 177 U. S. 172; 44 L. Ed. 721; 20 Sup. Ct. 617.
30. Texas & P. Ry. Co. vs. Nelson, 50 Fed. 814; 1 C. C. A. 688.

at any time to permit amendments in the process or pleadings upon such conditions as it shall in its discretion, and by its rule, prescribe. It follows that any amendments which would be allowable under State practice will be permitted by the Federal Court unless, perhaps, where their effect would be to violate some of the cardinal rules governing the jurisdiction or procedure of the Federal Courts. On the other hand, no State statute or practice can limit the power of the Federal Courts to permit amendments. Thus—

The California form of Lord Campbell's Act requires that the suit shall be brought by the legal representatives of the decedent for his next of kin.

In the United States Court for the Northern District of California such a suit was brought by the father of the deceased in his own name. He was the next of kin. The error was not discovered until after the time in which a new suit could be brought. It was held that he should be allowed to amend his old action in such manner as to substitute the administrator of the deceased as party plaintiff for the father.[31] It was immaterial that such substitution would not have been permitted in the State Courts.

468a. Revivor of Cause After Death of Party Regulated by Act of Congress.

Congress has provided that upon the death of any party to any cause in the Courts of the United States, at law, or in equity, or admiralty, his executor or administrator, by whatever State or Territory appointed, may take his decedent's place and may, at any time within two years after the death and before the final distribution and settlement of the estate, be brought into it by writ of scire facias, which may be served upon him by the

---

31. Reardon vs. Balaklala Consolidated Copper Co., 193 Fed. 189.

Marshal of any District in which he may be.   If he does not appear within twenty days after such service, the case may proceed against the decedent's estate as if he had done so.[31a]

469. Federal and State Pleading Nearly Identical—Federal and State Practice Similar.

For practical purposes it is sufficiently accurate to say that in most matters of pleading the procedure on the law side of the United States Courts, sitting in any State, is very nearly the same as in the Courts of that commonwealth, except that in the Federal tribunals the existence of facts necessary to jurisdiction must be averred and to some degree perhaps the line dividing equitable from legal remedies must be preserved.   Where it comes to what are more strictly matters of practice, the procedure of the United States Courts is in many respects identical with that of the State Courts, and in almost all others substantially similar thereto.   In all such matters, however, the prudent practitioner will always carefully examine the Federal Statutes and the rules of the particular United States Court in which he is practicing.

470. In Common Law States a General Issue Plea Does Not Traverse the Jurisdictional Averments.

In States which retain the common law system of pleading the general issue plea does not traverse the jurisdictional averments of the declaration.   In accordance with the Conformity Statute, if in the Federal Court sitting in such a State, the plaintiff alleges in his declaration the necessary jurisdictional facts, and the defendant does not traverse them by special plea in abatement, they are assumed to be true, although there may have been

31a. R. S. Sec. 955, as amended December 22, 1921.

no evidence upon the subject.[32] If in the course of the trial it should affirmatively appear that they are untrue it will be the statutory duty of the Court to dismiss the case, as one not really within its jurisdiction.

In Code States in which the general denial of the answer traverses the jurisdictional facts, the plaintiff must prove them. In most of the States in which the code system of pleading prevails, it is not necessary to plead specially in abatement. A general denial in the answer of all the allegations of the declaration or complaint that are not admitted, puts the burden of proving them upon the plaintiff. In such States it has accordingly been held that unless the defendant by its answer admits the jurisdictional allegations, the plaintiff must prove them, and if he does not, judgment must be given against him.[33]

471. Conformity Statute and Codes Applicable to Particular Counties Only.

In Maryland and perhaps in other States, there are separate codes for nearly every county. In some States, the legal requirements with reference to pleading and practice of the Courts differ in the different local subdivisions. The Act of Congress does not provide for the adoption of such local statutes.

472. Speedy Judgment Acts.

For example, in Maryland the Speedy Judgment Act applies to Baltimore City. There are acts, similar in purpose, but differing more or less in detail, in force in

---

32. Sheppard vs. Graves, 14 How. 505; 14 L. Ed. 518; Steigleder vs. McQuesten, 198 U. S. 141; 49 L. Ed. 986; 25 Sup. Ct. 616.

33. Roberts vs. Lewis, 144 U. S. 653; 36 L. Ed. 579; 12 Sup. Ct. 781; Lindsay-Bitton Live Stock Co. vs. Justice, 191 Fed. 163; 111 C. C. A. 525. The latter case overrules Hill vs. Walker, 167 Fed. 241; 93 C. C. A. 33, in which the whole subject and all the authorities are elaborately discussed.

quite a number of the counties of the State. No one of these regulates the practice of the District Court of the United States for the District of Maryland. That practice is necessarily uniform throughout the district. Conformity to the State practice as near as may be, is brought about by a rule of Court adopting the act effective in Baltimore City, with some modifications, the latter made in view of the fact that it is not quite fair to call on a defendant in Garrett or Worcester to plead in a clerk's office in Baltimore City quite so promptly as can reasonably be demanded of a resident of Baltimore.

473. Common Law Trials with Jury Unless Waived.

Every common law trial in the Federal Courts is to a jury unless the parties otherwise agree, as in civil, but not in criminal cases they may do. The agreement may be in writing or it may be by word of mouth. If it is not in writing, the right to a review of any ruling upon the admission or rejection of testimony or upon any other question growing out of the evidence, has been waived. The judgment of the Court is final. It has been held that the verbal agreement of the parties to submit the case to the Judge without a jury is as an agreement to abide by his arbitration.[34]

The statute, however, provides that the parties may stipulate in writing to try the case before the Court without a jury. When this is done, exceptions may be taken and writs of error issued in the same manner as if the trial was before a jury.[35]

474. Qualifications of Jurors.

The qualifications of jurors in the United States Courts are those prescribed by the law of the State in

---

34. Bond vs. Dustin, 112 U. S. 604; 28 L. Ed. 835; 5 Sup. Ct. 296.
35. Revised Statutes, secs. 649, 700.

which the Court is sitting. This rule has in some cases been very strictly enforced. Thus, a prisoner was indicted for having, while president of a national bank at Asheville, North Carolina, abstracted and embezzled its funds. His counsel and the district attorney stipulated in writing that the defendant might plead to the indictment, but should have the right on motion in arrest or for a new trial to take advantage of all matters and things available on motion to quash or by demurrer. After he had been four times tried and twice convicted, he attacked the competency of the Grand Jury by which he was indicted on the ground that two members of it were persons who had been assessed for taxes in North Carolina, but who had not paid their taxes for the preceding year, and who therefore were not, according to the State law, qualified to serve as jurors. The Circuit Court of Appeals held that this objection was fatal, reversed the judgment, and sent the case back with an order to quash the indictment. It was then about nine years since the offense had been committed. The Statute of Limitations was a complete bar to any further prosecution.[36]

475. Competency of Witnesses in Civil Cases Determined by State Law.

By Act of June 29, 1906,[37] the competency of a witness to testify in any civil action, suit or proceeding in the Courts of the United States is to be determined by the laws of the State or Territory in which the Court is held. The Act by its terms applies to cases at law, in equity[38] and in admiralty.

36. Breese vs. United States, 143 Fed. 250; 74 C. C. A, 388.
37. 34 Stat. 618; 9 Fed. Stat. Ann. 1421; U. S. Comp. Stat., sec. 1464.
38. Rowland vs. Bisecker, 185 Fed. 515; 107 C. C. A. 615.

476. Court Determines the Law, the Jury the Facts.

In civil as in criminal cases in the Federal Courts, the Court, that is to say, the judge, is the judge of the law; the jury of the facts. The judge is at liberty to comment upon the latter as fully as he sees fit, always provided he makes the jury understand that they are the final judges of the facts, and that they are at full liberty to disregard anything that he says on that subject, although they are absolutely bound to accept the law as laid down by him.

477. What Happens When Both Parties Ask for an Instructed Verdict.

Sometimes at the close of the trial, each party asks for an instructed verdict, and for nothing more, so far as the right of recovery goes. In the Federal Courts this amounts to an agreement that there are no disputed questions of fact which could operate to deflect or control the question of law. It is a request that the Court find the facts. The parties are bound by the finding upon which the resultant instruction is given, and the Appellate Court is limited to the consideration of the conclusion of law. If it be sound, and there is evidence to support it, the judgment must be affirmed.[39]

This rule, however, does not prevent either party from submitting a peremptory instruction, and does not prevent either party, after its request for a peremptory instruction has been refused, making a request that some issues of fact going to the right of recovery, be submitted to the jury. If he does and his request is denied, his rights upon writ of error will be the same as if he had not in the first instance sought a binding instruction.[40]

39. Beuttell vs. Magone, 157 U. S. 154; 39 L. Ed. 654; 15 Sup. Ct. 566.
40. Empire State Cattle Co. vs. Atchison, Topeka & Santa Fe Ry. Co., 201 U. S. 1; 50 L. Ed. 633; 26 Sup. Ct. 387.

To prevent misunderstanding, it is doubtless desirable in such cases to ask at the same time, but in the alternative, for the other instructions as well as for that seeking a directed verdict.

478. Exceptions to Charge Must Point Out Particular Error Complained of.

If counsel wish to reserve an exception of any value to the charge of the judge, it is necessary to point out to him specifically the very proposition alleged to be erroneous. The rule in this respect is the same in civil as in criminal cases.[41]

479. Federal Courts Will Direct Verdicts in Cases in Which in Courts of Some States Such Direction Could Not Be Given.

In the Federal Courts when the evidence points so unmistakably to one conclusion that no fair-minded and intelligent man could come to any other, the Court will instruct the jury to find a verdict accordingly. Such instruction will be given, although there may be a scintilla of evidence on the other side. The Court will direct a verdict for one party in those cases in which it would feel bound to set aside a verdict for the other.[42] This is contrary to the practice prevailing in some of the States.

Such direction has been given at the conclusion of the plaintiff's opening statement and before any evidence was offered. In the leading case on the subject the plaintiff, who had been consul general of Turkey, sued the Winchester Arms Co. for upwards of $130,000, which he alleged to be due him as a commission on a large sale of rifles to the Turkish Government. From

41. Section 127, supra.

42. Delaware, Lackawanna & Western R. R. Co. vs. Converse, 139 U. S. 469; 35 L. Ed. 213; 11 Sup. Ct. 569.

the opening statement of his counsel, it appeared that he had agreed for a commission to use his large personal influence with the Turkish officer detailed to select and buy the arms. The Court at once directed a verdict for the defendant. The Supreme Court said it was right in so doing.[43]

480. Actions on Bonds of Contractors for Public Works Must Be Brought at Law.

Under Acts of August 13, 1894,[44] and February 24, 1905,[45] the bonds of contractors for public works are to be so conditioned as to protect not only the United States, but all persons supplying the contractors with labor and materials in the prosecution of the work contracted for. The action upon such a bond must be brought at law,[46] unless the surety on the bond, availing itself of its statutory privilege, pays the full amount of the penalty of the bond into Court, in which case, the proceedings will be simply for the distribution of the fund, and therefore, in equity.[47]

481. When the United States Itself Brings the Suit.

If the United States itself brings suit upon such a bond, those who furnished labor or materials and have not been paid, have a right to intervene in the suit, and to have their rights and claims adjudicated therein, subject however to the priority of the claim and judgment of the United States. If there is not enough remaining after paying the United States to pay all other claims in

43. Oscanyan vs. Arms Co., 103 U. S. 261; 26 L. Ed. 539.

44. 28 Stat. 278; 8 Fed. Stat. Ann. 374; U. S. Comp. Stat., sec. 6923.

45. 33 Stat. 811; 8 Fed. Stat. Ann. 374; U. S. Comp. Stat., sec. 6923.

46. Illinois Surety Co. vs. Peeler, 240 U. S. 225; 60 L. Ed. 609; 36 Sup. Ct. 321.

47. Ibid.

full, whatever is left is distributed pro rata among the claimants.[48]

482. How Suit is Brought by Others than the United States.

If the United States does not bring suit within six months after the final completion and settlement of the contract, any person who has supplied labor and materials for the prosecution of the work, and has not been paid therefor, may apply to the proper department under affidavit for a certified copy of the contract and bond which will be furnished him. He may then sue, in the name of the United States. Only one action on a bond may be brought. Subject to the time limitations mentioned in the next section, all creditors entitled to the protection of the bond may intervene in that action. All known creditors shall be given such personal notice of the pendency of the suit and of their right to intervene as the Court may direct, and in addition thereto, notice, for at least three successive weeks shall be given by publication in some newspaper of general circulation in the State or town where the contract is being performed.[49]

483. Time Within Which Such Suits Must Be Brought.

No one other than the United States may sue on such bond until after six months from the final completion and settlement of the work, and suit must be brought, if at all, within one year after such final completion and settlement, and not later, so that there is only six months from the accrual of the right to sue until its expiration.[50]

---

48. 33 Stat. 812; 8 Fed. Stat. Ann. 374; U. S. Comp. Stat. Sec. 6923.
49. 33 Stat. 812; 8 Fed. Stat. Ann. 374; U. S. Comp. Stat. Sec. 6923.
50. 33 Stat. 812; 8 Fed. Stat. Ann. 374; U. S. Comp. Stat. Sec. 6923; Texas Cement Co. vs. McCord, 233 U. S. 157; 58 L. Ed. 893; 34 Sup. Ct. 550.

This period begins to run not from the date of final payment by the Government, but from the time when the contract being completed, the Government, according to established administrative methods, has determined what amount, if any, is due the contractor.[51] It does not depend upon the consent or agreement of the contractor that the amount awarded is correct.[52]

The unpaid furnisher of labor or materials may bring suit at any time within the six months allowed him by law. His time is not cut down by the provision of the statute, that he must give newspaper notice of the pendency of the suit once a week for three successive weeks, the last of which publications shall be at least three months before the time limited for intervention, and which is of course one year after the final completion and settlement.[53] That provision is directory and not jurisdictional.[54]

484. All Claims Under One Bond Should Be Tried Together.

The provision of the statute that all claims on a single bond shall be presented in a single suit is intended to "avoid the expense, confusion and delay incident to a multiplicity of actions, and to enable each claimant to be heard not only in support of his own claim, but also in opposition to the claims of others in so far as their allowance may tend to prevent the full payment of his claim, and generally to conserve the common security for the benefit of all who are entitled to share in it."[55]   No

51. Illinois Surety Co. vs. Peeler, 240 U. S. 218; 60 L. Ed. 609; 36 Sup. Ct. 321; Arnold vs. U. S., C. C. A., 4th Cir., Feb. 9, 1922.

52. Illinois Surety Co. vs. Peeler, supra.

53. 33 Stat. 812; 8 Fed. Stat. Ann. 374; U. S. Comp. Stat. Sec. 6923.

54. U. S. vs. New York Steam Fitting Co., 235 U. S. 327; 59 L. Ed. 253; 35 Sup. Ct. 108.

55. Miller vs. American Bonding Co., 257 U. S., decided Dec. 12, 1921.

claimant has a right to a separate trial. Ordinarily all claims should be submitted to a single jury, but when, under exceptional circumstances, there are special and persuasive reasons for departing from the practice, the trial Court, in the exercise of a sound judicial discretion, may do so.[56]

56. Ibid.

CHAPTER XVII.

PROCEDURE OF FEDERAL COURTS WHEN SITTING AS COURTS OF EQUITY.

485. General Equitable Procedure.

The procedure on the equity side of the Federal Courts requires separate consideration.

Originally equity had no jurisdiction in any case where a plain, adequate and complete remedy might be had at law. Such is still the rule in the Federal Courts.

486. Whether a Plaintiff Has a Remedy at Law Depends on Whether He Had Such Remedy in 1789.

Whether a plaintiff has such remedy at law depends not upon the state of the law at the time the suit is brought, but upon what it was when the Constitution drew the line of demarcation between legal and equitable jurisdiction. In many, perhaps in most, of the States, legislation has now provided legal remedies for many wrongs which formerly could have been redressed in Courts of equity alone. For example, the laws of Louisiana provide that, in a proceeding at law, a creditor may subject his debtor's property to the lien of his judgment, although before it was recovered the debtor, for the purpose of defrauding his creditors, conveyed such property to some one else. The existence of such a statute in no wise limits the equitable jurisdiction of the District Court of the United States for the District of Louisiana. In 1789 there existed no adequate and complete remedy at law, and the jurisdiction of equity to set aside such deeds and subject the property to the lien of the plaintiff's judgment was then thoroughly established.

487. Federal Courts of Equity May Enforce New Equitable Remedies for Equitable Rights.

The bounds of the equity jurisdiction of the United States Courts being fixed by the Constitution, can neither be extended nor restricted by State legislation.[1] As has been stated, Federal Courts can, however, avail themselves of any new equitable remedy for the enforcement of a right which is equitable in its nature.

Jurisdiction over proceedings to quiet title and to prevent litigation is inherent in equity. The Courts have imposed limitations upon its exercise by declaring that to maintain a bill to quiet title it is necessary that the plaintiff be in possession and, in most cases, that his title shall have been established at law or be founded on undisputed or long-continued possession. It is competent for the legislative power to remove such limitation.

A statute of Nebraska provided that an action might be brought and prosecuted to final decree by any person claiming title to real estate, whether in actual possession or not, against any person who claimed an adverse estate or interest therein for the purpose of determining such estate and interest and quieting the title to such real estate. It was held, the lands being wild and unoccupied and neither party in possession, that a bill to quiet title could be sustained in the Circuit Court for the District of Nebraska.[2] When, however, the defendant is in possession and the plaintiff claims a good legal title, the latter has a plain, adequate and complete remedy at law and no State statute will entitle him to proceed on the equity side of the Federal Courts.[3]

1. Mississippi Mills vs. Cohn, 150 U. S. 202; 37 L. Ed. 1052; 14 Sup. Ct. 75.

2. Holland vs. Challen, 110 U. S. 15; 28 L. Ed. 52; 3 Sup. Ct. 495.

3. Whitehead vs. Shattuck, 138 U. S. 146; 34 L. Ed. 873; 11 Sup. Ct. 276.

488. Federal Equity Procedure Uniform Throughout the Country.

While under the Conformity statute the pleading and practice of the Federal Courts on their law side are necessarily as varied as that of the States, precisely the opposite is true as to the conduct of their chancery business. Federal equity procedure and practice are uniform throughout the country.

It is well to remember, however, that a receiver in possession of property under order of the Federal Court must, under penalty of fine or imprisonment, manage and operate it according to the valid requirements of State law, in the same manner as its owner or possessor would be bound to do if in possession.[4]

489. Equity Rules of Supreme Court Regulate Federal Equity Procedure.

Under the provisions of sections 913 and 917 of the Revised Statutes, the procedure in equity in the Federal Courts is, in larger part, regulated by the equity rules prescribed from time to time by the Supreme Court. Such rules were first adopted in 1842. They remained in force for seventy years. During that time amendments and additions were made to them, but their general scheme remained substantially unaltered. On February 1, 1913, an entirely new set went into force. They made radical changes in equity pleading and practice.

490. The New Equity Rules.

They are published in full in Volume 198 of the Federal Reporter. They are intended to promote the prompt decision of causes and to insure, so far as possible, that they shall be decided in accordance with the substantial rights of the parties and not upon mere technicalities.

4. J. C. sec. 65; 5 Fed. Stat. Ann. 540; U. S. Comp. Stat. Sec. 1047.

491. Technical Forms of Equity Pleading Abolished.

To this end the 18th rule declares "unless otherwise prescribed by statute or these rules, the technical forms of pleading in equity are abolished."

492. The Bill.

A bill in equity should set forth the full name of every party when known, his citizenship and residence. If any party be under disability, that fact should be stated. The bill should contain a short and plain statement of the grounds upon which the jurisdiction of the Court depends, and of the ultimate facts upon which the plaintiff seeks relief. It is expressly directed that any mere statements of evidence shall be omitted. If from the bill it appears that there are proper parties to the litigation not made parties to the cause, the bill should explain why; as, for example, that they are without the jurisdiction of the Court or that they cannot be made parties without ousting its jurisdiction. If any special relief pending the suit or on final hearing is wanted, the bill must state it and ask for it. Relief may be sought in the alternative. Wherever special relief pending the suit is desired, as, for example, a preliminary injunction, the bill should be verified by oath of the plaintiff or by some one having knowledge of the facts upon which such relief is asked.[5] One of the objects of the Supreme Court was to get rid of unnecessary prolixity in equity pleading. It is the duty of the Courts to give effect to this purpose by requiring counsel to omit unnecessary allegations and to cut out all useless verbiage no matter how greatly it may have the sanction of centuries behind it.

493. Joinder of Separate Causes of Action.

If there is only a single plaintiff and a single defendant, the plaintiff may unite all his causes of action

5. Rule 25.

cognizable in equity in one bill. Where there is more than one plaintiff the causes of action joined must be joint. If there is more than one defendant the liability must be one asserted against all the material defendants or sufficient grounds must appear for uniting the causes of action in order to promote the convenient administration of justice. To further convenience, justice and dispatch, the Court is empowered to order separate trials of the various causes of action alleged if, in its judgment, all of them cannot conveniently be disposed of together.[6]

494. Process.

By the 12th Rule the clerk is required, upon the filing of a bill of complaint, to issue a subpœna for the defendant. It is returnable within twenty days from its issue.

495. Time in Which to Answer.

The defendant must file his answer or defense on or before the twentieth day after the subpœna is served on him,[7] unless for cause the judge extends the time for so doing. In counting these days, the day of service is excluded.[8] If he fails to answer in time the bill may be taken as confessed. These provisions greatly change the former practice. Under the old rules, all process was returnable to a particular return day; now it is returnable within twenty days of its issue. What is more important, the defendant no longer has so many days in which to enter his appearance and then so many additional days to answer. He is required to file his answer within twenty days after the subpœna has been served upon him.

6. Rule 26.
7. Rule 16.
8. Rule 12.

496. Pleas and Demurrers in Equity Are Abolished.

Pleas and demurrers in equity are abolished. If upon reading a bill filed against your client you are of opinion that upon the face of it you have a defense in point of law, whether it be for misjoinder of parties, non-joinder of an indispensable party, or insufficient allegations of fact to constitute a valid cause of action in equity, you may make a motion to dismiss the bill or you may set up your defense in your answer. Whether you do one or the other that portion of your defense may, at the discretion of the Court, be called up and disposed of before final hearing. Every defense formerly presentable by plea in bar or abatement should be made in the answer, and in the discretion of the Court may be separately heard and disposed of before the trial of the principal case.[9]

497. Must Answer Within Five Days After Denial of Motion to Dismiss.

If, representing the defendant, you move to dismiss the bill or any part thereof, your motion may be set down for hearing by either party on five days' notice. If it is denied your answer must be filed within five days thereafter or a decree *pro confesso* will be entered.[10]

498. The Answer.

The rules require the defendant, in his answer, to set forth, in short and simple terms, his defense to each claim asserted by the bill. He is to omit mere statements of evidence. He is to avoid any general denial of the averments of the bill. He must specifically admit or deny or explain the facts upon which the plaintiff relies. If he is without knowledge of them, he must say so; and the effect will be the same as if he had denied them.

9. Rule 29.
10. Rule 29.

Averments, other than of value or amount of damage, if not denied, shall be deemed confessed except as against an infant, a lunatic or other person *non compos* and not under guardianship. When justice requires, an answer may be amended by leave of the Court or the judge, upon reasonable notice, so as to put any averment in issue. The answer may state as many defenses in the alternative, regardless of consistency, as the defendant deems essential to his defense.[11]

499. Cross Bills Abolished, Counter-Claims in Answer Substituted.

Cross bills are abolished. There is no further necessity for them. The answer *must* state in short and simple form any counter-claim arising out of the transaction which is the subject-matter of the suit, and *may* set up any set-off or counter-claim against the plaintiff which might have been the subject of an independent suit in equity against him. Such set-off or counter-claim, so set up, has the same effect as a cross suit, and enables the Court to pronounce a final judgment, both on the original and cross claims.[12]

500. What Affirmative Claims May Defendant in His Answer Make Against Plaintiff?

The lower Federal Courts seem to be having some difficulty in determining just what the Supreme Court meant by saying that the defendant might set out in his answer any set-off or counter-claim which might be the subject of an independent suit in equity against the plaintiff. There is, of course, no question that even when taken in connection with Rule 23, providing if the suit be in equity and a matter ordinarily determinable at law

11. Rule 30.
12. Rule 30.

arises, it shall be determined in the pending suit, Rule 30 does not permit the setting up in the answer by way of counter-claim, of an entirely independent demand not having its origin in the same transaction, and in its nature, assertable at law only.[13]

The language of Rule 30 is admittedly broad, but with the inherent conservatism of the Courts, some judges have held that the defendant may not set up any claim which he could not, under the old system of pleading, have made the subject of a cross bill.[14] It is easy to conceive of two controversies which, although between the same parties, are so unconnected that they cannot with any advantage be tried together. Perhaps it is because they have had such instances in mind that some of the Courts have been so unwilling to give to the words of the rule their most natural interpretation. Even if the broadest construction be accepted, it is not necessary that two unrelated cases shall be tried together. Rule 26 expressly provides that where the plaintiff joins two or more causes of action in his bill, the Court may order separate trials when they cannot be conveniently disposed of together. Doubtless the same discretion may be exercised when the difficulty of trying all the issues at one time is caused by the defendant uniting in his answer two or more counter-claims. It will be quite possible to deal in one action, although if need be by separate trials, with all the equitable controversies between the same parties, provided they are all within the jurisdiction of the Federal Courts. In that way a final decree when drawn will dispose of all the controversies

13. Bankston vs. Commercial Trust & Savings Bank, 250 Fed. 985; 163 C. C. A. 235.

14. Williams Patent Brusher & Pulverizer Co. vs. Kinsey Mfg. Co., 205 Fed. 375; Terry Steam Turbine Co. vs. B. F. Sturtevant Co., 204 Fed. 103; Christensen et al vs. Westinghouse Traction Brake Co., 235 Fed. 898.

between the parties at one time and neither will be able to secure a decree against the other, while the other's equity suit is still pending against him. The whole subject, and all the authorities, up to the date of his decision, have been ably reviewed by JUDGE RELLSTAB.[15]

501. General Replication Abolished.

Where the answer does not rely upon a set-off or counter-claim the case is regarded as at issue upon the filing of the answer. No general replication is required. If the answer sets up a set-off or counter-claim, the plaintiff must reply thereto within ten days after the filing of the answer unless the judge allows a longer time. In default of a reply a decree *pro confesso* on the counter-claim may be entered as in default of an answer to the bill.[16]

502. Exceptions to Answer Abolished.

Exceptions to an answer are abolished, but if the answer set up an affirmative defense, set-off or counter-claim, the plaintiff, upon five days' notice, or such further time as the Court may allow, may test the sufficiency of the same by motion to strike out.[17]

503. Equity Suit May Be Turned Into a Suit at Law.

Rule 22 provides that "if at any time it appear that a suit commenced in equity should have been brought as an action on the law side of the court, it shall be forthwith transferred to the law side and be there proceeded with, with only such alteration in the pleadings as shall be essential."

15. Electric Boat Co. vs. Lake Torpedo Boat Co., 215 Fed. 377.
16. Rule 31.
17. Rule 33.

504. No Longer Necessary to Send Legal Issue to Law Court for Trial.

Rule 23 directs that "if in a suit in equity a matter ordinarily determinable at law arises, such matter shall be determined in that suit according to the principles applicable, without sending the case or question to the law side of the Court," and we have already seen that a statute now permits the interposition of equitable defenses in an action at law.[18] I do not understand that it is intended by these rules to break down the doctrine that in the Federal Courts, law and equity are to be kept separate and to be administered by distinct tribunals. All that is now purposed, I suppose, is that this doctrine while preserved in substance, shall not be enforced in such a way as to cause any unnecessary hardship to the parties.

505. Amendments.

Amendments may be allowed, at the discretion of the court, in furtherance of justice, at any stage of the proceedings, and the court may disregard any error or defect in the proceeding which does not affect the substantial rights of the parties.[19]

Whenever an amendment is made to a bill after answer filed, the defendant must put in a new or supplemental answer within ten days after that on which the amendment or amended bill is filed, unless the time is enlarged or it is otherwise ordered by a judge of the Court.[20]

506. Testimony to be Taken in Open Court.

A great revolution in the practice of the Federal Courts has been worked by the new rule which requires

18. 38 Stat. 956; 5 Fed. Stat. Ann. 1061; U. S. Comp. Stat. Sec. 1251b.
19. Rule 19.
20. Rule 32.

the testimony in equity causes to be taken orally in open Court. Where witnesses reside more than a hundred miles from the place of holding the Court, or where for other reasons prescribed by statute it is permissible to take their depositions out of Court, such depositions may still be taken and used, as they may be when in the case of particular witnesses good and exceptional cause for departing from the general rule is shown by affidavit.[21]

507. Time Within Which Depositions Must Be Filed.

It is provided that all depositions taken under a statute or under any order of Court shall be taken and filed, unless otherwise ordered by the Court or judge for good cause shown, within the following times, viz: "those of the plaintiff within sixty days from the time the cause is at issue; those of the defendant within thirty days from the expiration of the time for the filing of plaintiff's depositions; and rebutting depositions by either party within twenty days after the time for taking original depositions expires."[22]

508. Expert Testimony in Patent and Trade-Mark Cases.

In a case involving the validity or scope of a patent or trade-mark, the District Court may, upon petition, order that the testimony in chief of expert witnesses whose testimony is directed to matters of opinion, shall be set forth in affidavits and filed as follows—those of the plaintiff within forty days after the cause is at issue, those of the defendant within twenty days after the plaintiff's time has expired, and those in rebuttal within fifteen days after the expiration of the time for filing original affidavits. These are obviously to be *ex parte* affidavits, because the rule provides that, should the party

21. Rules 46, 47.
22. Rule 47.

desire the production of any affiant for cross-examination, the Court will, on motion, direct that the cross-examination and re-examination shall take place before the Court upon the trial, and unless the affiant is produced and submits to cross-examination in compliance with such direction his affidavit shall not be used as evidence in the cause.[23] So far as my personal experience goes, the filing of an affidavit of an expert is not very common. He is usually examined and cross-examined in open Court, although the other practice may be and sometimes is followed.

509. When Case Goes on Trial Calendar.

As soon as the time for taking and filing depositions under these rules has expired, the case is placed on the trial calendar. Thereafter no further testimony by deposition may be taken except for some strong reason shown by affidavit. In every application for permission to do so, the reason why the testimony of the witness cannot be had orally at the trial and why his deposition has not been before taken shall be set forth, together with the testimony which it is expected he will give.[24]

510. Postponements and Continuances.

After a cause has been placed on the trial calendar it may be passed over to another day of the same term by consent of counsel or order of Court. It shall not be continued beyond the term save in exceptional cases by order of the Court upon good cause shown by affidavit and upon such terms as the Court shall at its discretion impose. Continuances beyond the term by the consent of the parties shall be allowed on condition only that a stipulation be signed by counsel for all the parties, and

23. Rule 48.
24. Rule 56.

that all costs incurred theretofore be paid. Thereupon an order shall be entered dropping the case from the trial calendar subject to re-instatement within one year upon application to the Court by either party, in which event it shall be heard at the earliest convenient day. If not so reinstated within the year the suit shall be dismissed without prejudice to a new one.[25]

511. Reference to Special Masters Discouraged.

Before the new rules, special masters had been much used in the Federal Courts. Such references had become in many places so habitual as to result in much increased cost and in great waste of time. Rule 59, therefore, declares that, save in matters of account, a reference to a master shall be the exception and not the rule. Such reference will be made only upon a showing that some exceptional condition requires it.

512. Beginning Proceedings Before Special Master.

The party on whose motion the order of reference is made must cause it to be presented to the master for a hearing within twenty days succeeding the time when it was made, unless a longer time is specially granted by the Court or judge. If he omits to do so the other party is at liberty forthwith to cause proceedings to be had before the master at the cost of the party procuring the reference.[26]

513. Proceedings Before Special Master.

Under an order of reference a special master can compel the attendance of witnesses before him. He can go thoroughly into the facts and the law and is expected so

25. Rule 57.
26. Rule 59.

to do. When he prepares his report, the approved practice is for him to submit it, or copies of it, to the various counsel in the case and give them time to examine it and make objections to him. He considers these objections. He either does or does not change his report to meet them. He then returns it to the Court with his findings of fact and conclusions of law. He usually files with it a transcript of all the testimony taken before him and the originals of all exhibits filed with him. The report, after it is submitted, lies in the clerk's office for twenty days. If no exceptions are taken within that time it stands confirmed. If any are filed they stand for a hearing before the Court, if then in session, or if not, at the next sitting held thereafter by adjournment or otherwise.[27]

514. Frivolous Exceptions to Master's Report Penalized.

In order to prevent exceptions to reports being filed for frivolous causes, or for mere delay, the exceptant for every exception overruled pays $5 costs to the other party, and for every one sustained is entitled to a like sum.[28]

515. Weight to Be Given to Master's Report.

The weight to be given to a special master's report depends to a large extent upon the circumstances under which the reference is made and upon its terms. He is usually appointed to assist in the various proceedings incidental to the progress of the cause—as to take and state accounts, to take and report testimony, and to perform such duties as require computation of interest, the value of annuities, the amount of damage in particular

27. Rule 60.
28. Rule 67.

cases, the auditing and ascertaining of liens on property involved, and similar services.[29]

His report is merely advisory to the Court. The latter may accept and act upon it or disregard it in whole or in part, according to its own judgment as to the weight of the evidence. Even in references of this character the Court confirms the report as matter of course if exceptions are not taken to it. Unless the master's findings are found unsupported or defective in some essential particular, there is a presumption in their favor. It is this kind of reference, and this only, that can be made by the Court upon its own motion or upon the application of one of the parties without the consent of the other. Sometimes, however, both parties consent to a reference to a master to hear and decide all issues in the case and to report his findings both of the facts and the law. The determinations of the master so selected are not subject to be set aside and disregarded at the mere discretion of the Court. Such a reference is a submission of the controversy to a judge of the parties' own selection, to be governed in his conduct by the ordinary rules applicable to the administration of justice in tribunals established by law. His findings are to be taken as presumptively correct, subject indeed to be reviewed under the reservation contained in the consent and order of the Court, when there has been manifest error in the consideration given to the evidence or in the application of the law, but not otherwise. Such findings should not be disturbed unless they are clearly in conflict with the weight of the evidence upon which they were made.[30]

516. Preliminary Injunctions.

In at least one State, if a plaintiff sets forth, in his bill, a good cause for an injunction, the Court must give

29. Kimberly vs. Arms, 129 U. S. 523; 32 L. Ed. 764; 9 Sup. Ct. 355.
30. Kimberly vs. Arms, supra.

him one and that too, without hearing the other party, or at all events, without giving any weight to what the other party says. The refusal of such an injunction is ground for appeal.[31]

In the Federal Courts of Equity the rule is different. Before issuing an injunction they make every effort, reasonably practicable under all the circumstances, to hear the defendant's side. No preliminary injunction, technically so-called, ever issues from a Federal Court until after the party to be enjoined has been heard or has had an opportunity to be heard.[32]

517. Temporary Restraining Orders.

There are cases in which temporary restraining orders must be issued at once to prevent the situation being so radically changed before the parties can be heard as to make the hearing a rather academic performance. There have been some abuses, however, in the issuance of such restraining orders. While in form, temporary, they have frequently amounted, in fact, to preliminary, and sometimes almost to permanent injunctions. This happened when the time fixed for the hearing of the motion for the preliminary injunction was long postponed. In such a case the restraining order might remain in force as long as it was of any substantial use to the plaintiff or of any practical injury to the defendant.

Rule 73 was intended to prevent such abuse in the future. Its provisions have been incorporated in, and made somewhat more specific by sections 17 and 18 of the Clayton Act, which declare that "no temporary restraining order shall be granted without notice to the opposite party unless it shall clearly appear from specific

31. Articles 5, 31, Bagby's Maryland Code, 1912.

32. Sec. 17, Clayton Act, Oct. 15, 1914; 5 Fed. Stat. Ann. 983; U. S. Comp. Stat. Sec. 1243.

facts, shown by affidavit or by the verified bill, that immediate and irreparable injury, loss or damage will result to the applicant before notice can be served and a hearing had thereon.'' The order must define the injury and state why it is irreparable and why it was granted without notice. By its terms it must expire within such time after entry, not to exceed ten days, as the Court or judge may fix, unless within the time so fixed it is extended for a like period for good cause shown. The reasons for such extension, if granted, must be entered of record. Whenever a temporary restraining order is granted without notice the matter of the issuance of a preliminary injunction must be set down for hearing at the earliest possible time. It takes precedence over all matters, except older matters of the same character. ''When the same comes up for hearing the party obtaining the temporary restraining order shall proceed with his application for a preliminary injunction, and if he does not do so the Court shall dissolve his temporary restraining order. Upon two days' notice to the party obtaining such temporary restraining order, the opposite party may appear and move the dissolution or modification of the order, and in that event the Court or judge shall proceed to hear and determine the motion as expeditiously as the needs of justice may require.''

518. Hearings on Motions for Preliminary Injunctions.

Motions for preliminary injunctions were formerly heard almost exclusively upon affidavits. That practice is still common, although in some districts, judges prefer to have the evidence produced in open Court, and subject to cross-examination. In the order of Court setting down for hearing a motion for a preliminary injunction, unless the testimony is to be taken in open Court, it is usually provided that the plaintiff shall have so many

days to file affidavits in support of his motion, and that
the defendant shall have so many days thereafter to file
affidavits in reply.   Proper provision is also made for
the filing of rebutting affidavits by the complainant.

Section 18 of the Clayton Act requires that before a
restraining order or interlocutory injunction shall issue,
the applicant must give security in such sum as the Court
or judge may deem proper for the payment of such costs
or damages as may be incurred or suffered by any party
who may be found to have been wrongfully enjoined or
restrained.

519. Clerk May Make Orders in Course.

A Federal judge may not be as accessible as a State
judge usually is.   He may be required, in the discharge
of his duties, to be at some point quite remote from his
clerk's office.   The equity rules therefore authorize the
clerk to issue a greater number of orders in course than
is the practice in State Courts.[33]

520. Sales Under Equity Decrees of the Federal Courts.

The discretion of a Federal Court of Equity in the selling of real estate is more limited than is that of the Courts
of some States.[34]   The latter may under proper circumstances and with due care to prevent abuse, direct real
property to be sold at private sale.   Congress has withheld such powers from the Federal Courts.

Whenever real estate or an interest in land is sold
under an order or decree of any United States Court, the
sale must be public.   It has been held by the Circuit Court
of Appeals for the Fourth Circuit that this provision of

33. Rule 5.
34. Act March 3, 1893, 27 Stat. 751: 3 Fed. Stat. Ann. 241; U. S. Comp.
Stat. Sec. 1640.

law is mandatory.[35] Even after confirmation, a private sale may be set aside at the instance of the purchaser.

Moreover, the statute restricts the place at which sales may be made to the Court House of the county, parish or city in which the land is situated or to the premises. On the other hand, the Court is given power to direct in what other manner sales of personal property may be made. If no special direction is given the statutory provisions must be followed.

Before real estate can be validly sold under a judicial decree, notice of the sale must be given once a week for at least four weeks prior to the date fixed for it, in at least one newspaper printed, regularly issued and having a general circulation in the county and State where the real estate proposed to be sold is situated if such there be, and the statute has been construed to require that the first insertion shall be at least twenty-nine days before the day of sale.[36]

35. Cumberland Lumber Co. vs. Tunis Lumber Co., 171 Fed. 352; 96 C. C. A. 244.

36. Wilson vs. Northwestern Mut. Life Ins. Co., 65 Fed. 38; 12 C. C. A. 35; Walker vs. Stuart, 261 Fed. 427.

CHAPTER XVIII.

THE SUBSTANTIVE LAW APPLIED BY THE FEDERAL COURTS.

521. The Substantive Law Applied by the Federal Courts to Cases Within Their Exclusive Jurisdiction.

So far as concerns those subjects the control of which is by the Constitution given to the Federal Government, the substantive law applied is found in the statutes of Congress, in the decisions of the Federal Courts, in the general principles of admiralty and of international law, and in what is, in the view of the Federal Courts, the common law.

522. Substantive Law Applied by the Federal Courts to Cases in Which Their Jurisdiction is Concurrent With Courts of the States.

There are many cases which can be brought in either a State or a Federal Court. Some of these, if instituted originally in the State Court, may be removed to the Federal; as, for example, those in which Federal questions are involved or in which there is the necessary diversity of citizenship between the parties.

523. Federal Courts Apply State Law.

Generally speaking the substantive law applied to such controversies is the same as governs the State Courts of the State in which the Federal Court is sitting. Quite clearly it ought to be so. Most of the transactions which get into Court are entered into subject to the law of some State. Except in very peculiar cases there is no reason why that law should not be applied to the settlement of the controversy, whether the case, if in Baltimore, be tried in the State Court on the west side of Monument Square or in the Federal on the east side.

524. State Statutes Rules of Decision in Common Law Trials in Federal Courts.

Section 34 of the original Judiciary Act provided that "the laws of the several States, except where the Constitution, treaties or statutes of the United States shall otherwise require or provide, shall be regarded as rules of decision in trials at common law in the Courts of the United States in cases where they apply." This provision now constitutes section 721 of the Revised Statutes.

525. Federal Courts Are Bound by the Construction Given by the Highest Court of the State to Its Constitution and Statutes.

A part of the law of every State is its Constitution and its statutes. There may often be room for difference of opinion as to what particular provisions of either may mean. The interpretation put upon them by the highest Court of the State will be accepted by the Federal Courts as governing all transactions which originated after the announcement of the State Court decision. They will not inquire whether it commends itself to their judgment or not. The reasons for this rule were explained many years ago by CHIEF JUSTICE MARSHALL. He said:—

"This court has uniformly professed its disposition, in cases depending on the laws of a particular State, to adopt the construction which the courts of the State have given to those laws. This course is founded on the principle, supposed to be universally recognized, that the judicial department of every government, where such department exists, is the appropriate organ for construing the legislative acts of that government. Thus, no court in the universe, which professed to be governed by principle, would, we presume, undertake to say, that the courts of Great Britain, or of France, or of any other nation, had misunderstood their own statutes, and therefore erect itself into a tribunal which should correct such misunderstanding. We receive the construction given by the courts of the nation, as the true sense of the law, and feel ourselves no more at liberty to depart from that construction, than to depart from the words of the statute. On this principle, the construction given by this court to the Constitution and laws of the United States is received by all as the true construction; and on the same principle, the construction given by the courts of the several States to the legislative acts of those States, is received as true, unless they come in conflict with the Constitution, laws or treaties of the United States."[1]

526. Applicable State Statutes Will Be Enforced By Federal Courts Sitting in Equity Where the Demarcation Between Law and Equity is Not Affected.

The statute has reference to cases at common law only. It does not apply to chancery suits for reasons which have already been fully explained. Nevertheless, Federal Courts sitting as Courts of equity, do administer the statutory law of the State. Its applicable statutes are enforced by a Federal chancellor precisely as they would be in a common law case except where they in somewise affect the line of demarcation between law and equity. A State statute in force at the time of the delivery of a mortgage gave the mortgagor twelve months to redeem after foreclosure sale. It was held that such right could be exercised when the mortgage was foreclosed in a Federal Court.[2]

527. Section 721 Has Application to Substantive Law and Not to Procedure.

Back in the early twenties of the last century there were hard times in Kentucky. Creditors were insistent and were, moreover, not willing to take the notes of State banks in payment. The Legislature provided that if, upon execution, plaintiff would not accept them, the defendant, upon giving a bond, might replevy the property seized and thereby stay further proceedings for two years. It was contended that this statute was applicable to judgments rendered by the Federal Courts in Kentucky. The Supreme Court held that it was not, and

1. Elmendorf vs. Taylor, 10 Wheat. 152; 6 L. Ed. 289.
2. Brine vs. Insurance Co., 96 U. S. 627; 24 L. Ed. 858.

pointed out that section 34 of the Judiciary Act, now section 721 of the Revised Statutes, relates solely to rules of decision and has nothing to do with process.[3]

The real purpose of the 34th section was to recognize a principle of universal law, viz: that in every forum a contract is governed by the law with a view to which it was made.

528. When it is Claimed that the State Has Impaired the Obligation of a Contract the Decisions of the State Courts as to the Construction of a Statutory or Constitutional Provision Are Not Always Binding on Federal Courts.

Sometimes after a statute or a constitutional provision of a State has received a settled construction from its highest Court, and contracts have been made in reliance thereon, the policy of the State and the decisions of its Courts change. Under such circumstances the Supreme Court has sometimes held that the later construction by the State Court was itself a part of the State action and impaired the obligation of the contracts. Thus, for example—the Supreme Court of Iowa had in a number of decisions delivered between 1853 and 1859 upheld the right of municipalities of that State to issue bonds in aid of railroad enterprises. In 1857 the City of Dubuque issued such bonds which were taken in good faith by the public. In 1859 the Supreme Court of Iowa held that it had been wrong in its previous decision and that under the Constitution of the State a municipality had no right to issue bonds for any such purpose. The Supreme Court of the United States held that such change of decision could not impair the obligation of the contract between the city and the bondholders.[4]

3. Wayman vs. Southard, 10 Wheat. 1; 6 L. Ed. 253.
4. Gelpcke vs. City of Dubuque, 1 Wall. 175; 17 L. Ed. 520.

529. State Court Construction of State Statutes Made After a Case Has Been Brought in the Federal Courts Not Binding Upon It.

A creditor of a corporation brought suit in a State Court against a non-resident defendant to enforce a liability said to be imposed by a State statute upon him as a stockholder. He removed the case to the Federal Court. Up to the time the suit was brought the State Courts had never construed the statute. While the case was pending, the highest Court of the State interpreted it. Under the meaning thereby given it the defendant would have been liable. This construction was held not to be binding upon the Federal Courts, the Supreme Court saying:—

"The Federal courts have an independent jurisdiction in the administration of State laws, co-ordinate with, and not subordinate to, that of the State courts, and are bound to exercise their own judgment as to the meaning and effect of those laws." * * * "Since the ordinary administration of the law is carried on by the State courts, it necessarily happens that by the course of their decisions certain rules are established which become rules of property and action in the State, and have all the effect of law, and which it would be wrong to disturb. This is especially true with regard to the law of real estate and the construction of State constitutions and statutes. Such established rules are always regarded by the Federal courts, no less than by the State courts themselves, as authoritative declarations of what the law is. But where the law has not been thus settled, it is the right and duty of the Federal courts to exercise their own judgment; as they also always do in reference to the doctrines of commercial law and general jurisprudence. So when contracts and transactions have been entered into, and rights have accrued thereon under a particular state of the decisions, or when there has been no decision, of the State tribunals, the Federal courts properly claim the right to adopt their own interpretation of the law applicable to the case, although a different interpretation may be adopted by the State courts after such rights have accrued.　But even in such cases, for the sake of harmony and to avoid confusion, the Federal courts will lean towards an agreement of views with the State courts if the question seems to them balanced with doubt.　Acting on these principles, founded as they are on comity and good sense, the courts of the United States, without sacrificing their own dignity as independent tribunals, endeavor to avoid, and in most cases do avoid, any unseemly conflict with the well-considered decisions of the State courts.　As, however, the very object of giving to the national courts jurisdiction to administer the laws of the States in controversies between citizens of different States was to institute independent tribunals which it might be supposed would be unaffected by local prejudices and sectional views, it would be a dereliction of their duty not to exercise an independent judgment in cases not foreclosed by previous adjudication."[5]

530.　"Laws" of the State Do Not Always Include Its Unwritten Laws.

The word "laws" as used in section 721 does not necessarily include the decisions of the State Courts as to what their unwritten law is.　Many years ago the Supreme Court said:—

> "They are, at most, only evidence of what the laws are, and are not, of themselves,. laws.　They are often re-examined, reversed and qualified by the courts themselves, whenever they are found to be either defective, or ill-founded, or otherwise incorrect.　The laws of a State are more usually understood to mean the rules and enactments promulgated by the legislative authority thereof, or long established local customs having the force of laws."

5. Burgess vs. Seligman, 107 U. S. 33; 27 L. Ed. 359; 2 Sup. Ct. 10.

The Court went on to say in all the various cases which had hitherto come before it for decision it had uniformly supposed that a true interpretation of the 34th section limited its application to State laws, strictly local;

"that is to say, to the positive statutes of the State, and the construction thereof adopted by the local tribunals, and to rights and titles to things having a permanent locality, such as the rights and titles to real estate, and other matters immovable and intra-territorial in their nature and character. It never has been supposed by us, that the section did apply, or was designated to apply, to questions of a more general nature, not at all dependent upon local statutes or local usages of a fixed and permanent operation, as, for example, to the construction of ordinary contracts or other written instruments, and especially to questions of general commercial law, where the State tribunals are called upon to perform the like functions as ourselves, that is, to ascertain upon general reasoning and legal analogies, what is the true exposition of the contract or instrument, or what is the just rule furnished by the principles of commercial law to govern the case. And we have not now the slightest difficulty in holding, that this section, upon its true intendment and construction, is strictly limited to local statutes and local usages of the character before stated, and does not extend to contracts and other instruments of a commercial nature, the true interpretation and effect whereof are to be sought, not in the decisions of the local tribunals, but in the general principles and doctrines of commercial jurisprudence. Undoubtedly, the decisions of the local tribunals upon such subjects are entitled to, and will receive, the most deliberate attention and respect of this court; but they cannot furnish positive rules, or conclusive authority, by which our own judgments are to be bound up and governed."[6]

6. Swift vs. Tyson, 16 Peters, 1; 10 L. Ed. 865.

This was a case in which some persons in Maine had sold land, to which they claimed to have good title, to a citizen of New York. They drew upon him for part of the purchase money. He accepted the draft in New York. His acceptance was, therefore, a New York contract, and as the draft was to be paid in New York the contract was made and to be performed in that State. After the draft had been accepted it was endorsed over by the drawers to another citizen of Maine on account of a pre-existing debt owed by them to him. He had no knowledge of the circumstances. At the trial in the United States Court it appeared that the representations made by the original vendors of the land and drawers of the draft were materially untrue and fraudulent. The holder of the draft, the plaintiff in the suit, answered that he was a *bona fide* holder for value. Under the law of New York, he was not such holder, because according to the then rulings of its Courts, one who took a negotiable instrument on account of a pre-existing debt was not a holder for value in such sense that he could maintain an action when the original payee could not. The Supreme Court held, however, that this was a question of general commercial law; that they were not bound by the decisions of the State Courts of New York, and that such holder was a holder for value.

531. Reasons Why Supreme Court Will Not in Some Matters Follow State Decisions.

It is desirable that State and Federal Courts shall apply the same law to similar state of facts. It is also true that it is highly expedient that commercial transactions, frequently extending, as they do, across State lines, shall be governed by a law uniform throughout the nation. Only the Supreme Court of the United States is so situated that it may hope that its views will, in the long run, be accepted in all parts of the Union. It has therefore deemed it wise in such matters to follow its own opinion.

The law of negotiable instruments,[7] the construction of insurance contracts,[8] the liability of common carriers,[9] the validity of the stipulations in their bills of lading,[10] the measure of damages in suits against them,[11] the law of master and servant,[12] are among the questions of commercial law as to which the Federal Courts do not feel constrained to follow the State decisions. They, of course, are bound by any valid and applicable State statute, and the adoption by a number of the States of uniform laws on many such subjects has narrowed the field in which a divergence between State and Federal ruling is still possible.

The whole subject of when and how far the Federal Courts must follow the decisions of those of the States is reviewed in the case of Kuhn vs. Fairmount Coal Co.[13]

7. Railroad Co. vs. National Bank, 102 U. S. 23; 26 L. Ed. 61.

8. Carpenter vs. Providence Washington Ins. Co., 16 Peters, 495; 10 L. Ed. 1044.

9. Chicago, Milwaukee & St. Paul Ry. Co. vs. Ross, 112 U. S. 377; 28 L. Ed. 787; 5 Sup. Ct. 184.

10. Railroad Co. vs. Lockwood, 17 Wall. 357; 21 L. Ed. 627.

11. Railway Co. vs. Prentice, 147 U. S. 101; 37 L. Ed. 97; 13 Sup. Ct. 261.

12. B. & O. R. R. Co. vs. Baugh, 149 U. S. 368; 37 L. Ed. 772; 13 Sup. Ct. 914.

13. 215 U. S. 349; 54 L. Ed. 228; 30 Sup. Ct. 140.

CHAPTER XIX.

APPELLATE JURISDICTION OF THE COURTS OF THE UNITED
STATES—DIRECT APPEALS FROM DISTRICT COURTS TO
SUPREME COURT.

532. Two Methods of Initiating Appellate Proceedings.

A review of the rulings and conclusions of the lower Court may be sought in one of two ways—either by writ of error or by appeal. The former is the appropriate method of bringing to the attention of the reviewing tribunal mistakes which the lower Court made in hearing and determining a case at law. The latter is the proceeding by which a reversal or modification of an erroneous determination of a suit in equity may be secured. The circumstances under which each of them can be properly employed will be considered later. While discussing the appellate jurisdiction of the Federal Courts, in order to avoid unnecessary repetition, the word appeal will be used whichever is meant.

533. Courts Over Which the Appellate Jurisdiction of the Federal Courts May Be Exercised.

The jurisdiction of the Circuit Court of Appeals is limited to appeals from the District Courts of their respective circuits, and to the enforcement or review of certain classes of orders of the Interstate Commerce Commission, the Federal Reserve Board and the Federal Trade Commission.[1] The Supreme Court may sometimes entertain direct appeals from the District Courts. In some classes of cases it has, and must exercise, appellate jurisdiction over the determinations of the Circuit Courts of Appeals, and it may, if it deems best, by writ of *certiorari,* review any of their decisions. It, moreover, may under some circumstances, issue writs of error or of *certiorari,* to the Courts of the States. The last is the most important, though by no means the most frequently exercised, jurisdiction of the highest Court of the Union.

534. Jurisdiction of the Circuit Courts of Appeals.

Except as stated in the next preceding section, the Circuit Courts of Appeals exercise appellate jurisdiction only.

The rule is that from the final decision of a District Court, an appeal may be taken to the Circuit Court of Appeals of the circuit.[2] To this rule there are certain exceptions, viz: those in which an appeal lies directly from the District Court to the Supreme Court. Such cases are enumerated in the Judicial Code.[3] In order accurately to understand the limits of the jurisdiction of

1. Sec. 11, Clayton Act. Oct. 15, 1914; 9 Fed. Stat. Ann. 741; U. S. Comp. Stat. Sec. 8835j.

2. Judicial Code, Sec. 128; 5 Fed. Stat. Ann. 607; U. S. Comp. Stat. Sec. 1120.

3. Judicial Code, sec. 238; 5 Fed. Stat. Ann. 794; U. S. Comp. Stat. Sec. 1215.

the Circuit Court of Appeals, it is necessary to know when the Supreme Court may be asked to review directly a final decision of a District Court.

535. Jurisdiction of the Supreme Court Over Direct Appeals From the District Courts.

There are six classes of cases, or, more accurately, of questions of great importance which may be carried directly from the District to the Supreme Court. They are:—

1. Cases in which the jurisdiction of the District Court is in issue.

2. Prize causes.

3. Cases that involve the construction or application of the Constitution of the United States.

4. Cases in which the constitutionality of any law of the United States is drawn in question.

5. Cases in which the validity or construction of any treaty made under the authority of the United States is drawn in question.

6. Cases in which the Constitution or law of a State is claimed to be in contravention of the Constitution of the United States.

The reasons why it is expedient that they be promptly passed upon by the Supreme Court are obvious.

Apparently it has not always been easy for the profession to be sure whether certain concrete cases are or are not within any of them. A good deal of confusion and not a little profitless litigation has been thereby occasioned. It will be worth while to examine each of the classes separately and in some little detail, as well as to mention more briefly some other classes of cases usually of less moment in which an appeal lies directly from the District to the Supreme Court.

536. When the Jurisdiction of the District Court is in Issue.

The first class of cases which may be appealed directly from a District Court to the Supreme Court are those in which the jurisdiction of the former is in issue. There may be various reasons for questioning the jurisdiction of a District Court to entertain a proceeding instituted before it. The defendant may set up that no Court, whether of the State or the Nation, has any authority to pass upon such a controversy as the plaintiff raises, or he may say that the plaintiff has taken into a court of law a case cognizable only in equity or *vice versa,* or, while admitting that the dispute is one upon which it is fitting a Court should pass and that the plaintiff has as between the legal and equitable sides of the Court chosen rightly, he may contend that the case is not one over which the particular District Court of the United States has jurisdiction under the Constitution and the statutes.

537. The Issue Must Be as to the Jurisdiction of a District Court as a Court of the United States.

It is only when the jurisdiction of the District Court as a Court of the United States is challenged that an appeal can be taken directly to the Supreme Court. If the objection would be equally applicable to the jurisdiction of a State Court or of any Court of law or of any Court of equity, as the case may be, then no issue is raised which can be carried directly to the Supreme Court.

In the first and leading case on the subject, a bill in equity was filed, by a citizen of Rhode Island against a citizen of Massachusetts, alleging failure to pay royalties under a patent license and praying for an injunction and an accounting. More than the necessary jurisdictional amount was in controversy. The defendant objected to the jurisdiction on the ground that there was a plain,

adequate and complete remedy at law. The lower Court
so held. The plaintiff took an appeal to the Supreme
Court. It was there dismissed. The Court quoted with
approval what had been said in an earlier case by CHIEF
JUSTICE FULLER while presiding over the Circuit Court
of Appeals for the Seventh Circuit, to the effect that—

> "We do not understand that the power of the
> Circuit Court to hear and determine the cause was
> denied, but that the appellants contended that the"
> appellees "had not, by their bill, made a case
> properly cognizable in a court of equity. The objec-
> tion was the want of equity, and not the want of
> power. The jurisdiction of the Circuit Court was
> therefore not in issue within the intent and meaning
> of the act."[4]

"When the requisite citizenship of the parties appears,
and the subject-matter is such that the Circuit Court is
competent to deal with it, the jurisdiction of that court
attaches, and whether the court should sustain the complainant's prayer for equitable relief, or should dismiss
the bill with leave to bring an action at law, either would
be a valid exercise of jurisdiction. If any error were
committed in the exercise of such jurisdiction, it could
only be remedied by an appeal to the Circuit Court of
Appeals."[5]

In another case, the lower Court dismissed the bill because in its view the controverted questions had become
res adjudicata in consequence of certain prior decisions
of a State Court. The Supreme Court said that the jurisdiction of the lower Court as a Court of the United States
was not in issue and therefore that an appeal directly to
it did not lie.[6]

---

4. World's Columbian Exposition Case, 56 Fed. 656; 6 C. C. A. 58.
5. Smith vs. McKay, 161 U. S. 355; 40 L. Ed. 731; 16 Sup. Ct. 490.
6. Blythe vs. Hinckley, 173 U. S. 501; 43 L. Ed. 783; 19 Sup. Ct. 497.

In Louisville Trust Co. vs. Knott,[6a] the subject was rather fully reviewed. It was there held that the question as to whether a State or a Federal Court had first acquired jurisdiction of certain property did not raise any question of the jurisdiction of the Federal Court as such, but merely a question as to which of two Courts of concurrent jurisdiction had first acquired it in the particular case. The appeal was therefore dismissed.

The same conclusion was reached when the question at issue was, whether, the necessary diversity of citizenship existing, a suit could be maintained in a Court of the United States under the Employer's Liability Act of Massachusetts. The defendant contended that the Court had no jurisdiction to enforce the penal law of another sovereignty. The Supreme Court said that was a question of general law and not one peculiar to the Court below as a Federal Court.[7]

On the other hand, it is clear that where the jurisdiction of the District Court is challenged upon the ground that there is not the necessary diversity of citizenship to give it jurisdiction as a Federal Court a direct appeal will lie. A guardian of an infant brought suit in the Federal Court. The facts were such that if the citizenship of the guardian determined whether the diversity existed or not, the Court had jurisdiction; while, if the citizenship of the ward was the controlling circumstance, it had not. It was held that an appeal to the Supreme Court was properly taken.[8]

Quite obviously such an appeal is authorized where the jurisdiction of the Court below turns on the residence of

6a. 191 U. S. 225; 48 L. Ed. 159; 24 Sup. Ct. 119.

7. Fore River Shipbuilding Co. vs. Hagg, 219 U. S. 175; 55 L. Ed. 163; 31 Sup. Ct. 185.

8. Mexican Central Ry. Co. vs. Eckman, 187 U. S. 429; 42 L. Ed. 245; 23 Sup. Ct. 211.

the defendant or on the existence of a Federal question.[9]

A rather peculiar case was one in which the Italian ambassador intervened in a proceeding *in rem* against an Italian ship, by suggesting to the District Court certain facts which, in the judgment of the Court, if true, showed the ship to be immune from arrest. It therefore dismissed the libel.

On appeal the Supreme Court said that the Courts could not take cognizance of suggestions from the diplomatic representatives of foreign powers, unless they were made through the medium of our own State Department. If the Court below had ignored the suggestion, as it should have done, there would have been no question as to its jurisdiction. The appeal from the action of the Court below was properly taken directly to the Supreme Court[10] and could not be taken to the Circuit Court of Appeals.[11] It perhaps might have been nearly as easy to argue that the objection to the jurisdiction went not so much to the jurisdiction of the District Court as such, but would have been equally applicable to any American judicial tribunal, State or Federal.

538. Whether Defendant is Liable to Suit in the Particular District Raises a Question of Jurisdiction Which Can Be Carried Directly to the Supreme Court.

A controversy as to whether the defendant is or is not liable to suit in the particular district in which the action has been brought, when arising in a case in which there is a sufficient amount in controversy, and either a Federal

9. Davidson Bros. Marble Co. vs. U. S., 213 U. S. 10; 53 L. Ed. 675; 29 Sup. Ct. 324; Moyer vs. Peabody, 212 U. S. 78; 53 L. Ed. 410; 29 Sup. Ct. 235.

10. The Pesaro, 255 U. S. 216; 65 L. Ed. 339; 41 Sup. Ct. 308.

11. The Carlo Poma, 255 U. S. 219; 65 L. Ed. 340; 41 Sup. Ct. 309.

question is involved or diversity of citizenship exists, raises a question of jurisdiction directly appealable to the Supreme Court.[12]

In one case the plaintiff and the defendant were citizens of different States. Suit had been brought in a State Court in a district of which neither was a resident. The defendant removed the case to the Federal Court. The question of jurisdiction turned on whether or not the plaintiff had waived its right to object that the defendant was not suable in that particular Court. A direct appeal was properly taken to the Supreme Court.[13]

539. Whether Defendant Has Been Properly Served With Process Raises a Question of Jurisdiction Appealable to the Supreme Court.

It has been held that whether the Federal Court acquired jurisdiction over a defendant by a proper service may be reviewed by direct appeal to the Supreme Court,[14] although in principle whether it should be is admittedly a close question.

540. Direct Appeal to the Supreme Court as to Jurisdiction Carries Up That Question Only.

The statute provides that in any case in which the jurisdiction of the District Court is in issue, that question alone shall be certified to the Supreme Court. A defendant may believe that the lower Court was without jurisdiction, and may also be persuaded that it was wrong on other questions. If he carries the case directly to

12. Ladew vs. Tennessee Copper Co., 218 U. S. 357; 54 L. Ed. 1069; 31 Sup. Ct. 81.

13. Western Loan & Svgs. Co. vs. Butte & Boston Con. Mining Co., 210 U. S. 368; 52 L. Ed. 1101; 28 Sup. Ct. 720.

14. Remington vs. Central Pacific R. R. Co., 198 U. S. 95; 49 L. Ed. 959; 25 Sup. Ct. 577.

the Supreme Court he will be able to bring up the jurisdictional issue only, and if it should decide against him he would be unable to raise his other objections. On the other hand he may not wish to waive his protest against the assumption of jurisdiction. He therefore does not want to drop that contention and go to the Circuit Court of Appeals on the others alone. What he should do under such circumstances was elaborately discussed by the Supreme Court in United States vs. Jahn.[15] The following rules were there laid down:

1. If the jurisdiction of the Circuit (now District) Court is in issue and decided in favor of the defendant, as that disposes of the case, the plaintiff should have the question certified and take his appeal or writ of error directly to the Supreme Court.

2. If the question of jurisdiction is in issue, and the jurisdiction sustained, and then judgment or decree is rendered in favor of the defendant on the merits, the plaintiff who has maintained the jurisdiction must appeal to the Circuit Court of Appeals, where, if the question of jurisdiction arises, the Circuit Court of Appeals may certify it.

3. If the question of jurisdiction is in issue, and the jurisdiction sustained, and judgment on the merits is rendered in favor of the plaintiff, then the defendant can elect either to have the question certified and come directly to the Supreme Court or to carry the whole case to the Circuit Court of Appeals and the question of jurisdiction can be certified by that Court.

4. If in the case last supposed the plaintiff has ground of complaint in respect of the judgment he has recovered, he may also carry the case to the Circuit Court of Appeals on the merits, and this he may do by way of cross-appeal

15. 155 U. S. 109; 39 L. Ed. 87; 15 Sup. Ct. 39.

or writ of error if the defendant has taken the case there, or independently, if the defendant has carried the case to the Supreme Court on the question of jurisdiction alone, and in this instance the Circuit Court of Appeals will suspend a decision upon the merits until the question of jurisdiction has been determined.

5. The same observations are applicable where a plaintiff objects to the jurisdiction and is, or both parties are, dissatisfied with the judgment on the merits.

541. Same Party Cannot Take Two Appeals—One on the Jurisdiction, the Other on the Merits.

From these rules it appears that there cannot be two appeals by the same party, one to the Supreme Court on the question of jurisdiction and one to the Circuit Court of Appeals on the merits.[16]

Where the defeated party first appeals to the Circuit Court of Appeals on the merits and then to the Supreme Court on the question of jurisdiction, the appeal to the Supreme Court will be dismissed.[17]

542. When Appeal is Taken to the Circuit Court of Appeals on the Jurisdiction and Other Questions, the Circuit Court of Appeals May, But Need Not, Certify the Question of Jurisdiction.

Where an appeal is taken to the Circuit Court of Appeals generally, the question of jurisdiction, as well as the merits, being involved, if the Circuit Court of Appeals does not see fit to certify the jurisdictional issue to the Supreme Court, no appeal from its decision on that or the other questions in the case will be entertained by the Supreme Court, although, of course, the latter may in its discretion allow a writ of *certiorari*.[18]

16. United States vs. Larkin, 208 U. S. 333; 52 L. Ed. 517; 28 Sup. Ct. 417.

17. Robinson vs. Caldwell, 165 U. S. 359; 41 L. Ed. 745; 17 Sup. Ct. 343.

18. Weber Bros. vs. Grand Lodge, 171 Fed. 839; 96 C. C. A. 410.

543. District Court Must Certify to Question of Jurisdiction.

The statute provides that, in a case in which the jurisdiction of the lower Court is in issue, the question of jurisdiction alone shall be certified to the Supreme Court from the Court below for decision. The Supreme Court has repeatedly ruled that it cannot entertain the appeal unless there is a certificate of the kind specified in the statute or some sufficient equivalent therefor.[19]

It is not necessary that the certificate shall profess to be such. The Court is not required to use the word "certify"; nor is it essential that there shall be anything which on its face purports to be a certificate. It is sufficient if it appears from the lower Court's own statement in the record that its final decision turned on the question of jurisdiction. Thus, a final decree concluded "It is therefore ordered and decreed that said bill be and the same hereby is dismissed for want of jurisdiction." The order allowing the appeal contained the statement that it was allowed upon the final order and decree dismissing the suit for want of jurisdiction. The Supreme Court held that this itself constituted a sufficient certificate.[20]

544. Such Certificate Must Be Granted Within the Term at Which the Final Decree Was Made.

The Supreme Court has ruled that such a certificate must be given, if at all, during the term at which the final decision complained of was made.[21]

---

19. Maynard vs. Hecht, 151 U. S. 324; 38 L. Ed. 179; 14 Sup. Ct. 353.

20. Excelsior Wooden Pipe Co. vs. Pacific Bridge Co., 185 U. S. 282; 46 L. Ed. 910; 22 Sup. Ct. 681.

21. Colvin vs. Jacksonville, 158 U. S. 456; 39 L. Ed. 1053; 15 Sup. Ct. 866.

545. When Decree Constitutes Sufficient Certificate, Appeal May Be Taken at any Time Within Three Months.

The final decree is, of course, made during the term in which the case is decided. When it is itself a sufficient certificate, the defeated party has the statutory period of three months in which to appeal.[22]

546. Direct Appeal from Final Decree in Prize Cases.

Matters of prize almost necessarily have an international aspect. It is therefore expedient that there shall be an opportunity for a prompt and direct review by the Supreme Court of the final decree in all prize causes.

547. Direct Appeals in a Case Involving the Construction or Application of the Constitution of the United States.

In some senses the construction or application of the Constitution of the United States is involved in a very large proportion of the cases in the Federal Courts. If the language of section 238 were in this respect to be given the broadest construction, the large majority of cases decided by the District Courts would be directly appealable to the Supreme Court. In that event the Act of 1891 creating the Circuit Court of Appeals would largely fail of its purpose of lightening the burden of litigation pressing upon the Supreme Court.

548. In a Direct Appeal to the Supreme Court the Constitutional Question Must Be Controlling.

Very shortly after the passage of the act in question, the Supreme Court decided that in such cases a direct appeal to it will lie only when the construction or applica-

22. Herndon-Carter Co. vs. Norris & Co., 224 U. S. 498; 56 L. Ed. 857; 32 Sup. Ct. 550.

tion of the Constitution was the controlling question.[23] As, for example, a citizen of the United States and of South Carolina brought suit against the election officers of his precinct for wrongfully refusing to receive his vote for a member of the National House of Representatives. Here the controlling question was whether the Constitution of the United States gave him the right so to vote, he possessing all the qualifications required of a voter for the members of the most numerous branch of the State Legislature. A direct appeal therefore lay to the Supreme Court.[24]

549. When Construction or Application of Constitution Controls, Supreme Court Passes On All Questions in the Case.

When the jurisdiction of the lower Court is involved and the appeal is taken directly to the Supreme Court, it is the jurisdictional question, and that alone, which is brought up. But in the other classes of cases in which by the provisions of section 238 of the Judicial Code a direct appeal may be taken the rule is otherwise. In them the Supreme Court passes upon all the questions which, under the established principles of law, are upon the record reviewable upon appeal or writ of error, as the case may be.[25]

550. Where the Construction or Application of the Constitution is the Only Question in the Case No Appeal May Be Taken to the Circuit Court of Appeals.

A bank chartered by the State of Tennessee brought suit in the United States Court to enjoin the collection of

23. Carey vs. Houston & Texas Central Ry. Co., 150 U. S. 181; 37 L. Ed. 1041; 14 Sup. Ct. 63.

24. Wiley vs. Sinkler, 179 U. S. 58; 45 L. Ed. 84; 21 Sup. Ct. 17.

25. Horner vs. United States, 143 U. S. 570; 36 L. Ed. 266; 12 Sup. Ct. 522.

a municipal tax, the imposition of which it alleged was a breach of a valid contract between it and the State. The bill was dismissed. The bank appealed to the Circuit Court of Appeals. Here the Court below was affirmed. This was not, as we shall later see, one of the cases in which the decision of the Circuit Court of Appeals was final. The bank thereupon prosecuted a further appeal to the Supreme Court, as it was entitled to do, if the Circuit Court of Appeals had ever regularly acquired jurisdiction of the case. The Supreme Court, however, held that the sole matter in issue being the constitutional question the appeal should have been taken directly to it from the Court of first instance, and that the Circuit Court of Appeals was without jurisdiction.[26]

551. The Statute Does Not Permit Two Appeals From District Court.

In the case last cited, the familiar doctrine is reasserted, that the statute does not give to a party to a cause in the lower Court the right to two appeals, one to the Supreme Court on the constitutional question, and one to the Circuit Court of Appeals on the other issues involved. If the constitutional question is the controlling one in the case, the appeal must be taken directly to the Supreme Court. That Court has, as we have seen, the power to pass on all the other questions involved. If the constitutional question is only incidentally brought into the case, or is only one of two or more questions, any one of which, if decided in favor of the appellant, would entitle him to judgment or decree, an appeal lies to the Circuit Court of Appeals. That Court may then pass on the constitutional as well as on the other questions involved, subject, if the case is not one in which the

26. Union & Planters Bank vs. Memphis, 189 U. S. 71; 47 L. Ed. 712; 23 Sup. Ct. 604.

decision of the Circuit Court of Appeals is made final by statute, to a further appeal from it to the Supreme Court.

552. Constitutional Question is Not Involved Unless it is Clearly Raised Below.

The Supreme Court has said that in order to bring a case within this clause of the Act, the District Court must have construed the Constitution or applied it to the case, or must, at least, have been requested and have declined or omitted to construe or apply it. No construction or application of the Constitution can be said to have been involved in a judgment below, when neither was either expressed or asked for.[27]

553. Cases in Which the Constitutionality of Any Law of the United States is Drawn in Question.

A mere controversy as to the construction of an Act of Congress cannot be taken to the Supreme Court upon a direct appeal.[28]

554. Cases in Which the Validity or Construction of Any Treaty of the United States is Drawn in Question.

It is necessary that the construction or validity of a treaty be involved in other than a merely incidental or remote manner if such circumstance is to justify taking the appeal directly to the Supreme Court.[29]

Pettit vs. Walshe[30] is a good example of a case in which the construction of a treaty was drawn in question. There an alleged offender against the laws of Great Britain was resisting extradition. Both parties referred

27. Cornell vs. Green, 163 U. S. 75; 41 L. Ed. 76; 16 Sup. Ct. 969.

28. Spreckels Refining Co. vs. McClain, 192 U. S. 397; 48 L. Ed. 496; 24 Sup. Ct. 376.

29. Sloan vs. United States, 193 U. S. 614; 48 L. Ed. 814; 24 Sup. Ct. 570.

30. 194 U. S. 205; 48 L. Ed. 938; 24 Sup. Ct. 657.

to the treaty between the two countries and based their contentions in part upon the interpretation they gave its provisions. The Supreme Court held that the construction of that treaty was involved, although it might also be necessary to construe the acts of Congress which provided the machinery for carrying out the obligations imposed by it.

555. A Case in Which the Constitution or Law of a State is Claimed to be in Contravention of the Constitution of the United States.

The remaining class of cases under section 238 of the Judicial Code are those in which an attack was made below upon the constitutionality from a Federal standpoint of some provision of the Constitution or laws of a State. Either party, whose case in the Court below, as made by him, depended upon his being able to show that some State constitutional or statutory provision was in conflict with the Federal Constitution, has the right to appeal from a decision against him directly to the Supreme Court. It was the purpose of Congress to give opportunity, to an unsuccessful litigant, to come to the highest tribunal of the Nation directly from the Federal Court of first instance in every case in which a claim is made that a State law is in contravention of the Constitution of the United States.[31]

556. Direct Appeals by Government in Criminal Cases.

The Act of March 2, 1907,[32] creates another class of cases in which under some circumstances an appeal may be taken directly to the Supreme Court. Allusion has already been made to this statute in connection with the

31. Loeb vs. Columbia Township Trustees, 179 U. S. 472; 45 L. Ed. 280; 21 Sup. Ct. 174.
32. 34 Stat. 1246; 6 Fed. Stat. Ann. 149; U. S. Comp. Stat. Sec. 1704.

discussion of the criminal jurisdiction and procedure of the United States Courts. Appeals by defendants in criminal cases have long been common. They are taken to the Circuit Court of Appeals, and by statute its decision, in such cases, is final, subject, of course, to the right of the Supreme Court to issue a writ of *certiorari* if it sees fit.

The Act of 1907 for the first time gave an appeal to the Government. It is only from certain classes of rulings of the lower Court that such an appeal may be taken. They are: a decision or judgment quashing, setting aside or sustaining a demurrer to any indictment or any count thereof where such decision or judgment is based upon the invalidity or construction of the statute upon which the indictment is founded; a decision arresting a judgment of conviction for insufficiency of the indictment where such decision is based upon the validity or construction of the statute upon which the indictment is founded; and a decision or judgment sustaining a special plea in bar when the defendant has not been put in jeopardy. It is provided that no writ of error shall be taken by or allowed to the United States in any case where there has been a verdict in favor of the defendant.

The Act is constitutional. The objection made to it was that it authorized the United States to bring the case directly to the Supreme Court, but did not allow the accused the same privilege. The Supreme Court said:

"There is no merit in this suggestion. Except in cases affecting ambassadors and other public ministers and consuls and those in which a State shall be a party" * * * "we can exercise appellate jurisdiction, both as to law and fact, with such exceptions and under such regulations as Congress shall make in the other cases to which by the Constitution the judicial power of the United States extends. What such exceptions and regulations should be it is for Congress, in its wisdom, to establish, having of course due regard to all the provisions of the Constitution. If a court of original jurisdiction errs in quashing, setting aside or dismissing an indictment for an alleged offense against the United States, upon the ground that the statute on which it is based is unconstitutional, or upon the ground that the statute does not embrace the case made by the indictment, there is no mode in which the error can be corrected and the provisions of the statute enforced, except the case be brought here by the United States for review. Hence—that there might be no unnecessary delay in the administration of the criminal law, and that the courts of original jurisdiction may be instructed as to the validity and meaning of the particular criminal statute sought to be enforced—the above act of 1907 was passed. Surely such an exception or regulation is in the discretion of Congress to prescribe, and does not violate any constitutional right of the accused.''[33]

557. A Direct Appeal Under the Act of 1907 is Limited to a Review of the Special Questions Enumerated in the Statute.

The Supreme Court has said that the Act plainly shows that jurisdiction is given only to review the special kinds of questions mentioned in it. The whole case may not be opened up above.[34] Thus, for instance, where a demurrer was sustained on two grounds, one involving an appealable question, the other not, the Supreme Court considered only the first.[35] On such appeals the Supreme Court must accept the construction which the lower Court places upon the indictment.[36]

33. United States vs. Bitty, 208 U. S. 393; 52 L. Ed. 543; 28 Sup. Ct. 396.

34. United States vs. Keitel, 211 U. S. 398; 53 L. Ed. 230; 29 Sup. Ct. 123.

35. U. S. vs. Stevenson, 215 U. S. 190; 54 L. Ed. 153; 30 Sup. Ct. 35.

36. U. S. vs. Patten, 226 U. S. 535; 57 L. Ed. 333; 33 Sup. Ct. 141.

558. Direct Appeals Under the Tucker Act.

The Circuit Courts of Appeal have no jurisdiction over appeals from the District Courts in cases arising under the Tucker Act. They go directly to the Supreme Court,[37] in spite of some earlier decisions to the contrary expressly overruled in the case cited.

559. Direct Appeals Under the So-called Expedition Act.

In order to facilitate the prompt and authoritative disposition of a class of cases of great public importance, Congress has provided that in any suit in equity, in which the United States is complainant, brought in any District Court under the Sherman Act or the Act to regulate interstate commerce, or any other Acts having a like purpose, the Attorney-General may file with the clerk of the Court a certificate that in his opinion the case is of general public importance. It is made the duty of the clerk thereupon to furnish a copy of that certificate to each of the circuit judges of the circuit. The case is to be given precedence over others and in every way expedited. It is to be assigned for hearing at the earliest day practicable, and before not less than three of the circuit judges of the circuit, if there be three or more, and if there be not more than two, then before them and such district judge as they may select. An appeal is given directly to the Supreme Court from any case under any of such Acts wherein the United States is complainant, whether the Attorney-General has made the certificate or not. Such appeal must be taken within sixty days from the entry of the decision.[38]

It will be perceived that it is the District Court which

37. J. Homer Fritch, Inc. vs. U. S., 248 U. S. 458; 63 L. Ed. 358; 39 Sup. Ct. 146.

38. Act of Feb. 11, 1903, 32 Stat. 823; 6 Fed. Stat. Ann. 136; U. S. Comp. Stat. Sec. 8824.

is the Court of first instance. If there are any such cases in which the United States is a complainant and they are not expedited, the case is heard before the District Court as ordinarily constituted.[39] When the Attorney-General makes the certificate provided for in the Act, the Court is as a rule composed altogether of circuit judges, that is, of judges who now do not usually sit at *nisi prius*. It is only when it is not practicable to organize a Court of three without having a district judge among them that such a judge may sit. It is before Courts constituted as this Act requires that most of the more important anti-trust litigation of the last ten years has been conducted. The provision that such cases shall be heard ahead of others is intended, of course, to get a speedy decision in matters of much public interest and importance.

560. The Expedition Act is Not Repealed by the Judicial Code.

The Expedition Act was not incorporated in the Judicial Code. The claim was therefore made that it had been repealed by that enactment. The Supreme Court has decided that this contention could not be sustained.[40]

561. Appeals From Interlocutory Injunctions to Suspend State Statutes or Orders of Administrative Boards.

By the Act approved March 4, 1913,[41] section 266 of the Judicial Code is amended in such manner as to give a direct appeal to the Supreme Court from what is, at least nominally, a decision of a District Court in issuing an interlocutory injunction suspending the enforcement

---

39. U. S. vs. American Can Co., 230 Fed. 859.
40. Ex parte United States, 226 U. S. 420; 57 L. Ed. 281; 33 Sup. Ct. 170.
41. 37 Stat. 1013; 5 Fed. Stat. Ann. 983; U. S. Comp. Stat. Sec. 1243.

of a statute of a State, or of an order made by an administrative board or commission created by and acting thereunder. It is provided that no interloctutory injunction suspending or restraining the enforcement, operation or execution of any statute of a State by restraining the action of any officer of such State in its enforcement or execution, or in the enforcement or execution of an order made by an administrative board or commission acting under such statute, shall be granted by a Federal judge upon the ground of the unconstitutionality of such statute, unless the application therefor shall have been heard by not less than three judges, of whom at least one must be a justice of the Supreme Court or a circuit judge. When application is made for such an injunction, the judge to whom it is made calls two other judges to his aid. At least five days' notice of the hearing must be given to the Governor and the Attorney-General of the State, as well as to such other persons as may be defendants in the suit. A temporary restraining order may be issued by the judge to whom the application is made.

That Court is really very much the same as the Circuit Court of Appeals, although nominally it is the District Court. Strictly speaking, a Court, so constituted, cannot hear the case on its merits,[42] although of course very often the ground upon which the preliminary injunction is refused is that there is no equity in the case made by the bill.

From any order either granting or denying the interlocutory injunction, an appeal may be taken directly to the Supreme Court.

To prevent unseemly conflicts between the States and the Federal Courts, the statute provides that if at any time before the hearing of an application for such an interlocutory injunction a suit be brought in a Court of

42. Brown Drug Co. vs. U. S., 235 Fed. 603.

the State having jurisdiction, accompanied by a stay, in such State Court, of proceedings under such statute or order, pending the determination of the suit by the State Court, all proceedings in the United States Court shall be stayed pending the final determination of the suit in the Courts of the State. In order to prevent an abuse of this provision, the statute declares that the stay may be vacated upon proof, made after hearing, and notice of ten days served upon the Attorney-General of the State, that the suit in the State Court is not being prosecuted·with diligence and good faith.

It will be noted that the requirement of a Court of three judges applies to the hearing of a motion for a preliminary injunction only. If without such application the case proceeds to final hearing on the prayer for a permanent injunction, the statute does not apply and such hearing may be had by a single judge.[43]

To issue an interlocutory injunction to stay an order of the Interstate Commerce Commission also requires a District Court of three judges and from their decision an appeal may be taken directly to the Supreme Court.[43a]

562. Direct Appeals Under the Act Empowering the Secretary of War to Require the Removal of Bridges Obstructing Navigable Waterways.

The eighteenth section of the Act of March 3,[44] 1899, authorizes the Secretary of War to require the removal of bridges constituting unreasonable obstructions to the free navigation of navigable waterways, and provides penalties on the owners or controllers of the bridge if they do not remove it as directed, and provides that in any case arising under the section, an appeal or writ of error may be taken by either party directly from the District to the Supreme Court.

43. Republic Acceptance Corp. vs. Deland, 275 Fed. 632.
43a. Act Oct. 23, 1913; 38 Stat. 219.
44. 30 Stat. 1153; 9 Fed. Stat. Ann. 87; U. S. Comp. Stat. Sec. 9970.

CHAPTER XX.

APPEALS TO THE CIRCUIT COURTS OF APPEALS.

563. Jurisdiction of the Circuit Courts of Appeals.

Circuit Courts of Appeals have jurisdiction to review final decisions of the District Courts in all cases except those in which appeals may be taken directly to the Supreme Court or in which some special statute otherwise provides.[1]

564. The Appellate Jurisdiction of a Circuit Court of Appeals Does Not Usually Depend Upon the Amount in Controversy.

Ordinarily appeals may be taken from the District Court irrespective of the amount in controversy. To

1. Judicial Code, sec. 128; 5 Fed. Stat. Ann. 607; U. S. Comp. Stat. Sec. 1120.

this general rule there are some exceptions imposed by the terms of particular Federal statutes. Thus, a decision of the District Court allowing or rejecting, upon the facts, a claim in bankruptcy, is appealable, if the claim amounts to as much as $500, and not otherwise.[2] One who has sued the United States cannot appeal to the Supreme Court from a decision adverse to him unless his claim either exceeds $3,000, or has been forfeited to the United States for fraud under section 172 of the Judicial Code.[3] To avoid misapprehension, it should be stated that the United States may appeal in any case in which there has been a judgment against it, no matter how small is the amount in controversy.

565. Appeals on the Facts May Be Taken From Decisions in Bankruptcy Proceedings in Three Classes of Cases Only.

The right to appeal generally, as in equity, from decisions of the District Courts so as to secure a review both of the facts and of the law, is limited in bankruptcy proceedings to three classes of questions—adjudications, discharges and claims of $500 or upwards. No matter whether an adjudication be decreed or refused, a discharge granted or denied, or a claim for as much as $500 allowed or rejected, the party aggrieved may appeal as of right, precisely as he can from a final decree in equity.[4]

All proceedings of the District Courts in bankruptcy, whether interlocutory or final, other than the three just mentioned, may be superintended and revised by the Circuit Courts of Appeals as to the matters of law involved but not as the facts.[5]

Both the provisions cited have reference to proceedings

2. Bankruptcy Act, sec. 25, par. A, clause 3.
3. Reid vs. United States, 211 U. S. 529; 53 L. Ed. 313; 29 Sup. Ct. 171.
4. Bankruptcy Act, sec. 25a.
5. Bankruptcy Act, sec. 24b.

in bankruptcy proper as distinguished from controversies arising in bankruptcy proceedings. In the latter class of disputes there is the same right of appeal as in independent controversies originating otherwise than in bankruptcy. It is not expedient here to attempt to draw with precision the line which divides proceedings in bankruptcy from controversies arising in bankruptcy proceedings. "The former, broadly speaking, covering questions between the alleged bankrupt and his creditors, as such, commencing with the petition for adjudication, ending with the discharge, and including matters of administration generally, such as appointments of receivers and trustees, sales, exemptions, allowances, and the like, to be disposed of summarily, all of which naturally occur in the settlement of the estate." The latter, speaking with like breadth, involve "questions between the trustee, representing the bankrupt and his creditors, on the one side, and adverse claimants, on the other, concerning property in the possession of the trustee or of the claimants, to be litigated in appropriate plenary suits, and not affecting directly the administrative orders and judgments, but only the question of the extent of the estate."[6]

The whole subject is elaborately considered in the various standard text-books on bankruptcy.

566. In What Cases the Decisions of the Circuit Courts of Appeals Are Final.

The Circuit Courts of Appeals were created to lessen the burdens of the Supreme Court and to promote the prompt dispatch of business. Neither of these results would be attained if every party against whom they decided had a right to carry his case to the Supreme

---

6. In re Friend, 134 Fed. 778; 67 C. C. A. 500.

Court. The Judicial Code,[7] as amended, therefore provides that their decisions shall be final in all admiralty cases; in those in which jurisdiction is dependent entirely upon diverse citizenship, and in all cases arising under the patent, copyright, trade-mark, revenue or criminal laws, or under the Bankruptcy Act of 1898 and of all controversies arising in such bankruptcy proceedings and causes, and of all cases under the Railroad Employers' Liability, Hours of Service and Safety Appliance Acts or any supplements or amendments to any of them. For the most part, the statutory provisions as to the finality of the decisions of these Courts speak for themselves. A little may be profitably said about them.

567. In Cases in Which Federal Jurisdiction is Based Solely on Diverse Citizenship.

Whether jurisdiction depends solely upon diverse citizenship must be determined by an examination of the grounds upon which it was originally invoked. If from the plaintiff's statement of his own case, it does not appear that any ground of jurisdiction other than diverse citizenship exists, the decision of the Circuit Court of Appeals will be final, even though in the progress of the case other questions arose of which the Federal Courts would have had jurisdiction independently of the citizenship of the parties.[8] It is, not necessary, however, that the plaintiff shall in so many words base his claim that the Court had jurisdiction on anything other than diverse citizenship. If such other ground actually appears on the face of his pleadings, it makes no difference that he

7. Sec. 128; sec. 4, Act Sept. 6, 1916; 39 Stat. 727; 5 Fed. Stat. Ann. 607; U. S. Comp. Stat. 1120.

8. Colorado Central Consolidated Mining Co. vs. Turck, 150 U. S. 138; 37 L. Ed. 1030; 14 Sup. Ct. 35.

obviously did not appreciate its jurisdictional significance.[9]

When one of the parties is a corporation organized under the laws of the United States and is not a national bank, or a railroad company, the case arises under the laws of the United States. The decision of the Circuit Court of Appeals is therefore reviewable on appeal by the Supreme Court.

As has been explained, for the purposes of the jurisdiction of the United States Courts, the Federal statutes assimilate national banks to State corporations. The Federal Court may have jurisdiction of a suit to which a national bank is a party. That jurisdiction may rest solely upon the fact that the national bank is located in one State and its adversary is a citizen of another State or is an alien. It is held that, in such a case, the jurisdiction of the District Court rests upon diverse citizenship. The decision of the Circuit Court of Appeals, upon appeal from a judgment or decree of the District Court, is therefore final.[10]

568. In Criminal Cases it is Only the Defendant Below Who May Invoke the Jurisdiction of a Circuit Court of Appeals.

As has been already stated, the United States may under some circumstances carry up a criminal case. When it does, its appeal must go directly to the Supreme Court; on the other hand, an appeal of the accused is taken to the Circuit Court of Appeals. The decision of the latter is final unless the Supreme Court sees fit to grant a writ of *certiorari*. This writ is granted spar-

9. Union Pacific Ry. Co. vs. Harris, 158 U. S. 326; 39 L. Ed. 1003; 15 Sup. Ct. 843; Ex parte Jones, 164 U. S. 691; 41 L. Ed. 601; 17 Sup. Ct. 222.
10. Continental National Bank vs. Buford, 191 U. S. 119; 48 L. Ed. 119; 24 Sup. Ct. 54.

ingly, and the criminal cases in which it is allowed are few.

569. Decisions of Circuit Courts of Appeals Are Final in All Cases in Which the Amount in Controversy Does Not Exceed $1,000.

Section 241 of the Judicial Code gives a right of appeal from a judgment or decree of a Circuit Court of Appeals in every case in which the decision of the latter is not made final and in which the amount in controversy exceeds $1,000 besides costs.

570. How the Amount in Controversy is Determined for Purposes of Appeal.

It will be noticed that in stating the sum necessary to give a right of appeal, interest is not expressly excluded, as it is by section 24 in fixing the amount required to be in controversy in order to give jurisdiction to the District Court. It follows that interest accrued before the judgment of the Court below and disposed of by its decree, if in dispute, between the parties, is a part of the sum in controversy; as, for example, when the principal sum of $1,000 and seventeen years' interest thereon at six per cent was the matter in dispute, it was held that the amount in controversy exceeded $2,000,[11] then the amount necessary for an appeal.

The rule was well stated in a subsequent Supreme Court case in which it was said that

> "when the judgment is for the defendant or for the plaintiff, and for less than two thousand dollars, and the plaintiff sues out the writ of error, this court has jurisdiction if the damages claimed in the declaration exceed that sum; but that if the judgment is for plaintiff and not more than two thousand dollars,

11. United States Bank vs. Daniel, 12 Peters, 52; 9 L. Ed. 989.

and the defendant prosecutes in error, this court has not jurisdiction, for the amount in controversy, as to the defendant, is fixed by the judgment. In determining the jurisdictional sum or amount it is obvious that neither interest on the judgment nor costs of suit can enter into the computation, for costs form no part of the matter in dispute, and interest on the judgment can only arise after rendition, while the jurisdictional amount, if determined, by the judgment, is fixed at rendition.'"[12]

To give jurisdiction, the statutory amount must be really in controversy. At a time when the Supreme Court had jurisdiction in certain classes of cases only when the amount exceeded $5,000, there was a verdict for the plaintiff for $5,000. There were motions for new trial and in arrest, both of which were overruled. All this took some time, so that judgment was not entered upon the verdict until a trifle over four months after the latter was rendered. When the judgment was entered, it was for the precise amount of the verdict. Some days later the Court on motion of the defendant's counsel, increased it to $5,116.73, the $116.73 being interest on the amount of the verdict from the time of its rendition to the entering up of the judgment. The Supreme Court said that that amount of interest was not in controversy, as the plaintiff had not claimed it.[13] The motive of the defendant was to get an appeal to the Supreme Court.

571. Amount in Controversy Where Defendant Makes a Counter-Claim.

In cases in which the defendant has put in a counter-claim, the amount in controversy upon an appeal may depend on which party is the appellant. When there has

12. Walker vs. United States, 4 Wall. 163; 18 L. Ed. 319.

13. Northern Pacific R. R. Co. vs. Booth, 152 U. S. 671; 38 L. Ed. 591·
14 Sup. Ct. 693.

been a judgment for the plaintiff, and the defendant appeals, the amount in controversy is the judgment plus the counter-claim. If the defendant upon his counter-claim secures a judgment against the plaintiff, and the latter appeals, the amount in controversy is the sum of the claim and the judgment—as, for example, if the plaintiff claims $900 and the defendant counterclaims for $800, and there is a judgment for the plaintiff for $900, the defendant might appeal, because the amount in controversy from his standpoint would be $1,700. On the other hand, if the defendant recovered only $50, the plaintiff could not appeal, because the amount in controversy would be only $950.[14]

14. Harten vs. Loffler, 212 U. S. 397; 53 L. Ed. 568; 29 Sup. Ct. 351.

CHAPTER XXI.

WRITS OF ERROR FROM SUPREME COURT TO STATE COURTS.

31

572. Section 25 of the Judiciary Act of Sept. 24, 1789.

It is probable that section 25 of the Judiciary Act of September 24, 1789, has played a greater part in shaping the history of this country than any other enactment ever made by Congress. In a modified form, it now forms section 237 of the Judicial Code.[1] That section, as amended, provides, among other things, that "a final judgment or decree in any suit in the highest Court of a State in which a decision in the suit could be had, where is drawn in question the validity of a treaty or statute of, or an authority exercised under, the United States, and the decision is against their validity; or where is drawn in question the validity of a statute of, or an authority exercised under, any State, on the ground of their being repugnant to the Constitution, treaties, or laws of the United States, and the decision is in favor of their validity, may be re-examined and reversed or affirmed in the Supreme Court upon a writ of error."

If the Supreme Court had not been given such jurisdiction there would have been no way of insuring that the Constitution, laws and treaties of the United States should be the supreme law of the land in every part of the Union. There would have been very nearly as many constructions of some of their provisions as there are States. There would have been no way of reconciling these divergent views and no way of asserting the national authority against those prevailing in any particular State. Every State would thus have been able to nullify any law of Congress, if it had so wished, and at one time or another nearly every State has been anxious to press its opposition to some congressional action to the extreme limit of its power. It is, therefore, highly probable that without the provision in question, or some-

1. Sec. 2, Act Sept. 6, 1916; 39 Stat. 726; 5 Fed. Stat. Ann. 723; U. S. Comp. Stat. 1214.

thing very like it, either the Union would have been long since dissolved, or would today be very unlike the one under which we live. If it had not been embodied in the original Judiciary Act, there was probably no subsequent time, prior to 1861, at which it could have been enacted without raising a controversy, which would of itself have imperilled the continuance of the Federal Government.

In the view of a very large school of political thinkers, it extended the judicial power of the United States beyond the limits of the constitutional grant. For many years the Supreme Court of Errors and Appeals of Virginia denied its validity. A very dangerous situation would have resulted had not the original section, with great foresight, provided that when the Supreme Court reversed a judgment or decree of a State Court it might, in its discretion, in any case which had once before been remanded by it, proceed to a final decision and award execution. State Courts would have refused to obey its mandate, as, in fact, the Supreme Court of Errors and Appeals of Virginia did. There would have been no way, which public opinion would have sustained, of coercing the State Court into obedience. When, however, the Supreme Court issued execution directly against the individual parties to the cause, they had either to submit or take the responsibility of making armed resistance to the officers of the United States. The requirement that before execution may issue directly from the Supreme Court there must have been one remand to the State Court, is no longer law. Section 237 of the Judicial Code now provides that the Supreme Court may, at its discretion, either remand the case or award execution.

The argument for and against the constitutionality of this section need not be here considered. That question has, long ago, been settled beyond the possibility of controversy or appeal. While it still was open, there was, from the standpoint of a jurist who did not think nationally and who looked more to the past than to the future, much to be urged against its validity. Few better examples of great legal ability devoted to the discussion of a question of transcendent importance are to be anywhere found than the opinion of CHIEF JUSTICE MARSHALL[2] in support of the constitutionality of the provision, and that of JUDGE ROANE[3] of the Virginia Court of Appeals on the other side.

573. Right to Review is Confined to Questions Which Affect the Boundary Between Federal and State Sovereignty.

As the wording of the section plainly shows, its sole purpose is to make the Supreme Court the final arbiter of litigated questions, the answer to which depends upon the correct determination of the respective spheres of the State and Federal sovereignties. It was not passed to give the Supreme Court power to correct all the mistakes which it might think State judges had made. If such errors, real or imaginary, do not affect the distribution of power between the State and Federal Governments, the latter has no concern with them.

574. When the Federal Question is Involved, the Right of Review is Not Limited to Any Particular Kind of Suit, Nor is the Amount in Controversy Material.

As we have seen, that jurisdiction of the lower Federal Courts which is concurrent with the Courts of the States is limited to civil suits, although a few criminal cases of a peculiar and limited character may be removed from

2. Cohens vs. Virginia, 6 Wheat. 264; 5 L. Ed. 257.
3. Hunter vs. Martin, 4 Munf. (18 Va.) 25.

the State to the Federal Courts.[4] On the other hand, section 237 of the Judicial Code is equally applicable to criminal and to civil suits.[5] If one of the questions enumerated in it has been raised and determined adversely to the Federal right relied upon, the Supreme Court may issue its writ of error, or grant *certiorari*. None of the reasons which have withheld from the Federal Courts jurisdiction over special classes of legal controversies, such as divorce suits, probate proceedings, etc., here apply. Any one who in the State Courts claims a Federal privilege has, if it be denied him by the highest Court of the State to which he can carry that particular litigation, the right to invoke the judgment of the Supreme Court of the nation thereon. The Constitution, laws and treaties of the United States are thus made in fact, as well as in theory, the supreme law of the land.

The amount in controversy is not material. In the great case of Cohens vs. Virginia the plaintiffs in error were resisting the payment of a fine of $100 and costs amounting in all to $131.50.

575. The Various Classes of Cases in Which the Supreme Court May Issue Writs of Error to State Courts.

An analysis of what is now section 237 as amended[6] of the Judicial Code will show that there are six classes of cases in which the final decree of a State Court may be re-examined by the Supreme Court.

First, where the validity of a treaty or statute of, or an authority exercised under, the United States is drawn in question, and the decision is *against* its validity.

4. Sec. 33, Judicial Code, 39 Stat. 532; 5 Fed. Stat. Ann. 380; U. S. Comp. Stat. Sec. 1015.

5. Cohens vs. Virginia, 6 Wheat. 264; 5 L. Ed. 257; Twitchell vs. The Commonwealth, 7 Wall. 321; 19 L. Ed. 223.

6. Act Sept. 6, 1916; 39 Stat. 726; Act of Feb. 17, 1922.

Second, where the validity of a statute of, or an authority exercised under, any State on the ground of its being repugnant to the Constitution, treaties or laws of the United States is drawn in question and the decision is in *favor* of its validity.

Third, where the validity of a treaty or statute or of an authority exercised under the United States is drawn in question and the decision is in *favor* of its validity.

Fourth, where the validity of a statute of, or an authority exercised under any State on the ground of its being repugnant to the Constitution, treaties or laws of the United States, is drawn in question, and the decision is *against* its validity.

Fifth, where any title, right, privilege or immunity is claimed under the Constitution, or any treaty or statute of, or commission held or authority exercised under the United States, and the decision is in *favor* of the title, right, privilege or immunity especially set up and claimed under such Constitution, statute, commission or authority.

Sixth, where any title, right, privilege or immunity is claimed under the Constitution, or any treaty or statute of, or commission held or authority exercised under the United States, and the decision is *against* the title, privilege or immunity especially set up and claimed under such Constitution, statute, commission or authority.

A recent enactment[7] adds what perhaps may be called a seventh class, although in many cases it will probably be included within one of the others, and that is "in any suit involving the validity of a contract, wherein it is claimed that a change in the rule of law or construction of statutes by the highest court of a State applicable to such contract would be repugnant to the Constitution of the United States."

In the first two and the seventh of such classes, a writ

7. Act Feb. 17, 1922.

of error will issue; in the others, it will not, but the Supreme Court may, if it will, bring the case up by its writ of *certiorari*.

576. The Supreme Court May Now Review Decisions Sustaining the Claim of Federal Right, But it is Not Required To Do So.

For more than a century and a quarter, the right of the Supreme Court to review decisions of State Courts was limited to cases in which the decision below was in effect *against* the Federal right claimed. That is, it applied only in cases within the first, second and sixth classes enumerated in the preceding section. It was only by them that the supremacy of the Federal Constitution and the laws and treaties made under it could be challenged. When, however, the States began to deal in new ways with various economic, social and industrial problems, as for example, to require employers to compensate their workmen for the consequences of industrial accidents not occasioned by the neglect of those required to pay, it sometimes happened that State Courts of last resort held the enactments invalid as contrary to the prohibitions of the Fourteenth Amendment. The reasoning by which these decisions were sustained did not always approve itself to large and influential sections of public opinion, and there arose a demand that the Supreme Court should be given the power to protect the legislation of the States against too rigid a construction of the Federal Constitution by their own Courts. On the other hand, the Supreme Court was already burdened to the limits of its time and of the physical strength of its members. Disappointed and pertinacious litigants insisted on its hearing their frequently unjustified complaints that some Federal title, right, privilege or immunity claimed by them below had been improperly denied. The solution of the problem which suggested itself was to give to the Supreme Court the option, when it thought best, to re-examine State decisions which upheld the Federal right and to leave the Court equally free to decline to do so in cases under class 6 in which the defeated party had theretofore had a right to a writ of error, if he asked for it. So in 1916[8] while the classes of cases upon which the Supreme Court may pass was increased from three to six, those upon which it must do so was reduced from three to two. In the nature of things, the cases under class 6 are far more numerous than those under class 1 or 2, so that the net result of the statutory change has doubtless been to diminish the work the Court is compelled to do.

577. When is the Validity of a Treaty or Statute or an Authority Exercised Under the United States Drawn in Question?

The validity of a statute of the United States is not drawn in question merely because a dispute as to its construction is decided by the State Court. It is necessary that the treaty, statute or authority shall have been held invalid. Congress, by law, granted lands to the State of Alabama. Subsequently the State made conveyance of these lands and took a mortgage for part of the consideration. The State gave powers of sale to its grantee and mortgagor, to be exercised in accordance with the provisions of a section of the Act of Congress under which the State itself had taken title. The mortgagor granted some of the lands. The State afterwards foreclosed its mortgage and acquired the mortgaged property. The question arose whether a purchaser from the mortgagor took good title as against the State. Whether

8. Act Sept. 6, 1916, 39 Stat. 726; 5 Fed. Stat. Ann. 723; U. S. Comp. Stat. Sec. 1214.

he did or not, depended upon whether the grant made to him by the mortgagor was made in the way limited in the mortgage, which was, of course, that set forth in the section of the Act of Congress which the State had incorporated in its grant. It was held that no question involving the validity of an Act of Congress was in anywise involved.[9]

578. When is the Validity of an Authority Exercised Under the United States Drawn in Question?

Doubtless the primary purpose of that provision of the section which authorizes the Supreme Court to issue a writ of error to the highest Court of the State whenever the latter denies the validity of an authority exercised under the United States, is to protect the proceedings of the Courts and officials of the United States from State obstruction or interference. For example—State Court plaintiffs set up a lien on certain personal property under a judgment rendered by the Circuit Court of the United States for the Middle District of Tennessee. The defendant asserted a lien under a deed of trust from the judgment debtor. The Supreme Court of Tennessee held that the lien of the deed was paramount to that of the judgment. The validity of an authority exercised under the United States was therefore denied and the Supreme Court had jurisdiction.[10]

An illustration of another class of cases in which is drawn in question an authority exercised under the United States, is found in Railroads vs. Richmond.[11] At a time when grain coming from the West to Dubuque was necessarily taken out of cars, placed on ferry boats,

9. Miller's Executors vs. Swann, 150 U. S. 132; 37 L. Ed. 1028; 14 Sup. Ct. 52.

10. Clements vs. Berry, 11 How. 407; 13 L. Ed. 745.

11. 15 Wall. 3; 21 L. Ed. 118.

carried across the Mississippi and then again put into the cars, a railroad company made a contract, for a relatively long term of years, with the owners of an elevator, to elevate all such grain at so much per bushel. Subsequently, Congress made all railroads, post roads, authorized them to connect with other roads so as to form continuous lines of transportation and provided for the construction of a bridge across the Mississippi River at Dubuque. Upon completion of the bridge, the elevator service became unnecessary and the railroad discontinued its use. The owners of the elevator sued the railroad in the State Courts. The defendant contended that in not delivering the grain to the elevator it was acting under the authority of this Act of Congress. The highest Court of Iowa overruled this contention and gave judgment for the plaintiff. It was held that the validity of an authority exercised under the United States had been denied by the State Court and that a writ of error should issue.

579. When is the Validity of a Statute of a State or of an Authority Exercised Under Any State, Drawn in Question on the Ground that it is Repugnant to the Constitution, Treaties or Laws of the United States?

It is obvious that a litigant may be as effectually deprived of a right to which he is entitled under the Federal Constitution or laws by sustaining a State law in conflict with them, as by holding them invalid. The section therefore provides a way of securing the protection of the Supreme Court against such State legislation.

Plaintiffs brought suit in a State Court to enforce, against a vessel, a lien given by State statute. The defendants set up that the lien was a maritime one and enforcible only in the Courts of Admiralty of the United States. The State Court decided in favor of the plaintiff. The decision was reviewable on writ of error from the Supreme Court.[12]

Before the passage of the Fourteenth Amendment, the most frequent occasion for the exercise of this jurisdiction was the claim that State statutes, the validity of which State Courts upheld, had impaired the obligation of contracts. The famous case of the Trustees of Dartmouth College vs. Woodward[13] came before the Supreme Court upon a writ of error to the Superior Court of New Hampshire. For the last forty years or more numberless cases have gone to the Supreme Court upon the claim that some State statute has deprived a defeated litigant in the State Courts of liberty or property without due process of law, or has denied to him the equal protection of the laws.

580. Cases Where a State Court Decision is in Favor of or Against a Title, Right, Privilege or Immunity Especially Set Up or Claimed Under the Constitution or a Treaty or Statute of the United States or a Commission or Authority Held or Exercised Thereunder.

The first two classes of cases for which the section provides, are those in which the plaintiff in error has suffered because a State Court has declared invalid a statute or a treaty of the United States, or an authority exercised thereunder, or has held valid some State statute or authority which is in conflict with the Constitution, treaties or laws of the United States. Writs of error in such cases lie only when the decision is in favor of the validity of a State right or against that of a Federal one, although the writ of *certiorari* may be granted when the opposite conclusion has been reached. Mere

12. Edwards vs. Elliott, 21 Wall. 532; 22 L. Ed. 487.
13. 4 Wheat. 517; 4 L. Ed. 628.

questions of the construction of statutes, State or Fed
eral, are not, as we have seen, included in these classes.
Sometimes, however, whether a man shall or shall not
have rights to which he is entitled under the Federal
Constitution, treaties or laws, depends upon the construction which the State Courts put upon some one of
them. It is to guard against such possibilities that the
statute permits a writ of *certiorari* from the Supreme
Court to the highest Court of the State to which the
case can be carried in the fifth and sixth classes of cases,
namely, those in which any title, right, privilege or immunity is claimed under the Constitution, or any treaty
or statute of, or commission held or authority exercised
under the United States, and the decision is either in
favor of or against the title, right, privilege or immunity
especially set up or claimed by either party under such
Constitution, treaty, statute, commission or authority.

**581. In the Fifth and Sixth Classes of Cases Provided
for by Section 237, a Writ of Certiorari May Not
Be Granted Unless the Plaintiff in Error has
Specifically Set Up His Claim in the State Court,
and it Has Been There Denied.**

In cases in which the State Court has decided invalid
a statute or treaty of the United States, or an authority
exercised thereunder, or has held valid a State statute
or authority, it is not necessary that the defeated party
should have specifically set up a claim as to their validity
or invalidity, as the case may be. In such cases it is
sufficient if the Federal question appears in the record
in the State Court and was decided, or the decision
thereof was necessarily involved in the determination of
the case.[14]

14. Columbia Water Power Co. vs. Columbia Elec. Street Ry. Light &
Power Co., 172 U. S. 475; 43 L. Ed. 521; 10 Sup. Ct. 247.

Nevertheless, even in cases coming within the first and second classes, the right of review by the Supreme Court exists only when either the Federal question involved was brought in some proper manner to the attention of the Court and expressly passed upon, or the judgment rendered could not have been given without deciding it.[15] Where, however, the case falls either within the fifth or the sixth class, the Supreme Court has no jurisdiction unless the claim of Federal right was especially set up in the State Court. An illustration of a case in which such an immunity was specially set up was where a Pennsylvania corporation, sued in New York upon a cause of action arising in Pennsylvania, was held by the State Courts of New York to have been properly brought before them by service of process upon its agent authorized to accept services of process in that State against it over its objection that such service could only be made for causes of action arising in that State, and that to hold otherwise was to deny it the protection of the Fourteenth Amendment, the Supreme Court held that the case could not be brought there on writ of error, but must come, if at all, upon writ of *certiorari*.[16]

582. How Claim of Right Must Be Specifically Set Up.

In the Supreme Court the defendant in error frequently objects that his adversary did not, in the Court below, specifically set up the Federal claim. The authorities declare that the record itself must affirmatively show that such claim was so made. If the plaintiff in error, has in the regular pleadings in the case set up his Federal right as a ground of action or defense, it is, of course, sufficient. The pleadings may be silent on the question, if the opinion of the Court below shows that it was raised and decided. Originally this would not

15. Harding vs. Illinois, 196 U. S. 86; 49 L. Ed. 394; 25 Sup. Ct. 176.
16. Phila. & Reading Coal & Iron Co. vs. Gilbert, 245 U. S. 162; 62 L. Ed. 221; 38 Sup. Ct. 958.

have been enough. The opinion of the lower Court was technically not a part of the record,[17] and section 25 of the Judiciary Act expressly provided that the Supreme Court should consider no error except it appeared on the "face of the record." That phrase had a definite meaning at common law. It did not have the same significance where the procedure was under the civil law. Accordingly, at a comparatively early date the Supreme Court was constrained to hold that, under the Louisiana practice, the opinion of a Court of that State was part of the record.[18] The adoption of the Code practice in many States and other statutory changes in their methods of judicial procedure, increased the difficulty of determining with precision what was and what was not technically a part of the record. Section 25 was revised in 1867.[19] The express requirement that the error complained of must appear on the face of the record was omitted. The Supreme Court thereupon embraced the opportunity to hold that in future it would, if necessary, examine the opinion of the State Court to see whether the claim of Federal right had been there set up.[20]

As is stated in the opinion in the case last cited, the Supreme Court had long been in the habit of looking to a certificate of the presiding judge of the State Court, to aid it in determining what had been actually passed upon by that Court. Where such certificate is given, it is presumed to have been granted by the order of the State Court and to form part of its record.[21] The effect of such certificate is, however, quite limited. If it does

17. Williams vs. Norris, 12 Wheat. 117; 6 L. Ed. 571.

18. Grand Gulf R. R. & Bank Co. vs. Marshall, 12 How. 167; 13 L. Ed. 938.

19. 14 Stat. 386; 5 Fed. Stat. Ann. 723; U. S. Comp. Stat. Sec. 1214.

20. Murdock vs. City of Memphis, 20 Wall. 590; 22 L. Ed. 429.

21. Armstrong vs. Treasurer of Athens County, 16 Peters, 285; 10 L. Ed. 965.

not otherwise appear from the record that the Federal claim is necessarily drawn in question, the Supreme Court will not take jurisdiction.[22] This result will follow, although the Supreme Court has been careful to say that such certificate is always regarded with respect.[23] The claim of Federal right must be specifically set up or claimed at the proper time and in the proper way. What is the proper way and the proper time depends to a large extent upon the practice in the State Court or upon what the State Court in the particular case did.

After a State Court has announced its final decision the parties are not entitled as of right to a rehearing, and the denial of one does not necessarily involve any decision upon the claim of Federal right set up for the first time in the petition for rehearing,[24] but if the State Court does see fit actually to pass upon such question, the substantial requirement that there shall have been a determination below on the specific point is met.[25]

Sometimes a case is fought out in the State Courts without any Federal question being raised at all. After the final decision of the State tribunals has been rendered, it may occur to the defeated party that there was a Federal question involved. He tries to prolong the litigation. He applies to the Supreme Court for a writ of error or certiorari. Among his assignments of error he sets up the denial of the alleged Federal right. It is too late for him to do so. He must have claimed that right before the decision of which he complains.[26]

22. Railroad Company vs. Rock, 4 Wall. 180; 18 L. Ed. 381.
23. Powell vs. Brunswick County, 150 U. S. 439; 37 L. Ed. 1134; 14 Sup. Ct. 166.
24. Pim vs. St. Louis, 165 U. S. 273; 41 L. Ed. 714; 17 Sup. Ct. 322.
25. Mallett vs. North Carolina, 181 U. S. 592; 45 L. Ed. 1015; 21 Sup. Ct. 730.
26. Appleby vs. City of Buffalo, 221 U. S. 524; 55 L. Ed. 838; 31 Sup. Ct. 699.

A recent enactment[27] provides that in any suit involving the validity of a contract wherein it is claimed
that a change in the rule of law or construction of statutes by the highest Court of a State applicable to such
contract would be repugnant to the Constitution of the
United States, the claim will be good if made in the
highest Court of the State at any time before final judgment is entered.

583. Plaintiff in Error is not Entitled to a Writ from the Supreme Court Until He Has Carried the Case to the Highest Court of the State to Which He Can Take It.

In accordance with the salutary rule that Federal interference in State affairs shall be carried no further than
the exigencies of the situation require, a litigant will not
be allowed to take his case to the Supreme Court until
he has exhausted all the means open to him in the Courts
of the State itself to secure what he believes to be his
Federal rights. Every State judge is as much bound by
his oath of office to regard the Constitution of the United
States and the laws and treaties made under it as the
supreme law of the land, as is any Federal judicial officer.
So long as the highest tribunal in the State, to which the
question under the State laws and practice may be carried, has not spoken, the presumption is that when it does
speak, it will be to vindicate the Federal right.

On the other hand, the right of review would be in
large part ineffective, if it could be exercised only after
a decision on the question by the highest Court existing
in the State. In many States, the decision of Courts
inferior to the highest is final in certain kinds of litigation or upon certain questions.

The writ of error in the great case of Cohens vs. Vir-

27. Act Feb. 17, 1922.

ginia was issued to the Quarterly Sessions Court for the Borough of Norfolk, a Court which was composed of the Mayor, Recorder and Aldermen of that borough. The defendants, plaintiffs in error above, were there charged with selling tickets of a lottery not authorized by the law of Virginia, which then prohibited any traffic in lottery tickets not of its own creation. The defendants pleaded that Congress had incorporated the City of Washington and empowered it, among other things, to authorize the drawing of lotteries for effecting any important improvements which its ordinary funds or revenues would not accomplish, and that the tickets they were charged with selling were issued by the corporation of the City of Washington in pursuance of the authority there given. The Court decided that the plea was bad. The defendants were convicted and fined. They prayed an appeal to the next superior Court of law of Norfolk County. The prayer was refused on the ground that the decision of the Quarterly Sessions Court was final in such cases.

584. Rule in Cases in Which a Higher State Court May or May Not Allow an Appeal From a Lower.

Under the laws and practices of a number of the States, as, for example, in Virginia, a defeated litigant in a lower Court is not entitled, as of right, to a writ of error, from, or an appeal to, the highest Court of the State. If he wishes either, he must ask for it. It may be allowed or refused. Before he can carry the case to the Supreme Court of the United States, he must have sought its allowance.[28] If it has been denied him he can sue out the writ of error to the trial Court, for that, under the circumstances, will be the highest Court of

28. Fisher vs. Perkins, 122 U. S. 523; 30 L. Ed. 1192; 7 Sup. Ct. 1227.

32

the State from which he can obtain a decision.[29] It may be added that there are cases in which, although there has been a decision upon the question in the highest Court of the State, the writ of error may issue to the lower Court. Whether it should or should not depends upon whether or not under the State practice, the record of the case remains in the lower or in the higher Court. The writ should regularly issue to the Court in which the record is,[30] although, of course, the petition for it and the record must show that the highest Court of the State has given its decision.

585. The Supreme Court Has Jurisdiction to Pass On the Federal Question Only.

It was quite clear from section 25 of the Judiciary Act as originally enacted, that the Supreme Court could pass only on the Federal question involved. After passage of the Act of 1867[31] it was strongly contended that this rule had been changed; it was said that, thereafter, whenever a Federal question was in controversy, the Supreme Court had jurisdiction, and, having taken jurisdiction, was bound to pass upon all the issues in the case. That is the rule where the original jurisdiction of a District Court is invoked on the ground that the case arises under the Constitution, laws or treaties of the United States. In a characteristically able opinion, MR. JUSTICE MILLER, speaking for the Supreme Court, however, held that in this respect the Act of 1867 was as limited as that of 1789.[32] The Supreme Court will pass upon such errors

29. Western Union Tel. Co. vs. Crovo, 220 U. S. 364; 55 L. Ed. 498; 31 Sup. Ct. 399.

30. Norfolk Turnpike Co. vs. Virginia, 225 U. S. 264; 56 L. Ed. 1082; 32 Sup. Ct. 828; Wedding vs. Meyler, 192 U. S. 573; 48 L. Ed. 570; 24 Sup. Ct. 322.

31. 14 Stat. 386; 5 Fed. Stat. Ann. 723; U. S. Comp. Stat. Sec. 1214.

32. Murdock vs. City of Memphis, 20 Wall. 590; 22 L. Ed. 429.

of law only as the State Court is said to have committed with reference to the Federal question.

Even where the case below is in equity, the interposition of the Supreme Court is obtained by writ of error and not by appeal, and questions of law only are open for review.[33]

586. If Any Other Issue Adjudged by the State Court is Sufficient to Sustain Its Judgment, the Supreme Court Will Not Reverse, No Matter How the Federal Question Was Decided.

The Federal question may not be the only one at issue. Usually it is not. The party who denies the Federal right asserted by his adversary may say that he is entitled to a judgment even if his view of the Federal question is not sound. In such case, if the State Court upholds his contention as to one of the non-Federal issues, and that issue is sufficiently broad to sustain a judgment in his favor, no matter how the Federal question may be determined, the Supreme Court will not disturb the judgment below, even though the State Court has passed upon the Federal question and has reached a conclusion concerning it with which the Supreme Court cannot agree.[34]

To this rule there is an important and necessary qualification or exception, and that is when the State Court, although not denying the Federal right in express terms, has done so in substance and effect by putting forward non-Federal grounds of decision that are without any fair or substantial support. The Supreme Court itself said that this qualification was a material one and cannot be disregarded without neglecting or renouncing a jurisdiction conferred by law and designed to protect and

33. Murdock vs. City of Memphis, supra.
34. Murdock vs. City of Memphis, supra.

maintain the supremacy of the Constitution and the laws made in pursuance thereof.[35]

587. State Court Clerk May Be Compelled to Transmit the Record.

Sometimes State Courts which denied the constitutionality or applicability of the section of the Judiciary Act now under consideration, have directed their clerks not to furnish a transcript of the record. In such a case the Supreme Court will either issue a mandamus to the clerk requiring him to transmit the record, or it will, when under the facts it feels that it may safely do so, act upon what it is satisfied is a true copy of the record, though not formally certified by the clerk.

In the famous case of Ableman vs. Booth,[36] the question in controversy was the constitutionality of some of the provisions of the Fugitive Slave Act. The Supreme Court of Wisconsin held them unconstitutional. A writ of error was sued out to the Supreme Court of the United States. The Supreme Court of Wisconsin thereupon directed its clerk to make no return to the writ of error and to enter no order upon the journals or records of the Court concerning the same. These facts being made to appear to the Supreme Court of the United States, it laid a rule upon the clerk to make return to the writ of error on or before the first day of the next ensuing term of the Supreme Court. He was still disobedient. The Supreme Court then permitted the plaintiff in error to file a certified copy of the record of the Supreme Court of Wisconsin in lieu of the return the clerk should have made.

---

35. Ward vs. Love County, 235 U. S. 17; 59 L. Ed. 104; 35 Sup. Ct. 3.
36. 21 How. 506; 16 L. Ed. 169.

CHAPTER XXII.

FROM WHAT CLASS OF DECISIONS APPEALS MAY BE TAKEN AND HOW.

588. Only Final Decisions Are as a Rule Appealable.

In the Federal judicial system, as in that of many of the States, the rule has always been that appeals will not lie from any judgment or decree which is not final. From the practical standpoint there are imperative reasons for imposing such restrictions upon the right of appeal. To go to an Appellate Court is usually costly. It always takes time, often much time. If every decision of the trial Court could be made the ground of an independent appeal the waste of time and money would be ruinous. It would be frequently useless as well. Many a bitterly contested ruling of the Court below, in the subsequent progress of the case, becomes immaterial. Common sense dictates that before a litigant can invoke the protection of an appellate tribunal he must be certain that the decree of which he complains will, if carried into effect, hurt him.

On the other hand, neither Congress nor the people have ever been willing that in matters of any importance the trial Court shall have the last word. As to our judicial system we have always been idealists. We will not surrender the belief that, it is possible to administer justice so that it shall be free from error, both in form and in substance. We know that our lower Courts make mistakes. We create others whose sole business is to correct them. It may be that many of our experiments in this direction have not worked as we hoped. It is possible that better results would have been attained had we in matters of detail trusted more to the discretion and common sense of the Courts of first instance. However, that may be, all of us feel that before anything of real value, be it life, liberty or property, is taken from one man by the decision of another, the legality and justice of the determination should be passed upon by some one else.

In the course of actual litigation, and long before the final decision of the case below, there may be orders made which, if enforced, will alter the status of things so that no subsequent reversal can undo all of the harm which has been done. If appeals may be taken from every order which any of the parties dislikes, the case may last forever. If they may not be taken, until the Court below has finished everything it has to do in the case, many of its decrees will have been long executed, sometimes greatly to the prejudice of one or more of the parties. Where to draw the line between those decrees which are so far final in their effect that from them an appeal should lie and those which are so far interlocutory and tentative that they should be held not appealable, presents a problem which has difficulties both practical and theoretical.

589. What Are Final Decisions?

In a case at law there can seldom be much question as to whether the judgment is final or not, but in equity there may be and very often is. Though our equity practice is modeled on that of England, we early gave a different definition to the term "final decree" from that which was well established there. There every decree, whatever its nature, was considered interlocutory until it was signed and enrolled, and even then it remained interlocutory unless it completely determined every question which arose in the cause. If any matter was reserved for further consideration, the decree was not called final. Such a rigid definition was there possible because appeals could be taken from interlocutory decrees. As with us they cannot be, it has been necessary to relax considerably the English conception of finality.

Our Courts have tried to make the test a practical one. They are inclined to hold a decree or order final and therefore, appealable, if it requires something to be done which takes aught of substantial value from one of the parties, and if that which is commanded, cannot be undone by any subsequent reversal. When no such result will follow the enforcement of the order complained of, there is usually no sufficient reason why an appeal should lie. Such is the general principle. The actual cases are for the most part in harmony with it.

As always in such matters, there are, in its application, some anomalies; as, for example, it was early held that, a permanent injunction against an alleged infringer in a patent case was not appealable, if the decree left open for subsequent determination the question of damages or profits.[1] When the rule was first laid down, it was hedged about by limitations to prevent its working a hardship. It subsequently became crystallized. The limitations were dropped out of sight.[2] Speaking generally, however, whether a decree is final or not will be tested rather by what will be its actual working than by merely theoretical considerations. A decree for the sale of particular property is final, although it may leave undetermined many things—as, for example, the way in which the proceeds shall be distributed.[3] It is final because one of the parties asserts that the property is his and does not want it sold. The decree will if carried into effect change the status in a way which it will be impossible to undo.[4]

For the same reason a decree directing the immediate payment of money to any one and awarding execution therefor, is so far final that it is appealable.[5]

In one sense there is nothing final about an order of

1. Barnard vs. Gibson, 7 How. 656; 12 L. Ed. 857.
2. Humiston vs. Stainthorp, 2 Wall. 106; 17 L. Ed. 905.
3. Ray vs. Law, 3 Cranch, 179; 2 L. Ed. 404.
4. Whiting vs. United States Bank, 13 Peters, 14; 10 L. Ed. 33.
5. Forgay vs. Conrad, 6 How. 203; 12 L. Ed. 404.

Court authorizing the issue of receivers' certificates, even if it secures them upon property in the custody of the Court. But because it in fact imposes a lien upon the property, which a reversal of the order after it has been executed by the issue of the receivers' certificates and their sale might not discharge, it is held to be so far final as to be appealable.[6]

On the other hand, where the Court simply decrees that "A" is liable to "B" for the damage which "B" has suffered from some particular cause, or says that "A" should pay to "B" the profits which "A" has made in some particular way, but leaves the ascertainment of the amount of such damages or profits to future inquiry, no harm has been done to "A." None will be done to him until he is required to pay some sum. For that reason a decree in an admiralty cause that one of the parties is liable to the other for some tort, as, for example, the consequences of a collision, is not final. How much he will be forced to pay has yet to be determined. The final decree from which the appeal may be taken is that which, when such amount has been ascertained, directs the appellant to pay it.[7]

Theoretically the issue of an injunction intended to preserve the *status quo* during the litigation, or the appointment of a receiver merely to take charge of the property and hold it while the cause is pending, are interlocutory proceedings, and the Courts have always so held.[8] Practically, the damage which may be done by putting one of the parties under an injunction or by taking property out of his hands and putting it into those of a receiver are so great and may be so

6. Farmers Loan & Trust Co., 129 U. S. 206; 32 L. Ed. 656; 9 Sup. Ct. 265.

7. The Palmyra, 10 Wheat. 502; 6 L. Ed. 376.

8. Grant vs. Phoenix, 106 U. S. 429; 27 L. Ed. 237; 1 Sup. Ct. 414.

permanent that such orders stand in a class by themselves. The Courts have not felt free to hold that they were final. Congress has in consequence interposed by legislation.

590. Appeals From Interlocutory Decrees Granting, Refusing or Dissolving Injunctions or Appointing Receivers.

The law which created the Circuit Courts of Appeals attempted to make adequate provision on the subject. What was then done constituted the seventh section of the Act.[9] It is a matter not easy to deal with satisfactorily. The original section has already been four times amended,[10] sometimes by restoring something which an earlier amendment had stricken out or by striking out something which an earlier amendment had added. It now provides that an appeal may be taken from an interlocutory order or decree granting, continuing, refusing or dissolving an injunction or appointing a receiver. This appeal must in all cases be taken to the Circuit Court of Appeals, even although the case is one, in which, from a final decree, an appeal will lie directly to the Supreme Court. The decision of the Circuit Court of Appeals on an appeal from such interlocutory order is final in all cases,[11] unless the Circuit Court of Appeals directs a dismissal of the bill. In that event, the case being at an end, an appeal to the Supreme Court may be taken in those cases in which the decision of the Circuit

9. 26 Stat. 828; 5 Fed. Stat. Ann. 629; U. S. Comp. Stat. Sec. 1121.

10. 28 Stat. 666; 5 Fed. Stat. Ann. 629; U. S. Comp. Stat. Sec. 1121; 31 Stat. 660; 5 Fed. Stat. Ann. 629; U. S. Comp. Stat. Sec. 1121; 34 Stat. 116; 5 Fed. Stat. Ann. 629; U. S. Comp. Stat. Sec. 1121; Section 129, Judicial Code.

11. Mitchell Store Bldg. Co. vs. Carroll, 232 U. S. 379; 58 L. Ed. 650; 34 Sup. Ct. 410.

Court of Appeals is not made final by the statute.[12] Nor will the Supreme Court issue a writ of *certiorari*[13] unless under peculiar circumstances, as for example, where the District Court refused an interlocutory injunction because in its view an adequate remedy at law existed, but did not dismiss the bill, and the Circuit Court of Appeals affirmed the District Court.[14] An appeal under this section does not stay the proceedings of the Court below in other respects, unless the trial or the Appellate Court or a judge of the latter so orders.[15]

591. Time in Which Appeals Must Be Taken.

In all cases there are statutory limits upon the time in which appeals may be taken. They have been fixed by different acts, passed at different times, and drawn by different men, who, for the most part, apparently cared nothing for uniformity. As a consequence, some appeals must be taken within ten days. In others six months are allowed. An appeal to the Supreme Court must be taken more promptly than to a Circuit Court of Appeals.

Six Months. Unless otherwise provided, one aggrieved by a judgment of a District Court has six months in which to appeal to the Circuit Court of Appeals,[16] or to apply for a writ of certiorari to the Supreme Court of the Philippines.[17]

12. U. S. Fidelity Co. vs. Bray, 225 U. S. 214; 56 L. Ed. 1055; 32 Sup. Ct. 620.

13. U. S. vs. Beatty, 232 U. S. 463; 58 L. Ed. 686; 34 Sup. Ct. 392.

14. Union Pacific R. R. Co. vs. Weld Co., 247 U. S. 287; 62 L. Ed. 1110; 38 Sup. Ct. 510.

15. Smith vs. Vulcan Iron Works, 165 U. S. 518; 41 L. Ed. 810; 17 Sup. Ct. 407; U. S. Fidelity Co. vs. Bray, 225 U. S. 214; 56 L. Ed. 1055; 32 Sup. Ct. 620.

16. 26 Stat. 829; 6 Fed. Stat. Ann. 161; U. S. Comp. Stat. Sec. 1647.

17. Sec. 6, Act Sept. 6, 1916, 39 Stat. 727; 5 Fed. Stat. Ann. 917; U. S. Comp. Stat. Sec. 1228a.

Three Months. Writs of error, appeals, or writs of *certiorari,* except to the Supreme Court of the Philippines, intended to bring up any case for review by the Supreme Court, must be applied for within three months after the entry of the judgment or decree complained of.[18] One who has brought suit against the United States under the Tucker Act and has lost, has but ninety days in which to appeal.[19]

Sixty Days. In cases arising under the Interstate Commerce and Anti-Trust Acts, in which the Attorney-General has filed the certificate of expedition provided for by the Act of April 11, 1903,[20] an appeal must be taken within sixty days.

Thirty Days. When the United States seeks to appeal in a criminal case, it must do so within thirty days. Appeals in prize cases must be taken within the same time. A like limit is imposed upon appeals from interlocutory orders granting, refusing or dissolving injunctions or appointing receivers.

Ten Days. An appeal from a District Court to a Circuit Court of Appeals under section 25a of the Bankrupt Law must be taken within ten days.

The case of Grant Shoe Co. vs. Laird[21] shows what curious results may follow from the way in which the statutes regulating appeals have been drawn.

An alleged bankrupt against whom an involuntary petition has been filed may have a jury trial to determine whether he is insolvent or whether he has committed the act of bankruptcy charged against him. If he wishes it, he must ask for it, otherwise the case is tried

18. Sec. 6, Act Sept. 6, 1916, 39 Stat. 727; 5 Fed. Stat. Ann. 917; U. S. Comp. Stat. Sec. 1228a.

19. Judicial Code, Sec. 243; 5 Fed. Stat. Ann. 890; U. S. Comp. Stat. Sec. 1220.

20. 32 Stat. 823; 6 Fed. Stat. Ann. 136; U. S. Comp. Stat. Sec. 8824.

21. 203 U. S. 502; 51 L. Ed. 292; 27 Sup. Ct. 161.

by the Court. In the latter event an appeal from the order adjudicating or refusing to adjudicate may be taken to the Circuit Court of Appeals under section 25a, but if so it must be taken in ten days. In the Grant Shoe Company case a jury trial had been prayed. After the jury had been impaneled the bankrupt admitted its insolvency and the act of bankruptcy charged. There was nothing left for the jury to pass upon. The only disputed question was as to whether a petitioning creditor had a provable debt. That issue was one which the bankrupt had no right to have submitted to the jury. In any event, there was in the case in question no dispute about the facts. The only contention was that the claim was not provable because it had not been liquidated. The Court necessarily passed upon that precisely as it would have done had there been no jury, yet because a jury had been impaneled the provisions of section 25a of the Bankruptcy Act had no application. Review could be had by writ of error only. As the question raised went to the jurisdiction of the District Court, the case could be taken directly to the Supreme Court. It was held that the general law which then allowed two years for appeals or writs of error from the District Court to the Supreme Court applied. Doubtless if the jurisdictional question had not arisen and the writ of error had issued from the Circuit Court of Appeals, it could have been sued out at any time within six months of the entry of the order.

It would seem that in the vast majority of cases, thirty, or at most sixty, days would be quite sufficient in which to take an appeal from a District Court or a Circuit Court of Appeals. Such limitation, as has been stated, is already imposed upon appeals in some of the most important classes of litigation with which the Federal Courts are called upon to deal.

592. Ways in Which Review by Appellate Tribunal May Be Sought.

There are a number of different ways in which an appellate tribunal may be asked to review the judgments or decrees of a lower. As a rule, in any particular case only one of these is available and which that is depends on the character of the controversy and upon what has been heretofore done in it.

The two ordinary ways of carrying a case up are by appeal and by writ of error. Petitions for *certiorari*, for mandamus and for prohibition and to superintend and revise, in matters of law, proceedings in bankruptcy may also under some circumstances be used to bring before a higher Court a ruling of a lower.

593. Distinctions Between an Appeal and a Writ of Error.

A writ of error was the common law method of securing a review of the alleged mistakes of the trial Court in its conduct of a jury trial. If the issues of fact had been properly submitted to the jury, its findings were not open to further review.

The Seventh Amendment to the Constitution of the United States expressly provides that "no fact tried by a jury shall be otherwise re-examined in any Court of the United States than according to the rules of the common law."

The limits thereby imposed upon the right of appellate courts to review the facts in common law cases have been fully and learnedly discussed by the Supreme Court.[22]

For centuries important rights have been judicially determined by Courts which did not use the jury system. In them a judge or judges passed upon the facts as well

22. Capitol Traction Co. vs. Hof, 174 U. S. 1; 43 L. Ed. 873; 19 Sup. Ct. 580.

as upon the law. As a rule, they had before them, not the living witnesses, but merely the written depositions of such witnesses taken at another time and place. They might easily be mistaken in their conclusions as to what had happened as well as to the applicable law. The members of the appellate tribunal had usually as good an opportunity of getting at the truth. Presumably, those who sat in the higher Courts were abler and wiser than their brethren who presided in those of first instance. There can be little question that, on the average, they in fact are. They usually work under conditions more favorable to quiet and concentrated consideration of the really vital issues involved. There was no reason why they should not be free to consider and determine whether the Court below had not erred on the facts as well as on the law.

Speaking generally, a writ of error brings up for consideration the rulings on questions of law made in the course of a trial at common law. An appeal is used principally in equity and in admiralty. It carries up both facts and law. The original line of distinction still exists to the extent that no appeal can properly be taken in any case at law nor in any case in which the parties are entitled as of right to a trial by jury. In order that the Supreme Court shall not be called upon or permitted to review the decisions of State Courts in matters of fact, an appeal may not be taken, as we have seen, from a decision of the highest Court of the State to the Supreme Court even in an equity case. The only remedy is by writ of error and that brings up the rulings of law and only the rulings of law.

In the State practice in many States, writs of error are no longer used. One who wants a review by an appellate tribunal seeks it in the same way if what he complains of is the erroneous ruling of the Court in the course of a trial by jury, or the mistaken determination of a question of fact by a chancellor. He prays an appeal in each case. When he gets into the appellate Court, however, there is the same distinction as to the extent and character of the review there obtainable as exists in the Federal Courts; that is to say, in cases which have been tried by a jury, or by the Court sitting as a jury, the higher Court inquires merely as to the errors of law alleged to have been committed. It does not profess to consider whether there has been an incorrect conclusion upon the facts. If the case taken up is one on the equity side of the Court below, questions of fact as well as of law are open for the consideration of the higher tribunal.

In view of the experience of so many of the States, it would seem quite clear that two methods of invoking the jurisdiction of the appellate tribunal still prevailing in the Federal Courts are not necessary in order to preserve the essential distinction between the two kinds of review, and that the procedure under each of them could be greatly simplified without injuriously affecting any thing of substance, and Congress has now provided that no rights shall be lost because a writ of error has been sued out when an appeal should have been taken or vice versa.[23]

594. Writ of Error.

A writ of error to bring up the record of a State Court to the Supreme Court of the United States is not a writ of right. It does not issue until it has been allowed either by the chief judge of the State Court, if that Court have more than one judge, or by a justice of the Supreme Court.[24] It is occasionally refused and should be if the

23. Sec. 4, Act Sept. 6, 1916; 39 Stat. 727; 5 Fed. Stat. Ann. 607; U. S. Comp. Stat. Sec. 1120a.

24. Bartemeyer vs. Iowa, 14 Wall. 26; 20 L. Ed. 792.

judge or justice does not think the case comes within the provisions of the statute. If the application for it is made to a justice of the Supreme Court he may grant or refuse it, or he may refer the question to the Court as a whole.[25] In the case cited the litigation below had been initiated in the Supreme Court of the District of Columbia. It had been thence carried to the Court of Appeals of the District. The Supreme Court, however, said the same principles applied as in the case of a writ of error to the highest Court of the State. On the other hand, when the writ is to run from one Federal Court to another, it is not, strictly speaking, necessary to have it allowed at all.[26] It is the practice to obtain such an allowance which, however, is granted as a matter of course. It may be allowed by a judge either of the Court to which or from which it runs.[27]

595. From What Office the Writ Issues.

The writ is issued by a clerk of Court. Logically, it should come from the clerk's office of the appellate Court to which it is to be returned, and that was the original practice. For convenience, however, another provision has long been made. The clerk of the District Court may issue it, and since January 22, 1912, it may be issued by a clerk of a Circuit Court of Appeals.[28]

The Circuit Court of Appeals for the Sixth Circuit has construed the Act last mentioned. It holds that the writ may in all cases issue from the clerk's office of either the Court to, or the Court from, which it runs. That is, when the Supreme Court is asked to review a judgment of a Circuit Court of Appeals the writ may come from the

25. U. S. ex rel Brown vs. Lane, Sec'y of the Interior, 232 U. S. 598; 58 L. Ed. 748; 34 Sup. Ct. 449.

26. Davidson vs. Lanier, 4 Wall. 447; 18 L. Ed. 377.

27. Supreme Court Rules 36 and 40.

28. 37 Stat. 54; 6 Fed. Stat. Ann. 194; U. S. Comp. Stat. Sec. 1663.

clerk's office of either of those Courts. If a judgment of a District Court is in question, the clerk of either that Court or the Clerk of the Court to which it is to be returned may issue it. The clerk of the District Court may and usually does issue the writ when it is directed to the highest Court of the State. However issued, the writ is always returnable to the clerk's office of the appellate Court.[29]

596. Assignment of Error.

The law requires that there shall be annexed to and returned with every writ of error various other documents.

First, an authenticated transcript of the record.

Second, an assignment of errors and a prayer for reversal with a citation to the adverse party.

The assignment of errors tells the judge who is asked to allow the writ, what the errors are upon which the petitioner relies, and the opposing counsel and the appellate Court, what questions of law are presented for consideration and determination.[30] While the filing of the assignment is not a jurisdictional* requirement,[31] it is, nevertheless, an important document.

Supreme Court Rule 35 provides that neither a writ of error nor an appeal shall be allowed until such assignment has been filed. It should set out separately and particularly each error asserted and intended to be urged. When the error alleged is to the admission or rejection of evidence, the assignment should quote the full substance of the evidence admitted or rejected. When complaint is made of the charge of the Court, the assign-

29. In re Issuing Writs of Error, 199 Fed. 115; 117 C. C. A. 603.

30. Simpson vs. First Nat. Bank of Denver, 129 Fed. 257; 64 C. C. A. 503.

31. Old Nick Williams Co. vs. United States, 215 U. S. 541; 54 L. Ed. 318; 30 Sup. Ct. 221.

ment should set out the part referred to *totidem verbis*, whether it be instructions given or instructions refused. The assignment is to be included in the transcript of the record and printed with it. When this is not done, counsel will not be heard except at the request of the Court. Errors not assigned will be disregarded. The Court, however, reserves the option to notice a plain error not assigned. The rules of the Circuit Courts of Appeals contain similar provisions. The 21st rule of the Supreme Court and the rules of the Circuit Courts of Appeals require the counsel for the plaintiff in error or appellant to set up in his brief distinctly and separately the errors upon which he relies.

The preparation of the assignment of errors requires more skill than is in many cases expended upon it. The assignments should be precise and particular and not vague or general. On the other hand, they should not be too numerous nor should they include errors of a minute character. It is almost always a mistake to have a great number of assignments. It is exceedingly likely to suggest to the appellate Court that you have no great confidence in any of them. If you had, you would pick the one or the few upon which you really rely and omit the others.

597. Citation.

In the Federal practice it has always been thought essential that formal notice be given to the other side of the purpose to take the case up. In order to insure that this will be done, you are required to obtain from a judge authorized to allow the writ of error a citation upon your adversaries. The three important papers which are required in connection with a writ of error are therefore —

1. The writ itself, which is the order from the appellate Court to the lower Court to send up its record.

2. The citation, which is notice to the other side that you have taken the case up.

3. The assignment of errors, which tells both the other side and the appellate Court what it is of which you complain.

Curiously enough, the citation must be signed by the judge, though the writ of error never is, even although it be allowed by him.[32] As it has no purpose other than to notify the other side that the case is being taken up, there is no reason why the signature of the clerk would not do quite as well. Courts recognizing this fact, have held that any irregularity as to the signature of the citation or its service may be readily waived. For example, in the case last cited, the citation was signed by the clerk and not by the judge. It was, therefore, irregular. The defendant in error, however, entered his appearance in the Supreme Court. He took no other action at that term. When at the next he called attention to the absence of the judge's signature, it was held that he had waived his right to take advantage of that circumstance.

It should be regularly served as other writs, except that service upon the attorney or counsel of record of the defendant in error will do. Merely mailing it to a defendant in error is not sufficient.[33]

598. Appeals.

Where an appeal is the proper method of taking the case up, the defeated party is entitled to appeal. It is true that it is necessary for him to have his appeal allowed. Nevertheless, it is, in a proper case, a matter of right. The Supreme Court has said that its allowance is in reality nothing more than the doing of those things

32. Chaffee vs. Hayward, 20 How. 208; 15 L. Ed. 804.
33. Tripp vs. Santa Rosa Street R. R. Co., 144 U. S. 126; 36 L. Ed. 371; 12 Sup. Ct. 655.

which are necessary to give the appellant the means of invoking the jurisdiction of the reviewing tribunal.[34]

An appellant presents a short petition to the lower Court or the judge thereof stating his desire to appeal and asking that his appeal be allowed. With this he presents his assignment of errors and a citation to the other party, as he does when he sues out a writ of error. It is not necessary to obtain a citation when both the appeal is prayed and the bond given in open Court during the term at which the judgment or decree appealed from is entered. The presumption is that all the parties are present in Court.[35]

599. Appeal Bond.

Neither an appeal nor writ of error is complete until a proper bond is given with good and sufficient security that the appellant or plaintiff in error will prosecute his appeal or writ with effect, or if he fails therein will answer for all costs. Regularly this bond should be presented and approved at the time the appeal or writ is allowed and the citation issued, but the failure to do so at that time is not fatal to the jurisdiction. It may be presented and approved in the appellate Court.[36]

600. Summons and Severance.

In cases at law where a judgment is joint, all the parties against whom it is rendered must unite in the writ of error. In chancery cases all those against whom a joint decree is rendered must participate in the appeal. If one or more do not, the writ or the appeal, as the case may be, will be dismissed. The purpose of the rule is to insure that the successful party shall not be prevented by the appellate proceeding from enforcing his judgment

34. Brown vs. McConnell, 124 U. S. 489; 31 L. Ed. 495; 8 Sup. Ct. 559.
35. Hewitt vs. Filbert, 116 U. S. 142; 29 L. Ed. 581; 6 Sup. Ct. 319.
36. Brown vs. McConnell, 124 U. S. 489; 31 L. Ed. 495; 8 Sup. Ct. 559.

or decree against the parties who do not wish to have it reviewed, and to avoid the possibility of the appellate tribunal itself being required to decide a second or third time the same question on the same record. This it might have to do, if different parties could prosecute separate appeals.

The common law had worked out a method of proceeding when one would not take legal steps to secure a right which others jointly interested with him wished to enforce. It might be that two persons were the holders of a joint obligation; neither could legally sue without the other. Or, it might be, that a judgment had gone jointly against two persons and only one of them was willing to sue out a writ of error. In either case the party who wished to proceed caused a writ of summons to be issued. The unwilling one was thereby brought before the Court. If he then still refused to act, an order or judgment of severance was made against him. Thereafter his right to sue upon the claim was gone forever, and the other party might proceed without him. This somewhat elaborate mode of procedure has probably become obsolete. Strict compliance with it is no longer necessary. All that is required is that written notice of the desire of the other to appeal be served on him or that he enter his appearance in Court and there refuse to proceed. When either of these facts are shown, the Court may allow the other party to prosecute his appeal alone.

In one case an appeal had been taken in the name of two persons. One of them appeared and had the order of appeal, so far as he was concerned, stricken out. It was held that all the purposes of a summons and severance had been obtained. The other party could proceed without him.[37]

37. Farmers' Loan & Trust Co. vs. McClure, 78 Fed. 211; 24 C. C. A. 66.

The appellee can at once enforce his decree against the party who will not join and the latter will be estopped to appeal thereafter.[38]

601. Supersedeas.

If the plaintiff recovers a judgment below in a suit at law, or if a decree in equity requires one of the parties to pay money, to convey property, or to do or refrain from doing some other thing, it may be quite important to the person against whom the judgment or decree has gone that he shall have the right, pending the determination of the appellate proceedings, to have the enforcement of the decree below suspended or, in legal phrase, superseded. In order that he may have an opportunity to do this, the Revised Statutes[39] provide that where a writ of error may operate as a superseadas, execution shall not issue until after the expiration of ten days, exclusive of Sundays, from the entry of the judgment. It will behoove a defendant, therefore, against whom judgment has been given, to sue out his writ of error and to do the other things necessary to supersede the judgment within ten days. It is true that the same section gives him sixty days, also exclusive of Sundays, in which he may as of course supersede, but the plaintiff may at any time after the ten days cause execution to issue. The subsequent giving and approval of the bond will stop further proceedings. It will not undo anything which has been done. A judgment ousting the defendant from office and putting the plaintiff in had been given by a territorial Court. Ten days, exclusive of Sundays, after the entry of the judgment passed without the giving of any supersedeas bond. At the end of that period execution issued. Defendant

38. Masterson vs. Herndon, 10 Wall. 416; 19 L. Ed. 953.
39. Sec. 1007; Danielson vs. Northwestern Fuel Co., 55 Fed. 49.

was put out and plaintiff in. Thereafter, and within sixty days from the entry of the original judgment a supersedeas bond was filed and approved. The plaintiff below refused to vacate the office into which the judgment of the territorial Court had put him. The defendant below, the plaintiff in error above, thereupon applied to the Supreme Court for an order restoring him to the office, but that Court held that the supersedeas did not undo anything which before it was granted had been lawfully done. The appeal was thereupon dismissed by consent. The term of the office in dispute would have expired before the case could in its regular order have been heard by the Supreme Court. In such cases the importance of giving bond promptly is obvious.[40]

A judge or justice of the appellate tribunal may at his discretion allow a supersedeas even after sixty days, but only in the event that the writ of error has been issued within that time; that is to say, if the party aggrieved wishes to prevent his adversary from executing, he must sue out his writ of error and have his supersedeas bond allowed within ten days. If he wishes to be in a position to ask for a supersedeas at all he must obtain his writ of error within sixty days. If he does, he has the right within sixty days to supersede the judgment or decree. If he allows the sixty to elapse, he may even then be allowed to supersede if, in the discretion of a judge of the appellate Court, it is proper that he should, but if he has not sued out his writ of error within the sixty days he cannot in any way obtain a supersedeas.[41]

The exclusion of Sundays applies to all the periods mentioned in the section of the Revised Statutes under consideration. Sundays are not counted at all, so that the plaintiff in error or appellant has sixty secular days

40. Board of Commissioners vs. Gorman, 19 Wall. 661; 22 L. Ed. 226.
41. Kitchen vs. Randolph, 93 U. S. 86; 23 L. Ed. 810.

after the judgment or decree in which to obtain his writ of error and file his supersedeas bond.[42]

602. Amount of Supersedeas Bond.

An appeal bond is required in all cases. If, however, the appellant or plaintiff in error does not wish to supersede or is unable to give security in the amount required, his bond may be limited to a sum sufficient to cover the probable cost of an appeal. On the other hand, if he does wish his appeal to operate as a supersedeas, he must give bond sufficient, if he fail in his appeal to insure the payment of all damages and costs. The amount of the bond, where the judgment or decree is for the recovery of money not otherwise secured, must be for the whole amount of the judgment or decree, including just damages for delay and costs and interest on the appeal. Where the property in controversy necessarily follows the event of the suit, as in real actions, in replevin and in suits on mortgages, or where the property is in the custody of the marshal under admiralty process, as in the case of recapture or seizure, or where the proceeds thereof, or a bond for the value thereof, is in the custody or control of the Court, the bond will be required in an amount sufficient merely to secure the sum recovered for the use and detention of the property and the costs of the suit and just damages for delay, and costs and interest on the appeal.[43]

603. What Decrees Cannot Be Superseded as of Right.

There are many decrees in equity which the appellant has no absolute right to supersede. They may be important. They may grant an injunction or they may refuse or dissolve one, or they may appoint a receiver. Still

42. Danville vs. Brown, 128 U. S. 503; 32 L. Ed. 507; 9 Sup. Ct. 149.
43. Supreme Court Rule 29.

the party aggrieved, though he appeal, cannot demand that the enforcement of the decree shall be superseded.[44] In such matters the statute gives the trial or the appellate Court or a judge thereof the discretion to say whether in any particular case the order shall or shall not be superseded. Where appeals are taken from interlocutory decrees granting or refusing or dissolving injunctions or appointing receivers under section 129 of the Judicial Code the order appealed from is not suspended during the pendency of the appeal unless the Court which passed it or the appellate Court or a judge thereof shall otherwise order. The contention that language of the section implies a suspension of the order appealed from was held by the Supreme Court to be unjustified.[45]

By the 74th Rule, when a judge or justice who took part in the decision of the cause, allows an appeal from a final decree in an equity suit granting or dissolving an injunction he may in his discretion at the time of such allowance make an order suspending, modifying or restoring the injunction during the pendency of the appeal upon such terms as to bond or otherwise as he may consider proper for the security of the rights of the opposite party.

604. Certiorari.

A writ of *certiorari* was one of the writs habitually issued by the Court of King's Bench. It is not mentioned among those which the appellate Courts of the United States are authorized to issue, except in the Act of 1891, establishing the Circuit Courts of Appeals. Nevertheless, for some purposes, it is used by the Supreme Court and also by the Circuit Courts of Appeals. In their

44. Hovey vs. McDonald, 109 U. S. 150; 27 L. Ed. 888; 3 Sup. Ct. 136.
45. In re Haberman Mfg. Co., 147 U. S. 525; 37 L. Ed. 266; 13 S. Ct. 527.

practice, it is an auxiliary process only, intended to supply imperfections in the record of the case already before the Court which issued it. It is not used as a writ of error to review a judgment of an inferior Court.[46] It will never be granted where there is a plain and adequate remedy by appeal or writ of error.[47] It goes without saying, that it can never in any case be issued by a Court which has no right to review the action of the lower Court in the matter complained of.

605. Certiorari Granted When Necessary to Protect Appellate Jurisdiction.

There may be peculiar and exceptional circumstances which imperatively demand that the appellate Court shall issue the writ and by so doing put itself in a position to dispose promptly of the entire matter in controversy. It may be impossible otherwise effectively to protect its own jurisdiction.[48] In the case cited Chetwood had been carrying on some litigation in the State Courts of California against the officers of a national bank, which at the time was in receivers' hands. Subsequently, and while his litigation was still pending, the receiver having paid all the debts of the bank, its stockholders, in accordance with the provisions of a statute giving them the authority so to do, voted that the receiver should turn over the balance of its assets to an agent. Chetwood had been using its name in his litigation and about $27,000 had been paid into the State Court by some of the defendants in the cases he had instituted. At the instance of the agent of the bank, the United States Circuit Court for the District of California enjoined

46. American Construction Co. vs. Jacksonville R'way, 148 U. S. 372; 37 L. Ed. 486; 13 Sup. Ct. 758.
47. Whitney vs. Dick, 202 U. S. 132; 50 L. Ed. 963; 26 Sup. Ct. 584.
48. 165 U. S. 443; 41 L. Ed. 782; 17 Sup. Ct. 385.

Chetwood from further using the bank's name in any litigation and required him to turn over the $27,000 to its agent. The highest Court of the State subsequently decided against Chetwood. He, in the name of the bank, sued out a writ of error to the United States Supreme Court. For so doing he was attached and punished for contempt of the injunction of the Circuit Court. On petition for writ of *certiorari* the Supreme Court held that the question of whether he had a right to use the name of the bank in suing out a writ of error and all like questions were exclusively within its control; that he could not lawfully be enjoined from taking such action as he thought proper to bring his case before it, and that, therefore, it would grant the writ of *certiorari* to bring up the record if its actual grant should be necessary. It presumed, however, that the intimation of its opinion would be sufficient, and so it doubtless proved.

606. May Circuit Courts of Appeals Issue Writ of Certiorari?

The question whether such a writ may be issued by a Circuit Court of Appeals under similar circumstances has never been expressly decided. The reasoning of Supreme Court in a case in which the matter was discussed would seem to indicate that a Circuit Court of Appeals may grant it under circumstances which would, independently of the Act of 1891, justify its issue by the Supreme Court.[49]

607. Certiorari Will Not Be Issued to Review Administrative Acts.

Neither the Supreme Court nor a Circuit Court of Appeals will grant the writ of *certiorari* to review the

49. Whitney vs. Dick, 202 U. S. 132; 50 L. Ed. 963; 26 Sup. Ct. 584.

administrative decisions of public officers and boards not acting in a judicial capacity.[50]

In the case cited, the Supreme Court of the District of Columbia was asked to issue a writ of *certiorari* to review the action of the Postmaster General in forbidding the petitioners the use of the mails in furtherance of a scheme which he held to be fraudulent.

608. Certiorari From Supreme Court to the Circuit Courts of Appeals.

The Act of 1891, by a provision which in substance now forms the first sentence of section 251 of the Judicial Code, authorized the Supreme Court in any case in which the judgment or decree of a Circuit Court of Appeals was made final, to require by *certiorari* or otherwise any such case to be certified to it for its review and determination, with the same power and authority as if it had been carried by writ of error or appeal to the Supreme Court.

The Supreme Court is very often asked to exercise this right. It grants the request perhaps one time in six.

609. Supreme Court Will Grant Certiorari When Circuit Court of Appeals Has Been Improperly Constituted.

One of the classes of cases in which it will grant it is when the Court below was improperly constituted. The law provides that no judge before whom the cause or question may have been tried or heard in the District Court shall sit in the trial or hearing of such question in the Circuit Court of Appeals.

A district judge felt himself unable from pressure of

50. Degge vs. Hitchcock, 229 U. S. 162; 57 L. Ed. 1135; 33 Sup. Ct. 639.

business to give an important patent case the consideration it deserved. He entered a *pro forma* decree in favor of the defendants and at the same time set forth in writing that he had given the question no consideration whatever, and that the decree was signed merely for the purpose of expediting an appeal. The case was heard in the Circuit Court of Appeals before two circuit judges and the district judge who had signed the decree. Both parties consented to his serving. The Supreme Court held that no consent could qualify him to sit; that the error was so grave that it would allow the writ of *certiorari*. Then it pointed out that if it simply placed the case on its docket for hearing in due course it would do precisely what it would have done had the Circuit Court of Appeals been properly constituted and the writ of *certiorari* allowed for other reasons, or, to put it in another way, that it would hear the case in the first instance without any previous hearing having been had before a properly constituted Circuit Court of Appeals. The judgment of the Circuit Court of Appeals was thereupon at once reversed and the cause remanded to be heard again.[51]

610. When Writ Dismissed.

The Supreme Court may grant the writ on the assumption that the case involves an issue of importance sufficient to justify it in so doing, and at the hearing it may find that a mistake had been made and that no such question is raised at all. When that happens the writ will be dismissed.[52]

51. Cramp vs. International Curtiss Marine Turbine Co., 228 U. S. 645; 57 L. Ed. 1003; 33 Sup. Ct. 722.

52. United States vs. Rimer, 220 U. S. 547; 55 L. Ed. 578; 31 Sup. Ct. 596.

611. Certiorari is Extraordinary Writ—Circumstances Under Which it Will Issue Are Not All Definable.

The Supreme Court has said that the writ is an extraordinary one and that no attempt to define all the circumstances under which it will be granted will be made. It will usually be issued where Circuit Courts of Appeals of different Circuits have reached different conclusions, or where the question involved is one of great importance and difficulty, and upon which there should be an early and authoritative decision by the Court of last resort. Sometimes, but not frequently, it has been granted when there has been a marked difference of opinion between the judges below and the question is of general concern. The Supreme Court is so sharply pressed for time that it is granted very sparingly.

612. Certiorari Not Granted Unless Decision of Circuit Court of Appeals is Final.

It will not be granted in any case in which the decision of the Circuit Court of Appeals is not made final. When an appeal or writ of error lies from such decision *certiorari* will not be issued. The two remedies are not cumulative.[53]

613. How Certiorari Is Applied For.

The application for the writ is made to the Supreme Court itself. The petition sets forth the ground upon which its issue is asked. It must be accompanied by a certified copy of the entire transcript of record in the case, including the proceedings in the Court to which the writ of *certiorari* is asked to be directed. The petition should contain only a summary and short statement of the matter involved and the general reasons relied on for the allowance of the writ. The Supreme Court

53. U. S. vs. Beatty, 232 U. S. 463; 58 L. Ed. 686; 34 Sup. Ct. 392.

adds the significant reminder that a failure to comply with this direction to make the statement and summary short will be taken as sufficient reason for denying it. Thirty copies of the petition and transcript and of any brief deemed necessary shall be filed. Notice of the date of submission of the petition, together with a copy of it and the brief, if any, in its support, shall be served on the counsel for the other side at least two weeks before such date if such counsel resides east of the Rocky Mountains, three weeks if he lives west of them. If the respondent wishes to file a brief he must do so at least three days before the date fixed for the submission of the petition. The Supreme Court will not hear oral arguments on such petitions, and no petition will be received within three days next before the day fixed upon for the adjournment of the Court for the term.[54]

614. Mandamus.

In cases which are within its appellate jurisdiction the Supreme Court may issue writs of mandamus to inferior Courts. For example, if a judge of a Court, in a case in which a writ of error may issue directly from the Supreme Court, refuses to sign a proper bill of exceptions tendered to him, the Supreme Court will grant a mandamus to compel him to do so.[55] The dissenting opinion by JUSTICE BALDWIN, in the Crane case, is a very learned and interesting review of the old law as to the issue of the writ of mandamus by superior to inferior Courts.

The power to issue this writ in aid of its jurisdiction is also possessed by the Circuit Courts of Appeals.[56]

54. Supreme Court Rule 37, par. 3; 1 1919 Supp. Compiled Stat. Sec. 1217; 5 Fed. Stat. Ann. 854.

55. Ex Parte Crane, 5 Peters, 190; 8 L. Ed. 920.

56. McClellan vs. Carland, 217 U. S. 268; 54 L. Ed. 762; 30 Sup. Ct. 501.

If a judge of a lower Court refuses to take jurisdiction in a case in which his jurisdiction is clear, a mandamus may issue to require him to do so.[57]

It should be borne in mind, however, that if the case has proceeded to such an extent that a writ of error could be sued out, the writ of mandamus will not issue. It is granted, as a rule, only when there is no other adequate remedy.[58]

The writ will not issue to control the discretion of a lower Court. It will issue to compel the Court to exercise a discretion when it has refused to do so.[59]

615. Petition to Revise in Matter of Law.

Where a question arises in a proceeding in bankruptcy, as distinguished from a controversy in bankruptcy proceedings, section 24b of the Bankruptcy Act permits the filing of a petition to revise in matter of law. This petition may be used to review interlocutory orders and frequently is. It takes up questions of law only—not of fact. The petition is filed either with the clerk of the proper Circuit Court of Appeals or with the clerk of the Court appealed from. It should recite the proceedings in the Court below, should point out every question of law involved, and state the ruling of the District Court thereon. A certified copy of so much of the record as shows what the issue of law was and how it arose must accompany the petition. In the circuits in which there is no rule of the Circuit Court of Appeals fixing the time within which such petition must be filed, it may be filed at any time within six months.[60] In some circuits, the rules require it to be filed within ten or fifteen days. Due notice of it must be given to the other party.

57. In re Hohorst, 150 U. S. 653; 37 L. Ed. 1211; 14 Sup. Ct. 221.
58. In re Pennsylvania Co., 137 U. S. 451; 34 L. Ed. 738; 11 Sup. Ct. 141.
59. Ex Parte Morgan, 114 U. S. 174; 29 L. Ed. 135; 5 Sup. Ct. 825.
60. Kenova Loan & Trust Co. vs. Graham, 135 Fed. 717; 68 C. C. A. 355.

34

616. Prohibition.

Sometimes the most effectual way in which a superior Court may exercise its appellate jurisdiction is by a writ of prohibition directed to an inferior Court forbidding it to assume a jurisdiction to which it is not entitled.

Section 234 of the Judicial Code empowers the Supreme Court to issue writs of prohibition to the District Courts when sitting as Courts of admiralty and maritime jurisdiction. It is probable that this provision, which has come down from the original Judiciary Act, is a survival of the old practice of the Court of King's Bench, which was much in the habit of issuing prohibitions to the Courts of admiralty to keep them within the narrow limits of admiralty jurisdiction fixed by the English Courts of common law. This grant of power permits the Supreme Court in admiralty matters to issue the writ of prohibition to a District Court even in cases in which a direct appeal from the latter to the former would not lie. Sometimes fundamental questions of great importance are thus disposed of.[61] With this exception, the Supreme Court cannot, in any case in which it has neither original nor appellate jurisdiction, grant prohibition, mandamus or *certiorari*. Where the writ of prohibition is necessary to protect or further the appellate jurisdiction of the Supreme Court in a case in which that jurisdiction exists, the writ may issue; otherwise not. The same rule governs its issue by the Circuit Courts of Appeals.

617. Certification of Questions to the Supreme Court.

By section 239 of the Judicial Code, and the construction put upon it by the Supreme Court,[62] a Circuit

61. U. S. vs. Thompson, U. S. Supreme Court, Jan. 3, 1922.

62. U. S. ex rel Arant vs. Lane, 245 U. S. 166; 62 L. Ed. 221; 38 Sup. Ct. 58.

Court of Appeals is authorized, at any time, in any case in which its judgment or decree is not made final, to certify to the Supreme Court of the United States any questions or propositions of law for the proper decision of which it desires the instruction of that Court. When the questions are certified up, the Supreme Court may do either one of two things. It may give the instructions. If it does they are binding upon the Circuit Courts of Appeals, or it may require that the whole record and cause be sent up for its consideration. If it takes the latter course it is required to decide the whole matter in controversy in the same manner as if the case had been brought to it by a writ of error or appeal.

In this class of cases the Supreme Court is quite insistent that the Court below shall not evade its responsibility of decision. Not infrequently the questions certified by the Court below have been so framed that they practically asked the Supreme Court how to decide the cause, which might have been a more or less complicated one of mixed fact and law. Under such circumstances the Supreme Court invariably refuses to answer at all.

618. Only Substantial Rights of Parties to be Considered on Appeal.

By the Act of February 26, 1919[63] section 269 of the Judicial Code was amended so as to provide that upon the hearing of any appeal, *certiorari,* writ of error, or motion for a new trial, in any case, civil or criminal, the court shall give judgment after an examination of the entire record before the Court, without regard to technical errors, defects or exceptions which do not affect the substantial rights of the parties.

Doubtless the value of this provision of law depends

63. 40 Stat. 1181; Fed. Stat. Ann. 1919 Sup. 231; U. S. Comp. Stat. 1919 Sup. Sec. 1246.

upon the way in which it is applied, and that is likely to vary not a little, as different minds often differ to what is technical and what is substantial. It is to be hoped that the statute will receive a broad construction so as to accomplish the manifest intention of Congress.

APPENDIX

APPENDIX

APPENDIX

ART. III, SECS. 1 AND 2 OF, AND ELEVENTH AMENDMENT TO THE CONSTITUTION OF THE UNITED STATES.

Section 1. The judicial power of the United States shall be vested in one Supreme Court, and in such inferior courts as the Congress may, from time to time, ordain and establish. The judges, both of the Supreme and inferior courts, shall hold their offices during good behaviour; and shall, at stated times, receive for their services, a compensation, which shall not be diminished during their continuance in office.

Sec. 2. The judicial power shall extend to all cases, in law and equity, arising under this Constitution, the laws of the United States, and treaties made, or which shall be made, under their authority; to all cases affecting ambassadors, other public ministers, and consuls; to all cases of admiralty and maritime jurisdiction; to controversies to which the United States shall be a party; to controversies between two or more States, between a State and citizens of another State, between citizens of different States, between citizens of the same State claiming lands under grants of different States, and between a State, or the citizens thereof, and foreign States, citizens or subjects.

In all cases affecting ambassadors, other public ministers and consuls, and those in which a State shall be party, the Supreme Court shall have original jurisdiction. In all the other cases before mentioned, the Supreme Court shall have appellate jurisdiction, both as to law and fact, with such exceptions, and under such regulations, as the Congress shall make.

The trial of all crimes, except in cases of impeachment, shall be by jury; and such trial shall be held in the State where the said crimes shall have been committed; but when not committed within any State, the trial shall be at such place or places as the Congress may by law have directed.

In consequence of the decision of the Supreme Court in Chisholm vs. Georgia, 2 Dallas, 419, the Eleventh Amendment was adopted. It reads as follows:

Art. XI. The judicial power of the United States shall not be construed to extend to any suit in law or equity commenced or prosecuted against one of the United States by citizens of another State, or by citizens or subjects of any foreign State.

THE ORIGINAL JUDICIARY ACT.

(1 Stat. 73.)

AN ACT TO ESTABLISH THE JUDICIAL COURTS OF THE UNITED STATES.

Section 1. Be it enacted by the Senate and House of Representatives of the United States of America in Congress assembled, That the supreme court of the United States shall consist of a chief justice and five associate justices, any four of whom shall be a quorum, and shall hold annually at the seat of government two sessions, the one commencing the first Monday of February, and the other the first Monday of August. That the associate justices shall have precedence according to the date of their commissions, or when the commissions of two or more of them bear date on the same day, according to their respective ages.

Sec. 2. And be it further enacted, That the United States shall be, and they hereby are divided into thirteen districts, to be limited and called as follows, to wit: one to consist of that part of the State of Massachusetts which lies easterly of the State of New Hampshire, and to be called Maine District; one to consist of the State of New Hampshire, and to be called New Hampshire District; one to consist of the remaining part of the State of Massachusetts, and to be called Massachusetts District; one to consist of the State of Connecticut, and to be called Connecticut District; one to consist of the State of New York, and to be called New York District; one to consist of the State of New Jersey, and to be called New Jersey District; one to consist of the State of Pennsylvania, and to be called Pennsylvania District; one to consist of the State of Delaware, and to be called Delaware District; one to consist of the State of Maryland, and to be called Maryland District; one to consist of the State of Virginia, except that part called the District of Kentucky, and to be called Virginia District; one to consist of the remaining part of the State of Virginia, and to be called Kentucky District; one to consist of the State of South Carolina, and to be called South Carolina District;

and one to consist of the State of Georgia, and to be called Georgia District.

Sec. 3. And be it further enacted, That there be a court called a District Court, in each of the aforementioned districts, to consist of one judge, who shall reside in the district for which he is appointed, and shall be called a District Judge, and shall hold annually four sessions * * * ; and that the District Judge shall have power to hold special courts at his discretion. * * *

(*The specifications of the times and places of holding court are here omitted.*)

Sec. 4. And be it further enacted, That the before mentioned districts, except those of Maine and Kentucky, shall be divided into three circuits, and be called the eastern, the middle, and the southern circuit. That the eastern circuit shall consist of the districts of New Hampshire, Massachusetts, Connecticut and New York; that the middle circuit shall consist of the districts of New Jersey, Pennsylvania, Delaware, Maryland and Virginia; and that the southern circuit shall consist of the districts of South Carolina and Georgia, and that there shall be held annually in each district of said circuits, two courts, which shall be called Circuit Courts, and shall consist of any two justices of the Supreme Court, and the district judge of such districts, any two of whom shall constitute a quorum; Provided, That no district judge shall give a vote in any case of appeal or error from his own decision; but may assign the reasons of such his decision.

Sec. 5. (*Fixed the times and places of holding the Circuit Courts.*)

Sec. 6. And be it further enacted, That the Supreme Court may, by any one or more of its justices being present, be adjourned from day to day until a quorum be convened; and that a circuit court may also be adjourned from day to day by any one of its judges, or if none are present, by the marshal of the district until a quorum be convened; and that a district court, in case of the inability of the judge to attend at the commencement of a session, may by virtue of a written order from the said judge, directed to the marshal of the district, be adjourned by the said marshal to such day, antecedent to the next stated session of the said court, as in the said order shall be appointed; and in case of the death of the said judge, and his vacancy not being supplied, all process, pleadings and proceedings of what nature soever, pending before the said court, shall be continued of course until the next stated session after the appointment and acceptance of the office by his successor.

Sec. 7. And be it further enacted, That the Supreme Court, and the district courts shall have power to appoint clerks for their respective courts, and that the clerk for each district court shall be clerk also of the circuit court in such district, and each of the said clerks shall, before he enters upon the execution of his office, take the following oath or affirmation, to wit: "I, A. B., being appointed clerk of   do solemnly swear, or affirm, that I will truly and faithfully enter and record all the orders, decrees, judgments and proceedings of the said court, and that I will faithfully and impartially discharge and perform all the duties of my said office, according to the best of my abilities and understanding. So help me God." Which words, so help me God, shall be omitted in all cases where an affirmation is admitted instead of an oath. And the said clerks shall also severally give bond, with sufficient sureties, (to be approved by the Supreme and district courts respectively) to the United States, in the sum of two thousand dollars, faithfully to discharge the duties of his office, and seasonably to record the decrees, judgments and determinations of the court of which he is clerk.

Sec. 8. And be it further enacted, That the justices of the Supreme Court, and the district judges, before they proceed to execute the duties of their respective offices, shall take the following oath or affirmation, to wit: "I, A. B., do solemnly swear or affirm, that I will administer justice without respect to persons, and do equal right to the poor and to the rich, and that I will faithfully and impartially discharge and perform all the duties incumbent on me as   , according to the best of my abilities and understanding, agreeably to the constitution and laws of the United States. So help me God."

Sec. 9. And be it further enacted, That the district courts shall have, exclusively of the courts of the several States, cognizance of all crimes and offences that shall be cognizable under the authority of the United States, committed within their respective districts, or upon the high seas; where no other punishment than whipping, not exceeding thirty stripes, a fine not exceeding one hundred dollars, or a term of imprisonment not exceeding six months, is to be inflicted; and shall also have exclusive original cognizance of all civil causes of admiralty and maritime jurisdiction, including all seizures under laws of impost, navigation or trade of the United States, where the seizures are made, on waters which are navigable from the sea by vessels of ten or more tons burthen, within their respective districts as well as upon the high seas; saving to suitors, in all cases, the right of a common law remedy, where the common law is competent to give it; and shall also have exclusive original cognizance of all seizures on land, or other waters than as aforesaid, made, and of all suits for penalties and forfeitures incurred, under the laws of the United States. And shall also have cognizance, concurrent with the courts of the several States, or the circuit courts, as the case may be, of all causes where an alien sues for a tort only in violation of the law of nations or a treaty of the United States. And shall also have cognizance, concurrent as last mentioned, of all suits at common law where the United States sue, and the matter in dispute amounts, exclusive of costs, to the sum or value of one hundred dollars. And shall also have jurisdiction exclusively of the courts of the several States, of all suits against consuls or vice-consuls, except for offences above the description aforesaid. And the trial of issues in fact, in the district courts, in all causes except civil causes of admiralty and maritime jurisdiction, shall be by jury.

Sec. 10. (*Conferred upon District Courts for Maine and Kentucky the original jurisdiction of Circuit Courts.*)

Sec. 11. And be it further enacted, That the circuit courts shall have original cognizance, concurrent with the courts of the several States, of all suits of a civil nature at common law or in equity, where the matter in dispute exceeds, exclusive of costs, the sum or value of five hundred dollars, and the United States are plaintiffs, or petitioners; or an alien is a party, or the suit is between a citizen of the State where the suit is brought, and a citizen of another State. And shall have exclusive cognizance of all crimes and offences cognizable under the authority of the United States, except where this act otherwise provides, or the laws of the United States shall otherwise direct, and concurrent jurisdiction with the district courts of the crimes and offences cognizable therein. But no person shall be arrested in one district for trial in another, in any civil action before a circuit or district court. And no civil suit shall be brought before either of said courts against an inhabitant of the United States, by any original process in any other district than that whereof he is an inhabitant, or in which he shall be found at the time of serving the writ, nor shall any district or circuit court have cognizance of any suit to recover the contents of any promissory note or other chose in action in favour of an assignee, unless a suit might have been prosecuted in such court to recover the said contents if no assignment had been made, except in cases of foreign bills of exchange. And the circuit courts shall also have appellate jurisdiction from the district courts under the regulations and restrictions herein after provided.

Sec. 12. And be it further enacted, That if a suit be commenced in any state court against an alien, or by a citizen of the State in which the suit is brought against a citizen of another State, and the matter in dispute exceeds the aforesaid sum or value of five hundred dollars, exclusive of costs, to be made to appear to the satisfaction of the court; and the defendant shall, at the time of entering his appearance in such state court, file a petition for the removal of the cause for trial into the next circuit court, to be held in the district where the suit is pending, or if in the district of Maine to the district court next to be holden therein, or if in Kentucky district to the district court next to be holden therein, and offer good and sufficient surety for his entering in such court, on the first day of its session, copies of said process against him, and also for his there appearing and entering special bail in the cause, if special bail was originally requisite therein, it shall then be the duty of the state court to accept the surety, and proceed no further in the cause, and any bail that may have been originally taken shall be discharged, and the said copies being entered as aforesaid, in such court of the United States, the cause shall there proceed in the same manner as if it had been brought there by original process. And any attachment of the goods or estate of the defendant by the original process, shall hold the goods or estate so attached, to answer the final judgment in the same manner as by the laws of such State they would have been holden to answer final judgment, had it been rendered by the court in which the suit commenced. And if in any action commenced in a state court, the title of land be concerned, and the parties are citizens of the same state, and the matter in dispute exceeds the sum or value of five hundred dollars, exclusive of costs, the sum or value being made to appear to the satisfaction of the court, either party, before the trial, shall state to the court and make affidavit if they require it, that he claims and shall rely upon a right or title to the land, under a grant from a state other than that in which the suit is pending, and produce the original grant or an exemplification of it, except where the loss of public records shall put it out of his power, and shall move that the adverse party inform the court, whether he claims a right or title to the land under a grant from the state in which the suit is pending; the said adverse (party) shall give such information, or otherwise not be allowed to plead such grant, or give it in evidence upon the trial, and if he informs that he does claim under such grant, the party claiming under the grant first mentioned may then, on motion, remove the cause for trial to the next circuit court to be holden in such district, or if in the district of Maine, to the court next to be holden therein; or if in Kentucky district, to the district court next to be holden therein; but if he is the defendant, shall do it under the same regulations as in the before mentioned case of the removal of a cause into such court by an alien; and neither party removing the cause, shall be allowed to plead or give evidence of any other title than that by him stated as aforesaid, as the ground of his claim; and the trial of issues in fact in the circuit courts shall, in all suits, except those of equity, and of admiralty, and maritime jurisdiction, be by jury.

Sec. 13. And be it further enacted, That the Supreme Court shall have exclusive jurisdiction of all controversies of a civil nature, where a state is a party, except between a state and its citizens; and except also between a state and citizens of other states, or aliens, in which latter case it shall have original but not exclusive jurisdiction. And shall have exclusively all such jurisdiction of suits or proceedings against ambassadors, or other public ministers, or their domestics, or domestic servants, as a court of law can have or exercise consistently with the law of nations and original, but not exclusive jurisdiction of all suits brought by ambassadors, or other public ministers, or in which a consul or vice consul, shall be a party. And the trial of issues in fact in the Supreme Court, in all actions at law against citizens of the United States, shall be by jury. The Supreme Court shall also have appellate jurisdiction from the circuit courts and courts of the several states, in the cases herein after specially provided for; and shall have power to issue writs of prohibition to the district courts, when proceeding as courts of admiralty and maritime jurisdiction, and writs of mandamus, in cases warranted by the principles and usages of law, to any courts appointed, or persons holding office, under the authority of the United States.

Sec. 14. And be it further enacted, That all the before mentioned courts of the United States, shall have power to issue writs of scire facias, habeas corpus, and all other writs not specially provided for by statute, which may be necessary for the exercise of their respective jurisdictions, and agreeable to the principles and usages of law. And that either of the justices of the supreme court, as well as judges of the district courts, shall have power to grant writs of habeas corpus for the purpose of an inquiry into the cause of commitment. Provided, That writs of habeas corpus shall in no case extend to prisoners in gaol, unless where they are in custody, under or by color of the authority of the United States, or are committed for trial before some court of the same, or are necessary to be brought into court to testify.

Sec. 15. And be it further enacted, That all the said courts of the United States, shall have power in the trial of actions at law, on motion and due notice thereof being given, to require the parties to produce books or writings in their possession or power, which contain evidence pertinent to the issue, in cases and under circumstances where they might be compelled to produce the same by the ordinary rules of proceeding in chancery; and if a plaintiff shall fail to comply with such order, to produce books or writings, it shall be lawful for the courts respectively, on motion, to give the like judgment for the defendant as in cases of nonsuit; and if a defendant shall fail to comply with such order, to produce books or writings, it shall be lawful for the courts respectively on motion as aforesaid, to give judgment against him or her by default.

Sec. 16. And be it further enacted, That suits in equity shall not be sustained in either of the courts of the United States, in any case where plain, adequate and complete remedy may be had at law.

Sec. 17. And be it further enacted, That all the said courts of the United States shall have power to grant new trials, in cases where there has been a trial by jury for reasons for which new trials have usually been granted in the courts of law; and shall have power to impose and administer all necessary oaths or affirmations, and to punish by fine or imprisonment, at the discretion of said courts, all contempts of authority in any cause or hearing before the same; and to make and establish all necessary rules for the orderly conducting business in the said courts, provided such rules are not repugnant to the laws of the United States.

Sec. 18. And be it further enacted, That when in a circuit court, judgment upon a verdict in a civil action shall be entered, execution may on motion of either party, at the discretion of the court, and on such conditions for the security of the adverse party as they may judge proper, be stayed forty-two days from the time of entering judgment, to give time to file in the clerk's office of said court, a petition for a new trial. And if such petition be there filed within said term of forty-two days, with a certificate thereon from either of the judges of such court, that he allows the same to be filed, which certificate he may make or refuse at his discretion, execution shall of course be further stayed to the next session of said court. And if a new trial be granted, the former judgment shall be thereby rendered void.

Sec. 19. And be it further enacted, That it shall be the duty of circuit courts, in causes in equity and of admiralty and maritime jurisdiction, to cause the facts on which they found their sentence or decree, fully to appear upon the record either from the pleadings and decree itself, or a state of the case agreed by the parties, or their counsel, or if they disagree by a stating of the case by the court.

Sec. 20. And be it further enacted, That where in a circuit court, a plaintiff in an action, originally brought there, or a petitioner in equity, other than the United States, recovers less than the sum or value of five hundred dollars, or a libellant, upon his own appeal, less than the sum or value of three hundred dollars, he shall not be allowed, but at the discretion of the court, may be adjudged to pay costs.

Sec. 21. And be it further enacted, That from final decrees in a district court in causes of admiralty and maritime jurisdiction, where the matter in dispute exceeds the sum or value of three hundred dollars, exclusive of costs, an appeal shall be allowed to the next circuit court, to be held in such district. Provided, nevertheless, That all such appeals from final decrees as aforesaid, from the district court of Maine, shall be made to the circuit court, next to be holden after each appeal in the district of Massachusetts.

Sec. 22. And be it further enacted, That final decrees and judgments in civil actions in a district court, where the matter in dispute exceeds the sum or value of fifty dollars, exclusive of costs, may be re-examined, and reversed or affirmed in a circuit court, holden in the same district, upon a writ of error, whereto shall be annexed and returned therewith at the day and place therein mentioned, an authenticated transcript of the record, an assignment of errors, and prayer for reversal, with a citation to the adverse party, signed by the judge of such district court, or a justice of the Supreme Court, the adverse party having at least twenty days' notice. And upon a like process, may final judgments and decrees in civil actions, and suits in equity in a circuit court, brought there by original process, or removed there from courts of the several States, or removed there by appeal from a district court where the matter in dispute exceeds the sum or value of two thousand dollars, exclusive of costs, be re-examined and reversed or affirmed in the Supreme Court, the citation being in such case signed by a judge of such circuit court, or justice of the Supreme Court, and the adverse party having at least thirty days' notice. But there shall be no reversal in either court on such writ for error in ruling any plea in abatement, other than a plea to the jurisdiction of the court, or such plea to a petition or bill in equity, as is in the nature of a demurrer, or for any error in fact. And writs of error shall not be brought but within five years after rendering or passing the judgment or decree complained of, or in case the person entitled to such writ of error be an infant, feme covert, non compos mentis, or imprisoned, then within five years as aforesaid, exclusive of the time of such disability. And every justice or judge signing a citation on any writ of error as aforesaid, shall take good and sufficient security, that the plaintiff in error shall prosecute his writ to effect, and answer all damages and costs if he fail to make his plea good.

Sec. 23. And be it further enacted, That a writ of error as aforesaid shall be a supersedeas and stay execution in cases only where the writ of error is served, by a copy thereof being lodged for the adverse party in the clerk's office where the record remains, within ten days, Sundays exclusive, after rendering the judgment or passing the decree complained of. Until the expiration of which term of ten days, executions shall not issue in any case where a writ of error may be a supersedeas; and whereupon such writ of error the Supreme or a circuit court shall affirm a judgment or decree, they shall adjudge or decree to the respondent in error just damages for his delay, and single or double costs at their discretion.

Sec. 24. And be it further enacted, That when a judgment or decree shall be reversed in a circuit court, such court shall proceed to render such judgment or pass such decree as the district court shall have rendered or passed; and the Supreme Court shall do the same on reversals therein, except where the reversal is in favor of the plaintiff, or petitioner in the original suit, and the damages to be assessed, or matter to be decreed, are uncertain, in which case they shall remand the cause for a final decision. And the Supreme Court shall not issue execution in causes that are removed before them by writs of error, but shall send a special mandate to the circuit court to award execution thereupon.

Sec. 25. And be it further enacted, That a final judgment or decree in any suit, in the highest court of law or equity of a State in which a decision in the suit could be had, where is drawn in question the validity of a treaty or statute of, or an authority exercised under the United States, and the decision is against their validity; or where is drawn in question the validity of a statute of, or an authority exercised under any State, on the ground of their being repugnant to the constitution, treaties or laws of the United States, and the decision is in favor of such their validity, or where is drawn in question the construction of any clause of the constitution, or of a treaty, or statute of, or commission held under the United States, and the decision is against the title, right, privilege or exemption specially set up or claimed by either party, under such clause of the said Constitution, treaty, statute or commission, may be re-examined and reversed or affirmed in the Supreme Court of the United States upon a writ of error, the citation being signed by the chief justice, or judge or chancellor of the court rendering or passing the judgment or decree complained of, or by a justice of the Supreme Court of the United States, in the same manner and under the same regulations, and the writ shall have the same effect, as if the judgment or decree complained of had been rendered or passed in a circuit court, and the proceedings upon the reversal shall also be the same, except that the Supreme Court, instead of remanding the cause for a final decision as before provided, may at their discretion, if the cause shall have been one remanded before, proceed to a final decision of the same, and award execution. But no other error shall be assigned or regarded as a ground of reversal in any such case as aforesaid, than such as appears on the face of the record, and immediately respects the before mentioned questions of validity or construction of the said constitution, treaties, statutes, commissions, or authorities in dispute.

Sec. 26. And be it further enacted, That in all causes brought before either of the courts of the United States to recover the forfeiture annexed to any articles of agreement, covenant, bond, or other specialty, where the forfeiture, breach or non-performance shall appear, by the default or confession of the defendant, or upon demurrer, the court before whom the action is, shall render judgment therein for the plaintiff to recover so much as is due. according to equity. And when the sum for which judgment should be rendered is uncertain, the same shall, if either of the parties request it, be assessed by a jury.

Sec. 27. And be it further enacted, That a marshal shall be appointed in and for each district for the terms of four years, but shall be removable from office at pleasure, whose duty it shall be to attend the district and circuit courts when sitting therein, and also the Supreme Court in the district in which that court shall sit. And to execute throughout the district, all lawful precepts directed to him, and issued under the authority of the United States, and he shall have power to command all necessary assistance in the execution of his duty, and to appoint as there shall be occasion, one or more deputies, who shall be removable from office by the judge of the district court, or the circuit court sitting within the district, at

35

the pleasure of either; and before he enters on the duties of his office, he shall become bound for the faithful performance of the same, by himself and by his deputies before the judge of the district court to the United States, jointly and severally, with two good and sufficient sureties, inhabitants and freeholders of such district, to be approved by the district judge, in the sum of twenty thousand dollars, and shall take before said judge, as shall also his deputies, before they enter on the duties of their appointment, the following oath of office: "I, A. B., do solemnly swear or affirm, that I will faithfully execute all lawful precepts directed to the marshal of the district of   under the authority of the United States, and true returns make, and in all things well and truly, and without malice or partiality, perform the duties of the office of marshal (or marshal's deputy, as the case may be) of the district of   , during my continuance in said office, and take only my lawful fees. So help me God."

Sec. 28. And be it further enacted, That in all causes wherein the marshal or his deputy shall be a party, the writs and precepts therein shall be directed to such disinterested person as the court, or any justice or judge thereof may appoint, and the person so appointed, is hereby authorized to execute and return the same. And in case of the death of any marshal, his deputy or deputies shall continue in office, unless otherwise specially removed; and shall execute the same in the name of the deceased, until another marshal shall be appointed and sworn. And the defaults or misfeasances in office of such deputy or deputies in the mean time, as well as before, shall be adjudged a breach of the condition of the bond given, as before directed, by the marshal who appointed them; and the executor or administrator of the deceased marshal shall have like remedy for the defaults and misfeasances in office of such deputy or deputies during such interval, as they would be entitled to if the marshal had continued in life and in the exercise of his said office, until his successor was appointed, and sworn or affirmed. And every marshal or his deputy when removed from office, or when the term for which the marshal is appointed shall expire, shall have power notwithstanding to execute all such precepts as may be in their hands respectively at the time of such removal or expiration of office; and the marshal shall be held answerable for the delivery to his successor of all prisoners which may be in his custody at the time of his removal, or when the term for which he is appointed shall expire, and for that purpose may retain such prisoners in his custody until his successor shall be appointed and qualified as the law directs.

Sec. 29. And be it further enacted, That in cases punishable with death, the trial shall be had in the county where the offence was committed, or where that cannot be done without great inconvenience, twelve petit jurors at least shall be summoned from thence. And jurors in all cases to serve in the courts of the United States shall be designated by lot or otherwise in each State respectively according to the mode of forming juries therein now practiced, so far as the laws of the same shall render such designation practicable by the courts or marshals of the United States; and the jurors shall have the same qualifications as are requisite for jurors by the laws of the State of which they are citizens, to serve in the highest courts of law of such State, and shall be returned as there shall be occasion for them, from such parts of the district from time to time as the court shall direct, so as shall be most favorable to an impartial trial, and so as not to incur an unnecessary expense, or unduly to burthen the citizens of any part of the district with such services. And writs of venire facias when directed by the court shall issue from the clerk's office, and shall be served and returned by the marshal in his proper person, or by his deputy, or in case the marshal or his deputy is not an indifferent person, or is interested in the event of the cause, by such fit person as the court shall specially appoint for that purpose, to whom they shall administer an oath or affirmation that he will truly and impartially serve and return such writ. And when from challenges or otherwise there shall not be a jury to determine any civil or criminal cause, the marshal or his deputy shall, by order of the court where such defect of jurors shall happen, return jurymen de talibus circumstantibus sufficient to complete the panel; and when the marshal or his deputy are disqualified as aforesaid, jurors may be returned by such disinterested person as the court shall appoint.

Sec. 30. And be it further enacted, That the mode of proof by oral testimony and examination of witnesses in open court shall be the same in all the courts of the United States, as well in the trial of causes in equity and of admiralty and maritime jurisdiction, as of actions at common law. And when the testimony of any person shall be necessary in any civil cause depending in any district in any court of the United States, who shall live at a greater distance from the place of trial than one hundred miles, or is bound on a voyage to sea, or is about to go out of the United States, or out of such district, and to a greater distance from the place of trial than as aforesaid, before the time of trial, or is ancient or very infirm, the deposition of such person may be taken de bene esse before any justice or judge of any of the courts of the United States, or before any chancellor, justice or judge of a supreme or superior court, mayor or chief magistrate of a city, or judge of a county court or court of common pleas of any of the United States, not being of counsel or attorney to either of the parties, or interested in the event of the cause, provided that a notification from the magistrate before whom the deposition is to be taken to the adverse party, to be present at the taking of the same, and to put interrogatories, if he think fit, be first made out and served on the adverse party or his attorney as either may be nearest, if either is within one hundred miles of the place of such caption, allowing time for their attendance after notified, not less than at the rate of one day, Sundays exclusive, for every twenty miles travel. And in causes of admiralty and maritime jurisdiction, or other cases of seizure when a libel shall be filed, in which an adverse party is not named, and depositions of persons circumstanced as aforesaid shall be taken before a claim be put in, the like notification as aforesaid shall be given to the person having the agency or possession of the property libeled at the time of the capture or seizure of the same, if known to the libellant. And every person deposing as aforesaid shall be carefully examined and cautioned, and sworn or affirmed to testify the whole truth, and shall subscribe the testimony by him or her given after the same shall be reduced to writing, which shall be done only by the magistrate taking the deposition, or by the deponent in his presence. And the depositions so taken shall be retained by such magistrate until he deliver the same with his own hand into the court for which they are taken, or shall, together with a certificate of the reasons as aforesaid of their being taken, and of the notice if any given to the adverse party, be by him the said magistrate sealed up and directed to such court, and remain under his seal until opened in court. And any person may be compelled to appear and depose as aforesaid in the same manner as to appear and testify in court. And in the trial of any cause of admiralty or maritime jurisdiction in a district court, the decree in which may be appealed from, if either party shall suggest to and satisfy the court that probably it will not be in his power to produce the witnesses there testifying before the circuit court should an appeal be had, and shall move that their testimony be taken down in writing, it shall be so done by the clerk of the court. And if an appeal be had, such testimony may be used on the trial of the same, if it shall appear to the satisfaction of the court which shall try the appeal, that the witnesses are then dead or gone out of the United States, or to a greater distance than as aforesaid from the place where the court is sitting, or that by reason of age, sickness, bodily infirmity or imprisonment, they are unable to travel and appear at court, but not otherwise. And unless the same shall be made to appear on the trial of any cause, with respect to witnesses whose depositions may have been taken therein, such depositions shall not be admitted or used in the cause. Provided, That nothing herein shall be construed to prevent any court of the United States from granting a dedimus potestatem to take depositions according to common usage, when it may be necessary to prevent a failure or delay of justice, which power they shall severally possess, nor to extend to depositions taken in perpetuam rei memoriam, which if they relate to matters that may be cognizable in any court of the United States, a circuit court on application thereto made as a court of equity, may, according, to the usages in chancery direct to be taken.

Sec. 31. And be it further enacted, That where any suit shall be depending in any court of the United States, and either of the parties shall die before final judgment, the executor or administrator of such deceased party who was plaintiff, petitioner, or defendant, in case the cause of action doth by law survive, shall have full power to prosecute or defend any such suit or action until final judgment; and the defendant or defendants are hereby obliged to answer thereto accordingly; and the court before whom such cause may be depending, is hereby empowered and directed to hear and determine the same, and to render judgment for or against the executor or administrator, as the case may require. And if such executor or administrator having been duly served with a scire facias from the office of the hand, shall neglect or refuse to become a party to the suit, the court clerk of the court where such suit is depending, twenty days before-may render judgment against the estate of the deceased party, in the same manner as if the executor or administrator had voluntarily made himself a party to the suit. And the executor or administrator who shall become a party as aforesaid, shall, upon motion to the court where the suit is depending, be entitled to a continuance of the same until the next term of the said court. And if there be two or more plaintiffs or defendants, and one or more of them shall die, if the cause of action shall survive to the surviving plaintiff or plaintiffs, or against the surviving defendant or defendants, the writ or action shall not be thereby abated; but such death being suggested upon the record, the action shall proceed at the suit of the surviving plaintiff or plaintiffs against the surviving defendant or defendants.

Sec. 32. And be it further enacted, That no summons, writ, declaration, return, process, judgment, or other proceedings in civil causes in any of the courts of the United States, shall be abated, arrested, quashed or reversed, for any defect or want of form, but the said courts respectively shall proceed and give judgment according as the right of the cause and matter in law shall appear unto them, without regarding any imperfections, defects, or want of form in such writ, declaration, or other pleading, return, process, judgment, or course of proceeding whatsoever, except those only in cases of demurrer, which the party demurring shall specially set down and express together with his demurrer as the cause thereof. And the said courts respectively shall and may, by virtue of this act, from time to time, amend all and every such imperfections, defects and wants of form, other than those only which the party demurring shall express as aforesaid, and may at any time permit either of the parties to amend any defect in the process or pleadings, upon such conditions as the said courts respectively shall in their discretion, and by their rules prescribe.

Sec. 33. And be it further enacted, That for any crime or offence against the United States, the offender may, by any justice or judge of the United States, or by any justice of the peace, or other magistrate of any of the United States where he may be found agreeably to the usual mode of process against offenders in such state, and at the expense of the United States, be arrested, and imprisoned or bailed, as the case may be, for trial before such court of the United States as by this act has cognizance of the offence. And copies of the process shall be returned as speedily as may be into the clerk's office of such court, together with the recognizances of the witnesses for their appearance to testify in the case; which recognizances the magistrate before whom the examination shall be, may require on pain of imprisonment. And if such commitment of the offender, or the witnesses shall be in a district other than that in which the offence is to be tried, it shall be the duty of the judge of that district where the delinquent is imprisoned, seasonably to issue, and of the marshal of the same district to execute; a warrant for the removal of the offender, and the witnesses, or either of them, as the case may be, to the district in which the trial is to be had. And upon all arrests in criminal cases, bail shall be admitted, except where the punishment may be death, in which cases it shall not be admitted but by the Supreme or a circuit court, or by a justice of the supreme court, or a judge of a district court, who shall exercise their discretion therein, regarding the nature and circumstances of the offence, and of the evidence, and the usages of law. And if a person committed by a justice of the Supreme or a judge of a district court for an offence not punishable with death, shall afterwards procure bail, and there be no judge of the United States in the district to take the same, it may be taken by any judge of the supreme or superior court of law of such state.

Sec. 34. And be it further enacted, That the laws of the several states, except where the constitution, treaties or statutes of the United States shall otherwise require or provide, shall be regarded as rules of decision in trials at common law in the courts of the United States in cases where they apply.

Sec. 35. And be it further enacted, That in all the courts of the United States, the parties may plead and manage their own causes personally or by the assistance of such counsel or attorneys at law as by the rules of the said courts respectively shall be permitted to manage and conduct causes therein. And there shall be appointed in each district a meet person learned in the law to act as attorney for the United States in such district, who shall be sworn or affirmed to the faithful execution of his office, whose duty it shall be to prosecute in such district all delinquents for crimes and offences, cognizable under the authority of the United States, and all civil actions in which the United States shall be concerned except before the supreme court in the district in which that court shall be holden. And he shall receive as a compensation for his services such fees as shall be taxed therefor in the respective courts before which the suits or prosecutions shall be. And there shall also be appointed a meet person, learned in the law, to act as attorney-general for the United States, who shall be sworn or affirmed to a faithful execution of his office; whose duty it shall be to prosecute and conduct all suits in the Supreme Court in which the United States shall be concerned, and to give his advice and opinion upon questions of law when required by the President of the United States, or when requested by the heads of any of the departments, touching any matters that may concern their departments, and shall receive such compensation for his services as shall by law be provided.

Approved, September 24, 1789.

·THE JUDICIAL CODE.

(As amended to September, 1922.)

TITLE.

THE JUDICIARY.

CHAPTER ONE.

DISTRICT COURTS—ORGANIZATION.

Section 1. In each of the districts described in chapter five there shall be a court called a district court, for which there shall be appointed one judge to be called a district judge, except that in the Northern District of California, the Southern District of California, the Northern District of Illinois, the District of Minnesota, the District of Nebraska, the Eastern District of New York, the Northern and Southern Districts of Ohio, the District of Oregon, the Eastern and Western Districts of Pennsylvania, the Western District of

Texas, the Western District of Washington, and the District of North Dakota, there shall be an additional judge in each (except that whenever a vacancy shall occur in the office of the district judge for the District of North Dakota, by the retirement, disqualification, or death of the judge senior in commission, such vacancy shall not be filled, and thereafter there shall be but one district judge in said district), and in the District of New Jersey, two additional district judges, and in the Southern District of New York, three additional district judges. Provided, that there shall be one judge for the Eastern and Middle Districts of Tennessee, and one judge for the Northern and Southern Districts of Mississippi. Provided further, that the district judge for the Middle District of Alabama shall continue as heretofore to be a district judge for the Northern District thereof. Every district judge shall reside in the district or one of the districts for which he is appointed and for offending against this provision, shall be deemed guilty of a high misdemeanor. (36 Stat. L. 1087, March 3, 1911; 38 Stat. 580, July 30, 1914; 38 Stat. 961, March 3, 1915; 39 Stat. 48, April 11, 1916; 39 Stat. 438, February 26, 1917; 67th Congress (1st Session), Chap. 29, June 25, 1921.)

To which the Act of September 14, 1922, adds: That the President be and he is hereby, authorized to appoint, by and with the advice and consent of the Senate, the following number of district judges for the United States district courts in the districts specified in addition to those now authorized by law. For the District of Massachusetts, two; for the Eastern District of New York, one; for the Southern District of New York, two; for the District of New Jersey, one; for the Eastern District of Pennsylvania, one; for the Western District of Pennsylvania, one; for the Northern District of Texas, one; for the Southern District of Florida, one; for the Eastern District of Michigan, one; for the Northern District of Ohio, one; for the Middle District of Tennessee, one; for the Northern District of Illinois, one; for the Eastern District of Illinois, one; for the District of Minnesota, one; for the Eastern District of Missouri, one; for the Western District of Missouri, one; for the Eastern District of Oklahoma, one; for the District of Montana, one; for the Northern District of California, one; for the Southern District of California, one; for the District of New Mexico, one; and for the District of Arizona, one. A vacancy occurring, more than two years after the passage of this Act, in the office of any district judge appointed pursuant to this Act, except for the Middle District of Tennessee, shall not be filled unless Congress shall so provide, and if an appointment is made to fill such a vacancy occurring within two years a vacancy thereafter occurring in said office shall not be filled unless Congress shall so provide. Provided, however, that in case a vacancy occurs in the District of New Mexico, at any time after the passage of this Act, there shall thereafter be but one judge for said district until otherwise provided by law. Every judge shall reside in the district or circuit or one of the districts or circuits for which he is appointed.

Sec. 2. Each of the district judges, including the judges in Porto Rico, Hawaii and Alaska, exercising federal jurisdiction, shall receive a salary of seven thousand five hundred dollars a year, to be paid in monthly installments. (25 February, 1919, 40 Stat. L. 1156, c. 29.)

Sec. 3. A clerk shall be appointed for each district court by the judge thereof (or by the senior judge if there be more than one judge in the district). Act Feb. 11, 1921, 41 Stat. 1099.

Sec. 4. Except as otherwise specially provided by law, the clerk of the district court for each district may, with the approval of the district judge thereof, appoint such number of deputy clerks as may be deemed necessary by such judge, who may be designated to reside and maintain offices at such places of holding court as the judge may determine. Such deputies may be removed at the pleasure of the clerk appointing them, with the concurrence of the district judge. In case of the death of the clerk, his deputy or deputies shall, unless removed, continue in office and perform the duties of the clerk, in his name, until a clerk is appointed and qualified; and for the default or misfeasances in office of any such deputy, whether in the lifetime of the clerk or after his death, the clerk and his estate and the sureties on his official bond shall be liable; and his executor or administrator shall have such remedy for any such default or misfeasances committed after his death as the clerk would be entitled to if the same had occurred in his lifetime. [See §§ 67, 68.]

Sec. 5. The district court for each district may appoint a crier for the court; and the marshal may appoint such number of persons, not exceeding five, as the judge may determine, to wait upon the grand and other juries, and for other necessary purposes.

Sec. 6. The records of a district court shall be kept at the place where the court is held. When it is held at more than one place in any district and the place of keeping the records is not specially provided by law, they shall be kept at either of the places of holding the court which may be designated by the district judge.

Sec. 7. No action, suit, proceeding, or process in any district court shall abate or be rendered invalid by reason of any act changing the time of holding such court, but the same shall be deemed to be returnable to, pending, and triable in the terms established next after the return day thereof.

Sec. 8. When the trial or hearing of any cause, civil or criminal, in a district court has been commenced and is in progress before a jury or the court, it shall not be stayed or discontinued by the arrival of the time fixed by law for another session of said court; but the court may proceed therein and bring it to a conclusion in the same manner and with the same effect as if another stated term of the court had not intervened.

Sec. 9. The district courts, as courts of admiralty and as courts of equity, shall be deemed always open for the purpose of filing any pleading, of issuing and returning mesne and final process, and of making and directing all interlocutory motions, orders, rules, and other proceedings preparatory to the hearing, upon their merits, of all causes pending therein. Any district judge may, upon reasonable notice to the parties, make, direct, and award, at chambers or in the clerk's office, and in vacation as well as in term, all such process, commissions, orders, rules, and other proceedings, whenever the same are not grantable of course, according to the rules and practice of the court.

Sec. 10. District courts shall hold monthly adjournments of their regular terms, for the trial of criminal causes, when their business requires it to be done, in order to prevent undue expenses and delays in such cases.

Sec. 11. A special term of any district court may be held at the same place where any regular term is held, or at such other place in the district as the nature of the business may require, and at such time and upon such notice as may be ordered by the district judge. Any business may be transacted at such special term which might be transacted at a regular term.

Sec. 12. If the judge of any district court is unable to attend at the commencement of any regular, adjourned, or special term, or any time during such term, the court may be adjourned by the marshal, or clerk, by virtue of a written order directed to him by the judge, to the next regular term, or to any earlier day, as the order may direct.

Sec. 13. Whenever any district judge by reason of any disability or necessary absence from his district or the accumulation or urgency of business is unable to perform speedily the work of his district, the senior circuit judge of that circuit, or in his absence, the circuit justice thereof, may, if in his judgment the public interest requires, designate and assign any district judge of any district court within the same judicial circuit to act as district judge in such district and to discharge all the judicial duties of a judge thereof for such time as the business of the said district court may require. Whenever it is found impracticable to designate and assign another district judge within the same judicial circuit as above provided, and a certificate of the needs of any such district is presented by said senior circuit judge or said circuit justice to the Chief Justice of the United States, he, or in his absence the senior associate justice, may, if in his judgment the public interest so requires, designate and assign a district judge of an adjoining judicial circuit if practicable, or if not practicable, then of any judicial circuit, to perform the duties of district judge and hold a district court in any such district as above provided: Provided, however, That before any such designation or assignment is made, the senior circuit judge of the circuit from which the designated or assigned judge is to be taken shall consent thereto. All designations and assignments made hereunder shall be filed in the office of the clerk and entered on the minutes of both the court from and to which a judge is designated and assigned. (Act Sept. 14, 1922.)

Sec. 14. When, from the accumulation or urgency of business in any district court, the public interests require the designation and appointment hereinafter provided, and the fact is made to appear, by the certificate of the clerk, under the seal of the court, to any circuit judge of the circuit in which the district lies, or, in the absence of all the circuit judges, to the circuit justice of the circuit in which the district lies, such circuit judge or justice may designate and appoint the judge of any other district in the same circuit to have and exercise within the district first named the same powers that are vested in the judge thereof. Each of the said district judges may, in case of such appointment, hold separately at the same time a district court in such district, and discharge all the judicial duties of the district judge therein.

Sec. 15. Each district judge designated and assigned under the provisions of Section 13 may hold separately and at the same time a district court in the district or territory to which such judge is designated and assigned, and discharge all the judicial duties of the district or territorial judge therein. (Act Sept. 14, 1922.)

Sec. 16. Any such circuit judge, or circuit justice, or the Chief Justice, as the case may be, may, from time to time, if in his judgment the public interests so require, make a new designation and appointment of any other district judge, in the manner, for the duties, and with the powers mentioned in the three preceding sections, and revoke any previous designation and appointment.

Sec. 17. It shall be the duty of the senior circuit judge then present in the circuit, whenever in his judgment the public interest so requires, to designate and appoint, in the manner and with the powers provided in section fourteen, the district judge of any judicial district within his circuit to hold a district court in the place or in aid of any other district judge within the same circuit.

Sec. 18. The Chief Justice of the United States, or the circuit justice of any judicial circuit, or the senior circuit judge thereof, may, if the public interest requires, designate and assign any circuit judge of a judicial circuit to hold a district court within such circuit. The judges of the United States Court of Customs Appeals, or any of them, whenever the business of that court will permit, may, if in the judgment of the Chief Justice of the United States the public interest requires, be designated and assigned by him for service from time to time and until he shall otherwise direct, in the Supreme Court of the District of Columbia, or the Court of Appeals of the District of Columbia when requested by the Chief Justice of either of said courts. During the period of service of any judge designated and assigned under this Act, he shall have all the powers, and rights, and perform all the duties, of a judge of the district, or a justice of the court, to which he has been assigned (excepting the power of appointment to a statutory position or of permanent designation of newspaper or depository of funds); Provided, however, That in case a trial has been entered upon before such period of service has expired, and has not been concluded, the period of service shall be deemed to be extended until the trial has been concluded. Any designated and assigned judge who has held court in another district than his own shall have power, notwithstanding his absence from such district and the expiration of the time limit in his designation, to decide all matters which have been submitted to him within such district, to decide motions for new trials, settle bills of exceptions, certify or authenticate narratives of testimony, or perform any other act required by law or the rules to be performed in order to prepare any case so tried by him for review in an appellate court; and his action thereon in writing filed with the clerk of the court where the trial or hearing was had shall be as valid as if such action had been taken by him within that district and within the period of his designation. (Act Sept. 14, 1922.)

Sec. 19. It shall be the duty of the district or circuit judge who is designated and appointed under either of the six preceding sections, to discharge all the judicial duties for which he is so appointed, during the time for which he is so appointed; and all the acts and proceedings in the courts held by him, or by or before him, in pursuance of said provisions, shall have the same effect and validity as if done by or before the district judge of the said district.

Sec. 20. Whenever it appears that the judge of any district court is in any way concerned in interest in any suit pending therein, or has been of counsel or is a material witness for either party, or is so related to or connected with either party as to render it improper, in his opinion, for him to sit on the trial, it shall be his duty, on application by either party, to cause the fact to be entered on the records of the court; and also an order that an authenticated copy thereof shall be forthwith certified to the senior circuit judge for said circuit then present in the circuit; and thereupon such proceedings shall be had as are provided in section fourteen.

Sec. 21. Whenever a party to any action or proceeding, civil or criminal, shall make and file an affidavit that the judge before whom the action or proceeding is to be tried or heard has a personal bias or prejudice either against him or in favor of any opposite party to the suit, such judge shall proceed no further therein, but another judge shall be designated in the manner prescribed in the section last preceding, or chosen in the manner prescribed in section twenty-three, to hear such matter. Every such affidavit shall state the facts and the reasons for the belief that such bias or prejudice exists, and shall be filed not less than ten days before the beginning of the term of the court, or good cause shall be shown for the failure to file it within such time. No party shall be entitled in any case to file more than one such affidavit; and no such affidavit shall be filed unless accompanied by a certificate of counsel of record that such affidavit and application are made in good faith. The same proceedings shall be had when the presiding judge shall file with the clerk of the court a certificate that he deems himself unable for any reason to preside with absolute impartiality in the pending suit or action.

Sec. 22. When the office of judge of any district court becomes vacant, all process, pleadings, and proceedings pending before such court shall, if necessary, be continued by the clerk thereof until such time as a judge shall be appointed, or designated, to hold such court; and the judge so designated, while holding such court, shall possess the powers conferred by, and be subject to the provisions contained in section nineteen.

Sec. 23. In districts having more than one district judge, the judges may agree upon the division of business and assignment of cases for trial in said district; but in case they do not so agree, the senior circuit judge of the circuit in which the district lies, shall make all necessary orders for the division of business and the assignment of cases for trial in said district.

Section 2 of the Act of Sept. 14, 1922, is as follows: It shall be the duty of the Chief Justice of the United States, or in case of his disability, of one of the other justices of the supreme court, in order of their seniority, as soon as may be after the passage of this Act, and annually thereafter, to summon to a conference on the last Monday in September, at Washington, District of Columbia, or at such other time and place in the United States as the Chief Justice, or, in case of his disability, any of said justices in order of their seniority, may designate, the senior circuit judge of each judicial circuit. If any senior circuit judge is unable to attend, the Chief Justice, or in case of his disability, the justice of the Supreme Court calling said conference, may summon any other circuit or district judge in the judicial circuit whose senior circuit judge is unable to attend, that each circuit may be adequately represented at said conference. It shall be the duty of every judge thus summoned to attend said conference, and to remain throughout its proceedings unless excused by the Chief Justice, and to advise as to the needs of his circuit and as to any matters in respect of which the administration of justice in the courts of the United States may be improved. The senior district judge of each United States district court, on or before the first day of August, in each year, shall prepare and submit to the senior circuit judge of the judicial circuit in which said district is situated, a report setting forth the condition of business in said district court, including the number and character of cases on the docket, the business in arrears, and cases disposed of, and such other facts pertinent to the business dispatched and pending as said district judge may deem proper, together with recommenda-tions as to the need of additional judicial assistance for the disposal of business for the year ensuing. Said reports shall be laid before the conference herein provided, by said senior circuit judge, or in his absence, by the judge representing the circuit at the conference, together with such recommendations as he may deem proper. The Chief Justice, or, in his absence, the senior associate justice, shall be the presiding officer of the conference. Said conference shall make a comprehensive survey of the condition of business in the courts of the United States and prepare plans for assignment and transfer of judges to or from circuits or districts where the state of the docket or condition of business indicates the need therefor, and shall submit such suggestions to the various courts as may seem in the interest of uniformity and expedition of business. The Attorney General shall, upon request of the Chief Justice, report to said conference on matters relating to the business of the several courts of the United States, with particular reference to causes or proceedings in which the United States may be a party. The Chief Justice and each justice or judge summoned and attending said conference shall be allowed his actual expenses of travel and his necessary expenses for subsistence, not to exceed $10 per day, which payments shall be made by the marshal of the Supreme Court of the United States upon the written certificate of the judge incurring such expenses, approved by the Chief Justice. (Act Sept. 14, 1922.)

CHAPTER TWO.

DISTRICT COURTS—JURISDICTION.

Sec. 24. The district courts shall have original jurisdiction as follows:

First. Of all suits of a civil nature, at common law or in equity, brought by the United States, or by any officer thereof authorized by law to sue, or between citizens of the same State claiming lands

36

under grants from different States; or, where the matter in controversy exceeds, exclusive of interest and costs, the sum or value of three thousand dollars, and (a) arises under the Constitution or laws of the United States, or treaties made, or which shall be made, under their authority, or (b) is between citizens of different States, or (c) is between citizens of a State and foreign States, citizens, or subjects. No district court shall have cognizance of any suit (except upon foreign bills of exchange) to recover upon any promissory note or other chose in action in favor of any assignee, or of any subsequent holder if such instrument be payable to bearer and be not made by any corporation, unless such suit might have been prosecuted in such court to recover upon said note or other chose in action if no assignment had been made: Provided, however, That the foregoing provision as to the sum or value of the matter in controversy shall not be construed to apply to any of the cases mentioned in the succeeding paragraphs of this section.

Second. Of all crimes and offenses cognizable under the authority of the United States.

"Third. Of all civil causes of admiralty and maritime jurisdiction, saving to suitors in all cases the right of a common-law remedy where the common law is competent to give it, and to claimants for compensation for injuries to or death of persons other than the master or members of the crew of a vessel their rights and remedies under the workmen's compensation law of any State, District, Territory, or possession of the United States, which rights and remedies when conferred by such law shall be exclusive; of all seizures on land or waters not within admiralty and maritime jurisdiction; of all prizes brought into the United States; and of all proceedings for the condemnation of property taken as prize: Provided, That the jurisdiction of the district courts shall not extend to causes arising out of injuries to or death of persons other than the master or members of the crew, for which compensation is provided by the workmen's compensation law of any State, District, Territory, or possession of the United States." (Act of June 10, 1922.)

Fourth. Of all suits arising under any law relating to the slave trade.

Fifth. Of all cases arising under any law providing for internal revenue, or for revenue from imports or tonnage, except those cases arising under any law providing revenue from imports, jurisdiction of which has been conferred upon the Court of Customs Appeals.

Sixth. Of all cases arising under the postal laws.

Seventh. Of all suits at law or in equity arising under the patent, the copyright, and the trade-mark laws.

Eighth. Of all suits and proceedings arising under any law regulating commerce.

Ninth. Of all suits and proceedings for the enforcement of penalties and forfeitures incurred under any law of the United States.

Tenth. Of all suits by the assignee of any debenture for drawback of duties, issued under any law for the collection of duties, against the person to whom such debenture was originally granted, or against any indorser thereof, to recover the amount of such debenture.

Eleventh. Of all suits brought by any person to recover damages for any injury to his person or property on account of any act done by him, under any law of the United States, for the protection or collection of any of the revenues thereof, or to enforce the right of citizens of the United States to vote in the several States.

Twelfth. Of all suits authorized by law to be brought by any person for the recovery of damages on account of any injury to his person or property, or of the deprivation of any right or privilege of a citizen of the United States, by any act done in furtherance of any conspiracy mentioned in section nineteen hundred and eighty, Revised Statutes.

Thirteenth. Of all suits authorized by law to be brought against any person who, having knowledge that any of the wrongs mentioned in section nineteen hundred and eighty, Revised Statutes, are about to be done, and, having power to prevent or aid in preventing the same, neglects or refuses so to do, to recover damages for any such wrongful act.

Fourteenth. Of all suits at law or in equity authorized by law to be brought by any person to redress the deprivation, under color of any law, statute, ordinance, regulation, custom, or usage of any State, of any right, privilege, or immunity, secured by the Constitution of the United States, or of any right secured by any law of the United States providing for equal rights of citizens of the United States, or of all persons within the jurisdiction of the United States.

Fifteenth. Of all suits to recover possession of any office, except that of elector of President or Vice-President, Representative in or

Delegate to Congress, or member of a State legislature, authorized by law to be brought, wherein it appears that the sole question touching the title to such office arises out of the denial of the right to vote to any citizen offering to vote, on account of race, color, or previous condition of servitude: Provided, That such jurisdiction shall extend only so far as to determine the rights of the parties to such office by reason of the denial of the right guaranteed by the Constitution of the United States, and secured by any law, to enforce the right of citizens of the United States to vote in all the States.

Sixteenth. Of all cases commenced by the United States, or by direction of any officer thereof, against any national banking association, and cases for winding up the affairs of any such bank; and of all suits brought by any banking association established in the district for which the court is held, under the provisions of title "National Banks," Revised Statutes, to enjoin the Comptroller of the Currency, or any receiver acting under his direction, as provided by said title. And all National banking associations established under the laws of the United States shall, for the purposes of all other actions by or against them, real, personal, or mixed, and all suits in equity, be deemed citizens of the States in which they are respectively located. [See §§ 49, 64.]

Seventeenth. Of all suits brought by any alien for a tort only, in violation of the laws of nations or of a treaty of the United States.

Eighteenth. Of all suits against consuls and vice-consuls.

Nineteenth. Of all matters and proceedings in bankruptcy.

Twentieth. Concurrent with the Court of Claims, of all claims not exceeding ten thousand dollars founded upon the Constitution of the United States or any law of Congress, or upon any regulation of an Executive Department, or upon any contract, express or implied, with the Government of the United States, or for damages, liquidated or unliquidated, in cases not sounding in tort, in respect to which claims the party would be entitled to redress against the United States, either in a court of law, equity, or admiralty, if the United States were suable, and of all set-offs, counterclaims, claims for damages, whether liquidated or unliquidated, or other demands whatsoever on the part of the Government of the United States against any claimant against the Government in said court: Provided, however, That nothing in this paragraph shall be construed as giving to either the district courts or the Court of Claims jurisdiction to hear and determine claims growing out of the late civil war, and commonly known as ''war claims,'' or to hear and determine other claims which had been rejected or reported on adversely prior to the third day of March, eighteen hundred and eighty-seven, by any court, department, or commission authorized to hear and determine the same, or to hear and determine claims for pensions; or as giving to the district courts jurisdiction of cases brought to recover fees, salary, or compensation for official services of officers of the United States or brought for such purpose by persons claiming as such officers or as assignees or legal representatives thereof; but no suit pending on the twenty-seventh day of June, eighteen hundred and ninety-eight, shall abate or be affected by this provision: And provided further, That no suit against the Government of the United States shall be allowed under this paragraph unless the same shall have been brought within six years after the right accrued for which the claim is made: Provided, That the claims of married women, first accrued during marriage, of persons under the age of twenty-one years, first accrued during minority, and of idiots, lunatics, insane persons, and persons beyond the seas at the time the claim accrued, entitled to the claim, shall not be barred if the suit be brought within three years after the disability has ceased; but no other disability than those enumerated shall prevent any claim from being barred, nor shall any of the said disabilities operate cumulatively. All suits brought and tried under the provisions of this paragraph shall be tried by the court without a jury. Concurrent with the Court of Claims, of any suit or proceeding, commenced after the passage of the Revenue Act of 1921, for the recovery of any internal revenue tax alleged to have been erroneously or illegally assessed or collected, or of any penalty claimed to have been collected without authority, or any sum alleged to have been excessive or in any manner wrongfully collected, under the Internal Revenue Laws, even if the claim exceeds ten thousand dollars, if the collector of the internal revenue, by whom such tax, penalty, or sum was collected is dead at the time such suit or proceeding is commenced. (Act Nov. 23, 1921, § 1310c.)

Twenty-first. Of proceedings in equity, by writ of injunction, to restrain violations of the provisions of laws of the United States to prevent the unlawful inclosure of public lands; and it shall be sufficient to give the court jurisdiction if service of original process be had in any civil proceeding on any agent or employee having charge or control of the inclosure.

Twenty-second. Of all suits and proceedings arising under any law regulating the immigration of aliens, or under the contract labor laws.

Twenty-third. Of all suits and proceedings arising under any law to protect trade and commerce against restraints and monopolies.

Twenty-fourth. Of all actions, suits, or proceedings involving the right of any person, in whole or in part of Indian blood or descent, to any allotment of land under any law or treaty. And the judgment or decree of any such court in favor of any claimant to an allotment of land shall have the same effect, when properly certified to the Secretary of the Interior, as if such allotment had been allowed and approved by him; but this provision shall not apply to any lands now or heretofore held by either of the Five Civilized Tribes, the Osage Nation of Indians, nor to any of the lands within the Quapaw Indian Agency: Provided, That the right of appeal shall be allowed to either party as in other cases. (37 Stat. 46.)

Sec. 25. The district courts shall have appellate jurisdiction of the judgments and orders of United States commissioners in cases arising under the Chinese exclusion laws.

Sec. 26. The district court for the district of Wyoming shall have jurisdiction of all felonies committed within the Yellowstone National Park, and appellate jurisdiction of judgments in cases of conviction before the commissioner authorized to be appointed under section five of an act entitled "An Act to protect the birds and animals in Yellowstone National Park, and to punish crimes in said park, and for other purposes," approved May seventh, eighteen hundred and ninety-four.

Sec. 27. The district court of the United States for the district of South Dakota shall have jurisdiction to hear, try, and determine all actions and proceedings in which any person shall be charged with the crime of murder, manslaughter, rape, assault with intent to kill, arson, burglary, larceny, or assault with a dangerous weapon, committed within the limits of any Indian reservation in the State of South Dakota.

CHAPTER THREE.

DISTRICT COURTS—REMOVAL OF CAUSES.

Sec. 28. Any suit of a civil nature, at law or in equity, arising under the Constitution or laws of the United States, or treaties made, or which shall be made, under their authority, of which the district courts of the United States are given original jurisdiction by this title, which may now be pending or which may hereafter be brought, in any State court, may be removed by the defendant or defendants therein to the district court of the United States for the proper district. Any other suit of a civil nature, at law or in equity, of which the district courts of the United States are given jurisdiction by this title, and which are now pending or which may hereafter be brought, in any State court, may be removed into the district court of the United States for the proper district by the defendant or defendants therein, being non-residents of that State. And when in any suit mentioned in this section there shall be a controversy which is wholly between citizens of different States, and which can be fully determined as between them, then either one or more of the defendants actually interested in such controversy may remove said suit into the district court of the United States for the proper district. And where a suit is now pending, or may hereafter be brought, in any State court, in which there is a controversy between a citizen of the State in which the suit is brought and a citizen of another State, any defendant, being such citizen of another State, may remove such suit into the district court of the United States for the proper district, at any time before the trial thereof, when it shall be made to appear to said district court that from prejudice or local influence he will not be able to obtain justice in such State court, or in any other State court to which the said defendant may, under the laws of the State, have the right, on account of such prejudice or local influence, to remove said cause: Provided, That if it further appear that said suit can be fully and justly determined as to the other defendants in the State court, without being affected by such prejudice or local influence, and that no party to the suit will be prejudiced by a separation of the parties, said district court may direct the suit to be remanded, so far as relates to such other defendants, to the State court, to be proceeded with therein. At any time before the trial of any suit which is now pending in any district court, or may hereafter be entered therein, and which has been removed to said court from a State court on the affidavit of any party plaintiff that he had reason to believe and did believe that, from prejudice or local influence, he was unable to obtain justice in said State court, the district court shall, on application of the other party, examine into the truth of said affidavit and the grounds thereof, and, unless it shall appear to the satisfaction of said court that said party will not be able to obtain justice in said State court, it shall cause the same to be remanded thereto. Whenever any cause shall be removed from any State court into any district court of the United States, and the district court shall decide that the cause was improperly removed, and order the same to be remanded to the State court from whence it came, such remand shall be immediately carried into execution, and no appeal or writ of error from the decision of the district court so remanding such cause shall be allowed: Provided, That no case arising under an act entitled "An act relating to the liability of common carriers by railroad to their employees in certain cases," approved April twenty-second, nineteen hundred and eight, or any amendment thereto, and brought in any State court of competent jurisdiction shall be removed to any court of the United States. And provided further, That no suit brought in any State court of competent jurisdiction against a railroad company, or other corporation, or person, engaged in and carrying on the business of a common carrier, to recover damages for delay, loss of, or injury to property received for transportation by such common carrier under section twenty of the act to regulate commerce, approved February fourth, eighteen hundred and eighty-seven, as amended June twenty-ninth, nineteen hundred and six, April thirteenth, nineteen hundred and eight, February twenty-fifth, nineteen hundred and nine, and June eighteenth, nineteen hundred and ten, shall be removed to any court of the United States where the matter in controversy does not exceed, exclusive of interest and costs, the sum or value of $3,000. (38 Stat. 278.)

Sec. 29. Whenever any party entitled to remove any suit mentioned in the last preceding section, except suits removable on the ground of prejudice or local influence, may desire to remove such suit from a State court to the district court of the United States, he may make and file a petition, duly verified, in such suit in such State court at the time, or any time before the defendant is required by the laws of the State or the rule of the State court in which such suit is brought to answer or plead to the declaration or complaint of the plaintiff, for the removal of such suit into the district court to be held in the district where such suit is pending, and shall make and file therewith a bond, with good and sufficient surety, for his or their entering in such district court, within thirty days from the date of filing said petition, a certified copy of the record in such suit, and for paying all costs that may be awarded by the said district court if said district court shall hold that such suit was wrongfully or improperly removed thereto, and also for their appearing and entering special bail in such suit if special bail was originally requisite therein. It shall then be the duty of the State court to accept said petition and bond and proceed no further in such suit. Written notice of said petition and bond for removal shall be given the adverse party or parties prior to filing the same. The said copy being entered within said thirty days as aforesaid in said district court of the United States, the parties so removing the said cause shall, within thirty days thereafter, plead, answer, or demur to the declaration or complaint in said cause, and the cause shall then proceed in the same manner as if it had been originally commenced in the said district court.

Sec. 30. If in any action commenced in a State court the title of land be concerned, and the parties are citizens of the same State and the matter in dispute exceeds the sum or value of three thousand dollars, exclusive of interest and costs, the sum or value being made to appear, one or more of the plaintiffs or defendants, before the trial, may state to the court, and make affidavit if the court require it, that he or they claim, and shall rely upon, a right or title to the land under a grant from a State, and produce the original grant, or an exemplification of it, except where the loss of public records shall put it out of his or their power, and shall move that any one or more of the adverse party inform the court whether he or they claim a right or title to the land under a grant from some other State, the party or parties so required shall give such information, or otherwise not be allowed to plead such grant or give it in evidence upon the trial. If he or they inform the court that he or they do claim under such grant, any one or more of the party moving for such information may then, on petition and bond, as hereinbefore mentioned in this chapter, remove the cause for trial to the district court of the United States next to be holden in such district; and any one of either party removing the cause shall not be allowed to plead or give evidence of any other title than that by him or them stated as aforesaid as the ground of his or their claim.

Sec. 31. When any civil suit or criminal prosecution is commenced in any State court, for any cause whatsoever, against any person who is denied or cannot enforce in the judicial tribunals of the State, or in the part of the State where such suit or prosecution is pending, any right secured to him by any law providing for the equal civil rights of citizens of the United States, or of all persons within the jurisdiction of the United States, or against any officer, civil or military, or other person, for any arrest or imprisonment or other trespasses or wrongs made or committed by virtue of or under color of authority derived from any law providing for equal rights as aforesaid, or for refusing to do any act on the ground that it would be inconsistent with such law, such suit or prosecution may, upon the petition of such defendant, filed in said State court at any time before the trial or final hearing of the cause, stating the facts and verified by oath, be removed for trial into the next district court to be held in the district where it is pending. Upon the filing of such petition all further proceedings in the State courts shall cease, and shall not be resumed except as hereinafter provided. But all bail and other security given in such suit or prosecution shall continue in like force and effect as if the same had proceeded to final judgment and execution in the State court. It shall be the duty of the clerk of the State court to furnish such defendant, petitioning for a removal, copies of said process against him, and of all pleadings, depositions, testimony, and other proceedings in the case. If such copies are filed by said petitioner in the district court on the first day of its session, the cause shall proceed therein in the same manner as if it had been brought there by original process; and if the said clerk refuses or neglects to furnish such copies, the petitioner may thereupon docket the case in the district court, and the said court shall then have jurisdiction therein, and may, upon proof of such refusal or neglect of said clerk, and upon reasonable notice to the plaintiff, require the plaintiff to file a declaration, petition, or complaint in the cause; and, in case of his default, may order a nonsuit and dismiss the case at the costs of the plaintiff, and such dismissal shall be a bar to any further suit touching the matter in controversy. But if, without such refusal or neglect of said clerk to furnish such copies and proof thereof, the petitioner for removal fails to file copies in the district court, as herein provided, a certificate, under the seal of the district court, stating such failure, shall be given, and upon the production thereof in said State court the cause shall proceed therein as if no petition for removal had been filed.

Sec. 32. When all the acts necessary for the removal of any suit or prosecution, as provided in the preceding section, have been performed, and the defendant petitioning for such removal is in actual custody on process issued by said State court, it shall be the duty of the clerk of said district court to issue a writ of habeas corpus cum causa, and of the marshal, by virtue of said writ, to take the body of the defendant into his custody, to be dealt with in said district court according to law and the orders of said court, or, in vacation, of any judge thereof; and the marshal shall file with or deliver to the clerk of said State court a duplicate copy of said writ.

Sec. 33. When any civil suit or criminal prosecution is commenced in any court of a State against any officer appointed under or acting by authority of any revenue law of the United States now or hereafter enacted, or against any person acting under or by authority of any such officer, on account of any act done under color of his office or of any such law, or on account of any right, title, or authority claimed by such officer or other person under any such law; or is commenced against any person holding property or estate by title derived from any such officer, and affects the validity of any such revenue law, or against any officer of the courts of the United States for or on account of any act done under color of his office or in the performance of his duties as such officer, or when any civil suit or criminal prosecution is commenced against any person for or on account of anything done by him while an officer of either House of Congress in the discharge of his official duty, in executing any order of such House, the said suit or prosecution may, at any time before the trial or final hearing thereof, be removed for trial into the district court next to be holden in the district where the same is pending, upon the petition of such defendant to said district court, and in the following manner: Said petition shall set forth the nature of the suit or prosecution and be verified by affidavit, and, together with a certificate signed by an attorney or counselor at law of some court of record of the State where such suit or prosecution is commenced, or of the United States, stating that, as counsel for the petitioner, he has examined the proceedings against him and carefully inquired into all the matters set forth in the petition, and that he believes them to be true, shall be presented to the said district court, if in session, or if it be not, to the clerk thereof at his office, and shall be filed in said office. The cause shall thereupon be entered on the docket of the district court, and shall proceed as a cause originally commenced in that court; but all bail and other security given upon such suit or prosecution shall continue in like force and effect as if the same had proceeded to final judgment and execution in the State court. When the suit is commenced in the State court by summons, subpoena, petition, or any other process except capias, the clerk of the district court shall issue a writ of certiorari to the State court, requiring it to send to the district court the record and proceedings in the cause. When it is commenced by capias or by any other similar form of proceeding by which a personal arrest is ordered, he shall issue a writ of habeas corpus cum causa, a duplicate of which shall be delivered to the clerk of the State court, or left at his office, by the marshal of the district or his deputy, or by some other person duly authorized thereto; and thereupon it shall be the duty of the State court to stay all further proceedings in the cause, and the suit or prosecution, upon delivery of such process, or leaving the same as aforesaid, shall be held to be removed to the district court, and any further proceedings, trial, or judgment therein in the State court shall be void. If the defendant in the suit or prosecution be in actual custody on mesne process therein, it shall be the duty of the marshal, by virtue of the writ of habeas corpus cum causa, to take the body of the defendant into his custody, to be dealt with in the cause according to law and the order of the district court, or, in vacation, of any judge thereof; and if, upon the removal of such suit or prosecution, it is made to appear to the district court that no copy of the record and proceedings therein in the State court can be obtained, the district court may allow and require the plaintiff to proceed de novo and to file a declaration of his cause of action, and the parties may thereupon proceed as in actions originally brought in said district court. On failure of the plaintiff so to proceed, judgment of non prosequitur may be rendered against him, with costs for the defendant. (39 Stat. 532.)

Sec. 34. Whenever a personal action has been or shall be brought in any State court by an alien against any citizen of a State who is, or at the time the alleged action accrued was, a civil officer of the United States, being a non-resident of that State wherein jurisdiction is obtained by the State court, by personal service of process, such action may be removed into the district court of the United States

:in and for the district in which the defendant shall have been served with the process, in the same manner as now provided for the removal of an action brought in a State court by the provisions of the preceding section.

Sec. 35. In any case where a party is entitled to copies of the records and proceedings in any suit or prosecution in a State court, to be used in any court of the United States, if the clerk of said State court, upon demand, and the payment or tender of the legal fees, refuses or neglects to deliver to him certified copies of such records and proceedings, the court of the United States in which such records and proceedings are needed may, on proof by affidavit that the clerk of said State court has refused or neglected to deliver copies thereof, on demand as aforesaid, direct such record to be supplied by affidavit or otherwise, as the circumstances of the case may require and allow; and thereupon such proceedings, trial, and judgment may be had in the said courts of the United States, and all such processes awarded, as if certified copies of such records and proceedings had been regularly before the said court.

Sec. 36. When any suit shall be removed from a State court to a district court of the United States, any attachment or sequestration of the goods or estate of the defendant had in such suit in the State court shall hold the goods or estate so attached or sequestered to answer the final judgment or decree in the same manner as by law they would have been held to answer final judgment or decree had it been rendered by the court in which said suit was commenced. All bonds, undertakings, or security given by either party in such suit prior to its removal shall remain valid and effectual notwithstanding said removal; and all injunctions, orders, and other proceedings had in such suit prior to its removal shall remain in full force and effect until dissolved or modified by the court to which such suit shall be removed.

Sec. 37. If in any suit commenced in a district court, or removed from a State court to a district court of the United States, it shall appear to the satisfaction of the said district court, at any time after such suit has been brought or removed thereto, that such suit does not really and substantially involve a dispute or controversy properly within the jurisdiction of said district court, or that the parties to said suit have been improperly or collusively made or joined, either as plaintiffs or defendants, for the purpose of creating a case cognizable or removable under this chapter, the said district court shall proceed no further therein, but shall dismiss the suit or remand it to the court from which it was removed, as justice may require, and shall make such order as to costs as shall be just.

Sec. 38. The district court of the United States shall, in all suits removed under the provisions -of this chapter, proceed therein as if the suit had been originally commenced in said district court, and the same proceedings had been taken in such suit in said district court as shall have been had therein in said State court prior to its removal.

Sec. 39. In all causes removable under this chapter, if the clerk of the State court in which any such cause shall be pending shall refuse to any one or more of the parties or persons applying to remove the same, a copy of the record therein, after tender of legal fees for such copy, said clerk so offending shall, on conviction thereof in the district court of the United States to which said action or proceeding was removed, be fined not more than one thousand dollars, or imprisoned not more than one year, or both. The district court to which any cause shall be removable under this chapter shall have power to issue a writ of certiorari to said State court commanding said State court to make return of the record in any such cause removed as aforesaid, or in which any one or more of the plaintiffs or defendants have complied with the provisions of this chapter for the removal of the same, and enforce said writ according to law. If it shall be impossible for the parties or persons removing any cause under this chapter, or complying with the provisions for the removal thereof, to obtain such copy, for the reason that the clerk of said State court refuses to furnish a copy, on payment of legal fees, or for any other reason, the district court shall make an order requiring the prosecutor in any such action or proceeding to enforce forfeiture or recover penalty, as aforesaid, to file a copy of the paper or proceeding by which the same was commenced, within such time as the court may determine; and in default thereof the court shall dismiss the said action or proceeding; but if said order shall be complied with, then said district court shall require the other party to plead, and said action or proceeding shall proceed to final judgment. The said district court may make an order requiring the parties thereto to plead de novo; and the bond given, conditioned as aforesaid, shall be discharged so far as it requires copy of the record to be filed as aforesaid.

CHAPTER FOUR.

DISTRICT COURT—MISCELLANEOUS PROVISIONS.

Sec. 40. The trial of offenses punishable with death shall be had in the county where the offense was committed, where that can be done without great inconvenience.

Sec. 41. The trial of all offenses committed upon the high seas, or elsewhere out of the jurisdiction of any particular State or district, shall be in the district where the offender is found, or into which he is first brought.

Sec. 42. When any offense against the United States is begun in one judicial district and completed in another, it shall be deemed to have been committed in either, and may be dealt with, inquired of, tried, determined, and punished in either district, in the same manner as if it had been actually and wholly committed therein.

Sec. 43. All pecuniary penalties and forfeitures may be sued for and recovered either in the district where they accrue or in the district where the offender is found.

Sec. 44. Taxes accruing under any law providing internal revenue may be sued for and recovered either in the district where the liability for such tax occurs or in the district where the delinquent resides.

Sec. 45. Proceedings on seizures made on the high seas, for forfeiture under any law of the United States, may be prosecuted in any district into which the property so seized is brought and proceedings instituted. Proceedings on such seizures made within any district shall be prosecuted in the district where the seizure is made, except in cases where it is otherwise provided.

Sec. 46. Proceedings for the condemnation of any property captured, whether on the high seas or elsewhere out of the limits of any judicial district, or within any district, on account of its being purchased or acquired, sold or given, with intent to use or employ the same, or to suffer it to be used or employed, in aiding, abetting, or promoting any insurrection against the Government of the United States, or knowingly so used or employed by the owner thereof, or with his consent, may be prosecuted in any district where the same may be seized, or into which it may be taken and proceedings first instituted.

Sec. 47. Proceedings on seizures for forfeiture of any vessel or cargo entering any port of entry which has been closed by the President in pursuance of law, or of goods and chattels coming from a State or section declared by proclamation of the President to be in insurrection into other parts of the United States, or of any vessel or vehicle conveying such property, or conveying persons to or from such State or section, or of any vessel belonging, in whole or in part, to any inhabitant of such State or section, may be prosecuted in any district into which the property so seized may be taken and proceedings instituted; and the district court thereof shall have as full jurisdiction over such proceedings as if the seizure was made in that district.

Sec. 48. In suits brought for the infringement of letters patent the district courts of the United States shall have jurisdiction, in law or in equity, in the district of which the defendant is an inhabitant, or in any district in which the defendant, whether a person, partnership, or corporation, shall have committed acts of infringement and have a regular and established place of business. If such suit is brought in a district of which the defendant is not an inhabitant, but in which such defendant has a regular and established place of business, service of process, summons, or subpoena upon the defendant may be made by service upon the agent or agents engaged in conducting such business in the district in which suit is brought.

Sec. 49. All proceedings by any national banking association to enjoin the Comptroller of the Currency, under the provisions of any law relating to national banking associations, shall be had in the district where such association is located.

Sec. 50. When there are several defendants in any suit at law or in equity, and one or more of them are neither inhabitants of nor found within the district in which the suit is brought, and do not voluntarily appear, the court may entertain jurisdiction, and proceed to the trial and adjudication of the suit between the parties who are properly before it; but the judgment or decree rendered therein shall not conclude or prejudice other parties not regularly served with process nor voluntarily appearing to answer; and non-joinder of parties who are not inhabitants of nor found within the district, as aforesaid, shall not constitute matter of abatement or objection to the suit.

Sec. 51. Except as provided in the five succeeding sections, no person shall be arrested in one district for trial in another, in any civil action before a district court; and, except as provided in the six succeeding sections, no civil suit shall be brought in any district court against any person by any original process or proceeding in any other district than that whereof he is an inhabitant; but where the jurisdiction is founded only on the fact that the action is between citizens of different States, suit shall be brought only in the district of the residence of either the plaintiff or the defendant: Provided, however, That any civil suit, action, or proceeding brought by or on behalf of the United States, or by or on behalf of any officer of the United States authorized by law to sue, may be brought in any district whereof the defendant is an inhabitant, or where there be more than one defendant in any district whereof any one of the defendants, being a necessary party, or being jointly, or jointly and

37

severally, liable, is an inhabitant, or in any district wherein the cause of action or any part thereof arose; and in any such suit, action, or proceeding process, summons or subpoena against any defendant issued from the district court of the district wherein such suit is brought shall run in any other district, and service thereof upon any defendant may be made in any district within the United States or the territorial or insular possessions thereof in which any such defendant may be found with the same force and effect as if the same had been served within the district in which said suit, action or proceeding is brought. The word ''district'' and the words ''district court'' as used herein, shall be construed to include the District of Columbia and the Supreme Court of the District of Columbia: Provided further, That this Act shall be effective for a period of three years only, after which said section 51, chapter 4, as it exists in the present law, shall be and remain in full force and effect. (Act Sept. 19, 1922.)

Sec. 52. When a State contains more than one district, every suit not of a local nature, in the district court thereof, against a single defendant, inhabitant of such State, must be brought in the district where he resides; but if there are two or more defendants, residing in different districts of the State, it may be brought in either district, and a duplicate writ may be issued against the defendants, directed to the marshal of any other district in which any defendant resides. The clerk issuing the duplicate writ shall endorse thereon that it is a true copy of a writ sued out of the court of the proper district; and such original and duplicate writs, when executed and returned into the office from which they issue, shall constitute and be proceeded on as one suit; and upon any judgment or decree rendered therein, execution may be issued, directed to the marshal of any district in the same State.

Sec. 53. When a district contains more than one division, every suit not of a local nature against a single defendant must be brought in the division where he resides; but if there are two or more defendants residing in different divisions of the district it may be brought in either division. All mesne and final process subject to the provisions of this section may be served and executed in any or all of the divisions of the district, or if the State contains more than one district, then in any of such districts, as provided in the preceding section. All prosecutions for crimes or offenses shall be had within the division of such districts where the same were committed, unless the court, or the judge thereof, upon the application of the defendant, shall order the cause to be transferred for prosecution to another division of the district. When a transfer is ordered by the court or judge, all the papers in the case, or certified copies thereof, shall be transmitted by the clerk, under the seal of the court, to the division to which the cause is so ordered transferred; and thereupon the cause shall be proceeded with in said division in the same manner as if the offense had been committed therein. In all cases of the removal of suits from the courts of a State to the district court of the United States such removal shall be to the United States district court in the division in which the county is situated from which the removal is made; and the time within which the removal shall be perfected, in so far as it refers to or is regulated by the terms of United States courts, shall be deemed to refer to the terms of the United States district court in such division.

Sec. 54. In suits of a local nature, where the defendant resides in a different district, in the same State, from that in which the suit is brought, the plaintiff may have original and final process against him, directed to the marshal of the district in which he resides.

Sec. 55. Any suit of a local nature, at law or in equity, where the land or other subject-matter of a fixed character lies partly in one district and partly in another, within the same State, may be brought in the district court of either district; and the court in which it is brought shall have jurisdiction to hear and decide it, and to cause mesne or final process to be issued and executed, as fully as if the said subject-matter were wholly within the district for which such court is constituted.

Sec. 56. Where in any suit in which a receiver shall be appointed the land or other property of a fixed character, the subject of the suit, lies within different States in the same judicial circuit, the receiver so appointed shall, upon giving bond as required by the court, immediately be vested with full jurisdiction and control over all the property, the subject of the suit, lying or being within such circuit; subject, however, to the disapproval of such order, within thirty days thereafter, by the circuit court of appeals for such circuit, or by a circuit judge thereof, after reasonable notice to adverse parties and an opportunity to be heard upon the motion for such disapproval; and subject, also, to the filing and entering in the district court for each district of the circuit in which any portion of the property may lie or be, within ten days thereafter, of a duly certified copy of the bill and of the order of appointment. The disapproval of such appointment within such thirty days, or the failure to file such certified copy of the bill and order of appointment within ten days, as herein required, shall divest such receiver of jurisdiction over all such property except that portion thereof lying or being within the State in which the suit is brought. In any case coming within the provisions of this section, in which a receiver shall be appointed, process may issue and be executed within any district of the circuit in the same manner and to the same extent as if the property were wholly within the same district; but orders affecting such property shall be entered of record in each district in which the property affected may lie or be.

Sec. 57. When in any suit commenced in any district court of the United States to enforce any legal or equitable lien upon or claim to, or to remove any incumbrance or lien or cloud upon the title to real or personal property within the district where such suit is brought, one or more of the defendants therein shall not be an inhabitant of or found within the said district, or shall not voluntarily appear thereto, it shall be lawful for the court to make an order directing such absent defendant or defendants to appear, plead, answer, or demur by a day certain to be designated, which order shall be served on such absent defendant or defendants, if practicable, wherever found, and also upon the person or persons in possession or charge of said property, if any there be; or where such personal service upon such absent defendant or defendants is not practicable, such order shall be published in such manner as the court may direct, not less than once a week for six consecutive weeks. In case such absent defendant shall not appear, plead, answer, or demur within the time so limited, or within some further time, to be allowed by the court, in its discretion, and upon proof of the service or publication of said order and of the performance of the directions contained in the same, it shall be lawful for the court to entertain jurisdiction, and proceed to the hearing and adjudication of such suit in the same manner as if such absent defendant had been served with process within the said district; but said adjudication shall, as regards said absent defendant or defendants without appearance, affect only the property which shall have been the subject of the suit and under the jurisdiction of the court therein, within such district; and when a part of the said real or personal property against which such proceedings shall be taken shall be within another district, but within the same State, such suit may be brought in either district in said State: Provided, however, That any defendant or defendants not actually personally notified as above provided may, at any time within one year after final judgment in any suit mentioned in this section, enter his appearance in said suit in said district court, and thereupon the said court shall make an order setting aside the judgment therein and permitting said defendant or defendants to plead therein on payment by him or them of such costs as the court shall deem just; and thereupon said suit shall be proceeded with to final judgment according to law.

Sec. 58. Any civil cause, at law or in equity, may, on written stipulation of the parties or of their attorneys of record signed and filed with the papers in the case, in vacation or in term, and on the written order of the judge signed and filed in the case in vacation or on the order of the court duly entered of record in term, be transferred to the court of any other division of the same district, without regard to the residence of the defendants, for trial. When a cause shall be ordered to be transferred to a court in any other division, it shall be the duty of the clerk of the court from which the transfer is made to carefully transmit to the clerk of the court to which the transfer is made the entire file of papers in the cause and all documents and deposits in his court pertaining thereto, together with a certified transcript of the records of all orders, interlocutory decrees, or other entries in the cause; and he shall certify, under the seal of the court, that the papers sent are all which are on file in said court belonging to the cause; for the performance of which duties said clerk so transmitting and certifying shall receive the same fees as are now allowed by law for similar services, to be taxed in the bill of costs, and regularly collected with the other costs in the cause; and such transcript, when so certified and received, shall [t]henceforth constitute a part of the record of the cause in the court to which the transfer shall be made. The clerk receiving such transcript and original papers shall file the same and the case shall then proceed to final disposition as other cases of a like nature.

Sec. 59. Whenever any new district or division has been or shall be established, or any county or territory has been or shall be transferred from one district or division to another district or division, prosecutions for crimes and offenses committed within such district, division, county, or territory prior to such transfer, shall be commenced and proceeded with the same as if such new district or division had not been created, or such county or territory had not been transferred, unless the court, upon the application of the defendant, shall order the cause to be removed to the new district or division for trial. Civil actions pending at the time of the creation of any such district or division, or the transfer of any such county or territory, and arising within the district or division so created or the county or territory so transferred, shall be tried in the district or division as it existed at the time of the institution of the action, or in the district or division so created, or to which the county or territory is or shall be so transferred, as may be agreed upon by the parties, or as the court shall direct. The transfer of such prosecutions and actions shall be made in the manner provided in the section last preceding.

Sec. 60. The creation of a new district or division or the transfer of any county or territory from one district or division to another district or division, shall not affect or divest any lien theretofore acquired in the circuit or district court by virtue of a decree, judgment, execution, attachment, seizure, or otherwise, upon property situated or being within the district or division so created, or the county or territory so transferred. To enforce any such lien, the clerk of the court in which the same is acquired, upon the request and at the cost of the party desiring the same, shall make a true and certified copy of the record thereof, which, when so made and certified, and filed in the proper court of the district or division in which such property is situated or shall be, after such transfer, shall constitute the record of such lien in such court, and shall be evidence in all courts and places equally with the original thereof; and thereafter like proceedings shall be had thereon, and with the same effect, as though the cause or proceeding had been originally instituted in such court. The provisions of this section shall apply not only in all cases where a district or division is created, or a county or any territory is transferred by this or any future act, but also in all cases where a district or division has been created, or a county or any territory has been transferred by any law heretofore enacted.

Sec. 61. Any district judge may appoint commissioners, before whom appraisers of vessels or goods and merchandise seized for breaches of any law of the United States, may be sworn; and such oaths, so taken, shall be as effectual as if taken before the judge in open court.

Sec. 62. When any Territory is admitted as a State, and a district court is established therein, all the records of the proceedings in the several cases pending in the highest court of said Territory at the time of such admission, and all records of the proceedings in the several cases in which judgments or decrees had been rendered in said Territorial court before that time. and from which writs of error could have been sued out or appeals could have been taken, or from which writs of error had been sued out or appeals had been taken and prosecuted to the Supreme Court or to the circuit court of appeals, shall be transferred to and deposited in the district court for the said State.

Sec. 63. It shall be the duty of the district judge, in the case provided in the preceding section, to demand of the clerk, or other person having possession or custody of the records therein mentioned, the delivery thereof, to be deposited in said district court; and in case of the refusal of such clerk or person to comply with such demand, the said district judge shall compel the delivery of such records by attachment or otherwise, according to law.

Sec. 64. When any Territory is admitted as a State, and a district court is established therein, the said district court shall take cognizance of all cases which were pending and undetermined in the trial courts of such Territory, from the judgments or decrees to be rendered in which writs of error could have been sued out or appeals taken to the Supreme Court or to the circuit court of appeals, and shall proceed to hear and determine the same.

Sec. 65. Whenever in any cause pending in any court of the United States there shall be a receiver or manager in possession of any property, such receiver or manager shall manage and operate such property according to the requirements of the valid laws of the State in which such property shall be situated, in the same manner that the owner or possessor thereof would be bound to do if in possession thereof. Any receiver or manager who shall willfully violate any provision of this section shall be fined not more than three thousand dollars, or imprisoned not more than one year, or both.

Sec. 66. Every receiver or manager of any property appointed by any court of the United States may be sued in respect of any act or transaction of his in carrying on the business connected with such property, without the previous leave of the court in which such receiver or manager was appointed; but such suit shall be subject to the general equity jurisdiction of the court in which such manager or receiver was appointed so far as the same may be necessary to the ends of justice.

Sec. 67. No person shall be appointed to or employed in any office or duty in any court who is related by affinity or consanguinity within the degree of first cousin to the judge of such court.

Sec. 68. No clerk of a district court of the United States or his deputy shall be appointed a receiver or master in any case, except where the judge of said court shall determine that special reasons exist therefor, to be assigned in the order of appointment. But no clerk or deputy clerk or assistant in the office of the clerk of the United States district court shall receive any compensation or emolument through any office or position to which he may be appointed by the court other than that received by such clerk, deputy clerk or assistant, whether from the United States or from private litigants. (Act March 4, 1921, 41 Stat. 1413.)

Note.

[Chapter V, containing sections 69 to 115, both inclusive, is omitted as it deals only with the boundaries of districts and of divisions within them, with the places and times of holding court, and such like matters. These sections, or some of them, are amended at almost every session of Congress and the reproduction of them here would be of no substantial service.]

CHAPTER SIX.

CIRCUIT COURTS OF APPEALS.

Sec. 116. There shall be nine judicial circuits of the United States, constituted as follows:

First. The first circuit shall include the districts of Rhode Island, Massachusetts, New Hampshire, Maine, and Porto Rico. (38 Stat. 803.)

Second. The second circuit shall include the districts of Vermont, Connecticut, and New York.

Third. The third circuit shall include the districts of Pennsylvania, New Jersey, and Delaware, and the Virgin Islands. (39 Stat. 1133.)

Fourth. The fourth circuit shall include the districts of Maryland, Virginia, West Virginia, North Carolina, and South Carolina.

Fifth. The fifth circuit shall include the districts of Georgia, Florida, Alabama, Mississippi, Louisiana, and Texas, and the Canal Zone. (37 Stat. 566.)

Sixth. The sixth circuit shall include the districts of Ohio, Michigan, Kentucky, and Tennessee.

Seventh. The seventh circuit shall include the districts of Indiana, Illinois, and Wisconsin.

Eighth. The eighth circuit shall include the districts of Nebraska, Minnesota, Iowa, Missouri, Kansas, Arkansas, Colorado, Wyoming, North Dakota, South Dakota, Utah, Oklahoma, and New Mexico. (36 Stat. 565.)

Ninth. The ninth circuit shall include the districts of California, Oregon, Nevada, Washington, Idaho, Montana, Hawaii, and Arizona. (36 Stat. 576.)

Sec. 117. There shall be in each circuit a circuit court of appeals, which shall consist of three judges, of whom two shall constitute a quorum, and which shall be a court of record, with appellate jurisdiction, as hereinafter limited and established.

Sec. 118. There shall be in the second, seventh and eighth circuits, respectively, four circuit judges, and in each of the other circuits, three circuit judges, to be appointed by the President, by and with the advice and consent of the Senate. All circuit judges shall receive a salary of $8,500 a year each, payable monthly. Each circuit judge shall reside within his circuit, and when appointed shall be a resident of the circuit for which he is appointed. The circuit judges in each circuit shall be judges of the circuit court of appeals in that circuit, and it shall be the duty of each circuit judge in each circuit to sit as one of the judges of the circuit court of appeals in that circuit from time to time according to law. Provided, that nothing in this section shall be construed to prevent any circuit judge holding district court or otherwise, as provided by other sections of the Judicial Code. (Act Sept. 14, 1922.)

Sec. 119. The Chief Justice and associate justices of the Supreme Court shall be allotted among the circuits by an order of the court, and a new allotment shall be made whenever it becomes necessary or convenient by reason of the alteration of any circuit, or of the new appointment of a Chief Justice or associate justice, or otherwise. If a new allotment becomes necessary at any other time than during a term, it shall be made by the Chief Justice, and shall be binding until the next term and until a new allotment by the court. Whenever, by reason of death or resignation, no justice is allotted to a circuit, the Chief Justice may, until a justice is regularly allotted thereto, temporarily assign a justice of another circuit to such circuit.

Sec. 120. The Chief Justice and the associate justice of the Supreme Court assigned to each circuit, and the several district judges within each circuit, shall be competent to sit as judges of the circuit court of appeals within their respective circuits. In case the Chief Justice or an associate justice of the Supreme Court shall attend at any session of the circuit court of appeals, he shall preside. In the absence of such Chief Justice, or associate justice, the circuit judges in attendance upon the court shall preside in the order of the seniority of their respective commissions. In case the full court at any time shall not be made up by the attendance of the Chief Justice or the associate justice, and the circuit judges, one or more district judges within the circuit shall sit in the court according to such order or provision among the district judges as either by general or particular assignment shall be designated by the court: Provided, That no judge before whom a cause or question may have been tried or heard in a district court, or existing circuit court, shall sit on the trial or hearing of such cause or question in the circuit court of appeals.

Sec. 121. The words ''circuit justice'' and ''justice of a circuit,'' when used in this title, shall be understood to designate the justice of the Supreme Court who is allotted to any circuit; but the word ''judge,'' when applied generally to any circuit, shall be understood to include such justice.

Sec. 122. Each of said circuit courts of appeals shall prescribe the form and style of its seal, and the form of writs and other process and procedure as may be conformable to the exercise of its jurisdiction; and shall have power to establish all rules and regulations for the conduct of the business of the court within its jurisdiction as conferred by law.

Sec. 123. The United States marshals in and for the several districts of said courts shall be the marshals of said circuit courts of appeals, and shall exercise the same powers and perform the same duties, under the regulations of the court, as are exercised and performed by the marshal of the Supreme Court of the United States, so far as the same may be applicable.

Sec. 124. Each court shall appoint a clerk, who shall exercise the same powers and perform the same duties in regard to all matters within its jurisdiction, as are exercised and performed by the clerk of the Supreme Court, so far as the same may be applicable.

Sec. 125. The clerk of the circuit court of appeals for each circuit may, with the approval of the court, appoint such number of deputy clerks as the court may deem necessary. Such deputies may be removed at the pleasure of the clerk appointing them, with the approval of the court. In case of the death of the clerk his deputy or deputies shall, unless removed by the court, continue in office and perform the duties of the clerk in his name until a clerk is appointed and has qualified; and for the defaults or misfeasances in office of any such deputy, whether in the lifetime of the clerk or after his death, the clerk and his estate and the sureties on his official bond shall be liable, and his executor or administrator shall have such remedy for such defaults or misfeasances committed after his death as the clerk would be entitled to if the same had occurred in his lifetime.

Sec. 126. A term shall be held annually by the circuit courts of appeals in the several judicial circuits at the following places, and at such times as may be fixed by said courts, respectively: In the first circuit, in Boston; in the second circuit, in New York; in the third circuit, in Philadelphia; in the fourth circuit, in Richmond and in Asheville, North Carolina; in the fifth circuit, in New Orleans, Atlanta, Fort Worth, and Montgomery; in the sixth circuit, in Cincinnati; in the seventh circuit, in Chicago; in the eighth circuit, in Saint Louis, Denver or Cheyenne, and Saint Paul; in the ninth circuit in San Francisco, and each year in two other places in said circuit to be designated by the judges of said court; and in each of the above circuits, terms may be held at such other times and in such other places as said courts, respectively, may from time to time designate: Provided, That terms shall be held in Atlanta on the first Monday in October, in Fort Worth on the first Monday in November, in Montgomery on the third Monday in October, in Denver or in Cheyenne on the first Monday in September, and in Saint Paul on the first Monday in May. All appeals, writs of error, and other appellate proceedings which may be taken or prosecuted from the district courts of the United States in the State of Georgia, in the State of Texas, and in the State of Alabama, to the circuit court of appeals for the fifth judicial circuit shall be heard and disposed of, respectively, by said court at the terms held in Atlanta, in Fort Worth, and in Montgomery, except that appeals or writs of error in cases of injunctions and all other cases which under the statutes and rules, or in the opinion of the court, are entitled to be brought to a speedy hearing may be heard and disposed of wherever said court may be sitting. All appeals, writs of error, and other appellate proceedings which may hereafter be taken or prosecuted from the district court of the United States at Beaumont, Texas, to the circuit court of appeals for the fifth circuit, shall be heard and disposed of by the said circuit court of appeals at the terms of court held in New Orleans: Provided, That nothing herein shall prevent the court from hearing appeals or writs of error wherever the said courts shall sit, in cases of injunctions and in all other cases which, under the statutes and the rules, or in the opinion of the court, are entitled to be brought to a speedy hearing. All appeals, writs of error, and other appellate proceedings which may be taken or prosecuted from the district courts of the United States in the States of Colorado, Utah, Wyoming, and New Mexico to the circuit court of appeals for the eighth judicial circuit, shall be heard and disposed of by said court at the terms held either in Denver or in Cheyenne, except that any case arising in any of said States or Territory may, by consent of all the parties, be heard and disposed of at a term of said court other than the one held in Denver or Cheyenne. (39 Stat. 385.)

Sec. 127. The marshals for the several districts in which said circuit courts of appeals may be held shall, under the direction of the Attorney-General, and with his approval, provide such rooms in the public buildings of the United States as may be necessary for the business of said courts, and pay all incidental expenses of said court, including criers, bailiffs, and messengers: Provided, That in case proper rooms can not be provided in such buildings, then the marshals, with the approval of the Attorney-General, may, from time to time, lease such rooms as may be necessary for such courts.

Sec. 128. The circuit courts of appeals shall exercise appellate jurisdiction to review by appeal or writ of error final decisions in the district courts, including the United States district court for Hawaii and the United States district court for Porto Rico, in all cases other than those in which appeals and writs of error may be taken direct to the Supreme Court, as provided in section two hundred and thirty-eight, unless otherwise provided by law; and, except as provided in sections two hundred and thirty-nine and two hundred and forty, the judgments and decrees of the circuit courts of appeals shall be final in all cases in which the jurisdiction is dependent entirely upon the opposite parties to the suit or controversy being aliens and citizens of the United States, or citizens of different States; also in all cases arising under the patent laws, under the trade mark laws, under the copyright laws, under the revenue laws, and under the criminal laws, and in admiralty cases. (38 Stat. 804.)

Note.

[This section has been amended or added to by section 3 of the Act of September 6, 1916 (39 Stat. 727), by the declaration: That judgments and decrees of the circuit courts of appeals in all proceedings and causes arising under ''An Act to establish a uniform system of bankruptcy throughout the United States,'' approved July first, eighteen hundred and ninety-eight, and in all controversies arising in such proceedings and causes; also, in all causes arising under ''An Act relating to the liability of common carriers by railroad, to their employees in certain cases,'' approved April twenty-second, nineteen hundred and eight; also in all causes arising under an ''Act to promote the safety of employees and travelers upon railroads by limiting the hours of service of employees thereon,'' approved March fourth, nineteen hundred and seven; also in all causes arising under an ''Act to promote the safety of employees and travelers upon railroads by compelling common carriers engaged in interstate commerce to equip their cars with automatic couplers and continuous brakes and their locomotives with driving-wheel brakes, and for other purposes,'' approved March second, eighteen hundred and ninety-three; and, also, in all causes arising under any amendment or supplement to any one of the aforementioned acts which has been heretofore or may hereafter be enacted, shall be final, save only that it shall be competent for the Supreme Court to require by certiorari, upon the petition of any party thereto, that the proceeding, case, or controversy be certified to it for review and determination, with the same power and authority and with like effect as if taken to that court by appeal or writ of error.]

Sec. 129. Where upon a hearing in equity in a district court, or by a judge thereof in vacation, an injunction shall be granted, continued, refused, or dissolved by an interlocutory order or decree, or an application to dissolve an injunction shall be refused, or an interlocutory order or decree shall be made appointing a receiver, an appeal may be taken from such interlocutory order or decree granting, continuing, refusing, dissolving, or refusing to dissolve, an injunction, or appointing a receiver, to the circuit court of appeals, notwithstanding an appeal in such case might, upon final decree under the statutes regulating the same, be taken directly to the Supreme Court: Provided, That the appeal must be taken within thirty days from the entry of such order or decree, and it shall take precedence in the appellate court; and the proceedings in other respects in the court below shall not be stayed unless otherwise ordered by that court, or the appellate court, or a judge thereof, during the pendency of such appeal: Provided, however, That the court below may, in its discretion, require as a condition of the appeal an additional bond.

Sec. 130. The circuit courts of appeals shall have the appellate and supervisory jurisdiction conferred upon them by the act entitled ''An Act to establish a uniform system of bankruptcy throughout the United States,'' approved July 1, 1898, and all laws amendatory thereof, and shall exercise the same in the manner therein prescribed.

Sec. 131. The circuit court of appeals for the ninth circuit is empowered to hear and determine writs of error and appeals from the United States court for China, as provided in the Act entitled ''An Act creating a United States court for China and prescribing the jurisdiction thereof,'' approved June thirtieth, nineteen hundred and six.

Sec. 132. Any judge of a circuit court of appeals, in respect of cases brought or to be brought before that court, shall have the same powers and duties as to allowances of appeals and writs of error, and the conditions of such allowances, as by law belong to the justices or judges in respect of other courts of the United States respectively.

Note.

[Section 133 is obsolete as the result of the admission of New Mexico and Arizona as States.]

Sec. 134. In all cases other than those in which a writ of error or appeal will lie direct to the Supreme Court of the United States as provided in section two hundred and forty-seven, in which the amount involved or the value of the subject-matter in controversy shall exceed five hundred dollars, and in all criminal cases, writs of error and appeals shall lie from the district court for Alaska or from any division thereof, to the circuit court of appeals for the ninth circuit, and the judgments, orders, and decrees of said court shall be final in all such cases. But whenever such circuit court of appeals may desire the instruction of the Supreme Court of the United States upon any question or proposition of law which shall have arisen in any such case, the court may certify such question or proposition to the Supreme Court, and thereupon the Supreme Court shall give its instruction upon the question or proposition certified to it, and its instructions shall be binding upon the circuit court of appeals.

Sec. 135. All appeals, and writs of error, and other cases, coming from the district court for the district of Alaska to the circuit court of appeals for the ninth circuit, shall be entered upon the docket and heard at San Francisco, California, or at Portland, Oregon, or at Seattle, Washington, as the trial court before whom the case was tried below shall fix and determine: Provided, That at any time before the hearing of any appeal, writ of error, or other case, the parties thereto, through their respective attorneys, may stipulate at which of the above-named places the same shall be heard, in which case the case shall be remitted to and entered upon the docket at the place so stipulated and shall be heard there.

CHAPTER SEVEN.

THE COURT OF CLAIMS.

Sec. 136. The Court of Claims, established by the act of February twenty-fourth, eighteen hundred and fifty-five, shall be continued. It shall consist of a chief justice and four judges, who shall be

38

appointed by the President, by and with.the advice and consent of the Senate, and hold their offices during good behavior. Each of them shall take an oath to support the Constitution of the United States, and to discharge faithfully the duties of his office. The chief justice shall be entitled to receive an annual salary of eight thousand dollars, and each of the other judges an annual salary of seven thousand five hundred dollars, payable monthly, from the Treasury. (40 Stat. 1157.)

Sec. 137. The Court of Claims shall have a seal, with such device as it may order.

Sec. 138. The Court of Claims shall hold one annual session at the city of Washington, beginning on the first Monday in December and continuing as long as may be necessary for the prompt disposition of the business of the court. Any three of the judges of said court shall constitute a quorum, and may hold a court for the transaction of business: Provided, That the concurrence of three judges shall be necessary to the decision of any case.

Sec. 139. The said court shall appoint a chief clerk, an assistant clerk, if deemed necessary, a bailiff, and a chief messenger. The clerks shall take an oath for the faithful discharge of their duties, and shall be under the direction of the court in the performance thereof; and for misconduct or incapacity they may be removed by it from office; but the court shall report such removals, with the cause thereof, to Congress, if in session, or if not, at the next session. The bailiff shall hold his office for a term of four years, unless sooner removed by the court for cause.

Sec. 140. The salary of the chief clerk shall be three thousand five hundred dollars a year; of the assistant clerk two thousand five hundred dollars a year; of the bailiff one thousand five hundred dollars a year, and of the chief messenger one thousand dollars a year, payable monthly from the Treasury. .

Sec. 141. The chief clerk shall give bond to the United States in such amount, in such form, and with such security as shall be approved by the Secretary of the Treasury.

Sec. 142. The said clerk shall have authority when he has given bond as provided in the preceding section, to disburse, under the direction of the court, the contingent fund which may from time to time be appropriated for its use; and his accounts shall be settled by the proper accounting officers of the Treasury in the same way as the accounts of other disbursing agents of the Government are settled.

Sec. 143. On the first day of every regular session of Congress the clerk of the Court of Claims shall transmit to Congress a full and complete statement of all the judgments rendered by the court during the previous year, stating the amounts thereof and the parties in whose favor they were rendered, together with a brief synopsis of the nature of the claims upon which they were rendered. At the end of every term of the court he shall transmit a copy of its decisions to the heads of departments; to the Solicitor, the Comptroller, and the Auditors of the Treasury; to the Commissioner of the General Land Office and of Indian Affairs; to the chiefs of bureaus, and to other officers charged with the adjustment of claims against the United States.

Sec. 144. Whoever, being elected or appointed a Senator, Member of, or Delegate to Congress, or a Resident Commissioner, shall, after his election or appointment, and either before or after he has qualified, and during his continuance in office, practice in the Court of Claims, shall be fined not more than ten thousand dollars and imprisoned not more than two years; and shall, moreover, thereafter be incapable of holding any office of honor, trust, or profit under the Government of the United States.

Sec. 145. The Court of Claims shall have jurisdiction to hear and determine the following matters:

First. All claims (except for pensions) founded upon the Constitution of the United States or any law of Congress, upon any regulation of an Executive Department, upon any contract, express or implied, with the Government of the United States, or for damages, liquidated or unliquidated, in cases not sounding in tort, in respect of which claims the party would be entitled to redress against the United States either in a court of law, equity, or admiralty if the United States were suable: Provided, however, That nothing in this section shall be construed as giving to the said court jurisdiction to hear and determine claims growing out of the late civil war, and commonly known as "war claims," or to hear and determine other claims which, prior to March third, eighteen hundred and eighty-seven, had been rejected or reported on adversely by any court, department, or commission authorized to hear and determine the same.

Second. All set-offs, counterclaims, claims for damages, whether liquidated or unliquidated, or other demands whatsoever on the part of the Government of the United States against any claimant against the Government in said court: Provided, That no suit against the Government of the United States, brought by any officer of the United States to recover fees for services alleged to have been performed for the United States, shall be allowed under this chapter until an account for said fees shall have been rendered and finally acted upon as required by law, unless the proper accounting officer of the Treasury fails to act finally thereon within six months after the account is received in said office.

Third. The claim of any paymaster, quartermaster, commissary of subsistence, or other disbursing officer of the United States, or of his administrators or executors, for relief from responsibility on account of loss by capture or otherwise, while in the line of his duty, of Government funds, vouchers, records, or papers in his charge, and for which such officer was and is held responsible.

Sec. 146. Upon the trial of any cause in which any set-off, counterclaim, claim for damages, or other demand is set up on the part of the Government against any person making claim against the Government in said court, the court shall hear and determine such claim or demand both for and against the Government and claimant; and if upon the whole case it finds that the claimant is indebted to the Government it shall render judgment to that effect, and such judgment shall be final, with the right of appeal, as in other cases provided for by law. Any transcript of such judgment, filed in the clerk's office of any district court, shall be entered upon the records thereof, and shall thereby become and be a judgment of such court and be enforced as other judgments in such court are enforced.

Sec. 147. Whenever the Court of Claims ascertains the facts of any loss by any paymaster, quartermaster, commissary of subsistence, or other disbursing officer, in the cases hereinbefore provided, to have been without fault or negligence on the part of such officer, it shall make a decree setting forth the amount thereof, and upon such decree the proper accounting officers of the Treasury shall allow to such officer the amount so decreed as a credit in the settlement of his accounts.

Sec. 148. When any claim or matter is pending in any of the executive departments which involves controverted questions of fact or law, the head of such department may transmit the same, with the vouchers, papers, documents and proofs pertaining thereto, to the Court of Claims and the same shall be there proceeded in under such rules as the court may adopt. When the facts and conclusions of law shall have been found, the court shall report its findings to the department by which it was transmitted for its guidance and action: Provided, however, That if it shall have been transmitted with the consent of the claimant, or if it shall appear to the satisfaction of the court upon the facts established, that under existing laws or the provisions of this chapter it has jurisdiction to render judgment or decree thereon, it shall proceed to do so, in the latter case giving to either party such further opportunity for hearing as in its judgment justice shall require, and shall report its findings therein to the department by which the same was referred to said court. The Secretary of the Treasury may, upon the certificate of any auditor, or of the Comptroller of the Treasury, direct any claim or matter, of which, by reason of the subject matter or character, the said court might, under existing laws, take jurisdiction on the voluntary action of the claimant, to be transmitted, with all the vouchers, papers, documents, and proofs pertaining thereto, to the said court for trial and adjudication.

Sec. 149. All cases transmitted by the head of any department, or upon the certificate of any Auditor, or of the Comptroller of the Treasury, according to the provisions of the preceding section, shall be proceeded in as other cases pending in the Court of Claims, and shall, in all respects, be subject to the same rules and regulations.

Sec. 150. The amount of any final judgment or decree rendered in favor of the claimant, in any case transmitted to the Court of Claims under the two preceding sections, shall be paid out of any specific appropriation applicable to the case, if any such there be; and where no such appropriation exists, the judgment or decree shall be paid in the same manner as other judgments of the said court.

Sec. 151. Whenever any bill, except for a pension, is pending in either House of Congress providing for the payment of a claim against the United States, legal or equitable, or for a grant, gift, or bounty to any person, the House in which such bill is pending may, for the investigation and determination of facts, refer the same to the Court of Claims, which shall proceed with the same in accordance with such rules as it may adopt and report to such House the facts in the case and the amount, where the same can be liquidated, including any facts bearing upon the question whether there has been delay or laches in presenting such claim or applying for such grant, gift, or bounty, and any facts bearing upon the question whether the bar of any statute of limitation should be removed or which shall be claimed to excuse the claimant for not having resorted to any established legal remedy, together with such conclusions as shall be sufficient to inform Congress of the nature and character of the demand, either as a claim, legal or equitable, or as a gratuity against the United States, and the amount, if any, legally or equitably due from the United States to the claimant: Provided, however, That if it shall appear to the satisfaction of the court upon the facts established, that under existing laws or the provisions of this chapter, the subject matter of the bill is such that it has jurisdiction to render judgment or decree thereon, it shall proceed to do so, giving to either party such further opportunity for hearing as in its judgment justice shall require, and it shall report its proceedings therein to the House of Congress by which the same was referred to said court.

Sec. 152. If the Government of the United States shall put in issue the right of the plaintiff to recover, the court may, in its discretion, allow costs to the prevailing party from the time of joining such issue. Such costs, however, shall include only what is actually incurred for witnesses, and for summoning the same, and fees paid · to the clerk of the court.

Sec. 153. The jurisdiction of the said court shall not extend to any claim against the Government not pending therein on December first, eighteen hundred and sixty-two, growing out of or dependent on any treaty stipulation entered into with foreign nations or with the Indian tribes.

Sec. 154. No person shall file or prosecute in the Court of Claims, or in the Supreme Court on appeal therefrom, any claim for or in respect to which he or any assignee of his has pending in any other court any suit or process against any person who, at the time when the cause of action alleged in such suit or process arose, was, in respect thereto, acting or professing to act, mediately or immediately, under the authority of the United States.

Sec. 155. Aliens who are citizens or subjects of any government which accords to citizens of the United States the right to prosecute claims against such government in its courts, shall have the privilege of prosecuting claims against the United States in the Court of Claims, whereof such court, by reason of their subject-matter and character, might take jurisdiction.

Sec. 156. Every claim against the United States cognizable by the Court of Claims, shall be forever barred unless the petition setting forth a statement thereof is filed in the court, or transmitted to it by the Secretary of the Senate or the Clerk of the House of Representatives, as provided by law, within six years after the claim first accrues: Provided, That the claims of married women, first accrued during marriage, of persons under the age of twenty-one years, first accrued during minority, and of idiots, lunatics, insane persons, and persons beyond the seas at the time the claim accrued, entitled to the claim, shall not be barred if the petition be filed in the court or transmitted, as aforesaid, within three years after the disability had ceased; but no other disability than those enumerated shall prevent any claim from being barred, nor shall any of the said disabilities operate cumulatively.

Sec. 157. The said court shall have power to establish rules for its government and for the regulation of practice therein, and it may punish for contempt in the manner prescribed by the common law, may appoint commissioners, and may exercise such powers as are necessary to carry into effect the powers granted to it by law.

Sec. 158. The judges and clerks of said court may administer oaths and affirmations, take acknowledgments of instruments in writing, and give certificates of the same.

Sec. 159. The claimant shall in all cases fully set forth in his petition the claim, the action thereon in Congress or by any of the Departments, if such action has been had, what persons are owners thereof or interested therein, when and upon what consideration such persons became so interested; that no assignment or transfer of said claim or of any part thereof or interest therein has been made, except as stated in the petition; that said claimant is justly entitled to the amount therein claimed from the United States after allowing all just credits and offsets; that the claimant and, where the claim has been assigned, the original and every prior owner thereof, if a citizen, has at all times borne true allegiance to the Government of the United States, and, whether a citizen or not, has not in any way voluntarily aided, abetted, or given encouragement to rebellion against the said Government, and that he believes the facts as stated in the said petition to be true. The said petition shall be verified by the affidavit of the claimant, his agent or attorney.

Sec. 160. The said allegations as to true allegiance and voluntary aiding, abetting, or giving encouragement to rebellion against the

Government may be traversed by the Government, and if on the trial such issues shall be decided against the claimant, his petition shall be dismissed.

Sec. 161. Whenever it is material in any claim to ascertain whether any person did or did not give any aid or comfort to forces or government of the late Confederate States during the Civil War, the claimant asserting the loyalty of any such person to the United States during such Civil War shall be required to prove affirmatively that such person did, during said Civil War, consistently adhere to the United States and did give no aid or comfort to persons engaged in said Confederate service in said Civil War.

Sec. 162. The Court of Claims shall have jurisdiction to hear and determine the claims of those whose property was taken subsequent to June the first, eighteen hundred and sixty-five, under the provisions of the Act of Congress approved March twelfth, eighteen hundred and sixty-three, entitled "An Act to provide for the collection of abandoned property and for the prevention of frauds in insurrectionary districts within the United States," and Acts amendatory thereof where the property so taken was sold and the net proceeds thereof were placed in the Treasury of the United States; and the Secretary of the Treasury shall return said net proceeds to the owners thereof, on the judgment of said court, and full jurisdiction is given to said court to adjudge said claims, any statutes of limitations to the contrary notwithstanding.

Sec. 163. The Court of Claims shall have power to appoint commissioners to take testimony to be used in the investigation of claims which come before it, to prescribe the fees which they shall receive for their services, and to issue commissions for the taking of such testimony, whether taken at the instance of the claimant or of the United States.

Sec. 164. The said court shall have power to call upon any of the Departments for any information or papers it may deem necessary, and shall have the use of all recorded and printed reports made by the committees of each House of Congress, when deemed necessary in the prosecution of its business. But the head of any Department may refuse and omit to comply with any call for information or papers when, in his opinion, such compliance would be injurious to the public interest.

Sec. 165. When it appears to the court in any case that the facts set forth in the petition of the claimant do not furnish any ground for relief, it shall not authorize the taking of any testimony therein.

Sec. 166. The court may, at the instance of the attorney or solicitor appearing in behalf of the United States, make an order in any case pending therein, directing any claimant in such case to appear, upon reasonable notice, before any commissioner of the court and be examined on oath touching any or all matters pertaining to said claim. Such examination shall be reduced in writing by the said commissioner, and be returned to and filed in the court, and may, at the discretion of the attorney or solicitor of the United States appearing in the case, be read and used as evidence on the trial thereof. And if any claimant, after such order is made and due and reasonable notice thereof is given to him, fails to appear, or refuses to testify or answer fully as to all matters within his knowledge material to the issue, the court may, in its discretion, order that the said cause shall not be brought forward for trial until he shall have fully complied with the order of the court in the premises.

Sec. 167. The testimony in cases pending before the Court of Claims shall be taken in the county where the witness resides, when the same can be conveniently done.

Sec. 168. The Court of Claims may issue subpoenas to require the attendance of witnesses in order to be examined before any person commissioned to take testimony therein. Such subpoenas shall have the same force as if issued from a district court, and compliance therewith shall be compelled under such rules and orders as the court shall establish.

Sec. 169. In taking testimony to be used in support of any claim, opportunity shall be given to the United States to file interrogatories, or by attorney to examine witnesses, under such regulations as said court shall prescribe; and like opportunity shall be afforded the claimant, in cases where testimony is taken on behalf of the United States, under like regulations.

Sec. 170. The commissioner taking testimony to be used in the Court of Claims shall administer an oath or affirmation to the witnesses brought before him for examination.

Sec. 171. When testimony is taken for the claimant, the fees of the commissioner before whom it is taken, and the cost of the commission and notice, shall be paid by such claimant; and when it is taken at the instance of the Government, such fees shall be paid out of the contingent fund provided for the Court of Claims, or other appropriation made by Congress for that purpose.

Sec. 172. Any person who corruptly practices or attempts to practice any fraud against the United States in the proof, statement, establishment, or allowance of any claim or of any part of any claim against the United States shall, ipso facto, forfeit the same to the Government; and it shall be the duty of the Court of Claims, in such cases, to find specifically that such fraud was practiced or attempted to be practiced, and thereupon to give judgment that such claim is forfeited to the Government, and that the claimant be forever barred from prosecuting the same.

Sec. 173. No claim shall be allowed by the accounting officers under the provisions of the act of Congress approved June sixteenth, eighteen hundred and seventy-four, or by the Court of Claims, or by Congress, to any person where such claimant, or those under whom he claims, shall willfully, knowingly, and with intent to defraud the United States, have claimed more than was justly due in respect of such claim, or presented any false evidence to Congress, or to any department or court, in support thereof.

Sec. 174. When judgment is rendered against any claimant, the court may grant a new trial for any reason which, by the rules of common law or chancery in suits between individuals, would furnish sufficient ground for granting a new trial.

Sec. 175. The Court of Claims, at any time while any claim is pending before it, or on appeal from it, or within two years next after the final disposition of such claim, may, on motion, on behalf of the United States, grant a new trial and stay the payment of any judgment therein, upon such evidence, cumulative or otherwise, as shall satisfy the court that any fraud, wrong, or. injustice in the premises has been done to the United States; but until an order is made staying the payment of a judgment, the same shall be payable and paid as now provided by law.

Sec. 176. There shall be taxed against the losing party in each and every cause pending in the Court of Claims the cost of printing the record in such case, which shall be collected, except when the judgment is against the United States, by the clerk of said court and paid into the Treasury of the United States.

Sec. 177. No interest shall be allowed on any claim up to the time of the rendition of judgment by the Court of Claims, unless upon a contract expressly stipulating for the payment of interest, except that interest may be allowed in any judgment of any court rendered after the passage of the Revenue Act of 1921 against the United States for any internal revenue tax erroneously or illegally assessed or collected, or for any penalty collected without authority or any sum which was excessive or in any manner wrongfully collected, under the internal revenue laws. (Act of November 23, 1921, sec. 1324b.)

Sec. 178. The payment of the amount due by any judgment of the Court of Claims, and of any interest thereon allowed by law, as provided by law, shall be a full discharge to the United States of all claim and demand touching any of the matters involved in the controversy.

Sec. 179. Any final judgment against the claimant on any claim prosecuted as provided in this chapter shall forever bar any further claim or demand against the United States arising out of the matters involved in the controversy.

Sec. 180. Whenever any person shall present his petition to the Court of Claims alleging that he is or has been indebted to the United States as an officer or agent thereof, or by virtue of any contract therewith, or that he is the guarantor, or surety, or personal representative of any officer or agent or contractor so indebted, or that he or the person for whom he is such surety, guarantor, or personal representative has held any office or agency under the United States, or entered into any contract therewith, under which it may be or has been claimed that an indebtedness to the United States had arisen and exists, and that he or the person he represents has applied to the proper department of the Government requesting that the account of such office, agency, or indebtedness may be adjusted and settled, and that three years have elapsed from the date of such application, and said account still remains unsettled and unadjusted, and that no suit upon the same has been brought by the United States, said court shall, due notice first being given to the head of said department and to the Attorney-General of the United States, proceed to hear the parties and to ascertain the amount, if any, due the United States on said account. The Attorney-General shall represent the United States at the hearing of said cause. The court may postpone the same from time to time whenever justice shall require. The judgment of said court or of the Supreme Court of the United States, to which an appeal shall lie, as in other cases, as to the amount due, shall be binding and conclusive upon the parties. The payment of such amount so found due by the court shall discharge such obligation. An action shall accrue to the United States against such principal, or surety, or representative to recover the amount so found due, which may be brought at any time within three years after the final judgment of said court; and unless suit shall be brought within said time, such claim and the claim on the original indebtedness shall be forever barred. The provisions of section one hundred and sixty-six shall apply to cases under this section.

Sec. 181. The plaintiff or the United States, in any suit brought under the provisions of the section last preceding, shall have the same right of appeal as is conferred under sections two hundred and forty-two and two hundred and forty-three; and such right shall be exercised only within the time and in the manner therein prescribed.

Sec. 182. In any case brought in the Court of Claims under any Act of Congress by which that court is authorized to render a judgment or decree against the United States, or against any Indian tribe or any Indians, or against any fund held in trust by the United States for any Indian tribe or for any Indians, the claimant, or the United States, or the tribe of Indians, or other party in interest shall have the same right of appeal as is conferred under sections two hundred and forty-two and two hundred and forty-three; and such right shall be exercised only within the time and in the manner therein prescribed.

Sec. 183. The Attorney-General shall report to Congress, at the beginning of each regular session, the suits under section one hundred and eighty, in which a final judgment or decree has been rendered, giving the date of each and a statement of the costs taxed in each case.

Sec. 184. In any case of a claim for supplies or stores taken by or furnished to any part of the military or naval forces of the United States for their use during the late Civil War, the petition shall aver that the person who furnished such supplies or stores, or from whom such supplies or stores were taken, did not give any aid or comfort to said rebellion, but was throughout the war loyal to the Government of the United States, and the fact of such loyalty shall be a jurisdictional fact; and unless the said court shall, on a preliminary inquiry, find that the person who furnished such supplies or stores, or from whom the same were taken as aforesaid, was loyal to the Government of the United States throughout said war, the court shall not have jurisdiction of such cause, and the same shall, without further proceedings, be dismissed.

Sec. 185. The Attorney-General, or his assistants under his direction, shall appear for the defense and protection of the interests of the United States in all cases which may be transmitted to the Court of Claims under the provisions of this chapter, with the same power to interpose counterclaims, offsets, defenses for fraud practiced or attempted to be practiced by claimants, and other defenses, in like manner as he is required to defend the United States in said court.

Sec. 186. No person shall be excluded as a witness in the Court of Claims on account of color or because he or she is a party to or interested in the cause or proceeding; and any plaintiff or party in interest may be examined as a witness on the part of the Government.

Sec. 187. Reports of the Court of Claims to Congress, under sections one hundred and forty-eight and one hundred and fifty-one, if not finally acted upon during the session at which they are reported, shall be continued from session to session and from Congress to Congress until the same shall be finally acted upon.

CHAPTER EIGHT.

THE COURT OF CUSTOMS APPEALS.

Sec. 188. There shall be a United States Court of Customs Appeals, which shall consist of a presiding judge and four associate judges, each of whom shall be appointed by the President, by and with the advice and consent of the Senate, and shall receive salaries equal in amount to the salary provided by this act to be paid judges of the Circuit Court of Appeals of the United States, payable monthly, from the treasury. (40 Stat. 1157.) The presiding judge shall be so designated in the order of appointment and in the commission issued to him by the President; and the associate judges shall have precedence according to the date of their commissions. Any three members of said court shall constitute a quorum, and the concurrence of three members shall be necessary to any decision thereof. In case of a vacancy or of the temporary inability or disqualification, for any reason, of one or two of the judges of said court, the President may, upon the request of the presiding judge of said court, designate any qualified United States circuit or district judge or judges to act in his or their place; and such circuit or district judges shall be duly qualified to so act.

Sec. 189. The said Court of Customs Appeals shall always be open for the transaction of business, and sessions thereof may, in the discretion of the court, be held in the several judicial circuits, and at such places as said court may from time to time designate. Any judge who, in pursuance of the provisions of this chapter, shall attend a session of said court at any place other than the city of Washington, shall be paid, upon his written and itemized certificate, by the marshal of the district in which the court shall be held, his actual and necessary expenses incurred for travel and attendance, and the actual and necessary expenses of one stenographic clerk who may accompany him; and such payments shall be allowed the marshal in the settlement of his accounts with the United States.

Sec. 190. Said court shall have the services of a marshal, with the same duties and powers, under the regulations of the court, as are now provided for the marshal of the Supreme Court of the United States, so far as the same may be applicable. Said services within the District of Columbia shall be performed by a marshal to be appointed by and to hold office during the pleasure of the court, who shall receive a salary of three thousand dollars per annum. Said services outside of the District of Columbia shall be performed by the United States marshals in and for the districts where sessions of said court may be held; and to this end said marshals shall be the marshals of said court. The marshal of said court, for the District of Columbia, is authorized to purchase, under the direction of the presiding judge, such books, periodicals, and stationery, as may be necessary for the use of said court; and such expenditures shall be allowed and paid by the Secretary of the Treasury upon claim duly made and approved by said presiding judge.

Sec. 191. The court shall appoint a clerk, whose office shall be in the city of Washington, District of Columbia, and who shall perform and exercise the same duties and powers in regard to all matters within the jurisdiction of said court as are now exercised and performed by the clerk of the Supreme Court of the United States, so far as the same may be applicable. The salary of the clerk shall be three thousand five hundred dollars per annum, which sum shall be in full payment for all service rendered by such clerk; and all fees of any kind whatever, and all costs shall be by him turned into the United States Treasury. Said clerk shall not be appointed by the court or any judge thereof as a commissioner, master, receiver, or referee. The costs and fees in the said court shall be fixed and established by said court in a table of fees to be adopted and approved by

the Supreme Court of the United States within four months after
the organization of said court: Provided, That the costs and fees so
fixed shall not, with respect to any item, exceed the costs and fees
charged in the Supreme Court of the United States; and the same
shall be expended, accounted for, and paid over to the Treasury of
the United States.

Sec. 192. In addition to the clerk, the court may appoint an
assistant clerk at a salary of two thousand dollars per annum, five
stenographic clerks at a salary of one thousand six hundred dollars
per annum each, one stenographic reporter at a salary of two thousand five hundred dollars per annum, and a messenger at a salary of
eight hundred and forty dollars per annum, all payable in equal
monthly installments, and all of whom, including the clerk, shall
hold office during the pleasure of and perform such duties as are
assigned them by the court. Said reporter shall prepare and transmit to the Secretary of the Treasury once a week in time for publication in the Treasury Decisions copies of all decisions rendered to
that date by said court, and prepare and transmit, under the direction of said court, at least once a year, reports of said decisions
rendered to that date, constituting a volume, which shall be printed
by the Treasury Department in such numbers and distributed or
sold in such manner as the Secretary of the Treasury shall direct.

Sec. 193. The marshal of said court for the District of Columbia
and the marshals of the several districts in which said Court of
Customs Appeals may be held shall, under the direction of the Attorney-General, and with his approval, provide such rooms in the public
buildings of the United States as may be necessary for said court:
Provided, That in case proper rooms cannot be provided in such
buildings, then the said marshals, with the approval of the Attorney-
General, may, from time to time, lease such rooms as may be necessary for said court. The bailiffs and messengers of said court shall
be allowed the same compensation for their respective services as are
allowed for similar services in the existing district courts. In no case
shall said marshals secure other rooms than those regularly occupied
by existing district courts, or other public officers, except where such
cannot, by reason of actual occupancy or use, be occupied or used by
said Court of Customs Appeals.

Sec. 194. The said Court of Customs Appeals shall be a court of
record, with jurisdiction as in this chapter established and limited.
It shall prescribe the form and style of its seal, and the form of its
writs and other process and procedure, and exercise such powers con-

ferred by law as may be conformable and necessary to the exercise of its jurisdiction. It shall have power to establish all rules and regulations for the conduct of the business of the court, and as may be needful for the uniformity of decisions within its jurisdiction as conferred by law. It shall have power to review any decision or matter within its jurisdiction, and may affirm, modify, or reverse the same and remand the case with such orders as may seem to it proper in the premises, which shall be executed accordingly.

Sec. 195. The Court of Customs Appeals established by this chapter shall exercise exclusive appellate jurisdiction to review by appeal, as herein provided, final decisions by a Board of General Appraisers in all cases as to the construction of the law and the facts respecting the classification of merchandise and the rate of duty imposed thereon under such classification, and the fees and charges connected therewith, and all appealable questions as to the jurisdiction of said board, and all appealable questions as to the laws and regulations governing the collection of the customs revenues; and the judgments and decrees of said Court of Customs Appeals shall be final in all such cases. Provided, however, that in any case in which the judgment or decree of the Court of Customs Appeals is made final by the provisions of this title, it shall be competent for the Supreme Court, upon the petition of either party, filed within sixty days next after the issue by the Court of Customs Appeals of its mandate upon decision, in any case in which there is drawn in question the construction of the Constitution of the United States, or any part thereof, or of any treaty made pursuant thereto, or in any other case when the Attorney-General of the United States shall, before the decision of the Court of Customs Appeals is rendered, file with the court a certificate to the effect that the case is of such importance as to render expedient its review by the Supreme Court, to require, by certiorari or otherwise, such case to be certified to the Supreme Court for its review and determination, with the same power and authority in the case as if it had been carried by appeal or writ of error to the Supreme Court: And provided, further, That this act shall not apply to any case involving only the construction of section one, or any portion thereof, of an act entitled "An Act to provide revenue, equalize duties and encourage the industries of the United States, and for other purposes," approved August fifth, nineteen hundred and nine, nor to any case involving the construction of section two of an act entitled "An Act to promote reciprocal trade relations with the Dominion of Canada, and for other purposes," approved July twenty-sixth, nineteen hundred and eleven. (38 Stat. 703.)

39

Sec. 196. After the organization of said court, no appeal shall be taken or allowed from any Board of United States General Appraisers to any other court, and no appellate jurisdiction shall thereafter be exercised or allowed by any other courts in cases decided by said Board of United States General Appraisers; but all appeals allowed by law from such Board of General Appraisers shall be subject to review only in the Court of Customs Appeals hereby established, according to the provisions of this chapter: Provided, That nothing in this chapter shall be deemed to deprive the Supreme Court of the United States of jurisdiction to hear and determine all customs cases which have heretofore been certified to said court from the United States circuit courts of appeals on applications for writs of certiorari or otherwise, nor to review by writ of certiorari any customs case heretofore decided or now pending and hereafter decided by any circuit court of appeals, provided application for said writ be made within six months after August fifth, nineteen hundred and nine: Provided, further, That all customs cases decided by a circuit or district court of the United States or a court of a Territory of the United States prior to said date above mentioned, and which have not been removed from said courts by appeal or writ of error, and all such cases theretofore submitted for decision in said courts and remaining undecided may be reviewed on appeal at the instance of either party by the United States Court of Customs Appeals, provided such appeal be taken within one year from the date of the entry of the order, judgment, or decrees sought to be reviewed.

Sec. 197. Immediately upon the organization of the Court of Customs Appeals, all cases within the jurisdiction of that court pending and not submitted for decision in any of the United States circuit courts of appeals, United States circuit, territorial or district courts, shall, with the record and samples therein, be certified by said courts to said Court of Customs Appeals for further proceedings in accordance herewith: Provided, That where orders for the taking of further testimony before a referee have been made in any of such cases, the taking of such testimony shall be completed before such certification.

Sec. 198. If the importer, owner, consignee, or agent of any imported merchandise, or the collector or Secretary of the Treasury, shall be dissatisfied with the decision of the Board of General Appraisers as to the construction of the law and the facts respecting the classification of such merchandise and the rate of duty imposed thereon under such classification, or with any other appealable decision of said board, they, or either of them, may, within sixty days next after the entry of such decree or judgment, and not afterwards, apply to the Court of Customs Appeals for a review of the questions of law and fact involved in such decision: Provided, That in Alaska and in the insular and other outside possessions of the United States ninety days shall be allowed for making such application to the Court of Customs Appeals. Such application shall be made by filing in the office of the clerk of said court a concise statement of errors of law and fact complained of; and a copy of such statement shall be served on the collector, or on the importer, owner, consignee, or agent, as the case may be. Thereupon the court shall immediately order the Board of General Appraisers to transmit to said court the record and evidence taken by them, together with the certified statement of the facts involved in the case and their decision thereon; and all the evidence taken by and before said board shall be competent evidence before said Court of Customs Appeals. The decision of said Court of Customs Appeals shall be final, and such cause shall be remanded to said Board of General Appraisers for further proceedings to be taken in pursuance of such determination.

Sec. 199. Immediately upon receipt of any record transmitted to said court for determination the clerk thereof shall place the same upon the calendar for hearing and submission; and such calendar shall be called and all cases thereupon submitted, except for good cause shown, at least once every sixty days: Provided, That such calendar need not be called during the months of July and August of any year.

CHAPTER NINE.

THE COMMERCE COURT.

Note.

[Sections 200-214 all relate to the Commerce Court which was abolished by Act of Congress, of October 22, 1913 (38 Stat. 219), and all the acts, and parts of acts, relating to such court were thereby repealed. The act further provided as follows:

Nothing herein contained shall be deemed to affect the tenure of any of the judges now acting as circuit judges by appointment under the terms of said act, but such judges shall continue to act under assignment, as in the said act provided, as judges of the district courts and circuit courts of appeals; and in the event of and on the death, resignation or removal from office of any of such judges, his office is hereby abolished and no successor to him shall be appointed.

The venue of any suit hereafter brought to enforce, suspend or set aside, in whole or in part, any order of the Interstate Commerce Commission shall be in the judicial district wherein is the residence of the party or any of the parties upon whose petition the order was made, except that where the order does not relate to transportation or is not made upon the petition of any party the venue shall be in the district where the matter complained of in the petition before the commission arises, and except that where the order does not relate either to transportation or to a matter so complained of before the commission, the matter covered by the order shall be deemed to arise in the district where one of the petitioners in court has either its principal office or its principal operating office. In case such transportation relates to a through shipment the term "destination" shall be construed as meaning final destination of such shipment.

The procedure in the district courts in respect to cases of which jurisdiction is conferred upon them by this act shall be the same as that heretofore prevailing in the Commerce Court. The orders, writs and processes of the district courts' may in these cases run, be served, and be returnable anywhere in the United States; and the right of appeal from the district courts in such cases shall be the same as the right of appeal heretofore prevailing under existing law from the Commerce Court. No interlocutory injunction, suspending or restraining the enforcement, operation, or execution of, or setting aside, in whole or in part, any order made or entered by the Interstate Commerce Commission shall be issued or granted by any district court of the United States, or by any judge thereof, or by any circuit judge acting as district judge, unless the application for the same shall be presented to a circuit or district judge, and shall be heard and determined by three judges, of whom at least one shall be a circuit judge, and unless a majority of said three judges shall concur in granting such application. When such application as aforesaid is presented to a judge, he shall immediately call to his assistance to hear and determine the application two other judges. Said application shall not be heard or determined before at least five days' notice of the hearing has been given to the Interstate Commerce Commission, to the Attorney-General of the United States, and to such other persons as may be defendants in the suit. Provided, that in cases where irreparable damage would otherwise ensue to the petitioner, a majority of said three judges concurring, may, on hearing, after not less than three days' notice to the Interstate Commerce Commission and the Attorney-General, allow a temporary stay or suspension, in whole or in part, of the operation of the order of the Interstate Commerce Commission for not more than sixty days from the date of the order of said judges pending the application for the order or injunction, in which case the said order shall contain a specific finding, based upon evidence submitted to the judges making the order and identified by reference thereto, that such irreparable damage would result to the petitioner and specifying the nature of the damage. The said judges may, at the time of hearing such application, upon a like finding, continue the temporary stay or suspension in whole or in part until decision upon the application. The hearing upon such application for an interlocutory injunction shall be given precedence and shall be in every way expedited and be assigned for a hearing at the earliest practicable day after the expiration of the notice hereinbefore provided for. An appeal may be taken direct to the Supreme Court of the United States from the order granting or denying, after notice and hearing, an interlocutory injunction, in such case if such appeal be taken within thirty days after the order, in respect to which complaint is made, is granted or refused; and upon the final hearing of any suit brought to suspend or set aside, in whole or in part, any order of said commission, the same requirement as to judges and the same procedure as to expedition and appeal shall apply. A final judgment or decree of the district court may be reviewed by the Supreme Court of the United States if appeal to the Supreme Court be taken by an aggrieved party within sixty days after the entry of such final judgment or decree, and such appeals may be taken in like manner as appeals are taken under existing law in equity cases. And in such case the notice required shall be served upon the defendants in the case and upon the Attorney-General of the State. All cases pending

in the Commerce Court at the date of the passage of this act shall
be deemed pending in and be transferred forthwith to said district
courts except cases which may previously have been submitted to
that court for final decree and the latter to be transferred to the
district courts if not decided by the Commerce Court before December first, nineteen hundred and thirteen, and all cases wherein injunctions or other orders or decrees, mandatory or otherwise, have
been directed or entered prior to the abolition of the said court shall
be transferred forthwith to said district courts, which shall have
jurisdiction to proceed therewith and to enforce said injunctions,
orders or decrees. Each of said cases and all the records, papers,
and proceedings shall be transferred to the district court wherein
it might have been filed at the time it was filed in the Commerce
Court if this act had then been in effect; and if it might have been
filed in any one of two or more district courts it shall be transferred
to that one of said district courts which may be designated by the
petitioner or petitioners in said case, or, upon failure of said petitioners to act in the premises, within thirty days after the passage
of this act, to such one of said district courts as may be designated
by the judges of the Commerce Court. The judges of the Commerce
Court shall have authority, and are hereby directed, to make any
and all orders and to take any other action necessary to transfer as
aforesaid the cases and all the records, papers and proceedings then
pending in the Commerce Court to said district courts. All administrative books, dockets, files and all papers of the Commerce Court
not transferred as part of the record of any particular case shall be
lodged in the Department of Justice. All furniture, carpets and
other property of the Commerce Court is turned over to the Department of Justice and the Attorney-General is authorized to supply
such portion thereof as in his judgment may be proper and necessary
to the United States Board of Mediation and Conciliation.

Any case hereafter remanded from the Supreme Court which, but
for the passage of this act, would have been remanded to the Commerce Court, shall be remanded to a district court, designated by
the Supreme Court, wherein it might have been instituted at the
time it was instituted in the Commerce Court if this act had then
been in effect and thereafter such district court shall take all necessary and proper proceedings in such case in accordance with law
and such mandate, order or decree therein as may be made by said
Supreme Court.

All laws or parts of laws inconsistent with the foregoing provisions relating to the Commerce Court, are repealed.]

CHAPTER TEN.

THE SUPREME COURT.

Sec. 215. The Supreme Court of the United States shall consist of a Chief Justice of the United States and eight associate justices, any six of whom shall constitute a quorum.

Sec. 216. The associate justices shall have precedence according to the dates of their commissions, or, when the commissions of two or more of them bear the same date, according to their ages.

Sec. 217. In case of a vacancy in the office of Chief Justice, or of his inability to perform the duties and powers of his office, they shall devolve upon the associate justice who is first in precedence, until such disability is removed, or another Chief Justice is appointed and duly qualified. This provision shall apply to every associate justice who succeeds to the office of Chief Justice.

Sec. 218. The Chief Justice of the Supreme Court of the United States shall receive the sum of fifteen thousand dollars a year, and the justices thereof shall receive the sum of fourteen thousand five hundred dollars a year each, to be paid monthly.

Sec. 219. The Supreme Court shall have power to appoint a clerk and a marshal for said court, and a reporter of its decisions.

Sec. 220. The clerk of the Supreme Court shall, before he enters upon the execution of his office, give bond, with sufficient sureties, to be approved by the court, to the United States, in the sum of not less than five thousand and not more than twenty thousand dollars, to be determined and regulated by the Attorney-General, faithfully to discharge the duties of his office, and seasonably to record the decrees, judgments, and determinations of the court. The Supreme Court may at any time, upon the motion of the Attorney-General, to be made upon thirty days' notice, require a new bond, or a bond for an increased amount within the limits above prescribed; and the failure of the clerk to execute the same shall vacate his office. All bonds given by the clerk shall, after approval, be recorded in his office, and copies thereof from the records, certified by the clerk under seal of the court, shall be competent evidence in any court. The original bonds shall be filed in the Department of Justice.

Sec. 221. One or more deputies of the clerk of the Supreme Court may be appointed by the court on the application of the clerk, and may be removed at the pleasure of the court. In case of the death of the clerk, his deputy or deputies shall, unless removed, continue in office and perform the duties of the clerk in his name until a clerk is appointed and qualified; and for the defaults or misfeasances in office of any such deputy, whether in the lifetime of the clerk or after his death, the clerk, and his estate, and the sureties on his official bond shall be liable; and his executor or administrator shall have such remedy for any such defaults or misfeasances committed after his death as the clerk would be entitled to if the same had occurred in his lifetime.

Sec. 222. The records and proceedings of the Court of Appeals, appointed previous to the adoption of the present Constitution, shall be kept in the office of the clerk of the Supreme Court, who shall give copies thereof to any person requiring and paying for them, in the manner provided by law for giving copies of the records and proceedings of the Supreme Court; and such copies shall have like faith and credit with all other proceedings of said court.

Sec. 223. The Supreme Court is authorized and empowered to prepare the tables of fees to be charged by the clerk thereof.

Sec. 224. The marshal is entitled to receive a salary at the rate of four thousand five hundred dollars a year. He shall attend the court at its sessions; shall serve and execute all process and orders issuing from it, or made by the Chief Justice or an associate justice in pursuance of law; and shall take charge of all property of the United States used by the court or its members. With the approval of the Chief Justice he may appoint assistants and messengers to attend the court, with the compensation allowed to officers of the House of Representatives of similar grade.

Sec. 225. It shall be the duty of the reporter to prepare the decisions of the Supreme Court for printing and publication in bound volumes, as and when directed by the court or the Chief Justice; and when so directed to cause to be printed and published advance copies of said decisions in pamphlet installments. The reporter by requisition upon the Public Printer, shall have the printing and binding herein required done at the Government Printing Office. The quality and size of the paper, type, format (sic) proofs and binding shall be determined by the reporter subject to the approval of the Chief Justice. Authority is hereby conferred upon the Public Printer for doing the printing and binding specified herein. (Act July 1, 1922.)

Sec. 226. The salary of the reporter shall be $8,000 per annum, payable out of the treasury in monthly installments which shall be in full compensation for the services required by law. He shall also be allowed for professional and clerical assistance and stationery not to exceed $3,500 per annum, to be paid upon vouchers signed by him and approved by the Chief Justice. He shall be furnished a room in the Capitol, with suitable furniture, convenient to the space occupied by the Supreme Court and the law library thereof. (Act July 1, 1922.)

Note.

[Sec. 227. Provides for the distribution of a number of copies of the official reports to various public officials and libraries. (Act July 1, 1922.)

Sec. 228. Has reference to the price, character of volumes, etc., of the official reports. (Act July 1, 1922.)

Sec. 229. Provides for the furnishing of copies of Federal Reporter and Digest, etc., to various courts and officers.]

Sec. 230. The Supreme Court shall hold at the seat of government, one term annually, commencing on the first Monday in October, and such adjourned or special terms as it may find necessary for the dispatch of business. (39 Stat. 726.)

Sec. 231. If, at any session of the Supreme Court, a quorum does not attend on the day appointed for holding it, the justices who do attend may adjourn the court from day to day for twenty days after said appointed time, unless there be sooner a quorum. If a quorum does not attend within said twenty days, the business of the court shall be continued over till the next appointed session; and if, during a term, after a quorum has assembled, less than that number attend on any day, the justices attending may adjourn the court from day to day until there is a quorum, or may adjourn without day.

Sec. 232. The justices attending at any term, when less than a quorum is present, may, within the twenty days mentioned in the preceding section, make all necessary orders touching any suit, proceeding, or process, depending in or returned to the court, preparatory to the hearing, trial, or decision thereof.

Sec. 233. The Supreme Court shall have exclusive jurisdiction of all controversies of a civil nature where a State is a party, except between a State and its citizens, or between a State and citizens of other States, or aliens, in which latter case it shall have original, but not exclusive, jurisdiction. And it shall have exclusively all such jurisdiction of suits or proceedings against ambassadors or other public ministers, or their domestics or domestic servants, as a court of law can have consistently with the law of nations; and original, but not exclusive, jurisdiction, of all suits brought by ambassadors, or other public ministers, or in which a consul or vice-consul is a party.

Sec. 234. The Supreme Court shall have power to issue writs of prohibition to the district courts, when proceeding as courts of admiralty and maritime jurisdiction; and writs of mandamus, in cases warranted by the principles and usages of law, to any courts appointed under the authority of the United States, or to persons holding office under the authority of the United States, where a State, or an ambassador, or other public minister, or a consul, or vice-consul is a party.

Sec. 235. The trial of issues of fact in the Supreme Court, in all actions at law against citizens of the United States, shall be by jury.

Sec. 236. The Supreme Court shall have appellate jurisdiction in the cases hereinafter specially provided for.

Sec. 237. A final judgment or decree in any suit in the highest court of a State in which a decision in the suit could be had, where is drawn in question the validity of a treaty or statute of, or an authority exercised under, the United States, and the decision is against their validity; or where is drawn in question the validity of a statute of, or an authority exercised under any State, on the ground of their being repugnant to the Constitution, treaties, or laws of the United States, and the decision is in favor of their validity, may be re-examined and reversed or affirmed in the Supreme Court upon a writ of error. The writ shall have the same effect as if the judgment or decree complained of had been rendered or passed in a court of the United States. The Supreme Court may reverse, modify or affirm the judgment or decree of such State court, and may, in its discretion, award execution or remand the same to the court from which it was removed by the writ. It shall be competent for the Supreme Court, by certiorari or otherwise, to require that there be certified to it for review and determination with the same power and authority and with like effect as if brought up by writ of error, any cause wherein a final judgment or decree has been rendered or passed by the highest court of a State in which a decision could be had, where is drawn in question the validity of a treaty or statute of, or an authority exercised under the United States, and the decision is in favor of their validity, or where is drawn in question the validity of a statute of, or an authority exercised under any State, on the ground of their being repugnant to the Constitution, treaties, or laws of the United States, and the decision is against their validity; or where any title, right, privilege, or immunity is claimed under the Constitution, or any treaty or statute of, or commission held or authority exercised under the United States, and the decision is either in favor of or against the title, right, privilege or immunity especially set up or claimed by either party, under such Constitution, treaty, statute, commission or authority. (39 Stat. L. 726.) In any suit involving the validity of a contract wherein it is claimed that a change in the rule of law or construction of statutes by the highest court of a State applicable to such contract would be repugnant to the Constitution of the United States, the Supreme Court shall, upon writ of error, re-examine, reverse, or affirm the final judgment of the highest court of a State in which a decision in the suit could be had, if said claim is made in said court at any time before said final judgment is entered and if the decision is against the claim so made. (Act Feb. 17, 1922.)

Sec. 238. Appeals and writs of error may be taken from the district courts, including the United States District Court for Hawaii, and the United States District Court for Porto Rico, direct to the Supreme Court in the following cases: In any case in which the jurisdiction of the court is in issue, in which case the question of jurisdiction alone shall be certified to the Supreme Court from the court below for decision; from the final sentences and decrees in prize causes; in any case that involves the construction or application of the Constitution of the United States; in any case in which the constitutionality of any law of the United States, or the validity or construction of any treaty made under its authority is drawn in question; and in any case in which the constitution or law of a State is claimed to be in contravention of the Constitution of the United States. (38 Stat. 804.)

Sec. 238a. If an appeal or writ of error has been or shall be taken to, or issued out of, any circuit court of appeals in a case wherein such appeal or writ of error should have been taken to or issued out of the Supreme Court; or if an appeal or writ of error has been or shall be taken to, or issued out of, the Supreme Court in a case wherein such appeal or writ of error should· have been taken to, or issued out of, a circuit court of appeals, such appeal or writ of error shall not for such reason be dismissed, but shall be transferred to the proper court, which shall thereupon be possessed of the same and shall proceed to ·the determination thereof with the same force and effect as if such appeal or writ of error had been duly taken to, or issued out of, the court to which it is so transferred. (Act Sept. 14, 1922.)

Sec. 239. In any case within its appellate jurisdiction, as defined in section one hundred and twenty-eight, the circuit court of appeals at any time may certify to the Supreme Court of the United States any questions or propositions of law concerning which it desires the instruction of that court for its proper decision; and thereupon the Supreme Court may either give its instruction on the questions and propositions certified to it, which shall be binding upon the circuit court of appeals in such case, or it may require that the whole record and cause be sent up to it for its consideration, and thereupon shall decide the whole matter in controversy in the same manner as if it had been brought there for review by writ of error or appeal.

Sec. 240. In any case, civil or criminal, in which the judgment or decree of the circuit court of appeals is made final by the provisions of this Title, it shall be competent for the Supreme Court to require, by certiorari or otherwise, upon the petition of any party thereto, any such case to be certified to the Supreme Court for its review and determination, with the same power and authority in the case as if it had been carried by appeal or writ of error to the Supreme Court.

Sec. 241. In any case in which the judgment or decree of the circuit court of appeals is not made final by the provisions of this Title, there shall be of right an appeal or writ of error to the Supreme Court of the United States where the matter in controversy shall exceed one thousand dollars, besides costs. That no writ of error, appeal, or writ of certiorari intended to bring up any cause for review by the Supreme Court shall be allowed or entertained unless duly applied for within three months after entry of the judgment or decree complained of: Provided, That writs of certiorari addressed to the Supreme Court of the Philippine Islands may be granted if application therefor be made within six months. (39 Stat. 727.)

Sec. 242. An appeal to the Supreme Court shall be allowed on behalf of the United States, from all judgments of the Court of Claims adverse to the United States, and on behalf of the plaintiff in any case where the amount in controversy exceeds three thousand dollars, or where his claim is forfeited to the United States by the judgment of said court as provided in section one hundred and seventy-two.

Sec. 243. All appeals from the Court of Claims shall be taken within ninety days after the judgment is rendered, and shall be allowed under such regulations as the Supreme Court may direct.

Note.

[Sec. 244. Repealed. (38 Stat. 804.)

Sec. 245. Became obsolete on the admission of Arizona and New Mexico as States.]

Sec. 246. Writs of error and appeals from the final judgments and decrees of the Supreme Court of the Territory of Hawaii and of the Supreme Court of Porto Rico may be taken and prosecuted to the Supreme Court of the United States within the same time, in the same manner, under the same regulations, and in the same classes of cases, in which writs of error and appeals from the final judgments and decrees of the highest court of a State in which a decision in the suit could be had, may be taken and prosecuted to the Supreme Court of the United States under the provisions of section two hundred and thirty-seven; and in all other cases, civil or criminal, in the Supreme Court of the Territory of Hawaii or the Supreme Court of Porto Rico, it shall be competent for the Supreme Court of the United States to require by certiorari, upon the petition of any party thereto, that the case be certified to it, after final judgment or decree, for review and determination, with the same power and authority as if taken to that court by appeal or writ of error; but certiorari shall not be allowed in any such case unless the petition therefor is presented to the Supreme Court of the United States within three months from the date of such judgment or decree. Writs of error and appeals from the final judgments and decrees of the Supreme Courts of the Territory of Hawaii and of Porto Rico, wherein the amount involved, exclusive of costs, to be ascertained by the oath of either party or of other competent witnesses, exceeds the value of $5,000 may be taken and prosecuted in the Circuit Courts of Appeals. (38 Stat. 804; 39 Stat. 727.)

Sec. 247. Appeals and writs of error may be taken and prosecuted from final judgments and decrees of the district court for the district of Alaska or for any division thereof, direct to the Supreme Court of the United States, in the following cases: In prize cases; and in all cases which involve the construction or application of the Constitution of the United States, or in which the constitutionality of any law of the United States or the validity or construction of any treaty made under its authority is drawn in question, or in which the constitution or law of a State is claimed to be in contravention of the Constitution of the United States. Such writs of error and appeals shall be taken within the same time, in the same manner, and under the same regulations as writs of error and appeals are taken from the district courts to the Supreme Court.

Sec. 248. The Supreme Court of the United States shall have jurisdiction to review, revise, reverse, modify, or affirm the final judgments and decrees of the supreme court of the Philippine Islands in all actions, cases, causes, and proceedings now pending therein or hereafter determined thereby, in which the Constitution, or any statute, treaty, title, right, or privilege of the United States is involved, or in causes in which the value in controversy exceeds twenty-five thousand dollars, or in which the title or possession of real estate exceeding in value the sum of twenty-five thousand dollars, to be ascertained by the oath of either party or of other competent witnesses, is involved or brought in question; and such final judgments or decrees may and can be reviewed, revised, reversed, modified, or affirmed by said Supreme Court on appeal or writ of error by the party aggrieved, within the same time, in the same manner, under the same regulations, and by the same procedure, as far as applicable, as the final judgments and decrees of the district courts of the United States.

[The above has been in effect amended by section 5 of the Act of September 6, 1916 (39 Stat. 727), said section reading as follows:]

That no judgment or decree rendered or passed by the Supreme Court of the Philippine Islands more than sixty days after the approval of this act shall be reviewed by the Supreme Court upon writ of error or appeal; but it shall be competent for the Supreme Court, by certiorari or otherwise, to require that there be certified to it for review and determination, with the same power and authority and with like effect as if brought up by writ of error or appeal, any cause wherein, after such sixty days, the Supreme Court of the Philippine Islands may render or pass a judgment or decree which would be subject to review under existing laws.

Sec. 249. In all cases where the judgment or decree of any court of a Territory might be reviewed by the Supreme Court on writ of error or appeal, such writ of error or appeal may be taken, within the time and in the manner provided by law, notwithstanding such Territory has, after such judgment or decree, been admitted as a State; and the Supreme Court shall direct the mandate to such court as the nature of the writ of error or appeal requires.

Sec. 250. Any final judgment or decree of the Court of Appeals of the District of Columbia may be re-examined and affirmed, reversed, or modified by the Supreme Court of the United States, upon writ of error or appeal, in the following cases:

First. In cases in which the jurisdiction of the trial court is in issue; but when any such case is not otherwise reviewable in said Supreme Court, then the question of jurisdiction alone shall be certified to said Supreme Court for decision.

Second. In prize cases.

Third. In cases involving the construction or application of the Constitution of the United States, or the constitutionality of any law of the United States, or the validity or construction of any treaty made under its authority.

Fourth. In cases in which the constitution, or any law of a State, is claimed to be in contravention of the Constitution of the United States.

Fifth. In cases in which the validity of any authority exercised under the United States, or the existence or scope of any power or duty of an officer of the United States is drawn in question.

Sixth. In cases in which the construction of any law of the United States is drawn in question by the defendant.

Except as provided in the next succeeding section, the judgments and decrees of said Court of Appeals shall be final in all cases arising under the patent laws, the copyright laws, the revenue laws, the criminal laws, and in admiralty cases; and, except as provided in the next succeeding section, the judgments and decrees of said Court of Appeals shall be final in all cases not reviewable as hereinbefore provided.

Writs of error and appeals shall be taken within the same time, in the same manner, and under the same regulations as writs of error and appeals are taken from the circuit courts of appeals to the Supreme Court of the United States.

Sec. 251. In any case in which the judgment or decree of said Court of Appeals is made final by the section last preceding, it shall be competent for the Supreme Court of the United States to require, by certiorari or otherwise, any such case to be certified to it for its review and determination, with the same power and authority in the case as if it had been carried by writ of error or appeal to said Supreme Court. It shall also be competent for said Court of Appeals, in any case in which its judgment or decree is made final under the section last preceding, at any time to certify to the Supreme Court of the United States any questions or propositions of law concerning which it desires the instruction of that court for their proper decision; and thereupon the Supreme Court may either give its instruction on the questions and propositions certified to it, which shall be binding upon said Court of Appeals in such case, or it may require that the whole record and cause be sent up to it for its consideration, and thereupon shall decide the whole matter in controversy in the same manner as if it had been brought there for review by writ of error or appeal.

Sec. 252. [Has been substantially repealed by the provisions of section 3 of the Act of September 6, 1916 (39 Stat. 727), quoted under section 128, supra.]

Sec. 253. Cases on writ of error to revise the judgment of a State court in any criminal case shall have precedence on the docket of the Supreme Court, of all cases to which the Government of the United States is not a party, excepting only such cases as the court, in its discretion, may decide to be of public importance.

Sec. 254. There shall be taxed against the losing party in each and every cause pending in the Supreme Court the cost of printing the record in such case, except when the judgment is against the United States.

Sec. 255. Any woman who shall have been a member of the bar of the highest court of any State or Territory, or of the Court of Appeals of the District of Columbia, for the space of three years, and shall have maintained a good standing before such court, and who shall be a person of good moral character, shall, on motion, and the production of such record, be admitted to practice before the Supreme Court of the United States.

40

CHAPTER ELEVEN.

PROVISIONS COMMON TO MORE THAN ONE COURT.

Sec. 256. The jurisdiction vested in the courts of the United States in the cases and proceedings hereinafter mentioned, shall be exclusive of the courts of the several States:

First. Of all crimes and offenses cognizable under the authority of the United States.

Second. Of all suits for penalties and forfeitures incurred under the laws of the United States.

"Third. Of all civil causes of admiralty and maritime jurisdiction, saving to suitors in all cases the right of a common-law remedy where the common law is competent to give it and to claimants for compensation for injuries to or death of persons other than the master or members of the crew of a vessel, their rights and remedies under the workmen's compensation law of any State, District, Territory, or possession of the United States. (Act June 10, 1922.)

Fourth. Of all seizures under the laws of the United States, on land or on waters not within admiralty and maritime jurisdiction; of all prizes brought into the United States; and of all proceedings for the condemnation of property taken as prize.

Fifth. Of all cases arising under the patent-right, or copyright. laws of the United States.

Sixth. Of all matters and proceedings in bankruptcy.

Seventh. Of all controversies of a civil nature, where a State is a party, except between a State and its citizens, or between a State and citizens of other States, or aliens.

Eighth. Of all suits and proceedings against ambassadors, or other public ministers, or their domestics, or domestic servants, or against consuls or vice consuls.

Sec. 257. The justices of the Supreme Court, the circuit judges, and the district judges, hereafter appointed, shall take the following oath before they proceed to perform the duties of their respective offices: ''I, ——— ———, do solemnly swear (or affirm) that I will administer justice without respect to persons, and do equal right to the poor and to the rich, and that I will faithfully and impartially discharge and perform all the duties incumbent upon me as ——— according to the best of my abilities and understanding, agreeably to the Constitution and laws of the United States: So help me God.''

Sec. 258. It shall not be lawful for any judge appointed under the authority of the United States to exercise the profession or employment of counsel or attorney, or to be engaged in the practice of the law. Any person offending against the prohibition of this section shall be demed guilty of a high misdemeanor.

Sec. 259. The circuit justices, the circuit and district judges of the United States, and the judges of the district courts of the United States in Alaska, Hawaii, and Porto Rico, shall each be allowed and paid his necessary expenses of travel, and his reasonable expenses (not to exceed ten dollars per day) actually incurred for maintenance, consequent upon his attending court or transacting other official business in pursuance of law at any place other than his official place of residence, said expenses to be paid by the marshal of the district in which such court is held or official business transacted, upon the written certificate of the justice or judge. The official place of residence of each justice and of each circuit judge while assigned to the Commerce Court shall be at Washington; and the official place of residence of each circuit and district judge, and of each judge of the district courts of the United States in Alaska, Hawaii, and Porto Rico, shall be at that place nearest. his actual residence at which either a circuit court of appeals or a district court is regularly held. Every such judge shall, upon his appointment, and from time to time thereafter whenever he may change his official residence, in writing notify the Department of Justice of his official place of residence.

Sec. 260. When any judge of any court of the United States appointed to hold his office during good behavior resigns his office, after having held a commission or commissions as judge of any such court or courts at least ten years continuously, and having attained the age of seventy years, he shall, during the residue of his natural life, receive the salary which is payable at the time of his resignation for the office that he held at the time of his resignation. But instead of resigning, any judge other than a justice of the Supreme Court, who is qualified to resign under the foregoing provisions, may retire, upon the salary of which he is then in receipt, from regular active service on the bench, and the President shall thereupon be authorized to appoint a successor; but a judge so retiring may nevertheless be called upon by the senior circuit judge of that circuit and be by him authorized to perform such judicial duties in such circuit as such retired judge may be willing to undertake, or he may be called upon by the Chief Justice and be by him authorized to perform such judicial duties in any other circuit as such retired judge may be willing to undertake, or he may be called upon either by the presiding judge or senior judge of any other such court and be by him authorized to perform such judicial duties in such court as such retired judge may be willing to undertake. In the event any circuit judge or district judge, having so held a commission or commissions at least ten years continuously, and having attained the age of seventy years as aforesaid, shall nevertheless remain in office, and not resign or retire as aforesaid, the President, if he finds that any such judge is unable to discharge efficiently all the duties of his office by reason of mental or physical disability of permanent character, may, when necessary for the efficient dispatch of business, appoint, by and with the advice and consent of the Senate, an additional circuit judge of the circuit or district judge of the district to which such disabled judge belongs. And the judge so retiring voluntarily, or whose mental or physical condition caused the President to appoint an additional judge, shall be held and treated as if junior in commission to the remaining judges of said court who shall, in the order of the seniority of their respective commissions, exercise such powers and perform such duties as by law may be incident to seniority. In districts where there may be more than one district judge, if the judges or a majority of them cannot agree upon the appointment of officials of the court, to be appointed by such judges, then the senior judge shall have the power to make such appointments. Upon the death, resignation or retirement of any circuit or district judge, so entitled to resign, following the appointment of any additional judge as provided in this section, the vacancy caused by such death, resignation, or retirement of the said judge so entitled to resign shall not be filled. (40 Stat. 1157.)

Sec. 261. Writs of ne exeat may be granted by any justice of the Supreme Court, in cases where they might be granted by the Supreme Court; and by any district judge, in cases where they might be granted by the district court of which he is a judge. But no writ of ne exeat shall be granted unless a suit in equity is commenced, and satisfactory proof is made to the court or judge granting the same that the defendant designs quickly to depart from the United States.

Sec. 262. The Supreme Court and the district courts shall have power to issue writs of scire facias. The Supreme Court, the circuit courts of appeals, and the district courts shall have power to issue all writs not specifically provided for by statute, which may be necessary for the exercise of their respective jurisdictions, and agreeable to the usages and principles of law.

Note.

[Sec. 263 was repealed by section 17 of the Clayton Act (38 Stat. 737, etc.), which substitutes therefor, elaborate regulations as to temporary restraining orders and preliminary injunctions, but which also provides that nothing in this section contained shall be deemed to alter, repeal, or amend section two hundred and sixty-six of an act entitled "An Act to codify, revise and amend the laws relating to the judiciary," approved March third, nineteen hundred and eleven. (38 Stat. 737.)]

Sec. 264. Writs of injunction may be granted by any justice of the Supreme Court in cases where they might be granted by the Supreme Court; and by any judge of a district court in cases where they might be granted by such court. But no justice of the Supreme Court shall hear or allow any application for an injunction or restraining order in any cause pending in the circuit to which he is allotted, elsewhere than within such circuit, or at such place outside of the same as the parties may stipulate in writing, except when it cannot be heard by the district judge of the district. In case of the absence from the district of the district judge, or of his disability, any circuit judge of the circuit in which the district is situated may grant an injunction or restraining order in any case pending in the district court, where the same might be granted by the district judge.

Sec. 265. The writ of injunction shall not be granted by any court of the United States to stay proceedings in any court of a State, except in cases where such injunction may be authorized by any law relating to proceedings in bankruptcy.

Sec. 266. No interlocutory injunction suspending or restraining the enforcement, operation, or execution of any statute of a State by restraining the action of any officer of such State in the enforcement or execution of such statute, or in the enforcement or execution of an order made by an administrative board or commission acting under and pursuant to the statutes of such State shall be issued or granted by any justice of the Supreme Court, or by any district court of the United States, or by any judge thereof, or by any circuit judge acting as district judge, upon the ground of the unconstitutionality of such statute, unless the application for the same shall be presented to a justice of the Supreme Court of the United States, or to a circuit or district judge, and shall be heard and determined by three judges, of whom at least one shall be a justice of the Supreme Court or a circuit judge, and the other two may be either circuit or district judges, and unless a majority of said three judges shall concur in granting such application. Whenever such application as aforesaid is presented to a justice of the Supreme Court, or to a judge, he shall immediately call to his assistance to hear and determine the application two other judges: Provided, however, That one of such three judges shall be a justice of the Supreme Court, or a circuit judge. Said application shall not be heard or determined before at least five days' notice of the hearing has been given to the governor and to the attorney-general of the State, and to such other persons as may be defendants in the suit: Provided, That if of opinion that irreparable loss or damage would result to the complainant unless a temporary restraining order is granted, any justice of the Supreme Court, or any circuit or district judge, may grant such temporary restraining order at any time before such hearing and determination of the application for an interlocutory injunction, but such temporary restraining order shall remain in force only until the hearing and determination of the application for an interlocutory injunction upon notice as aforesaid. The hearing upon such application for an interlocutory injunction shall be given precedence and shall be in every way expedited and be assigned for a hearing at the earliest practicable day after the expiration of the notice hereinbefore provided for. An appeal may be taken direct to the Supreme Court of the United States from the order granting or denying, after notice and hearing, an interlocutory injunction in such case. It is further provided that if before the final hearing of such application a suit shall have been brought in a court of the State having jurisdiction thereof under the laws of such State, to enforce such statute or order, accompanied by a stay in such State court of proceedings under such statute or order pending the determination of such suit by such State court, all proceedings in any court of the United States to restrain the execution of such statute or order shall be stayed pending the final determination of such suit in the courts of the State. Such stay may be vacated upon proof made after hearing, and notice of ten days served upon the attorney-general of the State, that the suit in the State courts is not being prosecuted with diligence and good faith. (37 Stat. 1013.)

Sec. 267. Suits in equity shall not be sustained in any court of the United States in any case where a plain, adequate, and complete remedy may be had at law.

Sec. 268. The said courts shall have power to impose and administer all necessary oaths, and to punish, by fine or imprisonment, at the discretion of the court, contempts of their authority: Provided, That such power to punish contempts shall not be construed to extend to any cases except the misbehavior of any person in their presence, or so near thereto as to obstruct the administration of justice, the misbehavior of any of the officers of said courts in their official transactions, and the disobedience or resistance by any such officer, or by any party, juror, witness, or other person to any lawful writ, process, order, rule, decree, or command of the said courts. [Further elaborate provisions as to punishments for contempt are to be found in sections 21 et seq. of the Clayton Act (38 Stat. 738, etc.)]

Sec. 269. All of the said courts shall have power to grant new trials, in cases where there has been a trial by jury, for reasons for which new trials have usually been granted in the courts of law. On the hearing of any appeal, certiorari, writ of error, or motion for a new trial, in any case, civil or criminal, the court shall give judgment after an examination of the entire record before the court, without regard to technical errors, defects, or exceptions which do not affect the substantial rights of the parties. (40 Stat. 1181.)

Sec. 270. The judges of the Supreme Court and of the circuit courts of appeals and district courts, United States commissioners, and the judges and other magistrates of the several States, who are or may be authorized by law to make arrests for offenses against the United States, shall have the like authority to hold to security of the peace and for good behavior, in cases arising under the Constitution and laws of the United States, as may be lawfully exercised by any judge or justice of the peace of the respective States, in cases cognizable before them.

Sec. 271. The district courts and the United States commissioners shall have power to carry into effect, according to the true intent and meaning thereof, the award or arbitration or decree of any consul, vice-consul, or commercial agent of any foreign nation, made or rendered by virtue of authority conferred on him as such consul, vice-consul, or commercial agent, to sit as judge or arbitrator in such differences as may arise between the captains and crews of the vessels belonging to the nation whose interests are committd to his charge, application for the exercise of such power being first made to such court or commissioner, by petition of such consul, vice-consul, or commercial agent. And said courts and commissioners may issue all proper remedial process, mesne and final, to carry into full effect such award, arbitration, or decree, and to enforce obedience thereto by imprisonment in the jail or other place of confinement in the district in which the United States may lawfully imprison any person arrested under the authority of the United States, until such award, arbitration, or decree is complied with, or the parties are otherwise discharged therefrom, by the consent in writing of such consul, vice-consul, or commercial agent, or his successor in office, or by the authority of the foreign government appointing such consul, vice-consul, or commercial agent: Provided, however, That the expenses of the said imprisonment and maintenance of the prisoners, and the cost of the proceedings, shall be borne by such foreign government, or by its consul, vice-consul, or commercial agent requiring such imprisonment. The marshals of the United States shall serve all such process, and do all other acts necessary and proper to carry into effect the premises, under the authority of the said courts and commissioners. [Vide, however, Secs. 16 and 17, Act March 4, 1915, 38 Stat. 1184.]

Sec. 272. In all the courts of the United States the parties may plead and manage their own causes personally, or by the assistance of such counsel or attorneys at law as, by the rules of the said courts, respectively, are permitted to manage and conduct causes therein.

Sec. 273. No clerk, or assistant or deputy clerk, of any Territorial, district, or circuit court of appeals, or of the Court of Claims, or of the Supreme Court of the United States, or marshal or deputy marshal of the United States within the district for which he is appointed, shall act as a solicitor, proctor, attorney, or counsel in any cause depending in any of said courts, or in any district for which he is acting as such officer.

Sec. 274. Whoever shall violate the provisions of the preceding section shall be stricken from the roll of attorneys by the court upon complaint, upon which the respondent shall have due notice and be heard in his defense; and in the case of a marshal or deputy marshal so acting, he shall be recommended by the court for dismissal from office.

Sec. 274a. That in case any of said courts shall find that a suit at law should have been brought in equity or a suit in equity should have been brought at law, the court shall order, any amendments to the pleadings which may be necessary to conform them to the proper practice. Any party to the suit shall have the right, at any stage of the cause, to amend his pleadings so as to obviate the objection that his suit was not brought on the right side of the court. The cause shall proceed and be determined upon such amended pleadings. All testimony taken before such amendment, if preserved, shall stand as testimony in the cause with like effect as if the pleadings had been originally in the amended form. (38 Stat. 956.)

Sec. 274b. That in all actions at law equitable defenses may be interposed by answer, plea, or replication without the necessity of filing a bill on the equity side of the court. The defendant shall have the same rights in such case as if he had filed a bill embodying the defense or seeking the relief prayed for in such answer or plea. Equitable relief respecting the subject matter of the suit may thus be obtained by answer or plea. In case affirmative relief is prayed in such answer or plea, the plaintiff shall file a replication. Review of the judgment or decree entered in such case shall be regulated by rule of court. Whether such review be sought by writ of error or by appeal the appellate court shall have full power to render such judgment upon the record as law and justice shall require. (38 Stat. 956.)

Sec. 274c. That where, in any suit brought in or removed from any State court to any district of the United States, the jurisdiction of the district court is based upon the diverse citizenship of the par-

ties, and such diverse citizenship in fact existed at the time the suit
was brought or removed, though defectively alleged, either party
may amend at any stage of the proceedings and in the appellate
court upon such terms as the court may impose, so as to show on
the record such diverse citizenship and jurisdiction, and thereupon
such suit shall be proceeded with the same as though the diverse
citizenship had been fully and correctly pleaded at the inception of
the suit, or, if it be a removed case, in the petition for removal.
(38 Stat. 956.)

Note.

[The fourth section of the Act of September 6, 1916 (39 Stat. 727),
makes provisions which are actually, although not nominally, an
addition to the Judicial Code. It reads as follows:

That no court having power to review a judgment or decree rendered or passed by another shall dismiss a writ of error solely because an appeal should have been taken, or dismiss an appeal solely
because a writ of error should have been sued out, but when such
mistake or error occurs, it shall disregard the same and take the
action which would be appropriate if the proper appellate procedure
had been followed.]

CHAPTER TWELVE.

JURIES.

Sec. 275. Jurors to serve in the courts of the United States, in each State respectively, shall have the same qualifications, subject to the provisions hereinafter contained, and be entitled to the same exemptions, as jurors of the highest court of law in such State may have and be entitled to at the time when such jurors for service in the courts of the United States are summoned.

Sec. 276. All such jurors, grand and petit, including those summoned during the session of the court, shall be publicly drawn from a box containing, at the time of each drawing, the names of not less than three hundred persons, possessing the qualifications prescribed in the section last preceding, which names shall have been placed therein by the clerk of such court, or a duly qualified deputy clerk, and a commissioner, to be appointed by the judge thereof, or by the judge senior in commission in districts having more than one judge, which commissioner shall be a citizen of good standing, residing in the district in which such court is held, and a well-known member of the principal political party in the district in which the court is held opposing that to which the clerk, or a duly qualified deputy clerk then acting, may belong, the clerk or a duly qualified deputy clerk, and said commissioner each to place one name in said box alternately, without reference to party affiliations until the whole number required shall be placed therein. (39 Stat. 873.)

Sec. 277. Jurors shall be returned from such parts of the district, from time to time, as the court shall direct, so as to be most favorable to an impartial trial, and so as not to incur an unnecessary expense, or unduly burden the citizens of any part of the district with such service.

Sec. 278. No citizen possessing all other qualifications which are or may be prescribed by law shall be disqualified for service as grand or petit juror in any court of the United States on account of race, color, or previous condition of servitude.

Sec. 279. Writs of venire facias, when directed by the court, shall issue from the clerk's office, and shall be served and returned by the marshal in person, or by his deputy; or, in case the marshal or his deputy is not an indifferent person, or is interested in the event of the cause, by such fit person as may be specially appointed for that purpose by the court, who shall administer to him an oath that he will truly and impartially serve and return the writ. Any person named in such writ who resides elsewhere than at the place at which the court is held, shall be served by the marshal mailing a copy thereof to such person commanding him to attend as a juror at a time and place designated therein, which copy shall be registered and deposited in the post-office addressed to such person at his usual post-office address. And the receipt of the person so addressed for such registered copy shall be regarded as personal service of such writ upon such person, and no mileage shall be allowed for the service of such person. The postage and registry fee shall be paid by the marshal and allowed him in the settlement of his accounts.

Sec. 280. When, from challenges or otherwise, there is not a petit jury to determine any civil or criminal cause, the marshal or his deputy shall, by order of the court in which such defect of jurors happens, return jurymen from the bystanders sufficient to complete the panel; and when the marshal or his deputy is disqualified as aforesaid, jurors may be so returned by such disinterested person as the court may appoint, and such person shall be sworn, as provided in the preceding section.

Sec. 281. When special juries are ordered in any district court, they shall be returned by the marshal in the same manner and form as is required in such cases by the laws of the several States.

Sec. 282. Every grand jury impaneled before any district court shall consist of not less than sixteen nor more than twenty-three persons. If of the persons summoned less than sixteen attend, they shall be placed on the grand jury, and the court shall order the marshal to summon, either immediately or for a day fixed, from the body of the district, and not from the bystanders, a sufficient number of persons to complete the grand jury. And whenever a challenge to a grand juror is allowed, and there are not in attendance other jurors sufficient to complete the grand jury, the court shall make a like order to the marshal to summon a sufficient number of persons for that purpose.

Sec. 283. From the persons summoned and accepted as grand jurors, the court shall appoint the foreman, who shall have power to administer oaths and affirmations to witnesses appearing before the grand jury.

Sec. 284. No grand jury shall be summoned to attend any district court unless the judge thereof, in his own discretion or upon a notification by the district attorney that such jury will be needed, orders a venire to issue therefor. If the United States attorney for any district which has a city or borough containing at least three hundred thousand inhabitants shall certify in writing to the district judge, or the senior district judge of the district, that the exigencies of the public service require it, the judge may, in his discretion, also order a venire to issue for a second grand jury. And said court may in term order a grand jury to be summoned at such time, and to serve such time as it may direct, whenever, in its judgment, it may be proper to do so. But nothing herein shall operate to extend beyond the time permitted by law the imprisonment before indictment found of a person accused of a crime or offense, or the time during which a person so accused may be held under recognizance before indictment found.

Sec. 285. The district courts, the district courts of the Territories, and the Supreme Court of the District of Columbia may discharge their grand juries whenever they deem a continuance of the sessions of such juries unnecessary.

Sec. 286. No person shall serve as a petit juror in any district court more than one term in a year; and it shall be sufficient cause of challenge to any juror called to be sworn in any cause that he has been summoned and attended said court as a juror at any term of said court held within one year prior to the time of such challenge.

Sec. 287. When the offense charged is treason or a capital offense, the defendant shall be entitled to twenty and the United States to six peremptory challenges. On the trial of any other felony, the defendant shall be entitled to ten and the United States to six peremptory challenges; and in all other cases, civil and criminal, each party shall be entitled to three peremptory challenges; and in all cases where there are several defendants or several plaintiffs, the parties on each side shall be deemed a single party for the purposes of all challenges under this section. All challenges, whether to the array or panel, or to individual jurors for cause or favor, shall be tried by the court without the aid of triers.

Sec. 288. In any prosecution for bigamy, polygamy, or unlawful cohabitation, under any statute of the United States, it 'shall be a sufficient cause of challenge to any person drawn or summoned as a juror or talesman—

First, that he is or has been living in the practice of bigamy, polygamy, or unlawful cohabitation with more than one woman, or that he is or has been guilty of an offense punishable either by sections one or three of an Act entitled " An Act to amend section fifty-three hundred and fifty-two of the Revised Statutes of the United States, in reference to bigamy, and for other purposes," approved March twenty-second, eighteen hundred and eighty-two, or by section fifty-three hundred and fifty-two of the Revised Statutes of the United States, or the Act of July first, eighteen hundred and sixty-two, entitled " An Act to punish and prevent the practice of polygamy in the Territories of the United States and other places, and disapproving and annulling certain Acts of the legislative assembly of the Territory of Utah "; or

Second, that he believes it right for a man to have more than one living and undivorced wife at the same time, or to live in the practice of cohabiting with more than one woman.

Any person appearing or offered as a juror or talesman, and challenged on either of the foregoing grounds, may be questioned on his oath as to the existence of any such cause of challenge; and other evidence may be introduced bearing upon the question raised by such challenge; and this question shall be tried by the court.

But as to the first ground of challenge before mentioned, the person challenged shall not be bound to answer if he shall say upon his oath that he declines on the ground that his answer may tend to criminate himself; and if he shall answer as to said first ground, his answer shall not be given in evidence in any criminal prosecution against him for any offense above named; but if he declines to answer on any ground, he shall be rejected as incompetent.

CHAPTER THIRTEEN.

GENERAL PROVISIONS.

Sec. 289. The circuit courts of the United States, upon the taking effect of this Act, shall be, and hereby are, abolished; and thereupon, on said date, the clerks of said courts shall deliver to the clerks of the district courts of the United States for their respective districts all the journals, dockets, books, files, records, and other books and papers of or belonging to or in any manner connected with said circuit courts; and shall also on said date deliver to the clerks of said district courts all moneys, from whatever source received, then remaining in the hands or under their control as clerks of said circuit courts, or received by them by virtue of their said offices. The journals, dockets, books, files, records, and other books and papers so delivered to the clerks of the several district courts shall be and remain a part of the official records of said district courts, and copies thereof, when certified under the hand and seal of the clerk of the district court, shall be received as evidence equally with the originals thereof; and the clerks of the several district courts shall have the same authority to exercise all the powers and to perform all the duties with respect thereto as the clerks of the several circuit courts had prior to the taking effect of this Act.

Sec. 290. All suits and proceedings pending in said circuit courts on the date of the taking effect of this Act, whether originally brought therein or certified thereto from the district courts, shall thereupon and thereafter be proceeded with and disposed of in the district courts in the same manner and with the same effect as if originally begun therein, the record thereof being entered in the records of the circuit courts so transferred as above provided.

Sec. 291. Wherever, in any law not embraced within this Act, any reference is made to, or any power or duty is conferred or imposed upon, the circuit courts, such reference shall, upon the taking effect of this Act, be deemed and held to refer to, and confer such power and impose such duty upon, the district courts.

Sec. 292. Wherever, in any law not contained within this Act, a reference is made to any law revised or embraced herein, such reference, upon the taking effect hereof, shall be construed to refer to the section of this Act into which has been carried or revised the provision of law to which reference is so made.

Sec. 293. The provisions of sections one to five, both inclusive, of the Revised Statutes, shall apply to and govern the construction of the provisions of this Act. The words " this title," wherever they occur herein, shall be construed to mean this Act.

Sec. 294. The provisions of this Act, so far as they are substantially the same as existing statutes, shall be construed as continuations thereof, and not as new enactments, and there shall be no implication of a change of intent by reason of a change of words in such statute, unless such change of intent shall be clearly manifest.

Sec. 295. The arrangement and classification of the several sections of this Act have been made for the purpose of a more convenient and orderly arrangement of the same, and therefore no inference or presumption of a legislative construction is to be drawn by reason of the chapter under which any particular section is placed.

Sec. 296. This Act may be designated and cited as " The Judicial Code."

CHAPTER FOURTEEN.

REPEALING PROVISIONS.

Sec. 297. The following sections of the Revised Statutes and Acts and parts of Acts are hereby repealed:

Sections five hundred and thirty to five hundred and sixty, both inclusive; sections five hundred and sixty-two to five hundred and sixty-four, both inclusive; sections five hundred and sixty-seven to six hundred and twenty-seven, both inclusive; sections six hundred and twenty-nine to six hundred and forty-seven, both inclusive; sections six hundred and fifty to six hundred and ninety-seven, both inclusive; section six hundred and ninety-nine; sections seven hundred and two to seven hundred and fourteen, both inclusive; sections seven hundred and sixteen to seven hundred and twenty, both inclusive; section seven hundred and twenty-three; sections seven hundred and twenty-five to seven hundred and forty-nine, both inclusive; sections eight hundred to eight hundred and twenty-two, both inclusive; sections ten hundred and forty-nine to ten hundred and eighty-eight, both inclusive; sections ten hundred and ninety-one to ten hundred and ninety-three, both inclusive, of the Revised Statutes.

"An Act to determine the jurisdiction of circuit courts of the United States and to regulate the removal of causes from State courts, and for other purposes," approved March third, eighteen hundred and seventy-five.

Section five of an Act entitled "An Act to amend section fifty-three hundred and fifty-two of the Revised Statutes of the United States, in reference to bigamy, and for other purposes," approved March twenty-second, eighteen hundred and eighty-two; but sections six, seven, and eight of said Act, and sections one, two, and twenty-six of an Act entitled "An Act to amend an Act entitled 'An Act to amend section fifty-three hundred and fifty-two of the Revised Statutes of the United States, in reference to bigamy, and for other purposes,' approved March twenty-second, eighteen hundred and eighty-

41

two,'' approved March third, eighteen hundred and eighty-seven, are hereby continued in force.

" An Act to afford assistance and relief to Congress and the executive departments in the investigation of claims and demands against the Government,'' approved March third, eighteen hundred and eighty-three.

" An Act regulating appeals from the supreme court of the District of Columbia and the supreme courts of the several Territories,'' approved March third, eighteen hundrerd and eighty-five.

" An Act to provide for the bringing of suits against the Government of the United States,'' approved March third, eighteen hundred and eighty-seven, except sections four, five, six, seven, and ten thereof.

Sections one, two, three, four, six, and seven of an Act entitled " An Act to correct the enrollment of an Act approved March third, eighteen hundred and eighty-seven, entitled ' An Act to amend sections one, two, three, and ten of an Act to determine the jurisdiction of the circuit courts of the United States, and to regulate the removal of causes from State courts, and for other purposes,' approved March third, eighteen hundred and seventy-five,'' approved August thirteenth, eighteen hundred and eighty-eight.

" An Act to withdraw from the Supreme Court jurisdiction of criminal cases not capital and confer the same on the circuit courts of appeals,'' approved January twentieth, eighteen hundred and ninety-seven.

" An Act to amend sections one and two of the Act of March third, eighteen hundred and eighty-seven, Twenty-fourth Statutes at Large, chapter three hundred and fifty-nine,'' approved June twenty-seventh, eighteen hundred and ninety-eight.

" An Act to amend the seventh section of the Act entitled ' An Act to establish circuit courts of appeals and to define and regulate in certain cases the jurisdiction of the courts of the United States, and for other purposes,' approved March third, eighteen hundred and ninety-one, and the several Acts amendatory thereto,'' approved April fourteenth, nineteen hundred and six.

All Acts and parts of Acts authorizing the appointment of United States circuit or district judges, or creating or changing judicial circuits, or judicial districts or divisions thereof, or fixing or changing the times or places of holding court therein, enacted prior to February first, nineteen hundred and eleven.

Sections one, two, three, four, five, the first paragraph of section six, and section seventeen of an Act entitled " An Act to create a commerce court, and to amend an Act entitled ' An Act to regulate commerce,' approved February fourth, eighteen hundred and eighty-seven, as heretofore amended, and for other purposes,'' approved. June eighteenth, nineteen hundred and ten.

Also all other Acts and parts of Acts, in so far as they are em-braced within and superseded by this Act, are hereby repealed; the remaining portions thereof to be and remain in force with the same effect and to the same extent as if this Act had not been passed.

Sec. 298. The repeal of existing laws providing for the appointment of judges and other officers mentioned in this Act, or affecting the organization of the courts, shall not be construed to affect the tenure of office of the incumbents (except the office be abolished), but they shall continue to hold their respective offices during the terms for which appointed, unless removed as provided by law; nor (except the office be abolished) shall such repeal affect the salary or fees or compensation of any officer or person holding office or position by virtue of any law.

Sec. 299. The repeal of existing laws, or the amendments thereof, embraced in this Act, shall not affect any act done, or any right accruing or accrued, or any suit or proceeding, including those pending on writ of error, appeal, certificate, or writ of certiorari, in any appellate court referred to or included within, the provisions of this Act, pending at the time of the taking effect of this Act, but all such suits and proceedings, and suits and proceedings for causes arising or acts done prior to such date, may be commenced and prosecuted within the same time, and with the same effect, as if said repeal or amendment had not been made.

Sec. 300. All offenses committed, and all penalties, forfeitures, or liabilities incurred prior to the taking effect hereof, under any law embraced in, amended, or repealed by this Act, may be prosecuted and punished, or sued for and recovered, in the district courts, in the same manner and with the same effect as if this Act had not been passed.

Sec. 301. This Act shall take effect and be in force on and after January first, nineteen hundred and twelve.

TABLE OF CASES

TABLE OF CASES

(The References are to Sections.)

A

D

G

44

TABLE OF STATUTES CITED

REVISED STATUTES.

(References are to Sections.)

JUDICIAL CODE.
36 Stat. 1087.

INDEX

INDEX

(The References are to Sections.)

A

(The References are to Sections.)

(The References are to Sections.)

45

(The References are to Sections.)

(The References are to Sections.)

(The References are to Sections.)

(The References are to Sections.)

  46

(The References are to Sections.)

(The References are to Sections.)

(The References are to Sections.)

(The References are to Sections.)

(The References are to Sections.)

(The References are to Sections.)

(The References are to Sections.)

(The References are to Sections.)

(The References are to Sections.)

E

(The References are to Sections.)

(The References are to Sections.)

(The References are to Sections.)

H

Judge—Continued

Judge, Circuit

Judges, District

Judge, Presiding Judge of State Court

Judgment, Arrest of

(The References are to Sections.)

48

(The References are to Sections.)

(The References are to Sections.)

(The References are to Sections.)

(The References are to Sections.)

M

(The References are to Sections.)

(The References are to Sections.)

49

(The References are to Sections.)

(The References are to Sections.)

(The References are to Sections.)

Removal—Continued

(The References are to Sections.)

S

(The References are to Sections.)

(The References are to Sections.)

(The References are to Sections.)

(The References are to Sections.)

(The References are to Sections.)

(The References are to Sections.)

Venue—Continued

Verdict

Vermont

Virginia

Volstead Act

Vote

W

(The References are to Sections.)

[Total number pages, 800.]